SO-AZP-718

"An accurate and painstakingly detailed chronicle of the last great battle of World War II, the book is also a powerful antiwar statement that takes an unblinking look at the monstrous waste, pain and horror of modern war." — *Publishers Weekly*

"A 'must read' book . . . truly a landmark work. A superbly researched and extraordinarily detailed history of the battle." — *Sea Power*

"The grip of some books is so tenacious that the reader is transfixed by the tale past all reason, through meals, fire alarms and earthquakes far into the night. Told at the skin level . . . the book reads at times like a fine novel." — *Far Eastern Economic Review*

"This is military history at its best." — *Newport News*

"More than a military history, [this book] is also a supremely important, heartrending chronicle of the human condition." — *San Francisco Chronicle*

"A majestic, sweeping historical narrative . . . This book is an elegant testimony to the stark reality, horror and valor of war." — *Friday Review of Defense Literature*

"It is almost impossible to stop reading it to indulge in the necessities, such as food, work and sleep. It is an excellent piece of writing and research." — *The Press Enterprise*

"A skillful narrative of combat history . . . exceedingly vivid." — *New York Times Book Review*

"First-rate . . . A chilling chronicle of barbarism, unspeakable courage and suicidal bravery." — *Detroit Free Press*

"Short of having been there, Feifer's book is as close as we are likely to come to experiencing those terrible three months in the spring of 1945." — *Newsday*

"Read . . . and understand not only the horrors of war, but why American survivors who would have invaded Japan blessed the atomic bomb." — *Palm Beach Post*

"A classic history of a decisive portion of the Pacific war. Highly recommended." — *Rocky Mountain News*

"Simply one of the most affecting books I have ever read." — *Austin Chronicle*

"Brilliantly told . . . an uncompromising look at the inhumanity on both sides of the Pacific war." — *Houston Chronicle*

"Feifer masterfully choreographs his nearly ten years of research into a chorus of riveting testimonials about the land, sea and air combat on Okinawa. He brings back to life the ferocious ground action, which left 250,000 casualties (including 150,000 civilians) and weds the combat to the broader issues of where the war was headed and how to end it." — *Marine Corps Gazette*

"Magnificent." — *Leatherneck*

FROM VETERANS AND OTHER READERS

"Unless we know of Okinawa and its beleaguered people, we know precious little of World War II. They were war's classic victims, caught between the rock and the hard place, between the Japanese and the Americans. In George Feifer's encyclopedic though deeply moving work, we come to understand these survivors. They knew about the charnel house. They lived in it." — Studs Terkel

"One of the finest close-combat stories one will ever read. George Feifer has written an epic, and anyone who was involved from land, sea, or air units, or with the battle, will not want to put this down." — Bill Pierce, in *Military Chronicles*

"Marine veterans of the campaign who pick up [*The Battle of Okinawa*] will not want to put it down. For us, [*The Battle of Okinawa*] re-triggers the adrenaline and materializes some of our haunted submerged recollections, but it is a thoroughly fascinating read." — Jeptha J. Carrell (platoon leader in the battle of Okinawa), in *Marine Society Newsletter*

"A really great book. Exciting from beginning to end about one of the biggest battles of the Pacific war. . . . For the first time, this book blends the strategic, tactical and human side of the great land, sea, and air battle. It is destined to be a classic." — Rear Admiral R. La Rocclue, Center for Defense Information

"[*The Battle of Okinawa*]'s tremendous style of writing has produced without any question the most powerful antiwar book that I've ever read, and I've read a lot in the past forty-eight years." — Harold Young

"This is a terrific book. After reading much fiction and nonfiction about World War II in the Pacific, only these books on my list approach the reality of combat: *The Assault, Goodbye, Darkness* and [*The Battle of Okinawa*]." — Arlie Hunt

"[*The Battle of Okinawa*] is fantastic and will be around forever. It's a historical work of art." — Fred C. Poppe

"In my forty-two years, I have only felt compelled one other time to write a letter of praise to an author. [*The Battle of Okinawa*] was the most thorough and moving account of Okinawa I have ever read." — Keith Swogger

"My wife just finished reading [the] wonderful [*Battle of Okinawa*] aloud. It brought back many memories — memories that were proud, sad, and in some cases still numbing. It is the most definitive book on the peaks, fears, travails, and horrors experienced by combat infantrymen." — James Ahern

"The book certainly brought me back in time, and the accuracy of actions — on all sides of the conflict — was more than well done. I don't have to write my memoirs for my family. [*The Battle of Okinawa*] did it all!" — F. Raymond Hoeymans

"I was never able to tell my folks what their only child went through on Okinawa. Now *I* don't have to tell anyone at all because [*The Battle of Okinawa*] does a masterful job in recreating the vast, sprawling battle. Readers can truly imagine themselves there." — Donald Dencker

"George Feifer reveals the truth and then provides the reader with chilling insights and new perspectives on this last, epic battle of World War II. Even those who were there will learn from his exhaustive research and be awestruck by his words." — Richard Whitaker

THE BATTLE OF OKINAWA

Books by George Feifer

Red Files: Secrets from the Russian Archives (2000)
The Destined Hour with Barbara and Barry Rosen (1982)
To Dance with Valery Panov (1978)
Moscow Farewell (1976)
Our Motherland (1973)
Solzhenitsyn with David Berg (1972)
The Girl from Petrovka (1971)
Message from Moscow (1969)
The Challenge of Change (1967)
Justice in Moscow (1964)

THE BATTLE OF OKINAWA

The Blood and the Bomb

Originally published as
Tennozan: The Battle of Okinawa and the Atomic Bomb

George Feifer

THE LYONS PRESS

Guilford, CT

An Imprint of The Globe Pequot Press

Originally Published as *Tennozan: The Battle of Okinawa and the Atomic Bomb* by Houghton Mifflin, 1992

First Lyons Press Edition, 2001
Copyright © 1992, 2001 by George Feifer

ALL RIGHTS RESERVED. No part of this book may be reproduced or transmitted in any form by any means, electronic or mechanical, including photocopying and recording, or by any information storage and retrieval system, except as expressly permitted by the 1976 Copyright Act or in writing from the publisher. Requests for permission should be addressed to: The Globe Pequot Press, P.O. Box 480, Guildford, CT 06437.

The Lyons Press is an imprint of The Globe Pequot Press.

2 4 6 8 10 9 7 5 3

Library of Congress Cataloging-in-Publication Data
Feifer, George.
The Battle of Okinawa: the blood and the
bomb/George Feifer.
p. cm
Originally published: Tennozan. New York:
Ticknor & Fields, 1992.
Includes bibliographical references and index.
ISBN 1-58574-215-5
1. World War, 1939–1945 — Campaigns — Japan — Okinawa
Island. 2. Okinawa Island — History. 3. Atomic bomb.
D767.99.O45F45   2001
940.54'25 — dc21
2001029183

Printed in Canada

Book design by David Ford
Maps by George Ward

Quotations from E. B. Sledge's *With the Old Breed* are reprinted with permission.

Excerpts from *Typhoon of Steel: The Battle for Okinawa* by James H. Belote and William H. Belote. Copyright © 1970 by James H. and William H. Belote. Reprinted by permission of HarperCollins Publishers, Inc.

for the
Girl from the *Black Forest*
with thanks and love

Nothing is worse than war? Dishonour is worse than war.
Slavery is worse than war.
— Winston Churchill

KILL JAPS. KILL JAPS.
KILL MORE JAPS
You will help to kill the Yellow bastards
if you do your job well.
— A sign at the headquarters of
Admiral William F. (Bull) Halsey,
commander of the fleet that helped
devastate Okinawa

The battle for Okinawa can be described only in the grim superlatives of war. In size, scope and ferocity, it dwarfed the Battle of Britain. Never before had there been, probably never again will there be, such a vicious sprawling struggle of planes against planes, of ships against planes. Never before, in so short a space, had the Navy lost so many ships; never before in land fighting had so much American blood been shed in so short a time in so small an area: probably never before in any three months of the war had the enemy suffered so hugely, and the final toll of American casualties was the highest experienced in any campaign against the Japanese. There have been larger land battles, more protracted air campaigns, but Okinawa was the largest combined operation, a "no quarter" struggle fought on, under and over the sea and land.
— Hanson W. Baldwin, military historian

Okinawa retained importance for the Japanese only as a potential field of battle, a distant border area in which the oncoming enemy could be checked, pinned down, and ultimately destroyed.
— George Kerr, historian of Okinawa

Contents

Introduction

OKINAWA was the site of the largest land-sea-air battle in history. The Japanese called it a Tennozan, a decisive struggle on which, for a time, they staked everything. It was also a turning point in modern history. That first struggle on the territory of Japan — to which Okinawa belonged politically although not culturally — was also the last major one before the start of the atomic age. Surely some understanding of its nature is wanted for responsible assessment of the decision to use the atomic bomb, dropped some six weeks after the battle's end. Even accepting that no final judgment of the rights and wrongs of Hiroshima and Nagasaki can ever be made, condemnation of those horrors out of context — without knowledge of even greater devastation on Okinawa — makes the debate too easy.

Apart from a few sorties elsewhere, the entire Japanese kamikaze effort of World War II was directed against the American armada, also the largest in history, deployed off the Okinawan coast. It caused the Navy greater casualties than any previous engagement in either the Atlantic or the Pacific. The carnage was even greater on land, where the Japanese defenders were better fortified and armed than anywhere else in the Pacific. More than twice the number of Americans were killed and wounded than on Guadalcanal and Iwo Jima combined. While Washington's honored place for the statue of the famous flag-raising on Iwo Jima is entirely proper, the indifference to the longer, harder-fought, much more costly Battle of Okinawa is baffling.

The far greater American losses there were a particle of the total. The Japanese share, essentially unnoticed in America, was more gruesome, and even that was minor compared to the agony of Okinawa itself, a once independent kingdom of gentle farmers and traders. Americans tend to associate Okinawa with Iwo Jima — with which, however, it shares little except climate and geography. No resident civilians lived on the Japanese garrison island of Iwo, whereas Okinawa was the home of an ancient, tolerant civilization that had maintained no arms whatever for centuries before Japan swallowed it in 1879. The greatest suffering was borne by that peace-loving homeland, which ended in rubble and ash, its cultural heritage virtually obliterated.

Okinawa's civilian tragedy exceeded that of Hiroshima in most ways, including the number of noncombatants killed. Some 150,000 died, even more horribly than those seared and slaughtered under the mushroom cloud. They had weeks to witness their children's mutilation by "the typhoon of bombs and steel," as they called the colossal deluge of American firepower, or by Japanese troops when their morale collapsed after months of sacrificially courageous defense. And if innocence can be quantified, the Okinawans had more of it than the Hiroshima victims. They bore less responsibility — actually none — for the war in which they were massacred.

Although hundreds of books have been written about the atomic devastation, the far greater Okinawan one — cultural, material, and spiritual, as well as corporal — remains unknown to most Americans. I mention this at the start not to stake a claim in some ghoulish competition to crown the greatest catastrophe, but to point out that the Okinawan suffering has never been recognized; proportionately far smaller losses in Japan and America have always prompted much greater sorrow. That's among the puzzles of a campaign that never found its proper place in American history. Another puzzle is why so little is remembered — more precisely was never appreciated, even then — about the relatively huge American sacrifice. The whole nightmarish experience went into a kind of black hole of national memory.

Well over a million people were on the island and surrounding seas during the year or so of the 1945 battle and preparation for it. Nearly a quarter of them — Okinawan, Japanese, and American — were killed. It's of course impossible to tell the full story of the living or the dead. At first, I tried to omit no category of participant, but after reading my initial pages about a confusing array of regiments, crews, companies, platoons, and squads, focus on fewer soldiers and civilians seemed necessary. I felt I was following Lytton Strachey's rowing over "a great ocean of material" for *Eminent Victorians,* then lowering his "little bucket" that brought up "to the light of day some characteristic specimen." The only people more conscious than I of the categories my new approach excluded will be those excluded themselves: whole Army divisions in some cases, together with the entire crews of capital ships and hundreds of thousands of Okinawan farmers. I hope they'll recognize themselves in some of the people I *have* drawn, although I may risk offending some in attempting to convey a sense of the huge, complex whole through greater detail about what's intended as a representative selection.

War's horror exists partly because outsiders can't know it. "If people really knew, the war would be stopped tomorrow," said Prime Minister David Lloyd George in 1916, when trench warfare oddly similar to the Okinawan fighting was bleeding his Britain white. "But of course they don't know and can't know." Not even most servicemen know, since a minute proportion of them actually fight — and those who do are unlikely to describe their ordeal, partly because few are writers, partly because all rightly believe that no one who hasn't experienced combat can imagine it. As a historian of battle recently put it, combat is "too little related to anything recognizably human or natural."

Not having fought at Okinawa or anywhere else, I too don't know what is unknowable to outsiders. But the stories I heard during my research were close enough to horror for me. In any case, this book doesn't pretend to be a military history, of which more traditional ones exist in English and in Japanese, but sketches of elements of the battle and its background that may suggest what Okinawans, Americans, and Japanese endured. Even now, few survivors have more than a vague, often mistaken, impression of how the other participants shared their nightmare. It took me too long to see that all were victims, but when I did, that seemed another reason for not attempting a conventional account of the fighting, day by day, hill by hill, decimated platoon by decimated platoon. The Battle of Okinawa involved matters more important than its bloody heroism and anguish in the field and on the sea.

Among the combatants, it is chiefly infantrymen who are in "mortal contact with the enemy," in the same historian's phrase: roughly .0025 percent of Americans during World War II. Of the eleven million uniformed men in 1945 (some 7 percent of the national population), about 5 percent served in infantry combat divisions, of which roughly half went into the lines. Those who wore uniforms but never saw combat remained innocent of war's real misery, even if they were stuck on a mosquito-infested atoll. As Eugene Sledge pointed out in a gripping memoir of his fighting on Okinawa, the majority of servicemen behind the lines had almost as little notion as the civilians back home of the infantryman's war of "incredible cruelty," in which "decent men were reduced to brutish existence in their fight for survival amid the violent death, terror, tension, fatigue and filth." All that was "totally incomprehensible" to the uninitiated, as an artilleryman who fought from a mere few hundred yards from it discovered on Okinawa.

> After we . . . passed through the shambles of Naha [the island's largest city], we reached a rural area that had been under American fire for some time. We passed by a dead horse or mule and three dead Japanese soldiers. . . . The unforgettable memory is the stench of the rotting bodies. It's an unbelievably overpowering odor. Artillerymen didn't see that part of war often because we did our killing long distance. To see the results was horrible. . . . I survived Okinawa because I was artillery, not infantry.

This book was originally conceived as a record of the American hardship on Okinawa that never won rightful recognition. As the sixtieth anniversary of Pearl Harbor approaches, I hope it will give a new generation a hint of the fighting men's terrible ordeal of toil, terror, and misery. Their accomplishments in the face of appalling adversity remain hardly known by the general public — less forgotten than never appreciated in the first place, as I've suggested. When I sign books for veterans, I try to add some words of admiration and gratitude, which is what I'm trying to do here, as well, for those I'll never meet. I wish noncombatants of all generations could recognize what they endured, partly so that the surviving veterans, now approaching the end of their lives, might even now get some of the credit never given in 1945 or afterward.

The causes of the Pacific War were less clear-cut than most Americans believe. During the preceding decades, some of our forebearers and administrations periodically scorned Japan and her people with haughty insensitivity and racial prejudice, and few Japanese forgot the insults. Resentment nourished their determination to strike at America in 1941.

Still, the attack on Pearl Harbor, not to mention Japan's aggression against fellow Asians in Manchuria and China, went beyond any reaction that can conceivably be called justified. It was chiefly a pursuit of cruel self-interest, a "need" and "right" to grab other nations' land and food. Even in defense, as on Okinawa, Japan was a brutal aggressor. It's now clearer than ever that her victory in the war — closer to a right-against-wrong war than most others — would have been a calamity to her possessions and captured territories; and probably also to the militaristic homeland herself. The pride of American combat veterans therefore remains properly intact. Whatever wars Washington may wrongly have entered since, their effort on Okinawa remains as right and utterly necessary in retrospect as it seemed then. Although most fellow citizens never saw the light, the combatants' sacrifices and accomplishments in 1945 shine beautifully where it most matters, within themselves.

That's partly why the missing public acclaim doesn't ultimately matter to them: Their private rewards are more important. Dick Whitaker, my account's central American character, gave me my first hint of that some fifteen years ago when he said that nothing in life truly fazed him after his charge up a hill nicknamed Sugar Loaf. The self-respect that earned, he reflected, was enough to last a lifetime.

Whitaker, my neighbor on a sparse dirt road when most of this book was written, fought with the 6th Marine Division, which is one reason I chose to focus on it more than the other units on the American side. The larger reason is that it took the largest number of casualties while capturing some 75 percent of Okinawa's territory, including many of the best defensive fortifications. But Marines, while justifiably very proud of themselves and their feats, tend to be less justifiably dismissive of others, and I hope I don't give the impression that their Army counterparts displayed lesser valor or sacrifice. All combatants on Okinawa, especially at the

Shuri Line, one of the most formidable in the history of warfare, fought the same battle and endured the same hardships and losses as did the small number of Marine units I follow in some detail.

But while I continue hoping that those of us who have never been to the core of war will appreciate the full cost they paid, my research revealed a larger story than the one about unsung American valor. The veterans have every reason to feel good about themselves and what happened to them, even if so much of it was so terrible. Others don't. As they dug into the island's blood-soaked mud trying to stay alive, many Americans asked themselves what they were doing in that hell, a world away from home. For Okinawans, that *was* home, and it remains scarred by the war. Almost immediately after the battle, Washington and Tokyo began taking cruel advantage of the people who had already suffered so grievously. Their conspiracy continues into the twenty-first century.

To keep my quotes from the battle's participants authentic, I've retained the almost universal American wartime use of the now-offensive "Jap" and "Nip." They were a formidable enemy on Okinawa, as elsewhere in the Pacific War. Their accomplishments despite severe technological inferiority were stunning. Perhaps no army in the world could have labored and fought with such bravery, endurance, and sublimation of individual well-being for the sake of a national cause as the 32nd Japanese Army did on Okinawa. Perhaps no people were so driven by a desire to prove themselves, no matter what the hardships and consequences. It seems to me the Japanese goal was more than mere victory. Some deep national yearning impelled them to make horrific sacrifices and blinded them to what most other peoples considered reality. Although the nature of contemporary Japan lies well outside the scope of this book, the qualities displayed on Okinawa — extraordinary intensity, insularity, and a zealous capacity to endure pain in order to serve the nation and obtain rewards in a later life — may help explain the startling Japanese economic triumphs during roughly 1965 to 1990: triumphs to which the country may well return in the not-distant future, because some of her fundamental traits of course remain intact. There have been great national changes since 1945, but the samurai ethic lives on in many boardrooms, as does the willingness to sacrifice in many hearts. I believe Japan still embodies a mighty challenge, for reasons that became startlingly clear on Okinawa.

This is not to suggest that all her soldiers behaved badly there. It goes almost without saying many were not brutal — and most of those who were, like those who weren't, were themselves brutalized. Almost all survivors of the battle I interviewed had become deeply suspicious of militarism. (Despite the famous reluctance of most Japanese to say anything they fear might displease a listener, especially a foreign one, I don't think

I was much fooled, although interviewing through an interpreter is doubly tricky.) I can't say they appear to feel much remorse for the immeasurable suffering Japan caused other peoples in World War II, in particular Okinawans, whose pain many mentioned only when prompted. But they are appalled by war — and by leaders who take their people to it, journalists who lie to fire them up — as only people with their experience of hoodwinking and suffering can be. It was almost inevitable that many of those I saw, among them writers of memoirs and participants in Japanese-American memorial activities, formed a self-selected sample, more likely to be internationally minded and "liberal" than the average survivor. In any case, those elderly men, some of whom surely did gruesome things as young men, impressed me as wise, friendly, and kind.

Although it's hard for me to say what has and hasn't changed in my own country's national character, some of the qualities for which Americans are known — infectious optimism and dismal ignorance of other cultures, rare personal generosity and a stubborn inability to recognize the fact of American imperialism — were much in evidence during the Okinawan campaign. In some ways, it seemed a brighter time for the country, despite the hardships of the Depression that colored the childhood of almost every fighting man and despite the fighting itself. Perhaps inevitably, America of the relentlessly increasing materialism and ever-widening gap between those who make it incredibly big and those who remain appallingly poor has lost some of her bearings since 1945. She also hasn't been genuinely happy as the world's rich kid, a role World War II awarded her.

Still, the American survivors to whom I talked were also an inspiring collection, and on average more troubled by Okinawan suffering than were the Japanese. I'd argue that generalizations about those who fought in the front lines are valid, because the battle was the foremost influence on the young men and molded them all for life. The savage hardship was indelible, together with love for those who made it bearable by sharing its misery. Those unabashed patriots, whose middle-American lawns fly the Stars and Stripes on holidays, saw enough of real war to detest it, and are close enough to their natural deaths not to continue hiding what they know. Anyone who thinks life in the trenches leaves a good man fond of a good fight should talk to the survivors of Okinawa. They are justly proud of their feats but free of movie warriors' bravado and baloney.

Meeting a selection of those who fought one of America's proudest battles was this lengthy project's best personal reward. Even richer has been a packet of letters from readers, and from their wives and children. Some consist of no more than a paragraph of thanks in shaky handwriting. Others provide detailed accounts of horrific moments and days on the island. The ones I most treasure credit this book's original edition for prompting an emotional release that enabled the writers, at long last, to tell their families about what they endured in the hell of those fifty-plus years ago. A former professor of journalism named Brooks Hamilton was among those who explained why fighting men find that so hard to do.

> The fact is that even among writers, very few . . . who have experienced war on that basic combat level can write about it — or in fact hardly think about it. . . . There are parts of your book I still haven't read because as I got to some passages I became too emotional. I can write you tonight, in fact, only after a couple of stiff rum drinks have loosed things up!
>
> Let me illustrate by anecdote. In June of 1990, I visited my father on his 90th birthday. . . . As we sat and talked a bit that day, suddenly he looked at me, almost wistfully, and said, "You know, there is one thing I've never understood about you. You would never tell me anything about your experiences in the war. Why?" . . . I could not then, and cannot now, say "why." It is just impossible to do so to one who was not there.

Praise from such men for getting things right is surely the nearest I'll get to the approval all writers crave. And a bonus was bestowed in Japan, where most survivors were even less apt to tell their families what they'd endured. Shame for having lost and Japanese stoicism only add to the reasons why American veterans are unable to talk to outsiders who can't possibly understand.

Well after the war, Tadashi Kojo, the quintessentially dedicated infantry officer who serves as my chief Japanese character, took up a career that might have been his principal one — since he loved books as a boy — had it not been for Japanese militarism. Having learned English relatively late in life, largely by applying himself with his distinctive intensity, Kojo-san became a translator, especially of military history. And in a twist less curious than many that kept him alive during and after the murderous battle, he went on to translate this very book, in which he figures so centrally, into Japanese for its publication there. When I last met the former captain in Tokyo, I asked whether he'd ever told his wife about his Okinawa ordeal. No, he hadn't, he replied; she knew nothing about it. *Nothing at all?* I persisted, just to confirm the power of that constraint. "No, not a whisper." But had she seen any of his translation? Yes, she read much of his final draft while he was working on it. And what did she think about his part in it? The elderly but still scrupulously groomed veteran looked at me with more emotion than during the weeks when he'd recounted his story, years before. I wondered whether he, ordinarily still master of the absolute self-control he'd learned as a cadet, was actually almost faltering.

What was his wife's reaction? I repeated, no doubt impolitely. Now looking away from me, he continued suppressing a reply for several minutes until it came, at last, in a voice I hadn't heard from him before, even when he was telling me about his unimaginable hardships on Okinawa. "Many, many tears," he murmured, his own eyes almost betraying the same.

I was of course moved to learn that my account helped reveal some of the horror to Japanese families too. If only the larger civilian tragedy were acknowledged! Okinawans are hardly the first to endure a martyrdom of geography, but few have done so with less recognition. Before I visited the island, my journalistic travels had taught me something about the durability of national character. Formed by fundamental factors such as soil, climate, and centuries of common memories, most peoples' underlying attitudes and customs change far more slowly than their fortunes. But nothing supported that notion as did my impressions of Okinawans. Despite grave damage to so many bodies and minds, the majority remain largely as they were before the battle, easygoing and amiable. Having endured far more than the Japanese and American combatants, they are nevertheless as gentle and hospitable as in the descriptions of them I'd read before my visits. Long residence in Soviet Russia and other dictatorial countries left me impatient with leaders who preach peace and oppress the weak. But when Okinawans plead for peace, quietly, I shut up and listen.

It's worth repeating even here that more of their parents and grandparents died, and in greater agony, than in Hiroshima, and that the associated damage — the smashing of their world and culture — was incalculably greater. Measured by sheer anguish as well as by devastation of national life, the Battle of Okinawa was the greater tragedy, one that foreshadowed a yet more colossal horror had the war progressed to the next battleground on the Japanese mainland.

And if exact comparisons with Hiroshima's and Iwo Jima's suffering can't really be made, the central question now is a different one. Why does the Okinawan ordeal abide while the others have essentially ended? For Okinawans' punishment continues to this day as a direct result of the battle, even though they, the accommodating, exceptionally peaceful islanders, were its chief victims. That was one of the war's plentiful ironies — or inevitable consequences, since the weakest and poorest usually bear the greatest burdens.

A hundred Okinawans, Americans, and Japanese deserve my thanks. If only, I kept thinking during my interviews, they, whose first instinct was to "do good," could get to know one another. A small number are actually doing that now. After long preparation, a memorial to 6th Marine Division Americans killed during the campaign was unveiled in a Garden of

Remembrance on Okinawa, and it incorporated salutes to the Japanese and Okinawan casualties. American veterans who attended the ceremony, some so scarred by combat's torment and so full of hateful memory of the Japanese that they feared returning to the island, put their arms around their former enemies and wept. Together, they mourned all the dead — and felt cleansed and uplifted; some even felt a bond.

The inspiring memorial was unveiled in 1987, forty-two years after the battle. If the perception that emerged there of the other side as human beings had been earlier shared, much of the horror might have been avoided. "But I also came to realize that if our concept of . . . civilization was to mean anything, we had to acknowledge the humanity of even our misled and murderous enemies," John Hersey, ex–war correspondent, wrote later. Congratulations aren't yet deserved: To this day, care and concern for the chief victims are insufficient. Those chief victims, as anyone who has read this far will know, were Okinawans — who, characteristically, constructed their own memorial to *all* the 340,000 dead, Korean laborers and British sailors as well as Okinawan civilians and the combatants of both sides. That was in 1995, on the fiftieth anniversary of the battle's end. The names of the deceased were engraved in a stand of marble walls in a new Peace Park. "I guess it's like our Vietnam Wall," an American eager to demonstrate mutual understanding remarked to Masahide Ota, governor of the Prefecture of Okinawa, before its unveiling. "In a way," Ota responded dryly. "But there are no Vietnamese names on the Vietnam Wall."

The governor, whom I'd met years before, when he was a professor of sociology and journalism, happens to be my chief Okinawan character. If any one-liner can suggest the disparity between civilian and military perceptions of fields of battle — and, in particular, between American and native calculations of *this* battle's costs and rewards — his is a strong candidate. To say that much time will elapse before a Washington wall displays the names of Vietnamese dead, military or civilian, is to suggest an inexact parallel, since that war didn't take place on American soil. But that only makes the Okinawan stance even more admirable, because the battle that took so many of them ravaged *their* homeland — which explains most of the divergence between their view of it and ours. It also provides an introduction to the sense in which those much-abused victims of the war remain victims, even now. Just because the suffering of these profoundly antimilitary people is so little known, they continue to suffer as the fall guys in one of the war's last dirty deals. Against their will, much of their island that was razed by Japanese and American explosives remains appropriated by feared and loathed military bases of the same two powers.

Roxbury, Connecticut
March 2001

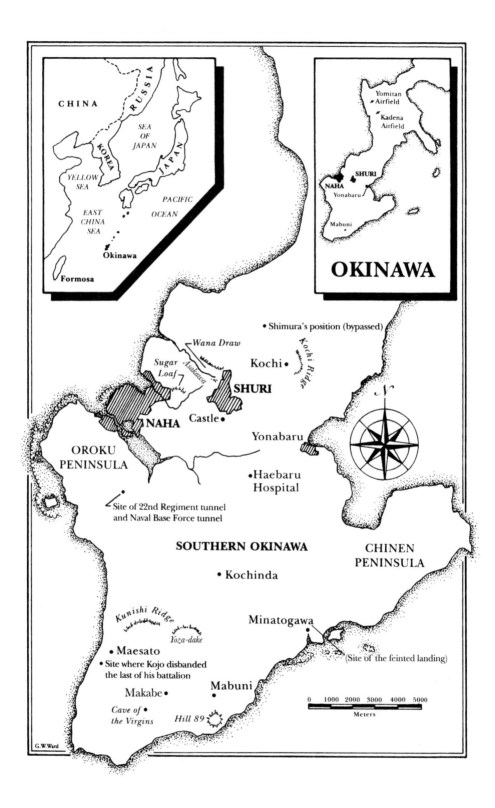

CHINA

RUSSIA

KOREA

SEA
OF
JAPAN

JAPAN

YELLOW
SEA

PACIFIC
OCEAN

EAST
CHINA
SEA

Okinawa

Formosa

Yomitan
Airfield

Kadena
Airfield

SHURI

NAHA
Yonabaru

Mabuni

OKINAWA

• Shimura's position (bypassed)

Wana Draw

Kochi Ridge

Sugar
Loaf

Asakawa

Kochi •

SHURI

Castle •

Yonabaru

NAHA

OROKU
PENINSULA

•Haebaru
Hospital

Site of 22nd Regiment tunnel
and Naval Base Force tunnel

SOUTHERN OKINAWA

CHINEN
PENINSULA

• Kochinda

Kunishi Ridge

Yoza-dake

Minatogawa

• Maesato
• Site where Kojo disbanded
the last of his battalion

Makabe •

Mabuni •

(Site of the feinted landing)

Cave of •
the Virgins

Hill 89

0 1000 2000 3000 4000 5000

Meters

G.W.Ward

Book I

1 · Operation Heaven Number One

What would we have done in olden times? We would have risked everything on one momentous gamble! Have we all become women? Hark back to history! Evoke the spirit of . . . [Admiral Isoroku] Yamamoto at Pearl Harbor.

. . . A show of spirit, that's what we want! The spirit of our glorious ancestors. The spirit of the Yamato people. The gods will come to our aid.
— The Combined Fleet's chief of operations, urging a sortie by *Yamato*

We die for sovereign and country. I understand that. But isn't there more to it than that? My death, my life, the defeat of Japan as a whole: I'd like to link them with something more general, more universal, something to do with values. What the devil is the purpose of all this?
— A reserve officer aboard *Yamato*

Isn't it enough to wear on your breasts the chrysanthemum emblem of the special attack force and to die with 'long live the Emperor' on your lips?
— The response of a regular *Yamato* officer

ON MARCH 25, 1945, an immense fleet of American warships closed on Okinawa, the largest pendant in the chain of Ryukyu Islands, which arcs gently toward Formosa from the Japanese homeland. The following day, hundreds of those ships began a final week of bombardment before invading the home of the once independent Okinawan dynasty. Three days later, Admiral Koshiro Oikawa, Emperor Hirohito's adviser on naval affairs, had an audience with the nearsighted monarch in Tokyo, some nine hundred miles northeast. His Majesty, deeply concerned, was eager to ensure his military leaders were ignoring no opportunity.

The meeting took place in the Imperial Palace, which lay in the center of Tokyo and at the heart of national beliefs. American pilots had been ordered to spare the serene grounds that occupied almost a square mile of the overcrowded city. Elsewhere, the bombing was less intense than in previous weeks only because so much of the capital had already been leveled. Air-raid sirens were again wailing when Oikawa was driven through the Imperial gates, and distant Okinawa was being pounded by wave after wave of planes from the American armada's carriers in addition to its heavy guns. Waiting with members of his staff in a damp bomb shelter near the Imperial library, the harried admiral tried to think how best to brief the Emperor about current operations.

Although Oikawa was the Imperial Navy's chief of staff as well as the Emperor's adviser, he was less than well informed. Intense rivalry with the commanders of the Combined Fleet kept him at arm's length from the vital decisions about operations. Imperial advisers now had an impossible task in any case. The Pacific War could no more be stopped than won. No one could acknowledge that the end was in sight, because the only possible end was the oblivion toward which the country was marching in lockstep.

The officers bowed deeply when the Emperor appeared, then seated themselves at a conference table. Hollywood would not have cast His Majesty for the role. Even in his field marshal's uniform, the "middle-aged guy with glasses," as a student of the period recently described the slight figure, looked more the shy academic than a belligerent empire's ceremonial leader. But Hirohito's people revered him as a direct descendent of the Sun Goddess, and Oikawa and his staff sat sideways in order to avert their gaze when they took their places at the table. Few Japanese permitted themselves a direct glance at the divine presence, let alone an opinion about his appearance.

If Hirohito had had the power to stop the war now, he may have considered it — not because he felt it had been wrong from the start but because it had taken such terrible turns. His Majesty hadn't always been the disapproving spectator of Japan's military adventures that the American occupation would pretend after the surrender. Never having seen anything shameful in the attack on Pearl Harbor, he relished victory even more than his cooks and his gardeners did, especially after the Pacific War began as well as it did for Japan. Nor was he as powerless or innocent as his postwar defenders would claim. On the contrary, he often studied battle plans attentively, sometimes making proposals for stronger action or asking questions that were interpreted as suggestions for altering tactics. That was particularly relevant to thousands of sailors now, for his questions to Oikawa were about to doom them.

The admiral's focus on preparations for Okinawa's defense was inescapable. If the enemy succeeded in landing troops there, the war would enter a stage of almost inconceivable menace. The island was a mere 350 miles from the southern tip of Kyushu, the southernmost of the four major Japanese home islands. And it was not an occupied territory but a sliver of the motherland, at least as a color on the map: The Ryukyus were one of the forty-seven Japanese prefectures.

The Emperor also worried that if the forthcoming battle there were lost, "the army and navy will lose the trust of the nation." Against those terrible threats, the need for what was called "special" measures was clear. The chief of staff informed the Emperor about provisions for kamikaze operations, which had already begun against the American fleet carrying out the pre-invasion bombardment. The Emperor urged him to "leave nothing to be desired" in executing those plans "with a hard struggle by all our forces, since [they] will decide the fate of our Empire." But Oikawa's assurance that two thousand planes were available for the suicide attacks troubled Hirohito. "Was that all?" he asked in his reedy voice. The admiral's hasty reply that the Army would contribute an additional fifteen hundred aircraft did not satisfy. "But where is the Navy?" His Majesty asked, his tone putting an edge to the question. "Are there no more ships? No surface forces?"

That sealed the fate of the Imperial Navy's *Yamato*, the world's biggest and best battleship. Horror of loss of face would grip Combined Fleet headquarters when they learned of the Emperor's query about why nothing had been planned for the surface ships. The same need to save face — in a war in defense of honor rather than of military advantage or territory — would cause much of the terrible waste at Okinawa. To the destruction would now be added a squadron of the last remaining operational warships, which Combined Fleet headquarters quickly undertook to send there.

A joyfully triumphant beginning made the war's current bleakness doubly difficult to accept. Few Japanese generals and fewer admirals had believed total victory could be won in a long struggle with America, but many had hoped swift, stinging blows would persuade Washington to permit Japan to pursue her interests in the Pacific rather than subject the American people to the hardships of war. The attack on Pearl Harbor that delivered the first one in December 1941 appeared successful beyond its proponents' wildest dreams. American brass, including the self-congratulating General Douglas MacArthur, had been almost unanimous in doubting that a nation inferior in every way their perceptions registered would contemplate risking such an "utterly stupid" and "almost fantastic" venture, which could only end in her own speedy destruction. "When the Japs come down here," an Associated Press correspondent allowed, conveying the pre-war self-assurance of the American garrison in the Philippines, "they'll be playing in the big leagues for the first time in their lives." That was shortly before the brilliantly daring raid, that Sunday morning of December 7, on the major U.S. naval base near Honolulu. Japanese planes killed and wounded four thousand Americans while sinking or severely disabling five of the eight battleships nestled in "battleship row."

It would later become common coinage that the tactical masterstroke at Pearl Harbor was a great strategic blunder, because it shook Americans from their pacifist isolationism — Hitler had invaded Poland two years earlier and now occupied most of Europe — and united them in hot resolve for vengeance. But at the time virtually every American saw the almost instant destruction of so much of the Pacific Fleet as a national calamity rather than a Japanese mistake. The near panic it prompted revealed more about America's susceptibility to paranoia than about the actual military situation — which, however, *was* gloomy in the short run.

The spectacular strikes and lightning landings that followed Pearl Harbor stunned Americans with disaster after disaster. In three months, Japan took vast areas of the Pacific by seizing island territories equivalent in size to half the United States. Her conquests soon extended to a near circle with a diameter of twenty-eight hundred miles, from Manchuria to China to Burma to the Dutch East Indies to New Guinea to five hundred miles west of Hawaii to the Bering Sea. Americans were particularly shocked by the fall of the Philippines despite her venerable U.S. garrison. The citadel of Corregidor, its fortifications protected by prodigious concrete, had been thought unconquerable. But nothing stopped the enduring, thirsting Japanese.

Their men were tougher and better trained. Many of their weapons were superior. The supposedly backward Orientals had better binoculars, range finders, and illumination devices, faster planes, and much more effective torpedoes. Their crack ships, relentlessly drilled under the most demanding conditions, were unequaled in seamanship and firepower. Their carrier pilots were the world's best. But the loss of great numbers of those pilots at the crucial Battle of Midway in June 1942 began turning the tide. Midway told virtually every Japanese admiral that the huge gamble of hard punches to persuade America to negotiate rather than fight was lost, for the Pearl Harbor strike had prompted a psychological effect opposite to the one intended. Instead of discouraging a people softened by democracy and luxury from shouldering the burdens of all-out war, it jolted the world's greatest economic power, whose industrial capacity was roughly ten times greater than Japan's, into unprecedented industrial and military action. Little could have better kindled righteous American wrath than the shock of the "sneak attack," as generations would know it (even after America began making her own such strikes against feeble states such as Grenada and Panama).

However, the Midway victory brought little relief to the Americans fighting in the Pacific, for whom the next thirty-three months might have been three decades. A succession of struggles, each more fierce than the last, was required to retake Japanese-captured territory. The Solomon Islands, Gilbert Islands, Mariana Islands, Bonin Islands . . . the names evoke images of supremely ferocious combat in atrocious conditions. Guadalcanal, Bougainville, Tarawa, Kwajalein, Peleliu, Guam, Tinian,

Saipan. . . . Not every island and atoll was host to progressively greater savagery, but the trend was clear: The nearer the site to the sacred Japanese homeland, the greater the resistance and blood. The first six days of fighting on Iwo Jima, about seven hundred miles south of Tokyo Bay, produced ten times the expected number of casualties. The total reached nearly twenty-six thousand Americans, most in their teens and early twenties, before some 250 Japanese launched a final suicide attack on the same March 26, 1945, when the American warships began their final pre-invasion bombardment of Okinawa.

It was time — as it had been for at least two savage years — for Tokyo to plan capitulation. But no matter how clear that was to Allied observers, the realization and logic were apparent to few Japanese. Their defense of honor, more important than the defense of any military position, could not be abandoned until many more could die suitably. Admission of defeat was so inconceivable to the military commanders who ruled the country that Admiral Oikawa wouldn't think of mentioning it to his Emperor that March 29, although the clearly futile defense of Okinawa the two discussed would almost inevitably be far costlier than all previous island bloodbaths. American troops headed there rhymed "the Golden Gate in '48," meaning they feared Japan's full defeat — and their homecoming — might take three more years. Although Okinawa would be the beginning of the end, the lost war was far from over for Japan, and thus for the Allies.

Yamato wasn't merely "the mightiest engine of destruction afloat," as the U.S. Naval Institute would call her. The masterpiece of naval design and construction was also a symbol and a legend, a source of immense pride for the Japanese people. Her supremely graceful profile belied her size. Even the most recently commissioned American battlewagons of the *Iowa* class looked bulky by comparison. A sweeping foredeck made *Yamato* a marine greyhound, eager to leap upon the enemy — and able to, thanks to an innovative hull shape that helped boost her speed well above what was expected from a ship of her size and firepower. Twelve engine and boiler rooms discharged their exhaust through a single funnel that swept back at a rakish twenty-five-degree angle. With her teak weatherdeck unbroken from streamlined stem to stern — a distance almost the length of three football fields — she was a singularly elegant structure, and the crew's quarters on "Hotel Yamato," as lesser ships' envious sailors nicknamed her, were positively indulgent by Japanese standards.

She even had revolutionary air-conditioning in many compartments, an extraordinary luxury in a navy that valued difficult conditions for their nourishment of the commitment to self-sacrifice inherent in *Yamato damashii,* "the Japanese fighting spirit." More to the point, she was not only one of the most intelligent and efficient capital ships ever built but also the most powerful and most heavily armored, fully 40 percent larger than the four ships of the same great *Iowa* class. With main armor of sixteen inches and protection of vital parts such as magazines by belts up to two feet thick, she was built to withstand the heaviest American naval shells and thousand-pound bombs dropped from eleven thousand feet.

Her own main armament consisted of nine 18.1-inch guns, compared to 16-inchers on the *Iowa*-class "wagons." They fired shells of 3,220 pounds — 30 percent heavier than America's new 16-inchers — a distance of nearly thirty miles, which meant the ship could hit the most powerful enemy vessels well before they could try to close within their range of her. Since heavier guns virtually guaranteed victory in surface battles with lesser ships, peerless *Yamato* seemed certain to destroy the best American battleship, even small groups of them, if she encountered them without carriers. Her armor and ingenious damage-control dispositions throughout her five decks made her nearly unbeatable and unsinkable by most surface opposition.

It said much about national priorities that such a superb vessel, with her enormous consumption of resources (including enough steel for a railroad line between Tokyo and Osaka, 250 miles apart), had been built at a time when the majority of Japanese panted to feed themselves. Only fierce ambition, matching sacrifice, and impassioned science permitted such a colossal construction project of such advanced conception, with dozens of major design and engineering triumphs and hundreds of components on the leading edge of naval technology, to be launched on such a relatively thin industrial base.

Yamato's keel had been laid in 1937, when Japanese military spending consumed 70 percent of government expenditure. The drydock was heavily screened by bamboo matting to keep her existence secret. She and a sister ship called *Musashi*, begun a year later, were to be the ace in the hole in a war with America, which, the Imperial Navy believed, wouldn't build battleships too large to use the Panama Canal. American bombs had sunk *Musashi* in October 1944, five months before the Emperor's fatal questions to Admiral Oikawa. The following month, American torpedoes sank giant *Shinano*, laid down in 1939 and later recommissioned as an aircraft carrier. The submarine that made that extraordinary kill had taken time off from her lifeguard patrol for downed B-29s because no air raids on the Japanese mainland were scheduled that night. Six torpedoes hit the converted supercarrier as she was on her way in internal waters to the great naval port of Kure.

But the first of her class was intact and fit. It didn't matter to most Japanese that that was because she'd so far done little fighting. What everyone could see was that the Imperial Japanese Navy's only surviving operational battleship remained silvery and spotless. *Yamato* was its "lucky ship," a survivor of the Battle of the Philippine Sea as well as Midway, and the only one to emerge from Leyte Gulf with only two insignificant bomb hits. It seemed even more natural that she remained magnificent even at that hopeless stage of the war, for she bore the national name: The Japanese often called themselves "the Yamato people," after the ancient kingdom on the Yamato Plain on Honshu, the largest mainland island. Thus the poetic, evocative synonym for Japan rang with symbolic significance, the very kind that sustained the Japanese people as the war turned toward disaster. The pride of the fleet was thought to have a special mission.

Her narrower one that first week of April, the planned foray to Okinawa, was supremely hazardous. For despite *Yamato*'s crushing power, she was on her way toward obsolescence the moment she was quietly commissioned, several days after Pearl Harbor — which, ironically, ended the battleship's reign as the king of naval power. The attack's triumph forever laid to rest the notion that surface ships would fight it out for control of the Pacific, with victory going to the behemoths with the biggest guns and toughest armor.

One of the old campaigners who best knew that was the "Japanese Nelson" who'd planned the tactically and technically masterful Pearl Harbor strike. Isoroku Yamamoto was also called the "reluctant admiral" because he'd long opposed war against the United States. "Do not uncover the teapot and release a typhoon," he warned when a staff officer first suggested the attack on Pearl Harbor. Yamamoto also vigorously opposed the building of the superbattleships. Asked how aircraft could possibly sink the new titans with their prodigious antiaircraft armament, he replied prophetically that "the fiercest serpent can be overcome by a swarm of ants" — just as the Pacific War would repeatedly confirm. As much as *Yamato*'s officers loved her, numerous sinkings of great capital ships by planes since 1941 led some to classify the vessel with the Great Wall of China and the Pyramids as "the world's three great follies, prize examples of uselessness."

Japanese admirals knew the new dominance of air power better than anyone. One of the most prominent was Minister of the Navy Mitsumasa Yonai, who was among the minority of senior admirals who had tried to avert war with America. Now Yonai regretted that the skeptics had allowed themselves to be convinced, against their better judgment, that quick, smashing defeats would persuade comfort-loving Americans not to make the sacrifices required for a lengthy struggle. The minister had become so appalled by the course of the war and his own complicity in extending it to America that he, a former prime minister, was holding secret talks, in fear for his life, with a few like-minded officers who hoped against hope to find a way to end hostilities.

Yonai was now less concerned with the debate over plans for *Yamato* than with trying to replace the present prime minister with someone who would permit a more open pursuit of peace. He felt obliged to work for the survival of Japan herself, not the fate of just one battleship, or even of a fleet. Still, he leaned against *Yamato*'s mission to Okinawa because it would be useless, even harmful, to the existence of the country as a whole.

The Navy's senior staff cleaved into factions. Many knew as well as Yonai that the war was lost but were afraid to say so. Others yearned for immediate action no matter what the odds or consequences. Better that the remnants of the fleet make a glorious final charge than they be sunk at their moorings by carrier-based American planes now hitting home-land bases, with the insufferable humiliation to naval and national self-respect. Although the proportion of "mystical" firebrands was distinctly smaller than in the Army, they used the same kinds of emotional appeal to honor and glory, to the Japanese spirit, and to obligations to the Emperor. "Even if the odds were only 10 percent in favor, the effort would be worthwhile," argued Captain Shegenori Kami, the Combined Fleet's chief of operations. "A true samurai doesn't ask whether his efforts pay. He merely seeks the opportunity to sacrifice himself."

Much lower in the command chain, the skipper of *Yahagi*, a light cruiser that would anchor *Yamato*'s screen, disagreed. Captain Tameichi Hara, one of the distinguished fighting officers who went against the grain of that Japanese appeal for sacrifice and more sacrifice, pointedly told his men that they should not hesitate to return alive. "Our mission appears suicidal and it is," Hara addressed his crew. "But I wish to emphasize that suicide is not the objective. . . . You are not to be slain merely as sacrifices for the nation." That that opinion had to be ventured said a good deal about the grip on the country by those who preached the value of precisely such sacrifices. "If the ship should be damaged or sunk, don't hesitate to save yourself," went Hara's key order — which he himself would follow in a rare reversal of the canon that Japanese commanding officers must go down with their ships.

Other skippers argued that the overriding consideration was the simple duty to fight. The Navy's commander in chief was swayed by one argument, then another. Of course the Imperial Navy must not lose more face, but which alternative offered more certainty of that? This time the Combined Fleet's staff did not ignore Naval Chief of Staff Oikawa. They interpreted the Emperor's questions to him as a reproach. It would have been impossible for the Navy not to carry out what His Majesty appeared to have suggested with characteristic Japanese indirectness: that surface ships must join the sacrifice of the kamikaze pilots. Even to admit to him the tiny number of fighting ships left would have been an intolerable loss of face.

It would be an exaggeration to say that at this stage of the war, the entire Yamato nation was preparing to do what *Yamato* had been ordered to at Okinawa, or that the same obligation to make the ultimate sacrifice would be expected of the Japanese people as a whole when the home islands were invaded. But the parallels were strong. When nothing was left but a supreme gesture of sacrificial defiance against an overwhelming force, that gesture had to be made. As a senior officer on one of *Yamato*'s escort ships remembered it, Hirohito's questions "implied essentially this: 'Others are dying. Kamikaze pilots are dying gloriously. Why are you doing nothing? You too should die!'"

When reports of the Imperial briefing reached the Combined Fleet's staff later the same day, the debate was resolved. Operation *Ten ichigo* — Heaven Number One — was assured, and *Yamato* was as good as sunk.

> *The time has come.* Kamikaze Yamato, *be a truly divine wind!*
> — *Yamato*'s executive officer

> *These days the entire nation shares the fate of having death on the doorstep.*
> — Ensign Mitsuru Yoshida of *Yamato*

> *Now came the first sextet of dive bombers from the* Bennington *under Lt. Cmdr. Ed De Garmo. . . . The* Dauntlesses *. . . came out of the clouds on radar and dove after the big battleship. The heavy bursts of flack were about one thousand feet short and below the altitude of the oncoming planes.*
> *"In pairs!" De Garmo screamed into his JV. "Let's get the big bastard!"*
> — Lawrence Cortesi, *Valor at Okinawa*

Another circumstance helped explain the naval chiefs' urge to act, even at the certain cost of the Navy's last and finest jewel. The destruction of Japan's major cities distressed them even more than the enemy's imminent landing on Okinawa. Operating from new bases on Saipan, Tinian, and Guam, those islands of the earlier bloodbaths, state-of-the-art American aircraft were virtually erasing urban targets. Night after night, the industrial centers and their civilian populations were being blasted by hundreds of B-29s loaded to their unprecedented limits with high-explosive and incendiary bombs. The awe-inspiring Superfortresses were commanded by Major General Curtis LeMay, father of the new strategy of saturation bombing. LeMay, who'd arrived from Europe in January to take over the 21st Bomber Command, promised to beat Japan "back into the Dark Ages." The shift from precision bombing of strategic sites to the destruction of entire cities led a Yokohama observer to report that looting presented no problem after a raid because nothing was left but rubble.

Tokyo's biggest turn had come three weeks before Oikawa's briefing of the Emperor, while American landing forces for Okinawa were en route on troopships or being assembled on staging islands. During the night of

March 9–10, 334 warplanes incinerated the capital's central districts with ten times the tonnage of the Luftwaffe bombs that had caused "the Great Fire of London" in September 1940. Tokyo's Great Fire Raid, as it became known in turn, roasted residents on the streets and in their homes as if entire city blocks had been shoveled into ovens. The horror in those congested sixteen square miles of wood and bamboo was unequaled anywhere on the home islands. By the count of the charred corpses, even the forthcoming atomic devastation of Hiroshima and Nagasaki would be lesser events.* Measured by numbers of torturous deaths or decibels of human pain, that tragedy would be exceeded only by what awaited the Okinawan people.

That night's strong wind whipped the flames of American incendiary bombs into a wall of fire roiling hundreds of feet in the air. A quarter of a million buildings were consumed. Before daylight, nearly a fifth of Tokyo's industrial areas and 63 percent of its commercial districts had disappeared. The heat ignited hordes at a distance; people running from the flames as fast as they could burst into balls of fire. Others jumped into canals for salvation and were boiled alive there. It was probably the greatest one-night disaster, with the largest sum of suffering, endured by any city in world history. When senior naval personnel debated the pros and cons of *Yamato*'s sortie three weeks later, the Navy Ministry's windows remained caked in black from the smoke and volunteers were cremating the last piles of carbonized corpses.

Kure, on the Inland Sea about two-thirds of the way from Tokyo to mainland Japan's southernmost city of Kagoshima — and about twenty miles from Hiroshima — had so far been spared major devastation, although it was home to Japan's largest naval base, including the yard where *Yamato* had been launched three years earlier. Kure's turn for destruction would come six weeks later, during the battle for Okinawa's Sugar Loaf Hill. Meanwhile, its food rations were approaching the starvation level, and cadets at the Naval Academy on the tiny island of Eta facing the port were jokingly dubbed moles because they were too busy digging caves and tunnels for refuge from the awaited bombing to learn much seamanship.

*Casualty statistics for the conventional and atomic bombings are more art than science. But although no single set of commonly accepted figures exists for those three cities, prudent averaging suggests the atomic bomb killed some 140,000 in Hiroshima, half within days, the other half from slower-acting burns and radiation. But the conventional bombs dropped on Tokyo that night of March 9–10 probably left about 197,000 dead and missing — "scorched and boned and baked to death," in General LeMay's description. And his operations were far from their climax. In late May, when the fighting on Okinawa would reach its apogee, American planes would drop thirty-two hundred tons of high explosives on Yokohama, the same on Osaka, and four thousand more on Tokyo, consuming new districts in another sea of flames.

While the enemy fleet's last pre-invasion salvos were pounding Okinawa, *Yamato* was awaiting routine repairs in Kure. Moored to an outer buoy, the great ship seemed to a twenty-two-year-old ensign named Mitsuru Yoshida "like a gigantic rock commanding all around her." Within hours of the American landing on Okinawa, some six hundred miles south, the rock was ordered under way. A detailed chart of Okinawan waters on the chart table showed an arc representing the range of *Yamato*'s big guns to the landing beaches. She didn't sail directly there, however, but to a safer anchorage behind an island some fifteen miles from Hiroshima while the plans for her sortie were made.

Combined Fleet headquarters' order to launch her unique operation came in Fleet Signal 607 to Vice Admiral Seiichi Ito, commander of Task Force II, as the 2nd Fleet battle group to be led by *Yamato* had been designated. Ito, a graduate student at Yale in the late 1920s, had opposed the mission from the start, certain that it held no hope without air cover. Although Combined Fleet headquarters had stopped communicating with its 2nd Fleet, perhaps out of embarrassment, it sent its chief of staff, Ito's classmate and close friend at the Naval Academy, to fly in to reassure him. Since no naval or military argument could accomplish that, the classmate used moral suasion: Task Force II was being requested to die gloriously, heralding the death of all Japanese who preferred that to surrender. "Sooner or later, it will come to a special [suicide] attack by the entire nation, the hundred million of us." Ito was asked to "die admirably" as a model for the hundred million.

The admiral agreed, but not all his captains did when summoned to a conference. After sometimes heated hours of discussion, the commander of the single cruiser among *Yamato*'s escorts told his crew they were participating in "a suicide mission pure and simple . . . but unlike those our Air Force is carrying out [the kamikazes], ours hasn't got the slightest chance of destroying an important target." The admiral in command of the entire nine-ship screen — that light cruiser plus eight destroyers — protested that "without air protection, we'll needlessly sacrifice the lives of five thousand sailors. . . . I'd gladly die at this very moment if I thought my death would help save our honorable homeland. But . . . the [screening ships'] officers believe they can accomplish more if allowed to go out alone as raiders to attack American ships. I agree with them." "This isn't even a kamikaze mission," the admiral in command of the squadron of the eight destroyers would add several days later, "since that implies the chance of chalking up a worthy target."

But in the end, Task Force Commander Ito broke a long silence at the conference by reflecting that all were being given an appropriate opportunity to perform their highest duty. "A samurai lives so that he is always prepared to die," he said. That unchallengeable declaration — although it skirted the salient question of whether that was the best *time* to die — ended the argument at the command level. "Orders are orders," a captain observed. "We must make the best of the situation."

As for *Yamato*'s officers, many were also aware — even while hoping otherwise — that the mission could only be a suicidal display of useless courage. Few knew precisely that there were *fifteen* American fleet carriers in Okinawan waters, plus a dozen smaller escort carriers and the help, if needed, of five more of the Royal Navy's best, which were operating nearby. But even a majority of the junior officers recognized the foray as an exercise in fantasy. With a casualty rate of over 90 percent among Naval Academy graduates, they accepted that little life remained for them too. It wasn't going to their deaths but going pointlessly that disturbed some of them. They wanted to die in a battle that might inflict damage on the enemy.

American air reconnaissance, they said in confidence among themselves, was too thorough for the ship to avoid being detected far before her surface guns were in range to fire a single shot. And once she was spotted, American air power was too overwhelming, just as American submarines had become too prevalent and efficient, for her to escape destruction. "Which country showed the world what airplanes could do by sinking the *Prince of Wales?*" an ironic voice asked. And even if *Yamato* did manage to reach Okinawa, so many enemy battleships and heavy cruisers would be waiting for her that she'd have no hope against their combined might.

Against that, the chief argument remained what it had been at higher levels: the duty, glory, and joy of dying for Emperor and country. At least one officer said aloud that their deaths would find purpose by contributing to defeat rather than victory. "How else can Japan be saved except by losing and coming to its senses? . . . We'll die as harbingers of Japan's new life. That's where our real salvation lies, doesn't it?"

But the expedition's operational plan was of course rooted in quite different notions, even if it was uncharacteristically ambiguous for Japanese practice. Task Force II's primary task was to serve as a decoy for weakening enemy defenses against a forthcoming mass kamikaze attack by luring away American carrier-based interceptors. The ships were to survive as long as possible and shoot down as many enemy planes as possible, after which any that managed to reach Okinawa were to charge a large enemy anchorage offshore at daybreak on April 8. *Yamato*'s huge guns would devastate enemy naval and shore targets, perhaps sinking enough transports and causing enough shock to force an American withdrawal from the island. Finally, the ship would beach herself and continue firing until all ammunition was expended, whereupon surviving crew members would disembark to fight on land.

During the ceremonial drinking of sake the evening before the sailing, the ship seemed overwhelmed by the immensity of her mission and possible tragedy. The men performed their roles like actors trapped in a morality play. A young ensign at one of the solemnly gay "drinking jamborees" dropped a glass raised to toast their departure, an unlucky omen in Japanese tradition. It shattered on the deck.

But there was also radiance in the ship's various divisions. Some young officers affectionately patted the bald head of Captain Kosaku Ariga, one of the Navy's most courageous and popular senior officers, who joined the fun instead of punishing that exceedingly uncommon display of liberty. Love for the captain and for his legendary bravery and skill filled every heart. There were tumultuous cheers for him and for the treasured ship, which, with her nine escorts, got under way the following afternoon, VOW TO DIE FOR THE EMPEROR chalked on a blackboard behind a main turret.

April 6 was a glorious spring day on the calm Inland Sea. His previous disapproval of the "suicide sortie" in the past, Tameichi Hara, the captain of the light cruiser, now felt "this beautiful homeland is worthy of our sacrifices." All hands assembled on the foredeck for the executive officer's reading of a farewell message from the Combined Fleet's commander in chief. They again heard the task force identified as "special," meaning essentially suicidal, and the attack described as "unparalleled in its heroic bravery." An urging to "exalt the glorious tradition of the Imperial Navy's surface forces" was intended to uplift spirits — and did. When the executive officer read, "The fate of the Empire truly rests on this one action," all instantly recognized the echo of Admiral Heichachiro Togo's almost identical exhortation to obliterate the Russian fleet at Tsushima in 1905 — which was indeed accomplished. That encouragement had been repeated often enough in the present war — including by Admiral Yamamoto to the attack planes about to take off for Pearl Harbor — to have become a cliché. But despite the almost pathetic note in evoking those glorious moments to a fleet steaming to certain annihilation, the celebrated words boosted spirits all the same. After all, stunning victories by naval forces *had* swung the balance for Japan in the past. "Fight gloriously to the death and completely destroy the enemy fleet. . . . Render this operation the turning point of the war!"

The crew bowed in the direction of the Emperor, sang the national anthem, and shouted "Banzai!" three times. The assistant radar officer, twenty-two-year-old Ensign Mitsuru Yoshida, was deeply moved, although he had no illusions about victory. The incomparable vessel on course for her sacred mission seemed the very soul of eternal, exalted Japan. Eyes watered and spines tingled as if the entire nation, present and past, were a military band playing a send-off march.

"Do a good job," officers encouraged. "Die a death worthy of you." Okinawa was six hundred miles away.

The Japanese public, when they finally learned of the mission's outcome, would long believe *Yamato* sailed with too little fuel for a round-trip, especially after the seeming confirmation by the two thousand tons of bunker oil noted in the official departure report. But young officers on the Combined Fleet staff could not leave the world's best ship with no chance to return. They knew the staggering odds as well as anyone. If the ship did have the inconceivably good luck to reach Okinawa undetected, she'd have a fighting chance against any two, possibly even three or four, American battleships and cruisers, but none against the dozen or more that would engage her — and that wasn't counting the enemy carriers and their planes, the critical factor in every major engagement at sea. Still, the junior officers rushed around Kure, frantically securing more precious fuel from overlooked storage places and ships not participating in the mission. Contrary to accounts by Japanese admirals and Western historians, *Yamato*'s bunkers held more than enough to bring her back to her base.

Now steaming outward, her majesty continued making it emotionally unthinkable that she would do otherwise. "Thanks to [her] incomparable seaworthiness," Ensign Yoshida recorded about the first hours under way, "there is no pitch or roll; even on the bridge we have the illusion of standing on firm ground." Yet the sea was deadly. With *Yamato* in the center and the cruiser *Yahagi* bringing up the rear, the force deployed in a formation for night sailing under threat of submarine attack. Although the Bungo Strait, which it entered from the Inland Sea, was part of what American submariners had dubbed the "Hit Parade" waters, that narrow passage had to be run because B-29s had just remined safer straits east and west.

The beautiful spring day was ending in glorious twilight. Sailors gazed at early cherry blossoms, ancient symbol of Japanese purity and evanescence, modern symbol of suicide volunteers. Lovingly observing Kyushu a few miles to starboard and Shikoku a few miles to port, the crew tried not to think that this was their last sight of the home islands, and to forget that "the enemy that controls the sky controls the sea."

He also controlled the radio waves. During the previous week, an American cryptanalysis center in Pearl Harbor had been working hard on secret Fleet Signal 607 and the accompanying flurry of intercepted radio messages. Intelligence analysts had put together an accurate summary of Task Group II's composition and intentions even before it set sail — and *Yamato* got no farther than the Bungo Strait before the first American sightings were made. In the late afternoon of April 6, *Hackleback* and

Threadfin, two submarines patrolling for the Japanese group, radioed an accurate description of it to Task Force 58, the American strike force at sea in the area. Trailing the formation by five miles, the submarines watched in fascination. The contact reports of American planes that took over the surveillance the following morning — a minute-by-minute record of the force's position, course, and speed — were monitored by *Yamato*'s radio personnel, but the captain could do nothing about them short of turning back. Hours after sailing, the great ship was doomed.

The men who manned their watches on the bridge that night worked with quiet intensity, the highest-ranking officers distinguished by fluorescent initials on their caps. Just before midnight, Ensign Yoshida climbed a ladder to the bridge for lookout duty. Facing his home in Tokyo, he bowed and said a brief prayer. Task Force 58 was roughly a hundred miles northeast of Okinawa when the submarine reports told it what it had been waiting to hear. A search plane from the carrier *Essex* found the *Yamato* group at dawn the following morning. From then on, it was relentlessly shadowed by aircraft flying just out of range of Japanese anti-aircraft armament, among them flying boats based at Kerama Retto, an island group fifteen miles west of Okinawa that Americans had taken a few days before landing on Okinawa itself.

Admiral Raymond Spruance, commander of the 5th Fleet, had intended to give his battleships first crack at the *Yamato* as a kind of combat training.* Adrenaline surged through the American crews when Spruance signaled them to prepare for a battle of behemoths that would surely be the war's last major surface action. But Task Force 58's vice admiral, Marc Mitscher, wanted to show that his planes could sink the world's most powerful ship, and Spruance yielded to his subordinate in direct command of the fighting unit. Mitscher ordered Task Force 58's four groups into launching positions. Reconnaissance planes from no less than a dozen carriers stalked *Yamato* while their strike craft were readied. In the unlikely event that those carriers and their escort of eight battleships and a dozen heavy cruisers would be unable to deal with the vastly weaker enemy group, older ships from the flotilla bombarding Okinawa also made ready to engage: six battleships (of the ten in the shore-bombardment force), seven cruisers, and twenty-one destroyers.

---

*While serving in Washington some twenty years earlier, Spruance had become quite friendly with Seiichi Ito, now commander of Task Force II, then assistant naval attaché at the Japanese embassy, where many other top Japanese admirals also served. Some Japanese observers held the romantic notion that Spruance might have favored using battleships rather than aircraft carriers in order to give his old friend the chance to go down fighting in a last surface action.

The 5th Fleet, so named when commanded by Spruance, became the 3rd Fleet when Admiral William Halsey, with whom Spruance alternated in 1945, took his turn.

Ninety minutes after the sighting of *Yamato* from the air, the task groups began launching their strikes from near Okinawa. The first main attack of 280 planes included dive-bombers with thousand- and five-hundred-pound bombs and torpedo bombers with the latest torpedoes. The flying boats, which had been shadowing the prey from a protecting overcast, guided them to their target, now just over halfway to Okinawa.

On board *Yamato*, there was some relief that the force had come so far without damage, despite the enemy search planes that were known to be plotting its position minute by minute. At noon, in the open waters of the East China Sea, a smiling force commander expressed confidence that all had gone well on the morning watch even though a radio report from a lookout on a Ryukyuan island north of Okinawa had announced that an estimated 250 enemy planes were headed in his direction. Half an hour later, a new radar contact was made and a hoarse voice reported the approaching aircraft's direction and range. The warning was so similar to hundreds of shipboard drills that the crew found it hard to accept as real. But the tension quickly surged as lookouts strained to see the enemy. At last two Grummans were spotted, then five, then thirty. *Yamato*'s huge number of antiaircraft guns had been bolstered by even more before she sailed. On Captain Ariga's order, six 6-inch secondary batteries, twenty-four 5-inch antiaircraft, and 150 machine guns commenced firing at the same instant, joined by the escorting destroyers' main and secondary batteries. The roar was as terrible as the sight of so many hostile planes.

No other Japanese force could come close to putting up so much flak. But although *Yamato*'s main batteries had once shot down an entire ten-plane formation, the force now faced far too many planes piloted by men with too much talent. A bomb hit one of the destroyers almost immediately. She exposed her crimson underbelly, lifted her stern into the air, and sank in less than a minute, leaving a few dozen survivors. And despite the black curtain of shell bursts and shrapnel from *Yamato*, despite desperate evasive maneuvers with her 150,000-horsepower engines straining mightily at full throttle, two Curtiss Helldivers penetrated the curtain. In minutes, they hit the ship with two bombs near the aft tower, destroying one of her radar rooms. Four minutes later, a torpedo bomber scored a hit on the port bow. A hot fragment killed a sailor near Ensign Yoshida. Through the deafening din of the explosions and antiaircraft fire, he heard "the dull thud of his skull striking against the bulkhead and sniffed fresh blood in the pall of smoke" rising from the hits.

After the first strike broke off, the chief of staff speculated that pilots of such fearless skill in bearing down to bomb and torpedo in the face of the ship's great antiaircraft fire must be of the enemy elite. But during the ensuing lull, some sailors assured themselves they'd survived the worst: The enemy carriers had surely exhausted themselves. Knowing a single torpedo couldn't seriously damage the great ship, her officers tried to make light of the hit. As medical corpsmen removed the body of a sailor from the bridge, Captain Ariga comforted the others. "We're still afloat and still fighting," the famous veteran declared.

The second wave, which arrived less than an hour after the first, had so many planes that a gunner likened the little spots under the clouds to sesame seeds. Bullets and shrapnel flew as thick as buckshot. Three sailors toppled simultaneously on young Yoshida. A fellow ensign tried to rise and bandage his thigh with a blood-soaked towel. As he was placed on a stretcher, he turned pale, smiled slightly, and fell back dead. The smell of human fat heavy in the air and the flocks of sailors blown apart by direct hits so that "not even the stench of their deaths [was] left to float in the air" created a kind of phantasmagoria. One of the first two bombs destroyed the compartment that housed the scopes for the air-search radar, a devastating loss.

Yamato's antiaircraft fire remained "without parallel" in the Japanese Navy. Her remarkable agility allowed her to dodge torpedoes as if she were a much smaller ship. She fired her 18-inch guns into the sea, presumably to down low-flying torpedo planes with the massive waterspouts. Still, the number of planes and their pilots' skill unnerved the Japanese gunners. No fewer than five torpedoes struck the port side during the second wave. The "invulnerable" ship began listing to port as more bombs rained on her, causing enormous casualties.

Even the near misses inflicted heavy damage. Their waterspouts were so fierce that they threatened to shatter metal high on the bridge. In the almost continuous attacks from 1300 to 1417 hours, the sailors lost track of the waves. The third one, of over a hundred planes, arrived on the heels of the second and scored several direct bomb hits near the stack and two more torpedo hits, again port amidships. Not even the least sinkable ship could take infinite damage. The six torpedo hits on the port side caused serious flooding, despite 1,150 watertight compartments designed to prevent it.

The list weakened morale and threatened fighting capability, which would be cut in half if it went to five degrees. Another ingenious engineering design allowed lists to be corrected by flooding the corresponding spaces on the opposite side. When the skipper ordered that measure, Ensign Yoshida immediately telephoned to warn the crews of the starboard boiler and engine rooms — but too late. Caught between the cold seawater rushing in and the steam of damaged boilers, several hundred men — who until that moment had "made the ship go, battling sweltering heat amid deafening noise, uncomplaining throughout" — were atomized.

Confined in the depths of the ship with no way of knowing how the battle is going, their bodies bathed in sweat and oil, they can converse and
communicate only by hand signals. . . . In the instant the water rushes in,
the black gang on duty are dashed to pieces, turned into drops of spray.
They see nothing and hear nothing; shattered into lumps, they dissolve.

At the price of those several hundred lives, the ship's trim was nearly restored, but her speed and maneuverability were much reduced. Low in
the water and moving slowly, *Yamato* was an increasingly easy target. The
fourth wave, of over 150 planes, landed at least ten more bombs topside
and gouged out more of the port side with new torpedo hits. Her steering
gear disabled, the ship was almost out of control. Still, professional
officers marveled at the flying skill that made the American planes so
different from practice targets. Yoshida noticed the flushed faces of the
pilots bearing down on him one after another, their eyes opened wide or
squeezed tight. "Coming in again and again on the ideal approach, precisely, exactly, calmly, they evoke in us a sense of exhilaration. Virtuosi.
Theirs is a strength we can't divine, a force we cannot fathom." At the
same time, Japanese officers were surprised that no pilot, even among the
few who were hit, thought to crash his plane into the ship, kamikaze-style.

The once peerless vessel was a nightmare of desolation. Everything
topside was a jumble of jagged steel and chunks of human flesh seared to
blackened lumps. Torrents of the crew's blood washed body parts along
the slanting deck. The convergence of torpedoes flooded the supposedly
impregnable communications department. The "watertight" radio room
had taken so much water that the ship had to rely entirely on light
bankers and flag signals to communicate with her screen. Without radio
capability, the giant vessel seemed to be disintegrating into separate parts
while she floated in the water "like a chunk of waterlogged wood."

Hope you will bring back a nice fish for breakfast.
— Signal from the commander of the American landing forces to the
    commander of the gunfire and covering forces just before the sighting of
    Yamato

*The rail's rivets are icy against my palms but inside my body I feel a flush of
warmth.*
*Father, mother, older sister, late brother-in-law lost in action a year ago. They
stand clearly before me.*
*And the faces of acquaintances, teachers and friends pass before my mind's
eye and face. . . .*
I am grateful to you, I whisper repeatedly, instinctively. . . .
I have gained the road to an easy death. Death is easy.
*You not blessed with death, you who are still forced to live. How will you
endure all the days after tomorrow?*
— Mitsuru Yoshida, *Requiem for Battleship* Yamato

When the final attack began at 1400 hours, the list was so great that it exposed the starboard side of the vulnerable belly. Severe damage to the rudder ended all evasive action, making the ship a nearly stationary target for more torpedoes. Seventy degrees of list. An incredible eighty degrees! Most ships sink at half that angle. Two years earlier, undergraduate Yoshida seemed destined to join Japan's elite from Tokyo Imperial University, its chief training ground. Now the ensign watched his "unsinkable giant ship" writhe in torment, "an ideal target for bombs, nothing more." Overwhelmed by fatigue, the living kept to their duty amid the fearful desolation until they joined the corpses strewn about them. To the living, Captain Ariga, renowned for his bravery, shouted, "Hold on, men! Hold on!" The encouragement of the burly, beloved Gorilla, as he was nicknamed, did as much and as little as any display could. Since great *Yamato*'s fate was certain, her amazing strength served only to prolong her agony.

With the ship helpless and her antiaircraft fire drastically reduced, the battle became a kind of exercise for the American planes. So many of the fourth wave's 386 were now circling above that they had to wait their turns for new runs, especially after rain squalls joined the low clouds to obscure the targets. Still, the enjoyment had its price: One Avenger's bombing run was so low that *Yamato*'s final explosion set it afire. The pilot bailed out, and two PBM seaplanes that had been among the first to locate Task Force II's position early that morning spotted his rubber raft. One served as a decoy for Japanese fire while the other neatly landed to pluck the pilot from a seaweed of Japanese corpses and survivors.* Those sailors and officers still able to see were dumbstruck by the American valor and pain to save an individual life.

(The rescue would be much written about, but seldom with a mention that the same crippled Avenger's two other crewmen had parachute trouble and drowned. If all men are equal in their Creator's eyes and families' hearts, the selection of those who are celebrated is as unfair as the tiny percentage who are chosen for combat during wartime and killed.)

But now there were thousands more unsung Japanese heroes than American, including Admiral Seiichi Ito. From his prestigious place on doomed *Yamato*'s bridge, the force commander who had helped devise the strategy of the war's every important naval battle silently watched the destruction and carnage he'd foreseen when opposing the operation. Now he ordered it broken off and directed the surviving ships to return to port after rescuing the living from their disabled sisters.

*Taking off again, the PBM delivered the pilot to an Okinawan airfield called Yomitan, which Marines had taken a week earlier, hours after their initial landing on Easter Sunday. See p. 108.

That order required great courage and resolve. Some senior officers in the group resented it bitterly, seeing cowardice in Ito's retreat from "a hundred million deaths rather than surrender!" Perhaps his decision to abandon the operation at that final moment was an expression of "I told you so." The admiral shook hands with officers who crawled to him through the slanting deck's wreckage and pleaded to stay at his side. He issued a final order to save themselves and retired to his private quarters just under the bridge. His door did not open again.

Universally admired Captain Ariga ordered all hands on deck. Even as the few still alive below struggled out of hatches, water cascaded into the openings, drowning others. Smoke too thick for flags to be seen required that the remaining destroyers be signaled by lamp to come alongside for removal of *Yamato*'s survivors. But the destroyers kept their distance, fearing the great hulk would suck them to the bottom together with herself. Many of the living on the battleship did not want rescue in any case. Some bound themselves together to lessen the possibility of floating or involuntarily struggling to the surface. A sailor who volunteered to stand guard at the battle flag earned an equally proud death by clinging unwaveringly to the staff as the flag dipped below the waves. When Captain Ariga suddenly remembered the portraits of the Emperor and Empress that had pride of place in the senior wardroom, he was assured they would not suffer the unspeakable disgrace of being captured after floating to the surface. The officer in charge of the sacred images was guarding them in his quarters, his hatch locked from the inside.

Ariga had no more wish to leave the ship than did Admiral Ito. To ensure that he wouldn't, he had a messenger — who could barely keep upright on the steeply slanting deck, slippery with blood — tie him to the binnacle in the antiaircraft command post atop the bridge. The captain cried, "Long live the Emperor," then awaited the end calmly eating biscuits while a half-naked officer on deck stabbed the air with his sword and screamed "Banzai!" at squads of enemy planes circling overhead, as if to symbolize the purpose of the mission and of continuing the war.

After her ten torpedo and five bomb hits and hundreds of near misses, the target with the list that now approached ninety degrees received the coup de grâce from her own munitions. Before she capsized, shells stored in the magazines slipped from their positions and began knocking their fuses against bulkheads and overheads. Most of the 1,080 monsters for the main batteries, each 18.1 inches, hadn't been fired. They began detonating as the derelict rolled over and plunged toward her grave, thus ending five centuries of naval warfare based on competition between surface ships. The flash of light and six-thousand-foot pillar of fire could be seen in Kagoshima, two hundred miles distant. Thick umber smoke bubbled from the ocean and into a mushroom cloud almost four miles high.

"The prettiest sight I've ever seen," noted a gunner in one of the American planes that had deftly disposed of the world's biggest and best battleship, just over a hundred miles off the Kyushu coast.

Although less passionate about offense over defense than the Imperial Army, the Navy favored speed and firepower over precaution and protection. For all *Yamato*'s superb innovations, her medical facilities hadn't been designed to cope with heavy casualties. Most of the wounded had had to fend for themselves during the battle. Most still alive when the hulk went down were lost immediately: She carried no lifeboats or rafts. Those who managed not to be sucked down by the enormous weight of metal struggled in water heavy with oil "as thick as melted caramels" and, in many places, on fire. Some sang to keep up their courage. Others went mad and consumed their last energy in wild thrashing. Hundreds choked and burned to death in the oil.

Paradoxically, the enormous final explosion saved several dozen men by blowing them back to the surface from the hulk that was taking them to the bottom. (The live-or-die margin was seconds here: Those blown up an instant too early, desperately gasping to relieve their bursting lungs, were sucked into the stack or killed by the explosion's downpour of fire and molten metal.) Among the chosen providentially shot to the surface at the last instant before they drowned, Ensign Yoshida tried to help the wounded, but the explosion had been so great that he could find no debris large enough to make a raft.

> *Yamato* — support of my life, now gone. Only bubbles, bubbles. The strafing fire of machine guns. Planes that skim past, hugging the water, carefree. . . . The faces, the heads near me. Jet black, monstrous. Like balls of charcoal the size of cantaloupes. . . . Teeth chattering, I groan with the cold.

Several American planes made final strafing runs at the survivors struggling in the oil, some chanting the naval song that begins, "If I go away to sea, I'll return a brine-soaked corpse." It was one of the rare times when gallantry lay with the Japanese, whose pilots often murdered Americans descending in parachutes but had refrained from shooting at the survivors of *Repulse* and *Prince of Wales*. One by one, those who had hung on until now, even with their entrails curling into the water from gashes, began slipping under.

The three surviving destroyers put boats over the side to salvage what they could of the human wreckage. The highest-ranking officer found alive, the admiral in command of the destroyer squadron, washed the oil from himself when pulled aboard, then wrote a signal to Combined Fleet headquarters that he was headed for Okinawa.

* * *

Operation Heaven Number One cost the American forces twelve fliers and ten of their 386 planes — of which several, according to Yoshida, were lost when *Yamato*'s final explosion engulfed them while they were circling to observe her end. It cost the Japanese seven ships and 4,250 men, almost as many as the American Navy's entire losses of killed and missing in action would be at and around Okinawa — a toll itself far heavier than any previous naval campaign of the war.

The attack on the light cruiser *Yahagi*, the largest of the screening ships, was second only to that on the main target. She took twelve bombs and seven torpedoes before going down. Not one man on the destroyer *Asashimo* survived. Although a bomb to the engine room of the destroyer *Kasumi* (spring mist) mortally wounded her, half her crew transferred to *Fuyutsuki* (winter moon), which bravely rushed alongside to save them. *Fuyutsuki* was one of four destroyers that escaped sinking. After they returned to their bases the following day, the crews were put in a kind of quarantine for several weeks in an attempt to keep the debacle of Task Force II from the public. The same reception awaited some of *Yamato*'s crew who survived the last American strafing: the 23 officers and 246 sailors of the complement of 3,332.

It's often been written that the end of *Yamato* marked the end of the Imperial Japanese Navy, now but a glorious memory. Actually, a heavy cruiser and a destroyer would engage five Royal Navy destroyers the following month, and a submarine would sink the cruiser *Indianapolis* in July. Several other capital ships that remained intact would serve more as targets for American planes than as offensive threats. Except for aircraft and feeble antisubmarine efforts off the coasts of the home islands, the Navy would contribute nothing further of operational significance. Immobilized by lack of fuel, the handful of surviving capital ships rode at anchor under heavy camouflage near their bases, relegated to floating antiaircraft batteries. In "a final revenge for Pearl Harbor," as one historian called it, American planes sank them almost to the last, after which their officers and sailors prepared to join the defense of the home islands — although many knew it would be just as futile as the last spurt of "glory" on April 7 — after the loss of Okinawa.

When the Emperor was informed of the destruction of *Yamato* and five of her escorts, he raised his hand to his temple and swayed in disbelief. "Gone?" he muttered. "She's gone?" When news reached Admiral Matome Ugaki — the commander of the 5th Air Fleet, which was mounting most of the kamikaze attacks on the American fleet off Okinawa — he noted in his diary that battleships were still needed for the day when "we resume the offensive," including a "general offensive" by the Japanese 32nd Army on Okinawa. When news reached General Mitsuru Ushi-jima — the commander of that 32nd Army — he snorted about the "infernal waste" and recalled that he'd advised the Navy against the adventure. "Banzai charges should be left to soldiers," he said.

When Japanese soldiers on Okinawa were informed — by BATTLESHIP YAMATO DESTROYED leaflets dropped from American planes — they admired the quality of the paper but guffawed in disbelief. A photograph of the sinking ship prompted some to scoff at the absurd measures American propagandists were taking to try to demoralize them. They, the fighting men in the field, knew *Yamato* could never be sunk any more than the Yamato people could be defeated. Like the sailors in Operation Heaven Number One, those troops on Okinawa would often be committed to actions that were useless for any rational military purpose. The percentage killed in action there would be only slightly smaller than on the *Yamato* mission, although the full Japanese design would consume three months rather than an hour and a quarter.

2 · American Participants

Maybe it was their training — or brainwashing. Our boys came over wanting to fight bad. They were a bunch of gung-ho kids itching to get into the field and beat the ass off the dirty Japs.
— An American who fought on Okinawa

That's what I was geared for at the time, adventure I guess you'd call it.
— A Marine who landed on Okinawa two years after managing to enlist at sixteen

Maybe there's glory in war but not for anyone fighting it. There's only fear and filth, shock and suffering. You see such blood, so many bashed bodies, so much gore. You're an animal, a barbarian, just like the enemy. No one who fought has illusions about glory.
— Dick Whitaker, another kid itchy for adventure

A LARGE HONOR ROLL dominated Main Street in Saugerties, a Hudson River town some fifty miles below Albany. Stalwarts' names were inscribed the moment they answered the call. The 1944 high school yearbook gave corresponding pride of place to photographs of graduates in uniform; admiration also suffused Broome's, a hotel, restaurant, and bowling alley whose clientele did not ordinarily ruminate about civic goals. George Broome kept a private honor roll of his warrior patrons over the fireplace of his saloon and looked the other way when skinny, underaged Dick Whitaker savored the bar's company of local workers and servicemen on leave. The national outpouring of patriotism had sharpened the itch of Whitaker's friends to take up Democracy's fight against her enemies. The fourteen-year-old himself yearned to join the boundless adventure of the Saugerties recruits already certified as heroes.

He couldn't forget Pearl Harbor or Franklin Roosevelt's Day of Infamy speech, which he heard with his parents on the radio in their modest living room. About the new enemy, he knew only that the sneaky little Japs bought lots of scrap and made cheap copies of American artifacts. But he hoped Roosevelt's outrage over their treachery might somehow speed him into the fighting. As tanks seemed a natural step up from tantalizing cars, war was an exciting progression from the best action movies.

The budding valiant in the world's finest cause went on to enlist in the Marines at the age of seventeen, but his father refused to sign the papers. So it was back to time-wasting high school. Despite his father's reduction to part-time work during the Depression, life in Saugerties and in the creek-filled countryside — perfect for fishing in summer, hockey in winter — was fine for a lad who loved the outdoors. Still, he couldn't be entirely happy. He was aging, and wars didn't last forever.

His luck changed when he graduated from high school in June 1944, nine months before *Yamato*'s final mission. Drafted immediately, the just-turned-eighteen-year-old took a bus to Albany to join a long line of fellow draftees shuffling slowly toward an Army induction counter in a post office until he was recognized by the Marine recruiter who'd arranged his vetoed enlistment the previous year. "Hey, Mac, still want the Marines?" Avid Dick did indeed, and so did the boy with him, an acquaintance from near Saugerties. The sergeant motioned them out of the line. Sworn "back" into the Marines, Whitaker boarded a train for his great adventure.

> *When I say fall out, all I want to see is dust and assholes.*
> — A drill instructor's greeting to Marine Corps recruits arriving at Parris Island

> *They made you feel like a piece of crap. It was worth it, although you didn't understand that then. They were making sure they could beat you down and you'd come up still able to do the job. The idea was that if you could get through boot camp, you could handle yourself anywhere.*
> — Norris Buchter of Connecticut

The Marine Corps's East Coast boot camp was on Parris Island, fifty miles below Charleston, South Carolina. Heads were shaved and dignity stripped instantly. Every last recruit was a worthless nothing. *"You are not Marines. You are stupid fucking civilian clowns! You're the fucking dregs!"* Many ardent boys deeply regretted their decision before the first sunset.

The training was dehumanizing as well as harsh. Its purpose was to undo everything the recruits had believed about themselves and reconstruct them mentally and emotionally as well as physically — to make them into *Marines*, the best fighters in the world. That belief was crucial. The best in the world would never let a buddy down no matter how deadly the enemy fire. The dregs could be made the best only by stripping away their individual egos and reassembling the remains as interchangeable members of fighting units. In body strong young men, the recruits were emotionally still boys — necessary for their remaking into unquestioning fulfillers of every order. Who else would feel compelled to undertake combat's otherwise mad acts, such as running up Okinawan hills honeycombed with Japanese gun emplacements? Only total indoctrinates in the glorious traditions they had to uphold would leave their cover to attack the enemy's murderous positions.

No living person had impressed most recruits, or ever would, as much as their amazingly tyrannical drill instructors. "Hey, you — shithead. Move your head again in ranks and I'll boot you so far up your fucking ass that you'll have to unbutton your fucking collar for your farts." Whitaker sometimes wondered whether the drill instructors were trying to kill the eighty members of his Platoon 452. When they incurred the milder wrath of their chief DI, a sergeant named Blackburn, he ordered them to place their scrubbing buckets over their heads and sing the Marine Corps hymn. Bellowing into that curious headgear, they couldn't hear him stalking the ranks. "Louder, you half-ass bunch of civilian scumbags. *Louder,* you fucking fuckups!" Anyone perceived as not shouting beyond the top of his lungs received a swagger stick's deafening whack on his bucket. Many singing more thunderously than they had believed possible got the whack anyway.

Punishment was administered to the entire bone-weary platoon for individual members' seemingly insignificant errors. In combat, the enemy would seek the single weak link to break the chain. The slightest slipup would jeopardize the dozens or hundreds who got it right. The recruits didn't yet understand they were being molded, brainwashed *never* to let the unit down in the slightest little anything. Each would have to be able to count utterly on every one of the others. Platoon 452 grew smaller. Better to learn on the drill fields that not all were cut out to be Marines than in a foxhole under attack in the dark of night.

Relentless physical hardening was the least of it for hardy specimens raised on outdoor labor or athletic conditioning, as a majority were. Learning how to kill took finer training. Marine Corps hype aside, the callow youths were made into excellent riflemen. Endlessly field stripping and reassembling their M1s blindfolded, they came to know them far better than their own bodies. The carbine, Browning automatic rifle, and several varieties of machine guns were also taught, but it was in use of "the piece" that they had to become maestros. ("Piece" was obligatory nomenclature. Any dog-tired unfortunate who called his M1 a "gun" was awarded extra hours of a testicle-centered drill that would keep him from ever repeating that mistake.) They learned to compensate for range when there was no time to adjust their sights. They became practiced in the art of "Kentucky windage" — making instant allowance for wind at various ranges. Every recruit became confident of being able to hit a head or chest at a hundred yards without kneeling or propping the piece against a support, which gave consistent accuracy at even greater distances. Should his ammunition run out, he knew how to kill quickly with his bayonet. The men of Platoon 452 graduated knowing they were damn good because that was what the Corps had made them. The grueling test passed together would link them forever, partly in contempt of lesser men, partly in trust that all other Marines would respond as instantly and unquestioningly to every order. None would let the Corps down because no Marine ever did. LET NO MOTHER EVER SAY HER SON DIED IN COMBAT FOR LACK OF TRAINING decreed a big Parris Island sign. Wondering why fathers had been left out, Whitaker felt certain neither parent would ever say that about him. Boot camp's overriding lesson — the purpose for the proficiency with weapons, utter reliability under extreme stress, and esprit de corps that would conquer fear of death — was how to close with the enemy and kill him, which the new Marines felt proud to have mastered.

The only redeeming factors were my comrades' incredible bravery and their devotion to each other. Marine Corps training taught us to kill efficiently and try to survive. But it also taught us loyalty to each other — and love.
— Eugene Sledge, who took boot camp in San Diego, July 1943

Battle is . . . to the young. Its physical ordeals — discomfort, loss of sleep, hunger, thirst, burdens — are not only better borne by men under thirty; so too are its terrors, its anxieties, its separations, its bereavements.
— Paul Fussell

After Edmund De Mar's father, a Brooklyn truck driver, lost his job during the Depression, the family left for humbler quarters in a Connecticut town. Ed quit school, did even smaller odd jobs than his father, and, with a few dollars earned cleaning up the mess of the 1938 hurricane, took off for Miami with friends in an old Plymouth. The nineteen-year-olds arrived with a nickel each. Back down to one nickel again two chancy years later, De Mar saw a Marine in dress blues promising ADVENTURE! on a post office poster. On his way to his physical in Savannah, he told himself that at least he'd be partway back to Connecticut if he failed.

The entry point for Parris Island was a profoundly hick town called Yamassee. When De Mar stepped off the bus there, a drill instructor was waiting. A fellow recruit extended his hand and politely introduced himself, in response to which the DI slapped him hard in the face. "I don't give a goddamn what your name is. You're a fucking pukey weakling, a nothing." De Mar considered getting back on the bus.

Fifteen months later, the boot camp graduate was back in Florida, now the corporal of the guard at a naval air station, when a jeep raced toward him, breaking the base speed limit and the Sunday peacetime slumber. "The Japs!" bellowed the driver. "Corporal De Mar, the Japs have bombed Pearl Harbor!"

"Those yellow bastards!" De Mar responded. "Where's Pearl Harbor?"

On Okinawa, he'd be among the few prewar regulars — and, at the age of twenty-six, one of the fighting Marines' older enlisted men. On the American side, it would never be more true than in the Pacific War's hardest encounter that wars made by older generations are fought by younger ones.

Thomas Hannaher's father was born in the Dakota Territory. The boy's body didn't accommodate his yearning to impress the girls with athletic feats. While his high school friends were entering various services, he, a freshman at North Dakota State, was classified 4F. The unlucky eighteen-year-old's second stab at joining the fighting men brought him up against the same medical captain who'd uncovered his asthma during his humiliating first examination. "What are you doing back here?" the doctor asked. "Because the colonel over there said I was okay," the ordinarily upright boy mouthed the instant lie that had somehow come to him. When the captain chose not to dispute his superior, Hannaher was in — and chose the Marines at the end of his final line. "Why'd you do that? Are you trying to commit suicide?" asked a friend determined to stay with the Army. Far from hero material, the unathletic Hannaher had never even fired a gun, something almost a little odd in the Dakotas. His choice of the Corps made no sense at all except in terms of his old desire to prove himself — for which he'd soon curse himself, for he hated where it took him. "First there was boot camp, a terrible experience for someone just out of high school who had been living at home in a quiet small-town community. Boot camp was . . . being treated like a criminal. It was like I had broken a law by joining the Marines and had been sent to reform school." But one of the war's million ironies would put him among the few Marines unwounded during the entire Okinawan campaign, whereas his more cautious Army friend would be blown to bits during the Battle of the Bulge in Belgium.

Pearl Harbor prompted John D. Rockefeller Jr. to prudent calculation of the danger of Axis bombs. Rockefeller, one of the five sons of the "original" John D., decided to relocate himself and his Park Avenue apartment's art treasures to his country estate. Joseph Bangert's family moved with him to Tarrytown, New York, for young Joe's father was one of five drivers who served John D. Jr.'s branch of the family. (The boss bickered with them over such matters as their laundry bills when they were on the road for him. Bangert once heard his father argue with Rockefeller over an expense item of a dime.)

Fearless Joe was the youngest and wildest of eleven Bangert boys, four of whom were overseas in various services by 1943. That was when the sixteen-year-old black sheep of the family, itching to do something other than screw up in school, enlisted in the Navy. The self-confessed "smart-ass" and "hell-raiser" was directed to report again after he turned seventeen, this time with his parents' consent. He bamboozled it by slipping in the form with others required for playing high school football.

With no medics of their own, combat Marines were assigned Navy corpsmen. Bangert took his first step toward that hazardous work at his induction, when he was told of a pressing need for medical corpsmen — who were automatically promoted to second-class seamen with a pay of fifty-four dollars a month instead of fifty dollars for third class. After boot camp and corpsman training, he was assigned to a California naval hospital, where he took his second step toward action in the field. An unsatisfactory inspection of some spaces for which he was responsible fired the wrath of his officer, a fastidious nurse.

"Are you through?" the second-class corpsman dared to ask the ensign after her harangue.

"No!" she screamed and resumed castigating until she ran out of breath.

"*Now* are you through?" Bangert repeated.

"Yes, I'm through."

"Then take this," said the smart-ass, gripping a broom handle, "and shove it up your gigi."

Given the Corps's great shortage of hands to tend the mounting number of wounded on the Pacific islands, his previous request for assignment to combat duty was now not to be denied.

Marines reached Okinawa in a variety of ways. A minority came from previous island battles after intervals of rest and rehabilitation. Others were graduates of more specialized schools, from which they were shipped to the Pacific. What almost all had in common, apart from their spirited training, was patriotic zeal.

Lenly Cotten, the son of separated parents (then a rare disgrace), managed to fool the examiners and enlist at sixteen, but his first duty on the Aleutian Islands disappointed him because there were no Japs to kill. "You wanted combat because that's what you were trained for from the first day in boot camp. All those months preparing to fight got to you; you wanted to *do* it." Back in the States at eighteen, Cotten knew replacement troops for Iwo Jima's combat were so badly needed that anyone caught AWOL was shipped there immediately. But since he was on the East Coast and would probably go to Europe, where Germany was almost finished, he hitchhiked west, careful to avoid military police patrols until he'd crossed the Mississippi — then gave himself up. "I knew I'd get sent straight to the Pacific from there. My only worry was that the war would be over before I could get there and be a hero."

The invading force would be made up of over half a million Americans. No more than a handful had any real knowledge of Japan. Whitaker knew "absolutely nothing until the sneak attack on Pearl." "If I had any impression of Japs at all," another Marine would remember, "it was that they were funny little people walking around in kimonos." A third thought of them as "gooks who were trying to peddle things to the States but didn't have a hope in hell, except for trashy souvenirs." A fourth classified them as "Oriental. Inscrutable. And nothing to do with us, so who cared?"

But virtually the entire half million cared very much that Japan was a sinister place populated by evil people. Those whose troopships stopped at Pearl Harbor on the way to their unknown destination knew that even better than the others. The sight of the sunken battleships' hulls and memory of the Japanese treachery fired their rage.

Fred Poppe loved sailing and volunteered for the Navy, but flat feet and astigmatism excluded him from all programs leading to a commission. Now he was a quartermaster third class on a brand-new landing craft converted to a floating rocket launcher. "Sometimes my buddies and I would cry when presenting arms to the flag. Actually cry — because of American goodness and virtuousness, all so beautiful and pure. Against that were the Japs, low-grade monsters who were totally inferior in everything, especially intelligence — but who fought savagely and committed terrible atrocities."

About Okinawa, they knew nothing whatever. Most would hear their first something aboard troopships bearing them there.

3 · Japanese Participants

Basic training caused many more deaths than necessary but it was effective for our way of fighting. Your beatings made you lose your mind and stop thinking even about self-preservation. You only trembled to obey.
— A Japanese soldier who fought on Okinawa

The Japanese soldier was a remarkable man. On Okinawa, he fought — and how he fought! — with no air cover whatever and amazingly little support. His resilience and endurance were tremendous.
— General James Day, who fought on Okinawa as a corporal and returned forty years later as commander of all U.S. forces there

What did I think about Pearl Harbor? As a regular Japanese Army officer, I never thought about anything except my duty and work.
— Tadashi Kojo, former captain

WHILE DICK WHITAKER was downing his pre-induction beers in Broome's, Tadashi Kojo was practicing the martial art of kendo across the Ussuri River from Siberia. Stationed in the bleak barracks settlement of Nishi-Toan, Kojo's 22nd Regiment of the Japanese 24th Infantry Division lived on hot resolve to crush the hated Russians.

The proud regiment was guarding Manchuria, the jewel of the Empire. After victory in the Sino-Japanese War of 1895, Tokyo claimed the Liaotung Peninsula, convinced heart and soul that the relatively small tract, tipped by Port Arthur, was among its just spoils. When Japan was forced to back down, patriots vowed to endure any privation — to "lie on kindling wood and lick gall" — to get back their own.

The humiliating retreat was coerced by France, Germany, and Russia, their own appetites upset by the Japanese aspiration to join their table of Asian snacks. In particular, the Russians were determined to keep Tokyo from establishing a power base in resource-rich Manchuria. Ever since Japan's deep isolation had ended in 1853, the poor, technologically backward nation worked sacrificially to industrialize and militarize in the pattern of her economic betters in the West. But instead of being welcomed into the imperialist club, as the Japanese naively hoped to be, they were given to know they were of the wrong race.

Memories of those insults remained fresh that June of 1944. The 22nd Regiment's officers revered the Army for its part in defeating the arrogant Russians in the War of 1905 — a victory that astonished the West, which had taken for granted the great bear would maul the little yellow upstart. A mere fifty years after her 1853 opening, feudal, agricultural Nippon mustered the astonishing effort to make herself at least partially industrialized, the proof of which was her defeat of a European power. But although that dressed her wounded honor with a rich balm, the country remained as sensitive as ever to others' snubs.

The Army restored more national honor in 1931 by taking not merely the "stolen" Liaotung Peninsula but all of Manchuria as well, to wild cheers at home. With a soaring population, scanty raw materials, and a Depression-crippled economy, most Japanese believed Manchuria was vital to the nation's survival. And although the country — renamed Manchukuo and ruled by a puppet government — had been a de facto colony for thirteen years, they remained convinced Russia still had evil designs on it. That was why the venerable, distinguished 22nd Regiment now kept unblinking watch on Soviet detachments across the river. Yes, the war with America was important. But the regiment's officers still saw their chief enemy in Japan's old rapacious competitor for Manchuria, which the great deceiver Stalin might well attack at any moment, despite the noninvasion pact with Moscow.

Actually, the senior officers were confident they themselves would do the attacking. The regiment trained relentlessly for an undeclared night strike across the river and through the Soviet marshes on the other side. Avid for the opportunity, the officers, overachievers in training as in so much else, kept their troops poised and ready.

The isolation helped. The soldiers' chief relief from their stark living conditions were prostitutes — some seized from Korea, another "protectorate." But women provided no relief from their regular soldierly beatings. Bullying noncommissioned officers went up and down the ranks, bashing faces. No one laughed when superiors had to stand on tiptoe to reach those of the tallest. The recipients learned to clench their teeth to keep them intact. Some toppled over, dazed and bleeding.

They were hardly the first or last cannon fodder to be both miserably treated and utterly loyal. As in other countries gripped by feudalistic patriotism, there may even have been a correlation between wretched treatment and devotion to the beloved homeland. The Emperor inspired awe and adoration. Although the barracks were full of whispered complaints against individual sadists, there was virtually no questioning of the Empire's uniqueness, rightness, and mission, or of the duty to suffer and die for them. Tokyo's leading newspapers explained why.

> The whole world searches for God but only Japan possesses Him. Japan
> is the divine country . . . therefore the Emperor's will is the only key to
> a new universal order.

All came to instant, unbreathing attention when the Emperor was
mentioned, as during the frequent readings of the Imperial Rescript
to Soldiers and Sailors, a document that predated the much less
relevant and (for officers) less important Constitution. The fundamental
rules and philosophy set forth in that self-described "Grand Way of
Heaven and Earth" and "universal law of humanity" had to be flawlessly
memorized. A recruit bound for Okinawa that June — who'd taken basic
training at about the same time as Dick Whitaker on Parris Island —
watched fellow recruits being beaten bloody for the tiniest mistake recit-
ing the Rescript's stilted, archaic phrases. Officers of other units killed
themselves to atone for the disgrace of a slip of the tongue or mispro-
nunciation of key words in their reading of it to their troops. No one
tried to stop them. Their shame was understood.

Much more minor infractions also earned blows, often to all members
of the units involved. Although the drive to establish collective responsibility had its parallel in American basic training, Japanese intentions differed tellingly. Bruised quarry who tried to supply a reason when asked
why they were being hit were hit even harder. The point was that they
weren't supposed to know the reason because their duty was never to
think. A native psychologist would conclude shortly after the war that the
violence was used in order to "implant the idea of absolute obedience,"
which was grounded in a lack of all thought, right or wrong. "Sometimes
it wasn't a matter of obeying or disobeying," a soldier who'd fight opposite Dick Whitaker on the Okinawan hill nicknamed Sugar Loaf would remember. "I was beaten for no justifiable reason and quite unexpectedly."

"I was hit almost every evening as a recruit," another infantryman on
Sugar Loaf would remember. "Utter obedience was demanded. If I was
shown a piece of black paper and told it was white, I'd have to agree." Another remembered being slapped every evening "for nothing." When he
actually committed a slipup — forgetting to hang his string-strung purse
from his neck — a senior private whacked his face with an old shoe.
Much later, another Japanese psychologist would dot the *i* of explanation for such behavior in a determination to instill "complete submis-
siveness." Subjecting young men to fear of violent punishment quickly
transformed them into "monsters of self-abasement, humiliation and
shrewdness."

Many recruits who'd be shipped to Okinawa lived in constant fear of
blows for "a bad attitude," which also meant for nothing. One man lost so
much weight that doctors grew concerned during a rare physical and or-

dered a ration of five eggs a week, all instantly confiscated by the veteran soldiers who administered the beatings. One day, his unit was told to jot down their candid thoughts about Army life. "Being neither cats nor dogs, we'd like to be treated like human beings," he wrote naively — and was beaten even more severely.

Fighting units like the 22nd Regiment conducted their own basic training, permitting noncommissioned officers to establish their tyranny from the start. The word of a superior even one grade up was likened to an Imperial order, giving noncoms the authority to warn that disobedience to them, even of an order to scrub latrines, was tantamount to disobedience to the Emperor himself. Such arrangements were much less onerous to Japanese soldiers than they would have been to American, for their upbringing was rooted in Emperor worship and a caste system based on strict submission. Conformity, discipline, hierarchy, loyalty, duty, and obedience were paramount in Japanese civilian life. The notions of individual rights and challenge to authority were remote to those whose earliest lessons focused on complying with group expectations in a culture where nonconformist behavior earned instant condemnation. Prewar Japan was so locked into hard work and instinctive bows to seniority and authority — and the belief that perseverance and endurance of suffering were among the most desirable qualities — that Army life, even in its tormenting first year, actually represented liberation to some.

In 1933, fourteen-year-old Kuni-ichi Izuchi, whose artillery battery would be annihilated on Okinawa, traveled to the ancient capital of Kyoto to be apprenticed to a respected painter. During the next five years, little Kuni-ichi's hands permanently ached from chilblains caused by scrubbing his master's floor with water that often froze in winter. He knew his relatively kind master liked him. His blows for not doing *exactly* as he was told were simply part of the accepted approach to training: Lessons were to be literally "beaten into the pupil's head," in a favored Japanese expression. In addition to the cleaning, which lasted into the night, the boy looked after the master's children and saw to a hundred household chores — without a single painting lesson during the full first year. Although Kyoto was but an hour away from his village by train, Izuchi endured four additional years of heavy toil and severe discipline without once going home to visit, despite his longing to indulge in that impermissible weakness. By the time he took basic training with his regiment, military discipline was a snap for him — and although he rated his chances of surviving the American war at no more than 20 percent, the confidence that everyone would do his job as told assured him Japan would win.

Still, Army life was sufficiently grimmer than the grinding apprenticeships to make many nonprofessional soldiers dream of returning home. The grueling physical training included "cold endurance" marches in winter and "heat endurance" in summer, both to physical limits — and beyond: Casualties were frequent. A Western expert before the war witnessed fortitude "little short of phenomenal." Rooted out of bed in the dead of night, soldiers were ordered to don huge packs and keep going, no matter what. The purpose was to build stoical disregard of pain and exhaustion. "Why don't you let them sleep?" a British observer asked during a forty-eight-hour marathon. The training officer's answer came almost before the question left his mouth: "They already know how to sleep."

There were no radios or movies on Tadashi Kojo's base in desolate Nishi-Toan. Day after day of bayonet practice served for sport. Bayonet charges also helped stress the supreme importance of *attack*. Officers relentlessly instructed their units that they could defeat the enemy only by disregarding all thought of their own lives — and by taking the offensive that had served so well from the Sino-Japanese Wars to the Russo-Japanese War to Pearl Harbor and Singapore.

> There is hell
> Under the falling blade.
> Jump into it and
> You will be saved.

and:

> Let your enemy cut your skin,
> You cut his flesh.
> Let your enemy cut your flesh,
> You sever his bones.

True grit helped make the Japanese soldier the country's supreme weapon, as promised by a manual issued to all recruits upon entering the Army.

> When you encounter the enemy after landing, regard yourself as an avenger come face to face at last with your father's murderer. The discomforts of the long sea voyage and the rigors of the march have all been but months of waiting for this moment when you may slay your enemy. Here before you is the man whose death will lighten your heart of its burden of brooding anger. Should you fail to destroy him, you may never rest in peace — and the first blow is always the vital one!

Regular Army field officers saw that opportunity to strike the first, vital blow as the full purpose of their lives. Those of the 22nd Regiment practiced kendo religiously. Evenings, they drank sake and discussed tactics, troop training, and preparing for the all-important Staff College examination. Boyish-looking Kojo himself, who was as tough as nails and as single-minded as prescribed, was a stickler for rules. The scrupulous twenty-three-year-old captain never hit his men, leaving that to his non-coms. He merely rapped his junior officers with his riding crop on occasion and they, in turn, slapped their men's faces. The men admired and feared their dashing battalion commander. Mistakes triggered his short temper. Arrogance was part of regular officers' professionalism.

In Kojo's case, it drew on patrician social stature. Almost a thousand years earlier, an important Japanese clan sent a young samurai to put down new roots in a remote, southern frontier called Satsuma. (*Samurai*, probably from a verb meaning "to serve," originally referred to a member of the sovereign's guard and later extended to high-ranking warriors privileged to ride a horse.) After the youth became a minor feudal lord, one of his sons was given the name Kojo, "small castle." The family's prominence endured in Tadashi's youth, when his grandmother acknowledged neighbors' deep bows with her own much shallower one. The clinic of his father, a distinguished surgeon who'd interned in progressive Nagasaki, had one of the prefecture's two X-ray machines, the other belonging to the major hospital. Even caring for his poorest patients without charge, he earned more than the prefectural governor, and was so keen on education that he sent a daughter to Tokyo to study, which was almost unheard of, especially in poor, backward Satsuma.

The affluent parents tried to keep their two daughters and six sons to the frugality more expected in spartan Satsuma than elsewhere in Japan. But Tadashi's father, who saw more than a hundred patients a day and devoured medical journals when not attending professional conferences in Tokyo, lacked time to apply the strict discipline also admired in that province.

His loving mother, the highly cultured daughter of a rich Nagasaki businessman, devoted herself to her children. Uncommonly free of rules and with positively indulgent exposure, by Satsuma's standards, to cosmopolitan influences, Tadashi climbed nearby mountains, swam in the local river, and rowed boats in Kagoshima Bay. Although most samurai legal privileges had been officially abolished in 1873, twenty years after the country's isolation ended, Satsuma schools still instilled the old ways of hierarchy, obedience, and stringent service — and pointedly favored the samurai boys.

Tadashi often postponed studying for reading, his love of which prompted thoughts of a literary career. But samurai boys were constantly exhorted to prepare for the life of few words and valorous deeds that characterized real Satsuma men. Partly out of warrior tradition, partly because the narrow Satsuma childhood retarded education for other professions, many top pupils applied for the military academies — which the ardently patriotic director of Tadashi's school urged also for him, an excellent if erratic pupil. After all, Army officers were a national elite as well as provincial heroes: Most of Japan's prime ministers had been generals. Tadashi's parents championed medicine, pointing out that an Army doctor would have the best of two worlds. But rare as it was in Satsuma, they left the decision to their boy — who now wanted to be a *real* soldier.

Entrance to the Imperial Military Academy, Shikan Gakko, remained extremely competitive in the mid-1930s, even while the academy was greatly expanding for Japan's deeper involvement in war. But Kojo easily passed the entrance exam and matriculated in 1937, at the age of seventeen. During his years there, Japan loathed the Western powers less than it later would, partly because confidence remained high during the Army's thrashing of China. Still, every youth received stiff daily doses of jingoism. The quick, happy gobbling of Manchuria had sharpened appetites. Further expansion was seen as the only answer to the Depression-caused collapse of Western markets and the doubling of the Japanese population in fifty years. The few who challenged the growing passion for military power were labeled *hikoku-min*, "noncitizens," and accused of endangering national security. Weaving a hold on the country of the samurai spirit and group mentality, prophets of national and self-fulfillment through conquest won more concessions the more violent they became.

The superpatriots excited poor peasants who yearned for better conditions for themselves and glory for their nation — and lacked all notion of the wretchedness that their aspirations caused other peoples. The most determined used intimidation and assassination to silence disapproving liberals and moderates. Especially after they yanked the country into war with China in 1937, the year Kojo became a cadet, their Imperial Way extremism established the national climate. "War is the father of creativeness and the mother of culture," began an Army pamphlet published three years earlier.

The population of Kojo's rugged native Satsuma — which had been renamed Kagoshima Prefecture, after its main city — remained top-heavy with samurai who felt superfluous in civilian life and happy for the national turn toward their soldierly outlook. Even the influence of Kojo's rich, relatively worldly parents didn't shake his acceptance of the axiom that the highest service was military. Having absorbed some of the academy's surging, unqualified love for the Army as the source of supreme honor and good, Cadet Kojo became convinced that sacrifice for Emperor and country was life's finest fulfillment.

The academy's curriculum was squeezed from four to three years as enrollment rapidly increased. Whole pages of its textbooks were crossed out, and those texts concerned military matters almost entirely. Shikan Gakko more resembled a superior officers' training school than it did West Point, which then offered science and humanities courses similar to those of ordinary colleges. All movies and plays, even Japanese, were forbidden, even on holidays. Most cadets were bright boys from poor farm families, very grateful for their chance to escape poverty while serving the nation. The few who had indulged in the dangerous distractions of nonmilitary interests were cured. It was an article of faith that any thought unrelated to training and fighting could only dull an officer's edge.

After the war, Kojo would realize that far from contributing to the Army's strength, the prized narrowness implanted a fatal weakness. But Cadet Kojo would not have believed that the Imperial Academy was actually training officers to be blind to critical realities. And just as the academy staff prided itself on having no background knowledge to consider anything nonmilitary, the high command was proud of its indifference to such political and economic factors as America's will to fight the costly war. It taught that discipline, field tactics, skill with arms, and inculcation of the crucial, indomitable Japanese spirit would destroy all enemies.

Kojo was less than a zealous student. While others awoke before reveille, leaping out of bed for a running start on morning duties, he slept until the last possible moment. The teenager missed his family's luxurious warmth and regretted that no book other than military texts and training manuals could be opened without permission. But in time, the restriction seemed natural; then it became natural not to *want* permission. Although sometimes so tired that he dozed in class, his face swollen from slaps for minor infractions, he became immensely grateful for his destiny. Privilege was merging with the unswerving elite of regular officers and their noble cause — their inspiration to strive for supreme integrity and unselfish loyalty, together with their contempt for outside interests. The Emperor conferred a blessing on the academy by attending its graduation ceremonies. Dismounting from his white horse, he stood beside the commandant during the presentation of the diplomas, the August Presence conferring on the graduates the highest conceivable honor. The awe and devotion that surged through young Kojo's body like an electric charge left him barely able to breathe.

Some of that supreme devotion and desire returned the first time he held his own sword in his hands. It wasn't from the family armory, because a gambling, womanizing grandfather had disposed of that magnificent collection in order to settle his debts. But a friend's grandmother gave him a graduation gift from *her* family's store: a Stradivarius of weapons, made by Sukesada, the master thirteenth-century swordsmith. Kojo's resolve to do his duty for sacred Japan was stronger than ever when he was assigned to the 22nd Regiment on the Manchuria-Siberia border. By the time he reported there, he knew he had the makings of a leader.

Regular officers recognized each other at a glance, supreme military bearing distinguishing them from reserve officers. They even walked differently, using their ramrod stiffness and total self-assurance to demonstrate the absence of interest in anything but military concerns. The academy had trained them never to show the slightest personal emotion. When very occasional entertainers visited from Japan, comedians told jokes and the regular officers' faces remained granite. They would never reveal the weakness of laughter in sight of the men. Rigid Kojo was becoming an exemplar of that single-minded elite.

Later in 1940, he was sent to a combat engineering course in Chiba, near Tokyo. More handsome than ever, the apprentice officer had hardly spoken to an unmarried female outside his family. When older classmates took him along to a geisha house, that mainstay of officers' entertainment, he found the women impossibly beautiful — literally impossible, because he couldn't think of a word to say to them. But the tongue-tied twenty-year-old was already learning to drink like a professional officer. When he was returning from the toilet during an evening's surfeit of sake, a lovely geisha leaped from a corridor in ambush. The tremulous excitement of his first kiss grew even greater because he still had no idea of what to say or do. "I liked you from the first evening," the geisha declared. "Why didn't you talk to me?" Kojo didn't explain that he hadn't dared look at the women long enough to distinguish one from the other.

Although a prostitute back in Manchuria taught him what to do, he repeated the pleasure rarely, preferring to sublimate his waxing desire to his duties. Even though young officers rarely discussed more than the military aspects of Japan's enemies, he knew what was daily reported: that Japan's ABCD encirclement — by America, Britain, China, and the Dutch — threatened to reduce her to permanent poverty and subservience. It seemed to him the height of hypocrisy for the European powers, fat on their own colonies, to criticize Japan's modest imperial efforts, whose wisdom and justice were of course guaranteed by the Emperor's presence at the center of governmental decisions. He also knew Japan to be utterly right in her foreign policy, with a "holy task" to settle her painful scores and take her proper place in the world as its leading race.

Kojo had no doubt and no capacity to doubt; only contempt for doubt. Fearing war with America might delay the settling of scores with Russia, he felt disappointed as well as exhilarated by Pearl Harbor. Still, he relished the prospect. His troops were invincible in hand-to-hand combat. He could no more believe that their ceaseless bayonet practice would be nearly worthless in the combat awaiting him on Okinawa than that his Army was capable of moral wrongs.

In 1943, two years into the Pacific War, First Lieutenant Kojo was sent to an intense, five-month course for battalion commanders, normally a major's billet. A severe shortage of field officers was developing in the still-expanding and now hard-pressed Army. When he returned to his regiment the following spring, he found most of the senior officers had been transferred to fighting units elsewhere. Appointed the regiment's youngest battalion commander, in command of fifteen hundred men, he was also promoted to captain. A sister battalion was soon detached and sent to a Caroline Islands atoll. But although that suggested the island battles weren't going easily, no academy graduate expected victory without sacrifice and setbacks.

His men also took victory almost for granted that summer of 1944. With virtually no information about the world apart from the Army's dollops, they knew next to nothing about America's control of the seas, the Empire's strangulation by submarines, even the loss of Guadalcanal, Tarawa, and other Pacific islands. They knew still less about the ruinous swing in arms advantage as American plants disgorged dizzying quantities of munitions while Japan's plants faltered for lack of fuel and raw materials. Even the handful of men who considered such larger realities doubted their country could be defeated. Japan had never been invaded. Her armies had not lost a war in twenty-three hundred years. More recently, the sanctified homeland had prevailed against Portuguese, Spanish, Dutch, British, Chinese, and Russian aggressors, teaching all those ill-wishers respect by breaking Western imperialism's "stranglehold" on Asia.

Their belief in Japanese invincibility was rooted in their image of themselves as a unique people whose ideals and values were unattainable by others. Their fighting spirit — the cherished *Yamato damashii* that engendered nobility, self-sacrifice, and purity — far surpassed the moral strength of other countries, especially the democracies. All but oddball civilians also believed the press reports about Japan's massive blows to the arrogant enemy, and genuinely accepted their leaders' assurances of eventual triumph. Even the tiny minority who suspected something had gone wrong in the Pacific couldn't imagine defeat. The final outcome would be determined by their transcendent spiritual strength, largely achieved by learning to endure pain.

That helped explain why punched and slapped Japanese soldiers remained confident; in part, it was precisely *because* they were punched and slapped. One man who would fight on Sugar Loaf Hill "suffered a very great deal" throughout his entire Army life, yet was convinced "the system was the basis of Japan's power. Officers were trained to lead, soldiers to carry out their orders. We all learned not to be discouraged but to persevere despite any hardship." In well-trained units like Kojo's 22nd Regiment, it was axiomatic that harsh discipline was vital to hone *Yamato damashii*. To the new captain himself, the possibility of defeat was as remote as the sun ceasing to rise.

4 · Okinawa

[Japan's] many suppositions that the Okinawan people were primitive . . . is a complete error due to ignorance of their true culture and to Okinawan humility. . . . The politicians simply regarded these small islands as a burden — so poor, so backward, so unimportant.
— Soetsu Yanagi, a Japanese artist, 1939

It was as pretty and gentle a sight as you ever saw. It had the softness of antiquity about it and the miniature charm and daintiness that we see in Japanese prints.
— Ernie Pyle, reporting from Okinawa over Navy radio

I left Okinawa knowing little more about it than when I arrived, except for how to use its terrain to kill Japs and try to stay alive.
— Dick Whitaker

Severely limited intelligence hindered American strategists' plans for the Okinawan campaign. The Ryukyus were among the world's least explored inhabited areas, largely because Japan had kept foreigners away for over sixty years. A secret War Department study established that fewer than 280 resided there in 1930, almost all of them Chinese and Koreans.

What would agents have found if they could have landed in 1944? Okinawa's landmass, roughly the size of Long Island's, was an ancient patchwork of tiny fields, sparsely inhabited mountains, and thousands of sharp ridges and rises that the troops soon to be pinned down in them would call "escarpments." The overwhelming majority of the population were farmers who lived in thin frame houses with thatched or tiled roofs. A Chinese lion protected against ill winds and evil spirits. Stone walls attempted the same against the typhoons. Clustered into South Sea island–like villages, the miniature houses helped make the island a pastoral delight, little spoiled since Commodore Matthew Perry saw it in 1854: "It would be difficult for you to imagine [its] beauties with respect to the charming scenery and the marvelous perfection of cultivation."

Most of all, however, the scouts would have sensed a prevailing good nature, even if that would have found no place in their reports.

Mixed origins may account for Okinawans' legendary and real hospitality. The earliest Ryukyuans, who probably descended from peoples who crossed a prehistoric land bridge from the Asian continent, were joined by Malayans and Micronesians carried from the south by the prevailing Black Current as well as by Japanese from the north (although recent ethnological and botanical research indicates the island was never physically linked to the home islands). Chinese visitors were later common, after Okinawans joined the many Asian peoples in Beijing's orbit. An eighteenth-century emissary found the island extremely poor but unfailingly gracious, as the Chinese name for it affirmed: *Shurei no kuni*, "the nation of constant courtesy." Another spoke of "an approach to the ideal society set forth in the classics, where all men knew their proper place and none violated the law."

Although Western visitors were likely to romanticize natives they hardly knew, enough were experienced travelers to give some weight to their reactions, especially since they were nearly unanimous. A Dutch scholar set the pattern in the late seventeenth century. "The inhabitants . . . are a good-natured, merry sort of people leading an agreeable, contented life, diverting themselves after their work is done with a glass of rice beer and playing their musical instruments, which they carry out with them into the fields for that purpose."

In 1816, the Royal Navy's Captain Basil Hall, one of the next European arrivals, found "an honest, peaceful, unassuming people, with neither money nor arms, kindly, hospitable and without guile." Hall's grandson added that Okinawans' most prominent characteristics were "their gentleness of spirit and manner, their yielding and submissive disposition, their hospitality and kindness, their aversion to violence and crime."

Okinawans may have been gentle because they had no choice. Until the establishment of the first lasting dynasty in the thirteenth century, warlords had battled one another there much as in Japan, if less fiercely. Now the people were squeezed by China and Japan, both competing to control them, and also helpless against the approach of hungry Western explorers. Still, observer after observer noted their "mildness, pliability, acquiescence and agreeableness," even in comparison to other subtropical islands. "Nothing can exceed the honesty of these good and kindhearted people . . . the greatest anxiety and every means [were] used to render our situation comfortable," noted a shipwrecked sailor. A surgeon on a British ship stated that they "displayed a spirit of intelligence and genius which seemed the more extraordinary . . . considering the confined circle in which they live . . . the kindness and hospitality of [the] inhabi-

tants have fixed upon every mind a deep and lasting impression of gratitude and esteem."*

The absence of arms astonished visitors. Stopping at St. Helena on his
way home, Captain Hall told a thunderstruck Napoleon that Okinawans
had no cannon, muskets, bows, arrows, or even daggers. On the other
hand, the Okinawan language, which had diverged into a separate one
from a common root with old Japanese, was rich in terms of hospitality.
The islanders startled ships by provisioning them without charge from
their meager stores. "No people we have met with have been so friendly,"
wrote Hall. "From the moment they came alongside, one handed a jar of
water to us, and another a basket of boiled sweet potatoes, without asking
for or seeming to wish for any recompense."

Of course there was a full share of nasty schemers who would endure.
Still, enough tenderness pervaded the landscape and people to make
men of both armies feel it almost palpably when they landed in 1944 and
1945. Together with fleas, flies, and superstition, the "delightful" island,
as *Life* magazine would call it, whose people and fields had an "earthly
beauty and idyllic charm," had a touch of paradise.

It was also a paradise for malaria and other tropical diseases, and the prewar Ryukyus had higher rates of tuberculosis and venereal diseases then any
other Japanese prefecture. Okinawans, with their laggard economic development and southern sense of time, had a stubborn resistance to industrial
discipline. Although most did their work well, their leisurely pace irritated
mainland Japanese. After the battle, a native would notice a contrast between his prisoner-of-war camp and the scrupulously neat Japanese camps
nearby. *Their* amateur shows boasted costumes ingeniously fashioned from
old parachutes, whereas Okinawan actors chose to "go back to ancient
times," appearing almost naked. (On the other hand, Okinawan theater
had always been more ribald and accessible than Japanese; also more fun.)

Okinawa's problems included an internal caste system and vigorous
snobbery. Just as most Japanese looked down on most Okinawans, rich
Okinawans, especially from the cities, tended to look down on the farmers, who did the same to inhabitants of the smaller Ryukyu Islands. More

---

*If other comments seem exaggerated, it may have been because they were made by peo-
ple very relieved to land, after a long, hard voyage, on a green island whose natives weren't
hostile. "A worthy, friendly and a happy race of people." ". . . the singular humanity of the
natives . . . behaving with a degree of politeness which rendered their company very pleas-
ing." "For gentle dignity of manners, superior advancement in the arts, and general intelligence, the inhabitants . . . are by far the most interesting enlightened nation in the Pacific
Ocean." The Russian writer Ivan Goncharov was skeptical when he arrived several decades
later. But "what a place, what people!" he found. "All exuded such a feeling of peace, simplicity, honest labor, and plenty that it seemed to me . . . a longed-for haven."

painfully, there was overcrowding. The island's southern third, where by far the hardest fighting would take place, was over four times more densely populated than Rhode Island. That would contribute to the coming battle's extraordinary toll of civilian deaths, as it had contributed to centuries of poverty.

So did the coral and limestone. The majority of the population eked out an existence on very thin soil. Nature took away almost as much as it gave. The chronicle of natural disasters, especially crop-ruining, house-flattening typhoons, reads like the drum rolls of a dirge to a little people also regularly decimated by drought, plague, and famine. "The whole fragile, minuscule structure survived throughout the centuries at bare subsistence level," a Western historian would summarize. The patch of meager land would never be a prize, except for its strategic position in other nations' plans.

Poverty remained widespread before the war. It was rooted in subtropical languor, agricultural backwardness, and those typhoons that regularly ravaged housing and crops. The 1940 population of about 475,000 owned 250 motor vehicles, one to every 2,000 persons. A quarter were buses. An average farmer in "poor" Japan, which felt compelled to seize other people's land, worked five *tan,* about one and a quarter acres. It was two *tan* on Okinawa, and average per capita income was about half the mainland's.

Farmers planted their tiny fields chiefly with sugarcane and sweet potatoes, the mainstay of their diet, which they fertilized with night soil — a rich source of typhoid, as American troops would discover. Despite great hunger for farmland, much of the island remained untilled. The mountain soil was too thin, large tracts were covered with sand, and thousands of coral escarpments had no covering at all — thus the even greater importance of the arable land. A long history of village responsibility for the common welfare bound the little hamlets in a deep sense of cooperation and community obligation. Rice was a luxury for many farmers. The sweet potatoes came with bean soup, a few garden vegetables, and very occasional pork and fish. Rain was considered good weather, since water was scarce despite heavy rainfall, most of which ran off the coral. But there was much laughter and song. There was an easygoing attitude toward one's time on earth, far easier than in intense, driven mainland Japan.

Soetsu Yanagi, the "father" of Japanese folk art, visited in 1939 and extolled Okinawa's simplicity, "naturalness," and freedom from the corruption of the machine — all of which helped keep the natives poor. But they were rich in literature, music, architecture, sculpture, dancing, and decorative arts, all woven into daily life like the vivid local cloth — which expressed a kind of comic sweetness that set, or mirrored, that of the island itself. "Okinawans possess a richness of artistic inheritance in arts and crafts such as to put cultural values above the economic," Yanagi concluded.

Much of the amusement came at *mo-ashibi,* village "field play-arounds" of singing, dancing, and flirting. "Musical life was in the streets, the homes, and the fields. . . . Everyone sings." Sexual mores were distinctly more relaxed than Japan's, and women's supervision of ceremonial and spiritual life gave them more status than on the mainland, while separate purses provided greater independence.

The relative lack of inhibition and stricture may have nourished Okinawans' ability to survive 1945. Struck by the rarity of mental breakdown despite their tremendous physical and mental strains in the coming battle, an American psychologist would suggest emotional security from prolonged breast-feeding on demand was strong enough to withstand even that holocaust. Another urged child-guidance experts to study Okinawa, because the young were raised in the bosom of community on top of abundant parental love.

> *Manifestations of extreme nationalism — the mass hysteria which swept Japan along the road to national defeat — were unpopular in Okinawa. The common people . . . had no traditions glorifying war. . . . [But] children at school were subjected to an intensive propaganda campaign and stirred to admiration for heroic deeds reported from the China warfront. . . . The youth of Okinawa were prepared to do their duty.*
> — Historian George Kerr, about the late 1930s

> *Throughout the Sino-Japanese War, the Russo-Japanese War and the China Incident to the Pacific War, Okinawan thought patterns and activities very well reflected their idea that the more they sacrifice themselves for the Japanese cause, the quicker they will reach their goal of attaining identity with Japan. Okinawan sacrifice in the . . . Pacific War disclosed the cruel result of this thought pattern more than sufficiently.*
> — Masahide Ota, who had been one of the youths eager to do his duty

The Otas of Kume Island were even poorer than their counterparts on Okinawa, sixty miles east. Like most of the lesser Ryukyus, little Kume lagged behind the larger island as the latter lagged behind the Japanese mainland. Masahide Ota grew up with the children who rose at dawn to help their mothers on tiny farms before setting off for school. His father was among the sixty thousand Ryukyuans who had emigrated in search of relief for their families, in his case to Brazil, just after Masahide's birth.

The tough lad was further hardened by his farming chores. Only tooth decay from chewing sugar threatened his robust health, and in the absence of dentists, he learned to endure the pain. He grew to adolescence without movies or thoughts of girls but enjoyed baseball on days not consumed by his domestic duties. The bat was whittled from a fence post. There were no gloves or masks. Masahide played catcher until a foul tip smashed his nose.

Gazing at the East China Sea from his little house, the tyke with the round face and big eyes dreamed of joining his father in the larger world. The little village school had no library and the Ota household had no books, but older sons of neighbors brought back a few when they returned from schools on Okinawa. Groping through one by a Japanese philosopher, Masahide was surprised by the discovery that people contemplated life's meaning and purpose.

In his own school, he learned that America, weakened and corrupted by something ugly called democracy, discriminated against Asians as well as blacks. The only ethnic Japanese he saw were school inspectors, to whom the student body bowed almost to the ground. On Japanese national holidays, such as the Emperor's birthday, bows were also made in the direction of the Imperial Palace in Tokyo, a thousand miles northeast.

The outer islands' best elementary pupils were awarded free places in Okinawa's Normal School, chief training ground for Ryukyuan schoolteachers. In 1941, sixteen-year-old Masahide, top in his Kume school, boarded a ferry for the eight-hour trip to the main island. He arrived in his school uniform, feeling nervous and extremely lucky for his chance to be educated.

Standing at the foot of Shuri Castle in Okinawa's former capital, the Normal School was the highest educational institution in the Ryukyus, the lone Japanese prefecture of the forty-seven without a university. Middle school pupil Ota learned that baseball had a third base; on Kume, they'd played with two. The dazzled farm boy heard recorded music for the first time — patriotic music, for Okinawa was being militarized: The village festivals had been banned and the singing of nonmilitary songs prohibited. The new ditty he learned about the days of the week — "Monday, Monday, Tuesday, Wednesday, Thursday, Friday, Friday" — marked the lack of weekends; the pupils were put to work restoring an old system of tunnels beneath Shuri Castle and helping with other military construction, in Ota's case, new airfields at Kadena and Yomitan, over twenty miles north. Walking there and staying overnight, the boys dug and carted earth during every spare moment.

Strict as the Japanese-imposed segregation of the sexes had become in ordinary middle schools, it was much more so for future holders of the high title of native teacher. Movies were prohibited. (Ota sneaked in just once.) Boys were forbidden to exchange a word with girls. But Ota had no such interests to suppress. The prestigious Normal School, half of whose teachers were mainland Japanese, realized his dream. Fairly aching with desire to be worthy of his honors and prove himself to his superiors, he excelled again and was appointed one of the three adjutants to the principal (who held a colonel's rank in the Army).

His great pride in his school's geographical and political position at the heart of Okinawan affairs swelled yet more after Pearl Harbor. The exciting war with America promised a chance of full approval for hewing to the strictest practice of mainland ways, for being supremely loyal to Japan and every little duty she demanded. His burning teenage patriotism embodied two of Okinawa's largest problems. The native elite that Ota would soon join hungered too much to prove itself to the mainland, which was as much an occupying power as a mother country. And the ordinary people had long been too trusting and submissive.

Seeing the war largely as an opportunity to at last win acceptance by their former conquerors, the upper crust toadied to rich and powerful Japanese on Okinawa itself. It also embraced the whole range of Uncle Toms who appear under colonialism and oppression — inescapably, since most good jobs and professional careers could be won only by shining in the Japanese-controlled schools, then going to the mainland for higher education or work. That showed even more clearly now in the atypically Japanese-oriented Normal School, and especially in its attitudes toward the war. When anxiety tightened around Japan in 1942 and 1943 and she tightened her hold on Okinawa, most natives felt a jumble of contradictions rather than the grateful patriotism of the elite that was eager to compensate for not being Japanese. The "ordinary" people too wanted victory for the Rising Sun, and almost inevitably so. Still, the great majority couldn't easily forget their history, little of which endeared Japan to them.

Okinawans hadn't always been so poor. In the fifteenth and sixteenth centuries, their trading ships were welcomed in China, Korea, Java, the South Sea islands, and Japan. At home, sporadic raids and incursions by Japanese pirates were only a minor threat to a culture that kept Naha, the principal port, bustling with foreigners and their goods. Open to the world, at peace with their neighbors, Okinawans flourished like Venetians of the Far East.

They drank too much — especially *awamori*, a potent liquor distilled from Thai rice. Too much of their trading profits went to rich town dwellers and to the court's elaborate ceremonies, derived from Beijing's. The Ryukyuan kings built and maintained their castle in Shuri, the hilltop capital four miles above Naha, on the backs of a very hard-pressed farming majority. But in addition to its beguiling crafts and culture, the "toy state" had essential decency and tolerance.

Near the end of the sixteenth century, Japan's most powerful feudal ruler ordered it to contribute men and arms to an invasion of China. But Shuri Castle disliked military ventures. It's generally believed that Okinawans had refused to support a huge Mongol invasion of Japan three centuries earlier, after which Mongol forces ravaged the little island in punishment. Now Japan was the aggressor, and Shuri still disliked invasions.

It didn't want to spoil its trade with Korea, through which the invaders would attack. It was even more reluctant to offend China, its cultural model and most valued trading partner. The Loochoo Islands — Chinese for the characters pronounced *Ryukyu* in Japanese — were officially recognized as a client state of the Chinese Empire. (Other transliterations for the Loochoos — "bubbles floating on the water" — are *Lu-chu, Lew Chew, Loo Choo,* and *Liu Chi'iu.*) So the king respectfully apologized that great distance and lack of funds had kept his "small and humble island kingdom" from rendering due reverence to the Japanese ruler, but now he was sending some gifts to show his "sincerity and courtesy."

That didn't work. And the death of the Japanese ruler (who attacked Korea without Okinawa's help) was even worse for the islanders. Probably misinformed about the extremely bloody struggle to succeed him, Shuri declined to send respects to the feudal lord who would eventually win.

A powerful family named Shimazu fought with the losers. The Shimazus were lords of the remote, mountainous province of Satsuma, where the Kojo family lived. While Japan's other provinces Westernized with astonishing speed after her opening, Satsuma's six hundred thousand clannish people clung to their traditions. Roughly 40 percent were samurai, many as poor as ordinary farmers in more prosperous provinces. Stoicism, obedience, and service to one's rulers — when not rebelling against them — were admired everywhere in Japan, but more so in Satsuma. In that sense, the generally narrower lovers of arms were right to consider themselves the most Japanese Japanese. It was Okinawans' bad luck that they were their closest Japanese neighbors.

The Shimazu lord coveted the island's maritime trade as much as he wanted to ingratiate himself with the new regime in Edo (the former name of Tokyo), which he had failed to support. To kill both birds, he requested permission to punish Shuri for not having paid respects to the same new regime — the one that would soon close Japan. The new rulers in Edo were happy to divert warlike Satsuma to a harmless enterprise at sea, in the opposite direction from themselves.

In 1609, the Shimazu lord dispatched three thousand men in over a hundred war junks from Kagoshima Bay. Satsuma warriors were renowned for their skill and ferocity. Okinawans' scattering of arms had been stored since their last use over two centuries earlier. The untrained islanders' frantic resistance was easily overcome. Shuri Castle was taken and looted. Irreplaceable national treasures were removed to Kagoshima, together with the king. The devastating expedition that ended the small country's separate development grew out of the very conditions that had made that development so promising: the Nation of Constant Courtesy's refusal to join big-power military conflicts.

The Shimazu lord then forced Okinawans to bear responsibility for their own pitiless persecution. After three years of imprisonment, the king pledged an oath recognizing an imagined "ancient" dependency on Satsuma and swearing eternal obedience for himself and his heirs. A royal adviser who refused to sign the documents was beheaded. Okinawa's Golden Age was over. The island would never again control its own destiny.

Satsuma overlords explained the lack of arms on Okinawa: They permitted none.* Their exploitation was so drastic that when the king returned and saw its effects, he refused to be buried in the royal tombs, a gesture of supreme significance in a culture where the highest spiritual goal was reunion with one's ancestors. New taxes reduced most of the people to terrible poverty. Much of the scant food left after paying them was lost to the droughts, fires, and earthquakes that continued to ravage the island, and the dreaded typhoons that destroyed hundreds of fishing craft and thousands of houses year after year. Nothing moved Satsuma to reduce its demands. The kingdom's income was cut in half.

Satsuma also seized total control of Okinawa's foreign trade, which became more profitable when Japan was closed in 1636 while non-Japanese Okinawans continued trading abroad. Since no other province had access to foreign goods, that large loophole for the Shimazu lords much boosted their profits. They ordered the Shuri court to maintain a fictitious independence so that the China trade would proceed undisturbed. Thus were Okinawans forced to fish, as a native scholar described the arrangement, but forbidden to eat the catch. Remorseless Satsuma patrolled everything through the sharp eyes of its concealed overseers and watchdogs.

Outside semisovereign Satsuma, the national opening sparked vast changes. Reformers argued that the only way to overcome the enormous crisis of foreign competition was to sweep away the old order. The Meiji

---

*That prompted cultivation of karate, the activity for which the West best knows Okinawa. Originally, that art of unarmed self-defense was borrowed from China, like so much else in Okinawan culture; it combined Chinese kung fu with hands and feet toughened by repeated pounding. Some Okinawans trained in secret for what they hoped would be a new means of resistance. Although karate proved useless against their oppressors' excellent swords and armor, they developed the art allowing "the small and weak to deal with a larger, better-armed adversary," as a devotee recently wrote.

Okinawans also used scythes and hairpins borrowed from well-groomed women. But as George Kerr put it, the Japanese "had been nurtured for centuries in traditions of war, which exalted skill in close combat and glorified the mystique of self-sacrifice. Not so the Okinawans."

Restoration, named for the Emperor whose reign began in 1867, is taken as the turning point between feudal and modern Japan. Four years later, Tokyo, which had assumed responsibility for the Ryukyus from the Shimazus, informed China that Okinawans were Japanese. Beijing also claimed them in a kind of defensive reflex. Okinawans played no part in the competition for their island.

The Chinese would have won a landslide victory in a referendum asking which court they least disliked. But Japan mounted an expedition, and weak China eventually recognized the sovereignty of expansionist Japan. Dismayed Okinawans watched new teams of overseers arrive from Tokyo to impose their will on the island. Loochoo was changed to Ryukyu in 1875. Four years later, troops occupied Shuri Castle. The monarchy was abolished, the islands annexed. The king's exile to Tokyo ended seven centuries of recorded history as an independent kingdom or kingdoms. The effect on national life and the national spirit was catastrophic.

Okinawa's subsequent history was essentially one of Japanization, for which it paid heavily in cash. Three years after annexation, the tax burden was twice that of the mainland prefecture closest in size and population. Forty-three years later, in 1925, the disparity between revenues paid to Tokyo and appropriations for island expenditures had tripled. Tens of thousands of farming families gasped and wept. On the mainland, prohibitions were posted against Koreans, Okinawans, and dogs. A pavilion outside a 1903 industrial exhibition featured women from a local brothel in a thatched-roof house. A guide — whip in hand, as if dealing with animals — passed them off as members of the Okinawan nobility. Protests from Beijing and Seoul put an end to similar displays of Chinese and Korean women, but the Okinawan show went on, despite imploring objections to the degradation of supposed fellow citizens. With their greater racial "deviance" than Koreans, Okinawans were made to suffer even more grievously for their failure to be pure Japanese, that most valued national quality.

Tokyo solemnly explained that the gap between Okinawan and mainland living standards could be closed only gradually — while it continued to widen. Even after Okinawa and more southerly Ryukyus were designated the Okinawa Prefecture, they continued to be treated like a colony. The prefectural governors generally despised the natives. Even during the best "reigns," most Japanese on the island considered native farmers laughable yokels and all Okinawans racially inferior, as proved by their lack of dedication to *bushido,* "the way of the warrior."

Some modernization was launched. Slowly, often reluctantly, Tokyo expanded the school system, that being where the fullest effort was made to convert easygoing Okinawans to devoted, disciplined subjects of the Empire. The Japanese language was made mandatory in schools and government offices, part of a campaign to suppress Okinawan dress, customs, and names along with the language. In the mid-1930s, some of Naha's best hotels and most fashionable streets remained reserved for Japanese officials and businessmen who arrived from the mainland to govern and control the commerce. Many considered the natives "little brown monkeys."*

After their annexation, many Okinawans opposed their youth serving in the Japanese Army as much as the Army opposed recruiting from such "inferior" material. They warned that maintaining an armed force on the island would invite invasion by foreigners with whom they had no quarrel. Many Okinawan boys were excused anyway, since far more than on the mainland were below the minimum height and weight. Poor, nonindustrialized Okinawa would contribute less to the war effort than any other prefecture.

By 1939, however, the Army had stopped rejecting most Ryukyuan boys. Okinawans were further trapped in the mainland's mutually exclusive policies of cultural assimilation (because they had to be made Japanese) and continued colonial treatment (because they could never make the grade). Genuine assimilation was almost impossible even for the rare native who intermarried across the wide gulf.

When the war began, a sharp intensification of the old campaign to impose Japanese order on loose native ways succeeded chiefly on the surface of urban life. With their rounder features and more relaxed movements, the islanders' very appearance belied the claim of some Japanese — when it suited them, usually in demands for more sacrifice — that Okinawans were as Japanese as they. The residents of the former kingdom differed from the mainlanders in a hundred cultural ways, from their gentle humor to their lack of concern for racial purity and Imperial divinity. The "yokels" continued producing their beautiful textiles — which irritated Prime Minister Tojo. "What do *they* have to do with the war effort?" he snapped.

The young and the elite, still struggling through the Japanese-regulated schools and Japanese-dominated institutions in order to achieve their ambitions in everything from medicine to business, provided most of the exceptions. Some thought the island as a whole could advance only through the mother country that controlled the economy and the influence. "To put it as clearly as possible," Okinawa's first newspaper had preached in devotion to total assimilation, "even our manner of

---

*Most Okinawans were darker and shorter than most Japanese. The average adult was then about five feet tall, wiry, and slightly bowlegged.

sneezing should be the same as that of Japanese main-islanders." Many educated, influential Okinawans joined the crusade to expunge their "peculiar" cultural diversity, the island's very identity. But although some of the brightest, like Masahide Ota, tried to prove their loyalty by becoming more Japanese than the Japanese, the great mass of farming families remained almost entirely in their old world of tiny fields and ancestral tombs.

Perhaps the most salient contrast with the Japanese was in the attitude toward life and death. Okinawans revered their ancestors but not as warriors. The landscape's most noticeable man-made feature was the great number of tombs, handsome dwelling places for eternal spirits on which most families spent as much money and effort as they could spare. One of the two most prominent designs was shaped like a little house, often built into a hill unsuited for cultivation. The gently beautiful other, probably imported from China, looked like a turtle's back, the turtle being a symbol of long life.

The family tomb was the site for picnics and holidays. Bones were preserved in a wonderfully colorful ceramic urn and their spirits were venerated — but with no glorification of death, let alone hunger to serve or sacrifice for a nationalist cause. Like Tadashi Kojo, many Japanese men who wanted to give their lives for the Emperor seemed less interested in a good life than in an honorable death, signifying superior moral commitment and the unconquerable Japanese fighting spirit. Even the minority of Okinawans who tried hardest to copy the Japanese ethic spoke of Okinawa as different, largely because the Emperor cult and world mission were artificial interests.

Stunning Japanese victories from 1931 to 1941 failed to convince most Okinawans that Japan was divine and destined to rule the world. Long skeptical of nationalist ambitions and military methods, they felt much goodwill toward the United States in particular. Many of the sixty thousand Ryukyuans who emigrated by 1930 went to Argentina, the Japanese mainland, and Brazil, with Ota's father. But many others were in Hawaii and California, and the savings sent back from their chiefly laboring wages represented riches to their families. Pearl Harbor wasn't enough to entirely squelch those good feelings, even in the Normal School, where Ota's best friend had a passion for English. When Japan began losing the war, however, propaganda about Americans' polluting lust and racism much intensified, especially in the schools. Cartoons of apelike Americans hung in classrooms and filled magazines. Endlessly warning that the enemy's deepest desire was to rule the world and to torture, rape, murder, or enslave all Asians, articles and broadcasts urged: "Annihilate your hateful foe!" In light of the triumph of equally outrageous propaganda in better-educated Europe in the 1930s and 1940s, it is not so surprising that the message often got through.

The effects of the war emergency grew relatively slowly — until 1944, when Prime Minister Hideki Tojo called the battle for Leyte a Tennozan, for the sixteenth-century battle in which a feudal leader staked his entire army and fate on a single victory. Okinawa's turn to become the site of decisive triumph came later the same year. Most of its small garrison had been manning shore batteries or servicing planes and ships for antisubmarine operations. Now, in March, Imperial General Headquarters activated the 32nd Army for its defense — but belatedly and with grudging supplies, for Okinawa was only one of many outlying islands that must not be lost. The first serious shipments of equipment arrived in April 1944, a year before *Yamato*'s end. Their meagerness puzzled schoolchildren raised on tales of Japan's invincible might, and troubled their parents. The first troops, chiefly airfield construction units, seemed a mere token force. That contributed to the ambivalence of most Okinawans. Many were proud to see their island transformed into a center of Japanese activity, happy to play that crucial role for the Empire after their long relegation to the most menial ones. Others resented the black market and lowered living standards, however, since money could no longer be sent in by émigrés abroad — as well as the inevitable rapes and the Army's commandeering of so many of the slim civilian resources. (Very few rapes were reported because Okinawan women, even if not caught up in the general patriotism, tended to be as intimidated by the mood of national crisis as by the soldiers themselves.) Still others, or the same people at different moments, felt themselves colonials trampled by Japanese combat boots and secretly hoped the potentially catastrophic battle could continue to be fought in the patriotic imagination.

Japanese officers were quartered in the homes of the rich and educated, and it was they and the schoolchildren, even those less elevated than Ota, who were most likely to link their fate to Japan's. Those families felt honored to drink sake with their guests. Here was a chance to prove that Okinawa wasn't the backwater for which it had always been taken.

After the war, many of the elite — if they survived — would prefer to forget how much they'd wanted Japan to win: how the teachers had exhorted their charges to compete for frugality by bringing to school the scantiest lunch (a rice ball with a pickled plum); how they feverishly praised Japanese ways. Anguished men and women would wonder how they could have abandoned Okinawa's culture for Japan's. But now nothing could have been farther from the yearning minds of Masahide Ota and his fellows. When the newly activated 32nd Army began arriving in mid-1944, it made its headquarters in Shuri's administrative centers, on the hill just above the Normal School. Thrilled to be so near their Japanese heroes, the students had not the faintest doubt that the immensely impressive senior officers who came and went from there would easily deal with the enemy if he was foolish enough to attempt an invasion. What could have been more certain than the promise of those splendid men to smash the American devils to smithereens?

"Ordinary" Okinawans were less exhilarated. Long defenseless against natural disasters and powerful foreigners, they had an old saying about smallpox, which had to be treated with courtesy and care if the wind brought the terror to the island, and with prayers that it would leave as soon as possible. Now those farmers and workers had no chance to resist the hostilities into which Japan was pushing them. The only escape was for their little homeland not to be invaded; but if the enemy did approach — whites craving to torture their families to death — he had to be defeated.

There was no alternative, which is why the military buildup worried them. Soon after a new commander named Masao Watanabe arrived in late March, a year before the battle's start, a story spread that the approach of an airplane caused him to interrupt a speech and dash, wincing, to a window. Relieved to recognize a "friendly" in the sky, he nevertheless told his audience that roars from above would no longer necessarily be Japanese. General Watanabe warned that the enemy would indeed surely land, in which case all Okinawans would share the Army's fate. "Be resolute and go down in *gyokusai*," he urged, repeating an insistent new Imperial slogan. *Gyokusai* — literally "a gem shattered into myriad pieces" — meant dying an honorable death for the Emperor. The mainland's cry for a hundred million *gyokusai* might be translated as "better we all die."

Watanabe's indignation over his inadequate supplies — "just so much junk" on "this rock pile" — and his linking an enemy landing with death for civilians as well as the garrison were predictably contagious. But the gloomy general was replaced after four months. Saipan's fall in July 1944 compelled Imperial General Headquarters to see Okinawa not as a rear base but a possible enemy target, where a top commander with a proper force was needed. That changed everything. In August, eight months before the battle's start, troopships and freighters began crowding Naha harbor while formations of warplanes flew overhead. Wide-eyed Okinawans watched a parade of tanks, trucks, and cannon crack their few asphalt streets. "Our island was turning into the mightiest fortress in all the Pacific — a fact that filled us with pride and apprehension," a native novelist recorded. "Many secretly prayed for deliverance from the horrible war — which, some of us felt, Japan was imposing on us."

The 32nd Army was becoming Tokyo's hope for the new Tennozan. "We will never permit a single enemy to step on the Emperor's soil," a Japanese colonel promised Okinawan conscripts. Whatever had happened on the Philippines and some South Pacific islands, "we will make Okinawa the last decisive battleground and destroy him. Defending Okinawa means defending the land of the Emperor. . . . Know that you will accept your fate in order to obey the Emperor's will." But all that still sounded unreal in the lovely setting. Even during the early fighting in 1945, Ernie Pyle would crowd his dispatches with descriptions of glorious vistas radiating an aura of gentle beauty. It would all seem "so quiet and peaceful" when the celebrated war correspondent camped one night on a hill overlooking a small river and terraced bluffs.

> Southern boys say the reddish clay and the pine trees remind them of Georgia. Westerners see California in the green rolling hills. . . . And the farmed plains look like our Mid-west. Okinawa is one of the few places I've been in this war where the troops don't gripe about what an awful place it is.

A young sailor on a battleship preparing to join the initial naval bombardment — which alone would ravage the land with over sixty thousand 5- to 16-inch shells — would gaze at the target and feel "I don't know, real enchanted by it [like] . . . a really beautiful painting." A lieutenant on a smaller ship would write his parents about "rich green hills . . . russet, jade hillsides above azure water, neath crimson and gold of setting sun. . . . Oh, what a setting!"

The memory would soon haunt. The scene of an ambush — piles of empty cartridge cases, bloody battle dressings, putrid corpses — would prompt an American to reflect on the peaceful land's hideous scourging. "As I looked at the flotsam of battle scattered along that little path, I was struck with the utter incongruity of it all. There the Okinawans had tilled their soil with ancient and crude farming methods; but the war had come, bringing with it the latest and most refined technology for killing. It seemed so insane, and I realized that the war was like some sort of disease afflicting man. . . . There on Okinawa the disease was disrupting a place as pretty as a pastoral painting."

Sensitive Japanese soldiers agreed. Many yearned to return to mainland "civilization," but most were moved by the Okinawan "dreamland" and "paradise." "I thought I'd never see anything so beautiful," said one with a sigh. "The people welcomed us so warmly. . . . Did they have the slightest idea of what would happen to them and their lovely homeland?"

After six wretched days on a troopship from Kagoshima, another arrival saw red roofs — Okinawan tiling was among the world's most beautiful — amid dazzlingly vivid greens: "a whole island shimmering like a gem in a dream world. . . . Who thought then that the whole of this fairy island would be burnt down in the flame of an inferno and turned into a pile of blackened rocks?"

5 · From Manchuria to Okinawa

We now knew that only Okinawa lay between the home islands of Japan and their invasion; so did our captors.
— An Australian dying in a Japanese POW camp

We were very confident we could beat the Russians. We knew almost nothing about American weapons, tactics or industrial power, but felt we could beat them too. Our training had blinded us to all reality.
— Tadashi Kojo, 1985

I still remember some Okinawan phrases I learned at that time. For some reason, all of them have to do with hospitality.
— Ikuo Ogiso, a Japanese soldier

CAPTAIN KOJO WAS TROUBLED. Apart from his stints in service schools, he'd served in Manchuria ever since his commissioning as an officer, but now his division was pulling out. Had the four years of fervent training to smash the Russians been for nothing? Was the Pacific War going so badly that the jewel of the Empire had to be exposed to the Soviet predators? Kojo didn't know that the fall of Saipan — breeching an Absolute National Defense Zone established less than a year earlier — had prompted Imperial General Headquarters to hurriedly shift forces, especially to Formosa. Still, he was disturbed by the order to withdraw.

The fifteen-thousand-man 24th Division would be the largest and best-equipped component of the Japanese force on Okinawa, but it traveled there light: Many transport and service personnel had to be left behind. Kojo's 22nd Regiment, less the battalion that had been shipped to the Carolines and some eight hundred men sent to China, boarded trains in July 1944, just as Dick Whitaker was entering boot camp and frail General Watanabe was spending his last days in command of the new 32nd Army on Okinawa. It was a thousand miles overland to Pusan in southern Korea, then only two hundred, most in relatively safe coastal waters, to the Kyushu port of Hakata, eighty miles north of Kagoshima, which was home for Kojo. But although he'd seen his family only three times since graduating, he didn't call them now: Troop movements were top secret. (His younger brother hadn't told him he was headed for Saipan before he died there.)

Hakata rumors about the Empire's various fronts were discouraging. When Kojo's men learned their destination, most were relieved that it wasn't a South Pacific island or the presumably doomed Philippines. Okinawa was Japan, however non-Japanese culturally. Still, many assumed they'd spend their last days in that outland. Noncoms distributed envelopes to each man for nail clippings and a lock of hair, the traditional mementos sent to families of the dead.

Kojo ignored his. Although it would honor him and his family to be among the great number certain to perish on Okinawa, he believed he would see them again. When his subordinate officers asked about their chances on Okinawa, his carefree "I don't know and don't care" was intended to boost their morale with a display of the supreme confidence required of Japanese command. But it was also the truth.

His men were less poised. Not that they doubted their eventual victory — if necessary ensured by a miracle, such as those that had saved thirteenth-century Japan from the militarily far superior Mongols. Two invading fleets were destroyed, the second of which may have been the world's largest naval force until then, five times larger than the Spanish Armada three centuries later. The agent was sudden typhoons, soon recognized as Divine Wind, or *kamikaze*. Japanese priests and flocks took them as proof that theirs was indeed a sacred nation, inviolable and unconquerable, a belief that would sustain the fervent people through many hardships foreigners considered impossible and pointless. Thus the troops awaiting transport to Okinawa were convinced that heavenly favor would again see the country through any and all grave crises awaiting her.

That didn't make their own lives sacred, however. Scratchy records broadcast the vaunting "Sinking Song," a current hit. "Instant sinking, instant sinking / That's the triumphant shout." But everyone suspected the droves of ships going down were no longer the enemy's. The Hit Parade waters of American submarines now included the Ryukyu stepping-stones that led straight to the homeland. Locals whispered about bodies washing up on nearby shores and about fishermen reluctant to put to sea because the cursed submarines prowled even Kagoshima Bay.

A stunning two thousand Japanese bottoms had already been sent down, most by American submarines, which were tearing the network of Imperial sea routes to ribbons. During the present year of 1944, no more than 5 percent of the production of conquered Asian oil fields reached Japan. After the Okinawan fighting would begin eight months later, not a single ship would arrive with supplies or reinforcements. But that too failed to dent Japanese combat resolve, despite all the talk among American noncombatants at home about why it should have.

* * *

Although even *Yamato* was occasionally pressed into service as a troop-ship, most forces headed for Okinawa traveled in a grab bag of inferior vessels. The 450-mile journey dragged on for four scorching days, passengers retching with nausea and foreboding although one or more of the Ryukyus was always in sight. The worst rumor about previous convoys was true. Six weeks earlier, a furiously overcrowded converted merchantman named *Toyama maru* had sailed from Kojo's native Kagoshima with the entire 44th Independent Mixed Brigade.

It had nothing in common with a pleasure cruise. Near the war's happier beginning, a poet had written of hellish suffocation alongside explosives in the "infernolike heat" of his ship's "dungeonlike" hold. Now an Okinawa-bound soldier claimed greater "agony" on his short voyage. "We were worse than caged animals . . . [we were] like criminals, ready to be tortured." He noticed yellowish streaks in a lead ship's wake.

> A ship transporting one to two thousand soldiers means that much waste. There was nowhere on an overloaded freighter to provide for that necessary function, so toilets were hung like birdcages on the side of the ship. . . . Rows and rows of boxes with a hole in the middle swaying like swings in the wind. We had no choice. There was no other place to do it. . . . To be on that swing and perform the necessary function exposed to all the world — the pity was that I got used to it.

Toyama maru's wake was a deeper yellow, for she was transporting six thousand men and one of her two engines was out of commission. Japanese soldiers were heroes of endurance, but the summer heat that stewed their vomit in the ovenlike compartments was as bad as anything this obedient group remembered. The ship used to serve the China trade. Squashed in three levels of what they called "silkworm shelves," the eleven soldiers in each six-by-twelve-foot area had no room to sit up and so little air that they feared suffocation. June sea winds blew some of the "birdcage" waste back on deck, where they had to step in it, then carry their soiled shoes into their berths to prevent theft. It was a life for beasts, one private observed — to himself, of course; such "subversive" thoughts were never breathed aloud.

A former health service clerk named Yoshizumi Waku went up on deck from the stinking inferno below but couldn't stomach breakfast even in the fresh air. Months earlier, Waku had felt safe from further fighting because he'd already served three turns in Manchuria and China. Then a draft call reached deep among grandfathers, feeble specimens, and other deferred categories, and there he was, hearing the dreaded, frenzied shout from the port side.

"Torpedoes!"

USS *Sturgeon,* a battle-tested American submarine, had fired four. Most Japanese troops were below during the moment of stupefying flash, thunder, and terror when all hit, tearing vast holes in the ship's sides. Thousands of drums of gasoline in the cargo turned the holds into crematoria. Most who survived the explosions drowned when the hulk went under almost immediately. Fighting to stay afloat and free of the flames in the water, twenty-seven-year-old Shigeo Yamaguchi, formerly an agricultural consultant, also fought the thought that he was about to join the seaweed forever. On the morning Yamaguchi had left his tiny home to answer his draft call, his four-year-old son grabbed him by the neck, shrieking, "Don't go, Papa! Don't go!" He regretted not having held the boy tight for a second, an urge he suppressed in order to keep visiting friends from seeing him commit such an unpatriotic act. To have comforted his child would have betrayed a spiritual weakness much disapproved of in the national dedication to wartime sacrifices.

Yamaguchi and Waku would be among the 10 percent of survivors. Some fifty-six hundred men — over a quarter as many as those soon to die on hellish Iwo Jima and almost twice as many as those who would go down with *Yamato* — were already dead. They wouldn't figure in Okinawa's grand tally, since the battle was still nine months away.*

The 22nd Regiment's turn for the Okinawa run came in mid-August 1944. The convoy hugged shallow water and zigzagged its short runs in the open. The ships delivered their twenty-eight hundred troops groggy but intact.

Captain Kojo's unexpected pleasure at his first sight of Okinawa was heightened by the contrast with stark Manchuria. Even in a Naha harbor clogged with transport ships, he saw exotic fish darting through translucent water. Vivid coral fringed a tranquil island beckoning with many hues of green. Ashore, he was further taken by stands of pine trees bordering roads and the luxurious vegetation. Even Naha's red-light district, when he was invited for dinner there, seemed another example of Okinawa's "beautiful culture." Although the poverty was much deeper than even his poor Satsuma's, Okinawans were easier going and more hospitable than any people he'd seen. All were so gracious in their rustic way, smiling and bowing to the "Yamato soldiers," that even his gruffer men were touched.

---

*Military postcards had been distributed when the 44th Independent Mixed Brigade was waiting for transport in Kagoshima, and all were ordered to inform their families of their safe arrival. Clutching those cards, frantic families would struggle to understand how their men had been lost at sea.

The 32nd Army ordered the soldiers to build their own barracks of bamboo and not to fraternize. (Some disobeyed.) Only battalion commanders and above could mix with civilians and choose their own quarters. Smartly uniformed Kojo rented a room in the house of a prosperous farmer with a sixteen-year-old daughter. The captain noticed that Okinawan girls were far less straitlaced than Japanese, perhaps because the subtropical heat matured them early. Beautiful, charming Yasu knocked on the handsome visitor's door at night, and he liked her very much. But he succumbed only twice, otherwise reminding himself that pleasure impaired the concentration of an Imperial Army officer preparing for combat.

The farmer's house bordered Kadena Airfield, south of Okinawa's neck — the work site to which Masahide Ota and other Normal School boys had been walking to and from for their weekly stints as laborers. Kojo's 1st Battalion had been assigned to defend the two miles between its dirt runways and the open beach where almost nothing had been prepared for the American landing expected precisely there. No antitank or antipersonnel mines were available, not even barbed wire. And Kojo sorely missed the regiment's horses, all but four of which had been left in Manchuria. As a battalion commander, he had one of those four, but the regiment lacked even carts for transportation — which meant the men would have to be worked harder than ever.

Okinawa was alive with feverish digging. Kojo's battalion joined to gouge out bunkers in rises that dominated the beach near the airfield. He kept the pace furious during round-the-clock shifts. An ordnance shop fashioned picks and shovels from wagon rails previously used for transporting sugarcane to refineries. Those without tools used their hands, and tried to maintain their energy on their diet of chiefly rice and miso soup with sweet potato greens: not quite enough of anything.*

Two months from now, American planes and surface ships would join submarines in totally severing Japan's sea route to Okinawa. Even in that late summer of 1944, the soldiers received almost no mail. Ships that managed to arrive until October were too packed with essential supplies to bother with letters. When American troops eventually landed, their mail would be delivered almost as regularly as ammunition and water. Units would sometimes receive their "tremendous," "terrific" boost to morale when they were only a few hundred yards back from the line. Letters sustained many American fighters who might otherwise have found

---

*Forty years later, Kojo would remember eating more or less what his men did, but their memory was of as wide a difference between officers and themselves in rations as in everything else, at least until the unit went into combat. Certainly not many enlisted men had the luxury of geishas from the red-light district, whom a few battalion commanders less single-minded than Kojo continued to enjoy, in some cases until the fighting approached their positions.

it impossible to continue. Those from Dick Whitaker's mother, who wrote every single day he was away, would come in bunches of three to half a dozen — from Saugerties, ten thousand miles away. But Japanese soldiers were virtually isolated in one of their own prefectures, 350 miles from the mainland. Many would get no more than one or two letters during the interminable ten months of digging.

Officers fared better. During breaks from inspecting his fortifications, Kojo sometimes retired to a patch of shade to read a letter from his wife for the nth time. He had married her ten weeks before he left Manchuria: the culmination of what had begun with little interest for the twenty-four-year-old captain who knew no women, let alone marriageable women, apart from occasional teahouse courtesans and prostitutes. That was not unusual for academy officers, with their disdain for civilian life. Most eventually settled into an arranged marriage. That was the intention of Kojo's elder brother, who worked in publishing. Disliking the thought of Tadashi never having a family, the Tokyo-based brother sent him a photograph of the daughter of a prominent engineer high in the Ministry of Communications. Despite the captain's certainty he'd never take time from his military duties for domestic life, he was enchanted — and even more so by the delicacy and refinement of the young woman's letters. Apart from some embarrassment over his own unpracticed writing style, their ease with each other in their correspondence charmed Kojo still further.

He arrived in Tokyo for his wedding in April 1944, dashing in his cape, proud of his position in the unconquerable elite of regular Army officers, but unable to sustain his pose of nonchalance when he caught sight of young Emiko. Even more attractive than her photograph, she was also, with her modern, citified face and traditional kimono and coiffure, a rare blend of contemporary chic and old Japanese virtues. Her large eyes expressed both subtlety and wholly unexpected femininity. He thanked his luck when she raised them to his.

Although Tokyo's saturation bombing was a year away, the city had much changed since his last trip there, when he was a candidate for a course for spotter officers, just a year earlier. All lights were blacked out, few nonbasic foods were available, and Kojo couldn't find a tailor to make a new uniform for the marriage. None of that grazed his certainty of Japan's victory — about which he actually forgot for moments. In the days before the marriage, Emiko's mother suggested the betrothed take walks in the wealthy family's elegant suburb. Although much more articulate than most regular officers, Kojo spoke with the reserve and in the dialect of his Satsuma, where real men used few words, while Emiko's voice shimmered with the sophistication of generations of Tokyo residence.

On the couple's trip to Nishi-Toan, the bride's beauty and cultivation showed in everything from her kimonos to her smiles. Kojo's delight and sharing of intimacy were new even to his imagination. The five days on the train and few weeks in a house just outside his desolate camp were by far the happiest of his life.

Now Emiko's loving letters confided she missed him powerfully. She promised a visit, hinting her influential father could arrange it. Kojo smiled at her naïveté, returned the letters to his pocket, and reassumed his academy-bred rigidity. Vast amounts of work lay ahead before he could mangle the American landing.

Much of the digging was completed by mid-December. Pride enlivened the exhausted soldiers' songs, which echoed from the hills in the evening. Kojo, still a quick-tempered stickler, was relatively pleased with his nearly finished fortifications, further protected by coral growth overhead. After five grinding months, he shifted his men to more training.

The immense power of American pre-invasion bombardments on previous islands had shown the terrible cost of exposure on or near the beach. This time the defenders would stay safely burrowed until the enemy bombardment stopped for his landing operations. The 24th Division's artillery would also remain in protected emplacements, opening fire only when the landing craft approached. The artillery and antitank guns had been intended for destroying the mechanized, heavily armed Soviets. Its concentrated firepower on top of the regiment's own guns would maul the enemy and prevent him from digging in on the beach.

As at Iwo Jima, it would tear the Americans to bits, at which point the poised infantry would appear from the safety of the refuges now being constructed for a massive counterattack. Kojo relentlessly practiced his battalion's thrusts and feints for that great slaughter. He knew his old-fashioned bolt-action rifles were no match for the enemy's great firepower. But Americans were amateurs. Japanese professionalism, training, and spiritual strength would win the day — as they had so often in China, where furious bayonet charges had often panicked the enemy. His own troops excelled in the hand-to-hand death struggle that would nullify American advantages in metal and matériel. Grateful for the luck that had placed him there to shatter them, Kojo relished his first chance for real combat.

Operational plans were reviewed at regimental headquarters, on a hill overlooking Kadena Airfield. At one meeting, the regimental ordnance officer demonstrated a charge with a delayed-action fuse that would demolish enemy tanks when men sneaked up and shoved it beneath their bellies. The ordnance officer opened a wooden box that housed the makeshift new weapon and disappeared except for the portion of his legs inside his boots. The accidental explosion also wounded the higher officers sitting in the first row. All were rushed to a hospital except for Kojo, who refused treatment, telling himself it was his solemn duty to remain composed in the face of all possible shocks. Personal pride and a desire to be worthy of his ancestry combined with his intense training to reveal no weakness.

He rode back to his battalion and held out for nearly a month. His headaches were unbearable, his fever was extreme, and pus from his ear stuck his head to his pillow. When he was finally taken to a hospital, his doctors hoped it wasn't too late to save his life.

6 · Early Damage

The Japanese Empire's strategic need to hold Okinawa was absolute.
— Thomas Huber, military historian

[Okinawa was] the most important operation of all, the logical conclusion to the historical Central Pacific campaign . . . the last important bastion guarding the homeland . . . a foot in the door for the final poke at the Japanese Empire.
— John Toland, *The Gods of War*

In the midst of the final military preparations, the bewildered ordinary citizens were left to make ready for the crisis as best they could. Families hurried to the countryside to conceal books and clothes and other goods in the family tombs or in pits dug in the ravines beyond the suburban settlements.
— George Kerr, *Okinawa: The History of an Island People*

ON OCTOBER 9, 1944, COMMAND OFFICERS of the 32nd Army, the (overwhelmingly Japanese) leaders of the prefectural government, and the cream of Okinawan society indulged themselves in a military ball. The imposing affair in the best Naha hotel lasted until early morning. But its high point had come earlier, when General Isamu Cho, the 32nd Army's blustery chief of staff, promised "complete destruction" of the enemy if he dared attack. When the pledge was tested hours later, Japanese troops and Okinawan civilians unknowingly glimpsed the future.

"I hope to God we won't have to go on any more of those screwy islands," one of the nineteen thousand Marines to be wounded on Iwo Jima would venture. He'd be among the lucky ones: Nearly seven thousand Americans and twenty-one thousand Japanese would die there, in one sense unnecessarily, for although B-29s would use Iwo's eight square miles for emergency landings after bombing Japan, it would never become the major base planned by American strategists. That dose of war's boundless bad luck wasn't shared by civilians, because none inhabited the garrison island. But Okinawa would surely never be operationally unnecessary. Just 350 miles from mainland Japan and 500 from China, the "piece of offshore rope," as the name meant, was well positioned to cut off Japan from her occupied territories on the

Asian continent while serving as an "unsinkable aircraft carrier" for attacks on the home islands.

It would also be a fine staging area for the American invasion of those islands, planned for late 1945. Large enough for assembling the necessary armies, Okinawa offered excellent anchorages in sheltered bays within easy striking distance of the mainland, and enough flat land for air bases within comfortable range of the targets. No one suspected that the first B-29 raid on the mainland would take off from the island on the war's very last evening because a new kind of bomb would obviate the need for more raids. For ten times as many people as on "screwy" Iwo Jima, Okinawa would be another unlucky draw, especially since a different "aircraft carrier" might have been chosen.

Admiral Ernest King, chief of naval operations, preferred Formosa, 380 miles southwest of Okinawa, as a base for simultaneously linking up with the weakening Chinese allies. Okinawa was doomed only six days before the grand ball in the Naha hotel, when senior Pacific admirals decided to take one or more of the Ryukyu Islands instead. Although Japanese strategists still guessed the enemy's choice would be Formosa, they continued reinforcing Okinawa too, where Tadashi Kojo's battalion was digging its bunkers above the beach near Kadena Airfield.

Task Force 58, as it would be designated, struck Okinawa just a week after the admirals' decision — while attendants were still cleaning up after the ball the previous evening and night. The 5th Fleet's awesome Fast Carrier Force, which would dispose of *Yamato* seven months later, comprised no fewer than ten carriers, six fast battleships, eight escort carriers, five light cruisers, and, on an average day, over sixty destroyers. It launched its heaviest single-day raid on October 10, 1944. Nearly fourteen hundred strikes dropped six hundred tons of bombs and fired thousands of rockets on that opening shot against Okinawa. On recently opened Yomitan Airfield, two miles north of the Kadena field, Japanese maintenance and service crews had just helped dispatch planes to Formosa and were breakfasting on the flightline. Although a high degree of air-raid readiness had been in force for a week, enemy planes were so unexpected, rather as at Pearl Harbor, that the men assumed their own were returning for some reason. Antiaircraft guns fired belatedly at the vapor trails of the attacking craft, all much too fast for them. Five Japanese fighters managed to take off; none returned. Among the debris on the ground — of warehouses, an engine plant, and field headquarters — a headless corpse bubbled blood.

Four more waves crippled additional airfields with fresh bombs and rockets from their carriers, then with strafing runs. Thousands of rounds of artillery shells were destroyed, as well as five million machine gun and rifle rounds and a month's supply of food for the entire 32nd Army. Eighty-eight Japanese aircraft, a serious threat to a landing fleet, were demolished, three-quarters of them on the ground. The raid was so successful and the photographic intelligence so useful for the invasion's preliminary planning that two months would pass before it was repeated — in January, with even greater duration and force.

Japanese failures contributed significantly. The main radar malfunctioned, the first American wave began its descent before it was recognized, antiaircraft performance was dismal, and interceptors were shot down almost immediately after taking off. "The enemy planes' nimble movements eluded our old-fashioned three-step shooting method and we couldn't sight at all," lamented an antiaircraft gunner. "But the real blow was the poor quality of our detection equipment, which kept us from knowing about the approach of such a huge enemy force until the very last moment. . . . Still, we all still firmly believed *our* airpower would retaliate for the enemy's treacherous attack. Our only hope hung on new planes arriving quickly, before the enemy task force could sail away."*

That first encounter with Americans was also the first combat experience for many Japanese. It shocked large numbers of them, and civilians even more. Despite the emergency's air-raid drills, training with bamboo spears, and the digging of shelters under Japanese direction, Naha remained a late-rising city. When the first wave of Grummans and Curtisses awakened residents that October 10, it was the sound of their engines that warned them. No siren sounded before the first bombs landed and explosions began literally shaking the city. Ammunition stacked amid supplies in the port blew up, extending the damage of the incendiary bombs. An October wind spread the conflagration through houses of paper and wood. Some of the feverish fire-fighting volunteers took refuge and prayed. Many were singed by racing flames on roads clogged by people trying to flee the city, by far Okinawa's largest, with a popula-

---

*The arrival of a formation of planes from the mainland three days later enthralled Japanese soldiers and many civilians, deep in foreboding after the American raid. "Riveted on the beautiful machines with the emblem of the rising sun," a soldier would remember, "our eyes became hot with tears." After furious preparation and throaty songs, a huge force took off the next day to avenge the raid. The antiaircraft gunner watched them circle over Naha's smoking ruins before heading toward an aerial battle on the Formosa Sea. Of the three hundred planes meant to return to the field where he waited, none appeared. Nevertheless, Imperial General Headquarters announced that a "highly successful" attack had destroyed TF 58 — which was now on its way, totally unscathed, to support the Leyte landings. The lie was enthusiastically believed.

tion of sixty-five thousand. At least 80 percent was destroyed. Roughly a thousand civilians, twice as many as military personnel, were killed.*

The old capital of Shuri on high ground above Naha took few hits. The hill complex containing the headquarters of the Japanese 32nd Army as well as several divisional and artillery command headquarters was completely undamaged. So was the Normal School, where the patriotic resolution and anti-Americanism of Masahide Ota and his classmates was further strengthened by the enemy's dastardly blow. But Naha lay in shock. When the attacks finally ceased in the evening, residents left the shelter of trenches, caves, and family tombs, some to climb surrounding hills. One described "the entire city" as "reduced to glowing embers. The setting sun blazed behind the writhing remains of the city, producing an illusion that the sun itself had set Naha on fire."

Ten days later, a Japanese medical corpsman disembarked from "the living hell" of a ship's hold. His voyage had taken a month because his wretched ship arrived as Naha blazed on October 10, and turned back to Kagoshima. Screams from torpedoed sister ships worsened the nightmare of the second trip still more, but the corpsman's joy at returning to terra firma lasted only until he saw that Naha was still smoldering.

Many evacuees returned to Naha when the ruins cooled, some to rebuild what they could of their houses or erect crude shacks for replacement. Classes resumed in the open, the children again singing, "Thank you, dear soldiers." A kind of military harem went up in the burned-down red-light district, some of the ladies impressed into service by the Army and paid almost nothing. But much of Naha, including schools, hospitals, and libraries, as well as factories, warehouses, and offices, could not be rebuilt. Six months before most American civilians had heard the name Okinawa, *October tenth* — or simply *10/10* — entered the Okinawan vocabulary as shorthand for tragedy.

Evacuations from the island — eventually to total some 160,000 people — had begun before 10/10. Mainland Japanese, some 5 percent of the population, were first to hurry home. Many officials of the prefec-

---

*Tokyo protested to Washington through Madrid that the "deliberate" bombing of the civilian population and nonmilitary targets violated international law and the principles of humanity. In light of Japan's instigation of the war and her even less discriminate bombing of Asian cities — starting in China in 1932, where terror bombing of a civilian population was first employed — that gesture was pathetic or outrageous, depending on one's humor.

Okinawan civilians also suffered heavily from continued kills by American submarines. On the very night of October 10, one sank a ship returning to Naha with some five hundred laborers who'd been conscripted to build a military runway on Yaeyami Island, one of the more distant of the Ryukyus. Their deaths too usually go uncounted in the campaign's casualty toll.

tural government that had been girding the natives for war were gone before it arrived. Parents hesitated when, on July 19, the prefectural government ordered native young and aged to join the evacuees. *Send our
precious children away? To Japan, with its anti-Okinawan prejudice?*

But schoolteachers were among the quickest to comply. Senior teacher
Seitoku Shinzato was, typically, both more Japanized and more concerned
with upholding authority than most Okinawans. Thirty-seven-year-old
Shinzato knew children would hinder military operations if the enemy
really did invade. And if, as some Okinawans whispered, the child-bayo-
neting American beasts slaughtered everyone on the island, Okinawan
blood had to survive somewhere, since nothing was more important than
perpetuating the family line. Besides, food was already scarce. Apart from
the government order, therefore — which *had* to be obeyed — Shinzato
felt it was right to take his mother, wife, and three young children to the
designated pier. His wife, also a schoolteacher, would be responsible for
forty children during their evacuation in Kyushu.

Three ships bearing some six thousand evacuees departed from Naha
on August 21, almost two months after the sinking of the *Toyama maru*
with the loss of nearly the entire 44th Independent Mixed Brigade.
Alone with his ambivalent feelings, Shinzato felt his distress increase with
each additional day without word from his family. After all, there was no
guarantee they'd reach Kyushu safely, and what would happen to them
there even if they did? Like the majority of the elite who strongly identified with Japan as the mother country, the schoolteacher nevertheless
thought of her as "alien."

The family had left on the *Tsushima maru,* a freighter that had sailed
from Shanghai with a cargo of silkworm cocoons for the home islands
and stopped in Naha to pick up the evacuees — as well as to discharge
soldiers transferred from China.* The dockside partings were full of
tears. "Papa, Papa, will we ever be able to see each other again?" Two
weeks later, rumors circulated that one of the three crammed ships that
had sailed together from Naha failed to reach Kagoshima. Full of foreboding now, Shinzato traveled north to his native city of Nago to ask his
terrible question of a police captain who might know the truth because
he worked with the 32nd Army, and might reveal it because he was a former pupil. No, nothing unusual had happened, the policeman stated —

---

*Those transferred soldiers had naively hoped they were heading home. Kenjiro Mat-
suki, once the first baseman for Japan's first professional baseball team, woke up to find
that he was about to be unloaded at Naha rather than Kagoshima, the final stop. The star
athlete would describe his great disappointment and cruel war in *Matsuki Ittohei no Okinawa
Horyoki* (Pfc. Matsuki's Tale as a Prisoner on Okinawa), which Tamako M. Yorichika translated for me, together with accounts by other Japanese survivors.

but his grimace betrayed him. Shinzato bit his lip until he was alone, then sagged with grief and anger. He tried to comfort himself with the thought that his wife and mother were brave women who would have managed to die together without becoming frantic. But he couldn't comprehend why he was alive and the children he'd sent away to save were dead.

The unmarked freighter had been torpedoed at 2 A.M. by USS *Bowfin* near Aku-ishi Jima (Bad Stone Island), roughly midway between Naha and Kagoshima. Shinzato's children were asleep, together with their mother, grandmother, and seven members of Shinzato's brother's family. One thousand, four hundred eighty-four women and children were killed, almost as many as in some of the American divisions that were about to fight the costliest battle in their history on Okinawa. The 177 survivors were warned not to talk about the sinking and to send postcards back to Okinawa saying all was well.

7 · Japanese Leadership

*Erect, lean-featured and composed, Ushijima exemplified the best in samurai
virtues. Even without noticing his insignia of rank, one would have been aware
of his exalted position in Japan's military hierarchy.*
— James and William Belote, *Typhoon of Steel*

*He was a true Japanese officer, a hero of the bravest kind, yet kindly. I wanted
nothing more in life than to be a little like him.*
— Tadashi Kojo

Tᴴᴇ ᴍᴀɴ ᴡʜᴏ ʀᴇᴘʟᴀᴄᴇᴅ Masao
Watanabe as commander of the 32nd Army was one of Japan's most
respected and liked general officers. After generations of inferior
prefectural governors sent from Tokyo, Okinawans were relieved and
flattered by the choice. It did not occur to them that strengthening the
losing side in war only prolongs the struggle, causing more pain to both
sides. They had no way of knowing that they themselves, the civilians,
would bear the heaviest price for the 32nd Army's great improvement
under General Mitsuru Ushijima, its excellent new commander.

The universal admiration for Ushijima was reinforced by his evocation
of Takamori Saigo, a soldier, statesman, and poet who had greatly contributed to Japan's modernization following her opening to the world.
Saigo the Great went on to disembowel himself in a sea of his followers'
blood after a catastrophic rebellion, precipitated by dissent to the 1876
invasion of Korea. But the whole political spectrum, from extreme militarists to liberal democrats, cherished the "peculiarly Japanese combination of qualities" that earned him his reputation as the last true samurai.
The frugal man, almost alone among his contemporaries to care nothing
for medals and honors, became the Meiji Restoration's only truly popular hero, not least for his death in defense of the national honor and
faith against corrupting Western ways.

A Japanese who somehow didn't know Saigo's origins might easily have
guessed: Such a stately mien and so few words were the Satsuma ideal.
Dedicated samurai families like Saigo's poor one raised their boys to
cherish simplicity and modesty as well as bravery and service. Young
Tadashi Kojo's uncles often recounted episodes of sacrifice from the life

of Saigo of Satsuma, as he was also known. "You must be a real man," they told him. "Like Saigo."

Ushijima now gave Kojo a living model of a true Satsuma samurai — and a special one, for he and his commanding officer were almost neighbors, from the same Kagoshima stock and caste. The general's association with Saigo was so strong that many thought he resembled the legendary hero physically. Tall for a Japanese, and emanating a commanding presence, Ushijima was so much the picture of a winning leader that his appearance alone inspired his troops. They revered him, and his officers did even more. The distinguished man seemed more an elder brother than a field officer, no common thing in an Army with piercing attention to rank and its trappings.

Ushijima once served as the military training officer at his alma mater, Kagoshima's First Middle School. He'd requested that post, which would have shamed many majors, because he liked teaching and cared little for furthering his career. Even after distinguishing himself with infantry units in the field, when he'd become known for his victories and bravery, he retained his easygoing modesty. Some liked him also because he didn't enjoy making speeches, and kept them short. Like Saigo, he seemed incapable of promoting his self-interest in the often fierce competition for advancement. When chosen for the staff of the minister of war in 1932, he at first declined the coveted appointment, explaining that he didn't feel up to the job, having served only in out-of-the-way places.

Japanese commanders were valued more as symbolic embodiments of strength than as hands-on strategists or policy makers. One of their primary functions was to radiate some of their Emperor's sublimity and benevolence, together with a resolve so strong that nothing on earth could shake it. Ushijima's field officers perceived the charismatic general as a kind of Mount Fuji, an immovable, unflappable guarantor of their victory — who, properly, stood above daily decisions, leaving all but the broadest strokes to his staff. In Kagoshima, where other strong but silent generals had grown up within a stone's throw of him, it was almost a motto that real men didn't bother with details. Even in high staff jobs, such as senior deputy to the Ministry of the Army, Ushijima seemed little interested in the give and take of intensely debated matters. Yet superiors were struck by his section's marked improvement, achieved largely because his subordinates admired his inability to quibble or nag.

His reputation having grown still more during his command of an infantry division in Manchuria, he was honored in 1942 by appointment to command the Imperial Academy, of which he was of course a graduate, as it strained to produce for a war racing to its zenith. Four years earlier, a fire in the cadet barracks had resulted in severe demotions. When another blaze destroyed some administrative offices, officers now braced for more wrath. Hideki Tojo, reviled by Americans as prime minister and minister of the Army, ordered severe punishment, including dispatch of the "offenders" in charge to the front, if appropriate. But Ushijima thanked the officers for their work containing the fire, argued that the full responsibility was his as commandant, and said he'd never send an officer to fight as punishment. He held firm against Tojo's fury and prevailed, adding to the fervent loyalty of his staff. The current minister of war was among many high officers eager to be appointed commander of the 32nd Army. Few grumbled when the prize went to Ushijima.

Most Okinawans were as cheered as the garrison itself by the arrival of "magnificent Ushijima" in August 1944. Those who caught sight of him saw an effortlessly friendly hero who — amazing for a Japanese bigwig — stopped to thank startled student volunteers who were helping dig fortifications. Field officers like Captain Kojo found him the commander under whom they'd dreamed of serving. His personal qualities were much more than a secondary matter: Subordinates were convinced that the "Japanese fighting spirit" with which he infused the 32nd Army counted for more than its armament.

When civilians encountered Ushijima's chief of staff, by contrast, they often saw a fierce countenance excoriating a quivering subordinate. It was fiery Isamu Cho who, the evening before the devastating October 10 air raid, had boasted the enemy would meet "complete destruction" if he dared attack Okinawa. Cho's reputation as a firebrand and intimidator was as deserved as Ushijima's as a father figure.

The notebook of fifty-one-year-old Cho, also a lieutenant general, was universally dreaded. His brushed record of his orders there included each project's completion date. Officers who failed to meet their deadline had the pages shoved in their faces as he roasted them. His temperamental likeness to Ushijima ended with his own reputation for extreme bravery. Many who saw nothing of the commander except a confident smile from an imposing presence endured outburst after thunderous outburst from his burly chief of staff. "You fool, can't you do *anything?*"

The "fools" included bright young officers whom Imperial General Headquarters had selected from its own complement to staff the 32nd Army. The best came to feel that Cho's bark was worse than his bite; their explosive mentor was simply unable to speak softly, especially now, when driven by fierce desire to complete his tasks before the possible invasion. Personally, Cho was outgoing and likable. More to the point, his charisma and rhetoric served to boost the 32nd Army's morale. Besides, if he demanded the dotting of every *i* in reports to him, that was his job as chief of staff, just as Commanding Officer Ushijima was supposed to hold himself above such details.

Still, the contrast between the two lieutenant generals went far deeper than billet or personality. In the best traditions of military officers everywhere, laconic, mild-mannered Ushijima was totally apolitical. In the worst tradition of Japanese militarism, eloquent Cho was immersed in the strident jingoism without which the Battle of Okinawa would never have taken place.

Cho's background is related to recently uncovered archival evidence that disproves some conventional wisdom about Emperor Hirohito. The Emperor did *not* hold no greater personal ambition than to pursue his love of marine biology. He *wasn't* an essentially peace-loving hostage to a clique of militarists who dragged Japan into the Second World War, despite his instincts and wishes. On the contrary, Hirohito took an active role in sanctioning Japan's conquests in the 1930s, secretly encouraging and supporting his seeming insubordinates. Still, the initial strikes upon Manchuria and China were remarkable for being planned and executed by a hotheaded faction of field officers who acted with wide latitude. Radical majors and colonels fabricated pretexts, mounted attacks, and presented Tokyo with faits accomplis the civilian authorities were unable to reverse, partly because they felt intimidated by the Army's fervent expansionist cliques, partly because the battlefield triumphs, glorified by the press, won wild cheers from most of the public. Those middle-level field officers counted on moderates being too weak to restrain the never officially authorized expansionist operations. With the blessings of some important politicians and generals in addition to the Emperor, it was they who thrust Japan into her greedy war by compelling support of their unprovoked aggression.

Cho was among the most passionate of them. The lover of strong drink and pretty women joined the notorious Cherry Blossom Society (Sakurakai) at its founding, in 1930. (The evanescent cherry blossom's disappearance after its brief life was an ancient symbol of the samurai's readiness to die for his sovereign at a moment's notice.) And together with self-sacrifice, the Sakurakai pledged to cleanse Japan of liberal democrats and other "decadent" Western influences that were polluting her traditional virtues. Their salvation was military dictatorship.

Isamu Cho stood out even among the ultranationalists who were utterly convinced that uniquely virtuous Japan had been grievously wronged by hypocritical evildoers and that right would be done only when the Army, sole repository of the national honor, wielded its sword to eliminate foreign enemies and domestic weaklings. The florid captain, prime mover of the society's most militant faction, was one of eleven members who prepared a coup d'état in January 1931. Their plan to murder the prime minister and install a general as dictator was abandoned at the last moment, but they did carry out the celebrated Manchurian Incident nine months later. Field-grade officers blew up a section of the Japanese-owned South Manchurian Railway, claimed that Chinese had done the insulting damage, and punished them by invading. The carefully prepared Kwantung Army (named for Canton Province) then tramped through the whole of Manchuria within months.

Most of Japan's great business and financial trusts (*zaibatsu*) initially opposed the adventure. So did much of the court aristocracy surrounding the Emperor and the elected government the Army supposedly served. All succumbed. But fearing that "weak-kneed" diplomacy would sacrifice the Army's glorious gains, Cho and a second ringleader led another attempt to replace the government with a military dictator — who was to appoint Cho himself to the crucial post of chief of Tokyo's metropolitan police. That plan called for the assassination of the prime minister. A conspirator later testified that Cho insisted on threatening the Emperor "with a drawn dagger" if he were reluctant to sanction the new cabinet. Higher officers thwarted that plot, perhaps because such incredibly blasphemous talk exceeded the bounds of even the superpatriots.

But although Cho was arrested, civilian judicial authorities were powerless to punish him amid the patriotic euphoria induced by the Army's easy devouring of Manchuria. For his episodes of blatant high treason, the stormiest of petrels was merely given a pro forma lecture by the inspector general of military education — who had been slated to be the conspirators' prime minister — and transferred to a pleasant post in the Kwantung Army: evidence of how thoroughly the most violent, disloyal "patriots" had already intimidated the Army and government. It had become dangerous to question even the most extreme acts proclaimed to have been taken out of "pure motives" for the nation's glory.

From Manchuria, Cho helped pressure the Army high command to support making it the puppet state of Manchukuo by circulating a rumor that the Kwantung Army might otherwise declare its independence. Again in 1938, he, now a regimental commander, was a ringleader inciting more "direct action," this time an attack on a Russian position on the Manchukuo-Soviet border. That would have drawn the Army into another border skirmish, but to the fury of many General Staff officers, the Emperor refused to sanction a major new conflict.

Ardent Cho persisted. During another desperate battle with Soviet border troops, he and a fellow officer urged their men to make suicide attacks against the enemy's tanks. Cho himself was said to have demonstrated Japanese coolness under fire by pulling down his breeches and standing exposed on a parapet. As chief of staff of the Japanese Army that later overran Thailand, he took it upon himself to press Vichy France to cede strategic territory, which Japanese troops quickly occupied. In all those actions, he exhibited contempt for anything not useful to Japan, an attitude that underlay the Army's often appalling treatment of non-Japanese soldiers and civilians. As a leading staff officer at Nanking in 1937, he faked a secret order — changing "Let them go" to "Finish them off!" — for disposing of thousands of Chinese prisoners. The subsequent brutalization of the Chinese capital was perhaps the world's greatest single act of willful cruelty until then: six weeks of maiming, raping, and murdering during which up to seventy-five thousand Chinese were shot, slashed, and burned to death, including many thousands of adult, aged, and infant civilians.*

Cho and the scrupulously neat Ushijima differed sharply even in dress; the chief of staff was wont to put his feet on his desk, unbutton his tunic, and enjoy a smoke. He would also remain fond of good drink and attractive women throughout the fighting. But no difference in personality or temperament, not even their opposite positions in political involvement, would come between the two or their model working relationship, the composed commanding officer acting as final arbiter for everything his excitable chief assistant prepared. Cho always shouted a smart "Yes, *sir!*" to his commanding officer's instructions and never contradicted him. And Ushijima, who had never attempted to stop the Imperial Way radicals, knew his zealous right hand, even more than the rest of his staff, shared his devotion to an impossible task, which is largely why he'd chosen him as his chief of staff. Their team excellence promised the worst for Okinawans, Americans, and Japanese together.

*The Tokyo War Crimes Commission would sentence Cho's commanding officer to hang for his part in the Nanking atrocities. Chinese scholars hold Ushijima, whose brigade was first to enter the capital, responsible for his troops' offenses but are otherwise silent about his role at Nanking. Japanese officers who knew him believe it "unimaginable" that he participated in atrocities — of which I found no evidence, not even in detailed Chinese accounts.

8 · The Boys in the Pacific

An endless stream of evidence ranging from atrocities to suicidal tactics could be cited . . . to substantiate the belief that the Japanese were a uniquely contemptible and formidable foe who deserved no mercy and virtually demanded extermination.
— John W. Dower, American historian of the war

Probably in all our history no foe has been so detested as were the Japanese.
— Alan Nevins, American historian

Goodbye, Mama, I'm off to Yokohama. . . . I'm going to slap a dirty little Jap.
— From a popular wartime song

DICK WHITAKER had a week's leave after boot camp, then two months of infantry training — through November 1944 — at North Carolina's Camp Lejeune. Shipped to the West Coast on December 1, the wiry lad was thus almost guaranteed to remain unsung even if he managed to become the hero he still hoped to be. War's meager proportion of glory to misery was much lower for Americans fighting in the Pacific than in Europe.

Location alone ensured them the worst fighting and least recognition. Europe was far more pleasant and closer to home, culturally as well as geographically. Rare Pacific liberties afforded little to take liberty with; sand and sun weren't much fun when the only change was monsoonlike rain. Even rear areas afforded only a tent for home, insect plagues attacking dirty skin, and plenty of disease. So much was nastier on the scorching or humid atolls and islands that a law of military life might have decreed the paradox: worse treatment for those who already had it worse — and more of it, since Pacific fighters' average tours lasted far longer.

Actually, a strategic decision made before Pearl Harbor was chiefly responsible for the imbalance. After the heads of the American services secretly agreed with their British counterparts to focus America's primary effort on Europe if and when she entered the war, President Roosevelt's and Prime Minister Churchill's first post–Pearl Harbor meetings confirmed that "only the minimum of force necessary for the safeguarding of vital interests" elsewhere should be diverted from the "decisive" Atlantic-European theater. The menace of the Third Reich in occupied Europe justified that decision. Given time, her U-boats might cut communications

between America and Britain. With more time, her scientists might produce devastating secret weapons — as they did, only slightly too late.

But sound as it was, the "Germany First" strategy necessitated less support for the "boys" in the Pacific, who were facing rougher conditions.
Those in Europe got more supplies, headlines, and applause for fighting their tamer war. Superb as he could be, the German fighting man
was an easier enemy than the Japanese, for he fought — the ordinary
Wehrmacht soldier, as opposed to members of the SS and other special
units — more or less according to the same dictates as the Allied soldier,
with more or less the same purpose and limits. With rare exceptions, his
goal was to kill others, not to die gloriously. He therefore surrendered
when the odds became hopeless. Whole divisions, entire armies of Germans surrendered, but virtually no Japanese.

Before Okinawa, only a statistically negligible scattering of Japanese
soldiers had been taken prisoner, even after stupefying bombardment
and even when there was no point in fighting on except death — which
was the point. They fought to it in the literal sense, often ending with a
suicide charge in pursuance of the remotest chance of killing an American before falling. Few veterans of the European theater could comprehend the implications without personal experience of it. *Think not of
death as you push through with every ounce of your effort, fulfilling your duties,* a
pamphlet distributed to all Japanese on active service instructed. *Fear not
to die for the cause of everlasting justice. Do not stay alive in dishonor. Do not die
in a way that will leave a bad name behind you.*

A year before, when Imperial General Headquarters had decided it
could no longer supply its Rabaul garrison, one hundred thousand
Japanese soldiers were left to fight or starve to death. The few captured
unconscious, a former Australian war prisoner recently wrote, "constantly attempted suicide when revived in an Allied hospital — by pulling
out IVs, tearing open newly stitched wounds, and even (when their hands
were tied) by trying to bite off their tongues."* When symbol-conscious
General MacArthur ordered the recapture of Corregidor, some two thousand of its three thousand Japanese defenders died by blowing themselves up in an underground arsenal.

Like his fellows unknowingly bound for Okinawa, Dick Whitaker
would have had great trouble crediting Japanese culture's very different
attitude toward "the last debt." In the West, death was an irreversible end

---

*Russell Braddon cites an Australian POW camp where 1,104 Japanese tried to kill them-
selves in atonement for having surrendered. "None had surrendered as we had surrendered,
with hands held high and an irrational optimism, and all had been treated with immense
consideration by their Australian guards. . . . Loathing the stigma of captivity, almost every
Japanese . . . positively dreaded meeting anyone who had known them in less painful days."

to a brief earthly appearance, a verdict feared because its sentence was unknown. Tears, repentance, sackcloth, and ashes naturally followed — whereas Japanese death was much more tolerable. In both the country's major religions, Buddhism and Shintoism, it was more a part of life than its end, and involved much less judgment, let alone final judgment to possible eternal damnation.

Actually, boot training gave Marines a better chance than most Americans to grasp Japanese attachment to the community. While Western religion, philosophy, and culture nourished a sense of self separate from all others, Japanese upbringing forged far more identity with the group. The cherished goal of *wa,* "harmony," could never be achieved by indulging in individual needs and rarely except through sacrificial pain. Especially in military affairs, Japanese men were prepared to believe that "death is lighter than a feather but duty heavier than a mountain."

Thousands of years on their cramped home islands had made the almost racially homogeneous Japanese members of one large family in some ways. The work patterns of their agricultural society also conditioned them to see themselves as members of a team. Farming, especially of the all-important rice crop, put a premium on cooperation. "If a nail sticks out," went one of the most repeated sayings about people who exhibited differences from the norm, "hammer it in." Almost all were brought up to feel that conformity to social expectations wasn't an unfortunate compromise but the only possible way to live.

Most Japanese were therefore snug in their own society, extremely uncertain and uncomfortable with outsiders, and habituated from their earliest years to think of what was defined for them as the common good rather than of self-assertion. That was the soil in which *bushido* grew. The Way of the Warrior was originally established as rules of conduct for samurai, retainers who wielded their swords for feudal lords. Elevating courage, valor, and loyalty, it corresponded in some ways to the chivalric codes for European knights. *Bushido* stressed self-discipline, reverence for nature, magnanimity, simplicity, modesty, and unquestioned obedience. It was pervaded with gratitude for the blessing of being Japanese.

To deter samurai from changing sides, which they'd done with some ease in medieval Japan, the notion was introduced that this brought loss of honor: strong discouragement in a "culture of shame," as a distinguished native social critic has called it. Surrender was also deeply shameful. Suicide was preferable, especially since Japanese culture included no prohibition against it. *Harakiri** came to be regarded as a

---

*Seppuku is ritual suicide, the rite of *harakiri* performed as remonstrance with prayer and pain, by cutting open one's abdomen. *Seppuku* has remained a solemn word while *harakiri* has become somewhat vulgar.

highly honorable act, reserved primarily for samurai, at the top of the commoners' social hierarchy.

But true samurai were never cowardly enough to court or hasten death. *Harakiri* was appropriate only when every resource had been exhausted and no hope remained to pass yet another test. Thus suicide was relatively rare — and even rarer in the seventeenth through nineteenth centuries, when central control became strong enough to stop almost all feudal fighting and samurai became more bureaucrats than warriors. Still, the practice was celebrated and idealized, chiefly by fervent noncombatants. When the act could be extolled in comfort rather than performed, legends, epics, and plays spread its virtues among armchair admirers, much as American Westerns would celebrate manly violence. *Bushido* was propagated far less by men who had to fight to the death or kill themselves than by comfortable fans of the drama. Although its roots went deep, its modern glorification arose after three centuries of peace, when, as Ian Buruma recently noted, the valorous "had little else to do but worry about rules, appearances [and] style . . . warriorhood without wars was soon reduced to a set of stylish postures."

A strong undercurrent of radical militarism ran close to the surface of Japan's relatively democratic 1910s and 1920s. When it broke through and pushed the country into her imperialist wars, ultranationalists menaced political, social, and cultural life — and held up *bushido* as a code of national behavior. Never mind that it had been devised for an elite in individual combat, that it mandated benevolence toward the weak and conquered, or that the feudal code could have rare application in modern combat. "The code of *bushido* says that a warrior lives so he is always prepared to die," the nonmystical captain of the light cruiser in *Yamato*'s screen told his crew as they got under way. "Nothing has been so abused and misinterpreted as this adage. It doesn't mean that a warrior must commit suicide for some slight reason. It means that we live so that we shall have no regrets when we must die. . . . We must not forfeit our lives meaninglessly." But few Japanese knew the origins or understood the concept. From the 1930s, it was exploited by the tyrannous twentieth-century obscurantism that overwhelmed the nation and hailed war.

That distortion elevated death from a slim possibility to a civic, or at least a military, duty. For half a century, all Japanese schoolchildren dedicated themselves to their Emperor every morning, bowing to His Imperial Majesty's photograph or in the direction of the Imperial Palace. Asked daily to state their dearest ambition, assembled classes thundered in unison: "To die for the Emperor."

A manual given each Army recruit spoke of "living and dying" with his fellow soldiers. *Read This Alone — And the War Can Be Won* lauded noble death — "Corpses drifting swollen in the depths of the sea / Corpses rotting in the mountain grass" — and extolled its rewards. All military life resounded with the need to die honorably. "Do not be afraid of combat and do not come home alive," was endlessly repeated. "Whether I float as a corpse under the waters or sink beneath the grasses of the mountainside," went a fighting man's hymn, "I will willingly die for the Emperor." As Russell Spurr put it recently, Johnny never came marching home. The martial songs "left him rotting on some foreign field or dying hopelessly in a futile suicide charge."

Troops were unceasingly reminded that *victory of honor* or *death of honor* were their only alternatives, that sublime willingness to die was essential to "the Japanese fighting spirit." "Do not disgrace yourself by being captured alive, but die," exhorted the Imperial Rescript for Soldiers and Sailors.

Of course there were degrees of belief in that. It was iron among the Army's backbone of academy graduates, men like Mitsuru Ushijima and Tadashi Kojo. One junior officer of that caste was wounded during the China War. A young Chinese officer recognized him as his instructor when he'd studied in Japan, and saw to it that the still-unconscious Japanese was delivered to a hospital. The rescued man killed himself after his release to atone for the shame of his capture — and Cadet Kojo thrilled to that admirable defense of honor.

The belief was weaker among reserve officers; still weaker among the drafted rank and file; and weakest among unmotivated nonconformists, softies, and recent conscripts who had hoped to escape the draft. One of the handful of a battalion's survivors on Okinawa would remember the Japanese people wearing two faces during the war's final years. "The one turned to others around them said, 'Fight and die for the country.' The other, turned inward and shared by the family, said, 'Don't die; survive at all costs and come home!'" Those who did return home to find tear-soaked telegrams mistakenly informing their families of their deaths realized that not all their parents were the uncompromising patriots they'd pretended to be.

Norio Watanabe, the antiwar and anti–Emperor cult draftee from Osaka, bought no part at all of *bushido*. Nothing in Army life or philosophy appealed to the former photographer. Just before Pearl Harbor, a fellow journalist risked a treason charge to urge him not to die in the likely imminent war with America, but Watanabe needed no such advice. Photographing for Osaka's General Motors division three years earlier, he'd viewed a company film. Images of its mighty Detroit plants were enough for the "misfit" to see immediately what the Army brass never could: Taking on America would be madness.

The diminutive Watanabe was thirty years old when his despised draft notice finally came, a year before the start of the fighting on Okinawa.

Clenching his teeth during basic training — partly to keep them from being broken — he quickly realized that the real reason for his beatings was the Army's conviction that fear was the best teacher of obedience. "The beaten lose their minds" — and loss of mind had taken Japan to the war in the first place.

Kenjiro Matsuki was another exception. His divergence from the norm began when he was a youngster in Honshu's impoverished north, where an uncle supplied him with baseballs fished out of a stream that ran from an athletic field to his little farm. Later, Matsuki's strapping size (by Japanese standards) and love of baseball — introduced to Japan in the 1870s by American visitors — won him a scholarship to Tokyo's Meiji University. The team's series against American universities in 1929 was a very exciting experience for the big first baseman, who went on to play on an All-Nippon team that hosted a series against Lou Gehrig and other stars. And during the summer of 1931, he actually danced with a young woman in Hawaii, something he might never have done in Japan outside dance halls, with their paid hostesses.

Matsuki played for Japan's first professional baseball team when it was formed in 1935, and he went on to captain, then manage the popular Hanshin Tigers. Happy memories of America deepened his sadness at the news of Pearl Harbor. What foolishness to extend the war, already far into China, to mighty America! But his firsthand knowledge of the enemy was exceptional among Japanese soldiers on Okinawa, and the uncommonly individualistic Watanabe would demonstrate that he was an even rarer exception. Although few ordinary Japanese soldiers believed the whole of their military indoctrination, most preferred death to the intolerable shame of surrender. The sullen, broken sprinkling who had surrendered in Pacific battles preceding Okinawa were convinced they could never return "disgracefully alive" to face the humiliation awaiting them at home, where their names would have been stricken from their villages' lists, their manhood forever effaced.

Americans took that for fanaticism, but it may have been closer to a poetic passion that welled up beneath the reserved Japanese countenance. It was a triumph of emotion over logic, like Japan's decision to attack America. But whatever its source, the heightened willingness to die was among the factors that made the Pacific War supremely brutal. Soldiers everywhere continued killing until they were beaten; the Japanese soldier wasn't beaten until he was killed.

Together with willingness to die, another important national trait helped ease the Army's way to its atrocities against Allied prisoners of war. Japanese children were raised to develop keen sensitivity to a complex web of duties, debts, and obligations that governed their society, all involving subtle rules and nuances that varied with time, place, and status. As Ian Buruma observed, it's almost essential to be brought up Japanese in order to acquire that sensitivity — "to have one's brains plugged into the social computer bank, as it were." But what of people who were outside the local and national communities — foreigners, in the first instance? The Japanese tendency was to feel no restraints when dealing with them, because the elaborate web didn't stretch that far. "When a Japanese is unplugged, by going abroad for instance, the computer can go berserk, for unlike Christian morality, the Japanese code isn't thought to be universal — it applies only to Japanese."

On top of that, many Japanese soldiers despised men for allowing themselves to be taken. Some believed beheading was an act of compassion that ended the prisoners' intolerable disgrace. How much better to give a prisoner a manly death than to prolong his "final degradation of the male spirit"!

It was easy for Americans in 1944 to see Japanese as inherently savage. The handful who knew something about their culture could cite the glorified barbarities — steel swords slashing human bone — that ran through Japanese history. But the country hadn't always mistreated prisoners of war. Defeated enemies sometimes received true *bushido* consideration and courtesy, as in the Russo-Japanese War of 1905, when treatment of Russian prisoners was often exemplary.* In *this* war, however, Japan was far more brutal than Germany to American POWs. However savage the Nazi occupation was to civilian populations, however monstrous the suffering imposed on Soviet and Eastern European prisoners, Germany treated many Western POWs tolerably, no doubt partly because the thousands of Wehrmacht soldiers in Allied hands were an incentive to observe her obligations as a Geneva Convention signatory. But Japan lost few prisoners to the Allies and cared little for those despicable cowards.

The Empire's prisoners were principally English and Dutch soldiers and colonial administrators captured during her lightning seizures of European colonies in the months following Pearl Harbor. Over a million had died or were painfully dying in their gruesome camps. Many were beaten, beheaded, and bayoneted, sometimes when tied between posts.

---

*At a model camp on Shikoku, Russian prisoners roamed the island, wandering into towns and houses. Early Japanese generals were of broad outlook and Confucian training, and at that time, Japan scrupulously adhered to international laws partly in her effort to win a revision of the unequal treaties imposed on her by the Western powers. Later generals became far more specialized and less in touch with nonmilitary interests of any kind, prompting some Japanese writers to attribute the shocking decline in humanity from 1905 to 1945 to the same narrowness that would cause so much military grief.

At Milner Bay, the penises of Australian prisoners were cut off and the foreskins sewn to their lips. Then a sign was left for when their comrades retook the territory: IT TOOK THEM A LONG TIME TO DIE.

> *Tokugawa Japan [in 1853], poor, proud and afraid, was about as different as a human society can be from plebeian, acquisitive, overconfident America.*
> — Murray Sayle, an Australian journalist who lives in Japan

> *We pray God that our present attempt to bring a singular and isolated people into the family of civilized nations may succeed without resort to bloodshed.*
> — Commodore Matthew C. Perry's journal entry the day after he arrived at Edo Bay in the same 1853

What caused such barbarity? Few Americans knew of the ripe hatred in the Japanese memory. American demonstrations of superiority, including opposition to Japan's wish for a racial equality clause in the 1919 Treaty of Versailles, seared and galled. Orientals were made ineligible for American citizenship. California and other states denied them the right to own land and segregated their schoolchildren. The 1924 Exclusion Act was directed specifically against Japanese immigration, despite a gentleman's agreement sixteen years earlier that had virtually ended it. The gratuitous insults demonstrated that the Yellow Peril was more in the American mind than in geopolitical reality.

The humiliations had begun earlier, at an episode hailed in American history and reviled in Japanese. When Commodore Matthew Calbraith Perry arrived to open Japan in 1853, the country had been closed almost hermetically for over two centuries. Sealed borders kept foreigners from entering and natives from leaving — or returning, if they'd been resident abroad. The entrenched isolation magnified the terrifying specter of Perry's warships in Tokyo Bay.

A letter from well-meaning President Millard Fillmore assured the Emperor that the democratic, peace-loving American Republic recognized Japan's right to govern herself without the slightest interference. But Japan's closure had led to occasional firing on foreign merchant ships in distress and to mistreatment of seamen shipwrecked on rocky coasts: aliens who'd violated the prohibition against entry. Perry had come to end those offenses — but more importantly to secure trading opportunities and coaling facilities and to awaken the Japanese to their "Christian obligation to join the family of Christendom," which the secretary of the Navy had confided was the mission's underlying motive. That was nothing to resent — presuming that good was served by opening a sovereign nation to *America's* economic and religious interests.

Enlightened Washington did not rely on moral suasion to convince the heathen. The good Christians brought big guns. Blinking at them, the

Japanese thought of the Westerners who had forced their way into China just fourteen years earlier. They included the British, who instigated the Opium War in annoyance at attempts to restrict the importation of the crippling drug and easily triumphed with their modern weapons. The Chinese Empire's virtual disintegration quickly followed, foreigners extracting concession after concession from the rump: "Slicing the Chinese melon," they called it.

Perry's demands were moderate, at least in comparison to those the British, Dutch, French, and Russians would make in his wake. Since *someone* was going to pry open the country very soon, better the young Republic than the cynical European powers that negotiated more arrogantly and mined concessions more greedily. But it was Americans who arrived first and began the process. An old Japanese folk song had warned of a "Black Ship . . . an alien thing of evil mien." Two of Perry's black-hulled ships also belched black smoke, the color by which the vessels instantly became known and remained so by every schoolchild of succeeding generations.

The Japanese had never seen steamships. Their shore batteries had no hope against Perry's cannon. The country was submerged in panic and dismay.

It would figure little in Japanese memory that Perry's squadron played a crucial part in the country's liberation from an often cruel feudalism whose borders were closed to tighten it. What most Japanese would remember was a devastating blow to national honor, with trespassers getting their way through superior might. The black ships became a national metaphor for affront to sacred Japan. The first sight of Western civilization — up the barrel of American guns — fed the Japanese sense of themselves as being under pressure from those who wished her ill, led by the United States.

Roots much deeper in their own history and national psyche fed their glorification of militarism and urge to subjugate others. An old Japanese saying has it that "the cherry is the first among flowers as the warrior is the first among men." Still, Perry's presumption and amazing cannon spurred their impatience to build their own. They had good reason to believe that unless they could copy the barbarians' military technology, they'd suffer more such humiliations, maybe even be carved up into economic colonies, as Western powers were doing elsewhere throughout Asia. Memory of the black ships helped feed an appetite for conquest that would end in the Pacific War, when the emotional people, overwhelmed by their rages and fears, perceived Americans as "provocative symbols of a detested past" rather than as human beings. A cartoon celebrating Pearl Harbor depicted a dismayed Uncle Sam uncorking a giant samurai from a bottle: revenge for the Black Ships.

From a barbarous prisoner-of-war camp, Laurens van der Post perceived Japan's response as "a kind of accumulated revenge of history on the European for his invasion of the ancient worlds of the East and his arrogant assumptions of superiority which had made him use his power . . . to bend the lives and spirits of the people of Asia to [the European's] inflexible will." Since Perry's arrival, the proud people had been forced to live "a kind of tranced life" in the presence of the European, who prevented them from being their own special selves, with their greatness and illusions. "But now the spell was broken," van der Post observed, "and the built-up flood of resentment had broken through all restraints. Out in full spate, in the open at last, it swept the Japanese, normally so disciplined, but now drunk on what . . . appeared to be invincible military power, into a chaotic mood of revenge."

But that couldn't fully explain the barbarity, because more of it was unleashed on impoverished fellow Asians than high-handed Westerners. Japan's slashing and conquering on the Asian continent in the 1930s and 1940s were as bad as the very worst of Western colonialism. The Greater East Asia Co-Prosperity Sphere, its hoaxing title for the conquered lands where it sloshed blood and sucked sustenance, spilled over with atrocities. "Japanization" of "inferior" Asians included slapping faces in public and murdering citizens: some ten million (mostly civilian) Chinese alone. The conquerors provided "an almost spellbinding spectacle of brutality and death," as a historian recently put it. In 1937, the best Tokyo newspapers reported a "friendly competition" between two officers to be first to behead 150 Chinese with their swords.

As for Americans, Japanese hatred waxed as the war situation worsened. By 1944, magazines were telling their readers that the more American beasts and demons who were sent to hell, "the cleaner the world will be." Classroom posters exhorted pupils to KILL THE AMERICAN DEVILS! Kill they did: Prisoners of the Japanese were seven times as likely to perish as prisoners in the European camps of the Axis, and the statistics were worse for Americans alone. One percent of American POWs of the Germans died; 40 percent died in Japanese camps. One of the living, who happened to be a knowledgeable admirer of Japanese culture, was made to watch soldiers taking bayonet practice on live prisoners tied between bamboo posts. "I would never have thought it possible that in our time there could still have been so many different ways of killing people — from cutting off their heads with swords, bayoneting them in [various] ways, to strangling them and burying them alive — but most significantly, never just shooting them."

The Imperial Army's Wake Island garrison shot over a hundred American construction workers who had been building airstrips there when the Japanese landed in 1941. Japanese pilots shot American pilots dangling in parachutes after bailing out. Their submarines sank a fraction of the tonnage sent under by American submarines, but Allied merchant sailors struggling in the water faced much greater danger. After a Japanese ship transporting American prisoners of war to the mainland was torpedoed, guards struggling to stay afloat machine-gunned prisoners nearby in the water. (Many of the prisoners would have died anyway in airless holds that drove them mad with thirst.) Within days of the October 10 raid on Naha, a Japanese submarine's crew laughingly fired pistols and machine guns into the lifeboats of a Liberty ship it had just sunk.

The historian John Toland has argued that the Japanese-American war would not have been fought if not for the mutual misunderstanding, distrust, and language difficulties — and racial prejudice, irrationality, honor, pride, and fear among both peoples. Toland produced much evidence to show that "both sides feared things they need not have feared . . . we were damn fools like they were damn fools, it's enough to make you sick." But even the disastrous American mistranslations of Japanese diplomatic communications he cites can't expunge what *did* have to be feared. Americans were indeed damn fools, full of rigidity and self-righteous ignorance of Asia, full of stupid, swaggering insults. But that wasn't the principal cause of the Pacific War, or of its most awful excesses.

After Whitaker's two months of infantry training in Camp Lejeune, he was sent to the West Coast in early December 1944, when the 32nd Army's crash program to build the fortifications he'd face on Okinawa was gaining momentum. The impatient eighteen- and nineteen-year-olds on the weeklong train ride believed no humans had ever been packed together so tightly — while outside stretched the West's awesome vastness, a new spectacle confirming their country as the world's most blessed and deserving. That strengthened their conviction that Americans were immeasurably more advanced and virtuous than the dirty little bucktoothed Japs. More than ever in love with their Land of the Free, the young warriors bitched about their living conditions but would never have traded places with the soft civilians who were going to miss the great fight.

Righteous vengeance beckoned. Several months after the Philippines had fallen to Japanese forces in April 1942, the U.S. Army learned the fate of prisoners taken there from three officers who managed to escape, but the information was kept secret for fear that its release would bring reprisals upon the surviving prisoners. Only in January 1944 did the American public learn that men dying of thirst were stopped alongside wells and forbidden to drink, that others barely able to stand were booted and beaten, that an officer's finger was hacked off when he refused to surrender his wedding ring, that prisoners were forced to bury their comrades alive . . . and that over six hundred Americans and at least ten times as many Filipinos too exhausted to keep pace on a march from Bataan to a prison compound were clubbed, shot, buried, bayoneted, and otherwise tortured to death.

American newspapers blistered with outrage and confirmation that the "inhuman," "barbarous," "depraved" enemy was a bestial force from some headquarters of evil. Everyone knew *some* Germans were good, but Japs were a racial menace as well as a dangerous enemy. Cartoons depicted them as mad dogs and hairy tarantulas rightly squashed by combat boots. Under a large photograph of Japanese corpses, a magazine for Marines called *Leatherneck* ran the caption: GOOD JAPS. KEEP 'EM DYING.

Whitaker had read about the Bataan Death March the previous year, but the details still gripped him as his train neared San Diego. Although he knew he'd be facing a "devious, cruel, bloodthirsty" enemy, he didn't yet know how they fought. He nurtured an assumption that the bow-legged runts in the sloppy uniforms — baggy trousers, ridiculous puttees — couldn't possibly be a match for his spit-and-polish, rough and very ready Marines, many of whom would sustain such bravado-laced illusions all the way to the front lines on Okinawa. Green replacements for badly shot-up companies would be rushed in during lulls; and with no time to acquire "combat smarts," a shocking number would themselves become casualties within hours.

Their platoon leaders would try hard to save them. One hurriedly lectured a new group of bewildered replacements as they huddled together against murderous Japanese fire from the hill nicknamed Sugar Loaf. Aching with exhaustion and shock from that day's loss of buddies, the young platoon leader, up from the ranks after all his officers had been shot, concluded by pointing his pistol at the greenhorns. "And if I hear any bullshit about the Japs being lousy fighters, I'll shoot you," he said. "If one of you motherfuckers says they can't shoot straight, I'll put a bullet between your fuckin' eyes before they do."

9 · Final Japanese Preparations

The Americans still don't seem to admit defeat. Their bombers are attacking the homeland. There are rumors . . . that Okinawa is about to be attacked.
— A nineteen-year-old gunner on *Yamato,* days before the American landing on Okinawa

Of course the tide must turn. The glorious spirit of our nation will overcome the enemy. Our brave young kamikaze pilots are sinking their ships and striking terror into their hearts. We shall fight on if a hundred million perish.
— The reply of the gunner's father

We don't have to fear Americans; they consider war a sport. With that mentality, they're certain to lose to the Japanese fighting spirit. Answer: *Yeah, a sports team against a suicide squad.*
— Two members of the Okinawan Home Guard on the eve of the American landing

WHAT CHIEF OF STAFF CHO whipped the 32nd Army to complete was an unprecedentedly effective complex of fortifications. Much of Okinawa's terrain of sharp rises overlooking flat plains was ideal for defense. Tens of thousands of Japanese soldiers and Korean laborers gasped all day in the sun to improve it with a network of strongpoints featuring integrated systems of observation, firepower, and reinforcement. Their number and scope far exceeded the much lesser works on Iwo Jima and other islands.

For 32nd Army headquarters, an ancient cave complex beneath Shuri Castle — atop the hill above the Normal School — was much enlarged and improved. The main tunnel was fifty feet below ground at its shallowest point. Thirty-two chambers and designated areas along its thirteen-hundred-yard length and side shafts accommodated a thousand men, the equivalent of a fighting battalion. They included a dispensary, a kitchen and pantry, a telephone switchboard chamber, weather and typists' sections . . . everything from General Ushijima's quarters to intelligence and operations rooms. (The well-stocked pantry was overseen by a chef whom General Cho had brought over from the mainland, together with a supply of fine Scotch whiskey.) American intelligence would locate that installation shortly after the start of the fighting, but even the heaviest air and naval bombardments would cause little damage except near one of its concreted entrances. The working spaces would prove virtually impervious to conventional explosives.

From the agony of the battle, Japanese soldiers would remember the months of preparation with nostalgia. But now their life was only sweat and tears. Bullying veterans monopolized water, food, and every perk. The beatings for slipups or "bad attitude" were even more severe than before because digging put the roughneck senior soldiers in a foul mood. When those "vicious, gangster-type" noncoms, as a junior private called them, were out of earshot, some victims comforted themselves with thoughts of retaliation if the Americans really did land. A few actually looked forward to battle in the hope that anything had to be better than their present misery.

Spring brought merciless heat. A large army prodigiously sweating while mixing vast amounts of concrete made water scarcer than ever on the island. "We couldn't wash our dishes, our clothes, even our hands after relieving ourselves," a soldier later lamented. The rapid spread of skin infections brought itchy torture even to the few who weren't performing heavy labor. The rations were so meager that men found picking and eating radish leaves "an indescribably happy occasion." Cooks ordered them to gather mulberry leaves for mixing into their rice, but the tough greens stuck in their throats. A thin soup, oily with pork fat and dressed with a few pieces of squash, completed the main meal. Still, ordure accumulated so fast that one artilleryman's turn to lug it to a swamp of sewage came every ten days. "Why so much waste? Because soldiers couldn't bear their hunger and secretly bought tapioca buns and steamed sweet potatoes from civilians" — although one little bun cost a private his daily pay.

During a regular "first-year soldier training" session, a senior private ordered a waste disposal team to fall in with their boots in their hands. The bully scrutinized them, then pointed to Norio Watanabe's. "What's this?" he thundered. Although Watanabe, the former photographer from Osaka, had cleaned and polished his boots with his usual frightened care, a speck of excrement remained on a heel. "Tell me," screamed the senior private, "from whom did you receive this item to keep and maintain?" As required, diminutive Watanabe replied that he kept and maintained his boots for the Emperor. "What? You know that and still put shit on it? Lick it off! Eat it!" Watanabe's hesitation increased his superior's rage. The senior private lashed out with his fists until Watanabe swallowed his new humiliation. "No matter what, we must blindly obey everyone of higher rank."

The troops were kept at their toil nights as well as days. Caves and more caves were needed for "barracks" and command posts, for supply and ammunition depots, for a whole strategy and existence based on counterattack from underground. Thousands of men worked around the clock for nearly a year, enlarging the natural grottoes and burrows with which the subtropical landscape abounded. The most elaborate holes had up to four stories, some supported by timbers and, when there was time, provided with cross-ventilation. Many of the tens of thousands of stone and concrete tombs that dotted the countryside were converted into makeshift pillboxes and fitted out with guns and supplies.

Okinawans dug too, some hired, some as conscripts. Thirty-nine thousand men — every fit male between sixteen and forty — were drafted, of whom about a third were used as laborers. Twenty-four thousand were issued rudimentary uniforms in the Home Guard, or Boetai. Teenage students assigned to units with no nearby living accommodations had to walk to their stations up to twelve miles every day, to and from home. In the fortified areas, most notable public and private buildings were taken over by the Army, the schools usually converted to barracks. Awed children watched growing numbers of soldiers drill on their dusty grounds while their parents wondered whether civilian life would disappear entirely. But there was no alternative to helping prevent Americans from bayoneting their children. Many Okinawans who volunteered, or *were* volunteered through their civic institutions, had only hand tools. The 32nd Army's full array of heavy construction equipment consisted of two bulldozers and one earth roller. A million tons of dirt were removed from caves in straw baskets balanced on heads and shoulders. New airfields were leveled with pickaxes and hoes. The laboring at Yomitan and Kadena Airfields, to which Masahide Ota and other Normal School students had been previously assigned, had been a minor preliminary to that massive effort.

Where tools couldn't be commandeered from farmers, Army officers told civilians to use their bare hands. Many did, including children. The limestone hills were relatively easy to dig into, but the coral, which in many places had a depth of twenty to sixty feet, was harder than concrete. Little dynamite was available. There was no iron for reinforcing concrete and too little concrete itself. Since the October 10 air raid had destroyed most of the gasoline allocated for the 32nd Army's handful of trucks, millions of timbers for shoring up the caves, tunnels, and entry shafts had to be brought down largely by hand from the mountains of the north, then loaded onto little native boats for transporting south.

With too little protein and fresh vegetables, civilians grew weak on the relentless labor. Many developed chronic colds and diarrhea, causing those previously exempted from physical work to be enlisted for the "slave labor," as an Okinawan later put it. Like real slave labor, this variety could kill. After months of grueling work in dank caves or under a burning sun with no rain, men began collapsing.

Isamu Cho oversaw the digging, but its mastermind was Ushijima's chief operations officer, Colonel Hiromichi Yahara. A talented tactician with a pragmatic bent, Yahara looked his part as a realist who relied more on his intellect than on a heart stiffened with "Japanese spirit." His broad range of planning experience included a year as an exchange officer in America, which helped make him more Western in outlook than the samurai traditionalist Ushijima or the mystically inclined Cho. It also helped make the 32nd Army's leadership Japan's best in the Pacific, although Yahara's dry personality and bent for facts and figures would incline him to clash with the romantically aggressive Cho, his superior.

But the two were now almost conspiratorial allies, for the overall strategy of digging deep and counterattacking from underground shelters was the 32nd Army's largely self-made response to what it knew would be overwhelmingly superior enemy firepower. That fundamentally defensive approach ignored both Japanese military tradition and Ushijima's disapproving superiors in Formosa and Tokyo. Why, the brass challenged, was the 32nd Army so committed to caution? Why was so little of the beach defended? But Ushijima stood his ground, and Yahara continued planning the defense in keeping with his view of war as more science than a test of the opposing armies' wills.

Colonel Yahara also knew that science started with acknowledging somber reality. During the 10/10 air raid, he'd had three divisions to work with, supplemented by some smaller armored, artillery, and service forces and the 44th Independent Mixed Brigade, partly "restocked" by local conscripts after most of it went down with *Toyama maru*. The strongest of those units was the crack 9th Division, whose high morale and long history of combat experience more than made up for its relative lack of heavy armor. The operations chief positioned that backbone of the 32nd Army in the backbone of the defensive position, behind a natural line of high ground protecting Shuri and Naha. That left the 24th Division above the beaches, where Yahara correctly foresaw the Americans would land, and where a heavy concentration of practiced artillery would devastate them when they'd be most vulnerable, while discharging their troops and equipment. Then infantry regiments, including Captain Kojo's, would emerge from their bunkers to hit fast and hard in the close combat where Japanese superiority would prevail.

Staff officers were supremely optimistic in public and fitfully so in private. No defenders of previous islands had thrown a landing force back into the sea, but none had been nearly so well prepared. Some understood that such a feat would make no difference in the long run. Eventually, a second or third landing by the enemy would have to succeed, since the defense had so few reserves and no way to replenish supplies that were short to begin with. But others hoped a bloody mauling of a major landing would compel America to seek tolerable peace terms instead of inviting worse by invading the mainland.

Such illusions soon vanished, however, together with the pleasurable anticipation of obliterating the landing force. The reason was an unlucky guess, or grave miscalculation, by Imperial General Headquarters, which removed the 9th Division to bolster the defense of the Philippines. The division's twenty-five thousand men were shipped in that direction via Formosa in December, but the Philippine cause seemed lost before they completed their trip. Not sent on, they weren't sent back either, partly in fear of more sea travel, partly because Formosa — which Japanese strategists still saw as a more likely next American target than Okinawa — had already been drained in vain support of the Philippine garrison. Ushijima's best division would remain on uninvaded Formosa throughout the rest of the war.

Through Yahara, Ushijima had tried to persuade IGHQ not to act on its devastating decision. The colonel argued with logic and passion that no effective defense of Okinawa could be guaranteed without the 9th — and if it had to be withdrawn because the Philippines was to be the decisive battle, General Ushijima preferred to accompany it and die in the fighting there. Ushijima couldn't be optimistic about his answer. During his own Tokyo tours, he'd helped draft telegrams with empty promises of heavy reinforcements to commanders fighting American forces on other islands. But with a chance for at least an interim stalemate if the 9th Division were sent back to anchor his defense on Okinawa, there was a faint hope this case might be different.

Tokyo held firm, however, and twice reneged on promises to send replacement divisions for the 9th. Eager as Japan's de facto rulers at Imperial General Headquarters were to prompt American thoughts of negotiating an acceptable peace, they were already girding for a decisive battle at home. Orders for the dispatch of the replacement divisions were therefore countermanded; better defend the mainland.

Although field commanders like Tadashi Kojo didn't permit the loss of the 9th Division to affect their morale, higher staff officers calculated that it represented almost half the 32nd Army's fighting strength and knew its transfer was a "shattering blow" to the defensive plan. Some would later speculate that it was also a personal blow to Ushijima: When the 9th sailed off, he began thinking about atoning for the "failure" of his inevitable defeat. Flouting an unwritten rule that generals appointed their adjutants from the elite of academy graduates, he chose a rough-hewn man up from the ranks: a master swordsman who would ensure a swift, sure beheading the instant after the time would come for the general's self-disembowelment.

Even now, Ushijima was utterly without illusion about his future. He remained the model commanding officer, radiating unshakable spiritual strength without the slightest outward sign of disappointment or doubt about the future. But the withdrawal of the 9th and the refusal to replace it were unmistakable evidence that Tokyo had already conceded Okinawa and saw the coming battle as a mere delaying action.

Yahara also had no illusions, even though some of the 9th Division's weaponry remained on Okinawa, giving the 32nd Army more of it, especially artillery, than the defenders of any previous Pacific island. Still, although that would stun and dismay the American forces, it changed little in the colonel's calculations. He estimated that the attacking force as a whole would have twelve or more times the firepower of the 32nd Army, not including their air and naval support. Therefore he scrapped his elaborate preparations for the massive counterattack in favor of a new strategy based on his sharply reduced resources. Instead of the cherished "decisive battle" in which winner takes all, Yahara prepared for a war of attrition based entirely on underground "sleeping tactics."

Much reorganizing of service, administrative, and engineering units into infantry battalions had to be undertaken for the diminished defense. As units moved to new sites during their massive repositioning in December, a gigantic explosion destroyed nearly half the 32nd Army's supply of munitions. Although small quantities of supplies were still arriving by air, Japanese shipping had nearly ceased after the 10/10 air raid. Now Yahara prepared a completely defensive campaign. Some staff officers calculated that a single battleship's firepower exceeded that of a full division. Knowing the enemy's control of the sea and air would give him an immeasurable advantage beyond his 12-to-1 firepower superiority on the ground, Yahara saw the sole solution as withdrawing from the bunkers above the beaches, burrowing even deeper into better fortifications inland, and waiting to engage the Americans seriously only from there.

The new strategy was not only defensive but also defeatist in the sense that it provided for no more than brief counterattacks with no hope of eventual victory. But although the great majority of Japanese lived on that hope, Yahara preferred pragmatic results to the comfort of fantasy. He had to plead his case, especially to calm the fervently aggressive Cho, against the grain of the Japanese upbringing on attack and more attack. But knowing there was no way to prevent the total destruction of the 32nd Army, the realist reckoned his only goal could be to make the outcome as costly as possible, for which protection from the enemy's supreme firepower was crucial.

Thus the pace of the digging increased even more, especially since the redeployment of the remaining Japanese forces required units to abandon their laboriously constructed fortifications and begin anew. Perhaps no digger in the world could keep at it longer and more intensely, with fewer tools and less nourishment, than the Japanese soldier. This was no supplementary effort to provide cover during battle but a fundamental approach, following the single most important Japanese decision of the campaign. It would result in the construction of over sixty miles of tunnels as refuges for the entire 32nd Army, with all its ammunition, weapons, and other supplies.

The diggers were more or less comforted by the ultimate reward spelled out in a slogan composed for them: "Confidence in victory will be born from strong fortifications." Knowledge that their safety would depend on their own efforts encouraged diligence. Some service units had occasional hours off to fish, drink in Okinawa's beauty, and take pleasure in the natives' kindness. The luckiest combat units had a few visits to Naha's famous red-light district, rebuilt after the 10/10 raid and closely supervised by the Army. (Okinawan courtesans and geishas were generally reserved for officers; Korean women, some brought from Korea and the Japanese mainland as comfort girls, serviced the men in the ranks. The Army had seized thousands of Korean girls, some only twelve and thirteen years old, by force.) Others had no time off whatever apart from a brief visit or two to houses of native volunteers. One man would remember only digging during his nine months preceding the battle. "We slept on rocks and gouged rocks. . . . We endured every conceivable suffering in a soldier's life while building our position."

More months of feverish work produced new shelters, the best of which were like railroad repair tunnels: well ventilated, equipped with drainage for the sour wetness underground, and protected by a hundred feet or more of earth above. Tracks were laid for mounting heavy artillery, and entrances were camouflaged: Iwo Jima had bitterly demonstrated the Americans' skill in detecting the source of incoming fire, then destroying the gun with savage shelling from their ships, planes, and artillery. Now Japanese gunners were forbidden to fire until the last minute, after which they'd quickly roll their guns back out of sight.

All that was preparation for exacting the highest price for territory to be surrendered foot by foot, which is what Yahara's final operational plan amounted to. Nevertheless, he wrote and distributed a pamphlet titled *The Road to Certain Victory,* and Japanese soldiers remained ignorant of his strategy's underlying pessimism. Civilians, although also disturbed by the loss of the 9th Division, suspected even less as they watched their ancestral tombs converted into bunkers and saw their pastoral hillsides turned into bastions bristling with machine-gun positions. Realizing that battle was imminent, they "shivered with their image of the enemy," although only a handful guessed there was no hope whatever of defeating him, much less that no sacrifice could do more than give the mainland more time to prepare for *its* Tennozan.

Book II

10 · The Landing

You cannot regard the enemy as on a par with you. You must realize that material power usually overcomes spiritual power in this war. The enemy is clearly our superior in machines. Don't depend on your spirits overcoming this enemy. Devise combat methods with mathematical precision, then think about displaying your spiritual power.
 — General Ushijima to the 32nd Army

The bombardment's gunsmoke and dust cloud changed the sky to yellow. The shells shot from hundreds of battleships, cruiser and destroyer batteries numbered thousands and tens of thousands a minute. . . . The Japanese army, on the other hand, kept silent and did not fire a single shot.
 — An unwilling Okinawan conscript

TO DISTINGUISH IT from earlier D-days, *L* — "love" in American military parlance — was chosen for the April 1 landing. Nothing as grim and breathtaking had been unleashed in the history of the Pacific. Nothing similar is likely to be seen again.

Most of the ships of the much-documented Normandy operation the previous June had to travel only the width of the English Channel. Operation Iceberg, an undertaking of the same immense scale, took place sixty-two hundred miles from San Francisco, four thousand from Pearl Harbor, and many days' sailing from supply depots and anchorages the Navy had established closer to the target. The movement of mountains of goods and equipment across the Pacific's breadth — from fighter planes to millions of candy bars — was an extraordinary feat in itself, and no secondary one, since the American way of war rested on colossal quantities of supplies. The twenty-two thousand tons that had been delivered daily to Iwo Jima during the fighting just ended there would be only 15 percent of Okinawa's daily total. Love-day's 1,457 ships and over half a million men were the consummation of a stunning exercise in military logistics.

Dick Whitaker first glimpsed its magnitude after his ship's convoy joined a larger one, but still saw only a fraction of the whole. "There were ships to the horizon, a truly awesome number. I couldn't have imagined that many ships existed in the world."

Four hundred thirty were troopships. Their union with the largest armada ever assembled in the Pacific awed everyone aboard. The vessels had sailed from eleven ports, from Seattle to Pearl Harbor to Ulithi, an atoll thirty-seven hundred miles west of Hawaii that provided a fine anchorage and base for forward operations (together with a sandy beach where Whitaker and his fellow passengers had enjoyed the luxury of an afternoon off their ship when she stopped there on her two-week passage from Guadalcanal). Although no man could see more than a sliver of the thirty square miles of ocean they covered, that was enough to bring relief that "someone somewhere knew what he was doing. Getting that unbelievable number of ships with their specialized equipment and personnel to arrive all at one time at a dot in the Pacific gave us confidence. Maybe we'd be all right."

"I felt myself smiling inside," another Marine would remember. "Maybe I'd be hit on this Okinawa where we were going, but there was no way we could lose with that incredible number of ships." The submarine fleet alone, Task Force 17, contributed over fifty vessels, some for landing advance parties to prepare the beaches. The 21st Bomber Command contributed over three hundred B-29s. The aircraft carriers of Task Force 58, which would engage *Yamato* a week later, supplied more than fifteen hundred additional planes, many of which would bomb targets on Okinawa for ten days before L-day. The fighting ships were the largest assembly in history: over forty carriers, eighteen battleships, scores of cruisers, and almost 150 destroyers and destroyer escorts.

They poured fire onto Okinawa, especially on and around the landing sites, for six full days and some of their nights. The pre-invasion bombardment by sea and air set a pattern for Japanese soldiers on the island that they'd follow until most of their deaths. As Colonel Yahara had planned, they hid underground during the day and sneaked out to do errands — later, to fight — at night. "Our activities begin in the evening, when the worst of the air raids are over," a survivor would record.

> Cooking, drawing water, washing and, more important, receiving more ammunition and moving our weapons . . . all that must be done when naval bombardments keep cutting into everything, making us break into a cold sweat when the shells hit. Still, it's a Garden of Eden when no planes are overhead.
> "Let's go! The demon's gone!"
> Out we jump from our cave, run the tiny path to the foot of the mountain to find the small trench where our ammunition is hidden.
> It's dark on the return trip. We trace our way back to the cave, heavy ammunition cases on our backs, frantic to make it back *fast*. Naval shells burst all around us [and] . . . I feel the whole time as if my soul is wearing out. It's totally unsafe outside the cave even when the demons aren't flying above.

Japanese soldiers who'd believed nothing could be worse than the air raid of the previous October 10 realized they were mistaken in January, when a series of equally powerful ones hit them day after day. Again they believed they'd seen the worst — until the pre-invasion bombardment, which was once more surpassed on L-day itself. In the small hours of April 1, the support ships and 564 carrier-based aircraft began raking eight miles of Okinawan beaches with by far the greatest bombardment in the history of the long Pacific campaign.

Japanese likened the start of the "ferocious" barrage to thousands of industrial plants switching on their machinery together — but, as another soldier specified, "with the magnitude of a hundred thunders striking at once." Soon the whole landing area was enveloped in smoke as if from a volcanic eruption: too heavy to make out the shore. Ten great battleships pounded it with their main batteries of 14- and 16-inch guns. Smaller broadsides from their secondary batteries and from nine cruisers, twenty-three destroyers, and almost two hundred gunships added to the enormous weight of metal: almost forty-five thousand shells, plus thirty-three thousand rockets and twenty-two and a half thousand mortar shells. Both sides felt the world was exploding. The ten battleships alone could send 120 tons of high explosive a minute onto Okinawa, and all sustained their ferocity for three hours, helping land some twenty-five rounds on every hundred square yards up to half a mile inland from the beach — which was also hit by planes, some using napalm. The smell, smoke, and head-splitting noise of previous amphibious landings had been stupendous. This was more.

Then it stopped, still in predawn darkness. At 0406 hours, the commander of the amphibious operation gave the traditional order to "land the landing force."

"We've all seen amphibious landings in the movies," a young naval officer whose landing ship was launching Sherman tanks in flotation collars would write home. "But the real thing is more spectacular than anything I ever dreamed of. The precision bombing of the beachhead by scores of planes, the monotonous shelling of the shoreline by the huge 'wagons,' the wave after wave of LVTs, small boats, etc., heading into the island constituted a display so formidable and awe-inspiring I shall never forget it."

The spectacle impressed the enemy too. A Japanese soldier reported from an observation post that he couldn't make out the ocean's color because of the enemy ships. A moment later, he conscientiously corrected himself. "I take that back. It's 70 percent ships, 30 percent ocean."

> *When I saw . . . the American fleet, I doubted my eyes. . . . They looked like sumo wrestlers, squatting and waiting without the slightest movement for their turn in a match on some stage. Just thinking of what would happen if all those warships started firing sent shivers down my spine. This tiny island of Okinawa would be completely plowed under.*
> — An Okinawan father two days before the landing

John Lardner reported the natives as "somewhat bemused" — nonsense prompted by ignorance of the bombarded in general and of Okinawans in particular, despite Lardner's success as a *New Yorker* war correspondent. They were actually full of foreboding. Since heavy American aerial reconnaissance had revealed almost nothing about the underground Japanese positions, most of the prelanding bombardment had no specific targets. The majority of shells therefore landed randomly to obliterate civilian buildings or "crater the fields of the Okinawan peasantry," as the naval historian Samuel Eliot Morison would put it — while Okinawans wondered whether "the whole island would be pulverized and blown away." The giant fleet's week of firing had been immensely more menacing than they'd expected. Their new routine too would last until the end of the campaign: hiding and sleeping by day, the luckiest in caves; seeking sustenance and better hiding places by night.

Shui Ikemiyagi, a Naha librarian now in the Home Guard, summed up the temper of the conscripted natives, who continued hoping for the promised Japanese victory — and that it wouldn't cost them everything. Most men in his generally "gloomy and miserable" cave wondered whether the imminent landing would bring their death. Some cried themselves to sleep, worrying about their families.

> We spent the last week of March like criminals on death row. The instrument of execution was there . . . all ready for us. The only difference was that it was the American fleet instead of an ax or noose. . . . We tried to suppress it and started to chatter a lot of nonsense. When no actual fear of death lurks nearby, we humans talk of it with composure, even laugh at it. But we stop mentioning death when it lies right in front of us.

Most Japanese soldiers were distinctly tougher — "full of apprehension," wrote an artillerist whose heavy gun was hidden deep in a hill and camouflaged with branches, "but it was mixed with eager expectation that swelled our chests." It was a tribute to their training, bravery, and supreme commitment that the sight of the enemy armada, while impressing them with its size and "impudence" for steaming so "nonchalantly" into Japanese waters, neither seized them with fear nor informed them of the battle's inevitable end. The same training, implemented amid the national hypnosis, was also what blinded virtually all to how Japan's war had been ravaging others and why it couldn't possibly be won — blinded them even to evidence before their eyes, for many gazed with satisfaction at the immensely powerful fleet. So many enemy vessels gathered for convenient destruction by Imperial planes and warships!

*   *   *

The spectacle was so massively more violent than anything the Americans had seen that most had moments of intense exhilaration. The smoke, smell, and thunder of naval salvo after earsplitting salvo were stupefying. To a man waiting for the order to enter his landing boat, just the din of brass shell cases clattering on one ship's steel deck deafened "like a thousand cymbals falling down stone steps." But the troops readying themselves to climb down the nets to the boats would have been happy to tolerate ten times worse. The first twenty-four hours on Iwo Jima six weeks earlier had cost fifty-five hundred American casualties. (The average casualty rate of Pacific landings was over three times greater than in the European fighting.) More were expected on Okinawa, whose strategically more valuable territory was a third closer to the mainland and also a Japanese prefecture rather than merely a possession. Rumor correctly had it that intelligence predicted L-day casualties of 80 to 85 percent, for which extra medical teams were going in with the first waves. Those troops were therefore grateful for every bomb, bullet, and rocket of the heaviest-ever bombardment in support of an amphibious landing.

Shouldering their weapons and backpacks, the infantrymen pulled themselves over the side, many carrying a hundred pounds of supplies and equipment. Sailors watched with a combination of camaraderie and relief that they didn't have to join them. "You bet I felt sorry for them," a twenty-year-old carpenter's mate on a repair ship would remember. "They didn't *show* fear, but how could they not have had it?"

As the huge roar of amphibious craft engines joined the gunfire thunder, sweat broke out on drawn faces. Even veterans of previous landings fought terror — or especially such veterans. This was John McMullin's fifth, "so I figured this had to be my time to get it; I'd been too lucky so far." "I don't know the words to explain how it is to be in combat," another veteran would later apologize. "I was afraid, frightened and scared each time we jumped off the landing boats." And another: "For myself, I must confess that from chow at 3 A.M. till I climbed into the landing craft, it seemed I'd explode from severe nervous tension." April 1 was Ed Jones's birthday. "I knew about Iwo. I thought I might have a very short nineteenth year."

Still, fear was only one of the emotions gripping the men as they squeezed into the bobbing landing boats and breathed their oily exhaust. Another was relief to leave the mother ships. Whitaker's crossing from the States to his Russell Islands staging area, then to Guadalcanal and Okinawa, was typical. In San Diego, he'd been packed into a Liberty troopship for a voyage whose first leg alone took a month. Steel decks turned scorching under the equatorial sun. The hastily built or converted tubs with their troughs for latrines were torture for men squeezed together in the reek of sweat, urine, and vomit. "You wouldn't treat sardines that way," a deck officer reckoned.

Many troops preferred landing to fight the Devil himself, and surely the devilish Japanese, to spending another twenty-four hours in buckets whose gagging conditions grew worse on the final leg to Okinawa, when the fringe of a typhoon made their lower decks a fetid mess. Most L-day breakfasts had been the traditional prelanding feast of steak and eggs — all they could eat! — but many men could manage only a few mouthfuls. At three or four o'clock in the morning, with the thunder of the naval guns reminding them that many would die during the next few hours, it was too much like a convict's last meal.

Some cocky teenagers without wives and children to cherish were impatient. Even without the torment of the voyage, as Paul Fussell pointed out, combat's compensations — "the thrill of comradeship, the excitements of the chase, the exhilarations of surprise, deception and the *ruse de guerre,* the exaltations of success, the sheer fun of prankish irresponsibility" — console young men more than older ones. And although "sheer fun" would be rare on Okinawa, older men shared with teenagers confidence in their training and certainty of victory. Deep pride in belonging to their units and an almost bodily satisfaction of righteous unity fed eagerness for the battle that was simultaneously feared. A mess sergeant in a tank battalion had paid fifty dollars to his first sergeant in order not to miss the fighting because he'd otherwise be stuck in his rear-echelon unit on Guam. A more impoverished buddy of his stowed away in order to be with his unit (and was later court-martialed for his initiative). After training endlessly for combat and absorbing all the indoctrination that went with it, not to join their buddies facing the test would have been a terrible letdown as well as a lucky break.

Fear that one's arms and legs might be among those soon to be blown off was usually surpassed by fear of failing in the eyes of the others. That had been the ultimate purpose of their training: to make them perceive the danger as less fearsome than the alternatives. An infantryman preparing to land in the first wave would later speak for almost everyone alongside him. "I think my biggest fear wasn't of getting hurt because like everybody else — until he's been in the line for weeks and knows that's pure bullshit — I was certain that's what happens to the other guys. This is crazy, but my biggest fear was whether the guy alongside me could tell what was happening in my stomach and whether I'd do something shameful when we hit the beach."

"I joined up to fight Japs and be a hero, but will I have what it takes?" a friend added. "I was scared out of my mind but also scared that the guy next to me would see that."

So the fear was private — shared but also covered up. "I wasn't just tense, I was scared half dizzy," a young infantryman would remember. "But even more than that, I was determined that nobody would see I was worried about anything. The main thing was not to show your buddy how frightened you were."

"You prayed you wouldn't panic," another added. "You hoped like hell your landing craft would somehow never reach the beach, yet also hoped it was already there so you could get it over with."

And most important: "You'd been trained never to let your buddies down. You knew how terrible that would be. So your fear of getting killed wasn't as bad as having to spend the rest of your life with your tail between your legs if you did let them down — a failure, a coward."

Buck Private Thomas Hannaher felt "dumb, dumb, dumb" for having voluntarily surrendered his asthma-caused 4F draft classification with the neat lie at his second medical examination in North Dakota — and choosing the Marines on top of that. "Dumb, dumb, dumb — one of the stupidest things I've done in my life . . . because you knew this would probably be even worse than Iwo. You knew you'd be a casualty soon, that was just the law of averages." But although Hannaher realized that day might be his last, another part of him "knew" that was impossible. Resolution grappled with self-pity. *Why* did he have to be there now? Nevertheless, he wanted to do his job. He still had to prove himself, and what better way? "I was scared as hell but also proud to be with those going into combat. . . . I was going to do this thing, and if I got through it, which I doubted, maybe life would be different when I got home."

Love of country was a given. All felt uplifted by belonging to their blessed, righteous homeland. But flag and country became abstract as the dawn approached. What now held mind and body together was a sense of duty to one's buddies squeezed in all around, and the unwillingness to lose face in their eyes.

On shore, an Okinawan conscript who felt the cannonade "compressed the hearts of Japanese soldiers with its elaborate cacophony" now watched the troop transport "spew forth small boats whose splendid formations traced white wakes in their arrowlike flight to the beach."

"Combat had offered no similar spectacle since the mass charges of the French knights in the Hundred Years' War," the American historians James and William Belote would write. "Here was the finest moment in the history of amphibious operations: an almost unbroken line of landing craft eight miles long simultaneously approaching one beach."

You don't think that much when you're going into the beach. . . . You want to get out and you don't want to get out. You're sitting there with all that energy and you're psyching yourself up. I mean, football players don't just sleep all day, they get ready and psyche themselves up. And that's what this was, if you want to be honest about it: a football game where you kill or get killed.
— Al Franks, a Marine who would be wounded five minutes after running ashore

Perhaps fear accounts for the discrepancy in memories of the weather that morning. Some would remember an overcast sky and choppy waves, others a "glorious sunrise" appearing above the hills and casting a glow over a tranquil East China Sea. One man saw a change from one to the other, reading into it the divine intervention for which all but the determinedly atheist were praying — just as Japanese were simultaneously praying for intervention on *their* side, remembering the Divine Wind that had helped defeat the seemingly all-powerful Mongols. American believers were comforted by the knowledge that April 1 happened to be Easter Sunday. "Even the sea changed from a raging turbulence to a peaceful, lapping water," a Marine gratefully observed. "It was as though God came on Easter Sunday to lay everything in readiness before us."

Trained to dig in for protection, the infantrymen felt vulnerable and helpless in their thousand-odd landing craft. In the tension, few remembered the small gunboats that had led the way, blanketing the beach to the last moment with shells, rockets, and mortars. But the memory of the landing itself would be universally joyous.

American intelligence hadn't even guessed that the landings would be virtually unopposed — even by artillery, for Japanese gunners had been ordered not to fire on the ships or landing craft for fear of revealing their positions and exposing them to devastating return fire. The Yahara-Ushijima strategy was still to delay all serious resistance for a better time and place. American aerial photographs had pinpointed some of the menacing fortifications constructed above the landing beaches, but didn't reveal that almost all were abandoned. Captain Kojo's battalion, for example, had been withdrawn more than three months earlier, shortly after Ushijima lost the 9th Division. Nor did the photos disclose the quality of the replacements for the highly trained 24th Division. The single regiment now protecting the beaches was composed of hastily organized service troops, chiefly airfield construction crews, reinforced by ill-trained, half-armed Okinawan Home Guard units.

The relief of the American brass was expressed in a radio message from Admiral Richmond Turner, commander of the landing operation, to his boss, Admiral Chester W. Nimitz, commander in chief of the Pacific Fleet: "Practically no fire against [landing] boats, none against ships. . . . Troops advancing standing up." The even greater relief of those making the swift advance turned from an immense sense of deliverance to the bafflement recorded in the battle diary of Taylor Kennerly, the leader of a machine-gun platoon:

> As our boats raced toward the rising sun there was no firing, all was quiet except for the roar of the boat's motor and the slapping of the waves against the open boat. . . . The ramp splashed down and I ran out into knee-deep water, followed by a boatload of Marines. Still there was no shooting. [I thought,] "They must be waiting to see the whites of our eyes. . . ." Scampering up the steep bank . . . I . . . then plunged through a narrow row of bushes. There were the Japanese gun emplacements — empty. Yes, empty!
> What kind of trick was this? The whole situation was eerie.

Japanese soldiers were no less baffled. Believing their Combined Fleet to be intact and their planes lying in wait on the mainland and Formosa, they thought it "simply incredible" that the American fleet was operating in broad daylight, right before their noses. "Looking at the fascinatingly beautiful battleships spitting fire, we still couldn't quite understand that they'd come to kill us." Through the dense clouds of smoke and dust left by the bombardment, they watched the landing in disbelief and confusion.

> From the transport ships that filled the ocean to the horizon, countless landing craft tracing white wakes set out, to disappear in the smoke. They kept coming relentlessly . . . in tens and hundreds, like arrows being shot in rapid succession and disappearing in the smoke. The vanguard reached the beach; tanks, other vehicles and infantry ran up onto Okinawan soil unharmed! What a great opportunity! Why didn't our Air Force come and attack them? . . . Finally, the enemy began landing in a leisurely manner, so to speak, and made our airfields into *their* unsinkable aircraft carriers!

A soldier assigned to defend the beach hurried to tell a friend positioned in a school two miles inland that his little unit had somehow survived the ten days of relentless bombing. "How tenaciously they cling to life!" marveled the friend — but the clinging was almost over. The entire unit at the landing site, including the member who immediately returned there, would be dead by midmorning.

Thus the operation became something of an exercise. Dashing anxiously from his landing craft, one Marine saw an earlier arrival flipping through a comic book. American fear shifted to amazement and jubilation all along the eight miles of beaches on the western (East China Sea) shore. Remembering his wounding on Guam, a young company commander named Owen Stebbins felt an inner joy that he was still in one piece. Other veterans of previous landings wondered where and when the Japanese would spring their trap: April 1 was April Fool's Day as well as Easter Sunday. "I've already lived longer than I thought I would," exulted an Army infantryman after running up the beach and making it to the top of a little hill. The opposition wasn't worse than at Iwo Jima, as expected; it was limited to occasional mortar shells and snipers' bullets, relatively no resistance at all.

Forty miles to the south, the 2nd Marine Division was faking a landing on another coast in order to deter Ushijima from rushing reinforcements to the real landing beaches, where four divisions, two Army and two Marine, were already rushing inland from the eight-mile stretch of beach. Okinawa's width at that point, just south of its narrowest neck, is some seven miles to the Pacific shore. On their way across, cutting the island in two, American units encountered two airfields, including Kadena, Captain Kojo's responsibility until the accidental explosion that drove him to a hospital. Both fields were less than half a mile from the landing beach, but American planners, with their experience of ferocious Japanese island defenses, had scheduled their capture for the third day. Defended only by a recently formed regiment of support troops with scant combat training, they fell easily the first morning. One Marine noticed that after the tumultuous American bombardment, nothing was alive — "not a goddamn grasshopper or snake or fly" — on the way to the fields.

The defenders of the slightly more northern Yomitan Airfield included Okinawan conscripts who had been issued uniforms but no arms. Shortly after it was secured, a Japanese Zero appeared directly overhead, almost transfixing the Marines below with its Rising Sun insignia. The pilot made a graceful landing, apparently with important papers from the mainland, then taxied across the field, climbed from his cockpit, and walked toward an airport building before realizing who the men gathered there were. They shot him as he tried to run back to his plane. The expected counterattack by a powerful parachute force didn't materialize. "This is hard to believe," wrote a correspondent who had covered previous landings, while bulldozers prepared to clear the runways of wrecked Japanese planes and clever dummies of sticks, straw, and cloth. By nightfall, Marine strike planes began landing, the first to operate from official Japanese soil since the war began.

That evening, a Marine artillery battery was fully ashore and ready to fire from a position near the beach. The men began digging in for the night, but found they were on solid coral that couldn't be dented. "We had to hope for no incoming fire, and luckily there wasn't any." Americans who reconnoitered the empty Japanese fortifications — the excellently positioned caves, gun emplacements, and pillboxes dug over the course of six months by Captain Kojo's 24th Division — realized they were even luckier than they'd thought. Despite the courageous feats of the Navy's underwater demolition teams,* many landing craft were stranded for hours on coral reefs about a thousand yards out: sitting ducks for enemy field artillery and heavy machine guns, had they been where originally positioned. And despite the heaviest pre-invasion bombardment in the long Pacific campaign, only civilian buildings had been demolished. Virtually intact defense works at the airfields and beaches testified to the unrealistic value Americans placed on weight of metal and explosives — as well as to the Japanese skill in choosing and fortifying sites.

If Ushijima hadn't lost the 9th Division, those sites wouldn't have been abandoned. Captain Kojo's replacement would have led a charge with professional ruthlessness and a poised, largely unharmed battalion from his original position above the beach. "The hardest part of all was trudging in," an American remembered with understatement. "The water was waist-deep. If we'd had to fight our way in, it would have been a job instead of a cinch." In other words, the invaders would surely have been the prey Kojo had envisioned.

The American Army, designated the 10th, had 541,866 men at its disposal: more than the Okinawan civilian population at that time, and almost five times more than the defending force. The smaller American landing force also represented a considerable numerical advantage over the Japanese, even beefed up by Okinawan conscripts. By nightfall, some 60,000 of the 10th Army's 183,000 assault troops were ashore, together with much armor, artillery, and supplies, and fifteen thousand service troops. The price was a fraction of what had been expected: twenty-eight killed, most by kamikaze crashes on land, twenty-seven missing, 104 wounded. Although kamikaze crashes into the sea had also squeezed the legs of some men in landing craft hard enough to crush their testicles, which had to be surgically removed, L-day had indeed brought a trace of love.

*Three days before the landing, a thousand frogmen smeared on silver body paint and swam to shore from landing craft some five hundred yards out. While naval shelling and a strike by carrier-based planes forced Japanese beach patrols to take cover, those "half-fish and half nuts" explored the rich coral reef that fringed the landing beaches. Although their exceedingly hazardous work didn't prevent that minority of landing craft from being caught on the coral, the teams managed to remove almost three thousand wooden stakes planted by Tadashi Kojo's men and others.

They risked their lives again the following morning by attaching charges to the stakes, setting fuses, and swimming seaward before a huge chain explosion disposed of the obstacles. Four months earlier, a submarine had performed the arduous, dangerous task of taking a survey at a range of only two miles with a new kind of sonar that also detected mines. That was followed by minesweeping for the fleet, which required less courage from each officer and sailor involved but was arguably as dangerous — and as essential, as the slogan "No sweep, no invasion!" suggested.

Marine losses in particular were trifling compared to previous landings: nine killed, a hundred wounded — including Alexander Franks,
whose platoon landed in a roaring amtrac (amphibious tractor).

> What are you thinking while you're waiting for your turn to land? . . .
> I'm thinking that I want to get out of the amtrac. . . . You've psyched
> yourself up because you've got to psych yourself up — and you want to
> get out and relieve the tension. Besides, you can get seasick. Or a mor-
> tar can hit the amtrac and you're all gone.
>   I'm also thinking, am I going to come out of this one alive? Is my
> buddy, sitting right there next to me, going to get killed — or am I? Yes,
> you actually think those thoughts while you sit there, trying to joke with
> your buddies. Trying to do a lot of talking, although you don't remem-
> ber what you've said the minute it leaves your mouth. . . . This was my
> second landing; I'd also hit Guam. And I was just as scared. Maybe
> more so, because on your first landing, you don't really understand. . . .
>   It seems like an eternity, circling and circling out there beyond the
> range of the shore batteries, waiting for your turn to land. *Am I going to
> come out of this alive?* I prayed. Believe me, lots of guys did. You ask the
> Lord to help you and your friends come out whole. Yes, your friends
> too — because you depend on that man next to you. If you can't de-
> pend on him and he can't depend on you, you're both gone, you're
> nothing.

When his amtrac at last headed in, Franks was much relieved to see no
incoming shells — and even more so to see no one falling around him
when the vehicle finally stopped and he ran up the pebbly beach. He
dashed up a little rise and dived to his stomach on top. A shell exploded
just to his left, killing the man next to him. Franks realized he too was hit
when he couldn't get up again.

"It's an awful thing to say, but I think it was one of our own — a short-
fall — because there were still no shells coming from the Japs.* My first
thought is, *Am I going to lose my leg?* And then: *I'm alive and I'll be going
home.* I'm deeply sorry to leave my buddies, I'm deeply sorry *for* them, but
there's nothing I can do for them anymore. That new guy right next to
me, two feet away, is dead, and I'm still alive. Still alive! And after the shot
of morphine from the corpsman, I realize my arm and leg are still on me,
so I probably won't be a cripple."

For Masahide Ota, the twenty-year-old native of Kume Island who'd been
appointed one of the three adjutants to the principal of his prestigious
school, L-day was almost unbearably exciting. Perhaps because it was as-

---

*The majority of the assault troops experienced nothing heavier than sporadic mortar
and sniper fire. Men who saw no incoming fire whatever shared the impression that so-
called own fire from misaimed American weapons caused many of the landing casualties.

sumed that the Normal School, so close to the 32nd Army's headquarters in the tunnel under Shuri Castle, must have been mobilized earlier, it was actually done only the day before the landing, March 31. By that time, over twenty thousand mostly teenage Okinawans were serving in the Home Guard. Although not all the boys of the island's various middle schools were among the conscripted, the Normal School's teachers and entire enrollment of 360 students were taken into the fifteen-hundred-boy corps called Blood and Iron Scouts for the Emperor. The top twenty-two students were formed into a subunit bearing the immensely proud name of a historical figure who had sacrificed his and his family's lives to protect the Emperor. Those enviable ones, including bright, diligent Ota, were assigned, sublimely, to staff intelligence at 32nd Army head-quarters. The students' years of military training had included no prac-tice firing, not even of small arms. Now a rudimentary, short-pants uniform was distributed, but there was no time for any substantive prepa-ration.

But the second-class privates were heady with the thrill of being near the highest-ranking Army officers on an observation platform at Shuri Castle. Looking down at the huge enemy landing, the boys delighted in the idiotic massing of so many ships marked for the bottom. Ota's un-qualified expectation of quick, total victory was further heightened when he saw the kindly, masterful General Ushijima calmly surveying the epic scene. The boys believed exactly what they'd been told: that Imperial General Headquarters had been clever enough to lure the large enemy force there in order to destroy it in one go. As one of their teachers put it, the noose into which the massive American fleet had been drawn would now be deftly closed. Ota felt a surge of exhilaration as he ob-served the stirring spectacle below. What an honor to participate in the glorious task of rapidly liquidating the sinister foe! He itched for his first assignment for staff intelligence.

Dick Whitaker was among the rich beneficiaries of the nearly unopposed landing. Had the assault force been met with the furious counterattack originally planned, he'd have been rushed in to replace one of the profu-sion of casualties, with a good chance of being killed or badly wounded then and there. As it was, the first wave of Americans penetrated so fast and deep that by the time he arrived, in the third wave an hour later, their greatest need was not more bodies but more matériel. The unimag-ined swiftness of the advance caused an instant crisis in supplies. Whitaker's replacement draft was among five thousand Marines formed into work details.

As his amtrac had circled in preparation for landing, he fell asleep — probably, he'd conclude years later (after taking a college course in psychology), in reaction to an overload of stress and apprehension. But now he worked through it by lifting and lugging, at which all Marines were old hands. Floodlights were rigged on the long beachhead so that unloading from landing craft could continue throughout the night, except for relatively rare interruptions when the men took cover from Japanese scouting planes. They bitched in good old military language. Fuck it, they didn't come to Okinawa to unload ships! The Marine Corps's invincibility had been confirmed. Whitaker believed himself invincible too. Some of the older, married men might have been happy to stay where they were, but the young bucks wanted off that goddamn beach where the fucking relentless fleas were a lot worse than the stupid Japanese Army. They wanted *combat* — to pull their triggers, become heroes, cop some good Jap souvenirs.

On the fourth day, half a dozen of them took advantage of some slack time to improvise a little scouting party. That was against regulations: No one in command would know where they were if they happened to get in trouble. But the ease with which the little Nips were being pushed back kept death an abstraction. A patch of woods farther inland had been "secured" days before, which is to say enough cleaned of the enemy for combat units to push on. But "Hey, get that!" shouted one of the party, pointing to a small rise a few hundred yards from the beach. Whitaker's first sight of a live Japanese soldier — of any living Japanese — brought a rush of excitement. *There* was the object of all his training, of the whole massive effort on the island. Joining the firing at the titillating target until its sloppy helmet disappeared over the ridge, he felt revved up even more.

The work parties were broken up a few days later and their members trucked to frontline units as replacements, but Whitaker saw few real targets even there. He was assigned to F (Fox) Company of the 2nd Battalion of the 6th Marine Division's 29th Regiment, which had advanced far north by the time he joined it. With the company's fighting up there almost over, American bullets now caused its worst wounds.

An air strike was requested one day when Whitaker's new platoon encountered a pocket of resistance on a mop-up patrol. The men were told to mark their own positions by making ground panels of ponchos and anything else easily seen from above. Several F-4Us soon appeared: the celebrated Corsairs that had already demonstrated their enormous value in the north, where Japanese artillery pieces fired once and pulled back into concealed emplacements on steep hillsides, making them almost invulnerable to naval gunfire. The Corsair, which carried more armament than a B-29, may have been the best close-ground-support aircraft ever designed, able to bomb or strafe as close as two hundred yards to delighted friendly troops. But one of the gull-winged beauts on that raid missed or misread the ground panels and strafed the wrong side, killing one Marine and wounding others. To be the target of one's own magnificent weapons was doubly anguishing. Hugging the ground in terror with the rest of his platoon, Whitaker viewed the great Corsair as a savage monster spitting murderous fire.

No list has been compiled of men killed and wounded on Okinawa by own fire, but it would surely run to hundreds, perhaps thousands — to which should be added those torn and blown apart by bulldozers, cranes, steam winches, and aviation fuel handled by young men necessarily in a hurry: the "industrial" accidents of a huge, extremely hazardous enterprise run under supreme stress with what otherwise would be called inordinate recklessness. The proportion of such deaths grew as armies acquired heavier machinery, more volatile fuel, deadlier armament, and more powerful explosives.

And in the field, it was impossible to have so many youths with so many never-predictable weapons without constant accidents and mistakes. Back south on Sugar Loaf Hill, where Whitaker would find himself in about three weeks, a second lieutenant would lose "a beautiful [eighteen-year-old] kid, a real fine, decent Marine" when a tank shell aimed at a Japanese target bounced off a tree stump and tore open his chest. On little Iheya Island, fifty miles north of Okinawa, Marines would be killed by rocket fire from ships that didn't know they were on the beach. It was inevitable that American bullets, grenades, mortar shells, artillery shells, and even flamethrowers would cut down American boys all over Okinawa because, as one veteran would put it, combat is "just too confusing for any kind of count of who killed whom."

Peacetime terrorist actions that take a single precious life are rightly emblazoned in headlines and abhorred. Infinitely worse losses on Okinawa were never mentioned in print or even to the families concerned, because few officers were willing to write that their men had fallen to own fire — "more than will ever be known," in the summary of one dismayed lieutenant, which is as accurate as any.

11 · The North

You know from your map we're nearly equidistant from Kyushu, Taiwan and China at Okinawa — all these Jap strongholds close to 300 nautical miles, yet such pathetic resistance. . . . We've surely got them where we want them now.
— An American naval officer, days after the landing

Having blinded us with countless airplanes and shells, the enemy were marching — no, walking leisurely ahead as if on a picnic. . . . Those soldiers functioned as feelers. One shot from us and they immediately used their portable radios to contact their artillery. Our small position would be blown up, hill and all, in two minutes.
— A Japanese soldier, at about the same time

That night, my detachment was sent to Miwashi Elementary School for lumber to support our cave. That meant demolishing the school building . . . and making off with its beams and joists.
— An Okinawan conscript, at about the same time

THE FIRST DAYS WENT SO WELL for the Americans that staff officers wondered whether Ushijima was a genius or a fool. Even if he now tried to "turn and make a stand," a seasoned correspondent predicted, the campaign would cost fewer casualties than any in the Pacific. Everyone asked where the Japs were. Cloud cover had interfered with prelanding reconnaissance flights, masking their positions — which remained hidden by nets and fresh branches.

In fact, the heart of the 32nd Army was just where Colonel Yahara's last plan had put it: waiting in its fortifications in the southern eighth of the island. The first strong line lay less than eight miles below the southernmost landing beach and only about a dozen above the island's southern tip. The two Army divisions that fought south from the landing encountered its outer edge toward the end of the first week, in valleys and draws protected by minefields and covered by well-camouflaged field guns. But although fortified hills dominating the lines of advance made them hard to take, the stubborn resistance there was considered normal. The honeymoon would be truly over only when the main body of the defense was reached.

Meanwhile, the two Marine divisions were still enjoying a relative holiday. The 1st was encountering much less resistance than expected while taking a large portion of the island's center; the 6th hurried north in what seemed a cakewalk, especially with Yomitan and Kadena Airfields already launching close-support strikes to speed it. Yahara and Ushijima hadn't expected those fields to fall so quickly.* When startling numbers of American planes began operating from them almost immediately, they had rueful second thoughts and wondered whether to counterattack.

Japanese regret at having given up the fields so easily — a consequence of the decision to not defend the beaches after the loss of the 9th Division — was deepened by belated recognition that the enemy's quick capture of Kerama Retto, a cluster of nine mountainous islands about fifteen miles west of Naha, was bringing more trouble. Those little islands had fallen during the week before the Okinawa landing, Ushijima having transferred most of their garrisons to Okinawa in the belief that they wouldn't interest the enemy. Easily defeating their few hundred remaining defenders, the Americans put them to immediate use as anchorages for repair ships and bases for patrol planes that would sink tens of thousands of tons of merchant shipping. They also became the final depots in the vast supply routes stretching from California.

A bonus was disarming a potentially serious threat to those routes. The Keramas had been a base for 250 Japanese speedboats armed with heavy depth charges that were to have severed the American supply lines with suicide charges at the larger ships. The little trap now failed: The tiny one-man boats were found in well-camouflaged coves, some being readied for surprise attacks they'd never make, others destroyed by their maintenance crews. Another surprise for the Americans was the bodies of some fifteen native women and children strangled by grieving husbands and fathers to save them from a worse fate at the hands of the invaders. Altogether, over five hundred civilians died on the Keramas, including many who were sent to meet the invaders when the Japanese force melted away. Serious thought about that tragedy by the American 10th Army staff would have helped lessen the larger one coming on Okinawa itself.

Other suicide craft berthed in the rough coasts of Okinawa's north** were also about to be disabled as the 6th Marine Division rapidly advanced to

---

*American tacticians would later point to that as Ushijima's single serious mistake: Even without the 9th Division, he should have redistributed his remaining forces to his original positions above the beaches, which would have enabled him to delay defeat even longer and cause more American casualties, his only attainable military goals. Otherwise, those American students ranked his tactical decisions after the start of the battle as sound to sometimes brilliant.

**In all, some seven hundred suicide craft had been hidden in the Ryukyus, about half on Okinawa. Some boats and swimmers based there did try to strike, the swimmers by leaving their craft for individual forays to blow up targeted ships. The dawn of a morning soon after the landing caught fifteen of them approaching a destroyer in a canoe and on a raft. All instantly blew themselves up with hand grenades.

occupy its remote ruggedness. The approximately fifty-by-eight-mile strip of rocky terrain north of the landing beaches contained two-thirds of Okinawa's territory but less than a quarter of its population. Apart from the Motobu Peninsula, which jutted like a large spur into the East China Sea, it was an inaccessible and essentially uninhabited mountain spine running northwest to the tip. Most of it was distinctly poorer than the south in 1945, even on the coastal roads, where almost everyone lived.

On the evening after the landing, a Marine detachment stopped after advancing a spectacular four miles from its landing site along the west coast road — a dirt track, like most of the island's arteries. The troops were some five days ahead of schedule, and veterans of earlier campaigns exchanged nervously joyful expressions of disbelief. Where were the Japs? Would their trap be really diabolical or was it possible that all Okinawa was going to be a picnic?

Still, the Americans cherished the most pleasant letdown of their lives. Some initiates to combat wondered about the veterans' talk and the war films. "Holy shit," a medical corpsman happily asked himself, "is all that hell and heroism stuff just more myth?"

The columns advanced up the coastal roads with the East China Sea on one side, terraced hills on the other — and no sign of snakes. Much worse had been expected of the island as well as its defenders. The prelanding briefings had warned about "all sorts of horrible results" from a microbe in the water that caused "liver fluke" (schistosomiasis), as well as about woods teeming with venomous adders, more frightening to some than the enemy. Habu snakes in particular were said to be a constant peril, but very few Americans would encounter one, now or later. (Some of those who did see snakes, especially after living days or weeks on cold rations, would make meals of their broiled meat.) Many men had already begun throwing away the puttees they'd been admonished to wear, together with their gas masks and, occasionally, even their helmets ("too heavy and not effective against bullets anyway"): anything to lighten the loads on their backs. So far, Okinawa had none of the sinister quality ascribed to it by the pre-invasion intelligence.

On that afternoon of April 2, Marines had taken photographs of the scenery, including gently curving white-sand beaches below the coast road. The spring day remained clear and pleasant when the sun went down, but all were extremely tired after marching very hard on very little sleep since the eve of the invasion. A unit that had started setting up in a cabbage patch was so tired and so relaxed that the men took their time digging their foxholes for the night — and were stunned by sudden fire from Japanese howitzers in a hill above.

Of course they'd been lectured and lectured to take cover fast whenever shelling started — no, *before* it started. But newcomers to combat saw the whole of their boot camp and infantry training as nothing compared to this terrible reality. ("I never repeated that mistake again," one of the targets would remember about his laziness in digging then. "On every one of my 80 evenings after that, I *first* dug my foxhole, then took a crap or had something to eat.") The first rounds whistled over their heads and landed in the sea, but unseen Japanese gunners instantly adjusted their range to hit jeeps and inflict casualties. Although a patrol sent into the hill managed to silence the howitzers before midnight, shock and fear kept most of the men awake during the night while corpsmen tended the wounded.

The same unit was more heavily shelled three nights later, when a nearby radioman was shot while his microphone switch was open. Other members of the group heard him calling for help for hours. "Come and get us!" "We're pinned down!" "Help us out of here!" Volunteers were trucked to where they might outflank the Japanese from behind. They climbed a hill, each with a hand on the belt of the man in front to keep from getting lost in the dark and the difficult terrain. Digging in at the top, they were told not to leave their foxholes: Anyone who did might be taken for a Japanese infiltrator. No one slept during the remainder of that night. Everyone fired at every movement. In the morning, two Americans were dead of own fire even before the others set out to neutralize the enemy artillery.

Each night as they pushed north, American battalions settled in whenever possible on high ground, where they employed an updated version of the wagon circle, setting up machine guns and BAR men on the position's outer ring. As an extra precaution, thin wires were strung some fifty to seventy yards out from the perimeter, across the footpaths leading down from the hills. Trip flares were rigged to go off when those wires were touched.

In such a position a few nights later, a radio operator's heart skipped a beat when a voice with a Japanese accent suddenly whispered into his earphones, "Americans die!" Then the line went dead.

To be cut off from regimental headquarters for an entire night was considered an unacceptable danger; the operations officer had no alternative but to send out a communications sergeant to lay a new line. One observer "never felt sorrier for anyone before or since" than he did for that man. Headquarters were a mile away, the night was black, Japanese were obviously in between, and he didn't know the location of other "trigger-happy" Marine outposts. "I think I'd have asked for a company of infantry to surround me." But the self-possessed sergeant took just two riflemen and two of his communications specialists into the terrifying blackness, where, they were certain, the same Japanese who had cut the line were waiting behind rocks, rifles poised, for the squeak of a roll reeling out a telephone wire to tell them when to shoot.*

Those slight episodes among thousands suggest that the push north was easy only in comparison to what would follow it. The luckiest units raced up the coastal roads at the speed of a motorized unit — sometimes actually in vehicles — still elated by the scantiness of the enemy fire. Some men found it "like a walk in the country, a picnic" — or, in a correspondent's richer image, a house that was expected to contain vicious gunmen but turned out to be only haunted. The luckier companies were accompanied by a destroyer escort or smaller ship steaming north at their pace to provide extra firepower from close offshore. Some Marines hooted at anyone who tried to warn them that Japs were savage fighters. Even when advance units entered Nago at the neck of the Motobu Peninsula — the largest town above the landing beaches, with a population of ten thousand — they rarely met more than rifle fire.

Other companies took only very scattered rifle, machine-gun, and mortar fire as they tramped ahead in single file, scouting the pine-covered hills and the terraces where the natives struggled to feed themselves. More harassment than serious opposition, the fire came from the hills or from behind sharp bends in the narrow, twisting roads of that "walking campaign." But unlucky units that happened to encounter defensive positions had to work and fight as hard as anywhere.

A veteran of island campaigns assured a medical corpsman that the Japs were hopeless shots except at long range. During the first five days, the same corpsman saw five Marines go down from single shots to the heart or head. After eight men in the platoon of a machine-gunner named Melvin Heckt were killed and nine wounded on April 14 and 15, Heckt proclaimed, "I only have God to thank for being alive." In another unit, four volunteers to cross a difficult ridge were picked off one by one as they tried. Two were killed, one crippled for life; the lucky one took shrapnel in every part of his body, including his testicles. Incidents like those prompted the commander of one Marine regiment to call the

---

*Although that group returned without casualties after several hours of hair-raising work, telephone maintenance continued to be a severe test of nerves. Old lines were never repaired, previous islands having revealed the Japanese tactic of putting a pin in them and waiting to ambush anyone sent out to troubleshoot. But the places for laying new lines in the same general direction were very limited, and the enemy was all but certain to be watching while they were being reeled out. At night, the operation was as frightening as combat — and the danger of being shot by other Marines hardly decreased. Some who ignored their solemn instructions not to leave their foxholes at night, usually to relieve themselves, were quickly cut down by unknowing others, nervous in the menacing darkness and apt to fire at every threatening sound, which often meant any sound at all.

northern operation "as difficult as I can conceive. . . . I wonder how it was accomplished." But the spotty resistance was better summed up by a young communications man in that regiment named Norris Buchter. "There were lots of very serious moments up there in the north. There were units shot to shreds. The whole thing seemed easy only later, look-ing back after what we went through in the south."

> *When I had a chance to look around, I was awe-struck by the beauty of the scene*
> *that stretched before me. I was on a fairly level plateau covered with green grass*
> *and pine trees. At one end was an old, partly decayed ruin of a Buddhist temple*
> *made from large rocks. A stone stairway led up to it. I followed the roadway,*
> *almost in a trance, through several flights of stairs until I stood on the highest*
> *point. . . . Below me about 200 meters away, a fire was rapidly licking up the*
> *fragile buildings in a town I think was Yami.*
> — Major Sam Reid, April 12

Colonel Takehido Udo commanded the defense. Unlike General Ushi-jima, his classmate at the Imperial Military Academy, Udo was considered bullying and ineffectual. The local population quietly despised him.

Udo's twenty-five hundred men assigned to defend 436 square miles re-vealed the slight importance Ushijima placed on holding the northern two-thirds of Okinawa's territory, where his predecessor originally thought to organize the bulk of the defense. Moreover, the "Udo force" consisted of bits and pieces of various groupings, including sixty survivors of *Toyama maru,* delivered to him in pitiful shape a week after the sinking. (Udo him-self had been the senior officer aboard. When the survivors finally arrived on Okinawa, they struck civilians as "stragglers without even fighting a bat-tle." Their condition — uniforms blackened with oil, heads bandaged, skin terribly swollen — surprised the islanders no more than their attempts to avoid attracting attention so that no one would learn what had happened to the ship and nine-tenths of the 44th Independent Mixed Brigade.) But Udo had an intimate knowledge of the tough terrain, including a moun-tain retreat that towered, on the Okinawan scale, to fifteen hundred feet. It was protected by well-placed outposts with good communications to his headquarters and a relatively adequate supply of mortars and machine guns in addition to well-hidden field guns and converted naval cannon.

Some of his works confounded Americans for days. Artillery emplace-ments dug into mountainsides were equipped with tracks used for rolling out the guns for a few quick rounds, then immediate withdrawal into the camouflage of surrounding vegetation. "When we finally took the terri-tory," one Marine remembered, "we'd find tremendous devastation all around but the gun inside, still intact."

Distant, demanding Udo's own redoubt was high on Yae-dake Moun-tain, which commanded the entire Motobu Peninsula, the only area he planned to defend in earnest. Covered by pine trees and a thick under-growth of vines and brambles, Yae-dake also concealed deep valleys that had to be crossed on the way to the top. Its defenders numbered roughly two thousand: most of the entire force. The most menacing to the Americans were several hundred soldiers manning a battery of heavy guns positioned on a steep face of the mountain. The colonel supervised his operations from a mat on the floor of his headquarters, where three local women waited on him, to the disgust of some of his noncommissioned officers. Native accounts pictured fear in his eyes as he complained about the impossibility of waging modern war without air support.

Marines attacked the sprawling mountain from two sides during the second week of the campaign, while American ships and planes pounded the heights. That was the start of four fierce days of fighting, during which the commander of the Japanese heavy-gun detachment became convinced the time was ripe to fire and frequently telephoned Udo for permission, but received no clear answer. After their Herculean labor of dragging the guns through the jagged terrain up to their vantage point, the gunners now suffered frustration. Americans discovered the position and attacked it heavily before it could do its full damage, while elsewhere on the mountain, violent clashes were taking place that required Marines to climb sheer cliffs under fire and engage in hand-to-hand combat on heavily forested ridges. One Japanese 75-millimeter gun had much more success than the heavier ones, emerging from its cave to fire with great accuracy, then withdrawing quickly enough to escape destruction by American naval gunfire, artillery, bombs, and napalm.

Udo counterattacked with his infantry only toward evening, when it was too close to nightfall for the Marines to risk mounting expeditions into the dangerous foothills, especially since their leadership was uncharacteristically wavering. The commander of the 29th Regiment, a rigid colonel who clung to ways learned in the First World War, had trained his men so severely on Guadalcanal that many felt worn out. Even after he was relieved on April 10, the results of his stodgy planning showed on Yae-dake. But after bitter hand-to-hand fighting for the peak, the full mountain was more or less taken on April 16, leaving no more objectives remotely as difficult anywhere in the north. By that time, other Marine units had already reached rocky Cape Hedo at Okinawa's northern tip.

Hiding somewhere on the Motobu Peninsula, Udo became an object of contempt to other Japanese, who knew neither his whereabouts nor why he hadn't died honorably at his headquarters. Other survivors formed small guerrilla groups that hid in Motobu's mountainous forests and elsewhere in the barely inhabited north, eluding American patrols. Young Okinawan soldiers who had been conscripted on the eve of the battle served those groups both as scouts and as small bands of their own,* their operations much more effectively commanded by a Captain Haruo Murakami than by the disliked Colonel Udo. A graduate of the Imperial Military Academy one year after Tadashi Kojo, Murakami shared Kojo's severe bearing, total dedication to military interests, and supreme confidence in ultimate victory — and his self-acquired expertise in guerrilla warfare made him more respected than many of his fellow regular officers. When Udo arrived one rainy night at a Murakami camp in civilian clothes and what was considered an unfitting manner, he found a sign posted at the captain's headquarters: UDO'S DEFEATED LITTLE REMNANT GANG NOT ADMITTED.

On April 20, the commander of American operations in the north declared it secure. The flag-raisers at 6th Division headquarters in Nago included a detachment from G (George) Company of the 2nd Battalion, 22nd Regiment, apparently because the company, having moved rapidly up the west coast road, made a final exploratory patrol down the east coast to ensure the collapse of enemy resistance. G–2–22, the company's designation in military shorthand, had suffered only two battle-fatigue casualties during the weeks of routing scattered groups of riflemen in their path. Their toughest "battle" had occurred when a hunter-killer squadron of American carrier-based planes repeatedly bombed and strafed them in the belief they were Japanese.

The 6th Division as a whole counted almost two thousand Japanese bodies, compared to their own casualties of 236 dead** and 1,061 wounded, roughly the "kill ratio" that would prevail during the full campaign. Compared to Marine experiences on other islands, as well as what had been expected here, the three weeks had been a cinch. One infantry

---

*A high school student named Yasuhara Agarie tried to keep fighting despite a grave bullet wound through his chest from an American patrol that killed some of his fellow guerrillas. The sixteen-year-old surrendered months later, only after his brother, who had spent years in America and returned to Okinawa with the invading forces, coaxed him from his hiding place. Agarie would become president of the University of the Ryukyus in rebuilt Shuri.

**Combat veterans tend to dislike the use of such statistics, because each death caused a kind of grief not easily understood by others. A medical corpsman asked a 6th Division radio operator named Austin Aria (a former batboy for the Philadelphia Phillies, then a major-league prospect himself) to hold a flashlight on a delirious teenager while he tried to keep him from becoming one of those 236 dead in the north. "Honey, you know I can't dance, so why do you keep asking me?" — the gravely wounded boy hallucinated an exchange with his wife. He stopped breathing before morning, and although Americans on Okinawa would grow almost numb to appalling outrages to the human sensibility and nervous system, few would take the deaths of their fellows any easier than Aria took that one, his first. Citing numbers can widen the gulf between those who know combat and those who don't.

battalion had marched all the way up the western coast road to the northern tip without suffering a single casualty.

With the April 20 pronouncement that organized resistance had ended in the north, the 6th Marine Division turned to mopping-up patrols and to savoring military life's little pleasures in the field: cleaning weapons, taking photographs, picking up toothpaste and cigarettes at the Red Cross tent, sacking in whenever possible during the days of heavy rain, and working on tans during the sunny ones. Manly recreation also beckoned. Ball games were organized, first of all football because "we were young, trained and spoiling for a fight," as one man put it. Soon many were hurrying to certain premises near the village of Unten. It was, in that straitlaced time, hardly a common practice of the U.S. Marine Corps to run a brothel, but there were reasons for an exception here. Of all the Pacific islands on which the Marines had fought, this was the first with a large civilian population, including many attractive women and girls. It seemed sensible to try to avoid venereal disease and get rid of camp followers, a sprinkling of whom had begun trading themselves for food. It also seemed a good idea to keep the men from wandering into the villages and to prevent rape, of which there had already been some complaints.

Unten, a site of captured nests for PT boats and midget submarines, was on the Motobu Peninsula, fifteen miles north of 6th Division headquarters. The volunteer girls worked in a large, well-cleaned house, putting in long hours and making very good money by local standards. The customers too had to put in considerable time, standing first in a long line to buy three-yen (thirty-cent) chits in scrip and condoms from corpsmen at a table, then in a shorter one at the entrance to the house. They waited again inside, now in little cubicles, while a madame assigned their partners. (One "older" man — of twenty-six — waited on his cubicle's cot until a girl entered who looked thirteen. He gestured for her to go back out and send in an older colleague with more curves, but she returned with the madame, who told him to take it or leave it. He took.)

The existence of the "cat house" was of course unannounced and unacknowledged, but the regiment's chaplains got wind of it and protested the disgrace. "If my men want to fuck, that's what they're going to do," countered the regimental commander with modern broad-mindedness. But the best recreation was fantasizing about getting the hell off Okinawa. Having secured the north, the victorious Marines told themselves that their job was done and that "our chances of being alive on V-J Day looked a little more promising," an infantryman wistfully calculated.

On clear nights in late April, some could make out the flickering of muzzle blasts forty or fifty miles south, from where a distant rumble also sometimes reached them. Private Eugene Sledge, who would write the great American memoir of the battle, tried to convince himself it was thunder, although he knew better. Since the first week after the landing, all 6th Division Marines had heard rumors about difficulties in the south.

But they had only a vague impression of what those difficulties really were and no idea whatever that many Japanese soldiers were still improving their fortifications there. It was never more true than among the happy Marines contriving to make life more comfortable for themselves in the sparsely inhabited north that men in the ranks rarely think beyond each day's assigned duties and possible perks. Some eagerly spread the only half-joking rumor that they were going back to Guam soon, then going home for Christmas.

In fact, they'd be going to the great Shuri defense line before the end of April. Their fighting had hardly begun.

12 · Civilians Flee

The [preliminary] bombardment was completely one-sided. . . . Planes and gunfire . . . wrecked most of the enemy aircraft on the island, which was all to the good. Apart from this, the principal results achieved . . . were the destruction of villages and isolated farmhouses that had no strategic value.
— Samuel Eliot Morison, after observing from an American ship

In the matter of civilians, [Marine officers] showed commendable restraint, especially considering that every Marine regarded Okinawans as Japs and would split no Oriental hairs whatever except to concede that these "Japs" looked very harmless and beaten down. The Okinawans we saw at first, cowering in the thatched houses of the little village of China — an apt name, since Okinawans are more like Chinese peasants than anything else — or hiding in nearby caves, were all women, old men, and children.
— John Lardner in *The New Yorker,* May 19, 1945

I thought I saw some bushes out there that weren't there that afternoon. So we called for flares and saw the bushes moving — but stop when the flare went zip. Then we threw about a dozen hand grenades from our foxhole right there and heard moaning all the rest of the night. In the morning, we saw that they were all young women, nurses or something, maybe Japanese, maybe Okinawan. One was beautiful, really beautiful — with only one arm and both legs dangling by just a little thread. She was still hanging on after her awful wounds and that full night of moaning. We had to put her out of her terrible misery.
— A medical corpsman

ALTHOUGH OKINAWAN CIVILIANS were far from Washington's greatest concern, their fate wasn't entirely ignored. The War Department, aware that this was the first time its Pacific forces would encounter a large unfriendly but noncombatant population, sought to minimize their inevitable casualties and lighten their inescapable distress while pursuing its main interests of keeping them from hindering American efforts or aiding the Japanese.

American servicemen themselves could not be informed of anything about civilians until their destination was revealed, which happened only when they were almost there. Four months earlier, at Christmas 1944, Okinawa's dot on a large map of the Pacific at the 6th Marine Division's bulletin board on Guadalcanal had a heavy smudge from countless fingers that had touched it while men speculated about their next destination. But none knew officially until they were at sea in their troop transports or landing craft, when a brochure distributed during prelanding briefings made the first mention of the "simple, polite, law-abiding" Okinawans. They were "not warlike," it informed, "and they resent the high and mighty ways of the Japanese from the big islands to the north."

> Under Japanese rule, it's kind of tough to be an Okinawa [*sic*], because as true Sons of Heaven they don't seem to make the grade. They are used as manual laborers by the Japanese and when they are drafted they usually go into labor battalions. There are practically no Okinawa officers in the Japanese army. Even the officials sent by Tokyo to run the islands have kept themselves aloof from the islanders.

Each of the four American divisions that landed on Easter Sunday was allocated seventy thousand pounds of rice and soybeans and instructed to protect as many civilians as feasible by handing them over to separate military government (milgovt) units composed of doctors, corpsmen, quartermasters, civil administrators, and engineers for building detention camps. Small teams of them were attached to the fighting units and moved up behind the advance, with drinking water and rudimentary medical supplies for the sick and wounded.

The milgovt mission was to evacuate unarmed natives from combat areas to assembly points in the rear. From there, women, children, and the elderly were taken to camps in villages with undestroyed houses, where attempts were made to supply them with farming tools as well as a roof. Those forward teams included Nisei — first-generation Japanese-American — interpreters essential for that humanitarian enterprise for reducing native aid to the Japanese 32nd Army.

Milgovt operations were generally carried out in accordance with orders, which were as charitable as might be expected in wartime, especially against so uncharitable an enemy as the Japanese. Apart from the exceptions of fools and sadists, personnel worked in good faith to ameliorate the harsh conditions of displaced civilians. The relatively few natives willing and able to work for the American 10th Army — chiefly as road laborers and mess and hospital attendants — were paid the going 1940 wage of one yen a day, roughly eighteen cents. Minimum supplies of food prevented starvation, and potentially destructive epidemic diseases were averted. Many tons of DDT were sprayed around the detention camps against the chronic scourges of mosquitoes, fleas, and flies, while staffs grappled with what one account called the chief discipline problem: getting the elderly women to use latrines.

On a personal level, many Americans felt deep sympathy for the desperate "Okies" and tried to help in every possible way. "They were crying and praying," said a young Marine whose platoon shot and killed "a lot" of civilians the first night. "They didn't know where our lines were and we didn't know who they were. . . . I remembered the movies of Japs butchering civilians in China and wondered whether we'd started doing the same." Such men sometimes wept over the bodies of civilians they'd mistakenly killed. They often showed consideration and generosity well beyond the call: medical attention for the wounded, transportation for the aged, rations and candy for the children. A thousand cans of peaches were spooned into the mouths of native grandmothers. Accustomed to worse from some Japanese and expecting infinitely worse from American "beasts," the beneficiaries bowed deeply in gratitude — those who believed the gifts weren't poisoned.

On the other hand, milgovt's primary goal was to control an enemy civilian population at minimum cost. "We did not come here to play Santa Claus for the inhabitants of these islands," specified its commander, a brigadier general. "Nor do we intend to raise the standard of their living higher than the prewar level." "Protection" meant herding as many as possible, eventually over a quarter of a million, into the extremely overcrowded detention camps, where Okinawans were grateful chiefly because their expectations were so low. For although the War Department recognized that they weren't racially or culturally Japanese, it didn't make the mistake of expecting them to welcome the landing forces as liberators. "But by and large, they are still loyal to Japan," its brochure continued. "All they know about Americans is what they get from Tokyo propaganda, so you can expect them to look at you as though you were a combination of Dracula and the Sad Sack — at first, anyway."*

And for all its good intentions, the brochure's first sentence revealed a smug disregard of what awaited the pastoral island. "There's no use giving you a sightseer's guide," it cheerfully began, "because after the navy and the air forces have blasted the way for a landing . . . [it] just won't look the same." This is not to blame those who did the blasting. Anyone about to hit the beach against the expected Japanese resistance deserved every softening-up shell he could get. In that sense, the horrific damage to the island wasn't their "fault." But Americans were also badly prepared to deal with their civilian prisoners. "Strange but simple people," a man mused about a grandfather and two young children who burst into tears

---

*Those who didn't get the brochure or a shipboard briefing were likely to know even less about Okinawa. A pilot named Samuel Hynes remembered that "no one had heard of Okinawa. [Squadron] intelligence knew nothing about it except for two striking 'facts'" in a mimeographed handout: "One was that the natives were not Japanese but a more primitive people called Hairy Anus. [That was probably a confused reference to the Caucasoid Ainu, a people indigenous to Japan, some of whom were among Okinawa's early settlers.] The other was that the island was infected with poisonous snakes."

when they thought they were about to be killed. For most Americans in 1945, "strange" usually came down to being non-American.

Still, even the few world travelers couldn't have predicted the power of the Okinawans' fear. Few people take alien ideology or indoctrination seriously, least of all when it seems patently absurd, as in the case of the Japanese anti-American propaganda. But while Americans knew they were the good guys who wished innocent natives no harm, Okinawans, like most people everywhere, believed what they'd been told: The invaders were thirsting to torture, rape, and kill. One of the first groups of prisoners taken on Easter Sunday emerged from a cave drawing trembling fingers across their throats to indicate they were ready to die. They'd surrendered only because a young woman among them — a student at UCLA who'd been on her way back to Japan when the war broke out — persuaded them that Americans weren't rapacious savages. (She happened to be extremely attractive, prompting a private's exclamation of "Boy, I'd like to fuck her!"; then his astonishment at her "Please don't do that" in perfect English.)

Sacred Japan was making much of not having lost a war in twenty-three hundred years, and blessed America had never lost one at all. But Okinawans were terrified by this war between the two powers that was being waged on their land. An artilleryman correctly observed in April that "there are hardly any young men left, only old men, women, and little kids." They were the ones — the scatterings too feeble or immobile to hide or flee the devil — who allowed themselves to be rounded up into the camps.

Fighting units began meeting such terrified groups within an hour of the landing — far more of them than anticipated, for the great speed of the advance that bisected the island cut off scores of thousands who had intended to evacuate to the rugged north. The first natives Eugene Sledge saw were "pathetic . . . totally bewildered by the shock of our invasion and . . . scared to death of us . . . [and full of] fear, dismay and confusion on their faces."

Aged grandmothers covered themselves head to foot with quilts and shrank deep inside caves. When Americans removed the quilts, the women would "kneel and bow their foreheads to the deck time after time," an officer observed. "Palms pressed prayerfully together before them, they beseeched their discoverers most piteously to spare their ancient lives." As it advanced a few days after the landing, a Marine platoon was strafing all holes large enough to be cave mouths, then lobbing grenades inside. Just as a member of the platoon was about to blast another such opening, a shrill cry sounded inside. The grenade was held back just in time. Two cowering young women with children eventually emerged, together with an old man. Bent almost in half, his white beard nearly touching the ground, he supported himself with a staff.

A platoon member took him by the arm to lead him to a roundup of civilians they'd just passed, destined for a camp. The old man broke away and shouted in terror to the women. As if the movement had been rehearsed, the three dropped to their knees in a neat line, the man using a chopping gesture at the back of his neck to plead for their quick beheading.

The memory of a Marine named Peter Milo of the children he encountered continued to haunt him forty-five years later. One trembled in his arms. He offered her a candy bar.

> She looked into my eyes but made no move to accept the candy. Trying to encourage her, I took a little bite and chewed it. She kept looking into my eyes. Suddenly I felt as though she was looking into my very soul. I found it hard to breathe and my eyes had a stinging sensation.
>
> When we reached the compound and they saw the other Okinawans, who were eating and laughing by now, the old man and the women relaxed and joined their conversation. I sat down on the ground with the little girl on my lap, and bit by bit she ate the whole bar, all the time her eyes never leaving mine. [Then] it was time to catch up with the outfit. I stood up, reached for my last Hershey bar, which would have been my dinner, and put it in the little girl's hand. After a few steps, I turned back to see her still looking at me.

On L-day evening, a Connecticut recruit named Irving Oertel dug in near Yomitan Airfield. A sharp-eyed platoon mate spied a Japanese infiltrator, with a pack on his back, creeping down a path to their clearing, and killed him with a burst from his Browning automatic rifle — after which the man was discovered to be a woman, her pack a child. "That really shook us up. We felt terrible. Then we got used to an awful lot worse."

For three months from that first night, shooting Okies by mistake was commonplace. The civilians contributed heavily to their own destruction by moving outside American positions at night, although repeatedly warned by leaflet never to do that. But their fear of the daylight blanket of bombs and shells, and of the immensely powerful invaders themselves, caused most to move *only* at night, and American units, unable to understand why civilians didn't get the vital message, continued firing blindly during that worst time for both. Once one began shooting into the dark, all joined to blast away at any noise in the terrifying dark. In the morning, the perimeter of their night positions had as many dead goats, rabbits, and civilians as Japanese soldiers.

Civilians also contributed by helping the Japanese. Each American who saw evidence of that became less concerned about discriminating between Japanese soldiers trying to sneak in and blow them up and local families trying to save themselves. A few nights later, Oertel's platoon, dug in near the beach, heard movement close by. They grabbed their weapons to defend against the dreaded nighttime banzai attack — until word came down to cease firing because the targets were civilians trying to return to their "huts," which the Marines had passed before dark. "Needless to say, we didn't cease firing," remembered Platoon Sergeant Edmund De Mar, the prewar Marine who had wondered where Pearl Harbor was. "Because how the hell did we know this? How the hell could anyone be sure they wouldn't banzai* and kill us?" The morning light revealed a cluster of female corpses mixed in with those of Japanese soldiers.

Since some of the women had hand grenades inside their kimonos, the platoon had reason to believe they'd been right to shoot them. But Americans didn't know that civilians often carried grenades for killing *themselves* to prevent their torture, for which Japanese soldiers had provided the means. Many didn't know what they'd do with them, only hoped a right decision would deliver them at the last moment.

But neither could the Americans know, and discoveries of weapons hidden in kimono sleeves helped many resign themselves to dead civilians. Their confusion was reflected in the first letter home of Thomas Hannaher, the young private from North Dakota. The natives, Hannaher wrote during an hour of rest from the push north, "don't like the Japs either because they have treated them poorly." But the letter also reported that "the natives here are Japs and cannot be trusted." Not entirely true, but true enough for Americans to shoot first and investigate later. Even farmers and fishermen with poles were perceived as threats.

The Doberman war dogs of a point squad pushing north along a coastal road on April 10 suddenly froze. Tense Marines heard rustling in the brush only fifty feet away. A glimpse of old-fashioned leggings through the brush told Lieutenant Taylor Kennerly that this was another ambush. "Fire, fire!" he yelled, and three rifles and one BAR opened up instantly. But female and juvenile screams set Kennerly shouting for the fire to cease. He ran in front of his men, knocking their weapons upward.

Rushing into the brush, the men found three dead enemy soldiers, one live one, and several women and children huddling together. The survivors' eyes bulged with fear until chewing gum, chocolate, and cigarettes were distributed. Kennerly felt relieved when he saw the natives sensing that his "kind, young Marines were no murderers of women and children."

---

*The banzai charge by outnumbered, desperate Japanese troops had become a dreadful reality for Americans on previous Pacific islands, especially Saipan, and an even more dreadful nighttime contemplation. Literally "may you live ten thousand years" — which was originally wished only for the Emperor — the word expressed total group resolution.

But a bullet had ripped the arm of an Okinawan boy almost from his body. The bones were in smithereens, the hand gone. Laying the child on a blanket, Kennerly fed him candy from his pack while desperately thinking of what to do. The company doctor was treating casualties far in the column's rear. The squad's medical corpsman had had no training in amputation and wouldn't try on the shattered little arm. Time pressed hard; the point squad was holding up the entire regiment and the child's wound would kill him very soon. Dismayed, Kennerly decided he himself had to amputate, but could find nothing sharp enough in anyone's pack. Since the child's only prospect was a lingering, agonizing death, the grieving lieutenant, praying for forgiveness from a merciful God, administered an overdose of the corpsman's morphine, then faced the harrowing duty of telling the parents.

> Who says that the nature and emotions of the Okinawan peasants are any different from those of middle-class Americans? The Oriental man is not prone to show his emotions in public. But there on that lonely mountainside, the husband placed his arm around his wife's shoulder and they both wept silently but bitterly, their bodies trembling in their anguish. Yes, I can sense that human nature is the same all around the world. As I watched the pathetic parents, my thoughts turned to my wife at home and our six-month-old son that I had never seen, and I breathed a prayer of thanks that they were spared the ordeals of war.

Late that afternoon, the weary company doctor found Kennerly digging in farther up the coast and told him the child would survive! The doctor had come across the family an hour earlier and amputated the dangling arm. The morphine hadn't killed the lad because it was old and had lost some strength. In fact, it had probably kept him alive — by mitigating his shock until the amputation. Kennerly's misery turned to joy.

Civilian groups cringed with fear until the barrier was broken, as often with a canteen of water as with a medical dressing or candy bar. Their plight prompted plentiful acts of individual kindness on the part of Americans who had the time and energy for thoughts about outsiders. The happy endings were cherished, especially in the midst of so many horrific ones. What those enormously burdened Americans didn't suspect — even they, who were right there — was the trifling proportion of them.

They didn't suspect it because they never saw the civilian majority. For the most part, they encountered only the very young and very old; the barefoot, blind, and crippled who inspired sympathy until the Americans had to duck the next bullet or shell whizzing toward them; the shrunken grandparents and the children with the hungry eyes who prompted fleeting reflections about the oneness of the human family. They rarely met the more or less healthy adolescents and adults with the stamina to avoid the American camps that would have been their best hope for survival, but which seemed to them the worst. Those with the strength ran, limped, and crawled to flee everything American, which is why only 126,000 civilians, slightly more than a quarter of the population, were in milgovt's custody by the end of April instead of the expected 300,000.

Forty years later, Taylor Kennerly would often think of the wounded boy, even search for him on a moving visit to Okinawa in 1987. He had no doubt why the child had been spared. "My honest conviction is that a gracious God is the giver and taker of life. How dare man assume that he can usurp this power?" But in 1945, Kennerly's frightened men, like so many others, would continue firing at movements in the night.* One morning not long after the child's miraculous survival, the same platoon found an entire family dead, including the children. The brave lieutenant's conviction of heavenly intervention doesn't explain why tens of thousands of equally innocent Okinawan children suffered precisely the agonizing death he couldn't countenance for his lucky boy.

> *The real war was tragic and ironic beyond the power of any literary or philosophical analysis to suggest, but in unbombed America especially, the meaning of the war seemed inaccessible. Thus, as experience, the suffering was wasted.*
> — Paul Fussell

> *It is apparent that the Okinawan people as a whole have not the remotest conception of the issues of this war as we see them.*
> — From an American naval officer's study, written soon after the battle

Many Okinawan civilians had resisted until the last moment the prefectural government's shouts for all "nonessentials" to evacuate. That last moment came with the arrival of the enemy fleet a week before L-day. March 24, the first day of the naval bombardment, choked the roads with traffic, starting at twilight. Scores of thousands felt that anything would be better than the unholy cascade of shells that reinforced the image of the enemy as wild beasts.

Throughout that week of pre-invasion bombardment, the central part of the island at night was like a giant anthill just destroyed. Bewildered families abandoned their tiny houses, most with nowhere to go and no

---

*Kennerly himself would be wounded just over a month later, as his platoon was approaching Sugar Loaf Hill on Mother's Day. Two machine-gun bullets tore holes in his jacket, inches from his heart. Another traversed his foot, and a fourth so shattered his ankle that he would leave a naval hospital only on April 1, 1947, exactly two years after the landing.

means of support away from their fields. Some eighty-five thousand — about the same number as in the Japanese 32nd Army — headed toward the far emptier north. Others scattered this way and that, seeking refuge in remote villages, changing directions for some new place glimpsed as a last-minute refuge.

Spying sprinklings of refugees two weeks later, Ernie Pyle would register Okinawans as "dirty" and "pathetic." Yes, and almost all families were slowed by their aged and infirm. Doubly hard pressed without their able-bodied men, women lugged all they could — pots and pans, meager supplies of food — toward the unknown. Many had never seen the villages of their destination. They bore bundles on their heads and infants on their backs while pushing disabled parents in carts — those lucky enough to have them. When they caught their breath, they tried to calm children whimpering with hunger.

Okinawa had an "excellent network of poor roads," as an American historian called it. Most were dirt trails for horse-drawn carts. On the east coast, almost directly across the island from the landing beaches, Yoshi Kamata, the wife of a soybean wholesaler, fled with her five-month-old infant on her back, pulling her three-year-old with one hand and encouraging her six-year-old to keep going on his own. Her destination was a village of relatives some fifty miles north, but an hour of staggering revealed the utter futility of her effort. Bravely ignoring his painful feet, the six-year-old stumbled on in silence, but his baby brother sobbed uncontrollably with fatigue. When they were incapable of another step, their mother panicked until she remembered that a bus went north from a village two and a half miles ahead. Two and a half miles seemed an impossible distance in the dark, but it was her sole hope of saving her dazed children. She grabbed them and tried to run.

Belching smoke from its charcoal engine, the bus was pulling away when Mrs. Kamata dragged herself and her children into the village. To her great good luck, people noticed the family's condition, and although the groaning bus was packed beyond imagination, the driver stopped. The passengers squeezed themselves in even more tightly, and the family was on its way to its relatives — with "the kind of luck," Mrs. Kamata soon realized, "that separated those destined to perish from those who would survive."

The village of Gushikawa, some seven miles due east of the landing, had been ordered to evacuate much earlier, but the Sonan family remained. Father Tosei Sonan too had been lucky until now. The name of his parents' infant son Tosei, who died four years before his namesake's birth, had never been removed from the family register. Taken for him, the "replacement" Tosei was considered too small and mentally undeveloped — "stupid," the examining officer pronounced — to be conscripted when he was called, four years too early. Actually, he was better educated than the average villager because his father, who had failed to amend the family register, was a municipal office worker. Young Tosei took a job in a mainland factory when he could find no work on the island. Since returning, he'd provided for the family relatively well on his fireman's wages.

The eldest daughter, having learned in school about subhuman Americans who killed unwanted infants by bashing their heads against a wall, was terrified when the pre-invasion bombardment jolted the island. Eleven-year-old Shigeko knew all about Americans' determination to destroy and depopulate Divine Japan. The little girl was even more terrified on L-day, when the invaders drove from the beaches on the opposite coast, past Yomitan and Kadena Airfields, and straight toward the Pacific coast. The sight of two "racist killers" in a jeep passing Gushikawa caused violent trembling. She escaped the American plane she saw on her way to draw well water two days later only by diving into bushes. The pilot, she was convinced, intended to fire at her.

That evening, father Tosei announced it was time to flee. The family set out after dark with all they could pack into a cart hitched to their horse. With her mother pregnant, Shigeko was treated as an adult who had to care for her three younger sisters, aged six, four, and eighteen months. Her grandfather's former wife, divorced only because she couldn't bear a child to preserve the precious family line, also joined the party. After hugging a neighbor who resolved to remain in her house, the Sonans departed. Terrified to stay, yet unable to accompany them, the old, ill woman who stayed behind embodied the civilian predicament: flee, stay, fight the incomprehensibly powerful enemy, or surrender to his bestiality? She was the kind most likely to be saved by American milgovt units — but when her son-in-law, a conscripted soldier, managed to leave his unit for a peek at the house several days later, he found her dead.

Weeping evacuees with similar burdens packed the roads leading north. Leaving their home and ancestral tomb, the family hoped their food would sustain them until the Americans were thrown back into the sea, but a bombed-out bridge over a nearby river forced them to unhitch their cart and leave it behind with the bulk of their provisions.

Hampered by the slowness of the grandfather's former wife, they followed the east coast road, hiding from the bombs and shells at daybreak and moving out again at twilight — as quickly as they could, for Americans were advancing fast behind them. When old Grandmother again fell far behind that second night, Shigeko was left to wait for her. Hours later, the eleven-year-old decided to go back to look for her. Just as she moved, a bomb or shell exploded in the spot where she'd been standing a second earlier. Grandma was less lucky; Shigeko's long search for her was in vain.

Unable to reach their assigned village, the family hid on Mount Tano, one of the north's most rugged and densely wooded mountains. To determine direction, a member had to climb a tree: dangerous exposure, because Americans often bombed and strafed any little movement. With the family's food almost entirely gone, they killed the horse and dried its flesh for eating. Shigeko's parents said she mustn't cry. She didn't, even when she was starving.

What she did do was help hunt for food, which was even more dangerous until nightfall. When the 6th Marine Division declared the north secure on April 20, its troops really controlled only the towns, villages, and coastal roads, from which patrols were sent into the interior to mop up the Japanese remnants still trying to fight. Looking for food and water from nearby streams, Shigeko and her cousins encountered several enemy groups. When hunger eventually throttled their fear, they accepted chocolate and C-rations — which their parents threw away, convinced anything Americans would give Okinawans had to be poisoned. At last, the famished children risked tasting new gifts on their own, but although they didn't die and some Americans actually seemed kind, Shigeko couldn't forget their lust to kill Asians.

Still hiding in remote parts of the lonely mountain, the Sonans and other families built straw huts, then abandoned them for fear they'd be spotted by American patrols. Besides, the proximate food supply, sometimes only boiled grasses and tree bark, was quickly exhausted. Some families prepared to kill themselves to avoid Americans torture. Others gave up the grim struggle after ventures to villages below, where locals assured them that Americans didn't kill civilians who surrendered, only took them to detention camps. But Tosei Sonan, his fear and loathing of Americans intensified by his years in Japan, remained convinced that any American he approached would shoot him on the spot.

Some civilian men *had* been shot, even though, or just because, they disguised themselves as women. Some women, in turn, cut their hair and dressed like men in the hope of escaping rape, of which there were enough incidents to nourish the fear. One day, two patrolling Americans* dragged a young woman from a hut they discovered near the Sonans'. Shigeko, hiding in a tree, heard terrified weeping while the Americans' backs moved in jerky motions. Together with her parents' constant warnings, the smearing of soot on adolescent girls' faces and

---

*They were almost certainly from the Army's 27th Division, which had by now replaced the 6th Marine Division. See p. 186.

their wearing of men's clothes when they left their shelters enabled her to guess what was happening to the woman.

Food was a greater problem. When nothing could be scavenged in deserted villages, Tosei sometimes boiled the safe parts of the sotesu, a primitive palm that had kept farming families of earlier generations alive after typhoons destroyed their entire crops. Days were spent high in the mountains, nights in makeshift huts regularly visited by Japanese stragglers, the remnants of Colonel Udo's force, some of whom threatened punishment for failure to supply food. The Sonans had heard they shot some such "unpatriotic" civilians.

At the same time, American patrols continued burning the huts they managed to find. Shigeko and her mother returned from a food foray one morning to find their own hut burned. Picking some charred bits of flesh from the ashes, they wailed for Shigeko's father and sisters — until the "dead" emerged from the woods demanding quiet, because the patrol that did the burning might still be near. Recovering from their hysterical laughter, the women helped prepare for yet another move. Building and abandoning thirteen huts in various forests, they were never dry in that spring's unusually wet rainy season. A night here, two nights there — and a critical debate as they drifted south again in search of sustenance. From a mountain called Ona-dake, they saw American ships stretching to the horizon. Perhaps to save the child she was carrying, miraculously not yet lost, Shigeko's mother argued that Japan could never defeat such a force: It was time to give themselves up.

Dismissing that "nonsense," Tosei Sonan insisted that unconquerable Japanese forces would soon arrive to smash the cowardly Americans and liberate Okinawa. Famished little Shigeko took her father's side because he knew far more about Japan and also because she would never forget her school-learned duty to "beat the Americans to death!" Now the skeletal children could climb the hills only with desperate effort. A virulent rash with a tormenting itch covered their bodies.

In June, although they couldn't be certain of the date, the family staggered to a small mountain somewhere in the south, where no tree remained standing. Japanese corpses sprawled on the blackened stumps, some in bits and pieces. Burying as many as they could, the exhausted Sonans could not dig deep enough to keep the feet from sticking out. The children put crushed leaves in their noses to block the stench when night fell. They had to sleep in the nearest clearing, together with rows of mortally wounded Japanese soldiers, rasping and moaning.

When Shigeko's mother gave birth, the Sonans had no idea the battle had been officially over for two weeks. The new baby somehow managed to live her first few days, but Shigeko's malnourished, malaria-ridden mother had no milk, and she finally persuaded her husband to surrender. Down from the mountains, the children, all bones and bloated bellies, were loaded onto an American truck, driven to a camp, fed, and sprayed with DDT. Ten months later, they were permitted to return to Gushikawa, which had been burned to the ground, together with their house and all their possessions. Still, the battle was kinder to the Sonans than to civilian Okinawans as a whole. In fact, they were still among the luckiest families: Everyone survived except Grandma and Shigeko's four-year-old sister, who died days after their flight's end, unable to swallow.

> *In Okinawa, we say* Nichi do takara: *Life is the treasure. Whatever the reasons to fight and kill, however profound the causes or pretexts for war, they can't justify the result. Human lives are too precious to sacrifice.*
> — Masahide Ota, forty-six years later

For the Normal School students turned auxiliary soldiers, L-day's thrill lasted hours. Senior staff members of the 32nd Army — and of the 62nd Division and 5th Artillery Command, coordinator of all heavy artillery — spent much of that long day observing the American armada from the observation post at Shuri Castle, appreciating the enemy's colossal strength and landing skills but showing no concern. General Ushijima's smiling composure continued to reflect Japan's invincibility and the Emperor's inviolability. Ota continued believing clever Japanese tactics had lured the invasion fleet to Okinawa, the better to sink it.

The confidence of the Normal School's complement, all enrolled in the Blood and Iron Scouts, could not have been higher as they took up their tasks. Every morning, those in the prized subunit assigned to staff intelligence at 32nd Army headquarters walked the two hundred yards from the mouth of their cave to the headquarters under Shuri Castle, where they were briefed on battle victories and how wobbly the faint-hearted enemy's morale had become. The boys took notes. Then their little unit's commander, who happened to be a mean-spirited Japanese intelligence officer, dispatched them in groups of two or three to disseminate the fictions to towns and villages south of the Shuri Line.

The boys shouldered their rifles and made their way on foot to spread their glad tidings to local military authorities and civilians as far away as the island's southern tip. The mostly female and elderly civilians welcomed them joyfully even before hearing the news and promises of a prompt American defeat. Taking the communications soldiers as substitutes for their own boys, almost all of whom were fighting with Army or Home Guard units, mothers and grandparents fed them rice, already gone from their own cave in Shuri. They stayed a night or two, depending on the distance from Shuri, then returned for their next assignment.

Before the first week was over, they traveled only by night: Enemy reconnaissance planes and firepower made daylight movement too risky.

Soon they were ordered not to leave their cave for any purpose whatever except after dark. But their confidence remained unshaken even when the fierce American bombardment leveled their beloved Normal School and caused their first serious casualty — on April 12 (the day of President Roosevelt's death). Ota and a close friend disobeyed orders by racing outside to relieve themselves there instead of in their cave. Dashing back, they stood at its mouth to watch Japanese tracer bullets reach for the enemy planes that buzzed Shuri like flies. A chunk of shrapnel knocked Ota's friend flat.

The hospital cave to which the others quickly carried him was packed with a number of patients they could scarcely believe — so full of severely wounded soldiers that the boys were refused entry until one remembered he knew a doctor inside. He was found and persuaded to treat the first student casualty, but the wounded boy had to be taken back to his own cave because the wards were overflowing. Having no mother, he called for his sister throughout his classmates' all-night vigil. The startling reality of his death on top of the hospital cave's frightening scenes put the first chip in the unit's morale.

But it also fed the boys' patriotic resolve. Swearing their own lives to repay the brutal Americans, the classmates reminded themselves that Imperial General Headquarters and the 32nd Army command had attracted the arrogant enemy to the island as a tactical move. *"Let your enemy cut your skin / You cut his flesh. / Let your enemy cut your flesh / You sever his bones."* Repetition of the famous lines made sense of their friend's death.

They'd been digging a separate little chamber in their cave for the Normal School's principal, who, unlike many Japanese civilians on Okinawa, had neither escaped to the mainland when invasion seemed imminent nor tried to curry favor with the 32nd Army. Students and teachers loved and trusted Principal Sadao Noda even more than before the emergency. As the grim days passed, Noda fashioned a memorial tablet to each student killed while delivering a message. In mid-May, when the tablets covered an entire wall of his chamber, his despondency worried the survivors more than their own precarious safety.

But the towns and villages to which they traveled continued greeting them as family. Their inhabitants, almost entirely cut off from other sources of information, thirsted for encouraging news. As their skepticism of the reports of great victories grew, however, the boys came to feel guilty about conveying them. The trips took ever longer under the intensifying bombardments — especially for Kume-raised Ota, easily lost on the unmarked Okinawan roads. They also became ever more dangerous. Several boys who walked south with Ota one night were killed just after they'd dispersed for their assigned villages. Things were also worse at each return to Shuri. From one rice ball a day in early April, their food ration dwindled to nearly nothing. The lice-infested lads learned to feed themselves by scavenging in fields on their travels. The tension of confinement in their cave interspersed with the constant danger from the relentless bombardment during the missions snapped some young nerves. So many deaths! So little hope of escaping it, of even getting something to eat! The music teacher composed a song for them, its lyrics from a poem full of love for the old, peaceful days under the shade of Shuri's ancient trees. Some boys fought tears when they sang it, visions of their own deaths in their eyes. Screaming about the enemy in their sleep, several slowly became useless. (Curiously, those who had led their class in military training were more likely to break under the pressure than the quiet and meek.) Yet all remained proud to sacrifice for the highest ideals. It would have been treason to imagine that they, the trusted Okinawans, would stop doing their duty for Japan.

13 · Ruriko Morishita, Nurse's Aide

What really gets me angry is . . . that I had chances, plenty of them, to get [a Jap flag]. These Nips aren't carrying them anymore and Mom are they fanatical. They'd rather kill themselves than surrender. The women are just as bad as the soldiers and when I first hit this rock it hurt me to see them killed. You know . . . I naturally [considered] women as a little bit better than men and more or less put them on a pedestal. But these Keisha girls are like dogs. . . . After seeing some of [their] work . . . it don't bother me at all anymore to see them killed.
— From a letter home of a Marine who would devote much of his later life to reconciliation with Japanese and Okinawan survivors

I can't describe the worst. The worst was indescribable.
— Ruriko Morishita, forty-three years later

OKINAWANS' COMMITMENT TO Japanese goals remained uneven, the young generally much more enthusiastic than their parents and grandparents. Although many soldiers conscripted to serve with fighting units longed to drop everything and return to their families, boys as young as fourteen happily polished their new arms, and native girls served with equal pride, many as nurse's aides. Six high schools supplied students for that work, which virtually all saw as a sacred honor and trust. Among them were 155 girls from the elite Himeyuri (Princess Lily) Girls High School and Himeyuri Teachers College in Shuri, the Normal School's female counterpart, selected for the most responsible student assignments.

The Student Medical Corps was destined to enter the literature of martyrdom as the Himeyuri Girls. Although their lot was no harder and their casualties scarcely greater than among Okinawan women as a whole, the young daughters of the island's privileged families would make captivating characters for romantic literature and prettified Japanese films, cast in the glow of their pre-invasion purity. Since the Confucian teaching to separate the sexes after the age of seven had arrived on Okinawa only with the Japanese school system in the 1880s, much of the island outside its few cities observed it less than rigorously until the general tightening of discipline during the war emergency after Pearl Harbor. The strictest adherence had always been for the young "princesses" in the Himeyuri schools, where such lapses as exchanging a spoken or written word with a boy earned quick expulsion.

The most envied place to serve was the Haebaru Army Hospital. Although many Japanese fighting units down to regimental level had their own field hospitals and lesser medical installations, that new facility for a thousand patients, directly subordinate to 32nd Army command, boasted the best. When the 10/10 air raid demolished its Naha building, staff officers took the point about enemy airpower and decided to rebuild in a safer place, behind the Shuri Line. They chose a country site some five miles southeast of Naha, three miles due south of Shuri. The Okinawa Military Hospital, as it was officially called, was a series of caves dug into the sides of a large, grassy ridge bordering the farming village of Haebaru.

Hospital staff members lived in the village while military engineers supervised the digging. Failure to complete the main tunnel by the time the fighting began left most of the twenty-one caves isolated instead of the planned wings of an integrated system. When Himeyuri dormitories were also destroyed in an air raid four months before L-day, many girls were moved to shacks thrown up at the construction site. But seventeen-year-old Ruriko Morishita, whose parents owned a small trading company, remained at Shuri in order to finish her studies at the prestigious Teachers College, which culminated in hasty graduation ceremonies a week before the American landing. Still hoping to become a teacher when the crisis ended, fervently patriotic Ruriko moved in with the others at Haebaru, helping with the hospital's now-frenzied preparations.

She was assigned to one of Ward Three's half-dozen caves for infectious diseases. (Ward One was for general medicine; Two for surgery.) Ward Three had quite enough to deal with even without further casualties. Japan's tuberculosis rate was very high, partly because girls who'd caught the disease while working in textile factories spread it to their villages when they were sent home. Attempts earlier in the war to send young male carriers among the troops back to Japan from the conquered territories ended when American submarines began ripping Japanese shipping lanes to shreds. Now Okinawa's dank caves served as hatcheries for the bacillus.

When Ward Three was declared ready, Ruriko and fellow aides began working light eight-hour shifts. Besides tuberculosis, the principal infectious diseases were amoebic dysentery, typhoid, and malaria, but some patients were still recovering from the 10/10 air raid. Within days of the landing, however, Ruriko's cave was filled beyond capacity with newly wounded, and the shelling and bombing were so intense that the girls were forbidden to go outside except to fetch food from the mess cave, water from the well at one end of the ridge, and medical supplies from stacks deposited near the cave mouths. But conditions inside became so foul that some started breaking the rule for the sake of brief relief from them. A number of girls were killed on those ventures outside. The survivors took to sleeping near the patients rather than in their dormitory cave. Surrounded by bodies ripped apart by bombs and shells, some prayed for instant death if they too were hit.

By mid-April, the medical staff stopped cheering the news of "victories" delivered by messengers the likes of young Masahide Ota. Many of the wounded were finished off by bombing, shelling, and strafing as they waited in long lines of stretchers outside, or on their comrades' backs. Desperate screams of "Please let us in!" sounded when planes and gunfire attacked. Soldiers who had braved the heaviest American fire to carry battlefield mates to the hospital wept to see their lives ebb away, but there was simply nowhere to fit more patients inside.

The girls slept in a tangle of arms and legs, with hardly enough room to draw breath. Every square foot of floor space was packed with grievously wounded soldiers, squeezed in there even more tightly than on the troopships that had brought them to Okinawa. Relatively few had been hit by bullets. Shell fragments caused most of the damage: bones crushed, flesh gouged out, hands and legs blown off. Without the cross-ventilation from the unmade connection to the central tunnel, the only air, from the caves' narrow mouths, penetrated no more than a few yards inside.

Otherwise, the caves were fit only for bats. The walls and ceiling oozed condensation. Unremoved stalactites hung down like grotesque icicles. Sour smells of mildew and wet earth were joined by the stench of blood, pus, urine, feces, and rancid sweat from combat-broken bodies. When Japanese personnel distributed hand grenades for personal use and showed the nurse's aides how to use them, Ruriko longed for two tastes before her time came: of fresh air and clean water.

She learned to snatch seconds of sleep standing up, then even while groping in the clammy, stinking dark toward patients moaning for help, or when holding candles during surgery. The aides had three hours off in every twenty-four. Ward Three dropped infectious diseases almost entirely in favor of surgery. (Its doctor, an Okinawan pediatrician, had begun training himself in surgery after the 10/10 raid, which convinced him his island would not escape more devastation.) Except in the niches used for surgery, the lighting came from bottles of kerosene with wicks of twisted rag. Their flickering flames, half starved for oxygen, barely penetrated the murkiness. Day and night were indistinguishable. Weeks became a seamless nightmare.

The now-filthy cream of Okinawan maidenhood were infested by lice from the men with whom they were squeezed together. The only hot water was in the surgical areas, and there it was barely enough to wash the instruments. Inexplicably heavy limbs, amputated without anesthetic, had to be carried outside to holes or bomb craters. Numbing themselves, Ruriko and a friend also lugged the heavier corpses outside, one by one. Other wards fell far behind in that work, so that the barely living had to spend long intervals with corpses, from which many were too weak to wriggle away. The staff rarely had the time or strength to help them, especially during bombardments.

Inside, men mad with thirst howled relentlessly. The girls were happy not to understand some of their babbling and curses. During lulls in the bombing, however, they did hear maggots wriggling into the wounded — like silkworms crunching mulberry leaves, they imagined. Although the ravenous larvae supposedly prevented tetanus by consuming pus, even the bravest soldiers moaned and screamed when their flesh was munched. The face of one whose jawbones had been crushed to a pulp so teemed with them that dozens fell onto Ruriko's hand when she worked to trickle rice gruel down his throat. Then she tried to see through the murk in order to pick the wriggling creatures from his oozing wounds with crude wooden chopsticks. The men for whom the aides performed that service were profoundly grateful. Watching a girl quietly work to free his wound — "open like a ripe pomegranate" — of its maggots, one saw her as "an angel in the midst of hell."

The teenagers also had to deal with every natural function of men, from whom they'd previously been segregated so assiduously. Ruriko had touched the hand of no man or boy apart from her father and brother since she was seven. Now she had to help strangers defecate and hold the penises of double amputees so they could urinate. To control her trembling, she issued orders to herself. "This must be done. You're doing it for your country."

In despair over the ghoulish overcrowding, Ward Three's former pediatrician no longer worried about cleanliness or his primitive supplies — only about his patients, who were in urgent need of recuperation after surgery but had to be evicted because there was simply no room in the cave. Soon the self-taught surgeon was able to treat only the very worst cases, if they had a chance to be saved; otherwise they weren't admitted. The less critically wounded were ordered directly back to the front.

But despite everything, including her own horror, Ruriko remained certain that "the good side" must win against the demon enemy. The Divine Wind would return to save sacred Japan.

While many patients were eager to return to their units, some of the most gravely wounded were resigned. A few whispered to the student aides — although never to their bosses, the military nurses — that they knew Japan couldn't win because they'd seen the enemy's overwhelming power and supplies. Through her exhaustion, Ruriko objected. "You're just talking like that because you're a little hurt," she scolded men lacking arms and legs. "You'll be better soon and come to your senses."

Worsening conditions served only to strengthen the girls' resolve. They were the ones, they told themselves, who must save Okinawa. "Anyway, once we're dead," Ruriko reminded the others, "we'll go to Yasukuni Shrine." Patients still able to smile coined a nickname for her: Miss Victory Day.

14 · Kojo Returns

Where on earth are our planes? Escaped somewhere? They didn't show up during the October raid and now either — no sign of even a single plane with the Rising Sun.
 — A conscripted Okinawan laborer

There is talk that the Combined Fleet will come and destroy the enemy by Navy Memorial Day.
 — From a diary found on a Japanese corpse

THE FIELD HOSPITAL to which Tadashi Kojo was taken after the accidental explosion of the homemade antitank charge was a converted schoolhouse. He hovered near death during the December week following his operation. During the following months, his head throbbed and his hearing was severely impaired, but even totally deaf, he'd have had no trouble registering the pre-invasion bombardment three months later, during the last week of March 1945. Bombs and shells shook the earth throughout the center of the island, including the fields where the patients lay, having been moved from the schoolhouse because all relatively prominent buildings presented likely targets. Kojo's recuperation was approaching a hundred days when that thunder announced the imminence of the enemy landing. He rose from his cot, pulled on his clothes, and set out to return to his cherished regiment.

A doctor stopped him. Lifting his heavy head bandages, he indicated the large, unhealed hole behind his left ear. "Captain, this goes straight to your brain. Infection here — and you're in great danger of it — means fairly certain death." When the doctor moved on, Kojo instructed his orderly to fetch his horse after dark. He slipped out and rode to regimental headquarters.

Regular transfer of field officers to new duties was standard practice in the Japanese Army. A new commander of his 22nd Regiment had been flown in from a high staff job on Formosa just days earlier, the plane managing to land during a lull in the enemy's air operations. Lieutenant Colonel Masaru Yoshida had barely managed to meet his senior officers by the time Kojo reported back for duty, but a new commanding officer was the least of the changes awaiting the captain. In the redeployments following the loss of the 9th Division, the 22nd Regiment had been shifted to a different position.

The men were digging new projects, having started from the beginning again. They were eleven miles south of their original fortifications, protecting the beach near Kadena Airfield. The regiment was now in a kind of reserve, its new area of responsibility covering from just below Naha Airfield on the Oroku Peninsula — itself about two miles southwest of the capital — to the city of Itoman, some four miles farther down the island's west coast.

When Kojo rode in from the hospital that evening, a tunnel had been almost completed in a hill below Naha Airfield. That large new project housed the 22nd's regimental headquarters, which had just been connected to a far larger bastion — headquarters of the Navy's Okinawa Island Command — deep beneath the same hill. The Naval Base Force, as it was better known, was a conglomerate of all naval units on the island, including construction, shipbuilding, and engineering, midget and suicide submarine service personnel, and the crews of land-based naval guns. A third of its ten thousand men were regulars; the others were Home Guards and assorted Okinawan conscripts. Although its overall commander, Rear Admiral Minoru Ota, was a specialist in land defenses, only several hundred of his troops had taken armylike basic training, and even they had no combat experience.

The Okinawa Island Command was responsible for defending the six square miles of the Oroku Peninsula, which reaches out toward China at the island's widest point. Its headquarters were much more impressive than its potential as a ground fighting force. The three-hundred-yard main tunnel cut entirely through the hill in a sweeping curve three stories high in some places. Power lines ran to a central station in Naha. The deeply sunken complex had its own operations, communications, cipher, and signal spaces, and medical rooms with hot water — even repair facilities and roosts for carrier pigeons. The dank concrete refuge, second only to 32nd Army headquarters below Shuri Castle, was packed almost solid with sailors completing the installations, who would soon turn to manning them.

With a replacement now commanding Kojo's old 1st Battalion, Colonel Yoshida appointed the captain his operations officer. Since a skilled second lieutenant already in charge of the operations department made the assignment nominal, he used the time for more recuperation, telling no one he still felt shaky. As serene Ushijima gazed at the enemy fleet from his observation tower at the castle, Kojo observed the same scene from six miles southwest, at the top of the hill above the two underground headquarters of the Naval Base Force and 22nd Regiment. The twenty-four-year-old captain felt almost honored by the immense parade of power assembled to challenge them. At last the alien ships were there, far more numerous and mighty than he'd imagined, but he remained utterly confident in General Ushijima's leadership and Japan's ultimate victory. Abandoning the almost finished strongpoints above the landing beaches had depressed him after the furious work to complete them in time to crush the enemy there. But now he laughed at the Americans' even more furious bombardment of that same area — for it was empty! Let the big, fat enemy go on wasting effort while they, the military professionals, prepared for the kill.

Almost immediately after the landing, the 22nd Regiment's 2nd and 3rd Battalions were transferred from the 24th Division to the 62nd, Ushijima's only other full division, and ordered to join the main Japanese line on high ground protecting Shuri. That left the 22nd Regiment with a single battalion: the 1st, formerly Kojo's. It also left only two horses at regimental headquarters: Lieutenant Colonel Yoshida's and Kojo's — which he permitted a passionate horseman on the staff of the adjoining Naval Base Force headquarters to ride. Although Japanese officers of the separate services tended to keep their distance from one another, the shared equestrian interest, and perhaps the approaching danger, drew those two unusually close in a matter of days.

When regimental operations officer Kojo read a copy of the order from Imperial General Headquarters informing that the battleship *Yamato* was being readied for its foray to Okinawa, he assumed it was part of the great naval strike for obliterating the American fleet anticipated by the entire 32nd Army. But something puzzled him, and he inquired about it in a way that would have been inappropriate for a mere captain if the naval staff officer hadn't become a friend.

"Why just *Yamato* and her screen?" he asked with uncustomary directness. "Why not the Combined Fleet?"

Kojo's generosity with his horse prompted the older man to reveal a momentous secret. "There is no Combined Fleet; the Americans have finished it. All we have left is *Yamato* and a few destroyers."

"I mean the rest of our ships," Kojo replied, thinking his new friend's jest rather tasteless. "Why leave our carriers out of the attack?"

On that April day in 1945, Kojo learned of the Battle of Midway in June 1942, where the modern Imperial Navy suffered its first crushing defeat. Scores of Japan's best warships had steamed for the showdown at the western approach to the Hawaiian Islands, certain of annihilating America's Pacific Fleet. When that great gamble ended in the loss of four heavy carriers and their air groups — hundreds of the country's best pilots — most Japanese admirals immediately recognized it as the beginning of the end. The Imperial Navy could no longer protect the Empire,

let alone regain its supremacy. (Isoroku Yamamoto, Japan's most respected admiral since he planned the masterly Pearl Harbor strike, commanded the Japanese force at Midway from his flagship *Yamato,* which
was participating in her first serious engagement. After the sinking of the
cream of his carrier fleet, he wept in his cabin.)

But now, almost three years later, many high-ranking Army officers
even in Tokyo still knew nothing of the war's sharpest turning point,
for the Navy had taken great pains to conceal its fatal wounds and humiliation. Tens of thousands of field officers, not to mention the civilian population, knew even less. Until that April day, Kojo too had been
utterly unaware of both the Midway disaster and the Navy's subsequent
decimation, resulting in the collapse of the Empire's lifelines. As after
Tsushima maru's sinking while she was evacuating women and children
from Okinawa, survivors of the stricken warships were ordered to say
nothing about the losses. That was partly for the sake of Japanese
morale in general, but also to protect the Navy's pride. Admission of
defeat, difficult for every military service in every country, was especially difficult for the Japanese brass during that period when victory
was essential to sustain the massive illusions with which the war was
being pursued.

The ignorance of 32nd Army officers of Kojo's rank and higher would
remain intact throughout the Okinawan campaign. Yet had they known,
only the most perceptive would have understood the consequences, and
that knowledge would have scarcely diminished their commitment. Even
Norio Watanabe, the freelance photographer from Osaka who'd considered the war with America huge folly from the first, was now caught up in
the spirit of battle.

Watanabe's artillery unit was positioned just northwest of Naha, some
five miles above where the two detached battalions of Kojo's regiment
had been sent into the line, but part of the same defensive core centered
at Shuri. From there, the hater of everything military watched a few hit
enemy planes hurtle into the sea, and felt deep envy when American flying boats rescued their pilots from the water. His unit could easily have
shot the downed pilots from its vantage point, but the company commander did not give that order because no time could be spared from
destroying enemy planes themselves. Besides, the battery was still trying
to conceal its guns except during their firing, and shooting pilots would
have brought swifter, more severe retaliation than shooting at planes.
Headquarters announced that Watanabe's unit had accounted for fourteen. He believed the real score was four or five, but despite his contempt
for official lying and conviction that Japan couldn't possibly win — which
still made him almost an aberration — he found the downing of enemy
planes gave him some professional satisfaction.

Weak as he still was, Kojo, with none of Watanabe's doubt or cynicism, eagerly looked forward to reassuming the work for which he'd trained his entire adult life. What did aircraft carriers really matter anyway, or the Imperial Navy as a whole? Not fully believing the naval staff officer's fantastic story of the Midway debacle, he in any case remained convinced the decisive struggle would take place on land. The massive enemy landing made him more than ever aware that the struggle for Okinawa would be extremely hard and costly. But he also knew that the 32nd Army's main defenses hadn't yet been tested, because the new plan was to defeat the Americans well after they'd landed.

General Ushijima was naturally less sanguine. He was in his headquarters deep below Shuri Castle when he was informed, days after the Easter Sunday L-day, that the Imperial Navy's last great ship was about to come to his aid. The secret signal included instructions for him to take advantage of *Yamato*'s sortie to counterattack on the ground as she approached the following morning. Ushijima disapproved of the idea and radioed advice to stop Operation Heaven Number One. He believed the first week of the land war was too early for counterattacks; the Army's best hope of doing the greatest damage to the enemy lay in biding its time in its best fortifications. He also felt he better appreciated the enemy's air domination and naval strength than did the mainland strategists. Combined Fleet headquarters seemed to be living in a dream world.

The general's impatient chief of staff, by contrast, was confident that the *Yamato* operation would help turn the tide on land by catching the enemy off balance. Isamu Cho knew in his bones that defense had never been the Japanese way. The "attack and more attack" that had created the Empire would now save the day against the Americans by confusing and confounding them. Those characteristic reactions of the commanding general and his chief of staff would soon sharpen the debates about the kind of war they should wage on Okinawa itself. When Ushijima heard about *Yamato*'s end on April 7, he snorted about the "infernal waste" and recalled his urging to cancel the adventure. "Banzai charges should be left to soldiers," he said — and he would use them sparingly in his own command because they were too wasteful, no matter how much they terrified the enemy. However, the chief of staff would continue to press for more operations in the spirit of Heaven Number One.

Ironically, the superpatriots like Cho, having helped provoked the war, were now helping shorten it with gambles that squandered the remaining resources, while the nonpolitical warriors like Ushijima helped protract the agony with their sober professionalism. Soon *Yamato* would be gone and Okinawa's north would be falling with disturbing speed. But there were other ways to deal with America's extravagant material advantages. The kamikazes were in full flight.

15 · Kamikazes

To blossom today, then scatter;
Life is so like a delicate flower.
How can one expect the fragrance to last forever?
— Admiral Takajiro Onishi, father of the kamikazes

Living, to be overwhelmed with the immeasurable blessings of Imperial goodness.
Dead, to become one of the country's Guarding Deities and as such to receive
unique honors in the temple.
— A choice put to Japanese pilots

When I fly the skies
What a splendid place to be buried
The top of a cloud would be.
— A kamikaze volunteer before setting out on his mission

IN THE END, the primary objective of *Yamato*'s last mission was to scatter the defenses against an air assault on the American invasion fleet. The great battleship had been chosen both as the best decoy for luring away the greatest number of enemy interceptors and as the stoutest target for withstanding their attacks for the longest possible time — giving Japanese planes a turn against the American fleet. Some nine hundred aircraft took part in that offensive of April 6 and 7.

Launched from a ring of airfields on the mainland, Formosa, and occupied Shanghai, the effort was mounted in weak coordination — the best the Japanese High Command could manage — with Operation Heaven Number One. Wave upon wave of Japanese planes sank three destroyers, two ammunition ships, one LST, and one minesweeper, as well as damaging a light carrier, eleven destroyers, two destroyer escorts, and eight other craft off and near Okinawa. On the April 7 of *Yamato*'s sinking, more strikes hit a battleship, carrier, destroyer, destroyer escort, and one other vessel.

That use of Japanese aircraft defied logical explanation. While American dive-bombers were having their way with the Imperial Navy's greatest prize, her appeals for air cover went unanswered. A mere two hundred miles away, however, the nine hundred Japanese planes were swarming over the very ships that had launched the *Yamato*-hunting Hellcats, Helldivers, and Avengers. Just after the veteran carrier *Hancock*'s first such launch, a Zero slipped through her screen of battleships, cruisers, and destroyers in one Task Force 58 battle group and headed straight for her starboard bow. It dropped a bomb on her flight deck, then put a twenty-foot hole there by crashing farther aft. Seventy-two men were killed and eighty-two wounded by explosions that set fire to her hangar deck and twenty parked planes.

That Zero was suicidal, like more than a third of the planes dispatched on April 6 and 7 and roughly the same proportion throughout the Okinawan campaign. Altogether, the Japanese would mount just under nine hundred air raids on the island and the American fleet, by far the war's greatest effort. Compared to five thousand to six thousand sorties by conventional dive-bombers and torpedo planes — that is, by pilots who didn't intend to crash — nineteen hundred were flown by kamikazes. (That's the American tally; official Japanese records document the loss of 2,944 kamikaze planes.) It was those "special" missions that prompted the greatest American consternation and fear, and not only because they caused some 80 percent of the damage to the fleet. Kamikazes greatly increased tension — even from the extreme pitch of ordinary air attacks — because every sailor on every ship was convinced they were aiming for him. A British historian saw the kamikazes reintroducing an element of personal threat that "had been absent from naval warfare since the days of boarding and hand-to-hand fighting."

The April 6 attack was the first massive one on American ships at Okinawa, but individual Japanese planes and small groups had been dogging them even before L-day. Kamikazes crashed a battleship, two destroyers, and a destroyer-minesweeper on March 27, when the fleet was bombarding the island and taking Kerama Retto, the cluster of little islands the Americans had wisely seized before L-day. A landing craft was hit the next day. On March 31, carrier-based American fighters "splashed" two planes attacking the heavy cruiser *Indianapolis* — flagship of Admiral Spruance, commander of the 5th Fleet — and antiaircraft fire from the nearby *New Mexico* downed a third. But a fourth managed to scrape a wing against the cruiser before careening into the sea. Its bomb crashed through several decks on the port side and exploded in an oil bunker, killing nine men and wounding twenty.

Half of the more than seven hundred planes that attacked the fleet on L-day itself were kamikazes. Before dawn that morning, two explosions in quick succession awoke the Marines still fitfully sleeping below decks on *Hinsdale*, flagship of a troop transport division. Frightened passengers frantically dressed in pitch darkness, the ship having lost electrical power immediately. One Marine managed to control his trembling hand enough to light a cigarette on the third try. After ten infinitely long minutes, an order was shouted down the hatches for all hands to proceed to their abandon-ship stations.

The predawn grayness had hidden the plane from straining lookouts and its low altitude over the water had allowed it to evade radar, so no one aboard the ship, or the three dozen others in her squadron, saw the attacker visually or electronically until the last moment. The plane itself was also unusual. Most that crashed intentionally were obsolete models that had been stripped of usable instruments, loaded with explosives, and fueled for a one-way trip. The pilot of this first-line Tony fighter may have decided on his own not to return from his mission.

But in other respects, *Hinsdale'*s trial was much like that of scores of ships sunk or severely damaged in that unfathomable way. The Tony crashed into her port side amidships at the waterline. Flames shot high enough to severely burn men on the bridge some fifty feet above. More of the sixteen killed and thirty-nine wounded were in the engine room, into which the plane telescoped. The living passengers, "strung tight as violin strings," abandoned ship.

Twenty-four sailors and Marines on an LST participating in the fake landing in the far south joined the L-day dead. The regular Japanese submarine force was too weakened to pose much threat; the surface fleet could muster only enough strength for the last effort by *Yamato* and her screen; the scattered Okinawan shelters of most suicide submarines and suicide boats would be captured before their craft could get under way. It was left to the kamikaze pilots to do almost all the sinking and killing, and they would keep at it throughout the campaign; the Navy's ordeal was only beginning.

That twenty-two ships were hit and eleven sunk in the attack of April 6–7 was particularly dismaying to Americans because carrier strikes on mainland airfields on the morning of the sixth were thought to have destroyed virtually all Japanese planes able to reach the fleet from there. That would not be the campaign's last expression of American optimism stiffened with poor intelligence of Japanese camouflage, dispersal, and digging — in this case, of vast systems of underground hangars, tunnels, and barracks being completed at many mainland installations.

Crews of American ships also tried to convince themselves that the Japanese had "shot their bolt" with their kamikaze attacks; only isolated bases could still get a few craft into the air. "Christ, we must have knocked out every plane they had left on those home islands!" a lieutenant in a carrier's recreation room assured fellow players in a pinochle game. But late the same afternoon, the radar screen of the destroyer *Leutze* revealed dozens of bogeys some ninety miles west and closing at two hundred knots, their pilots pleased to be attacking out of twilight's blinding setting sun.

The first lookouts spotted the formation thirteen minutes later. Pandemonium reigned on and above *Leutze* and *Newcomb*, a sister destroyer that joined the antiaircraft firing with her every gun but couldn't stop one plane from crashing into her aft stack and another from hitting her amidships with a large torpedo or bomb that demolished her vital parts. As *Newcomb*'s stores of ammunition and petroleum products fed her fierce blaze, a third plane hit her forward stack, spraying enough additional aviation fuel over decks and sailors to send flames hundreds of feet into the air. Gallantly going to her aid, *Leutze* was crashed by a fourth plane among the dozens that were shot down or missed on their own.

The two destroyers' fire-control crews fought the damage in searing heat. Sailors struggled to shore up bulkheads, secure steam lines, extinguish fires in magazines. Some were burned to death trying to fight flames and reach trapped fellow crew members, while *Newcomb*'s surgeon operated through the night in her wardroom, surrounded by destruction and carnage. Forty-seven were killed or missing, fifty-eight wounded — but both scorched wrecks were eventually towed to Kerama Retto and saved, whereas even more intense attacks sank *Bush*, with a loss of thirty-five killed and missing and twenty-one wounded.

No fewer than forty to fifty planes attacked *Bush* that afternoon. One crashed between her stacks, allowing its bomb to explode in an engine room; another hit her port side, starting a fierce fire that killed all the wounded who'd been taken to the wardroom. Casualties on *Calhoun*, a fourth destroyer that had to be abandoned and eventually sunk by American guns, were seven of twenty-six officers killed and eighty-seven of 307 men. *Calhoun* had fought off eleven raids before dawn that morning, five in the space of fifteen minutes. Two previous kamikaze crashes that afternoon damaged her so severely that the last one, by a pilot who persisted although his plane was ablaze, made little difference. Of the nine more destroyers hit that day, one was sunk, two had to be scrapped, and three went unrepaired until after the war.

The Japanese goal was to cut off American supplies and naval support so their Army could better deal with the enemy ashore. That was wishful thinking: Even with sufficient supplies of planes and aviation fuel, the hot kamikazes — Divine Wind — wouldn't have melted Operation Iceberg, as the Americans had code-named the Okinawan invasion. But they did cause the American Navy by far its greatest terror and torment of the

war. Nothing of the kind had ever been mounted by one force or endured by another.

> *The feeling of utter helplessness that wraps around you when you are aboard a*
> *ship crippled by enemy action [hit us] . . . on Easter morning. . . . We had been*
> *warned to be ready for such a possibility but when it happened, it was startling,*
> *unbelievable and more than a little fearsome.*
> — Herbert Shultz, a combat correspondent

The knowledge that pilots were intent on killing themselves in order to
kill others was terrifying in itself. The act was "incomprehensible" and
"inhuman" to many American sailors, who wondered whether the Japanese who were resolved to blow themselves to bits were religious fanatics
or simply drunk or drugged. To the fighting men, nothing did more to
confirm their enemy's singularly sinister nature. "The whole idea is
eerie," one lieutenant told another on the carrier *Belleau Wood*. "I just
can't figure out how anybody can just commit suicide without feeling
anything. It's against human nature."

"It doesn't matter to those Nips," his fellow officer answered. "They
don't think the same way we do." An American admiral who observed
kamikazes plunging at Okinawa waxed more theoretical: "I doubt if
there is anyone who can depict with complete clarity our mixed emotions
as we watched a man about to die in order that he might destroy us in the
process. There was a hypnotic fascination to a sight so alien to our Western philosophy."

In fact, the kamikaze phenomenon wasn't *quite* so alien to Western
practice, if not philosophy. Occasional German pilots had used suicide
attacks against Allied planes, although their superiors never organized a
special force of them. American and British leaders, Winston Churchill
and Douglas MacArthur among them, ordered some of their commanding officers never to surrender in certain circumstances. In addition,
Britain as well as Italy and Germany had very small units manning "special attack" weapons, chiefly small boats and planes that made some
nearly suicidal missions. American pilots of obsolete torpedo planes in
the Battle of Midway knew they'd probably be killed or gravely wounded
attacking the Japanese carriers, and reprieves were few in some instances: Eight of eight from the carrier *Hornet* were downed, ten of
fourteen from *Enterprise,* and ten of twelve from *Yorktown*. The brave
squadrons that lost every one of their planes came close to being
kamikazes in some ways, and the crews knew the odds when they took off.

Every nation cherishes its tales of wounded heroes who know they'll
probably die charging the enemy but remain determined to do their utmost to stop him. "Give me liberty or give me death" might be seen as the

philosophical and emotional underpinning of the American Navy's experiments with near-suicidal submersibles during the War of Independence and the Confederate Navy's similar interest during the Civil War. And a kind of suicidal desperation prompted Pickett's Charge. The Alamo, so elevated in the folklore celebrating American bravery, had something in common with Japanese resolution. Perhaps because everything Japanese seemed sinister or demented, it occurred to few Americans — even those who'd loved *They Died with Their Boots On,* an extremely popular Hollywood tale on the eve of Pearl Harbor — that their own myths sanctified warriors' sacrificial deaths. Many more Americans might have been eager to die for honor and country, or at least applaud those who did, if their nation had ever faced the shock of total national defeat now confronting the Japanese. For the kamikaze movement can't be understood without taking into account Japan's unwillingness to accept the enormity of the prospect looming before her. In a similar situation, self-sacrificing American pilots might have been acclaimed as heroes.

> *The special attack operations were truly impossible to bear in terms of our*
> *natural human feelings but Japan having been put in an impossible position,*
> *those unreasonable measures were all that was left to us.*
> — Emperor Hirohito, a year after the end of the war

The kamikaze institution was founded — as much as any single event can qualify for that distinction in a country with a long tradition of honorable self-sacrifice — six months earlier, when a rear admiral commanding an air flotilla in the Philippines deliberately crashed a dive-bomber on an American carrier. That fine officer was known for his Western attitudes — understandably so, because he'd begun his naval training with the Royal Navy after an English public school education. However, he despaired over the Imperial Navy's defeats and the decimation of his squadrons. His pilots, replacements for a great corps of aces shot down or lost in sunken Japanese carriers, were so ill trained that a third of them flying out from Japan never reached the Philippines.

The admiral believed two dozen lucky ones could stem the entire American advance by sinking its big carriers — not an absurd idea, especially after the whole Japanese advance had been stopped largely by the loss of the Imperial Navy's four carriers at Midway. It would be simplistic to call him the usual "Japanese fanatic" for his own dive onto USS *Franklin* in October 1944. In any case, he posthumously won a gifted ally. Although his crash, a deliberate violation of orders, horrified most Japanese staff officers almost as much as it did *Franklin*'s crew, Takajiro Onishi, a high-ranking admiral who arrived from Tokyo days later to assume command of all naval aircraft in the Philippines, was moved.

Onishi had earlier encouraged pilots to perform just such crashes as a last resort. Now he, who had the bluntness of warriors utterly dedicated to purpose and corresponding contempt for compromising politicians, launched a campaign to make them a regular practice.*

Onishi's intention shocked much of the naval brass, who much more approved of the man he had relieved in Manila, a skilled professional who would fight to the death in suitable equipment but saw no value in needlessly sacrificing his precious pilots. "When you can show me how to bring the men back from special attacks, I'll listen," Onishi's more prudent predecessor had told his raised-in-England colleague when he arrived to replace him. But the resourceful, fearless Onishi quickly organized a small volunteer force resolved to put the major enemy carriers out of action for a week. That was the first organized use of suicide missions in the Pacific War, although there had been isolated attacks before, some by damaged planes, a few premeditated. Even though Onishi's initial mission hit two carriers, and later ones also achieved some striking successes, the Imperial High Command did not approve the special attack philosophy until the enemy fleet was massing for L-day — partly because air attacks had sunk only one ship and damaged a dozen-odd others off Iwo Jima. But now Onishi had the satisfaction of seeing his once highly controversial approach incorporated into the defense plan, then elevated to an essential plank, as the highest Army as well as Navy officers convinced themselves that this last resort would change the course of the war.

In that view, what happened on Okinawa itself wouldn't much matter. In fact, many in the High Command now saw Ushijima's task as no more than delaying the enemy so that as many enemy warships and supply vessels as possible could be finished offshore. Ivan Morris, perhaps the most careful student of Japanese attitudes toward sacrifice, would call the kamikaze operations "the principal manifestation of the country's will to resist . . . during Japan's death throes." The Battle of Okinawa, Morris would write, "more and more assumed the character of a culminating suicidal explosion."

Onishi, who was given overall charge of mass kamikaze attacks against the fleet at Okinawa, represented certain profoundly Japanese qualities — which, however, included some that all peoples would be proud of. It was no accident that the dynamic maverick, who despised talk as a

---

*Although *kamikaze* acquired quick notoriety in the West, the proper name was *shimpu*, a different reading of the same characters with a more dignified, solemn ring, more befitting the pilots' heroic undertaking. Like *harakiri*, *kamikaze* later became vulgar in Japan: a moniker for assorted daredevils, from taxi drivers to breakneck skiers, as Ivan Morris pointed out.

substitute for action, was Japan's leading naval aviator and chosen collaborator of the best naval brains — or that he'd helped Admiral Yamamoto, the "Japanese Nelson," plan his Pearl Harbor attack. The model of personal courage was an impressive combination of traditional selfless virtues and mastery of technological advances. Many of his most idealistic junior officers adored him.

Most of the "treasures of the nation," as he called the kamikaze pilots, would have been any nation's treasures. A majority were in their early twenties — university students until their recent call-up. More had studied the humanities than the natural sciences or engineering. Still gripped by poetry, they filled their last thoughts with symbols of beauty. One volunteer saw his commitment in the images of an eighteenth-century nationalist writer's verse: "What is the spirit of Yamato's ancient land? / It is like wild cherry blossoms, / Radiant in the rising sun." Just as those blossoms scattered without regret after dispersing their short-lived radiance, the young hero explained, "so must we be prepared to die for Yamato without regret."

As Morris pointed out, most kamikaze pilots, far from the "fierce, superstitious, jingoistic fanatics" foreigners usually imagined, were in the upper ranks of university students in intelligence, sensitivity, and culture, including Western culture. As the Okinawan garrison was being bludgeoned toward its inevitable defeat, driven superiors pressed a small but growing number of young pilots and trainees to join "volunteer" suicide units. Nevertheless, superior officers who actually selected pilots for the flights were likely to have more genuine volunteers than they could accommodate.

Straight to the end of the war, many units had twice as many eager candidates as planes. Most were driven less by a desire to kill than by their wish to perform a lofty deed that would win admiration at their bases and a place among the country's heroes at the Yasukuni Shrine. Most of all, they wanted to sacrifice themselves for a cause more noble than personal advancement. Part of that cause was protecting their families and sacred Japan from foreign intrusion, especially since most truly believed their cherished nation and people would be forever destroyed unless they gave their utmost, including the utmost self-denial. On top of the great debt almost all Japanese youth felt to their parents for having conceived and raised them, many of the young heroes' final poems, diary entries, and letters to their families so abounded in love and desire for virtue — if also in ignorance of their beloved country's Asian and Pacific atrocities — as to seem nearer the limit of human goodness than evil.

> Dearest Parents,
>   Words cannot express my gratitude to you. It is my hope that this last act of striking a blow at the enemy will serve to repay in small measure the wonderful things you have done for me. . . . I shall be satisfied if my final effort serves as recompense for the heritage bequeathed by our ancestors. . . .

My dear parents . . . I shall be leaving this earth [tomorrow morning] forever. Your immense love for me fills my entire being down to my last hair. And that is what makes this so hard to accept: the idea that with the disappearance of my body, this tenderness will also vanish. But I am impelled by my duty. I sincerely beg you to forgive me for not having been able to fulfill all my family obligations. . . .

My greatest regret in this life is the failure to call you *"chichiue"* [revered father]. I regret not having given any demonstration of the true respect which I have always had for you. During my final plunge, although you will not hear it, you may be sure I will be saying *"chichiue"* to you and thinking of all you've done for me.

The world in which I lived was too full of discord. As a community of rational human beings, it should have been better composed. Lacking a single great conductor, everyone let loose with his own sound, creating dissonance where there should have been melody and harmony.

We're going to die. . . . I will fight for my country or for my personal honor, but never for the Navy, which I hate! . . . It is dominated exclusively by a clique of Naval Academy officers. [Another pilot called the Navy a "beast!" but willingly died for his honor and country.]

This is my last day. The destiny of our homeland hinges on the decisive battle in the seas to the south, where I shall fall like a blossom from a radiant cherry tree. . . . I am grateful from the depths of my heart to the parents who reared me with their constant prayers and tender love. And I am grateful as well to my squadron leader and superior officers, who have looked after me as if I were their own son and given me such careful training.

The Japanese way of life is indeed beautiful and I'm proud of it, as I'm proud of Japanese history and mythology, which reflect the purity of our ancestors. . . . And the living embodiment of all wonderful things from our past is the Imperial Family, which is also the crystallization of the splendor and beauty of Japan and its people. It is an honor to be able to give my life in defense of these beautiful and lofty things.

Letter after letter expressed gratitude for the chance to repay parents and the nation. Nor did the volunteers stop valuing their own lives during their final days. Air raids on their bases, where some lived in miserable conditions despite their honored status, multiplied throughout the Okinawan campaign, terrifying even some of the pilots scheduled to die on the morrow. Yet many were indeed radiant that following morning when they made their sacrifice.

Of course there were exceptions. Not all the thousands of kamikaze pilots were the studious, considerate, idealistic souls their parents would remember as their best, kindest sons. Scores spent their final hours drunk on sake rather than on lofty thoughts. Others made the gesture less from heroism than calculation: Since everyone was going to die in the war anyway, better to die a pilot, with its rewards — perhaps including a warship to one's credit. Amid the laughter and song, some wept with fear, regret, or frustration for having to sacrifice themselves to a hopeless cause when they'd only begun to live. At least one strafed his command post before flying off toward the enemy fleet. A larger number masked their resentment — but they were a small minority. Most young men experienced joy and elation when chosen for the honor — and impatience, bitterness, or self-hatred when rejected. Some burst into tears and cried unashamedly when not permitted to join comrades on their final missions. Onishi promised the Divine Wind would be ushered in by the "purity" of the youth he loved, and there it was, in the hearts of highly educated, lovingly raised young men, trembling with desire to attain the highest patriotic virtue.

But if most kamikaze pilots were far from the moronic or drugged robots imagined by the bluejackets on the strained targeted ships — in fact, distinctly better educated and more refined than almost all the Americans who degraded them — the stark ignorance of the culture from which the movement grew doesn't invalidate the sailors' and infantrymen's gut reaction that their enemy was in some way "nuts." A former kamikaze pilot — the sole survivor of his group of twenty-one officers — argued in 1989 that "this so-called suicide mentality" was hardly specific to the Japanese. "The spirit of self-sacrifice exists in all countries among all peoples, particularly among the young who are innocent and free of cynicism when they are in a wartime, life-or-death situation."

Yes, in a way — as argued too several pages earlier. Still, the larger truth is that the kamikaze phenomenon as practiced in 1945 could not have taken place elsewhere.

The American infantrymen who threw themselves on Japanese hand grenades in order to save their buddies were expressing an impulsive, unthinking surge of camaraderie, not an intentional desire to kill themselves. The Alamo's defenders didn't intend to die, except, perhaps, when it was too late for another choice. Jimmy Doolittle's pilots knew it would take luck to land in China after bombing Tokyo from the carrier *Hornet* in April 1942, but they had at least a hope and a chance. Those rare exceptions were no more the counterparts of kamikaze pilots than the swashbuckling Onishi was a naval officer like heroic naval officers elsewhere.*

---

*Commanding ever fiercer loyalty for his courage and boldness, the dashing but kindly looking Onishi would become an object of an intense cult by passionate junior officers until — and after — Japan's surrender prompted his agonizing, eighteen-hour suicide. He's reported to have said, "There will probably not be anyone, even in a hundred years, to justify what I've done," but his remorse came only after the inconceivable surrender. His every action having been based on that "impossibility," it could now seem he'd sent thousands of young men to a useless death — but not a meaningless one, as they'd had the joy of dying beautifully for a cause they believed to be just.

An uneducated American footslogger on Okinawa summed up the difference as tellingly as any historian or sociologist, revisionist or otherwise: "Our infantrymen landed on Pacific islands knowing they might die but hoping they wouldn't. Kamikaze men knew the outcome in advance."

Perhaps defeat was more shameful to Japanese. Perhaps their long tradition of fighting to the death against impossible odds explained the existence of an organized, mass force for such military waste. The country's equally long veneration of mythical young heroes whose destruction guarantees society's survival also surely played a role. (Ivan Morris noted that it was almost a prerequisite of Japanese tales that their young heroes died achieving their lofty aims — or failing to.) Whatever the practice's origin and however realistic its initial purpose — stopping the enemy's onslaught by sinking his carriers — it swelled into an escape to mystical salvation, in which sense it *was* characteristically Japanese. The mainland slogan about a hundred million *gyokusai,* the jewel shattered into myriad pieces, was now much more insistent than when General Ushijima's glum predecessor on Okinawa had cited it a year earlier. "Better we all die."

By now, young Japanese were dying in a panoply of special attack weapons, including crash boats, human mines, and human torpedoes. Simplified midget submarines designed in 1943 by three young naval officers failed to achieve significant results at Okinawa. It was chiefly their hidden pens, carved out of cliffs, that had been captured in Kerama Retto and the Okinawan north, where Americans gaped at the little boats in which men were prepared to head out on a one-way trip toward a selected ship. A few did manage to score in nearby waters, their targets never knowing what hit them. Sailors on ships loaded with munitions, dynamite, and aviation fuel needed no second order from their captains to "shoot at anything larger than a cigarette butt" that moved in the water at night.

The most important of such weapons was the *ohka* (exploding cherry bomb), an aerial cousin of the midget submarines conceived in disappointment that even the very small percentage of kamikazes that managed to hit home often failed to sink American ships because their impact speed was too slow. Promising to crash half a ton of high explosives at six hundred miles an hour, the 1944 *ohka* touted by Radio Tokyo as a guarantee of American defeat was essentially a rocket-powered bomb released by a converted bomber. It had just enough fuel for a short, sharp dive, just enough wing area for slight maneuvering on the way down, and just enough cockpit space for a man to squeeze into — for it too was manned, like a German V1 rocket with a pilot.

Americans called that weapon *baka* ("idiot bomb" or "screwball"), as if in search of comic relief from the apprehension it generated. Pilots and antiaircraft gunners found the speedy rockets almost impossible to hit once they were launched. But their weight made their mother planes sitting ducks for American interceptors. In their raids, too, *ohka* kamikazes maintained their gratitude for the chance to die honorably. The crew of one mother plane reported that its *ohka* pilot, a twenty-two-year-old lieutenant, slept peacefully as they approached the target on April 12 — but that was the only mother plane in a squadron of eight that managed to return to its base.

One hundred eighteen of the 185 planes used in *ohka* attacks would be destroyed, at a cost of 438 Japanese airmen. On one occasion, sixteen of sixteen Betty mother planes dispatched toward American carriers were shot down in ten minutes, despite a fighter escort of fifty-five planes (many of which developed mechanical trouble before the force approached its target). Still, improved versions, including a final one with an engine adapted from a German jet, were designed and produced right up to the end of the war for use against the fleet that would take part in the invasion of the mainland.

The kamikaze pilots embodied the peculiarly Japanese attitudes of the time even more than the engineers who designed so many special attack weapons. Many prized their death for its own rewards, almost as if it were more important than its purpose. Although the call was for "death simultaneously with a mortal blow to the enemy," the former was often the chief objective, which helps explain why the net results of the raids were pitifully disproportionate to their enormous expenditure of equipment and first-rate men. The human waste was the greater folly: Months or years of pilot training were squandered on the single, usually futile charge in the flying coffins. Yet Imperial General Headquarters became so convinced of salvation by suicide attacks that it issued an order implying that all armed forces should employ that "lunacy," in the later assessment of the commander of an air flotilla that dispatched them from the mainland.

> That proved the High Command, utterly confused by a succession of defeats, had lost all wisdom . . . and degenerated to the point of indulging in wild gambling. The order was nothing less than a national death sentence. Like every military order, it was issued in the name of the Emperor and therefore not open to question or criticism, no matter how outrageous.

The young heroes had been girded by the long history of Japanese literature that elevates death as "the only pure and thus fitting end to the perfection of youth," in Ian Buruma's summary. Perhaps their longing was less for death than for what Buruma called "a supremely sensual state of unconsciousness" remembered from early childhood, when Japanese boys were powerfully indulged by their mothers. Whatever the cause, the greater the likelihood of defeat, "the more certain it was that the Japanese would fight to the death in battle or kill themselves following defeat," as a former kamikaze pilot put it in 1989. The impossible odds at

Okinawa enhanced rather than diminished the romance with exquisite death. The more obvious the futility, the more noble the sacrifice.

That would be far from universally true in the 32nd Army on land. Many of its more educated reserve officers, responsible for their men's lives as well as their own, would be caught between the military code's absolute requirement to be ready to die and humanistic feelings much intensified by their men's suffering. Besides, dispatch on suicide missions on Okinawa was usually not an honor but a punishment, meted out to men in bad favor — who were often just such liberal officers. But there were far fewer complications for young kamikaze pilots. "If I go away to sea, I shall return a brine-soaked corpse," pledged the old anthem that often ended the pretakeoff ceremonies. Gunning their engines, the youth were as enticed by self-destruction as destruction of the enemy.

Although assurances that *Yamato damashii* would triumph in the end continued sounding, many pilots, by now often barely trained, appeared to believe it no more than that their sacrifice would help alter the course of the war. Too bright and skeptical to swallow the promises or to respond to military fanfares, they'd pleaded for their opportunity to die because their objective was as much gesture as military tactic — like much of Japanese thinking as a whole. It was as important, perhaps more important, to express utter sincerity in a just cause, no matter how hopeless — or precisely *because* it was hopeless — as to damage the enemy's gargantuan navy. Tale after folktale about young heroes dying for doomed causes had taught that life's meaning couldn't be realized by calculating military advantage any more than by anything else attainable through mere reason. The ultimate goal was higher, purer.

The last letters also reflected a fervent desire to surmount petty, earthly interests. Attaining the longed-for spiritual victory over material comforts probably accounted for much of the young men's joy on the eve of their final flights. Such victory often required a "Zen-like suppression of reason and personal feelings, a blind devotion to direct action, and an infinite capacity for hardship and pain." Takajiro Onishi called the lucky men "already gods without earthly desires." Many penned their letters in eager anticipation for their "splendid" death, "as sudden and clean as the shattering of crystal." With "no remorse whatever," they truly "never felt better."

> We were bubbling with eagerness. . . . I thought of my age, nineteen, and of the saying "To die while people still lament your death; to die while you are pure and fresh; this is truly *bushido*."

> Yes, I was following the way of the samurai. My eyes were shining as I stepped on board [my plane] once more. I remembered with pleasure [a fellow officer] quoting from a poem and telling me I would "fall as purely as the cherry blossom" I now held.

Defeated but unconquered, men of the 65th Fighter Squadron were born separately but die together.

Warmest greetings [to a brother]. I hope you are all well. As for me, duty calls more and more. What a fine reward determination is. It gives one peace of mind. After all, the body is only an attachment of the spirit.

I know that no purpose can any longer be served by my death but I remain proud of piloting a suicide plane and it is in this state of mind that I die. . . . Tomorrow a man in love with liberty will leave this world. I may have given you the impression of being disillusioned but at the bottom of my heart I am happy to die.

Dear Parents:
     Please congratulate me. I have been given a splendid opportunity to die. . . . How I appreciate this chance to die like a man!

Looming military defeat *increased* the appeal of a death that demonstrated denial of self-interest and even community advantage. Belief counted more than reason, the purity of the motive more than the result. The ability to defy rationality and logic was itself a triumph, which was surely why many young pilots felt disgust and disgrace when they crashed without dying — and why others were plunged into depression when their missions were aborted; in their own words, they felt "deprived" of death. The disappointment of one group that returned to its base alive because bad weather near Okinawa had concealed the targeted ships became acute when it learned another had nevertheless pursued the attack that day, its pilots accomplishing nothing apart from their sublimely noble deaths.

> *If in doubt whether to live or die, it is always better to die.*
>   — A saying repeated to kamikaze pilots and other Japanese warriors

> *Once a Japanese man decides to do something, he carries it out to the bitter end, and at all costs.*
>   — A father-mentor to his son in a contemporary comic book for boys called
>   *I Am a Kamikaze*

Many kamikaze pilots, even knowing they couldn't seriously damage the American fleet, hoped their demonstration of sublime dedication might shock the spiritually inferior enemy into defeat. Actually, however, it prompted the reverse reaction, reinforcing Americans' conviction that the demented Japanese had to be prostrated utterly. In the end, the supreme self-sacrifice of the suicide missions was also an expression of supreme selfishness. Yes, the pilots achieved their self-denying feats by heroically suppressing their own feelings, but they also ignored or discounted the feelings of others. To hell with the larger consequences of proving their utter purity — such as their enemies' frightened loathing of Japan.

Even if the men of the 10th Army and 5th Fleet had known that what attracted many kamikazes was less killing others than dying well themselves, precious few would have been interested. So much stark evidence of "degenerate" thirst for blood at such "inhuman" cost nipped any desire — slight to begin with among most Americans — to probe deeper into the unfathomable Oriental mentality. The cost ineffectiveness of kamikaze operations also comforted few Americans. Well after the campaign, the Navy would reveal that thirty-three ships had been sunk, well over half by kamikazes, and 368 ships and craft damaged, more than fifty seriously. (As with calculations of the bombing damage to Japanese cities, various reports give different casualty and damage figures. These are probably accurate to within a ship or two.)

Carriers also lost 539 planes — but the Japanese cost was staggering. On some days, up to 90 percent of the planes delivering mass attacks, conventional and kamikaze together, were destroyed — a total of 7,830 for the three months of the Okinawan campaign. The kill ratio of the kamikazes alone was naturally far higher, and most of the tiny percentage that managed to crash on ships instead of into the sea did so on superstructures, causing relatively superficial damage. Huge as the attack of April 6–7 was, the fleet comprised more ships than the nine hundred Japanese planes — and none larger than a destroyer was sunk that day or later. Some four thousand treasures of the nation died for that strategically minor wounding off Okinawa, most of them less than twenty-one years old.

But what mattered to American crews was their own hell, not the enemy's irrationality. When their ships weren't under attack, their life was tolerable, at least by Pacific War standards. There was often far too much rain and too little usable water: Tense watches at General Quarters under deluges in April and May were followed by days and nights of blistering heat that turned ships into furnaces. The sun was so strong by mid-May that a careless touch of a plane parked on a flight deck could cause a burn, and the stifling heat intensified the rashes, diarrhea, and outbreaks of boils in the overcrowded quarters. Still, most crews had dry clothes, relatively clean beds, and three squares on most days — unimaginable luxuries to combat infantrymen.

During the air attacks, however, supreme terror gripped. There was also fear of suicide boats and rumors of Japanese swimmers attaching charges to ships' bottoms, which prompted the posting of guards with submachine guns around the deck and men packing carbines or .45s when they went topside. "At night, anything that moved got riddled," Fred Poppe would remember. "Any sound, any sight including whitecaps — we were plain scared. And when one guy opened up, everybody fired at everything. So there were lots of ricochets and accidents." Transfer to a larger LST on the opposite coast, near Naha, did nothing to lessen Poppe's fear. "Kamikazes just poured at us, again and again. It scared the shit out of us, far more than on L-day. We'd get warnings about half an hour before they appeared, and the waiting was scary too, the knowing what was coming when those pilots' one wish in the world was to kill you."

The Japanese called their April 6–7 operation Floating Chrysanthemum Number One. In addition to almost daily missions of one to twenty planes, they would stage nine more such mass attacks at weekly intervals, each launched from a variety of airfields and lasting from two to five days. The ten Floating Chrysanthemums provided "shows" awe-inspiring enough to momentarily divert combat troops on land from their anxieties. The spectacle of an armada firing ten thousand guns faster than seemed possible at swarms of attackers was mesmerizing. Norris Buchter spent L-day night on a slope several hundred yards from the beach where he'd come ashore. The sky above the invasion fleet riding in the darkness offshore was so full of tracer shells from the thousand-odd ships' antiaircraft fire that it glowed like coals. "It was like a hundred July Fourths together. What a terribly magnificent carnival!" William Marshall ran to the top of a coral hill on a night later in April to see two sections of a severed destroyer emanating an eerie glow as they drifted apart, burning fiercely. When both sections sank, a "gigantic" explosion sent shock waves up through the hill and a blinding light flashed "as though several suns had detonated" into the night. When a kamikaze hit an ammunition ship a few evenings earlier, John Grove blinked at "a huge multicolored fan of fire and shells" on the horizon. The macabre sight was also "magnificent, except that I knew it had to mean the death of maybe hundreds of Americans."

Medical Corpsman Joseph Bangert, the wise-guy son of John D. Rockefeller's driver, was "on the throne" — a hole in the Okinawan ground — one May evening when he saw two kamikazes attack *New Mexico*. One of the battleship's five-inch shells exploded directly under the first plane, lifting it just clear of her mastheads, but the plane's bomb detonated in a stack, turning it into a giant blowtorch. The second plane, also hit several times, held on and crashed into the gun deck. "That wagon took off like a shot," Bangert remembered in amazement. "I guess to avoid other strikes. I couldn't believe a big ship could move that fast." (Although fifty-four were killed or missing and 119 wounded, *New Mexico* wasn't listed among the badly damaged ships because she was able to continue fighting.)

Dick Whitaker watched "the daily and nightly spectacle" when his company was pulled back for rest and replenishment on high ground, from which both the Pacific Ocean and East China Sea, where ships still extended to the horizon, were sometimes visible. "During the day, the ships threw up so much ack-ack that daylight almost disappeared in a million black puffs. During night attacks, the concentration of fire made a kind of twilight — incredible. So much fire would have seemed truly impossible if you didn't see it."

When Navy construction units nicknamed the Seabees landed soon after the combat troops to begin bulldozing roads for American traffic, they erected a large movie screen on top of a hill. Betty Grable vehicles were favorites, some repeated so often that the audience said the lines along with the actors. But the alternate show of suicide pilots diving on frantic ships, also visible from there, sometimes beat the competition.

Although American troops would best remember the night attacks that floodlit the sky, the Japanese usually timed their flights to arrive at twilight, when their planes were most difficult to see. Whitaker noticed independently that twilight was the hour of the most awesome shows. It seemed to him inconceivable that a single attacking plane could penetrate a sky solid with smoke from antiaircraft bursts long enough to reach its target. He watched in amazement as some managed the feat, then crashed into an oily fireball of their bombs, their fuel, and themselves.

Ordinarily, he felt little sympathy for swab jockeys. At least they had good chow and could take a shower at night. (He didn't know how rare showers actually were; most ships had to maintain severe water rationing.) They could jump into a clean sack — while he and his platoon slept, or couldn't sleep, in a hole in the ground "soaked to the skin, freezing our asses off and without the protection of a ship or anything else." But when kamikazes struck, Whitaker felt pity for the crews. Sailors had no foxholes. They couldn't dig in during their moments, or hours, of terror. Infantrymen nearer the shore who saw the wreckage of ships blown to bits — sometimes with a dozen or so sailors' bodies — were even more aware of the price being paid at sea.

The same extravaganza prompted very different reactions in 32nd Army spectators. For the beleaguered defenders, the first reward was a brief suspension of the shelling of their positions while the attention of the American fleet turned skyward. Many Japanese who profited from that blessed break felt guilty toward the young heroes who provided it. Still, the temporary cessation of the enemy's barrages enabled them to relax and enjoy some brief moments "watching the Ryogoku." (Tokyo's Ryogoku district held a captivating fireworks display every year.)

A single master switch seemed to turn on the sirens* and searchlights of the American ships, "a brilliant show in itself." Then the Japanese planes

---

*Hearing the sirens one day, Kenjiro Matsuki, the star of Japan's first professional baseball team, reckoned he had half an hour of safety and left his cave for a nearby well, planning to wash his face for the first time in over a month. But for some reason, perhaps because that particular kamikaze attack didn't materialize, the ships quickly turned their searchlights off and resumed their bombarding. A shell landed so close to Matsuki that fragments hissed like hot pokers when they splashed into the well — into which he too jumped for protection. Rushing back to his shelter, he swore never again to take such a risk.

approached with their metallic roar. Picked up by the searchlights, they became the targets of "millions of antiaircraft bullets and shells . . . a panorama of incomparably gorgeous display." Another Japanese soldier remembered the American fleet's nonessential lights going out "in a blink" when the kamikazes approached, "and the blazing stream of anti-aircraft fire gushing upward with a terrifying explosion. Then we'd catch a glimpse of [a plane] hurtling down from the sky like a pebble lit up in the beam of a searchlight . . . or sometimes wrapped in its own flame."

The ships' rapid-fire pompoms awed Japanese soldiers. They threw up tens of thousands of rounds to crisscross the lower sky like some cosmic fireworks display beneath explosions of higher-caliber automatic shells, beneath, in turn, bursts of flak that blanketed the upper sky. The trans-fixed soldiers prayed the planes would stay up until they could crash into the targets at which they were aiming with such stunning bravery. When they succeeded, joy surged through the otherwise tormented watchers before they dashed back to cover, often in tears of gratitude.

Soon the quick ventures from the caves to watch the spectacle acquired a more formal description: "To go worshipping the Special Attack Forces."

> Come evening, the mountain rumbles. A thunderous sound can be heard in the cave — from which we leap out, shouting, "Yea! Our Tokkoki [special attack] planes have come!" We go up the mountain and see . . . that the clouds over the sea are red. The enemy fleet is fir-ing its antiaircraft guns, all of them. Tens of thousands of tracers criss-cross like a fountain, turning the sky fiery above the ships. . . . Shining like a single grain of rice, our Tokko braves this barrage. The minute we catch sight of it, it hurtles toward the water in flames . . . or goes straight for an enemy ship, releasing a gigantic pillar of fire. . . . The sound of the firing, like the beating of a colossal drum, suddenly stops. . . . Some of us go down on our knees and worship toward the sea, worship the Tokko. "Well done! Thank you!"

Inside the caves, maniacally exaggerated reports of the success of the air attacks provided additional exaltation. Masahide Ota and other mes-sengers from 32nd Army headquarters at Shuri Castle distributed uplift-ing news about kamikaze victories, mainly in the form of a one-sheet newspaper. "Our brave eagles" sank twenty-one enemy ships, it reported on April 7. Two days later, thirty were supposedly sunk and eighteen crip-pled; on April 13, nineteen sent down. "Our Air Force continues attack-ing . . . with fierce intensity," the paper added.

> Since April 12, our results include, as far as we could determine:
>   Sunk: Carriers — 1, Cruisers — 2, Cruiser or Transport ship — 1, Destroyer — 1, Transport ship — 1
>   Damaged: Battleships — 1.

The arrival of such misinformation filled the caves with loud cheers. The tiny newspapers went from hand to hand, surrounded by soldiers who bent over them to read the great tidings for themselves. Few doubted that the (virtually nonexistent) Japanese submarine fleet was in the process of strangling the land enemy by destroying his overextended supply lines. Soon, their wonderfully successful Air Force would turn to helping them on land.

By the campaign's end, it would be claimed that kamikazes sank forty-nine carriers, battleships, and cruisers. But although the actual total in those categories was zero, the logic that the Americans couldn't continue to lose ships as they reportedly were lifted the dejection caused by the Japanese retreats on land and the wretchedness of cave existence. Cheeks shone with optimism in the darkness. Shigemi Furukawa, a former high school teacher, later saw that as part of "a curious battlefield psychology [in which] we took whatever 'information' fed our wishful thinking for certain fact, no matter how often we were disappointed."

The wishful thinking extended to some of the highest commanders. Staff officers of Vice Admiral Matome Ugaki, commander of the 5th Air Fleet based on the home island of Kyushu, spoke of huge enemy losses after each Floating Chrysanthemum. The admiral thought it "almost certain" that special attack forces of the first one, on April 6–7, destroyed four American carriers. "In the light of so many reports of crashes on enemy carriers," he noted in his diary on April 11, "there can't be many undamaged ones still operating." Evidently Ugaki — who would himself take off in a plane and disappear, an almost certain suicide, after the Emperor's call for surrender in August — was genuinely convinced the American Navy would soon be "finished off."

Crashes on the carriers did force a few to suspend operations. The damage and losses were terrible in comparison to what the American Navy had suffered anywhere previously in World War II. But no carrier was put permanently out of action, let alone sunk, during the entire Okinawan campaign. On the second day of the Sixth Floating Chrysanthemum, a kamikaze suddenly dived from some low clouds toward *Bunker Hill,* one of the carriers whose planes had disposed of *Yamato* five weeks earlier. The Zeke hit the flight deck, setting parked planes alight in a huge conflagration. Just as its bomb penetrated the deck, a Judy dived almost vertically and did the same, its bomb also exploding below. In moments, three decks were ablaze almost the full length of the ship, the inferno fed by more parked planes and aviation fuel in hangar and working spaces. Three hundred ninety-three of her crew were killed and missing and another 264 were wounded, but *Bunker Hill* survived.

Three days later, in the interval between the Sixth and Seventh Floating Chrysanthemums, fighter-interceptors and antiaircraft guns shot down twenty-five of the twenty-six planes attacking *Enterprise,* but the approach of the twenty-sixth made throats go dry on the carrier.

> All the batteries were firing: the 5-inch guns, the 40mm and the 20mm, even the rifles. The Japanese aircraft dived through a rain of steel. It had been hit in several places and seemed to be trailing a banner of flame and smoke but it came on, clearly visible, hardly moving, the line of its wings as straight as a sword.
> The deck was deserted; every man, with the exception of the gunners, was lying flat on his face. Flaming and roaring, the fireball passed in front of the "island" superstructure and crashed with a terrible impact just behind the forward lift. The entire vessel was shaken, some forty yards of the flight deck folded up like a banana skin.

The worst damage came from a bomb exploding deep in a lower deck. Fourteen men were killed, sixty-eight wounded. The "Big *E*" had been hit twice before, most recently by two planes within an hour. This time she had to retire for major repairs in a navy yard, not to return to sea — like *Bunker Hill* — until after the war.

Royal Navy carriers consistently suffered less damage when hit. Five of them formed the core of a British fleet that, together with surface-support and supply and service vessels, was designated Task Force 57. Its appendage to Iceberg a fortnight before L-day had been less than an example of heartwarming Anglo-American cooperation. After catastrophic losses early in the war, senior British officers were keen to return to the Indian Ocean, where their former possessions in Burma, Malaya, and Indonesia awaited liberation from the Japanese. Suspicious of the old colonial interest, however, their American counterparts strove to keep the Royal Navy out of the Pacific anywhere west of Hawaii or, failing that, to relegate it to sideshows. They wanted John Bull to share the glory of Japan's final defeat even less than they wanted American resources drained to supply British ships. In the end, however, the political leaders surmounted the military-strategic rivalries. Churchill offered Roosevelt the British fleet for Pacific island campaigns rather than for any Indian Ocean operation, and the president quickly accepted.

But although American staffs then turned characteristically generous with supplies, some high-ranking officers continued nudging the Royal Navy as far aside as possible in order to "forestall any possible postwar British claim that they had delivered even the least part of the final blows which demolished the remains of Japanese seapower," as an English historian would see it. Nevertheless, the British worked unsparingly to make Task Force 57 a balanced, self-supporting force.

Its main assignment was to neutralize Sakishima Shota, a small archipelago of islands between Formosa and Okinawa. TF 57 repeatedly bombed and shelled those islands, some of which had important military airfields repaired by sedulous Japanese soldiers and native workers after every strike. The fleet's peripheral location, some three hundred miles southwest of Okinawa, guaranteed it would have little chance for publicity and every chance of being attacked from enemy airfields on the Chinese mainland as well as nearby Formosa, where many Japanese pilots were more experienced and skilled than the mainland's young graduates of crash courses. Beginning on L-day, when they acted as a decoy to divert attention from the vastly larger American force off the landing beaches, the British ships served as a shield across the approaches to the battle site from Formosa and China. But although they were occasionally the principal raid targets, naval design rooted in national attitudes kept their damage relatively minor and casualties relatively few. Working in an atmosphere of determination to avoid World War I's catastrophic casualties, British naval architects had given their carriers flight decks of three inches of armor plating instead of teakwood.

American designers disliked armored flight decks because their weight reduced stability and striking power. TF 57's five carriers together provided only 244 planes, slightly more than half the number on American carriers of equivalent size. (Their steel decks also made the crews' quarters even more like infernos after weeks under the fierce sun.) They were also slower, less maneuverable, and less protected by antiaircraft armament than their American counterparts. Still, their better damage control proved crucial for withstanding kamikaze attacks. All five carriers were hit at least once, often with spectacular impact. But the same aircraft that often penetrated wooden American decks and exploded into havoc below usually "crumpled up like a scrambled egg," in an American observer's simile, against British steel. "When a kamikaze hits a U.S. carrier, it's six months' repair in Pearl [Harbor]," observed another American. "In a Limey carrier, it's 'Sweepers, man your brooms.'"

Although it was never quite that easy for the Limeys, virtuoso pilots whose crashes would have put an equivalent American carrier out of action for months merely slowed the British quarry for several hours or reduced their rate of launching planes. When a Zeke with a five-hundred-pound bomb crashed on *Indefatigable*'s flight deck from an almost vertical dive, the blast killed eight ratings but left only a three-inch dent in the heavy steel. Even some multiple fires caused by several nearly simultaneous crashes were extinguished within a quarter of an hour. The chunks of the smashed Japanese planes — and of their pilots, in the form of skull splinters or a single finger stuck to a bulkhead — were pushed over the side, together with the incinerated British ones that had been parked on the flight deck, mostly American-made Avengers, Hellcats, and Corsairs. The carriers were fully operational again.

At one point, TF 57 set a Royal Navy record since Nelson and the era of sail: thirty-two continuous days at sea. Throughout them, they diverted a share of the Japanese planes from the vastly larger American fleet, and every diverted kamikaze was a blessing to TF 58. When senior American officers counted their own casualties, their coolness toward the "Forgotten Fleet," as a chronicler later dubbed it, inched toward respect and even a little affection.

Of the seventy-eight hundred Japanese planes lost, thousands were piloted by youths with barely enough training to get them into the air and attempt the quick dive they prayed would crown their deaths with the additional glory of a hit. Thousands crashed into the sea without coming close to their targets. As is so much in war, it was a matter of chance. Men on unluckier ships became deeply impressed with their attackers' patience and cunning — and with reason: Some were skilled pilots. The experts dived "with the velocity of a comet" for their targets' vulnerable parts, such as carrier elevators, and chose the most vulnerable moments, during plane launching and recovery, when quick maneuvering was extremely difficult. Captains had learned, as one put it, that it was "fatal" to hold a steady course during an attack.

Artful Japanese timing also delivered carrier pilots waiting to take off in their own planes into a special chamber of hell: Strapped into their cockpit seats, they saw kamikazes approaching and every sailor, except gun crews, racing for cover. Ships could rarely tell whether approaching aircraft were conventional or kamikaze until almost the last moment, when the dives began. When two or more kamikazes dived in a coordinated attack from varying points at varying angles, they much increased the chances of a successful crash no matter how brilliant the maneuvers to avoid them.

Apprehension on the ships increased even further because the crews could also rarely tell until that last moment whether the planes coming in were piloted by experts or novices. Looking up at five-hundred-pound bombs strapped to bellies or extra fuel tanks under each wing, they tried to guess. Even an almost empty plane could be lethal. In one case a wheel bounced off a kamikaze and decapitated a gunner, who had been firing furiously until the moment of the crash he was desperately hoping to prevent. Near misses too could cause significant damage. Another kamikaze totally disabled its target ship by hitting the water hard and close enough to flood both boiler and engine compartments.

Get the destroyers. Without their radar warning of our approach, we will enjoy great success.
— Admiral Matome Ugaki, commander of the 5th Air Fleet

Although your historian himself has been under kamikaze attack and witnessed the hideous forms of death and torture inflicted by that weapon, words fail him to do justice to the sailors on the radar picket stations.
— Samuel Eliot Morison, naval historian

Attacks against the capital ships naturally attracted the most attention, but the tin cans and other attendant vessels suffered proportionately more. Human resources are almost always more strained on smaller naval ships, and many of those in particular were intentionally stationed directly in harm's way: "sitting ducks of Okinawa," as one observer called them.*

To protect the main body of the fleet, the Americans established a ring of sixteen early-warning radar picket stations in the most probable approaches of the attacking planes, ranging out to about seventy-five miles from Okinawa. (That was in addition to Task Force 58's own picket group and to some seventy-five American planes always orbiting in concentric circles above the island and the picket ships during daylight. Those carrier-based combat air patrols shot down hundreds of easy pickings but also risked flak from their own side's ships with daredevil courage during the thick of the Floating Chrysanthemums.) Destroyers and destroyer escorts did most of that dangerous picketing in slow-speed circles, although minelayers, smaller gunboats, and landing craft were soon added in the effort to increase antiaircraft firepower against the swarms of attackers.

Since many shaky pilots were unable to keep their rickety planes aloft long enough to reach the choicer targets of the carriers and transports, those unarmored little craft took a disproportionate share of the dives. Although kamikazes badly damaged thirteen American carriers, ten battleships, and five cruisers off Okinawa, only smaller ships, with their skimpier antiaircraft armament, went down: a dozen between late March and the end of June, in addition to three sunk by conventional air attacks. Naval historian Samuel Eliot Morison concluded that destroyer crews living in daily and nightly terror of them were probably under greater stress for a longer period than had previously been experienced by any seamen serving in a surface fleet.

> Men on radar picket station, to survive, not only had to strike down the flaming terror of the kamikaze, roaring out of the blue like the thunderbolts that Zeus hurled at bad actors in days of old; they were under constant strain and unusual discomfort. In order to supply 650-pound steam pressure to build up full speed rapidly in a destroyer, its super-

---

*Merchant ships manned by civilian crews were also fat targets. One Liberty ship struggling to off-load was attacked by seventy-two kamikazes. The hospital ship *Comfort* was also hit, although probably in error, by a plane in flames and out of control. Six nurses were among the twenty-eight killed.

heaters, built only for intermittent use, had to be lighted for three and four days' running. For days and even nights on end, the crew had to stand general quarters and the ship kept "buttoned up." Men had to keep in condition for the instant reaction and split-second timing necessary to riddle a plane bent on a crashing death. Sleep became the rarest commodity and choicest luxury, like water to a shipwrecked mariner.

That drew a greater distinction between kamikaze and conventional attacks than most Japanese themselves would have made. Many veteran pilots considered too valuable for the former flew strikes that were suicidal in all but name; they wore no parachutes and didn't expect to return. By the sixth week, the demarcation between suicide missions and ordinary ones was increasingly blurred. "They were all human bullets," Denis and Peggy Warner argued, "whether they chose to die in kamikaze aerial attacks, in banzai charges, in *ohkas,* or on small boats loaded with explosives." And although most of the less publicized Japanese infantry was not specifically suicidal, its night attacks, especially by units that had been reduced to near inoperative, were almost the same. Very few of Ushijima's eighty thousand regular troops expected to return to Japan, nor did the twenty thousand to thirty thousand Okinawans conscripted in the Home Guard expect to live, though a far larger percentage of them wanted to.

Besides, chroniclers understandably overwhelmed by the shipboard terror had little notion of the suffering on Okinawa itself. It is probably true that "never in the annals of our glorious naval history have naval forces done so much with so little against such odds for so long a period," as the commander of the radar pickets claimed. But the land battle was harder, and many Japanese units did a lot more with a lot less against incomparably greater odds for a longer period. Americans on ships hit by kamikazes had only a brief taste of the experience of Japanese soldiers on the island, who for months faced an almost constant rain of bullets, shells, and bombs.

Still, the ordeal of the radar picket vessels was indeed unprecedented in many ways. On and on went the kamikaze attacks, bringing dread to sailors who didn't want to believe the "crazy Japs" had more planes left after so many had been shot down. But they had thousands left — never mind their condition — and the grim drama with the spectacular sights and unequaled intensity played again and again: the pilots' half-hypnotic last minutes in their planes, the tension on the ships below, the guns with the glowing barrels, the sky red with tracers and "almost literally black" with bursts of antiaircraft shells, the sea churned up by spray from the shorts, the crew members' rush to toilets to cool feet seared by their decks. The absence of relief from shooting down any part of an attacking force, because it was always the last plane that scored; the hope that no crash would come amidships to make the ship go dead in the water and become a sitting duck; the gun crews' unflinching fire as planes did hit, engulfing them in flames. The jettisoning of anchors, torpedoes, guns, and all other possible weight to try to save listing vessels; damage-control crews operating as bucket brigades when all power was lost and the fire hoses were useless; burned survivors struggling to stay afloat in a sludge of sea, oil, and blood around crippled and sinking hulks — into which new bombs fell. Knots of sailors using their last energy for an excited burst of swimming toward rescue vessels and dying of exhaustion, other knots drowned by big seas, crushed by the hulls of sister ships come to help, or wriggling from their life jackets and letting themselves slide under, even though possible rescue was near, because they could stand no more agony . . .

The destroyer *Laffey*'s picket station during the Third Floating Chrysanthemum was on a straight line between Kyushu and Okinawa. Enemy planes filled her radar screen — up to fifty closing bogeys at one point — from first light of April 16. During one eighty-minute period, at least twenty-two planes dived at her from all points of the compass. Her decks were repeatedly strafed. One bomb scored a near miss; four others hit. One kamikaze splashed almost alongside; six others crashed home. (Eight hit another tin can on another day.) Ton for gross ton, the attack was probably more intense than even *Yamato* had experienced, and *Laffey*'s trial, until being taken in tow by a sister ship, lasted almost as long. Despite the explosions, flames, and casualties — thirty-one missing and killed, seventy-two wounded — no gun was abandoned, although only four of her 20-millimeters were operable when the Japanese broke off.

Those small-caliber guns proved little use in stopping a determined pilot. Even direct hits by the larger ones often failed to do that. One of the most remarkable scenes of the whole remarkable tableau was of Japanese planes lurching forward on their collision courses even when repeatedly hit and in flames — even when their pilots were riddled and parts of the planes had broken off and spun into the sea. No amount of fire from a ship under attack ensured her safety until the attacker, or swarm of them, fell into the sea. The strain from that enemy bravery added further to the anxiety. A Japanese writer's recent claim that "the sight of a single Japanese plane raised terror in the hearts of men on the enemy vessels" conveyed an essential truth.

The desperation of nearly all combatants to take out the enemy in battle had an added edge when nothing but shooting down the relentless planes *in time* and *far enough away* could save the targeted ships from fierce damage. (Such furious firing of course led to even more mistakes than usual when masses of young men were operating an immense assemblage of complex guns. "I saw something today which made my blood run cold, something I shan't soon forget!" said an officer on a landing ship medium on April 6, during the First Floating Chrysanthemum. American gunners had shot down a Hellcat — a blunder that would be repeated regularly in the frenzy of defense.) When a ship's power was knocked out, as often happened, gun crews operated their guns manually — work so arduous that healthy young men with adrenaline pumping could keep it up for only two minutes. Nothing better illustrated the old Asian proverb about dying twice when one knows one is about to die.

Permanent General Quarters would have exhausted the crews beyond ability to function reasonably. With hundreds of extra duties to keep the ships as ready and as free of inflammable materials as possible, steaming day and night under the usual normal high-condition watches was depleting enough. On top of that, nerves were "exposed and quivering like wires stripped of insulation," in the image of one sober chronicler.

Despite fire- and damage-control skills honed in repeated encounters, the new repair berths in Kerama Retto swelled with gutted ships and hulks. The final toll of naval casualties over the course of the campaign would be 4,907 killed or missing and 4,824 wounded, far more than in any previous battle of the war, including one-sided Pearl Harbor, where fewer than half that number died. (It was extremely rare for the number of deaths to exceed the number of wounded, as here: testimony to the infernos ignited by the crashes.) Nearly 20 percent of the Navy's total casualties in the Pacific, Atlantic, and all smaller seas throughout the war were inflicted off Okinawa.

Only forty-five kamikazes would participate in the Tenth Floating Chrysanthemum on June 21–22, down from the First's 355. On average, the eight in between involved progressively fewer planes but without proportionate relief of strain in the fleet. And those Japanese numbers decreased partly because officers on the home islands had already begun husbanding for the struggle there, for which they'd be able to muster ten thousand or more planes for kamikaze use. When B-29s joined TF 58's carrier strikers bombing mainland fields in mid-April, many Japanese planes were transferred from the Navy to Operation *Ketsu* (last resort) under overall command of the Imperial Army. The honor of its chiefs — who also controlled the government — unconditionally required a final battle on the mainland, whatever the odds, even if (or precisely because) there was no hope of winning. The specter of ultimate defeat increased rather than diminished the commitment to special attacks. "I see the war situation becoming more desperate," a squadron leader wrote in his cockpit moments before following five of his pilots in their final dives at Okinawa. "All Japanese must become soldiers and die for the Emperor."

16 · The Shuri Line

The Japanese [in Okinawa's south] were in extremely well-thought-out, well-prepared positions, in terrain superbly suited for defense units. They were determined to . . . [make] American infantry and its support units pay dearly for every advance, and advances would usually be measured in yards rather than miles.
— Ian Gow, *Okinawa 1945*

It's going to be really tough, there are 65,000–70,000 fighting Japanese holed up in the south end of the island. I see no way to get them out except to blast them out yard by yard.
— Major General John Hodge, commander of the American Army's divisions

ON THE MORNING of May 9, thirty-nine days after L-day and nineteen after the north had been officially secured, Platoon Leader Paul Dunfrey huddled with forty-five men on the northern bank of a small river twenty miles south of the landing beaches. The brackish Asakawa (Asa River) runs almost due west from Shuri heights, oozing its way into the East China Sea a few miles above Naha. Lieutenant Dunfrey's platoon, which had been delivered there from relatively easy antiguerrilla patrols in the north only the day before, had been ordered to scout across the river.

Crossing at low tide, it pushed several hundred yards farther south to two low hills, making note of the defensive positions that dotted them. They would make the territory "sheer hell" to take, Dunfrey reckoned.

He was impressed by the enemy's fire discipline. His men saw Japanese soldiers ducking back into caves and observing them from machine-gun nests in well-placed vantage points, but all held their fire. The scope and ingenuity of their positions impressed him even more. Many caves had entrances on both slopes; others housed artillery pieces covered by branches or canvas. Dunfrey had been promoted to lieutenant after his platoon leader was killed on Guadalcanal, then acquired more combat experience in Okinawa's north — but he'd never seen such defensive skill and strength. His unhappy scouting completed, he tried to hurry his men back to relative safety. The enemy opened fire when the unit was most vulnerable, back at the Asakawa. Many Japanese kept their positions concealed by firing only when his men's backs were turned.

A little like the Japanese Army, Marines were much more practiced at advance than withdrawal. Crossing in chest-high water with rifles over their heads, that group made fine targets, especially Dunfrey himself, at whom much of the fire was concentrated. The loss of his young runner inches beside him caused an additional problem: A buddy of the dead man began hauling the body back, despite the additional risk to himself and Dunfrey. The lieutenant had to "kick ass" on the weeping corporal — one of his best men — and order his platoon sergeant to get everyone the hell back across the river *now*. A second man was killed in the ninety-minute struggle to do that.

Later that day, Dunfrey was summoned to 6th Division headquarters in a former Japanese command post. Some forty officers were there, underground, including Major General Lemuel Shepherd, the 6th Division's commander, and his boss, Lieutenant General Simon Buckner, commander of the entire 10th Army. Dunfrey answered their questions and was dismissed. He started to leave, then turned back to ask permission to add something. He wanted to say the questions hadn't allowed him to paint the full grim picture of what he'd observed. When the Japanese artillery at last opened up on his men, there were not merely very many more guns than he'd expected, but they were also positioned to give them meshed lines of fire down on all lines of advance and excellent protection from American counterfire. "Dis-*missed!*" a staff officer roared before Dunfrey could reopen his mouth. But a second officer called him back and he was permitted to wonder aloud whether a frontal assault could take such excellent positions.

At three o'clock the following morning, his weakened platoon was the second to cross a rope bridge strung across the Asakawa by engineers earlier that night. So much for his misgivings! His men had orders to hold their fire, light no cigarettes, move soundlessly. They hoped a dense fog blanketing the little valley would conceal an attack planned for dawn, three hours hence. But Japanese flares kept lighting the night, and when the leader of the first platoon to cross the bridge reached its far side, just ahead of Dunfrey, two enemy rifles were pointed at him from close enough to be seen through the fog. They shot down the American hope for surprise.

Still, Dunfrey's group moved out on time, at 6 A.M., almost blindly in the fog — whereas the defenders had clearly taken great pains to pinpoint the only possible lines of advance. It was no surprise to the lieutenant that extremely heavy fire pinned down his men in minutes. Half an hour later, he felt a great thud in his stomach. Machine-gun bullets and fragments of his belt buckle had severed his bowel. Although a corpsman risked his own life to reach the exposed platoon leader with sulfa, it was almost seven hours of desperate gasping for breath before he could be evacuated. The Japanese who had so scrupulously held their fire the day before were now delivering much too much of it to allow a stretcher to be brought out.

Paul Dunfrey didn't know he'd played a bit part in the campaign's feature attraction, set at the main Japanese defensive line. If he'd gotten through that morning without serious injury, his chances for the same during the rest of May would have been negligible. A mile south of his wounding, the terrain of terraces, steep escarpments, and rugged ravines approached perfection for defense.

The 32nd Army had carved the limestone and coral of each commanding hill there into a kind of land battleship. Outdoing themselves in excavation and construction, the men had fashioned "defensive masterpieces" largely impervious to the fire of the American fleet offshore as well as of the land artillery and the bombers. Many were contiguous or had protected access from one to another. Where possible, they'd been tunneled with bends just inside the entrances to limit the fire entering the interiors. A single sector of well less than half a square mile would be found to contain sixteen hidden light mortars, eighty-three light machine guns, forty-one heavy machine guns, seven antitank guns, six field guns, two mortars, and two howitzers.

The most extensive works were in the high ground protecting Shuri, which would have been difficult to take even with less shrewd and elaborate preparations. Centuries of Okinawan kings had built forts on those natural defensive sites, where Shuri Castle was now the keystone of Ushijima's attrition strategy. Not even sixteen-inch naval shells could disturb the deep, vast tunnel beneath it — almost thirteen hundred feet long, with blower-assisted ventilation shafts — that served as 32nd Army headquarters. The castle stood on a high knob near the city's southern edge. East and west from there, the line was carved and constructed across the island's full twelve-mile width. Anchored by the Asakawa on the west coast, the Shuri heights in the center, and a hill mass at Yonabaru on the east (Pacific) coast, the mighty system of artfully placed fortifications was like a Corregidor for the bulk of the 32nd Army. For all the late start, logistical difficulties, interference by American air raids, loss of the 9th Division, and other setbacks, the defenders' prodigious labor had built their most formidable positions of the Pacific War on terrain best suited for them.

Americans who'd later inspect the works would hardly credit that they'd been completed in under a year. "I couldn't believe those underground forts," one Marine marveled for thousands. "Two-tiered quarters, running water, everything beautifully engineered — that's why you never saw a Jap most of the time. They'd be bombed, bombarded, napalmed —

and safe inside those thousands of caves. Some with mouths so small you wouldn't see them until you were almost right on them and they started shooting. *Bingo!*"

In and out of the caves, hidden positions were placed for the best flat-trajectory fire directly on areas where attackers would have no cover or concealment. Major and minor strongpoints were integrated to provide intersecting, interlocking fields of fire for artillery, mortar, machine-gun, and small-arms fire, and the vantage points from the heights facilitated their coordination for rare accuracy, economy, and effect. Mounted on tracks, artillery pieces could be rolled to the mouth of their camouflaged cave or emplacement, fired once or twice, and rolled back out of sight, before their positions could be fixed — as in the north, but with thirty times more firepower. Little zeroing in was required because that had been done on a tight grid for everything significant, down to boulders and clumps of trees. The attackers would have to advance exposed or marked.

Some complexes in the network of trenches, galleries, caves, and tunnels were almost two miles long. While protecting the Japanese infantry from all but the heaviest and most accurate air strikes and naval and artillery fire, it provided the best possible firing positions and concealment for *their* weapons, and the system's depth would enable withdrawals to be made with maximum secrecy and safety. The full advantage of exits at both the front and rear of caves, and sometimes on the flanks of the hills, was about to become clear. They would much facilitate the shifting and concentrating of limited resources to meet changing battle needs. The defenders would be able to reinforce units on their forward slopes by sending fresh troops and supplies from the rear exits, or even from adjoining hills, from where they couldn't be expected. Colonel Yahara, the brilliant operations officer, and General Cho, the fiercely goading chief of staff, had devised a defensive tour de force and contrived to get their troops, the indefatigable movers of earth, to build it during the year of preparation. And once again, American reconnaissance had failed (as it would again, even using its much-improved technology, in the Vietnam War) to uncover the nature and magnitude of the defenses — even the number of defenders, which it underestimated by almost 40 percent.

Military histories rightly dwell on the 32nd Army's "maze of caves, interconnecting tunnels well stocked with grenades, [with] approaches well mined and covered by barbed wire [and] supported by fierce mortar, artillery, and machine gun fire." However, it may be enough to say here that Americans began speaking of the "Little Siegfried Line." By early May, the nature of the Japanese resistance on the island's southern third had become clear, and it was the worst possible kind for the offense, fought entirely from the skillful underground complexes under commanders whose ultimate purpose was to die in combat. The Americans' early-April optimism was replaced by an acceptance that Okinawa would be no exception to the Japanese rule of savage fighting for every rise, hill, tomb, and cave. Now it promised to be the war's harshest confirmation of that rule — until the even bloodier fighting that would have to follow on the mainland.

Against such opposition, it seemed sensible to take one's time, blasting and blasting again with every available shell before advancing with bodies — which is what the forty thousand troops of the Army's 7th and 96th Divisions had been doing almost since L-day. While the 6th Marine Division had been racing for the north, the Army had been bearing the brunt of the Japanese power on a hard grind south. The first serious barrier, the northernmost from Shuri, stood only a few miles below the landing beaches. Five days after L-day, strongpoints there stopped the advance of many Army units, which were forced to attack Cactus Ridge and the Pinnacle again and again before taking them, with heavy casualties. (Although hills and rises were identified by numbers on the map, the customary American nicknaming began immediately.) The forty-odd-foot Pinnacle, atop which Commodore Perry's party may have planted an American flag ninety-two years earlier, served as an introduction to rises that seemed piddling until the attackers' approach prompted fire from concealed caves, bunkers, and a collection of stone and concrete tombs converted to pillboxes. Interlocking fire from adjacent rises and hills left no weak point to attack.

Those small fortresses gave a taste of what lay ahead. On April 9, two battalions of the 96th Division's 383rd Infantry Regiment launched a major attack on seemingly unimpressive Kakazu Ridge, which actually anchored a major defensive line some four miles north of the main Shuri Line. It took units of one Army division seven days and over eleven hundred casualties to advance six thousand yards. Units of the other needed three days of intense attack to capture a single small hill in a line studded with them.

The Army tried again a week later as part of a general offensive against the whole line, after softening up Kakazu Ridge in particular with the biggest bang of the entire Pacific War so far. Three hundred twenty-four American artillery pieces fired nineteen thousand shells at enemy positions. Eighteen warships joined the bombardment; 650 planes dropped bombs and napalm and also fired rockets and machine guns. That was the "industrial" aspect of American warfare: Before the end of the campaign, Army and Marine field guns alone would fire 1,766,352 rounds.

But they were far less effective than ordnance statistics implied against the Japanese there, who remained underground, ignored casualties, and rushed out to fight when the bombardment let up. However restricted and weakened by the heavy guns, Japanese soldiers retained the power to fire rifles, machine guns, mortars, and artillery pieces at chosen moments. Perfectly positioned antitank guns wreaked havoc. In one small action below Kakazu Ridge, those guns and squads armed with satchel charges — like the one whose accidental explosion had wounded Tadashi Kojo — swiftly destroyed or immobilized twenty-two of thirty American tanks. The situation was so favorable for counterattack that Ushijima ignored his own prohibition of them and ordered a small one. Soon nearly sixty American tanks were blown up or captured.

When Americans managed to gouge openings in the line, the defenders used their network of tunnels and hidden trenches to seal them, day after day. "You can't bypass a Jap," an Army officer lamented, "because a Jap doesn't know when he's bypassed." Kakazu Ridge wasn't taken until April 24, when Army commanders discovered its defenders had withdrawn during the previous night's fog and an unusually powerful artillery barrage — but only to the next series of even more formidable hills, about a mile farther south.

Still, the Americans were advancing, however slowly and painfully. Prudent minds still considered it safest and surest to tread ahead cautiously, relying on sheer weight of metal. That was the conviction of most of the 10th Army's staff, including General "Buck" Buckner, commander of the 155,000 American troops on the ground. Simon Bolivar Buckner Jr. was a stolid man who liked to take as few risks as possible. If it had been up to him alone, Okinawa might have been less costly in American infantry casualties — but only at the expense of the greater naval losses a slower advance would have brought. (The welfare of the native population, whose suffering was bound to increase with the length of the campaign, was not a consideration.)

The American commander had soldiered for thirty-seven years since graduating from West Point, in 1908. Exemplary service before, during, and after World War I earned him regular promotions. As much as a parallel was possible in two countries of such contrasting culture and traditions, Lieutenant General Simon Buckner was an American version of Lieutenant General Mitsuru Ushijima. The upbringing and training of both seem to have pointed them toward their commands on Okinawa almost from birth. Buckner's father, a Civil War hero, attained the rank of lieutenant general, and later had a distinguished civilian career that included the governorship of Kentucky.

Buckner may have been a shade less prominent in the American military establishment than Ushijima in the Japanese, but he was equally devoted to soldiering and only soldiering, and among the most respected and popular of the Army's top brass. As Ushijima had had the honor of commanding the Imperial Military Academy, punctilious Buckner had the same at West Point, in the late 1930s. He too was the picture of a general, down to rugged good looks topped by thick white hair. At fifty-eight, a year older than Ushijima, he kept himself in excellent shape.

More to the point, the "leading Army schoolmaster," as he was known for his years of studying and teaching in the highest staff schools, had a firm command of battle strategy and tactics. He'd led the American campaign in the Aleutian Islands in 1943, and his decoration for "exceptionally distinguished and meritorious service" was more than the standard Army boilerplate. Although a commanding officer's personal example was generally less important to American troops than to Japanese, GIs generally admired the "big, handsome, ruddy, strong-bodied" man, as one saw him now. He trained them hard but his commanding presence was free of arrogance. As much as fighting troops could have positive feelings about anyone at headquarters, most of the 10th Army's felt the commander and his staff were a skilled collection.

He'd assumed its command in August 1944, the month when Ushijima took command of the much smaller 32nd Army. If the campaign against Formosa hadn't been canceled, he would have led it with the same force. On Okinawa, he was commanding three Marine divisions as well as four Army ones — but to the considerable extent that he went by the book, it was the Army book. His instinct was to defeat the enemy by applying the Army's standard use of superior force. Moreover, he naturally leaned toward the conservative side of the generally conservative Army; except for a brief tour in aviation, he was an infantryman with special skills in tanks. "We'll take our time and kill the Japanese gradually," he'd told correspondents about his intentions for May. And now, *during* May: "You will see many Japanese killed. You will see them gradually rolled back . . . but you won't see spectacular advances because this isn't that kind of fighting."

But the "Old Man of the Mountain," as he was also called, was now under pressure to fight a more imaginative campaign than the step-by-solid-step that came naturally to him. Among others, it was being applied by his superior, Fleet Admiral Chester W. Nimitz, who'd urged making Okinawa rather than Formosa the next target after Iwo Jima. That gave the admiral an extra measure of concern about the progress of the campaign, about which he hadn't shared the early optimism. After the first week's relative ease, capped by the sinking of *Yamato*, Vice Admiral Richmond Turner, Iceberg's overall commander, sent him a jocular radio signal: I MAY BE CRAZY, BUT IT LOOKS LIKE THE JAPS HAVE QUIT THE WAR, AT LEAST IN THIS SECTION. Nimitz's succinct reply reflected his character: DELETE ALL AFTER "CRAZY." It was the following day that Army units first encountered the Little Siegfried Line in the unassuming shape of Kakazu Ridge. And now Admiral Turner's overconfidence had switched to hot-tempered criticism of General Buckner.

Buckner couldn't have pleased everyone. Campaign commanders everywhere had to reckon with a fundamental difference between the Army's and Marine Corps's fighting styles, the Army generally attacking much more deliberately with heavier weapons than the leaner Marines, who moved out faster with less equipment and more initial risk. Army forces usually had the wherewithal for campaigns of attrition and tended to fight them as long as the defense remained organized and powerful. Marine leadership, always hurried by limitations of time and supply, believed fewer men would be lost in the end by constant advance, using flanking movements if possible, instead of burrowing into foxholes while softening up the enemy — and allowing *his* artillery and mortars to do their damage at the same time.

The Marine credo had been developed in smaller campaigns than this one, and against less entrenched opposition. There the men did what they were best trained for: storm beachheads, win quick victories in small areas, ship out to the next destination. And it wasn't logically certain that units moving forward rapidly suffered fewer casualties than those that waited in position until weather, support, and other factors were favorable. But rapid advance did boost morale, on which the Corps heavily depended.

Words like *assault, take,* and *capture* tripped even from Dick Whitaker, no master of strategy or tactics. But he'd been a Marine long enough to know that "our philosophy was advance, advance, advance. It became a battle only when the advance was stopped for some reason." Since every teenage private knew he wasn't winning if not advancing, it was almost inevitable that when the strongpoints stopped the Marines now, in early May, some staff and higher field officers proposed outflanking them with another amphibious operation well south of the Shuri Line. A few high Army officers, including Major General John Hodge, commander of the XXIV Corps that comprised the 7th and 96th Divisions, had already pressed Buckner to do the same. But the Marine leadership was even more outspoken in the effort to move the land commander from his slug-it-out strategy.

Unhappy with what they saw as Buckner's lack of appreciation for maneuver, the dissenters, who included General Shepherd, the commander of the 6th Marine Division that had taken the north, wanted to shorten the campaign with a daring end run.* They specified it should be made by the 2nd Marine Division, which was in reserve on Saipan after L-day's sham landing in the south in order to deter Ushijima from moving reinforcements to the real landing beaches. That division, a veteran of amphibious assaults, should now return to the place of its feint, the southeast beaches of Minatogawa on the Pacific coast, which were promising enough to have been an alternative site for the real landings. Supported by those arguments and by the Marine Corps commandant, General Alexander Vandegrift, on a visit to Okinawa, the Marines pressed their case. They were convinced Buckner's predictable frontal assault took more time and cost more lives in the end than quick, hard strikes that would stop the enemy from making his skillful retreats to the next prepared barriers, as at Kakazu. Such nighttime withdrawals at the last moment before the besieged barriers were overwhelmed were allowing the Japanese to sustain their defenses just as they'd planned.

Buckner's rejection of those proposals was grounded in soldierly resolve — he'd made up his mind — and in the very caution of which he was accused. Kamikazes had cost the 10th Army two ammunition supply

---

*Douglas MacArthur's use of a Marine division for a more daring amphibious strike behind the enemy lines in Korea five years later led to the quick retreat of the powerful North Korean forces, although that doesn't prove General Shepherd and the others were right on Okinawa. Coming from the Army school, MacArthur was cautious, but the same General Shepherd worked closely with him in planning and executing the bold Inchon landing. Shepherd was assisted by an exceptionally resourceful staff officer named Victor Krulak, now his chief of operations on Okinawa.

The strategic issues in Vietnam twenty years later were not precisely parallel: There it was less territory than the peasants' allegiance that had to be won. Still, some elements of the Army-Marine conflict remained the same, especially the determination of General William Westmoreland, the commanding officer — a man much in Buckner's educational and professional mold — to win with pulverizing firepower. The Marine generals, including Victor Krulak, tried to convince Westmoreland that the standard Army approach couldn't work in Vietnam. But "for Westmoreland to have conceded they were right," Neil Sheehan observed, "would have been to deny himself the war he wanted to wage of mass troop movements, artillery barrages, skies filled with helicopters and fighter-bombers, and the thunder of B-52s."

On Okinawa, over fourteen million tons of bombs alone were dropped on Japanese positions by mid-May — without significantly denting the heart of the defense. Stubbornly hoping to hit the enemy so hard that infantry would eventually be able to advance easily, most Pacific Area planners overestimated the value of massed artillery fire and naval bombardment, assisted by air strikes. They also consistently underestimated the enemy's acuity, resourcefulness, and thoroughness of preparations, together with his bravery and endurance — an error perhaps furthered, as in Vietnam, by assumptions of racial superiority over the Japanese. Buckner's intelligence reports in particular consistently overstated the damage to installations. For all the terror the bombardments struck in the Japanese and misery they caused by keeping them underground, enemy soldiers were relatively safe if they remained in their caves and fortifications until American infantrymen came within shooting range.

ships. The commander and his staff insisted that another fighting front would break down his supply system (although the 2nd Marine Division said it had enough logistical support to sustain itself for at least a month of fighting on Okinawa). Buckner also wanted to keep the 2nd fresh for the July landings planned for a tiny Ryukyu island midway between Okinawa and the Japanese mainland.

Besides, the general argued, the 32nd Army's tactics and artillery strength and the steep cliffs dominating the possible southern landing sites would have made a new amphibious operation "another Anzio but worse." Japanese guns did have a direct line of a fire to the coral-strewn beaches below, and a few high naval officers also doubted proper cover could be mounted for another landing there. However, high-ranking Japanese officers, including Colonel Yahara, thought Minatogawa would make a good landing beach for the Americans, and such an operation would be their most damaging move.

Buckner surely wouldn't have changed his mind if he'd known that a landing below Shuri might have averted the coming catastrophe for Okinawan civilians. He might have reconsidered had his intelligence suggested what more the Little Siegfried Line had in store for the 10th Army itself. But it didn't; his confident prediction of hard but not overly hard victory was based on the optimism of ignorance. Taking the bull by the horns at a press conference now, he opened it by comparing a new landing to a general's navel: "You'd look totally stupid without one, but it serves no purpose." That disarmed most of the reporters, but not Homer Bigart of the *New York Herald Tribune*. Bigart's almost aberrant criticism of the failure to stage that second landing and catch the Japanese in a pincer movement would spark a heated postmortem controversy in the States. Although politicians and journalists knew but a fraction of the hardship caused by the Shuri Line, that was enough for American newspapers to begin criticizing Buckner's conduct of the campaign, surely encouraged by the Marine Corps commandant after he'd returned to Washington.

Newspapers complained about Buckner's devotion to wooden frontal tactics. Some went further, suggesting the "ultraconservative" campaign had been a "fiasco" and "a worse example of military incompetence than Pearl Harbor." Admiral Nimitz, conciliatory by nature, would join those who deplored the criticism, going out of his way to applaud Buckner and praise the Army's "magnificent performance." But that admirable exercise in team play was intended to mask interservice friction, and it too would come after the fact. Now, when it mattered, his reaction to Buckner's leadership was quite different. The advance was stalled. The four hundred planes of the Third Floating Chrysanthemum had just swarmed over the fleet. Leadership wrangling was threatening to break out into the open. So Nimitz flew to Okinawa for some straight talk with Buckner.

Like the Marines, the modest admiral wanted faster results in order to reduce the kamikazes' unprecedented damage to his fleet. He may also have been having second thoughts about the whole campaign — the "ill-considered decision to take Okinawa by storm," as one historian would describe it, that left "no other way for Buckner but straight ahead into the sausage machine." In any case, the relatively huge toll in American ships and crews deeply disturbed him, and he was uncharacteristically sharp in a meeting with Buckner on April 23, ordering the general to speed things up. Buckner countered that the ground campaign was an Army operation, *his* business. Nimitz restated his point without mincing words. "I'm losing a ship and a half a day. So if this line isn't moving in five days, we'll get someone up here to move it so we can all get out from under these damn kamikaze attacks." (Although that of course went unreported to 10th Army troops, the magic of scuttlebutt quickly apprised them of the conversation's substance. "Perhaps Nimetz [*sic*] put a spark up Buckner's but [*sic*]," a lowly Marine speculated in his diary a few days later.)

Whatever the merits of the conflicting strategies, however many thousands of lives might or might not have been saved by dropping characteristic Army caution, it must be said that lack of information and imagination played a large part in the ultimate decision, together with the tendency to underestimate the Japanese that had been present from the start. Some of the bloodiest weeks in American history were approaching, and when the results are compared to the planning, the latter appears seriously inadequate. As so often in war, the larger possibilities and potential consequences, which ought to have been clear from previous wars, were set aside or not raised at all. Buckner had already chosen his tactical objectives, and his resolve to reach them with firepower and more firepower remained unchanged.

But he did try to get the line moving again, partly by exchanging one of his Army divisions for the 6th Marine Division. His order for that came on the fifth day of the five Nimitz had given him. That is what delivered Paul Dunfrey's platoon down from the north to the defensive fury at the Asakawa on May 9 and 10, ten days after all Okinawa was supposed to be in American hands, according to the plans.

The Army got the best food, best equipment, best weapons, best artillery. The Marines got all the crap left behind. Sometimes the only way to get replacements and ammunition was to go into Army supply dumps and scrounge — practically steal the stuff. They tried to fight by relying on all their supplies because they weren't going to use their lives — and when that failed, the Marines had to go in and clean out the enemy.
— Norris Buchter, 22nd Marine Regiment

We believed, probably correctly, that we were put in the field to do more at less cost than other servicemen. But maybe Marines took a perverse pleasure in being so Spartan.
— Clyde McAvoy, 4th Marine Regiment

The Army division exchanged for the 6th Marines was a National Guard unit from New York that had been sent into foreign combat — a rare exception in American practice — with little reorganization. No one who hasn't fought in the "killing zone," within rifle range of the enemy, has a right to criticize those who have. But the record shows that the 27th Division also went into combat with a higher-than-average percentage of inexperienced officers. On Saipan, where it had fought the year before, its failure to match the achievements of other units in the bloody line had led to controversy. Marine General Holland (Howlin' Mad) Smith, the corps commander, sent it back into reserve and swore never to use it again.

The 27th's sixteen thousand troops were roughly of the same human stuff as the other divisions. Even most Marine leaders acknowledge that the man-to-man difference between Marine and Army troops in action is insignificant. If anything, therefore, that proves only the importance of training — especially, in this case, of senior officers. On Okinawa, the 27th had been sent into the line on April 9, after the going in the south got rough. It saw heavy action during the rest of the month, principally at Kakazu Ridge and two deadly strongpoints of the next major Japanese barrier south. One was Item Pocket, a large rise located in the *I* or Item grid square on the American battle map. It was one of Okinawa's best natural defensive positions and most cleverly prepared, a lethal citadel of skillfully mounted armament with no approach except by exposure to its many bands of fire. Taking the interlocking ridges required repeated feats of arms and bravery. The progress had been slow, perhaps necessarily so, but many companies distinguished themselves. However, two fled in disarray from intense fire, one of the rare such instances during the entire Okinawan campaign.

Few Marines knew anything specific about the record of the 27th on Saipan or on Makin or Eniwetok, where it had also fought. Even fewer knew that it had originally been in "floating reserve" status at Okinawa, earmarked for garrison duty after the island's taking. Or that, despite the setbacks at the deadly positions against which it had been hurriedly committed, it often fought hard and well. Sixth Division Marines in particular had no idea that Ushijima's real defense had been prepared in that southernmost eighth of the island from which they were most distant. But the facts would have made little difference to most Marines, because they had an "underlying contempt," as a critically admiring corpsman who tended their wounded put it, for everyone else. "If you weren't a Marine, you weren't much of anything."

Special contempt for the Army in particular was built into their elite training, one of the prods that charged them to advance faster against more seemingly unassailable positions than miserable soldiers. William Manchester has claimed that several Marines sent two souvenir-hunting Army officers to their almost certain deaths on Okinawa by pointing them in the direction of Japanese snipers. If that was true, it was an "awesome example," as Dick Whitaker would call it, of the bad feelings between the 6th Marine Division and 27th Army Division in particular — but not an entirely unbelievable example. Every Marine considered every soldier a "doggie," and barked at him, Manchester added. Most Marines more or less despised doggies all the way up to their top one in the Pacific, General of the Army Douglas MacArthur.*

Although Marines had taken higher casualties on many islands, here so far it was the reverse. When the 6th Division Marines were sent south in late April and early May, Army casualties were seven times greater than theirs. The many dangerously weakened Army units included the sterling 383rd Regiment, which, although badly mauled during its attacks on Kakazu Ridge, had to relieve the 382nd Regiment because the latter was down to half strength, while the 305th was even more depleted. And the 27th Division's casualties during its hardest two weeks in April were almost as great as both Marine divisions suffered during the full month. Its losses at Item Pocket, still three miles above the main Shuri Line, were proportionately the highest of the entire campaign.

If Marines knew none of that, they fumed with the knowledge that they were indeed less well supplied than their larger sister service. The grudge they nursed served as more inducement for showing up the fat, dumb doggies, and as justification for appropriating their treasures. One June evening, Dick Whitaker would come upon an Army tank unit setting up its mess tent — itself a startling extravagance to Marines in combat, who lived entirely in holes and ate rations. Whitaker and a company mate named Jack Crary entered the tent to find a mess sergeant inside, together with a stack of canned hams: wild luxury after months of fighting on Marine subsistence. Crary asked for a can, and the sergeant told him to fuck off. The former unslung his rifle and pointed it. "Too bad you feel that way, but we're taking that fucking ham anyway!"

The sergeant handed him the can and the two typically rabid Marines, as he obviously saw them, backed out of the tent like bank robbers — until Whitaker saw his favorite weapon, a Thompson submachine gun,

*Marines were convinced the theatrical supreme commander and national hero gave them the most dangerous assignments but inadequate equipment and supplies. Manchester also told of coaching Okinawan children to beg from passing Army units — except that they weren't saying "Give me a cigarette," as they thought, but "General MacArthur eats shit."

hanging on the tent's center pole. "Well, as long as Jack's taking the ham," he reasoned with impeccable Marine logic, "I'm taking that." The two then made their escape into the Okinawan night.

Even Marines with the least interest in military philosophy had a practical sense of the differences in fighting styles. They knew they were not only trained but also organized and supplied, or undersupplied, for fast assaults as opposed to the "ponderous" Army's "plodding" advances, attempted only when an overwhelming numerical advantage had been assembled. Until then, Marines sneered, "those lumps just stayed in their foxholes — and what foxholes! like houses! — and hoped artillery would do their jobs for them." Wrong as that often was, grave as shortages of supplies could be for Army units too, it remained generally true that the Marines' determination to advance with relatively small forces against all opposition was usually fiercer than the Army's.

That push had been amply illustrated during the race to take the north. When the commander of the 29th Regiment was relieved on April 10 (see p. 120) his slowness in taking Yae-dake Mountain wasn't the full cause. After bitter hand-to-hand fighting, the colonel asked his boss, the divisional commander, for a twenty-four-hour break to give his tired men a rest and a chance to change their socks. The heavily decorated veteran of many hard battles was gone the following day — and although that angered his men, they were also proud of the relentlessness with which they were driven.

Finally, the Marines up north had heard many rumors about the performance of the "useless" 27th Division, and the nearness of mortal danger gave rumors the advantage over the unavailable truth. The stories ranged from the division being pinned down and unable to move, which was partially true, to having such low morale and integrity that it couldn't even recover its dead — the most unforgivable failure to Marines, since honoring *their* dead fused their half-mystical comradeship. "So the 27th's behavior was inexcusable — and that's not rumor because I was one of the Marines who recovered some of their dead for them under enemy fire. Simply notorious!" But other rumors were silly, and cocky Marines, ignorant of what the Army had been facing in the south for almost a month, loved spreading them. Admiral William Halsey, who alternated commanding the 5th Fleet, had supposedly "told Buckner that he was going to pull his Navy and Marines out of Okinawa if he couldn't get the Army to move its fat ass." What most bothered 6th Division Marines with access to real news from the south were reports that Japanese firepower, especially artillery, was devastating, and that their own brothers in the 1st Marine Division were being killed unnecessarily because the 27th Division was leaving them exposed on the flanks (as they heard it had done to Marines on Saipan) by not advancing on schedule to silence that artillery. Besides, the 6th Division also feared that this would mean the end of that other, "good" rumor — that they'd soon be out of Okinawa and back on Guam.

> *We passed the 27th Army Division as we went in to relieve them. Every one of us felt the only reason we were going south and they were going north was that they'd fucked up again.*
> — Dick Whitaker, 29th Marines

> *When we were up north, we knew the Army was getting the shit kicked out of them and we said it was because they just wouldn't get up out of their holes and move. We used to joke that one Jap machine gun was holding up a whole damn Army division. That was before we knew how bad it was down there.*
> — Joseph Bangert, medical corpsman with the 22nd Marines

The transfer itself might have provided a war movie's comic relief. Marine wags posted road signs reading MARINES AND MEN pointing south, and ARMY or 27TH DIVISION pointing north, together with USO and REST AREA. When their trucks passed each other, sometimes within inches, they shouted abuse at the "retreating" doggies, and flung back the candy bars a few friendly GIs had tossed them with insulting barks. But other soldiers pretended to film the Leathernecks, mocking them as gung-ho savages who craved glory at any cost. "Go ahead and bark; you bastards live like dogs anyway." The greenest Marines were likely to shout the loudest; combat veterans tended to be quieter. But all cast an envious eye at Army riches. When a 27th Division truck tipped over the shoulder of a meager road, a band of Marines stole their better carbines and ran off.

Forty years later, 6th Division veterans would dwell on the exchange. What really made the memory durable was that it marked the trauma of returning to battle from the relative comfort and safety of the mopping-up patrols and other occupation duties up north. "I'd never been in combat before, so our fighting in the north surprised me," one Marine would recall. "I mean, the pretty weak opposition and few casualties. We thought we were done with Okinawa and would be leaving soon, so going back into the slog down south was a shock." A much-mellowed veteran would venture in retrospect that the taunting of GIs was "all bravado" to mask anxiety: Instead of the fantasy of going home for Christmas, they were going in to take over from the fucking 27th. Another would remember that resentment of the Army really took root only after the Marines arrived in the south "and began getting the crap kicked out of them." For it wasn't merely more combat they were returning to, but hardship that surpassed almost all they'd experienced.

17 · Sugar Loaf Hill

The biggest and fiercest battle in the post V-E world was in progress last week in Okinawa. U.S. troops were advancing in the old-fashioned, inescapable way, one foot at a time against the kind of savage, rat-in-a-hole defense that only the Japanese can offer.
— *Time*, May 21, 1945

The terrain is just right for the Nips and many American boys are falling. I thank the Lord that I am in artillery. We have it bad, but not as bad as the Marine Infantry.
— Thomas Hannaher, in a letter home, May 21

THREE MAIN DEFENSIVE LINES crossed Okinawa's south. The first, anchored by Kakazu Ridge and a collection of contiguous rises including Item Pocket, had been broken, chiefly by Army units, but at a cost that had started the wrangling about Buckner's judgment. The Okinawan campaign was already longer than those for Saipan and Iwo Jima, and although its casualties were still about a quarter less than Iwo Jima's, the brass now knew the greatest bloodletting lay ahead. It was time to shorten it by breaking the back of the defense. The ventures of Paul Dunfrey's platoon across the muddy Asakawa on May 9 and 10 were feelers for a general offensive the following day, General Buckner's response to demands that he get moving again.

The full-scale attack on May 11 was intended to penetrate the second and best line, which guarded Shuri. It would take place across the full width of the island where the 10th Army was stalled, about twenty miles south of the landing beaches. The 7th Army Division was enjoying a brief rest after a brutal month taking the Pinnacle and another defensive system at a group of hills near Kochi (where it unknowingly engaged Captain Kojo's battalion). Each of the other four divisions faced extremely formidable barriers at their places in the line. A large hill mass called Conical Hill confronted the 96th Army Division on the Pacific coast. The heights of Shuri itself awaited the 77th Army Division. On those heights' other flank, the 1st Marine Division faced Wana Ridge and Wana Draw, a giant moat that might have been created for the slaughter of anyone mad enough to enter it. The obstacles in the path of General Shepherd's (and Paul Dunfrey's) 6th Marine Division, just down from the north, seemed comparatively less difficult. It remained on the west coast facing the East China Sea, where the Asakawa and the Asato, another river farther south, rimmed some three miles of relatively flat land.

Most of the 6th Division began the May 11 offensive a day earlier in order to cross the Asakawa and some fairly open ground to the main fortifications. For G (George) Company of the 2nd Battalion, 22nd Regiment, May 10 started in the predawn darkness, at a point where the Asakawa was shallow enough to wade across. G–2–22, comprising green men and savvy veterans of earlier Pacific combat, was a typical Marine company typically convinced it was far better than typical. Its young commander, Captain Owen Stebbins, had fought on the Marshall Islands and Guam after graduating from Officer Candidate School. Having been wounded on Guam, he was as relieved as anyone at the ease of the company's landing on L-day and relatively painless April in the north.

Good-natured Stebbins, who'd played football for Fresno State College, seemed to take everything in stride. Admiring him for his combat experience and fairness, his men were confident that "nothing ever fazed him." But after crossing the Asakawa in the morning's dense fog, he was no less amazed by the scope and skill of the Japanese preparations than Paul Dunfrey had been. "Their camouflage was so superb even in fairly open territory that some of my men were hit by machine-gun fire from five yards away. And in the back because they had the terrific discipline to hold their fire until our patrols passed. Or until our men came almost right up on top of them — so near they couldn't use mortars or grenades to knock out the machine guns or get back the wounded, who were just too close."

When two of Stebbins's three infantry platoons were pinned down almost immediately, he was faced with one of the decisions that torment company commanders in the field. A scout cut down by a hidden Japanese machine gun lay within yards of it. Stebbins felt he couldn't attack the emplacement with grenades or mortar fire, because his man might be alive. He risked using his binoculars, whose glint in the sun now rising over the Japanese position would make him a special target. From two hundred yards away, he saw the body wasn't moving — but still hesitated to use heavy armament until he could be sure. Now entered the element of chance that always determined life and death on the line. A medical corpsman who'd already saved several men by braving pinpointed hostile fire crawled out to rescue the scout while the machine gun still chattered. The wounded man *was* alive, because he happened to have fallen into a crease in the ground, where further bullets whizzed over him — but now killed the corpsman.

When Stebbins later had time to think beyond the demands of the field, he saw that twist of fate as yet another confirmation that combat was a constant roll of dice. "The element of luck is enormous. One guy's miracle is the next guy's death."

Two long days later, Stebbins's company was again pinned down by heavy, accurate fire from a hill in its path. It had been assigned a platoon of tanks to attack with it by Lieutenant Colonel Horatio Woodhouse, the commander of the 2nd Battalion. After encountering increasing fire as they neared that hill, the four tanks waited some eighty yards back. Stebbins himself was in an unprotected observation post some three hundred yards forward of the company's command post, where First Lieutenant Dale Bair, the executive officer, or second in command, was positioned with the machine-gun officer. Stebbins's 1st Platoon was on his right, the 2nd on his left, and the 3rd in a reserve position, just behind the company command post. Dashing to consult with him in his observation post, Second Lieutenant Edward Ruess reported that heavy fire had pinned down his platoon, the 1st, and was inflicting casualties. He hoped the tanks would help.

Rising for a better look at how they should use the terrain, Stebbins was quickly hit by three machine-gun bullets. He would recuperate for several months in a hospital and then go home, whereas the same burst that raked his little observation post, no doubt aimed at him, the officer, killed his runner — by that time, the single surviving rifleman in his forward observation post. His other runners had all been hit earlier.

Meanwhile, Ruess had sprinted back to his men, dodging, ducking, hitting the ground every ten yards. Platoon leaders were the officers who stood or crawled beside, or in front of, their men in battle. Known as one of the best, Ruess was virtually idolized by his men for his leadership. Two days earlier, Stebbins had noticed a dirty bandage the lieutenant was trying to conceal. Shot through the hand the day before, shortly after crossing the Asakawa, he went without treatment in a battalion aid station because he wouldn't leave his men when things were getting difficult. Stebbins also knew Ruess would never let his platoon stay pinned down long, which is why the captain had chosen it to lead the way onto the troublesome hill ahead. Fearless, "tiger-quick" Ruess liked to fix the positions of machine guns that were pinning down his men by showing himself to draw their fire. But this hill had too many concealed machine guns firing too great a volume of fire. Trying his daring move again, Ruess was killed.

The body of the runner who'd been killed beside Captain Stebbins tumbled into a decline. Unable to find his walkie-talkie radio, the captain crawled toward the rear until he was spotted by one of the tanks. It radioed the company command post, and stretcher bearers were dispatched to bring the captain farther back. While he was being bandaged, he told Lieutenant Colonel Woodhouse, who'd run back from his battalion's forward observation post, that the tanks were needed quickly.

Woodhouse took First Lieutenant Bair, who replaced Stebbins as company commander, to where they could coordinate another go at the hill. Runners were sent to inform the three platoons to ready themselves for a tank-supported attack to be led by Bair. The obstacle had to be taken quickly. Its fire was holding up the entire advance in the area.

Casualties among the lieutenants serving as platoon leaders had been especially heavy in the two days following the crossing of the Asakawa. Stebbins had also lost the leader of his 3rd Platoon on that same advance — to mortar fire in the morning fog of May 10. His place was taken by Platoon Sergeant Edmund De Mar, the Brooklyn boy who'd ventured a spell in Miami before enlisting in 1940. Now twenty-five years old, De Mar was called not Pops, like so many men over twenty, but Mommy, thanks to his regular admonitions to his teenage charges during their training. "Do I always have to be a mother and father to you?"

When the runner arrived with the message from Bair, Mommy was in a protected little position near the company command post, several minutes' run behind where Captain Stebbins had been hit. Despite the delay during the previous hours and the casualties to the company's two other platoons, the new obstacle gave no indication that it would be uglier than others in the two-mile lake of fire since the Asakawa. The "prominent hill," as the Americans referred to it, stood beyond a slight draw that formed a corridor leading up to it. A similar rise called Charlie Hill had fallen the day before to the 1st Battalion, after a day and a half of tank and infantry assault supported by naval gunfire. There was no reason to expect the new hill, barren except for a few scrubby trees, would be more difficult. De Mar, studying it again from a few hundred yards north, saw it as "just another lump, a brownish incline with a little knoll on top."

G Company's return to combat had been hard. After suffering only two battle-fatigue casualties during its weeks in the north, it lost nine men to exceptionally heavy artillery, mortar, and small-arms fire in just two days in the south, including five killed on the first day alone. De Mar's 3rd Platoon had escaped from one action only with the aid of a smoke screen. But the company would soon look back to those two days pushing south to here as almost easy going. At least everyone could still keep track of the killed and wounded.

Actually, De Mar was reassigning the functions of the missing men in his weakened platoon when the runner arrived with the order to meet with Lieutenant Bair for coordination. De Mar had twenty-eight men left of a full complement of forty. According to the plan, they would be joined by nineteen men still fit for action from dead Ed Ruess's 1st Platoon and be supported by the tank platoon. The hill had to be taken quickly, because its machine guns and mortars were badly chewing up everything in sight, including other companies.

The tanks were waiting in a depression not visible from the hill. When Lieutenant Bair gave Platoon Sergeant De Mar and the replacement for Ed Ruess the plan of attack, they took the usual precaution of squatting far enough apart so that one mortar round couldn't hit them all. They were eager to learn one another's names to avoid calling out "Lieutenant!" or "Sergeant!" — another way of making themselves priority targets for snipers. The plan was straightforward: De Mar and his men on the left, Bair and the reduced 1st Platoon on the right, and the tanks moving out at the same time, while a machine-gun section would give additional fire support as they advanced.

The tank commander wanted assurance that he wouldn't be left "high and dry." Tanks were a great advantage to the infantry they supported, and the American 10th Army had vastly more of them than the Japanese 32nd Army. But enemy fire of such intensity and accuracy turned even the best American Shermans into a danger too, as targets for concentrated salvos. Veterans learned to control their first instinct to crouch behind them for protection and to mistrust the false sense of security they provided. Especially when antitank guns and other armament zeroed in on their whistling and clanking, the instinct of troops at their sides was to scramble as far from them as quickly as possible, leaving them vulnerable to dreaded Japanese infantrymen with satchel charges.

Against powerful defenses, therefore, tanks needed the protection of infantrymen as much as infantrymen needed the extra punch from tanks. De Mar urged the lieutenant in command of those four Shermans not to worry: "We'll stick to you like flies on shit." They synchronized watches. Jump-off time would be 1600 hours on a signal from Lieutenant Bair.

De Mar returned to his platoon and gave the word. Final preparations were made for the attack. Waiting was a miniature prelanding limbo, the men hoping the moment would come soon and that it never would. De Mar worried about them, about the steady Japanese fire from both flanks, and about communications because his radio had been knocked out. It would be nice, he mused, to be somewhere else. At 1600 hours, the lead Sherman's hatch cover closed and it started off with the 3rd Platoon.

It was only minutes to the hill. Starting the climb, De Mar and the others suddenly saw it was thick with guns. Tank fire had ripped down camouflage, exposing dozens, maybe hundreds, of emplacements now showing gun barrels and muzzle flashes. They didn't yet know that some of the most damaging fire pouring down on them was from other hills. De Mar had no time to look at anything other than his men, some of whom were already down. The tanks were being hit just as fast by concealed, expertly placed mines and antitank guns. Two were put out of action almost immediately.

The crest was only a few hundred yards away. Hoping audacity would compensate for their lack of deception, the two platoons charged straight up and reached it, but with a much-reduced complement. Bair spread his remaining dozen-odd men into shell holes, but the Japanese fire was so intense and the American already so diminished that the lieutenant, his radio communications also out, sent a man back to report that G needed help to hold the summit. Racing and dodging down, that messenger could see little movement among De Mar's group, which was "getting the hell beaten out of them."

Nothing De Mar had seen in combat, let alone in films, had prepared him for such concentration of incoming fire. It very quickly killed many of his men and left others unable to function as fire teams. Soon only a handful remained unhit, most prominently Bair. The big, burly first lieutenant was a man of few words who, like Ed Ruess, had been among the noncommissioned officers selected for officer training as the Marines' need for more officers to replace casualties grew. He presented a fine target — but also served as an inspiration to the men — as he tried to see to the wounded and rally the others. He motioned to De Mar: something about one of the disabled tanks. Then he was violently spun around and De Mar saw a large chunk had been ripped from his upper leg. But powerful Bair picked up a .30-caliber light machine gun from alongside its two dead operators, threw a belt of ammunition over his shoulder, and, like a John Wayne character, laid out lead in the enemy's direction — *one* of the directions. It wasn't long before he took a second hit, this time in the arm cradling his machine gun. The lieutenant continued producing covering fire so that some men could crawl to help others who'd been wounded going up the hill until his third hit, in the buttocks, sent him spinning out of sight.

De Mar quickly threw some grenades and started crawling toward Bair. Then he felt as if someone had taken a log from a fire and slammed it with all his might into his leg. He went down flat and couldn't get up. Still down, he saw one of his 3rd Platoon men spring up and bang on a disabled tank with his rifle, after which the crew fired furiously for a moment — against what looked like "thousands of Japanese coming at us," as a crew member would later put it — until they ran out of ammunition and escaped through the tank's emergency hatch. Other tank crews continued firing although their vehicles were burning, then leaped out to help wounded riflemen.

There was no place anywhere to make a stand. Much later, in the sweet luxury of being alive to remember, De Mar would quip it was a situation from which General Custer would have cut and run. Dirt had jammed his rifle. He had no cover or protection. Knowing a sniper was poised somewhere on his left, maybe the one who'd already hit him, all he could do was hug the ground for all he was worth. He heard cries — from about ten yards away, he guessed — from a private named James Davis, whose size had earned him the nickname "Little Bit." Strong and tough nevertheless, Davis was only eighteen years old and his wounds were obviously very bad; he was crying for his parents to come get him. De Mar grunted for him to shut up: Any noise there would probably be a fatal noise. When Davis eventually did fall silent, De Mar hoped it was because he'd heard him.

Disabled in the extremely precarious position on the crest, De Mar thought of his own parents. He looked at his watch. It was 1645 hours. Forty-five days, not minutes, seemed to have passed. Now no Americans at all seemed still to be firing, and he could see none except dead and wounded. "What am I going to do?" he asked himself, trying to stay calm. He decided to wait, head as flat on the ground as he could push it. It would soon be dark. His leg was numb and he'd lost a lot of blood, but he knew he could crawl. A figure slithering down the hill in the dark would most likely be finished off by his own troops, who would take him for a Jap, especially at night when they were the only ones to move. He didn't even have that night's password. But those were problems for later; now he could only lie where he was, still surprised and dismayed by the dense, accurate Japanese fire from big guns, small arms, hand grenades, and mortars.

Some time later, he heard a whisper. "De Mar, you hit bad? Can you crawl?" Although he didn't recognize the voice of the man risking his own life for his, the sense of comradeship gave him an incredible lift.* "Can I crawl?" he whispered back, his head still half buried in the mud. "I can crawl back to the States."

A good smoke screen was laid down — from smoke shells fired by the surviving tanks, De Mar would later learn. He started down. Someone joined him from behind and cut off his pack to ease his crawling. Finding a little ditch, he squeezed into it for cover and kept crawling until his hand touched the body of a rifleman from his platoon — who had a bullet hole between the eyes. He tried to pull the body with him, but the helper behind urged him to just get down off the hill for now. Although it would have been a four-minute stroll from summit to bottom, the incomprehensibly intense enemy fire made their progress painfully slow.

---

*That was too common among Marines to deserve mention except to restate that their training's most important product was a sacred sense of comradeship. Medical corpsmen who tended the Marines developed the same sense of obligation and almost never failed to respond to calls from the wounded except when ordered not to because the fire was too intense. In many such instances, the officers and noncommissioned officers who issued those orders themselves went out into the killing zone to reach the wounded.

Soon he came upon Lieutenant Bair, badly bleeding from his wounds but trying to get his machine gun operating. De Mar tossed him his pistol because he believed he had some hand grenades left for any Japanese who might try to hurl satchel charges against the tank he hoped would take him back. Reaching it, he saw Little Bit's body lying alongside, where it had been pulled by Jim Chaisson, the man who'd run to the command post for reinforcements, then run back up the murderous hill to help his buddies. A tank man quickly dressed De Mar's wound, but Mommy refused to move until all known wounded had been brought down from the hill.

Then he was hoisted up onto the turret, where another wounded man was soon placed beside him. Recognizing the youthful voice of the "tanker" who'd rescued him from the hill, De Mar took out his battle dressing, leaned toward him, and asked where he'd been hit. Five fast rounds cracked out. Four hit the "expeditionary can" — five gallons of spare water or oil on the turret inches from De Mar's head. The fifth hit his savior behind the ear, splattering blood and brains all over De Mar. Gripping the now grievously wounded boy as the tank roared off, he reached for his grenades and found he had none; his pouch had been shot off.

When the tank made it back to Fox Company's command post, the young tank driver was dead. A sergeant asked how things were going. "Pretty rough on that goddamn hill," answered Mommy, not suspecting how much rougher it would become. The full strength of the defenses was still beyond his imagination — or that of any American, including General Buckner.

Those were the first assaults on Sugar Loaf Hill, as it would be christened two days later (when Lieutenant Colonel Woodhouse would call it by a name he'd used for objectives during training exercises on Guadalcanal). No more were made that day, for the battalion commander, now aware that the objective was far more difficult than originally believed, withdrew G Company and called for air strikes. Starting the next day, the sequence of attacks became so confused, with so many Americans cut off from their units, that it was impossible to keep track of who reached the summit before he fell.

Besides, holes from both sides' shelling were so large that men who crouched in them couldn't see members of other units yards away. What was known for certain was that five of De Mar's 3rd Platoon were killed and ten wounded on May 12, a casualty rate of 50 percent. Other platoons lost even more men. On May 14, G Company's three rifle platoons with their machine-gun sections had to be consolidated into a single platoon — whose lieutenant would be killed that night. Sustained losses like this would quickly prostrate the 6th Division.

The 6th Division was up against the Sugar Loaf, main western anchorage of the Shuri line, where there took place a combat not exceeded for closeness and desperation . . . by that at . . . Iwo Jima or any other.
— Fletcher Pratt, military historian

[Sugar Loaf is] the most critical local battle of the war . . . the bloodiest battlefield in the world.
— *Newsweek*, May 21 and 28

The hated hill looked to most Americans less like anything involving sugar than a rectangular loaf of coral and volcanic rock. Stebbins and De Mar weren't alone in wondering how such an object, seemingly less significant than the Kakazu Ridge finally taken by the Army, could cause such slaughter. To the 6th Division staff, it was merely a minor midway station wanted as a platform for fire support against a higher hill called Kokuba about a mile farther south.

Sugar Loaf's three hundred or so yards of frontage rose abruptly to a height of sixty feet from an area of plain before it, an unhappy feature to those who had to cross that open country, about the size of six football fields. The hill itself was low enough, especially in relation to the others in view of it, including the Shuri heights, to appear almost negligible — a "pimple of a hill," as one Marine would call it forty years later, still trying to fathom how it could have been so evil. A young man in the good shape of all infantrymen could run to its crest in three or four minutes. Yet it would cost more casualties than any other single Pacific battle, on Iwo Jima or elsewhere.

The next assaults were prompted not only by the continued need to take the hill for the sake of the advance but also to stop its defenders from rolling hand grenades down on American wounded lying at the base. But "shot-to-shit" G Company was losing its power to attack on its own. Of the 215 men with which it had started on May 12 — down from a full complement of about 250 — only seventy-five, including just three officers, were fit to fight by nightfall.

The summit was reached again the next day, but rapid counterattacks drove the attackers off. On May 14, Sugar Loaf became the focus of the entire stalled division. The 22nd Regiment was ordered to take it before nightfall at any cost, but more Japanese artillery from Shuri and deadly fire from unapproachable antitank guns repulsed every attempt. All approaches to the hill that gave the slightest protection of defilade were covered by intense mortar fire.

In the late afternoon, the commander of the 2nd Battalion ordered the remnants of G Company to try again, this time together with F Company. When the force of 150 reached the base of the hill two bloody hours later, 106 had been disabled, together with three of their four supporting tanks. Amazingly, the intensity of the mortar and machine-gun fire seemed to have increased.

Although riflemen normally carried almost two hundred rounds in their rifles, belts, and bandoliers, the counterattacks from the reverse slope and flanks depleted their supply in minutes. The open killing field was now littered with smoking hulks of tanks* and casualties who couldn't be recovered while it was still more or less light: Snipers were everywhere. But twenty-six men from a supply echelon now arrived with replenishment, and Major Harry A. Courtney Jr., the battalion executive officer (or assistant commander), had an idea. Courtney had spent the day and previous night with the forward units to bolster their morale after the loss of so many of their senior officers, especially G Company, which, after the wounding of Stebbins and Bair, was under its third commander. Now he formed up the new arrivals with the survivors of F and G Companies. Pressed against the base under devastating fire, the twenty-eight-year-old major told the group that he wanted volunteers for a banzai of their own: Otherwise, the Japanese would be down with a counterattack in the morning. "That hill's got to be taken and we're going to do it. What do you say?"

All said yes, and they stormed up after dark, comrades near the base braving continuing fire to collect the dead and wounded from the earlier attacks. At the same time, the exchange of grenades near the crest was at such close range that members of Courtney's group could hear Japanese grunting as they tossed theirs uphill. When Marines answered, their grenades raised so much dust that the hill slope was obscured. The dust turned to mud when a drenching rain resumed a few hours later. Then the rain of Japanese grenades and mortars grew more accurate. Courtney was killed by one or the other shortly after he reached the crest. (He would be one of four 6th Division Marines awarded the Medal of Honor, three posthumously; Dale Bair received the Navy Cross.) The leadership passed to Ed Pesely, another first lieutenant up from the ranks, who'd taken over F Company earlier in the day when its commander was shot in the hip. The thinning force dug in and threw grenades to try to avert an imminent counterattack by Japanese seen gathering in the light of illumination shells fired by American ships.

A Japanese grenade in a steady barrage of them shot fragments into Pesely. Bleeding from the chest, he radioed Colonel Woodhouse, who

---

*One man would count thirty-three of them after Sugar Loaf was finally taken. A battalion farther east that had approached the Shuri Line with sixty tanks ended with six operables. Mechanical problems disabled a few of the lost fifty-four, but Japanese fire accounted for most, some where they'd roared out to protect and recover wounded riflemen in exposed areas.

told him to try to hang on; he'd get as much fire as he could from every possible artillery battery, Marine and Army. The lieutenant colonel stayed on the radio with him all night, calling in coordinates for that artillery. Shortly after dawn, a handful of survivors — some fifteen of the sixty men who had stormed the crest with Courtney — withdrew, slightly protected from the severe Japanese fire by a morning mist.

One of the lucky fifteen was Wendell Majors, a G Company rifleman who realized sometime after midnight that he was the only man left alive on the hill's left flank. Private Majors began inching closer toward what he hoped would be friends in the center when a Navy star shell burst into light overhead. He dashed for the cover of a shell hole, jumped in, and felt a searing jolt. A bayonet fixed to a rifle, one of many weapons abandoned in earlier seesaw charges by both sides, had entered the back of his right thigh and was protruding from the front.

Another lucky one was Irving Oertel, whom De Mar had given command of a machine-gun platoon in the emergency of the soaring casualties. "Guys were all over the place, wounded, bleeding, dead — and the living could hardly move because you simply *couldn't* without getting hit. . . . Then it got dark and I stayed [below the crest] all night because the air was still really thick with Japanese fire. The platoon was down to a few men. We just didn't have any guys left."

Those who *were* left had reached the limit of endurance. Corporal Dan Dereschuk had been assigned to protect the right flank with two machine guns and eight G Company Marines — all sunken-eyed with exhaustion after five days with almost no sleep since crossing the Asakawa. The corporal had actually fallen asleep while digging his foxhole the previous night. He was even more spent now, and his face ached from shrapnel wounds suffered the previous day, but there could be no sleep. Mortar fire knocked out one machine gun and steady firing burned out the barrel of the other. Dereschuk's eight men dwindled to three, one alternately crying out and moaning from a stomach wound, which brought more grenades down on the three survivors. But they managed to evacuate at dawn.

After the seesawing of May 14, the 2nd Battalion was a skeleton and the entire 22nd Regiment was down to 62 percent of combat efficiency. May 15 was no better. The pitch of that day's fighting probably exceeded any in the division's history. Furious artillery and mortar barrages met the units that moved out early in the morning. The Japanese counterattack that had driven the last of Major Courtney's group from the hill pushed forward until early afternoon, retaking some precious ground just north of it. By the end of the day, the 2nd Battalion had to be withdrawn because it had taken more than four hundred casualties, almost half its normal complement. (Owen Stebbins's G–2–22 was down to one officer, a lieutenant who'd become the company commander, and a scattering of enlisted men.) Further reduced by sickness and exhaustion, the battalion could field 282 effectives out of its normal complement of roughly one thousand men.

Two boys had returned to combat that afternoon, their wounds from up north patched on a hospital ship and in Hawaii. Not finding their unit before dark, they tried to wait out the night in the safety of a cave. But since all were too packed with other Marines sheltering from the fire to squeeze in, they lay down just outside one of them, under a tepee formed by two huge rocks. A shell found its way even into what seemed that perfect cover and killed them before they could rejoin their buddies.

Only the Shuri Line in general has been more studied by military analysts than its Sugar Loaf segment — attention well deserved, for the skill and sweat of Japanese groundworks were in dramatic evidence here.

The terrain favored them almost by the nature of things; defenders almost always fortified the high ground, toward which attackers had to fight from below, along predictable routes. In this case, the Japanese had a better view of the attackers than usual, especially from the Shuri heights that dominated the entire area. Their cave exits on the rear slopes and the flanks as well as the forward slope allowed defenders protected from American shells to rush out to counterattack Marines who had reached the summit — and in force, because the unusually elaborate network of tunnels provided safe access for reinforcements. In addition, their machine-gun emplacements, hidden mortars, and other defensive arrangements had been sited with particular care, probably under General Cho's personal direction.

The crux was that Sugar Loaf Hill, or Heights 51.2, as the Japanese designated it, didn't stand alone in the defensive scheme, although the Marines began by attacking it alone. Much to the contrary, it was one component of a triangular system including Horseshoe Hill on the right and Half Moon, or Crescent, on the left. Those two formed a funnel for pouring dense fire down on Sugar Loaf, especially on every square yard of the summit whenever Americans approached it, as Sergeant De Mar and those who followed him discovered. The chance of surviving without a hit was measured in minutes rather than hours. Additional heavy artillery from the Shuri heights behind Half Moon was less accurate on individuals but more devastating to groups. More voluminous and more accurate than any previously encountered in the Pacific, the linked fire also ravaged troops attempting to flank Sugar Loaf from either side. And since many of the mortars were on the reverse slopes of Horseshoe and Half Moon, they were largely protected from American artillery and mortar fire until Sugar Loaf could be taken.

Few Americans there, as elsewhere in the best Japanese positions, saw the defenders at all. "We were fighting an underground enemy the whole time," one of them realized after catching on to their strategy. But the Americans could advance only by showing themselves. "Hell's half-acre" — the flat, bare ground beneath Sugar Loaf and the other hills — exposed them to simultaneous crossfire from the several interlocking sources, unseen and unreachable positions causing half to three-quarters of the American casualties.

"At first we were totally unaware of the power of the whole defensive line and Sugar Loaf's part in it," Captain Stebbins would put it with restrained regret. "It took several days to begin grasping the extent to which it was fortified with pillboxes, tunnels, mazes, and interlocking automatic weapons. It took another day before the mutually supporting system would become apparent: the key to the defense of that whole side of the island."

From the air, the full line bore a resemblance to a series of spokes radiating down and out from the hub at Shuri. Sugar Loaf was at the end of the one that reached farthest toward the western coast and Naha. That made it the key to the barrier protecting both Shuri and Naha, and explained Cho's personal interest in the preparations there and special reinforcements now ordered by Ushijima.

The American response was less well conceived. "No matter how heavy the supporting fire," a historian of Pacific combat has put it, "a moment arrived when men had to stand up and run across naked ground into a level stream of bullets." But that moment might have been better chosen than on Sugar Loaf, whose punishing triangular "fort" was further argument for devising something more imaginative than the 10th Army's bludgeon; for outflanking by the line with a second landing in the far south, as General Buckner's critics advocated. However, the pain at Sugar Loaf and almost everywhere else in the Shuri Line evidently didn't prompt the commander to reconsider.

A few infantrymen in the fighting units began to wonder, when off the line for breaks between their maulings, why they seemed to be fighting a Japanese fight, almost hand to hand, despite their huge advantage in equipment and firepower. The much-vaunted, perhaps congenitally overoptimistic American intelligence had again failed, in this case to give unit commanders like Captain Stebbins and Sergeant De Mar any idea of the deadliness of the Japanese preparations.

Japanese forward observers happened to use Hill 51.2 for spotting during their months of artillery training. Thus their knowledge of the terrain was such that "they often didn't have to adjust because they fired on the right spot the first time. . . . We couldn't have done them a better favor than attacking there," according to General James Day, who fought on Sugar Loaf and studied it during many later tours on Okinawa. "They had us beautifully zeroed in." Sergeant De Mar knew that without later study. "It was like target practice for them from all those damn hills. They had every foot covered with grids." Above all, it was pounding from Shuri's big 150-millimeter guns — hardly seen before in the Pacific — that made the battle horrendous for the Marines.

As the crow flies, Sugar Loaf was about a mile from the 32nd Army head-quarters in the tunnel deep beneath Shuri Castle. The battles being waged simultaneously along the rest of the eight-plus miles of the main Shuri Line — separate pitched battles into which Buckner's general of-fensive had broken down almost immediately — were equally ferocious, though they seesawed less between attack and counterattack.* The Shuri Line was accomplishing for the Japanese much of what the French had hoped from their Maginot Line, and that was far more Ushijima's feat than Imperial General Headquarters', since their support of him had been minimal for a campaign of such importance. Clinging to their fundamental belief in attack, IGHQ had resisted the Ushijima-Yahara strategy of a war of attrition fought from underground. Besides, they had already decided that the Tennozan of Tennozans, for which all pos-sible arms and equipment had to be husbanded, would take place on the mainland. Thus the Shuri Line was essentially the 32nd Army's own creation.

Almost a quarter of a million men faced each other there: "two great armies," in William Manchester's telling image, "squatting opposite one another in mud and smoke . . . locked together in unimaginable agony." In World War I's deepest combat, Manchester continued, battalion frontage (the length occupied by the battalion's thousand-odd men) was approximately eight hundred yards. "Here it was less than six hundred yards . . . about eighteen inches per man." The military analyst Thomas Huber would agree. "The fighting on Okinawa had features that were all its own, but even so its dynamics bore a startling resemblance to the fierce no-man's-land fighting of World War I."

Almost without exception, the Japanese had constructed a fortified po-sition on every hill and ridgeline, with other positions heavily covering their approaches. Taking each little knob and crease, even when only ten yards away, was an operation in itself. A rear-echelon Army colonel who visited one of the line's easier sectors during a relative lull in the fighting was almost as overwhelmed as a civilian would have been.

*Although American unit commanders on Sugar Loaf had little knowledge of the fight-ing elsewhere on the Shuri Line, the battle-torn Wana Ridge and Wana Draw area, on the 6th Division's left flank, was an exception. The 1st Marine Division's inability to take those objectives for another week further hampered the 6th Division because it enabled the de-fenders to keep firing heavy artillery at them from the west side of the Shuri heights. Thus the 6th Division's persistent concern about the progress at Wana.

There is nothing colorful about such an engagement. The rapid stac-
cato of machine gun fire continued along with the crack of .30-caliber
rifles and carbines. The plop of mortar shells as they left their muzzles
punctuated the incessant hail of other hardware. The whole valley was
covered with a thick pall of smoke that completely obscured the sky
overhead. . . . On the road, several hundred meters away, stood one of
our disabled tanks that could not be recovered due to the enemy artillery and mortar rounds falling in the vicinity. The burst of our own
artillery shells was clearly discernible as they landed on the hill in bil-
lows of flame and smoke and the whistle that accompanied them and
then the boom of the guns in the rear. Our ears were filled with the din
of battle and the smell of gunpowder penetrated our nostrils with a
burning sensation. This, however, was almost overcome by the stench of
rotting flesh while the sting and stickiness of the flies became almost
unbearable. The . . . dirty, slimy troops around us seemed somewhat
oblivious to most of these happenings, only concentrating on their particular job.

It was no miracle that two such congregations of men could cause each
other so much torment. By that time, both had absorbed lessons that
made the fighting harder. The Americans, among other things, had
learned how to keep getting water and supplies to the front so their men
could stay there. The Japanese had learned that the banzai attacks to
which they'd resorted on other islands were far less effective than the methodical warfare they were waging here.

Despite the Marines' conviction that they were being used for "target
practice," the Japanese agony was greater than theirs. Sugar Loaf's defenders were remnants of the 62nd Division, which had opposed the
American attacks in most of the south, reinforced by the 15th Independent Regiment, airlifted to Okinawa the previous July to supplement the
44th Independent Mixed Brigade that had been largely lost on *Toyama
maru*. Led by a highly skilled colonel named Seiko Mita, the 15th Independent Regiment was also suffering heavy losses. But the Sugar Loaf
complex had to be held as long as possible, and Ushijima committed
some of his last reserves of well-trained infantry troops to reinforce the
defense during the night of May 15. They included a farmer named
Masatsugu Shinohara.

When the Americans had landed, Shinohara was stationed about fifteen miles east on Tsuken Island in the Pacific. Tiny Tsuken controlled
the entrance to large Nakagusuku Bay, which the invaders needed for an
anchorage and landing supplies. Some 250 Americans set out in ten yellow rubber boats to take the little dot on the morning of April 6, roughly
when *Yamato* was setting out for Okinawa. Its little garrison had a field
gun, two heavy machine guns, and four mortars. As the enemy boats ap-

proached, Shinohara, leader of a mortar section, chased them off with some deadly rounds, after which American bombs shook the island for days, preparing for a second landing led by amphibious tanks. Of the defending force of sixty, twelve survived to follow their orders to find a way to rejoin the rest of the regiment on Okinawa. Crossing the fifteen miles on diminutive fishing boats, they snuck through the American force already controlling the Okinawan coast where they landed.

On Sugar Loaf's rear, southern slope, Shinohara and other Tsuken survivors crept through trenches to carry mortar shells to their positions. To avoid the enemy observation planes that seemed to be always hovering over them, they worked at night and tried not to move in daylight except to fire their mortars. Their rations consisted of dried biscuits only. They had no sleep during their seventy-two hours on or beside the hill.

Although the prodigious defensive works and their firepower dismayed the Americans, the Japanese saw themselves as children fighting giants. Still, Hill 51.2, the anchor for nearby Shuri, had to be held, no matter how impossible that seemed. Some remembered the feats of arms, courage, and endurance on the 203 Heights, a key hill in the high ground around Port Arthur that the Japanese had simply *had* to take in the 1905 war with Russia — and did. Few hated the Americans now; there was no energy for that. But all knew the enemy, as obsessed with Sugar Loaf as he was, must be killed because failure would lead directly to the loss of Okinawa, then the same kind of vicious assault on the homeland. Meanwhile, short rounds from the heavy artillery at Shuri inevitably killed many Japanese too. When Shinohara was at last withdrawn from Sugar Loaf, fifty-five of the original Tsuken group of sixty, including its commander, were dead.

The Americans, even those who had landed on Okinawa loathing everything Japanese, retained no more energy than their enemy for the luxury of hatred. "We were past that, past bitterness. This was simply the ultimate athletic contest that you had to win. A contest with literal sudden death and no overtime."

The same machine gun that got Captain Stebbins got me too. . . . I don't know what happened to the other guys because the concussion busted my right ear drum and I couldn't see or hear for a couple of hours.
— Marvin Zimmerman

When you got to the top, the Japs were just waiting for you and cut loose; all hell was being kicked out of our units. I was very, very lucky, one of the few to come down — by crawling over bodies.
— Joseph Bangert

A buddy and I were told to man a machine gun about 30 yards away. . . . A mortar and hand grenade barrage interrupted us about halfway there and

pinned us down. . . . A grenade went off in front of my face and blew my helmet to the back of my head. . . . I don't know if I'd been unconscious for any length of time. I looked over at the machine gun we were headed for and saw two dead Marines by it and thought . . . if we do get there, we'll be two more dead Marines. . . . Suddenly I heard a "poof" behind me. I turned around and saw that my platoon leader, a first lieutenant, was killed instantly by a direct mortar hit and the body was a black hulk. A little later, a Marine ahead of me began calling for a corpsman. I found out later the corpsmen were all dead or wounded. The Marine finally gave up calling and crawled [out]. . . . As he passed, I saw that his right foot up to the middle of the calf had been blown off.
— Declan Klingenhagen, about some thirty minutes on the morning of May 15

After ninety-six hours, most Americans were too depleted to remember what happened with much clarity. Some could hardly tell in which direction they were looking. The mental exhaustion led to many extra casualties, because not enough adrenaline continued pumping to maintain the concentration that would have prevented stupid mistakes.

Most of the 22nd Regiment was approaching that state on May 16, which some felt exceeded May 15 as the 6th Division's hardest day of the campaign and the war. Several companies of the 29th, including Dick Whitaker's, had recently joined the battle. Units of both regiments launched a general assault on the hill from the front and both flanks, and were met by crippling defensive fire. Replacements had replaced replacements, and re-formed units were again so badly shot up that some survivors had to take their organization into their own hands. The day's huge losses had again produced no territorial gain.

Before dark on that May 16, Anthony Cortese of Company I–3–22 ran to the top of a little hill called Chocolate Drop and looked at Sugar Loaf through his lieutenant's binoculars. He "couldn't believe what I saw; it was covered with dead Marines. A few enemy too, but mostly our guys, maybe a few hundred in my view alone." Cortese also saw some Japanese rebuilding their positions and ran back to tell his lieutenant that Sugar Loaf had to be softened up with more artillery before they went in. "But the next day, up we go into the slaughter, just like the others."

That next day, three battleships moved in close to blast Sugar Loaf, Horseshoe, and Half Moon with their heavy guns while aircraft carriers launched waves of bombing strikes. Then all three hills were attacked. Cortese's company of 245 men ended with three fit to fight. Two of them, including Cortese, quickly set up a machine gun to stop a counterattack until yet more reinforcements could be rushed in.

Dick Whitaker was told his go at Sugar Loaf was the eleventh. When his stint unloading invasion supplies on the landing beaches ended and he was assigned to F Company, 29th Marines, Private Whitaker was made a helper in a machine-gun squad, charged with lugging ammunition to the gun and protecting it with his rifle. Both his cans of .30-caliber ammunition, carried in addition to his pack and his own M1 ammunition, weighed about twenty pounds. But the hill seemed to him, as to all the others in the previous ten or so charges, almost insignificant in size, especially in its present blackened, denuded condition.

His platoon began attacking it shortly after seven o'clock on the morning of the seventeenth, single file, Whitaker third in line. Mortar fire cascaded on the little column as if the Japanese had been preparing for them alone throughout the night. Running, panting, sweating, thinking of nothing, not even of what his body was doing, Whitaker pushed forward and upward as if the absurdity were happening to someone else. Three squads with three water-cooled machine guns followed a lieutenant whose name he couldn't remember, the young replacement having appeared only hours before to take over the platoon.

The attack plan — to move right at the crest — never had a chance. Whitaker couldn't tell where the bullets and shells were coming from, only that he now understood the expression *withering fire*. As the men neared the crest, enormous and stunningly accurate fire from mortars, machine guns, and rifles deluged them, shaking the ground. When they reached it, they were showered with hand grenades from unseen positions on the reverse slope.

The next minutes seemed years. At the crest, the platoon couldn't unlimber their guns. Even if the right targets could have been found, it was impossible to set up the machine guns because each move out of a shell hole or scar in the ground brought another deadly burst of fire. Whitaker's gunner was hit. The new lieutenant was killed four steps in front of him. When the platoon finally did manage to set up despite the casualties, it was so outgunned that the men hardly knew where to shoot. Desperate nonstop firing burned out the barrels of all three machine guns. Whitaker realized that even if they somehow held on, the Japanese on the reverse slope would continue pinning them down indefinitely. He was frightened out of his mind yet impervious to fright because the scene was beyond his ability to grasp.

Down the line from him, more men kept getting hit as they sought cover until someone, Whitaker thought a sergeant, yelled, "Let's get the hell out of here!" But getting out would prove harder than getting up. Whitaker and another private named John Senterfitt picked up their gunner, groaning from a bad stomach wound, and tried to take him down to safety. Fierce mortar fire resumed the moment they started. Panting from the strain and from exhaustion, they took a measure of refuge in a shell hole. Other men passed them, carrying and supporting their own wounded through the smoke. "Corpsman!" they yelled. *"Corpsman!"*

A corpsman was found only when the two crawled to the bottom and across a portion of the open killing area to the marginal protection of the back of a small elevation north of the hill. Without glancing back, Whitaker carried the noise of Sugar Loaf's ferocious fire in his ears. It was not yet 8 A.M. on the fifth day at the hill. His fifteen minutes going up, taking fire, and coming down had been beyond belief. It would later strike him that "war is hell" was a silly metaphor because "no one has been to hell with the possible exception of Dante." He would prefer "hell is war" — but such conceptual notions did not come to him in the filth and fear themselves, when nothing mattered that wasn't immediate, instant. One of Ernie Pyle's last observations on Okinawa was that "life up there [at the front] is very simple, very uncomplicated, devoid of all the jealousy and meanness that float around a headquarters city." Men continued worrying about their buddies after coming down from Sugar Loaf. *Did we get everyone off? Did we leave anyone up there in that hell?* Slowly, immense relief that his duty there was over for now began washing over Whitaker, together with a vague hope he wouldn't have to go up again. It was up to his officers to think and to order that the hill must be taken. He only felt profoundly happy to have made it down.*

Attack, counterattack, attack, counterattack . . . each time units were pushed back, it was with many or most of their men killed or missing. The wounded were pulled into craters until corpsmen or fellow fighters chose a time to risk slipping out to them. Scatterings of unhit men left behind in holes fell asleep from exhaustion that conquered even fear of their hopeless situation out there all alone. Part of F Company would go up again, but without Whitaker's decimated platoon. Later on May 17, E Company of the same 29th Regiment was driven off three times, the remnants by bayonet charges. Although a fourth attempt might have succeeded, their ammunition was exhausted and too few men were left to spare help for the wounded.

The Japanese didn't know the attackers could not persist much longer because no more replacements were available. But their own casualties had

---

*Later, too, he would join those who idly wondered whether it might have been a mistake to assault Sugar Loaf. Wasn't something wrong in having to charge it so many times at such cost only to keep being beaten back? Actually, had his regimental commander known or suspected how strongly and skillfully the hill complex was defended, he might have tried to bypass it by advancing farther to his right, closer to the beach — which, however, would have left Japanese guns to control a larger area. The drawbacks of both alternatives strengthened the case for another major landing to outflank the whole of the Shuri Line.

been so heavy that the general in command of the defending force doubted he could hold on another day. Assembling the last of his reserves from the caves of Horseshoe and Half Moon, he told them that fresh troops would arrive in three days; meanwhile, they must defend Sugar Loaf to the death. After dusk, he sent them to reinforce the shredded units there.

But Americans had taken enough of the little rises to detect their movement. No fewer than twelve battalions of Marine artillery fired violently on the intended reinforcements, probably killing and otherwise disabling all but a dozen. (In all, 6th Division artillery fired 92,560 shells in the Sugar Loaf engagement.) That helped quicken the end for the Japanese the following morning, May 18. The commander of D–2–29 Company sent half his men around the right side of the hill with tanks. When they had engaged the defenders' attention, he sent the other half, also with close tank support, around the left flank. That turned out to be the final charge. The 1st Marine Division's taking of Wana Draw and Wana Ridge at last had silenced some of the artillery fire from there, two miles northeast. Here, enough damage had been done to the Japanese guns on the triangle's other two hills to enable the tanks to work their way ahead while eighty men from D Company ran up the forward slope to the summit.

Although six tanks were quickly knocked out, the other flankers encircled the hill from both sides and fired into the Japanese positions on the reverse slope while the infantrymen showered them with grenades. An hour of savage fighting followed, desperately brave Japanese squads attacking with satchel charges. By then, the defenders had been weakened enough for the Marines to properly dig in. By nightfall, the organized defense system had at last been cracked, after the hardest single battle in the Pacific War and, by some measures, the hardest for Americans anywhere in World War II.

The next day, General Shepherd, commander of the 6th Marine Division, received a dispatch from his immediate boss, a Buckner subordinate. RESISTANCE AND DETERMINATION WITH WHICH ELEMENTS OF YOUR DIVISION ATTACKED AND FINALLY CAPTURED SUGAR LOAF IS INDICATIVE OF THE FIGHTING SPIRIT OF YOUR MEN X MY HEARTY CONGRATULATIONS TO THE OFFICERS AND MEN CONCERNED. That night, a newly deployed Marine sat in "one of the deepest foxholes I'd ever seen," atop Sugar Loaf. Now that there was time to look, Naha's smoking ruins, only two miles southwest, could be seen from the crest. The stench of Japanese corpses, piles of which had been collecting for days — and of American ones too — was "indescribable." His own squad was down to four men. Flares from nearby warships "kept the area as light as day, all night long. We lost many men that night and the next day."

So did other American units; the battle still wasn't over. Sister companies D and E of Whitaker's F Company took heavy casualties on May 19 and 20 from fire from Sugar Loaf's rear slope as well as neighboring hills. "Taking a hill was a very loose term there," Whitaker's company commander would explain, "because our men hadn't gone *inside* it, where many Japs were still fighting from all those caves. . . . My own company had a night of terrible casualties after Sugar Loaf was officially secured. There seemed no end to it." Certainly not that night of May 20, when a machine-gun squad was included in reinforcements sent out at 10 P.M. — one of the rare American advances after dark — to support an infantry company that had suffered heavy casualties repelling a counterattack. The squad's sergeant had just managed to find cover in a trench when "all hell broke loose between Sugar Loaf and Horseshoe Ridge."

General James Day's studies of Sugar Loaf during his tours of duty on Okinawa — most notably forty years after the battle, when he would command all U.S. forces on the island — were prompted by his old fighting days, when he, a young corporal, was wounded on the hill. Day would conclude that more men were killed per square foot there — mostly in the open killing area beneath the hill — than anywhere else, including the larger and longer battles. The profusion of casualties stunned even the toughest veterans. Nearly three thousand were killed and seriously wounded, roughly the same as on all of Tarawa and more than at Casino, and up to 50 percent more than the worst battle for a single position on Iwo Jima. An additional 1,289 men were lost to sickness and combat exhaustion — but the numbers can't convey their effect upon the survivors. There was little hyperbole in a Marine's lament that "battalions melted away, companies vanished."

Parts of four battalions were mangled. Several rifle companies ended with a dozen men from their normal complement of roughly 250. In two, not a single officer or staff noncommissioned officer survived. In many others, privates ended in command of their shattered platoons. In Marine Evacuation Hospital Number 2, four or five men receiving transfusions in shock positions on litters learned they were their entire rifle companies' only known survivors. Medical personnel observed that their dismay was exceeded only by that of the green troops who'd still been in boot camp on L-day, seven weeks earlier, and were introduced to combat at Sugar Loaf.

So many tanks were knocked out that some companies alternated crews on the remaining ones. In the infantry, eleven of eighteen company commanders, including Captain Stebbins, had been killed or wounded. Scarcely an original platoon leader escaped. Mommy De Mar was G–2–22's only exception, and he was a substitute. "For the men who'd been pushed into this fierce cockpit for eight days," a survivor would remember, "it seemed like an eternity."

18 · Close Combat

Okinawa had a thousand Sugar Loafs. Everyone in combat had his Sugar Loaf.
— Dick Whitaker

Boot camp was designed to see if you could take it, then to make you take much more, far beyond your normal limit, so nothing would faze you in combat. It was amazingly grueling, but it was also nothing compared to the real thing. There it was physical and mental endurance; on Okinawa it was death.
— Norris Buchter

SUGAR LOAF'S SEIZURE opened the way to other strongpoints. Something snapped for the Japanese, as they knew it would, when the pivotal hill finally fell. Now the campaign would move more swiftly toward the American victory that had never been in doubt.

But that's the historical view, reached in retrospective examinations like this one, which are as distant from the war as the daring new swimsuit advertisements installed in New York subway cars during the weeks when the Shuri Line was mangling twelve thousand Americans. No one who dragged himself out of a foxhole at dawn knew that a climax had been reached around May 20. The fighting remained equally desperate, if smaller in scope, at the hundreds of other fortifications that gave the campaign "a fury, a storm of devastation . . . that surpassed the ground fighting seen anywhere else in the war," as Geoffrey Perret, a historian of U.S. Army operations during World War II, would write. Together, the two Army divisions east of Shuri took almost as many casualties as the 6th Marine Division on Sugar Loaf to the west. The 1st Marine Division suffered more during the first two weeks of May than the 6th during the two weeks that included Sugar Loaf.

Okinawa's southern landscape was studded with hill turrets that repelled assaults like the posts of a pinball machine. There was the Chocolate Drop–Wart Hill–Flattop Hill complex, the Tiger–Charlie–Oboe Hill complex; there were Hen, Hector, Conical, Red, Nan, Mabel, William, How, and Dick Hills, Rocky Crags, Kakazu West, Hills 60 and 178, Skyline Ridge, Ryan's Ridge, Gaja Ridge; hundreds of ridges and rises festooned with hidden gun emplacements, scores of escarpments where the Japanese positions were just as murderous to those hit by a howitzer shell or machine-gun bullet. The struggles for those places differed chiefly in their duration. The colonel commanding the Army's 383rd Infantry Regiment, which took Sugar Hill, eight miles east of Sugar Loaf, saw "the greatest display of courage of any group of men I've ever seen."

Radio Tokyo caught the incongruity of the lethal obstacles' colorful nicknames. "Sugar Loaf Hill . . . Chocolate Drop . . . Strawberry Hill . . . gee, those places sound wonderful! You can see the candy houses with the white picket fences around them. . . . But the only thing red about [them] is the blood of Americans." Perhaps that broadcast intentionally omitted such ridge names as Hand Grenade, Hacksaw, Bloody, and Tombstone. There was also ironically named Easy Hill on the Oroku Peninsula, where units attempting an encircling movement would take fire from fellow units, and Lenly Cotten, the boy who'd schemed himself into combat by going AWOL, couldn't fire for fear of helping cut down Americans. Cotten's platoon leader shouted for binoculars and someone handed him a pair. A bullet shattered his head before he could focus.

On Charlie Hill, just before Sugar Loaf, a squad of sixteen flame-thrower operators was cut to five. Two of those five were again advancing when a stunning barrage of mortar fire landed a shell between them, killing one and tossing the other through the air, the flamethrower ripped from his back. The following day, the latter was resting below the hill, nibbling at a C-ration. A shell from a smaller mortar hit the boy next to him in the back of his neck, blowing off his head and shooting his bloody brains all over the previous day's survivor and his can of hash. The rugged volunteer for the dangerous flamethrowing duty vomited uncontrollably.

The fiercest artillery fire to hit Melvin Heckt's machine-gun section came at 7 A.M. on May 21. When it missed his trench by yards, Heckt joined an attack on a ridge slightly south of Sugar Loaf, which had been more or less secured three days earlier.

> *Donvito* was first to be hit. Shrapnel in the hip. *Dunham* was next. He received a concussion and possible broken collarbone. . . . Next *Ward Bowers* was killed by Nip artillery. . . . We were in a couple of bomb craters. *Cullen* was passing by with a piece of shrapnel in his back. *Andriola* was helping him walk back when a Nambu [machine gun] opened up and wounded Andriola in buttocks and Cullen in leg. *Hassell* . . . ran out to drag them in out of the fire land and was hit in nose, mouth and arm. *McGee* and *Congdon* ran out and drug Cullen, Hassell and Andriola to safe positions. The artillery and mortar fire became heavier and more intense so I took my section and ran across the open field to *Baumhard's* 3rd platoon. It is lucky we moved out for Congdon was killed in the location from which we came and probably more of us would have been killed had we not moved. *Maritato* was hit in buttocks

and testicle. *Acuna* was hit. . . . Supposedly this [a ditch in which the survivors took cover] was the safest position anywhere. But the Nips lobbed a mortar right in the ditch and killed instantly 3 of my men, *Jennings, Ablett* and *McGee. Simmons* was sitting with the other three and received shrapnel in the leg, arms and side . . . that makes 6 men killed out of my squad. Too damn many boys to lose for any damn land. Poor Red McGee was blown all over the side of the hill. Only his red hair and scalp remained where he had been sitting.

May 23, when the unit pushed toward the outskirts of Naha, was similar, except that several survivors "cracked up" under the strain and one of the KIAs was "good old Al, a staff sergeant who carried ammo when he could have been in rear echelon — a boy who volunteered for everything." One of that day's wounded had a leg blown off. "They carried him into [a] wrecked hut and amputated with a kabar and pocket knife. *Davis* took it like a man and only screamed once. *Tex Durisoe* sharpened the knife and off came the stub." Now five were left in Heckt's machine-gun section, eight having been killed, nine wounded, and one more or less permanently deranged. So it went for many fighting units. While it was strategically downhill from the breaking of the Shuri Line's cornerstones, and historically inevitable, very few fighters had any notion of that at the time.

> *You were always wondering what the next five minutes would be like. Words like "tomorrow" and "next week" had little meaning. Life was all about now.*
> — Dick Whitaker

Most men in the lines on Okinawa knew little more than what was happening in their line of sight: what threatened from the next cave or rise or tree stump. Those who lived a week or more became marvelously expert in that, the constant proximity of death honing animal instincts and senses into a new nature. By the time Dick Whitaker's company reached Sugar Loaf on May 17, he well knew that "the difference between life and death often depended on what we smelled and heard."

Officers and noncommissioned officers learned to take special precautions because they were priority targets. When Owen Stebbins was hit on May 12, it was almost certainly after Japanese machine-gunners spotted Ed Ruess running to his forward observation post for their quick parlay. Following the runner, they aimed for the captain, the top man. The Japanese were expert enough in eliminating leaders to generate privates' compassion for their superiors. Day after day, single shots took down sergeants and second lieutenants crouched with their men — and also communications specialists carrying radios, and everyone involved with command. Night after night, infiltrators found their way to the foxholes of Americans who'd been carefully selected during the day. "I can't tell you how many lieutenants we went through," a Company G–2–22 private would commiserate.

That was why distinguishing armament such as .45-caliber pistols were tucked out of sight, why Captain Stebbins and all other officers rarely risked using their binoculars, and why "you never, ever mentioned rank in the field," as Ed De Mar would put it. Japanese snipers seemed uncannily patient and skilled at selecting anyone whose loss was likely to hurt more than that of an ordinary rifleman. "It was amazing how they could pick out anyone in command, sometimes just from the way they talked to others. That's why everyone tried to look as dumb and dirty as everyone else."

Americans also learned to hide everything — maps, binoculars, stripes or bars of rank — that would distinguish them from footsloggers. Salutes were anathema. "Any rifleman who saluted an officer on the line, targeting him for an enemy sniper, would have been in deep trouble," William Manchester would note.*

Marine contempt for Army leaders who supposedly put themselves in peril by maintaining rank's rituals on the line actually revealed as much about their snobbery as the reality. For despite the Army's generally greater distance between fighting officers and men, its combat units fought the same war and learned the same lessons as the Marines. De Mar would remember laughing at (probably apocryphal) Army officers who wore their insignia in combat. "The day before *we* went in, anything and everything came off that could single you out. If you didn't know a captain or a major by sight and he came up to you, you wouldn't know who he was — and if you guessed, you didn't show it to those Japs out there watching to see who gave the orders. That became second nature."

Similarly, medical corpsmen tried to be known personally by the units they attended so wounded men would call "Jones!" or "Bangert!" instead of "Corpsman!" or "Doc!" Japanese soldiers sometimes shouted the generic titles in order to pick off the men who ran out to help.

New replacements, however, often had no time to learn their corpsmen's names. Their failure to know and sense a great deal more accounted for the high proportion killed or wounded on their first days and even hours. Thousands came up to the front full of expectation and

---

*Almost all other manifestations of "chicken shit" also disappeared among fighting units. "And they didn't dog you to do the things you knew you had to do," a Marine private would recall about his officers, "unless you were a green replacement and hadn't had time to learn." When things were going well, the relation between officers and men was closer to that of coaches and players than anything learned in basic training — and the officers who risked their lives with their charges were more loved than resented. Dick Whitaker sympathized with those who had to exercise command, "an incredible burden when just taking care of your own ass was a twenty-four-hour-a-day job."

anxiety, saw the truth of combat, for which none was truly prepared, did something without the necessary artfulness, and — all in their first day — were delivered to a medical facility with grievous wounds and eyes still dumb with shock and disbelief.

No matter how rigorous Marine infantry training tried to be, only combat itself could teach real combat smarts. The training had made much of never bunching up so that no single mortar shell could hit more than one or two men, but green men kept being killed in bunches formed of fright. It was only after they saw this happen that an instinct to stay apart developed — yet not too far apart, because riflemen needed each other's protection on every flank. Then that instinct was further refined, and they kept the optimal distance in varying terrains of plains, hills, woods, and escarpments.

American infantrymen who survived a month in the line became as professionally skilled and personally cauterized as infantrymen anywhere. From the positioning of canteens to the placement of an extra knife under their shirts, everything they wore and carried was readied for the best chance to kill before being killed. Experience had taught that in this, all the skill in the world counted less than good luck, especially during an assault against a fortified position, when no one had any control over what ground a hidden Nambu light machine gun would spray or where a mortar shell would fall. Everyone knew that some of the most reckless men went miraculously unscathed and some of the most prudent and expert were blown to bits, that practicing every measure of protection couldn't prevent one's own number from coming up. Still, expertise offered slightly better odds of surviving. Men had seen the slack of rifle slings spell the difference between life and death.

(Needless to say, they disagreed about such fine points as whether or not to tape down hand grenades. Many hung them on the handiest place, their pack straps, but others, having seen the terrible accidents they inevitably caused, feared they might explode there, or one would fall off. The trade-off — added safety versus a second's delay using them — was disputed, but not by those whose experience brought them firmly down on one side or the other — like those who *did* tape, but forgot to remove it in time and were almost finished by that tiny delay in throwing one. "Usually you didn't have a chance to learn from your mistakes," Norris Buchter would reflect, "because they got you killed.")

As in all modern wars, ears became acutely sensitive to menaces broadcast by sounds, especially of the varieties of incoming fire. Each whoosh, whine, and whizz identified a bullet or shell type, with its individual trajectory and proximity. One low-velocity shell could actually be seen approaching, tumbling end over end. It was the new Japanese "screaming meemie" or "box car" or "garbage can," a 320-millimeter spigot mortar detonated by a propellant charge struck with a mallet. The 32nd Army had twenty-four of them. Their launching shriek — "like a locomotive from hell" — and earthshaking thunder when the 650-pound shells hit shredded the stretched nerves even of the veterans who knew they were extremely inaccurate, unlike the little Japanese knee-mortar, a simple, deadly weapon that gave almost no warning.

Many veterans were also convinced they could smell the enemy, just as the enemy could surely smell *them,* the consumers of so much animal fat. "Nip smell" was said to be "sweetish," a little like talcum powder. If you sniffed it in your foxhole at night, "every nerve quivered until dawn," an infantryman would remember. "And sure enough, you'd find evidence that your perimeter line had been penetrated. But you didn't need evidence; you had your senses."

Combat also sired a kind of medical wisdom. "Even at the tender age of eighteen," another infantryman would recall, "you learned a lot about the different aspects of wounds and what reaction to expect." A wounded man able to walk with help or talk clearly prompted smiles: Those were signs that he wasn't in serious shock. But calls for mothers were ominous. "People who called 'Mama!' didn't survive."

The sharpened senses and new powers of observation and analysis instantly assessed the relative dangers of new strongpoints and terrain. A silent counter recorded the number of Japanese rounds expended, since the dreaded Nambu light machine gun, for example, almost always fired bursts of six to eight rounds. Eyes almost automatically registered possible evidence of mines and booby traps. Bodies purged themselves of superfluous movement.

A new, semiconscious process considered each movement before it was made. Should the window of that half-standing "hut" be peeked through from the left or right? Should the next grenade be held an extra two seconds to prevent the targets from throwing it back? Should it be thrown with the right hand or left, which would allow quicker operation of the trigger finger? Should the rock ahead be jumped over in one bound or two? Is it time to move *now?* Is a sniper or machine-gunner zeroing in?

Bodies tuned themselves for supreme silence and stealth, which meant reducing combat gear to a minimum. "Every day you learned more," as one Marine would put it, "and the more you learned, the more you chucked from your kit. You lived by your wits, which meant traveling light." Gas masks had been discarded on the landing beaches, and the bulkiest nonessential equipment, such as supply packs with the extra pair of boots, quickly followed. "Experience has shown that a soldier will not carry equipment for which he has no apparent need," a confidential Army report titled "Principal Lessons Learned in the Okinawa Operation" would confirm. Every essential item was fixed on the body or in the pack so that it wouldn't make a noise by moving or shattering. "If you had to move quickly, even with full gear, the only sound would be your muffled footsteps," Whitaker would remember.

With some of their self-inflation also discarded, the Marines came closer to their image of themselves as the best fighters in the world, although the more worldly would later doubt whether they'd been better than the best Japanese. Veteran infantrymen would realize how much combat had changed them — almost into a new species with vastly developed physical senses, and almost everything else, including ethical considerations, shed like hazardous baggage. Although that was nothing new in war, this longest, largest, most intense land campaign in the Pacific reduced more participants to such a primitive state.

Infantrymen on Okinawa came to feel that their changed muscles, senses, instincts, *everything* had been designed for war and savage war alone, and that this was almost natural. Norris Buchter's first view of combat veterans on Guadalcanal, where the 6th Marine Division was being formed, had frightened him. "They were jungle animals, nothing we could relate to, nothing to fool around with — really tough and probably on the verge of going wacky from battle fatigue. You knew they belonged to another world." After his six weeks on Okinawa, he heard a replacement speak of his own group just that way — and realized they'd *had* to become those same new creatures. "It's from living on the edge too long, using your wits each minute to survive. It's watching, listening, thinking of what to expect next — not like just an animal but a hunted animal. You've seen so much horror. It's just a different life, indescribable."

> *Time had no meaning. Life had no meaning. . . . I had retired from the human race. I just wanted to kill.*
> — An anonymous American veteran

> *The only glory was in surviving, in staying alive.*
> — Robert Sherer, Dick Whitaker's company commander

Heightened instincts or not, men in the lines had a more limited perspective than almost anyone farther removed, perhaps because ignorance of events outside the immediate environment was necessary to free minds for the requisites of survival. Owen Stebbins felt his men's real life was generally twenty yards on either side of their foxholes, and Manchester agreed: "No Marine in the middle of a firefight, however clever he may have been, knew any more about the foe than the rifleman in the next foxhole." Many on Okinawa literally didn't know where they were during the fighting. "I obviously knew when we got into Naha," one would recall. "Otherwise, I had almost no idea. We weren't told and maybe we didn't want to know, or couldn't know; our minds were full of other things."

Without ever hearing Napoleon's saying about the combat soldier seeing only the pack of the man in front of him, Dick Whitaker knew exactly what it implied. "Maybe the Japanese knew more than we did. At least they might have recognized some landmarks: This was the hill they used to watch the stars from; that was the road they used to take to the beach. We didn't even know where we were or what lay beyond the nearest trees. All we had was a grunt of 'Follow me' from somebody in front — and a hope that he knew where the hell he was going, which he often didn't."

Hundreds of men died on Sugar Loaf never having heard its nickname. Many survivors never learned details that would roll from the tongues of war buffs. Superiors didn't necessarily keep information from the participants out of calculation; it was just as likely to be a sharing of ignorance. "I think one of the reasons we were never told anything was that nobody *knew* anything," Stuart Upchurch, who turned eighteen five days after L-day, would conclude.

"I followed orders, not knowing what they meant," a Sugar Loaf survivor from another company would recall. "When my platoon sergeant said we were taking Hill 63 tomorrow morning, that meant nothing to me. Hill 63 was just another ugly mound with blackened tree stumps that you and your guys had to crawl up, hoping it wouldn't be your last."

Private Thomas Hannaher of Minnesota would become one of the campaign's more thoughtful veterans, remembering with horror the cost to his friends and to Okinawans. But during the fighting itself, he was almost wholly unaware of most concerns larger than keeping his head down and his weapon oiled.

> I was one of many know-nothings on Okinawa. . . . I knew absolutely nothing about the overall battle plan, much less the plans for my battalion and battery and gun section. I was in my own very tiny world. Eat, sleep, work and wonder — *What am I doing here? Will I be killed? Why me?* And even if I do live through it, what next, the great battle of the Japanese mainland? How long could my luck hold? And there was nothing, absolutely nothing, I could do about it.

Hannaher's private world was his battery of 75-millimeter pack howitzers, which operated closer to the infantry than any other artillery apart from the 37-millimeters and heavy mortars. Still, that was a precious few hundred yards from the much more awful front lines. One ridge made a huge difference. "It was no lark for us," another artilleryman would remember. "We lived with quite enough danger even when we weren't being shelled — a man on the gun next to mine was killed by muzzle blast, for example. But we didn't have that constant feeling of imminent death, counting your days because they're numbered. When we saw those ragged, groggy infantrymen trudging somewhere, we felt real admiration for them. *They* were on the fighting edge, the real war — and we felt proud to support them, but from a different world."

American infantry got huge support from those close-range howitzers in addition to long-range artillery, the naval flotilla's massive guns, and the swarms of Army, Marine, and naval aircraft. But as the writer Bill Ross said about Iwo Jima two months earlier, the ultimate weapon on Okinawa remained a young man with a rifle. That was why infantry officers, those most perishable creatures, looked a little down on all others, even those in tank units. "Land had to be seized and held," said Owen Stebbins. "That was the only way the war could be won — on the ground."

The proximity to the Japanese on the ground depended on whether they'd fortified an area and when they decided to make a charge. At the moments of contact, it was often close enough for Whitaker to hear Japanese songs, whispers, the clatter of utensils — and, once, a shout of "Babe Ruth eat shit!" "If you left your foxhole and advanced, sooner or later you'd meet a Jap who was out there with a single purpose, to kill you. That's how close, the twenty or thirty paces you could lob a grenade. Sometimes you didn't have time to aim your weapon, you just fired and fired from any possible position and hoped your buddies kept pouring it on while you reloaded. Close was what it was all about. That's how you took ground."

The infantrymen who did that also often hugged the ground as tightly as they could. Very occasionally, something drove a sprinkling of them to the kind of feat dramatized in war movies: an unmanageable surge of adrenaline or exhaustion even beyond the ordinary, or nerves snapping because they couldn't stand the terror of being pinned down any longer. Sometimes it was a saintly calculation that all would die unless one took an otherwise lunatic risk. Okinawa's heroes disagree about why they performed their wild acts of gallantry. Some mention devotion to their beloved unit, whom an evil enemy was trying to kill. One former sergeant who charged Sugar Loaf although dazed with exhaustion swears it was all a mistake because he'd intended to run away from the fire instead of toward it. Then, when all the Americans near him were shot, he lay down, "absolutely quivering with terror."

Mistakes, lack of imagination, and stupidity were indeed among the explanations for supreme courage. Some men couldn't imagine themselves dead. Or the decisions to risk everything were made because the fighters "just became too utterly disgusted with the battlefield's unspeakable existence," as one would modestly interpret his action. "They became so full of revulsion against that hideous life that anything was preferable."

Some heroes appeared "unnatural" to average infantrymen. When one future winner of the Navy Cross "stood up like a bear with his BAR, shouting, 'Come on out, you sons of bitches!'" a machine-gunner who would later offer that description watched in wonder. "A man who stood up on the front line day after day almost looked like he *wanted* to get killed. He must have had a screw loose. No sensible man would do those things." Some of that species of hero would become problems back in civilian life.

Whatever the reasons, a handful bolted from their cover on a few occasions and charged enemy positions, shouting and firing. Those rare exceptions fill much of the standard American accounts of the battle, such as a lore-filled homage by James and William Belote titled *Typhoon of Steel,* which is rich in give-'em-hell action scenes where the good guys stand tall and "dish it out." "Let's go, men," reads a typical passage describing a officer leaping to his feet and running into a deadly ravine.

> This time the attack burst right through, with the flamethrower men dousing the caves with liquid fire as they passed. Emerging Japanese toppled to the riflemen. One cried weakly, "Banzai." "Banzai, hell," a Marine retorted, knocking him sprawling with a burst from his Browning automatic rifle.

When superiors heard of such exploits, a medal was possible, even the Congressional Medal of Honor, of which twenty-three, the largest number of any campaign in the war, were awarded for conspicuous gallantry on Okinawa. They served as the material for the bulk of traditional battle literature, filled with "storybook" warriors shouting inspirational challenges or curses as they wielded their weapons like figures from manly dreams, down to grins as they "took on" the enemy and "stopped them with a blaze of glory." But battlefield men knew that bravado, even without the comic-book dialogue, was no more typical than decorations were an accurate record of heroism. While a top-heavy percentage went to officers in command posts two hundred yards behind the line, many heroic acts out in front went unrewarded because no one survived to witness them. "I saw men do braver things than those who got the highest decorations but were never cited," an Okinawa veteran would recall. Besides, decorations tend to "romanticize the hellish misery called war."

Combat infantrymen learned the luck that helped determine who won medals was as unfair as in the matter of who survived and who didn't. Some of the bravest men walked away after their heroic acts, wanting and getting no reward other than saving their comrades. Major Courtney, as mentioned, assigned Corporal Dan Dereschuk to protect his right flank on Sugar Loaf, and Dereschuk's eight men dwindled to three, one with a bad stomach wound. All night, the two utterly exhausted and partially wounded "fit" heroes kept the Japanese at bay with rifles and hand grenades. After their evacuation at dawn, Dereschuk was patched up and returned to combat without rest or citation.

Whatever the merits and demerits of awards, the rare courage of the standouts represented a tiny fraction of the total man-hours on the line. A military historian's study concluded that only a quarter of men under fire in World War II and the Korean War fired back. The majority were too frightened to put into practice their intense training focused on precisely that. Although Army and Marine infantrymen surely performed far better on Okinawa, they spent much more time taking cover than leaping up from it. The Whitakers dug into the ground, vision restricted to the patch of charred terrain they could see from the lips of their foxholes, with no glimpse of the larger picture. In that sense, this account is as misleading as all others about the war in the killing zone, because "the real war will never get in the books," as Walt Whitman, a hospital nurse during the Civil War, declared. Those about combat are in a way its reverse, and to the degree that the Battle of Okinawa was harder than its predecessors, that's more than ordinarily true about this one.

News of Nazi Germany's collapse and of V-E Day had reached Okinawa the day before Paul Dunfrey scouted beyond the Asakawa, four days before Sugar Loaf. Many of the ships in the bays held services of thanksgiving, and battleships and cruisers joined field artillery in sending a huge salvo at enemy positions. The Japanese had no idea what prompted the earthshaking thunder* — but neither did many Americans on the ground. And even those who did know didn't much care. To men soaked with rain, covered with mud, and peering ahead for a glimpse of a rifle pointed at them, Europe meant little more than a place that was draining off the best supplies. "To hell with that war. *This* is the one I'm worried about."

Dick Whitaker felt the defeat of Nazism "was happening on another planet. We didn't think much about what was happening on the next hill, not to mention Germany." "They told us it was all over in Europe but it sure as hell wasn't all over for us," another Sugar Loaf survivor would remember. "The thing we really cared about was how soon some troops would be here from Europe to help us out."

The death of Franklin Roosevelt on April 12, almost a month earlier, had had greater significance for many fighters, most of whom had known

---

*Some nonmilitary items in the eight million American leaflets dropped on Japanese positions during the campaign — NIGHT BASEBALL REVIVED IN AMERICA, SHIRLEY TEMPLE ENGAGED — brightened otherwise wretched cave life for a few. But almost all continued dismissing the war news as attempts to weaken their morale, even while appreciating the fine quality of the paper. Far cruder Japanese leaflets composed for the Americans stressed the uselessness of their fight and the death it would bring them, together with suffering for their families. What a pity it was that American fighters were allowing their women to be ravished by men back in the States! "Don't you know that this operation to Okinawa is destroying your glorious mother land?" read a handwritten scrawl on a V-mail form that had evidently been taken from an American body. "Your useless battle will fat the dogs in Okinawa by yourselves's corpse. Imagine your wife crying at the sad news."

Meanwhile, Tokyo Rose kept broadcasting. "I got mine last night, your best girl got hers," Whitaker heard. "Did you get yours?"

only one president in their lives. But it was on the anchored or patrolling ships that the greatest grief was felt, or in the supply and reserve forces. Still, while many wept who weren't in the line, those who *were* felt only some pangs of sadness between dodging bullets and shells. They were too busy trying to catch their breath, catch some sleep, and stay alive.

In America, Roosevelt's death and V-E Day were among the events that helped keep the desperate hardships on Okinawa from reaching the public consciousness. The president's funeral, daily new evidence of the collapse of German defenses, and Harry Truman's early weeks in the White House seemed more important and relevant news. Throughout the first month of fighting on Okinawa, editors who'd long given greater prominence to the European War kept that up by allotting much more space to the dramatic assault on Berlin and the German surrender. MUS-SOLINI DEAD! YANKS MEET RED ARMY ON THE ELBE! BERLIN FALLS! HITLER SUICIDE IN HIS BUNKER! Compared to that, the Okinawan campaign was just another slog on a remote island; the greatest land-sea-air battle in history was usually reported on inside pages. And attention quickly shifted to new, again more dramatic stories of the Nazi death camps, Europe's future, and the imminent invasion of the Japanese mainland. Although Okinawa was now what a historian would call "the vortex of the war," that recognition would never enter the public consciousness.

Few dispatches from the island offered clues to the nature of the fighting. Almost all conveyed an optimistic summary of its overall progress and provided color about men interviewed behind the lines. Reporters weren't exactly prevaricating in that. It's worth repeating that most military "service" in 1945 was quite different from actual fighting. Combat, the real thing, had always been a relatively small part of military life, involving far fewer soldiers for far fewer days than its planning. Armies prepared by drilling, conferring, and cleaning latrines; only the men on their outer edges fell to bludgeons, swords, scimitars, and arrows — and since more sophisticated weapons required more personnel to transport and service them, technological development further reduced actual combat's proportion. "The worst of war is hell, but there isn't much of the worst . . . and not many soldiers experience even that much," a journalist-veteran recently summarized. Or, as Edward N. Luttwak put it, "Battle is no more characteristic of war than copulation is of marriage." (Luttwak, a student of military affairs, argued that this helps explain why combat remains part of the human experience "instead of being swept away by the outrage of those who have been in its hell and have come back to tell the tale.")

The Americans who fought their way past the deadly Okinawan caves represented a tiny fraction even of those serving in the Pacific at the time. On average, each was supported by nineteen others, usually from a considerable distance. Most of those nineteen endured varying degrees of discomfort but were as spared from the real horror as civilians. It was only within rifle range of the enemy where life became unlike anything previously imagined. Most reporters ventured no closer than five hundred yards.

It is largely as a result of the misinformation supplied by reporters that Americans have been led to think of themselves as the great saviors of the world. . . . The public is forced to swallow whole the idiotic stories of utterly uninformed men on so vital a matter as the enemy we have been fighting.
— Lieutenant j. g. Donald Keene, a Japanese-language specialist who served on Okinawa

Most men didn't talk about it. It was not that they did not want to talk about it, it was that when they did, nobody understood it. It was such a different way of living, and of looking at life even, that there was no common ground for communication in it.
— James Jones, a former combat soldier

Ernie Pyle went farther than most. World War II's most celebrated American correspondent landed on Okinawa on L-day afternoon and quickly began filing stories with his flair for the intimate. Almost singlehandedly, he'd compelled Congress to award mud-slogging doughboys the Combat Infantryman's Badge and extra pay. (The Marine establishment declined both, asserting that *all* Marines were combat troops.) As in the European theater, where he'd won his name and affection by writing from ground level rather than command heights, Pyle appeared to tell it like it was.

"Infantry's Friend" even toured a sideshow on the little island of Ie Shima, just four miles from the Motobu Peninsula in the north, where the Marines had overcome Colonel Udo's mountain artillery. Ie Shima, one of several offshore islands close enough to be almost extensions of Okinawa, accommodated Asia's largest airfield on its eleven square miles. Photographic evidence indicated it was undefended, which seemed confirmed by an absence of fire on attacking American planes. Actually, a strongly fortified mountain overlooked the field.

Pyle stepped ashore on April 17. The next morning, a machine gun fired on the jeep taking him toward the fighting. It killed "the most famous and beloved civilian of all the United States services."

According to a respected military historian, the shock brought the Okinawan campaign to the attention of millions back home. Not really. The loss of that single life simply became news while battles that were taking thousands, and locking tens of thousands in daily agony, remained nearly unknown. (In six days of fighting on Ie Shima, 240 Americans were killed and a thousand wounded. *The New Yorker*'s John Lardner called it a "quick and otherwise unnoteworthy little special campaign" except for Pyle's death.)

The irony is that Pyle's dispatches from Okinawa, as elsewhere, were far too pretty to convey any real sense of the fighting. Although his stories came a tad closer to the filth and pain than most others, they still missed by a mile — as they had to. "It's humiliating to look back at what we wrote during the war," a Canadian reporter would later admit. "It was crap — and I don't exclude the Ernie Pyles. . . . I suppose there wasn't an alternative at the time. It was total war. But for God's sake let's not glorify our role. It wasn't good journalism. It wasn't journalism at all."* As for Pyle in particular, Paul Fussell recently and fairly likened his copy to "emissions from the Office of War Information."

Dispatches from Okinawa outdid themselves in masking rather than conveying the hardships, partly because they were so extreme. Whatever few facts they supplied, their tone and assumptions fed the usual cheerleading prevarications. A few nonprofessionals who took the trouble to jot down their impressions got much closer to the truth — as in an officer's notes about the "demolished" village of Gusukuma.

> I was surprised to feel that the ground was soft and soggy under my feet. I looked down to see the knee of a dead Japanese soldier protruding from the dirt. As I stood, somewhat horrified, maggots oozed from the remains. The stench was terrible . . . green flies were everywhere, blowing the bloated bodies. I stepped into the entrance of a large cave and saw . . . the half-clothed body of a Japanese soldier. A rat scurried away to hide beneath a pile of rubbish. I noticed the body had a ghastly hole in the stomach where the rat had burrowed, feeding on the dead flesh. The soldier had been dead for several days and had swollen to an abnormal size. His legs burst his wrap leggings and a bulge protruded over his shoe tops where the shoe would not permit it to swell further . . . his eyes were bulging from his head and his close-cropped black hair seemed ready to pop from his head.

Accredited correspondents omitted almost all such details, and without the "almost" when describing the home team. Most of their "human interest" stories and "Hi, Mom!" features about hometown boys could only mislead readers about life in the field, not to mention Japanese behavior. There was no mention of all-night retching with disease and fear, no moans or screams or mental disintegration, let alone shot-off faces and testicles.

Despite Pyle's half step closer to some aspects of the real thing, his outlook helped explain why Europe's less grueling and cruel fighting got

---

*Quoted by Phillip Knightley in *The First Casualty,* his compelling exposé of war reporting.

more recognition. Sent to the Pacific in late 1944 under heavy official pressure, he continued to believe the European war was more important. And his treatment of Okinawan civilians helps explain why the major story of the campaign, measured in *real* human interest, wasn't told at all to the good folks back home. His little vignettes had Okinawans going their Oriental-inscrutable ways while they were actually suffering horrendously.

Even the best journalism in the most authoritative pages now reads like fluff. Battle hardships were couched in images of a hard-fought but essentially sane sporting event. "Leathernecks and doughboys of the 10th Army held the Japanese key fortress of Shuri in a giant cup-shaped pincers today as they turned both ends of the Okinawa battle line." Pyle's accounts of Americans' misery ventured all the way to the infernal biting of Okinawan fleas and mosquitoes, as if that was what distinguished infantrymen's ordeal from normality. The reality later revealed in the memoir of Eugene Sledge, a pious eighteen-year-old Marine, would have almost nothing in common with the dispatches filed at the time. "I felt sickened to the depths of my soul," Sledge wrote of his first taste of combat. "I asked God, 'Why, why, why?' . . . I had tasted the bitterest essence of the war . . . and it filled me with disgust."

The why of ignoring war's bitterest essence is easier to explain than the why of war itself. Reporters played on the same team as the fighters or didn't get to the game. Having provided exclusive access to the material, the military exercised tight control on how it was written up. A maverick convinced the truth was more important and courageous enough to defy all convention of supporting the American side wouldn't have lasted long. The great war correspondent John Steinbeck knew that "the foolish reporter who broke the rules would not be printed at home and in addition would be put out of the theater by the command. . . . We were all part of the War Effort." David Lloyd George had put the reality in a nutshell: "The correspondents don't write and the censorship would not pass the truth."

Whitaker's cheery letters home also left the bitter essence unmentioned. Even with the talent to convey it to outsiders, he'd not have wanted to attract the censors' attention or distress his parents. Other letter writers tried to hint that there was much to tell, but despaired of communicating its immensity. "So far I have been very lucky," went a typical passage on Red Cross stationery, "and I know it is because of all your prayers and . . . mine. I have a lot to tell you when I am in a position to and that isn't right now." But that writer, like most survivors when they returned, would never be able to tell his family, despite their great closeness. "There was no way to describe it because it was beyond every imaginable aspect of life." Or, in Dick Whitaker's take: "It's really very hard to describe what it was like on Okinawa. Almost anything you did could get you killed, including absolutely nothing."

You could always tell whether men were moving up or coming off the line. Usually those coming off . . . had a different look — dull, sightless eyes showing the strain, misery, shock, sleeplessness, and in veteran fighters, the supreme indifference of young men who have lost their youth and will never forget it.
— William Manchester

I arrived as a replacement in the middle of May and boy, was I happy to get off that miserable troopship and rocking landing craft! But I was already ducking by the time the ramp came down. Okinawa didn't have a landscape, it had a glimpse of hell on earth. . . . I spent my first night in the replacement area, awaiting assignment. There were screaming dogfights above, kamikazes crashing into ships and artillery fire I couldn't tell whether was ten miles or ten yards away. I was scared. And just miserable.

In a few hours, the rain water was up to my waist. . . . The casualties were tremendous. Near us was a huge mound of personal belongings — of the dead. I was never a thief, but this was survival: My boots were all mush and I had to get some dry socks. And that gave me another fright because a big Marine at the mound, maybe who'd just lost a buddy, almost shot me for reaching into it for a pair. And I hadn't even seen the fighting yet.

Then I was rushed to Sugar Loaf and couldn't believe the look of the guys coming down from there. I don't mean the wounded or the dead but the living, who didn't look alive either.
— Buzzy Fox, machine-gunner on Okinawa

All of that gave the home front, less equipped to picture Pacific conditions to begin with, a much vaguer notion of the fighting on Okinawa than it had of more familiar Europe. The American public was further disadvantaged because generations had been protected from bombing, shelling, and mutilation. Apart from the minority who fought, they were largely conditioned to assume war's victims to be mostly the enemy, who'd brought things on themselves. But even if reporters had lived on the killing edge and could have reported honestly, the battle's ways differed too greatly from anything their audience could have imagined from newspaper or radio copy. Almost all infantrymen at the Shuri Line periodically felt the experience wasn't happening because it couldn't, it was too unnatural.

Most of Okinawa's heavy annual rainfall came during the four weeks or so that usually began in May, when skies could deposit ten inches a day. The spring of 1945 happened to be much wetter than usual. Low-lying clouds delivered ceaseless deluges, day after day. One writer claimed all previous rainfall seen by Americans was "reduced to the status of Scotch mist." Even without a sharp wind lashing their faces with drops, they were often too dense to make out fellow platoon members in neighboring foxholes — and they made fires for coffee and hot food impossible.

Ponds of ochre floodwater on the lowlands became lakes that swallowed eight-wheel trucks. Replacement troops dug their first foxholes, took cover in the souplike mud, and were in water to their waists within an hour. Elsewhere, the ground was everywhere so slippery that some men used their precious rifles as walking sticks.

No one on the line had a moment's escape from the all-submerging mud. "You were knee-deep in it," Joseph McConville would remember. "Sometimes you slept standing up in it." Day after day, men shivered in their puckered skin. An outbreak of typhoid occurred during those downpours. "Jungle rot" spread from feet to the crotch. Ringworm in the belt area was sometimes so painful that combat troops couldn't wear their packs or cartridge belts.

In World War I, a painful condition caused by prolonged exposure to wet and mud was called trench foot. Now it was "immersion foot," and dry feet became a longed-for luxury. Dick Whitaker's reeked of mud and the sweat of exertion and fear. He wore the same socks, and the same underwear, for weeks. Men who found streams for washing on their breaks from fighting had to cut off their socks. When a jeep towed up a large tank of water one day to where Whitaker's platoon had been pulled back from the line, each man was allotted a helmetful. Whitaker had a bath with his and felt gloriously clean. Then he dressed, saving for last a pair of treasured clean socks he'd been carrying in his pack. Standing on a tall rock, he lost his balance pulling on the second one and fell into a pond of muck.

It was much more tragic than funny at the time — too much like the rifles that fell into the same stuff when a bullet or shell knocked their users flat, then wouldn't fire. When enemy soldiers on Sugar Loaf approached one man whose rifle was useless with mud, he frantically kicked the bolt home with his foot, then had to hope it wouldn't explode in his face when he fired. He was lucky. He kept kicking and firing.

The battles for Sugar Loaf and all the Shuri Line's other strongpoints took place during the most torrential deluges. Sleepless pilots would hear the rain beating down and wonder whether it would ever stop. They lived "in a world of water and mud," their feet stuck in the gluey bog of the "company street" of tents, their clothing and bedding never dry. Those were the lucky pilots in the rear who *had* tents and bedding to get wet, so unlike the infantrymen. After charges at those strongpoints, clusters of survivors huddled not only in mourning for their dead and fear for themselves but also in the cold rain's soaking, incessant "misery beyond description."

Battlefield mud compounded it. Vehicles using Okinawa's dirt-track roads during the dry months produced a blinding cloud of thick red dust — which now turned to sludge that clung to everything. Men without a suction-breaking covering of burlap bags on their boots needed help to pull themselves out. Jeeps got mired. The trucks, tractors, and bulldozers that came to the rescue were swallowed. Tanks disappeared in lakes of ooze. The need for ammunition and other supplies being insatiable, infantrymen, often near exhaustion from combat's physical demands and mental tension, had to take on the extra work of carrying as much as they could on their shoulders and backs, wading through quagmires impassable by motorized transport.

Most of war's literary and cinematic dramatization blithely ignores that "grueling facet of the infantrymen's war," as Private Sledge would later call it. It implies that ammunition happens to be at hand whenever needed for giving the enemy hell. Every time veteran Whitaker would see a movie hero who never ran out of ammunition, he'd remember the way Okinawa's few moments of intense firing could exhaust the precious supply and leave him defenseless.

The average infantryman, even those not lugging extra weapons like machine guns, BARs, flamethrowers, or satchel charges, was a small arsenal. He heaved his way through the mud with his rifle, backpack, and a cartridge belt containing eight to ten clips of eight rounds each, a considerable burden in itself. Two to four hand grenades dangled from his belt, and since that supply could be exhausted in minutes during emergencies, only the weight kept most from carrying more. (Whitaker had a constant fear that an enemy bullet would hit one of the grenades he clipped to his cartridge belt or pack strap.) The combined load made very heavy exercise of combat's running, dashing, and crawling under fire.

Whitaker's two steel boxes of .30-caliber ammunition were in addition to his other burdens. Although he and other machine-gun carriers improvised cushions and shoulder straps, their arms felt as if they were coming out of their sockets after twenty minutes of lugging — which lasted hours, on and off.

They were weakened by lack of food, sleeplessness, and at least a touch of dysentery. Hauling was even harder when much of the front was a morass — and when Japanese artillery, zeroed in on every road near the Shuri Line, forced them into rice paddies. Carrying the wounded was harder still, and more nerve-racking. Strong young men became so exhausted that they hesitated to put down their loads for fear they wouldn't be able to pick them up again. An ammunition carrier in another machine-gun platoon would bear his load across one large rice paddy farther south, then fall to the ground. "If a Jap had come around a tree and aimed at me, I truly wouldn't have been able to move. It wasn't exhaustion but stupefaction." Melvin Heckt, leader of the decimated machine-gun platoon, found some humor in it. "Here I am now twenty years old and I don't feel a day over forty."

In keeping with Murphy's Law of War, mandating that those who have it worst should also be worst sustained, fighting men on Okinawa ate wretchedly. Combat so strained the nervous system that many couldn't swallow much anyway, despite their enormous expenditure of energy. All had almost constant thirst, and worried about supplies of water only less than of ammunition. The oily-tasting liquid was brought up in five-gallon tanks. The grateful recipients dropped a purification pill — not always effective against dysentery — inside the "slimy green shit" and drank as if in the desert. But many had to force themselves to eat.

Basic nourishment was almost always available in the form of a K-ration in one's pack. The little box contained a sardine-size can of "ungodly" hash and cheese or ham and eggs, soluble coffee or lemonade, and some hard biscuits. The larger C-ration offered a slightly more tempting can of pork and beans but was heavier to carry, an important consideration to men who lacked the energy to be hungry and whose appetites were further depressed by constant fear and revulsion of the battlefield's sights and smells. Starting out thin, Whitaker could hardly afford his loss of twenty pounds, which was average. He lived for days on cigarettes, included in the rations, and on "dog turds," fortified fruit-and-chocolate bars that provided quick energy and didn't melt in heat. "You carried them in your pack until you thought you were starving. You took one bite and felt stuffed."

Whitaker ate his single hot meal during the Shuri Line fighting about a week after Sugar Loaf, when word was passed down that everyone should assemble with his mess kit because a truck was expected with mess hall chow. No one in the platoon had a mess kit by then, the metal being too given to dangerous rattles. Whitaker did have his canteen cup, into which a scoop of hamburger meat was plunked when he reached the truck. Then an orange was pushed at him to cap his feast.

Another man's single hot meal arrived by parachute. But some had no hot food at all in two months of savage fighting. Kitchens were closed when the going got tough. Mess staffs were shifted to combat duties as riflemen and stretcher bearers.

Near the end of the campaign, a mobile kitchen was opened for a Marine unit that had had no hot food in nearly two months. A radio operator salivated as he speared a piece of hotcake, but he couldn't eat it, this time not for lack of appetite. Fearless flies twice the size of any he'd seen in America flew into his mouth before he could rush his first bite in. He didn't try again.

Lice and fleas were separate, additional scourges. The fleas, generously hosted by native goats, infested the beaches, houses, villages — and now the foxholes too. Few infantrymen on either side were spared. The May 3 entry of a diary found on a dead Japanese soldier noted the lucky break of being assigned no night duty. "But it was hot [in his cave] and there were so many fleas and lice that I couldn't sleep a wink." However, those two insects that increasingly tormented the occupants of the caves and foxholes played second fiddle to monster flies. Japanese soldiers had been harried by tenacious, seemingly angry clouds of them even before the fighting began. "They were as big as horseflies," one would remember, "with red heads and fierce, glaring eyes. They swarmed all over our faces whenever we came close to the piles of garbage."

Flies had previously fed on native night soil and other decay — but not extravagantly, since prewar Okinawa threw out little. Growing piles of rubbish and untreated wastes that accumulated while the Japanese soldiers were digging the fortifications greatly increased their number, but they were nothing compared to the treats of combat's effluents that now littered the landscape. Ever larger and more relentless swarms feasted on the garbage, excrement, and rotting corpses now strewn over the battle sites. When Americans were lucky enough to be pulled off the front line for rest and regrouping — only a few hundred yards back, but with less likelihood of being hit — hot coffee often waited. Flies would attack it even as it was being poured, although the hand not holding the cup was fighting them off with maddened waves. Whitaker was one who craved coffee — anything liquid — despite his dead appetite. "But if you put down a cup for one second, you could hardly see it when you looked again. The surface was covered solid by huge black insects. Or green ones."

(When Marine units passed the ruins of a sugar refinery in late May, the grotesque specimens feasting on a thick, dark ooze that had run from smashed vats of molasses and now stuck to the boots of the advancing troops prompted fear of an epidemic. Planes sprayed the area with disinfectant. The Japanese, probably suspecting the spray marked the start of chemical warfare by the racist American beasts, began shelling furiously with the remains of their artillery. The Americans, having left their gas masks on the beach on L-day, were equally frightened that the Japanese beasts would use the incident as a pretext to deploy their own chemical weapons.)

Americans believed the flies' trips from the corpses to their coffee helped spread the dysentery that plagued nearly everyone. (There was also a mild outbreak of typhoid, caused by bacilli that fed in the native and military night soil.) Weakness and loose bowels prompted some Marines on the line to leave their precious cover to run to a corpsman for paregoric. Many who wouldn't take that risk had to mess their pants. Whitaker was among the majority who had at least a touch of dysentery much of the time. On bad days, he'd vomit when he lay on his stomach and lose control of his bowels when he lay on his back. He "tried to do neither — to *live* — by finding a position on my side. Not always easy in a foxhole filled with mud and water."

One product of the endemic dysentery lay before everyone's eyes and noses. Combat fronts had no sanitation facilities. When there was time and the risk was acceptable, a hole was dug several inches into the ground. During action on the line, however, the surface of the ground had to do for the hurried functions, the rain, shelling, garbage, dysentery, and rotting corpses in their various colors making the land on which infantrymen lived all day and night worse than open cesspools.* The pus and puke and slime and shit of a quarter-million harrowed men mixed into the battlefield's seas of mud.

John Keegan would point out that battle, always unpleasant for a minority of its participants, "has increasingly become an intolerable experience for the majority." Modern warfare has transformed its environment into a hellhole even without the fighting. Okinawa veterans make the same point by suggesting that anyone truly interested in combat's reality can glimpse it in peacetime simply by living a week or two in a hole in the ground filled with water, mud, excrement, and gore, and listening to a recording of ceaseless artillery thunder. Without dysentery to drain your strength and swarms of flies feasting on the product of feverishly running bowels, without the maggots and stink of decaying corpses and the near impossibility of proper sleep, without even the shells, bullets, exhaustion, and fear, a short spell there, in a drenching rain and filthy wet clothes and without proper food, will begin providing an inkling of an existence not conveyable by words or film.

Eugene Sledge, whose searing memoir of Peleliu and Okinawa comes closest, fought with the 1st Marines at Wana Draw, two miles northeast of Sugar Loaf. The stink of one area's "half-flooded garbage pit" a little farther south was worse than most, but Sledge's life depended on digging into it for cover. At eight inches, he encountered "a mass of wriggling maggots that came welling up as though those beneath were pushing them out." He had to keep digging. Minutes later, his spade hit a rotting Japanese corpse — "dirty, whitish bone and cartilage with ribs attached" — with an overwhelmingly nauseating odor. "How I managed not to vomit . . . I don't know. Perhaps my senses and nerves had been so dulled by constant foulness for so long. . . . Having to wallow in war's putrefaction was almost more than the toughest of us could bear."

---

*Buddies often sent off men picked for lone missions — to scout a ridge, secure a building, or check a radio wire — with a reminder to "keep a tight ass." Unconsciously or otherwise, that good-luck wish and admonition to come back alive derived from the prevalence of messing one's pants when bullets and shell fragments hit. Forty-five years later, one perfectly sane veteran packed toilet paper even when traveling to luxury hotels. "I just can't leave the house without it. I can't forget how we lived."

When volunteers to retrieve Sugar Loaf's dead found the body of Major Courtney on May 15, they had to break the future winner of the Medal of Honor's legs to make a smaller "package" that would lessen the danger of the dash back down through the Japanese fire. That afternoon, the exhausted litter bearers hitched a ride back to their units in a raucous amtrac with about twenty corpses and eight inches of sloshing water in its well. One eighteen-year-old who had to ride above that well supported himself on a handle, but lost his grip when the vehicle climbed a knoll. He fell into the water, now full of maggots and body pieces. The putrid liquid rushed back at him whenever the amtrac again made a climb — and the vehicle's roar drowned out his hysterical screams, so that his swallows and wrestles with the corpses continued until he blacked out. "What I was thinking then and all through these years [until the 1980s] was 'Enough, enough! We've been abused enough!'" But he was unable to mention such episodes for forty-one years, until he fought to a breakthrough with the help of an enlightened veterans' hospital.

Men didn't talk about such things at the time because, Sledge would explain, "They were too horrible and obscene even for hardened veterans. The conditions taxed the toughest I knew almost to the point of screaming. . . . It is too preposterous to think that men could actually live and fight for days and nights on end under such terrible conditions and not be driven insane. But I saw much of it there on Okinawa and to me the war was insanity."

Recent films that have begun to show young men gripped in combat's pandemonium of shocking noise, confusion, and terror necessarily leave out combat's largest dirty secret: the pervasive filth and decay. Replacements making their way toward the front lines heard a rumbling like a distant thunderstorm. It grew louder and more ominous as they approached the heavy guns and the clamor of battle itself: the roar of tanks, whump of mortars, shriek of rockets, whoosh of shells streaming through the curtains of flame, and dense dust of cordite. Men in amtracs sometimes couldn't hear their roaring engines over the din, which was heightened by shouts and explosions. But the smell hit before the noise began to daze. Manchester would call it "a stench of piss and shit and rotting human flesh. . . . You are with men, all of whom, like yourself, have some shit in their pants and otherwise stink of battle. It was not an animal life but worse."

Sledge found his only way of bearing "the monstrous horror of it all" was to look away from it — upward to the rain clouds — and repeat again and again that he'd soon awaken from his nightmare. "But the ever-present smell of death . . . the overpowering stench . . . saturated my nostrils. It was there with every breath I took."

*It was always "one more hill." You were always told it was the critical one till
you took it, then there was one more.*
— Mitchell Zampikos, 22nd Marine Regiment

*Everybody expected to be hit sooner or later. Almost everybody had been hit
already, we ended with over 100 percent casualties in our platoon and company.*
— Stuart Upchurch, 22nd Marine Regiment

Coming from a culture that valued individual life, infantrymen took time
to comprehend a world whose purpose was to extinguish it. But death became so common that they soon felt an odd dichotomy. They'd come to
treasure the lives of their fellows, who could be lost at any moment, more
than they had treasured any other. Yet all their lives together seemed of
little consequence to the forces that had delivered them there.

Especially heavy casualties among young platoon leaders kept the men
from remembering their names or even faces, as when Dick Whitaker
went up Sugar Loaf. Those officers came and went too fast. Only two of
the twenty-one Company I–3–22 officers who landed on L-day weren't
killed or seriously wounded. Several companies replaced some of their
officers three and four times.

Second lieutenants in rifle companies seemed to Sledge a species made
obsolete by modern warfare, wounded or killed with such regularity that
"we rarely knew anything about them." When the platoon tended by Corpsman Joe Bangert, the erstwhile wiseguy, went up Sugar Loaf, he "couldn't
tell you my own lieutenant's name because we lost him so fast — and so
many others." Stuart Upchurch's platoon went through so many that "we
started to just ignore the new ones. They really couldn't tell us anything we
didn't know. The smart ones did well to learn from us."

The second lieutenant in command of the platoon of James Day, the
corporal destined to become a general, was killed in the field. His replacement died of wounds in a hospital. Most of the company's other
officers fell, together with many of their superiors. His battalion commander and the battalion executive officer died in action. His regimental commander, a replacement for one seriously wounded on Sugar Loaf,
was killed days later. Nearly the entire regimental command structure
was lost — and most of the troops. Day's battalion started with 1,145 men
on April 1. When its fighting finished in June, some three thousand past
and present men were listed as having belonged — which meant each
man had been replaced twice.

On the day before Christmas 1944, a furious football game had been
played in the Mosquito Bowl, a field pounded out of Guadalcanal's coral.
Thanks to the Corps's appetite for recruiting athletes, the teams were
studded with former college and professional stars (some of whom con-

sidered that game, played without shoulder pads or helmets, the roughest of their careers). Fourteen weeks later, at least twelve of the sixty players — including All-Americans and other captains of college powerhouses — had been killed on Okinawa, and the other forty-eight wounded or injured almost to a man; thirty-one received the Purple Heart. The spectators fared better only by comparison. Casualties among the nine infantry battalions that watched the game reached 75 percent: four hundred officers and 7,822 enlisted men killed and wounded.

After a few weeks on Okinawa, a college graduate who'd been haunted by not making officer realized how lucky he was. He'd be the sole member of his eleven-man machine-gun section not killed or wounded seriously enough for evacuation. He'd started as an ammunition carrier like Whitaker, but all ten men in front of him were shot "like ducks in a row. I was the last duck, but the campaign ended just in time." That was common; Melvin Heckt's sixty-two-man platoon ended with two lucky ones. Sledge's company finished with twenty-six of the 235 officers and men who'd made the landing. The same percentage was left of Owen Stebbins's G-2-22 Company, two platoons of which ended with only three men from L-day, one of whom was seriously wounded twice.

Army infantry units suffered similarly, prompting efficiency experts who later analyzed the campaign to recommend attaching a Graves Registration platoon to each regiment because the personnel who dealt with the bodies "proved insufficient . . . and necessitated the employment of frontline troops to evacuate the dead."

What men endured on Okinawa was so frightening and painful that many try to make light of it, even joke about it. Just in terms of eating, sleeping, staying dry and evacuating, it was as tough a 24 hours as anyone could imagine.
— Dr. Edmund Shimberg, who served as a nineteen-year-old corpsman

The mud was knee-deep in some places, probably deeper in others if one dared venture there. For several feet around every corpse, maggots crawled about in the mud and then were washed away by the runoff of the rain [that] poured down on us. . . . The scene was nothing but mud; shellfire; flooded craters with their silent, pathetic, rotting occupants; knocked-out tanks and amtracs; and discarded equipment — utter desolation. . . .

I existed from moment to moment, sometimes thinking death would have been preferable. We were in the depths of the abyss, the ultimate horror of war. I believed we had been flung into hell's own cesspool.
— Eugene B. Sledge, on the ten days of fighting at Wana Draw, two miles from Sugar Loaf

It's not quite true, as Marines like to remember, that they were stalwart to a man. One young private shot himself in the toe as his company advanced toward the Shuri Line. His company had only two officers for some critical fighting a few days later because a junior one "mysteriously disappeared," in the company commander's words, after four of his six fellow officers had been hit during the first day at Sugar Loaf. The missing officer was found to have turned himself in "sick" to his battalion aid station. An officer of another company with shocking casualties stayed behind to cover his men's retreat one day until volunteers ran back with a poncho to drag him out from where he lay wounded. A corpsman later noticed his leg wound bore signs of powder burns.

Of the thousand men who were pinned down by machine-gun fire on the way to Sugar Loaf and waiting for the order to push on again through it, one burst out crying, threw away his rifle, and began crawling to the rear. Also during the assault on the Shuri Line, a fine regimental commander's failure lost him his command. After the admirals' pressure on General Buckner to advance more rapidly, General Shepherd ordered Sugar Loaf taken "at any cost." When the cost became horrendous, the regimental commander in question — a tough, fully battle-tested Marine colonel — told the general he couldn't order his decimated regiment to carry out another attack on the hill. As with the colonel previously in the north, he was relieved, and his replacement did give the order.

East of Sugar Loaf, a 1st Marine Division battalion commander who had been ordered to take a fiercely fortified hill objected that his men were "all used up . . . half of them belong in sick bay." The assistant divisional commander replied that the battalion commander, a lieutenant colonel, had his orders and that heads would roll if they weren't obeyed. The latter saluted and left, eyes tearing. "We'll take the fucking hill," he told an intelligence officer, "but I don't care if I come off it or not." The hill was taken (and the battalion commander wasn't wounded until later).

The men obeyed. Incidents of refusal, even of corporals' orders, were astonishingly few. Whitaker was among the overwhelming majority who never saw or heard of one, or of cowardice. Not to advance when ordered was inconceivable for all but a statistically negligible minority.

Almost no one *wanted* to charge the frightening danger, and only a small minority volunteered for especially hazardous assignments. A young Marine named Declan Klingenhagen was lucky enough to be skipped by his sergeant for what may have been the twelfth assault on Sugar Loaf.

> I was sitting in a trench dug out of the bottom of a small hill and I was apprehensive. . . . I wasn't hiding because there were other Marines around but I hoped no one would see me. I guess I was feeling fear. . . .
> At one point, a longer-time member of my squad saw me and asked why I wasn't going with the assault. The sergeant was nearby and told the member to leave me alone; it was all right.

The sergeant knew Klingenhagen's very first action as a replacement on Sugar Loaf three days earlier had put him in a kind of shock. A mortar barrage killed his lieutenant and so ravaged his squad that only four men were able to withdraw. One of the four was badly wounded; another lasted only until he reached the bottom of the hill, when he fell dead at Klingenhagen's feet with a bullet hole in his chest. Yet although the eighteen-year-old private "sure hoped" it wouldn't happen, he also knew he'd go up again if ordered.

A seasoned military maxim posits that a combat unit that has taken casualties of 30 percent or more can't sustain its fighting spirit. Many frontline units on Okinawa went far above that, Whitaker's 29th Regiment to 82 percent. However true it was (as many Japanese survivors later saw it) that Americans won their assured victory largely by applying their greatly superior resources, it's thus also true that those at the killing edge behaved exceptionally. Another old adage that war is 90 percent logistics didn't diminish their record of surpassing courage and esprit de corps.

Dick Whitaker was among the majority to whom it never occurred not to obey every order, and his wounds had been relatively trifling so far. Two days after his charge up Sugar Loaf on May 14, he and his platoon's other survivors were on the back slope of a little rise a hundred yards north. Exhausted and numb, they'd lost all their machine guns on the hill. Whitaker knew the wasted platoon would be ordered up again soon — but maybe not now, maybe not until tomorrow. That was all the future they could contemplate.

Whitaker dug his foxhole deeper and stuck his shovel in the mud to light a cigarette. He leaned down toward a buddy's match, his left hand remaining on the shovel's handle. A sniper's bullet caught it there, exactly where his heart had been a second earlier.

He made his own way to his battalion aid station, about half a mile to the rear. Cleaned and dressed, his wound seemed less serious than when the bullet struck. Three days later, a doctor pronounced him fit for duty, and he returned to his unit, which was even smaller because it had charged Sugar Loaf again in his absence. (A month to the day after Whitaker was hit, Marine Corps headquarters in Washington wrote his parents that he'd been wounded in action against the enemy on — this was mistaken by two days — May 18. "Your anxiety is realized and you may be sure that any additional details or information received will be forwarded to you at the earliest possible moment." That moment came more than a month later, when the campaign was over and Whitaker was back on Guam. The new note informed that he'd been returned to duty on May 20.)

Two weeks later, the 4th and 29th Marine Regiments attacked the Oroku Peninsula, site of Naha Airfield and of the tunnels of the Naval

Base Force and Captain Kojo's regimental headquarters. The day after their amphibious landing there, on June 4, Whitaker's platoon dodged small-arms fire while advancing along the top of a ridge. When they came upon a forward artillery spotter peering through his binoculars, Whitaker asked what his objective was. The lieutenant handed him his glasses, through which he made out three Japanese soldiers studying a map on the next ridge. "Watch this!" said the spotter, calling in some co-ordinates by radio. Moments later, the platoon heard American shells whizzing overhead. The three Japanese disappeared, together with the entire top of the ridge.

Whitaker woke up in an amtrac about half an hour later with no memory of how he got there. (It might have been after being hit by a short round from an American gun.) His head ached badly, blood flowed from his nose, and he couldn't hear. He supposed he was in the hands of a Graves Registration team, since the vehicle was also transporting poncho-wrapped bodies. In fact, he was being evacuated to a hospital ship (where he had his second hot meal). He'd never find out what had caused his concussion.

He told his shipboard examiners that he didn't feel "too bad" and was returned to a regimental hospital ashore. After a night there, he was checked again at his battalion aid station, which turned him loose to return to his outfit. Part of him "knew" he'd come through alive and without a disabling or disfiguring wound. Another part accepted how unlikely that was. "All those people around you were getting hit. Your turn just had to come too." Although every infantrymen still secretly believed he was the exception whose turn would *never* come, all knew the heavy odds against that. "You do get letters from home and you keep reading them," Norris Buchter of Connecticut would reflect. "But you've lost the feeling that you'll ever be back in that other world. . . . You get to a time when you're resigned to your own [death] coming sooner or later, that only makes sense."

Evan Regal, a lad from a struggling New York farm, felt certain "it was a question of time. You might survive this battle or that, but sooner or later they'd get you; that was unavoidable. I tried not to think about it. I knew guys who had premonitions they were going to get it the next day — and often enough that's when they actually did get killed." Regal was the classic combat schizophrenic operating on reason, which told him the odds, and faith, which obscured them.

But solicitous Mommy De Mar observed his men gradually tilting toward pessimism. "After a while, you've seen so much death and you expect your own has got to come sooner or later. You're there for just one thing: to kill until you get killed." "Until you get killed" wasn't fanciful, since Americans in the Pacific (like Soviets in World War II) didn't go home after serving a year or two but stayed "for the duration" — which usually ended in their death or wounds serious enough to merit their evacuation. Or in breakdown, for although their spirits very rarely refused to obey an order, their nervous systems failed more often.

> *There is no such thing as "getting used to combat." . . . Each moment of combat imposes a strain so great that men will break down in direct relation to the intensity and duration of their exposure . . . psychiatric casualties are as inevitable as gunshot and shrapnel wounds.*
> — From "Combat Exhaustion," an official American report

> *I was scared shitless most of the time and probably had some form of battle fatigue from April 1 till the day we quit and went to Guam.*
> — Dick Whitaker

> *It's a good thing the Lord helps block out unpleasant memories. I don't think one could vividly remember those feelings and still have his sanity.*
> — Robert H. Jones, 4th Marines

Few Americans considered how demoralizing their resources and firepower were to the Japanese. Fewer Japanese questioned the assumption that the Americans' material superiority gave them an easy time. The truth is that the relentless defense of a well-fortified enemy determined or resigned to fight to the death strained the attackers to their limit and beyond. The horrendous weather alone would have been enough to cause some battle fatigue. Tough young bodies that could have coped for six or seven days with the extremely abnormal demands succumbed after weeks — in some cases months — of cumulative misery and exertion, adding nervous breakdown to fever, pneumonia, malaria, and a range of respiratory infections from the exposure. Combat's additional demands hugely augmented the strain, and the tension couldn't be dissipated, because units pulled back the usual two hundred yards or so remained under artillery fire.

Even L-day had been too much for a scattering of Americans, including a few in the boats who remembered the blood of earlier landings. But most who came apart did so after combat's chaos and dread, where death was "as fantastically near" as a man inches away, or that man, usually a buddy, was disintegrated by a shell. Such gut-wrenching sights were often the straw that broke the backs of their nerves.

Well after the war, the American Army conceded that as many as one in ten of its soldiers suffered battle fatigue. Psychologists had learned that the number of shell-shock or battle-fatigue casualties increased in geometric proportion to the intensity of incoming fire and the length of exposure to it — which, again, is what distinguished Okinawa from previous campaigns. The report "Principal Lessons Learned in the Okinawa

Operation" would stipulate that "troops should not remain in the front lines for more than two weeks."

The first great concentration of enemy firepower at Kakazu Ridge produced the first surge of "walking dead," for which the 10th Army soon had to allocate an entire field hospital. The evacuation of battle-hardened veterans of earlier island campaigns confirmed that longer pounding from Okinawa's more elaborate fortifications caused higher levels of strain. Sugar Loaf claimed no fewer than 1,289 shell-shocked Marines, almost half as many as the killed and wounded. The campaign cost the 10th Army as a whole almost twenty-six thousand "nonbattle" casualties, most psychiatric. An extraordinary fourteen thousand occurred at the Shuri Line, the heaviest concentration of incoming fire predictably producing the highest rate. (The resilience of youth no doubt kept those numbers from being even higher. Roughly 80 percent of the Marine troops were under twenty-one.)

Some sufferers babbled incoherently or suddenly leaped up and tried to charge a machine-gun nest of "dirty yellow bastard Japs" who had been decimating their units. Others trembled, sobbed, or wet their trousers. A few screamed weirdly, fought wildly, and had to be restrained by their fellows, sometimes with fists. That happened to the most hardened, admired veteran officers and to some of the bravest men who had performed the most valorous feats, here or on previous islands. Their buddies recognized they'd reached the breaking point.

But most battle-fatigue cases simply stopped functioning as fighters — a condition the others also recognized, and led them to help in a battalion aid station. Their glazed eyes, slowed movements, and "witless" expressions announced their nervous systems could absorb no more; they didn't care any longer. Over twenty-five hundred would be discharged, many to remain more or less detached from reality in civilian life.

Sometimes doctors and corpsmen designated the exhausted as "blast concussion" cases to get them off the line for rest before they cracked. But breakdowns also came later. One ammunition carrier in a machine-gun squad became its leader after all the others had been killed and wounded, mostly one by one. In the end, he'd be the only man in his squad to have lasted the entire campaign. Despite the tremendous pressure of its eighty-two days, he remained cool, full of combat wisdom, and very helpful to replacements — many of whom took him for twenty-five years old, not his actual nineteen — straight through to the end. "His toughness and savvy saved me," one would remember. "His skill and leadership held us all together" — until he was back on Guam, where he cracked during preparations for the invasion of the Japanese mainland. "The last thing I remember about him was carrying him out of his tent on all fours."

I now duck at every shell, whereas I used to laugh as they went over. . . . We who
remain have God and only God to thank for our being alive.
— Mevin D. Heckt during his fighting

The only thing you could feel good about was surviving. You felt good for that
day by day, hour by hour, which is how you lived.
— Buzzy Fox

Fear caused most of the battle fatigue. It was so pervasive and its causes so
obvious that discussing it would be superfluous if not for the combat
literature and dramatization — the kind on which most Marines like
Whitaker had been raised — that fail to mention it. Veterans looking
back from the perspective of forty-plus years, and with the candor
prompted by the approach of their natural deaths, rarely hide the terror
that squeezed their throats and stomachs.

Fear gripped even when the most gallant deeds were being done; that
was inevitable, since there could be no gallantry without it. "We were all
out there afraid, and the fear bound us together," a company commander would observe. No minute of any day was entirely free of it. "You get
scared, you remain scared," Whitaker would remember. "Anyone who
isn't is lying or a fool. It's terrifying — and you learn to live with it."
Whitaker's company commander never retired even to battalion headquarters during his months of fighting — and remained scared. "There's
no way a man can prepare for the horror of advancing into an area where
an enemy he can't see may end his life any second. No one grows up expecting to face that stark terror. It's beyond description."

No notice was taken of messed pants, especially under artillery bombardment. Whitaker's first taste of that came the night after he was delivered from the north to the south, where his platoon hadn't had time to dig
in well. He later guessed the Japanese had learned that the Marines were
relieving the Army's 27th Division and wanted to rattle them — which they
did, with a barrage that became accurate and furious in minutes.

Unless stymied by coral, Marines liked to dig their holes about eighteen inches deep and just wide enough for two bodies. (When there was
time, they'd dig deeper pockets at the four corners into which enemy
hand grenades could be kicked before they exploded.) That first night in
the south, Whitaker and others had to use the 27th Division's foxholes,
whose greater width left them feeling miserably exposed. Protection was
further reduced by the low-trajectory Japanese fire that caused some
shells to bounce off the ground and detonate in the air. Two men in
Whitaker's company were blown to bits. The others huddled for much of
the night in dismay and terror.

Prolonged shelling is the hardest trial for most men in combat. Again,
the Shuri Line, with its greater concentration of Japanese heavy guns in

greater variety than in any earlier Pacific campaign, made it harder than on other islands. That the Japanese endured far worse doesn't diminish the American ordeal. The 32nd Army's heavy artillery had only a thousand rounds of ammunition per barrel to expend, and their operation was further restricted by what the Americans would have considered woeful communications and coordination. But the big guns were commanded by one of Japan's most respected artillerists, General Kosuke Wada.

From field officers to new replacements, Americans were awed and shaken by Japanese skill in zeroing in on them. Heavy shells would land forty yards away, then thirty, then closer, until — as an Army doctor described it — they found a neighboring foxhole and spilled the brains of a man's buddy all over him. Sledge found the "whistle and scream of the big steel package of destruction" almost unendurable. Bombardment was "an invention of hell . . . the essence of man's inhumanity to man. . . . I often had to restrain myself and fight back a wild, inexorable urge to scream, to sob and to cry [with] terror and desperation." To Private Gilbert Kanter, the pounding on the way to Sugar Loaf was "beyond the imagination of anyone who hasn't experienced it. I was still in a supposedly safe place, but my body was shaking. I had only four days of fighting, but that was enough; it was too terrible. I looked up and saw some birds, miraculously, alive in that insanity and even chirping. I wondered which of us was really the intelligent species." (Kanter's fear would go up a notch even from there after his wounding in the throat near Sugar Loaf's crest. "After I was hit . . . I wanted to hide, to duck every time a plane went overhead. I was terrified.")

The pilot Samuel Hynes identified two kinds of fear of shelling. The first, constant and inescapable even in the relatively secure rear, was of not knowing the moment when a shell with your name on it would land: the unrelenting subliminal fear that "soon now — right now — as you crossed the road, exposed and helpless, the shriek would sound and the shell would fall, carrying your death." But that was mild compared to the periods of tactical bombardment, when the bravest men couldn't stop trembling. Far as he was from the concentrated Japanese barrages at the front, Hynes in his tent at Yomitan Airfield nevertheless felt pure terror.

The earsplitting pandemonium alone was unbearable. The approach of heavy shells that could be heard from a far distance prolonged unholy suspense; battle-hardened men came to feel that the whistle alone could achieve the enemy's goal. The inability to do anything to save oneself was probably the most intolerable feature. A Navajo named Mike Kiyaani was in a foxhole near Sugar Loaf when a bombardment began from nearby Shuri. He'd seen the results before: much uglier wounds than those made by bullets. Now screams sounded as the shells advanced toward him. Then a friend was blown out of his foxhole, ten feet away. Kiyaani didn't realize he too was hit, only that his friend was dying — and he was impotent. "If you'd get up and run, you'd be shot up even quicker — so you wait there and go crazy."

Even the shells that missed shook the ground, shocking the ears and brain and sending hot fragments through the air, sometimes with body pieces. The young Marine who shot himself in the toe did so after a dazzlingly accurate barrage of Japanese 150-millimeter guns had landed a hit on a nearby foxhole, blowing its two cowering occupants into little red chunks. Some men, including a few who'd performed the bravest exploits during firefights when they could shoot back, were driven over the edge of sanity.

During its eight weeks in the south, Whitaker's company was pulled back half a dozen times to several hundred yards from the front. Since Japanese snipers could be accurate at five hundred yards and more, constant checking of the surroundings became second nature. Still, life at that distance from the edge was tolerable by comparison — except when the company took fire from artillery, boosting their fear to another pitch.

> *When you get scared is in your foxhole at night, remembering what happened to guys you knew, thinking of what's going to happen to you. It was so bad that some men couldn't sleep and others couldn't do anything but sleep. Lots of men hated nighttime long after the war.*
> — Joseph Bangert, medical corpsman

> *It's pitch black and you smell that unmistakable smell of a Jap. You don't say anything to the man in the hole with you, just make a sniffing motion with your nose and maybe throw a pebble to the next foxhole if it's near enough. For the rest of the night, your senses are like springs and your heart feels like it might run out of control.*
> — Dick Whitaker

> *Night was the worst. They might launch a banzai attack and even if we killed one with every round, we couldn't kill them all. Knowing that when you're in that foxhole with only one other man was a terrific psychological strain.*
> — Major General James Day, U.S. Marine Corps

> *The day was never long enough because the night was the longest, loneliest time of your life. From sunset to daybreak nobody moved. Your heart pounded. You prayed for daylight. You were just SCARED all the way through.*
> — Buzzy Fox

A final trial for the Americans surpassed the others. For all its repetition, darkness never became easier to endure.

The infantrymen who managed to stay unhit and unevacuated the full eighty-two days of the campaign dug some seventy foxholes as they advanced. They occasionally stayed two nights in the same hole or spent one in a tomb or the ruins of an Okinawan house. Otherwise, no one had to order them to dig. No sane man would spend a night on the surface.

The units tried to set up by late afternoon. Each company's three infantry platoons spread out, giving the machine-gun squad a favored position and a bit more protection on the highest ground. In the Marine divisions, the "poor sonofabitch" who operated the backpack radio was often a Navajo, like Mike Kiyaani, who communicated with tribesmen in his native language with code words that were as unintelligible as the best coding devices to anyone outside the Navajo culture. That was to foil the significant number of Japanese who understood English. Each Marine division had eight to ten Navajo, most so tough that they'd taken boot camp in stride. They worked in teams, switching from the holes designated company command points to stations farther in the field. Their bravery impressed other Marines. Radio operators could hide their antennas under their arms when moving during daylight, but had to extend them at night: a magnet for sniper fire.

A manual issued to each conscripted Japanese jeered that "Westerners, being . . . very cowardly and effeminate, have an intense dislike of fighting in rain, mist or darkness. . . . They can't conceive of night as a proper time for war. IN THIS, if we seize upon it, lies our great opportunity." The Japanese indeed made excellent use of night attacks throughout the war. The 32nd Army in particular speculated that the enemy's great advantages in numbers and equipment made him overconfident. And noticing less discipline than their own in such duties as watch standing, they sought to take advantage of the lapses when the enemy closed up shop each evening. (U.S. Army postmortem operations reports, such as the one that concluded most troops "lacked confidence in their ability to accomplish night missions efficiently," would tend to validate Japanese sneers at Americans for fighting "like office workers.")

But night excursions soon became more a necessity than an opportunity. Since leaving their caves for close combat — the only kind in which they stood a chance — was usually foolhardy during daylight, Japanese soldiers were all but forced to fight in the dark. They still heard pep talks about how effective *kirikomi* — penetrating the enemy for hand-to-hand combat — had been in previous battles, but current observation told them the contrary. They knew they'd be likely to set off "torrential" firing on themselves by touching the trip wire Americans rigged around the perimeter of their night positions. Still, they attacked as ordered — sometimes with enthusiasm, feeling they had to try *something* after hiding in their caves all day, more often with resignation, because "night attacks became synonymous with suicide attacks," as one man noted. "I'm sorry," an officer told him on the eve of an outing, "but resign yourself to being slain."

When the time came, the selected men crept from their caves with as many grenades as they could tie around their waists and sometimes twenty-two-pound explosive charges on their backs. Another soldier who watched such parties leave night after night saw them begin to take their deaths for granted, accepting their fate "of summer bugs that fly into the fire and burn themselves."

The Japanese kept a finger raised as they crawled toward American positions. When able to detect the protective wire without setting off the trip flares, they straddled the wire, got in closer, and used their grenades and satchel charges — or bayonets and knives. Few of their American targets stopped to think that the enemy's preference for night came chiefly from a need to avoid their own devastating firepower. Most thought operating in the dark, where men were certain to make mistakes and kill themselves, was a stupid way of fighting that confirmed the low-life Japanese as bloodthirsty fanatics. Their motivation mattered as little to American infantrymen as the ideals of kamikaze pilots mattered to American sailors; all they had to know was that the sneaks liked to do their slaying at night, so "you stayed in your hole, waiting and hoping. You had a better chance if you didn't make a mistake," but even the sharpest eyes often couldn't see the killers coming.

Each foxhole seemed to its pair of occupants a lone sanctuary. The other body pressed up against theirs contained the only friendly soul in a demented universe. It didn't have to belong to a buddy with whom they spent free time; the Corps forged transferable trust. It was enough that he was a Marine and had come that far, and therefore served as a link — the only one — to hope in the madness of the tyrannically malevolent dark.

The watch-standing norm was four hours on, four off. The general practice was to stay awake as long as you could, then wake your mate, who stayed awake as long as *he* could. They strained to interpret every sound out there, strained to see — often through heavy rain — the cleverly camouflaged killers before they struck. It was like a game of hide-and-seek, one Marine would recall, "except with the ultimate stakes." The Japanese knew the terrain better. Especially at night, they knew where *you* were, but you could only guess about them. What you did know was that they'd spend hours stalking you with infinite patience. Some crawled to within inches without being heard. Sometimes all the way, despite your precaution.

In those cases, the percentage of deaths was high and the wounds grievous because many were inflicted from directly above the foxhole or actually in it. The difficulty of wielding rifles there led to a great demand for .45 pistols. When Whitaker managed to obtain one, he slept with it in his hand or tucked into his belt. Despite a fear of "shooting my balls off while half asleep," he always kept a round in the chamber, the hammer half cocked and the thumb safety off.

On the second night after the landing, an infiltrator's grenade exploded between two of Melvin Heckt's platoon mates in a hole six feet away and killed both instantly. Several nights later, a Japanese team sneaked up on a foxhole of Captain Stebbins's G–2–22 company. A pair in another hole mere yards away heard nothing until one of the attackers had crawled almost on top of his target with a satchel charge. "The waiting for them to repeat that on every night! Hearing the noises, feeling the tension — *every night!*"

An infiltrator crept up unheard to the hole of a Marine from Chicago named Ray Eustace during the night of May 12–13. His bayonet entered the back of Eustace's neck, pierced his throat, sliced down through his chest and one lung, and exited at the armpit. Few infantrymen failed to see such casualties with their own eyes, within ten or twenty yards. Paul Gibson set a trip flare in the bottom of a drainage ditch into which Japanese had crawled on previous nights before lobbing grenades into his platoon's foxholes. Gibson heard his trap go off in the middle of the night, but no flare went up. In the morning, he found it lodged in a Japanese throat.

So the watch standers had reason to sense hideous death in the thousand countryside sounds they heard or imagined. Drenched with cold rain, those off watch shivered in muddy puddles — and not only muddy, for if sanitation was bad during the day, it was worse at night, when few were crazy enough to leave their holes for anything. Nor did dysentery's effects abate after dark. And on any given night, a number of the men were also vomiting from stress and ordinary sickness. Many were reluctant to bail slop from their holes for fear of the noise. Even with a good poncho, even after the hardest day's fighting, most found sound sleep almost impossible until their exhaustion approached infirmity. The buddies of eighteen-year-old Declan Klingenhagen thought him dead because he slept through one night's long, fierce mortar barrage without moving a muscle.

Merely maintaining mental equilibrium in the mire was an ordeal. Whitaker "never found a comfortable position" for weeks on end. Men also worried about deadly snakes slithering into their foxholes. Besides, although each one knew he could count on his foxhole mate, some watch standers did doze off. However great their exhaustion, the off-watchers rarely got more than snatches of sleep.

On many nights, neighboring foxholes more than an arm's length away might as well have been "on the next planet," in Whitaker's image. "You can't be absolutely certain they're not asleep over there. You can't communicate with them anyway because a whisper can get you shot. There was a special fear of being cut off from one's unit and left alone with Japanese brutality — but even greater fear of giving away one's position. Everyone knew a whisper traveled like a bugle at night."

Platoon leaders had wider communications. Fine black wires were strung from their radios to the hole that served as the company command point. Every half hour or so, an operator there checked the other positions, blowing into his microphone as softly as he could and murmuring "1st Platoon." The acknowledgment was even fainter, the barest trace of a whisper. "1st Platoon." Then 2nd and 3rd Platoons — but those slightest possible sounds were sometimes enough to attract a bullet in the hand or face of the communicator at either end. After one man Whitaker called answered in his whisper, Dick heard the instant high-pitched chatter of a Nambu machine gun — then, over the wires, the operator's muffled moan.

An unanswered call might mean the man on the other end had heard something and was afraid to give away his position, but it was usually treated as evidence of enemy penetration. In that case, the company commander sent a man out to inch toward the silent platoon, using the wire as a lead. That man knew Japanese soldiers might have the same wire in their hands while crawling toward *him* from out there in the blackness. When Whitaker was dispatched on the terrifying mission one night, he was only yards out of his hole in the direction of the mute platoon when heavy fire suddenly broke out there. He realized the man hadn't answered because the infiltrators had crept so close that a whisper would have "sealed his doom."

Although Whitaker now had all the psychological defenses necessary to live as a combat animal, they didn't ease the dark hours for him. "The quiet out there. So much more terrifying than any horror-movie score. You're so lonely, so isolated. The world consists of you and your foxhole buddy. He's the only other human being in the world, the only thing you have to keep you sane."

One evening, two of his hardened buddies gouged out their hole several yards forward of the line in a kind of point position. One was killed during the night, and the other had to spend the rest of it alone. At dawn, he was confirmation of the general rule that "to feel alone in combat is to cease to function; it is the terrifying prelude to the final loneliness of death." Whitaker helped lead the incoherent man with the petrified eyes back to an aid station.

"You can't understand what night was like. To be in a foxhole and hear something in the pitch-black void was the most terrifying of all possible experiences. Nobody cared what they shot at out there as long as it stopped those terrifying noises. You got up in the morning and saw a collection of dead things where they were, from goats to rats to Japs to civilian children. That too was terrible, but there was no way to tell what was coming at you hours before."

Infiltrators often used a noisy movement or quick burst of their own fire as a lure to locate enemy positions, which was why Americans were instructed to hold their nighttime fire except when absolutely necessary. "But terrified of everything that moved," as one put it, "we fired at everything." "Somebody fires at a rattle of leaves," another explained. "And when one person fires, everybody fires."

The jittery fusillades swelled the number of own-fire casualties because the tendency was "to shoot anybody on his feet first and *then* inquire. You just couldn't distinguish friend and foe in the split seconds you had." Kenny Geiman's closest call came when a clank of metal against a helmet woke him — enemy grenades had to be armed with such a tap after their pins had been pulled — and he saw Japanese eyes staring at him. Screaming, he rolled out of his hole into some brush. The screams set off a volley from neighboring holes and Geiman was saved, but he'd forgotten the night's password and had to spend its remaining hours in the brush, motionless except for his quivering. In the morning, sixteen bullets were counted in the Japanese corpse. Geiman knew he too would have been shot to pieces at the first sound he made.

When they had time, Americans rigged their wires around the perimeter of their clustered foxholes — the wires Japanese tried to detect by crawling with a raised finger — then strung them with trip flares and pebble-stocked tin cans. A machine gun set up to fire in a wide arc would blast everything at the first sound of pebbles dancing in the can, indicating the wire had been touched. The trip flare — "a thing of beauty" because "it was like having someone else on watch in addition to your foxhole buddy" — provided slight reassurance against dreaded surprise. It would freeze the infiltrator for a few seconds, long enough for an accurate rifle shot.

Few nights went without incident. One Marine put the average number of crawlers at half a dozen — "lots female," who may or may not have been just natives trying to survive. Platoon Leader Mitchell Zampikos spotted a tiny mound near his hole one daybreak after a night during which he kept hearing faint noises but could see nothing. Soon he saw movement inside and was certain a small animal was about to emerge. Zampikos ordered his men to hold their fire, then watched an elderly Okinawan woman pull herself out. "What a sight! She really did live like an animal all night in that tiny hole and in that rain." But the Americans had to assume crawlers were trying to sneak in for kills.

They could also use walkie-talkies to call for larger flares from the mortar section; these were relatively less dangerous when foxholes had been dug without telltale mounds of earth around the rim to reveal their positions. (That's why mortar gunners loathed firing flare shells: A trail of flame from the tubes revealed *their* positions.) Soon an amazing luminescence was in the air, lighting everything. "Everything" included oneself: Whitaker felt flares were like "a thousand searchlights thrown on you." They also lit up sheets of slanting rain and scatterings of corpses. The phosphorous light — stark but greenish, garish yet ghostly — was a final eerie touch.

Hallucinations were frequent, given the macabre setting and exhausted men. Sledge saw dead Marines rise from waterlogged craters and try to tell him something. Floating down in its parachute, the freakish light nevertheless seemed to stay up forever, an eternity. The blackened tree stumps, disabled field guns, and burned-out tanks seemed to confirm that some great natural calamity had recently destroyed the area. The dreaded infiltrators were also usually there, running, dodging, and ducking for cover at almost every flare — "*always* out there," Whitaker specified, "always on their way to penetrate us."

Japanese flares seemed to hang in the air terrifying minutes longer. In either case, Marines froze; the slightest movement in the light would make them targets. But Japanese soldiers also knew to freeze and often passed for corpses. Flares could work as well for the other side, and although it was "really nice to catch a dozen Japs out there," the advantage was reversed when a well-prepared enemy had time to see where to toss a grenade before he could be shot. While all hated the darkness, they hated that unearthly light too.

And although the nights grew shorter in May and June, each additional ordeal seemed to last longer than the previous ones. Men bolted up from their semisleep, saw their buddies peering out for the menaces, and closed their eyes again but couldn't shake their fear. "I lived through some days nobody would believe. The blood, the filth, the deaths — but the nights were worse. You can't see what's out there and you don't know anything except that you can die any minute. The suspense is fantastic."

"Tropical sunsets are beautiful, right? But when you knew what was coming, you hated them, *hated* them."

"From sunset to daybreak, nobody moved. You just waited for dawn, couldn't wait for it, your heart pounding, your finger on the trigger. You never got used to it. Know what I mean by looking forward to the kinds of days we were having? But at least you could *see* during the day; it didn't have that constant terror."

Whitaker's worst night after his first artillery bombardment in the south took place on the Oroku Peninsula, which his regiment invaded by amphibious landing two weeks after Sugar Loaf. With his company taking heavy sniper fire as evening approached, he and his mate — John

Senterfitt, with whom he'd come down from Sugar Loaf — had to scrape a hurried foxhole alongside the shoulder of a dirt road at the bottom of a hill. The moonless night was pitch black. Other foxholes were only yards away, but that was too far for communication — and the other men probably couldn't hear the careful sounds on the narrow road. But Whitaker and Senterfitt heard them: whisperings and tiny noises of concealed movement that suggested the Japs were massing for a banzai attack. Convinced they'd be shot if they called for mortars or a flare, they tried not to move a single muscle so as not to give themselves away to whoever was making those preparations, mere yards away. "'A night of horrors' isn't just a saying; there *is* such a thing. You never got used to it."

In closing this diary, I would like to say this much about my service in the Corps.
I wouldn't take a million for the experiences or give a penny to do it again.
— Melvin Heckt, 4th Marines, after the Okinawan campaign

War is a brutal, deadly game, but a game, the best there is. And men love games.
You can come back from war broken in mind or body, or not come back at all.
But if you come back whole, you bring with you the knowledge that you have
explored regions of your soul that in most men will always remain uncharted.
— William Broyles Jr., a veteran of Vietnam

Evan Regal had hated his Parris Island drill instructor so passionately that he swore to kill him — "I mean *kill* the sadistic bastard" — if he ever managed to see him in combat. After the DI became one of the stateside Marines corralled to replace the unexpected casualties on Okinawa, Regal did see his torturer — and thanked him for saving his life "again and again" by "teaching me right. Because Okinawa was so much worse than the worst day of boot camp that there was no way to guess until you were there. You won't believe either if I tell you. You have no way to understand, like I didn't."

Yet profound satisfactions partially compensated Regal and almost all other Americans for their torment. For all but the handful who enjoyed killing, some of the reward came from the exhilaration of having survived a trip to the far edge of human experience. When Dick Whitaker would think of Sugar Loaf years and decades later, he'd feel great pride, mixed with some well-deserved conceit, in having been among the few who fought on the cursed hill. The one trip up, the charge from his fifteen minutes of terrified bedlam there, gave enough to last a lifetime. "Just to know I did it is enough." Okinawa's hundred other battles endowed almost all survivors, apart from those who would never recover from battle fatigue, with a similar reserve of self-esteem. "The best thing that ever happened to me." "Nothing can ever dim what we did there." "The proudest moments of my life."

Everyone who saw actual combat cherishes lifelong memories, terrible but also sublime.

(Naturally, that pertains far more to American participants than to Japanese, most of whom would be ashamed of having survived. Even without their obligation to die rather than surrender, surviving on the losing side was emotionally very different. Very few Japanese who did would share the American gratitude for the experience.)

The netherworld of combat offered other rewards. Living on the edge afforded a heady freedom from many of civilization's restraints, an intoxicating sensation for most young men. That made them high when not driving them low with fear and misery. Combat's supreme intensity dominates everything, cutting away all unrelated problems. It delivers its participants to hell on earth, but simultaneously to utopia, which largely explains why "thoughtful, loving men can love war even while knowing and hating it," as William Broyles recently wrote. In World War II as never later, righteousness strengthened the impulses feeding that love. Most Americans on Okinawa drew great satisfaction from fighting for God, democracy, and what they felt was an ultimate goodness. Utterly secure in their conviction that victory was vital to civilization, they were sustained by moral purpose even amid the filth and torment.

When Emil Rucinski, a gunnery sergeant turned platoon leader, was gravely wounded on May 11, he was given absolution, as he requested. On his first stretcher, he supposed he wouldn't make it, but the thought didn't depress him. "I had some morphine in me by then, but I think I was at peace with the idea anyway. Because I had a patriotic conviction, remember that? I was doing something important for my country, so I took it as an honor if I was going to die."

Forest Townsend was uneasy because he, a replacement, hardly knew anyone in his new squad. And he was "scared to death" by the intensifying artillery fire as it pushed south with its company. "You just can't live through those shells raining down on you without fear." Still, Townsend knew he was doing what had to be done, surrounded by the world's best fighting men. On a late-May morning, his squad had to cross an open field on its way to leveled Naha. Two men made it to cover on the far side, but an enemy soldier popped up from a hole in the ground when Townsend was halfway across, and a burst from his Nambu machine gun spun Townsend around and down. An inner voice had time to comment that that was the way it was when you were hit, even as training and instinct issued commands: Find cover fast, any cover; don't let him finish you off. He slid into a shell hole and was shocked again by rainwater rising to his waist, his bleeding chest, his armpits. The eighteen-year-old knew he'd been hit very badly.

"*Am I going to die here?* Well, Mother wouldn't want it, but she and Dad will be proud of me. Very sad, but also very proud, the whole family — so it's okay."

Tens of thousands took similar comfort. A corpsman in a surgical tent tended a parade of casualties whose fierce pain seemed not to faze them, whose composure, the product of their pride and sense of reward, helped many recover. "Whatever their individual resources," the corpsman would conclude, "all of them had a fantastic support system. They had constant nurturing — at least rhetorical — not only from their comrades but also their families, communities, government, all of society. America had only one face, and that face told them they were on God's side, fighting the good fight. No one questioned the rights and wrongs because all knew they were right. Therefore no one really questioned the need for the suffering."

At the critical moments, your heart feels what it's been trained to: that you can't let your buddies down. Because you're nothing without them, you've learned that's not just pep talk. You depend on that man next to you absolutely and he depends on you, which is why you're more than family. You pray as much for him to come out alive as you pray for yourself.
— Al Franks, 22nd Marines

The only other glory besides surviving was seeing people stripped bare of all their artificiality and developing feelings for them unknown anywhere else. Respect, affection, loyalty, love — everything came out of need, as in all human relations, except that here it was far greater than in normal life.
— Robert Sherer, Dick Whitaker's company commander

Would you do it again?
Sure.
Even knowing the horrors and misery — and that you'd have a good chance of not making it a second time?
Sure.
Can you explain why?
For the right country and the right cause. I think every one of us would have.
Despite everything?
Sure. And for what we shared. Nobody worried about who you were and how much money you were making — or weren't making. You had real friendship, real closeness for maybe the first and last time. You weren't making an impression by telling everybody you were a millionaire because that didn't make a damn bit of difference. All you knew was you depended on that guy next to you and you loved him. I never found that again.
— Answers by Joseph Bangert, one of the flag-raisers on Okinawa's southern tip

For Marine infantry, their fellows were it, *the only family they had.*
— James Day, the corporal who became a general

But Americans' uplift from fighting for the highest national cause usually remained in the background. In the foreground was a handful of beloved comrades. Another combat reward was a love as difficult for outsiders to know as the horrors that sired it.

The love fed on trust. Unlike that of ordinary friendship and romantic attachment, this one was total, since one's life was constantly in the hands of one's platoon mates. The bond could not be broken "by a word, by boredom or divorce or by anything other than death," as Philip Caputo would write. Ordinary life's usual mean motives and jockeying for personal advantage vanished in the mutual reliance on and concern for one's fellows. Those who endured the grime and gore together felt themselves elevated toward absolute selflessness.

Thus all combat offered some of the kamikaze pilots' exhilaration at being liberated from petty considerations. It compelled but also freed men to act more unselfishly, lovingly, and nobly than they ever had or would. The intensity of their devotion was comparable only to the surge parents feel for their young children when they're endangered. But here the emotion was reciprocated, prompting an intoxicating gratification.

Class position and social origins counted for nothing in the world of instant death and ubiquitous maggots. Marines in particular were Marines, not members of other groups. "It was all the same who you were and where you came from because you *were* the same, struggling with higher forces."

Blacks remained the exception. Still not acknowledged as "the same" on Okinawa, they served in segregated Army units — some fighting, a majority in support services such as transportation and laundry — and nowhere at all in the Marines, apart from a scattering of orderlies. But Okinawa would break down even some of those barriers, as in a Marine medical unit that returned to Guam in July, after the campaign, and was led to a common mess until it could set up its own. Base personnel directed a handful of black stewards who'd served in the officers' mess on Okinawa to a separate, segregated table, but those officers refused to eat there under those arrangements. "Because when the fighting got furious," a white corpsman would remember, "those stewards also served as litter bearers under fire. If they were good enough to be shot at with the rest of us, they were good enough to eat with us. That's what we learned, including our large sprinkling of Southern rednecks — and we prevailed in the end."

The Navajo who served as communications specialists tended to seek their own company when not on the line. Many years later, after Dick Whitaker had learned about racial minorities' sensitivities, he'd regret having called them all "Chief" without a thought. But that practice was grounded more in innocent ignorance than prejudice. There was little overt discrimination against, and much affection for, the Indians, those buddies under fire. As for Jews, some had encountered coarse anti-Semitism during their training and on their troopships coming over — even, occasionally, in some rear areas on the island itself. In the strain and compensatory unit embrace of combat itself, however, ethnic and religious antagonism evaporated. And when pulled back into temporary reserve, men of all faiths almost indiscriminately attended services held by Catholic, Protestant, and Jewish chaplains. ("Even the atheists prayed," one man would remember with only marginal exaggeration.)

Infantryman Gilbert Kanter, who'd be shot in the throat near Sugar Loaf's crest six weeks later, was surprised that a man he'd splattered with his vomit as they approached the shore in their L-day landing craft "never said a thing, not even 'You dirty Jew.' From then on, there was no hint of anti-Semitism; we were like one." Jews were such a small percentage of the Marines on Okinawa that some companies had none, although one Jewish platoon leader carried "a little black book," evidently the Kaddish, and asked some of his men to read a few paragraphs in case he was badly hit. About an hour later, one of his men inched to his officer's corpse in order to fulfill the request.

Battle makes brothers of men who had previously had very little in common, and their intimacy and love are not quite understandable to people outside the family. Even for men like Whitaker, whose home lives had lacked nothing in affection, their combat family of total partnership and interdependence brought more intense commitment than anything in civilian life. Returning after the war to peacetime's individual strivings, the brothers would go their divergent ways, departing more and more from what had been the common interests of unformed teenagers in uniform. Still, when Marine veterans of Okinawa would meet at reunions half a century later, their durable love filled the vapid motel banquet rooms. The "fierce male tenderness that men feel for flesh and blood in war," as Laurens van der Post called it, remained almost palpable.

Van der Post likened the bond of devotion to fire. It spread over Okinawa together with the devastation — no hotter than on other Pacific islands but igniting more souls in the war's largest, most difficult campaign. Each man fought to keep his inner group alive. Letting one down would haunt him forever.

That too was different for the Japanese. Their courage had to be greater than the Americans', if only because they faced so much more firepower in encounters made more deadly by it — and with little rest, no replacements. And they couldn't even hope to keep their buddies alive. Brotherhood was harder to sustain in units that were disintegrating, as many Japanese units soon would be. For a people who view themselves primarily as members of a group, that calamity was especially demoralizing. The ultimate loneliness of being cut off from one's fellows was even more frightening for Japanese than Americans. Still, many units did hold together as they were being destroyed, engendering a multitude of kindnesses that would never be recorded because every man in many units died.

When one of Captain Kojo's companies faced what promised to be total annihilation, a group of friends dug a hole outside their cave to make red bean soup, a delicacy. The fire under the pot had to be minuscule lest the approaching enemy see it and finish them there and then. The very old beans remained stone hard even after a long period of anxious boiling. American mortars were landing within yards of the tent by the time the treat was finally rushed inside the cave. Each of some thirty men slowly licked his cup of it, savoring its sweet taste. "No one said as much, but we all knew this was our farewell party."

Japanese soldiers expressed some of their fierce male tenderness in attempts to respect the dead, a large number of whom, however, could not be buried. Incoming fire made it impossible to recover most bodies, a more difficult task for the retreating side in any case because the dead often lay in enemy territory. Still, thousands of Japanese took huge risks to bury friends. Battlefield camaraderie — sealed, perhaps, by a higher degree of love while there was little hope of anything but joining those bodies — was many units' only joy.

Kuni-ichi Izuchi, the artist whose grueling apprenticeship to the master had made basic training seem easy, almost missed the Okinawan ordeal. He was in an Army hospital in Beijing, his leg gashed by a mortar, when he heard his unit was being transferred. He begged permission to join them and it was granted.

Arriving with another surname — his original one — the passionate patriot developed a close friendship with a fellow soldier named Izuchi, who was killed soon after L-day. Kuni-ichi fought to find his body, then severed the left hand and found some wood to cremate it. The two had promised each other that whoever survived longer would bring some of the other's bones to his family. But when Kuni-ichi too was very badly hit and dragged himself around for days without help, he became so weak that Izuchi's few bones were nearly more than he could carry. Still, his promise remained sacred even when he came a breath from death. When he returned to Japan in 1946, he presented the bones to Izuchi's family — and took Izuchi's sister's surname when he married her the following year, a fairly common practice when the bride's family lacked a male heir.

But although Japanese soldiers performed ten thousand such acts of heroic devotion to their buddies and their memory, the losers in the battles also lost some of the sense of compensation for their misery. Their veterans' reunions are much more somber and spiritual than the victors'.

Dodging enemy shells and bullets, we carry the stretchers south, weak from our long unnatural life underground, gasping from the weight. On one stretcher, Takai tosses and babbles. . . .

We finally reach Asato village but can't find the hospital cave. Takai complains his hip is stiff and Takagi, a close friend, stoops to massage it. Looking comfortable now, Takai closes his eyes. . . . I touch his forehead. It's very cold. . . . Each time it gets colder. No pulse. Can't hear his breathing.

"Ah, his life is ebbing away!" No matter how you try to fend it off, life mercilessly dwindles, second by second. We grasp his hands, put our faces on his chest, tremble as time passes relentlessly. . . .

Takai's face has death written on it. His unfocused eyes stare at a corner of the sky. The dirt and sand blown on his pale cheeks from the enemy's howitzer fire look like freckles.

"Takai, Takai!" An old buddy of his from Manchuria can't bear it any longer and cries out loud. . . . We take clippings from his hair and nails. Always very neat, he has no extra growth of either. We bury him at the foot of the mountain and place a green branch in his canteen on the spot.
— Shigemi Furukawa

I remember the . . . narrow path to the tree line rising beyond the rice paddies. This was a no man's land. He was on that path, lying face up with his throat cut, never going back to Detroit. Tony Marinelli, Marine private. 1945.

Day dreaming, 1981 . . . a fat man is sitting by the pool, in shorts, looking at the water, puffing a big cigar. Tony smoked cigars, big cigars. With that name he should have played shortstop for the Tigers instead of smoking cigars on Okinawa and getting killed. . . .

Harry is the man in charge [of the bar]. The maker of fine drinks in the sun. The opener of beer cans, the hot dog chef, the man who knows all about this Everglade town. . . .

Around the pool, three couples are sunbathing, stretched out, feeling that Florida sun. . . . The fat man at the pool flicks cigar ashes and bites down, looking at the pool.

Would Tony have been fat now? No, don't think so. He was lean and dark and short with coal-black hair and a tricky little smile that made you like him.

Hard to remember him alive. Too easy to remember him dead, with a cut across his throat, wet blood running like a river down the side of his neck.

No more cigar for Tony.

No chance to be fat, to sit in the Florida sun.

"Harry! Two beers."

One for Tony and one for me.
— Thomas Hannaher

Every Marine still loved the Corps, with its honorable bloodline and heroic ancestors, now his own. Each still believed he was part of "the best damn fighting outfit in the world." But thoughts about that extended family dwindled. When the going got toughest for the 6th Marine Division in mid-May, as it had been tough for Army units since early April, most men in the line came to feel they were fighting not for the Corps, let alone for God or Democracy, but for the handful of fellows at their side. "My world was the ten guys in my squad," Edward (Buzzy) Fox would remember. (The squad was down to ten because replacements for their casualties were unavailable.) "And maybe my company to some extent. To tell the truth, I didn't really care about anything else. There just wasn't enough strength or imagination."

Whitaker would reflect that generals perceived the world as masses of men and equipment, captains as deployments of companies, sergeants as movements of platoons. The ordinary Joes like himself had all they could do to cope with the welfare of their own fire teams of five or six men. Stripped of their privacy and social skins, that half dozen fought, slept, and performed all natural functions, as well as battle's unnatural ones, in total togetherness. Fire teams now lived more like wolf litters than human brothers.

Their ages drew them further together. "We were physically tough, really, truly tough," eighteen-year-old Walter Kaminski quickly discovered. "But inside, we were just teenagers who needed our families. And the guys in your unit were the only family you had and maybe the last you'd ever see."

Kaminski, who'd grown up in a close Chicago family, needed that support as much as anyone.

> When we joined up, we thought the Marines would be all storming
> beaches, charging up hills, maybe blood running into the sand. But
> Okinawa was just as much about friendship and loyalty. It was about
> kinship, trust, loving other people more than anyone before or maybe
> since. . . . You need your buddies because they're the only thing be-
> tween you and that hell. It sounds corny but you're eager to give to
> them — totally. . . . And when you see a brother killed, nothing's more
> terrible.
>
> Yes, you like some men in your platoon more than others, they're a
> mixture of good and bad like anywhere else. But when Joe Smith over
> there is taking fire, it doesn't matter if you don't have a great affinity
> for him. He's your brother and that's a very precious thing. I knew
> there was nothing anyone could do for me if I was killed. But I also
> knew that if I was captured, my buddies would come get me out — the
> whole U.S. Marine Corps, if necessary.

Wounded the day before the start on Sugar Loaf, gregarious young Kaminski made his way back about a mile to the tent of a field hospital. Without his platoon brothers there, he was suddenly a vulnerable teenager alone in the alien world, feeling cut off from everything, even his beloved Corps. His depression threatened to disable him longer than his wrist wound, until a priest named Eugene Kelly saw it during his rounds to comfort patients.

"What's your name, son?"

"Kaminski, Father."

"No, your first name."

"Walt."

"Hey, Walt, two guys were looking for you, just before we started talking. They went out there."

Knowing the visitors could only be his buddies, Kaminski leaped up and continued feeling better even after other patients near where Kelly pointed said they'd seen no "two guys." Later, he lovingly called him "the Lying Priest. . . . But if there ever was a good lie, that was it. He snapped me out of my stupor because he knew what buddies mean to a combat rifleman, something different from anything else in the world."

Human virtue fell short of perfection even there. Congenital braggarts, cowards, and hoodlums didn't change much. A sprinkling of thieves stripped bodies of their wristwatches because "the grave digger will get this stuff otherwise and I know he'd rather it went to me." But the few rotten apples didn't spoil the barrel. Thousands of wounded Kaminskis and Whitakers hurried back to the front as fast as they could, even lying to their doctors to do so, instead of staying a deserved extra day or week under care. "Lots of men with bad wounds begged to be patched up and sent back to their units," Corpsman Bangert would remember. "Unfortunately, we had some of the most patriotic boys in the world — but mainly they couldn't bear the thought of their buddies still in danger out there. That's what drew them back to combat even after they'd lived with its unbelievable awfulness."

Of course everyone wanted to go home. At the same time, many wanted to continue sharing their buddies' burden, even knowing it would probably end in grave wounds or death. Such loyalty helps explain their obsession with recovering their dead, which was driven by more than respect for the remains. Every Marine's resolve to honor a slain buddy's memory and reputation made an unrecovered body, deprived of its proper treatment, the worst possible loss. "It was part of the bargain we all made, the reason we were to willing to die for one another," Michael Norman recently wrote of the same commitment in Vietnam. Men crawled into the killing zone because "each believed that if his had been the body . . . other Marines would have come for him." A man who performed many recoveries on Okinawa specified that it was essential not for the corpses but for the living, "who could count on a decent burial just like he would count on his buddies never letting him down in any hell."

Some tried to sustain the emotional ecstasy even from back in the States. A secret part of them had dreamed of a "million-dollar wound" serious enough to make them unfit for combat but not for civilian life. After Sugar Loaf, however, a few who were back home with that lucky degree of damage — and who felt alienated from everyone who hadn't been in on the edge with them — began writing their buddies about rejoining them. Only the glow of the purest manly selflessness could lure them back to the madness of shock and fatigue.

> *My heart pounded inside whenever I saw a buddy get hit and even more so when they died. We were taught to carry on and we knew we could not stop and dwell on the tragedy around us.*
> — Robert Jones

Two weeks after the end on Sugar Loaf, William Manchester was in the courtyard of a tomb with a man named Rip Thorpe. They heard the shriek of an approaching screaming meemie mortar, but the chances seemed remote that the huge shell could clear the top of the hill and land on its safer back slope, where the tomb was located. But this one fell into its courtyard, and Thorpe's disintegrating body sent fragments of bone into Manchester. His "flesh, blood, brains and intestines encompassed me."

Most infantrymen who fought a week or two on Okinawa had that same supreme shock and horror — seeing a combat friend instantaneously destroyed inches away. If many wept openly when their buddies were killed out of their sight, the effect was predictably worse when cubs in the litter were dismembered or atomized *in* their sight — with the crunch and squish in their hearing. Two days after Sugar Loaf, a direct hit of an artillery shell killed a man who was covering others with his body. One buddy's grief spiraled further when the dead man was listed as "missing in action" because the chunks of leg and hip that could be found weren't enough to identify the corpse.

A screeching shell passed no more than a foot over Eugene Sledge's head when he was sheltering in a foxhole on Half Moon Hill, then exploded two holes down, where a man had been drinking hot chocolate. It also instantly killed the two youngsters in the hole next to his.

Irving Oertel enjoyed a break in Naha's outskirts after fighting through its rubble. No one felt fully safe within a thousand yards of the front, because nothing that close was reliably free of metal slicing the air. But in that area, believed to be "pretty secure," Oertel and a mortarman named Prince were sitting on their helmets, playing cards on an ammunition box. A single shot rang out. The bullet imploded Prince's head, and he died before he could utter a sound. Although Oertel had seen a great deal of death, especially during his charge up Sugar Loaf weeks earlier, this was his time for the screws to come loose. "Usually when someone was hit, you shouted once or twice for a corpsman and tried to stop the bleeding until he came. But this was too much, I guess. Although I didn't know it then, I kept screaming over and over for a corpsman — even though nothing could help my friend Prince."

Few infantrymen were spared splattering by their friends' blood and tissues. Ed Jones — known as "Teeth" because he smiled so much — saw a man catch a bullet full in the face, also south of Naha. "His whole mouth was simply gone. It was just *terrible*. I wasn't so good at forgetting that."

A month after Anthony Cortese saw the sea of dead Marines on Sugar Loaf from nearby Chocolate Drop Hill, his platoon again took heavy fire while advancing up another hill farther south. Its leader, a green lieutenant just arrived from the States, ordered him to scout the enemy positions with two other men. They started up the hill. A shell landed nearby, killing one of his young companions and blowing off the legs of the other. "How can I forget that? He tried to pick himself up and couldn't believe what he saw: He had no legs. He died right there. How can I ever forget?"

Anyone not hit after a week or two had "a horseshoe in his hip pocket," as Robert Sherer, Whitaker's company commander, put it. Everyone remembered incidents of missing death by an instant — of a man taking a step away and, before his foot came down, seeing someone else killed in the spot he'd just vacated. But what invested the experience with too much emotion for normal nerves to bear was that the other man was likely to be a combat friend, loved more deeply than all but the luckiest lovers. Inches away, bullets and shells turned the dearest creatures on earth, the objects of their fierce male tenderness, into offal and ooze that stuck to their own helmets and faces. The shock and dismay, trauma and bereavement topped the general loss of much that distinguishes human beings from lower forms of life.

I was in a large cave with lots of tunnels branching off the main "hall." The whole thing was full of Jap corpses, but suddenly I saw one breathing, although his eyes were closed. "Hey, we've got a live poggie here," I shout as I release the safety on my submachine gun. Then I drill a pattern right into his chest — and think nothing of it! That's pretty gruesome. That's how it was.
— Ed Jones

One of the things I learned [as a war correspondent] was that war makes no national or racial or ideological distinctions as it degrades human beings.
— John Hersey

Although so much savage death numbed combat infantrymen, few could jettison their moral sense entirely. They were further dehumanized by the "bestial, monstrous and vile" things they had to do.

The sight of mutilated bodies alone was often enough. One eighteen-year-old saw a pair of "nonchalant" Japanese legs standing beside a low wall, and the torso, sliced off by an artillery shell, on its other side. He laughed. But another part of him kept asking why he himself was still alive; bullets surely intended for him had killed his buddies. He would continue asking *Why? Why? Why?* for fifty years. Sledge once saw a Japanese gunner sitting upright with his eyes wide open, although the top of his head had been shot off. A night of rain had filled the skull with water, into which a buddy of Sledge was flipping chunks of coral and watching the splashes, like a child tossing pebbles into a puddle. "It was so unreal. There was nothing malicious in his action. This was just a mild-mannered kid who was now a twentieth-century savage."

When heavy fire stopped Dick Whitaker's company near Sugar Loaf one day, his platoon leader called for help from a flamethrowing tank, one of America's most fearsome weapons, which saw its first major use on Okinawa. The tank moved up to shoot streams of napalm into the cave from which machine-gun fire had been hitting Whitaker's platoon. Japanese soldiers who ran from the furnace were squirted with napalm — which, however, failed to ignite. One of the tankers saw to that with a tracer bullet, turning a fleeing man into a torch — which prompted a throaty cheer from the platoon. "That was our war," Robert Sherer would remember. "Yes, that Jap had been machine-gunning our people moments before — but he was a human being. And we cheered that incredibly horrible sight, the burning of another human. Whatever the justification, we'd become savages too."

Buzzy Fox registered the spiritual metamorphosis the day before he joined the line as a green replacement, when he saw a fellow Marine testing his rifle on a cow. "I think that's terrible," he said, but the shooter explained that the incessant rain and inescapable mud made it vital to test his M1. "I still think killing an animal unnecessarily is stupid — until *my* time in foxholes," when "I'd have been happy to test my rifle on a live animal if any more existed on the island."

> Because every tiny little advantage, every *anything* you can do to stay alive, is worth it. What do you care about animals anymore when you've seen stacks of dead buddies and you know you can join them in one second? One day, I thought I'd try to get down some food, so I sat down on a log. Then I noticed it wasn't a log but a charred Jap corpse. And I didn't move; it didn't faze me a bit. A dead body, another human being, meant nothing to me — because it was Japanese and I myself had become something less than human.

Civilized values may have been the ultimate loss. "You can't ask a man who's been in combat how he feels about those things when he does them," reflected John Townsend (no relation to the Forest Townsend who took comfort from his family's pride). "If you want to know that, go to a slaughterhouse and ask the men there what they feel about their jobs. You're dealing in meat, not lives."

"I resigned from the human race. . . . I just wanted to kill," another Marine would recall. A very small percentage were sadists who enjoyed it, but most were ordinary American boys, raised on the Ten Commandments. However they'd relished the thought of zapping Japs during their training, what they had to do in reality degraded them. Sledge knew no combat infantryman would ever be the same. They weren't just living in conditions that taxed "the toughest I knew almost to the point of screaming" but also contributing to depravity, an acceptance that human life was not at all sacred.

Book III

19 · Kojo at the Shuri Line

We fought hard on Okinawa, maybe harder and better than any Americans before. But would we have won without our enormous superiority in numbers, firepower and supplies, our control of the air, our ability to replace men and equipment? If the Japanese say that's what licked them, I think they're right. We didn't win because our fighting men were superior; the Japanese were as good or better.
— Clyde McAvoy, 4th Marines; later a businessman in Tokyo

We had firepower of all types right down to Fox Company. We could deliver a withering, concentrated field of fire that would take out anything within 100 yards. Looking back, I realize it was mainly that superiority that enabled us to win.
— Dick Whitaker

The American soldier fights largely to save his ass. When you corner him, he's tough, but when things go badly, he thinks of how to get the hell out of there. The Japanese soldier was very different.
— John Toland, historian

TADASHI KOJO'S FIGHTING began in late April, while the 6th Marine Division was still in the north and the five other American divisions, one Marine and four Army, were making their unacceptably slow progress against the main fortifications. Kojo joined the battle on the Shuri Line, just northeast of Shuri itself. To the participants, the four miles to Sugar Loaf on the west might have been forty: The battles for the major strongpoints seemed like separate wars.

Ushijima's other division — in addition to Kojo's 24th — was the 62nd. Lightly armed to begin with, it had borne the brunt of the defense, which drained half its fighting strength. No longer fearing a second major American landing in the deep south, the commander now ordered the 24th's 22nd Regiment out of reserve to reinforce it. Kojo wasn't with Colonel Yoshida, the recently arrived regimental commander, when he established his field headquarters on a hill a mile behind his forward troops. Still recuperating as the regimental operations officer, he handled paperwork and attended Shuri briefings. With only his small operations staff to command, he nevertheless considered the tropical uniform insufficiently officerlike and dressed like Ushijima, in his regular uniform with breeches and a pith helmet.

Actually, only the 22nd Regiment's 1st Battalion was available to respond to Ushijima's order, the other two having been detached earlier and severely mauled. On April 26, two days after that essentially hale 1st Battalion was committed, a naval shell's direct hit on its headquarters killed its commander. Captain Kojo was ordered to replace that major — that is, to return to the unit that had been his before the accidental explosion that nearly finished him.

Leaving his personal effects in the regimental tunnel south of Naha, he resumed command of the men he'd trained in Manchuria and led during their early months on Okinawa. They were now defending a long ridge behind the village of Kochi, a critical high point guarding Shuri and 32nd Army headquarters, some two miles behind them.

They were attacked the following morning. After so much digging elsewhere, including the abandoned fortifications commanding the landing beaches, they'd here had time only for foxholes slightly forward of their caves. Kojo's cave was a small one fifty yards behind the main ridge, on the rear slope of another small rise. After nearly eight single-minded years girding for combat as a cadet and an officer, this would be his first engagement. The fastidious captain felt no fear. His confidence in General Ushijima and unvanquishable Japan remained absolute.

He had the same confidence in his training, which is why it took him disastrously long, as he'd learn when it was almost too late, to correct his mistakes. Among American misconceptions about Japanese soldiers was the conviction that they were born jungle fighters. Combat veterans associated the "absolutely atrocious, murderous" climate of previous islands with the "Jap jungle rats," assuming, as one put it, that "Nips lived from birth in that awful, miserable unhealthiness." Even the respected war correspondent John Hersey believed Japanese "take to the jungle as if they had been bred there." The truth was that most were trained for quite different conditions and had to learn as painfully as any novice to adapt. The notion that they were "natural" defenders was equally misconceived. Kojo's constant training for *offense* had begun at the Imperial Military Academy, whose cadets were assured that a single spirited Japanese division properly fired with dedication to all-out, decisive attack could defeat three better-equipped Soviet ones. Professionally and emotionally, the Army relegated defense to something almost unnecessary, if not actually shameful. Although the 24th Division was a partial exception because it had expected to face heavy Soviet armor, that didn't substitute for training. Kojo's occasional defensive exercises in Manchuria took place on paper, never in the field or with a belief they'd be needed. The reserve officers who now served as his company commanders knew even less about defense.

Starting at Kochi with slightly less than his full complement of eleven hundred men, Kojo instructed those company commanders to position them on the ridge's forward slope, from where they could observe the American advance and rush out to meet it at opportune moments. They were in sight of a host of enemy warships anchored in a bay less than five miles away. That first day, naval guns joined American mortars and artillery in delivering what felt like a horizontal squall of shells. American fire was ten to twenty times heavier than the Japanese barrages that would decimate the Marines at Sugar Loaf and the other strongpoints. Kojo registered to himself that it was "unbelievably" more powerful than anything he'd expected — almost a new kind of warfare entirely.

As on subsequent days, he saw little more because the barrage kept him in his cave until it let up at twilight, when he found a startling number of men had been killed without having fired a shot. At intervals, his weary survivors, eyes already bloodshot, would fire their machine guns and small arms at advancing Americans, who usually retreated. Moments later, however, enemy shells would burst above them, "red lights flickering in their black smoke. Then the fragments rain down on us and we can't lift our heads."

Hit that way day after thunderous day, soldiers at all the strongpoints like Kochi became convinced their sector had been selected for special fury. "The ferocity of the bombing is terrific," a superior private recorded in his diary. "What the hell kind of bastards *are* they? Bomb from six to six." Massive concentrations of additional artillery, heavy mortars, and naval fire — a battleship or cruiser provided gunfire support for each American Army regiment — reduced even some American troops to "stupefaction or numbness," as one put it, before they advanced into the "wreckage of earth" where the explosives had landed. Just like Americans, Japanese were consumed with the frustration of being unable to do anything against the firing from long range. A private in Kojo's battalion would remember "no dead angle or safe place anywhere. . . . Bombs and shells came from land, from the sea, from the sky. . . . If you were in a valley, trench mortars did the job. One step out of your cave and your fate was in God's hands." Another put it more directly: "It's sheer wonder that any foot soldiers managed to live."

The supremely professional Kojo was less concerned. "So this is real combat," he said to himself. "Very costly." But he didn't react to the cost, and his noncommissioned officers never dreamed of complaining. Reckoning the time must soon come for the bayonet charge for which the battalion had practiced so long and ardently, he anticipated his chance to make the Americans panic, as his predecessors had done to the Chinese in the Sino-Japanese War. (What did such practice have to do with *this* war? What good were bayonets against flamethrowing tanks? But he'd ask himself that only after the war, when he at last fully accepted that fire-power, in which deluded Japan was pathetically inferior, was the critical determinant.)

Meanwhile, he kept his men on the forward slopes, where they could see — and be seen by — American observers. Almost a week passed and nearly half his men were lost before he "woke up," in his own phrase. Now he ordered his company commanders to keep only one or two men from each platoon in the forward slope's foxholes. All others were to re-main under cover on the rear slope until the enemy's big guns let up and his infantry approached. Although Japanese forces had deployed simi-larly on other islands, Kojo was so unpracticed in defense that he con-sidered himself something of an originator when he at last put his new tactics into practice.

Days later, his force of nearly a thousand had been reduced by about two-thirds. But now casualties were much diminished; his new deploy-ment worked well. His attackers were the 17th Infantry Regiment of the Army's veteran 7th (Hourglass) Division, which had been in some of the bitterest fighting in the south from the first week in April. They'd move out every morning after their breakfast, sometimes supported by tanks, including the new flamethrowing model that shot its napalm well into caves. Kojo's skeleton crew of spotters on the forward slope would relay their coordinates to those waiting on the rear one, and mortar crews would fire until the Americans pulled back. The same sequence was usu-ally repeated in the afternoon, after which the defenders would take cover for the enemy's late-afternoon artillery and naval bombardment.

Kojo's strongest contribution to the surprisingly powerful defense was a novel use of the knee-mortar, as it came to be known from its height. (Early in the war, Americans erroneously thought it was braced against the leg or knee for firing, which may also account for the name.) Because the very light, simple weapon could fire its two-inch projectile almost straight up and down, it could be used at extremely close range and al-most any angle. It was deadly just where American mortars, of which the smallest was almost twice the size, had to stop firing for fear of hitting their own troops.

American infantrymen on Okinawa had already developed a hatred for Japanese mortars, which could be carried anywhere by a single man, fired from safe positions, and quickly moved to avoid retaliation once their location was spotted. Knee-mortars, the clever little version that could "drop their shells right on your head, that's how accurate they were," rated special loathing. "Whenever we evacuated wounded over open ground," an American would remember, "we ran like hell because they could almost pinpoint the stretcher."

Each Japanese infantry platoon had a squad of four knee-mortars, and there were three platoons in a company, three companies in Kojo's battalion. But instead of the usual deployment under the platoon leaders, he concentrated the thirty-six weapons into one unit under his personal command, producing what American military historians would call "an exceptionally effective system" of concentrating fire.

Although some 24th Division artillery was still operational, each firing revealed the gun's position, provoking far heavier return fire from American planes and rocket launchers as well as the land and naval cannon. The guns were also virtually immobile in the caves into which they were pulled back after their scant few rounds, because the 32nd Army was unable to shift troops, let alone trucks, anywhere during daylight. By early May, the planes would "pounce on a single soldier who moved" — not to mention gun crews trying to take up new positions. That lack of support from other units made Kojo's knee-mortars even more important to him.

His machine guns, easily concealed and fired from very low to the ground, were also highly effective. Day after day, ten- or fifteen-second bursts from his dozen skillfully deployed guns cut down lead Americans, after which the main body of the advance generally retreated. Unless American tanks joined the push, the defenders sometimes achieved brief equality in equipment in such encounters because the attackers had only the armament they could carry — and heavy artillery support had to cease for fear of causing own-fire casualties. Americans had been repeatedly assured they were superior to the enemy in every way, able to "lick them hands down when it comes to the fighting," as their pre-invasion briefing assured them. But it wasn't nearly so easy when it came closer to a fair fight of man against almost equally armed man.

Kojo's men learned to rush to the surface and prepare for those close encounters the instant bombardments let up. On May 3, the battalion helped shred a major assault on the ridge. The captain reckoned he could check the advance of an entire battalion if just two or three machine guns remained operable, for the Americans seemed attached to fighting by the clock — and with great caution and concern for their lives. It was, he thought, as if they were engaged in some gigantic industrial operation instead of mounting the all-out, go-for-broke attack that would have won them quick victory. What a gift to his tactics!

Lower-ranking Japanese shared his puzzlement over American prudence. A soldier at the eastern anchor of the same line, also under siege by an Army unit, observed that Americans never made surprise attacks. "First of all, they provide a protected zone, construct roads, put up a bridge if it's down, level a wide area for parking their vehicles, which are loaded with weapons and supplies. Once that solid base of operations is established, they start advancing one step at a time" — in what an American military historian would compare to the movement of "the tireless inchworm." (Such "creeping" advances usually pertained more to Army than to Marine tactics, but not on the Shuri Line in May.) Still, "the advance is like a mountain moving slowly at you. Against that, our resistance is like a child playing with a little firecracker, so we have to retreat."

Kojo, however, was unimpressed with anything American apart from the lavish matériel. He speculated that any Japanese unit on the offensive there would have gone for the jugular, whatever the casualties.

The perceived American unwillingness to sacrifice lives also surprised his men. Many Japanese elsewhere on Okinawa were taken by American bravery — of pilots who dived through antiaircraft barrages, for example — and silently noted the falseness of their teaching about their enemy's softness and weakness. At Kochi, however, even Kojo's privates considered them too cautious. At the same time, they were envious that the only time Americans did seem to take risks was to recover their dead and wounded. They themselves were so short of supplies that they were forced to look at corpses, their own as well as American, as sources of useful items, from weapons to rations.

Apart from the few forward observers, the men lived in their unimproved caves during daylight. Two miles southwest, the thousand occupants of the less crowded and incomparably better-equipped 32nd Army headquarters under Shuri Castle lived like a higher species of underground animal. Night barely differed from day in the deep, dank tunnel, with its warren of companionways and smell of disinfectant from the medical center. The air was foul. The lights were permanently on; disorientation was inevitable. Half-naked off-watch soldiers snored in shared berths or on moldy bales of rice. Underground water soaked the lowest berths, but some who shared them liked the relief from the stifling heat. Even Colonel Yahara, Ushijima's gifted operations officer who had planned the defense from underground, began to feel he was "being dragged to the bottom of hell." But everyone derived some strength from the lantern-lit slogans on the walls: BE A SHIELD TO YOUR EMPEROR! DON'T DIE UNTIL YOU ANNIHILATE YOUR FOES! STICK TO YOUR GUNS UNTIL YOU DIE!

Kojo's troops were doing the latter from suffocating caves that made all those behind the lines luxurious by comparison. They reeked of smoke, gunpowder, and the human odors of men long unwashed and under supreme stress. The purgatory's final physical and psychological touches were scores of moaning, severely wounded men inside and hundreds of corpses just outside. But the living soldiered on with little surprise. Surrender was never considered. Even if they could somehow arrange to meet Americans for that, it would only bring a more hideous death, most Japanese remaining convinced that the enemy yearned to kill them in monstrous ways. Some believed bestial Marines, whose special purpose in Asia was to rape and murder Asian women, had qualified for the Corps by murdering their parents. The "demons" and "beasts" got their laughs castrating prisoners.

And if Japan lost the war, Americans would torture, mutilate, and drastically depopulate the homeland.* Even the one in a thousand who disapproved of Japanese militarism knew *prisoner of war* was "an abominable phrase," as one such rare exception put it: dishonor that would make him afraid to face friends and relatives — if he'd ever have that chance, given that he might be taken to America for a life of hard labor. A few bold thinkers speculated that surrender's shame might be lessened if Japan lost the war, in which case the Emperor too would become a prisoner. But 99 percent remained convinced that surrender would hasten the rape of everything sacred by barbarians who hated beautiful Japan. Such a life would not be worth living.

Captain Kojo's stoic men had been conditioned, since at least their first years in school, to obey authority without question, to suffer any amount of hardship in necessary silence, and to believe that a display of will would overcome all obstacles in the end. Many were natives of the northernmost main island of Hokkaido, whose inhabitants were considered slow to learn but extremely tenacious. Kojo supposed they were glad to be fulfilling their duty, even knowing it would end in death. Few shared their elite commander's belief in their happiness, but most were proud that their knee-mortars were exacting such a toll on the enemy. Even fewer cried, "Long live the Emperor!" when hit, but most were convinced that the bravest possible stand on Okinawa, with the greatest damage to the Americans, might prevent an invasion of the mainland, where their families would be at the evil enemy's mercy. And since Tokyo surely knew better than anyone that the loss of Okinawa would open the way to that nightmare, they continued bolstering themselves with talk of the massive reinforcements on their way to relieve them and/or help launch the long-awaited counterattack.

The 9th Division was returning from Formosa for a landing in the far south! The Combined Fleet was steaming from Singapore or waiting to pounce from one of the Ryukyu Islands farther north! New secret weapons were about to be introduced; the Americans' supply lines were fatally overextended and they were running desperately low on men and

---

*That notion was less farfetched than it may seem, since many winning sides in Japan's feudal wars had done unspeakable things to losing sides, sometimes torturing and butchering every survivor, including servants and children, when they were present in some of the besieged fortresses and settlements. At one such complex of fortified temples and shrines, a contemporary writer saw "the whole mountainside" as "a great slaughterhouse and the sight was one of unbearable horror."

arms; Washington was poised to sign an armistice on terms favorable to Japan! . . . and so on. Very few soldiers suspected Okinawa had already been written off as a sacrifice to gain time for the decisive battle in the homeland.

Those illusions accompanied a refusal to accept that the battle elsewhere on Okinawa wasn't going well. Even more than when *Yamato* was sunk, no bad news was believed unless accompanied by direct proof.

Circumstances enhanced the Japanese capacity to believe in the nation's divine invincibility. The great majority of civilians, raised on their isolated islands with deep mental barriers to the outside world, honestly and genuinely accepted their leaders' bizarre accounts of the war's progress. With even less information and more urgent need to trust, the 32nd Army had reason to deny the evidence of their eyes. Of course some troops merely followed orders without much patriotism until their time came to die. Of course there were doubts at the bottom of many hearts. But to air them "would have invited certain trouble," a soldier of another unit would remember of that period, "so we all talked bravely. Looking back at that time now, it was as if we were on death row, talking about a possible reprieve."

The hugely unfair American advantage in numbers and equipment reinforced the sense of mission. (Hadn't Japan *always* been treated unfairly, after all? Always been threatened, since the arrival of Perry's black ships? Hadn't her need to expand been fired by foreigners' oppression?) It also stiffened the conviction that *Yamato damashii* would be decisive in the end, which was as deep as the 10th Army's conviction of the superiority of the American way of life. That didn't free Kojo's men from a quaking fear of death or stifle their constant hope that their turn would come tomorrow rather than today. But much more than Americans, they were prepared not to return from Okinawa.

Their endurance at Kochi and elsewhere was also bolstered by a desire to serve a better cause than individual advancement. With fortress Okinawa seen as not only the home islands' best protection from invasion but also essential to Japan's survival, this "most important stand of the war," as Ivan Morris would call it in *The Nobility of Failure: Tragic Heroes in the History of Japan*, "became virtually synonymous with kamikaze."

Virtually everyone felt he should indeed be willing to die for the Emperor without regret. Their emotions, though not easily expressed, ran deep. In fact, their tendency to act on emotion rather than on reason helped condition them to accept the idea of extreme sacrifice. On top of that came the group pressure to do one's duty. Every American training officer knew men were able to function in battle because they feared failure in their comrades' eyes more than they feared death. That was even more true of the Japanese, whose dread of ignominy had long played a greater role in society, and to whom subservience of individual interests to group discipline was far more natural. An American battalion too might fight to its last man's death if its members felt their families' existence depended on it — but alternatives would surely be discussed, including surrender in order to fight another day. However, even the least fervent among Kojo's men accepted that this life had to end before a better one could begin. A soldier who was later amazed that he'd survived summed up the mood: "I never thought I'd come home alive. It was clear to us all what would happen. [But] we could do nothing else."

The American offensive of May 11 to crack the Shuri Line was still a week away, but 10th Army headquarters already accepted that a major undertaking was needed to break the back of the defense that was so much stronger than anticipated. In particular, the Americans' appreciation of the skills of the "Jap fanatics" at Kochi Ridge increased. Kojo's concentration of accurate fire was too serious a menace to try to overcome in one attack; the policy of steady destruction with superior firepower would be maintained.

But the Japanese showed no signs of being destroyed, despite pressure on the 7th Division to do that from the Army Corps's headquarters. In the second week of May, the "utterly exhausted" 7th was replaced by the 96th, reinforced and fresh from a ten-day rest. The new troops continued probing mornings and afternoons, and Kojo's mortars — now used only when the attackers were fully exposed — continued cutting them down. Tank-supported American penetration proceeded on both flanks of Kochi Ridge, but the 1st Battalion held on, now inflicting more casualties than it was taking.

It was the kind of defense by attrition Colonel Yahara had dreamed of, with Japanese tactics and tenacity almost a match for American equipment and might. The enemy would pound the position much of the day, shaking the earth and threatening to collapse Kojo's little headquarters cave. But however miserable that made the recipients, most were protected and ready to move out the moment the bombardment stopped for the small-arms skirmishes in which they stood a chance, because the Americans couldn't make use of their roughly 50-to-1 advantage — including naval and air support — in firepower.

The 1st Battalion was reinforced by an understrength rifle company commanded by a Captain Kiguchi, a friend of Kojo's from the Imperial Academy and service in Manchuria. Kiguchi, a typical academy graduate devoted wholly to military life and thoughts, was exceptionally eager, cool, and brave. Despite his pleas to join the fighting, however, Kojo insisted

the slightly junior officer was his guest and kept his 180-odd men in reserve — until a week's attrition of the battalion left him little choice. Exuberant Kiguchi utterly ignored all danger, dashing to his machine-gun
positions and occasionally to confer with Kojo. His requests for permission to blow up American tanks with satchel charges were so insistent
that Kojo reluctantly succumbed, even knowing how badly a commander's loss damaged unit morale. Kiguchi succeeded in blowing up one
tank, but a close escape on a second attempt prompted Kojo to withdraw
permission.

As for Kojo's men, massive fatigue as well as the reduced but regular
daily casualties were weakening them. When the enemy's evening shelling
ceased, they dragged themselves to complete tasks that could be undertaken only in the relative safety of darkness: repairing their trenches, carrying their wounded to an underground first-aid station, and supplying
themselves. The work details would continue until the resumption of the
shelling at dawn.

All were incessantly thirsty. There was so little water that they had trouble swallowing the biscuit that supplemented their rations, and some
risked leaving their positions in daylight to sneak to wells below the
ridge. Otherwise, they carried in water at night from supply caves in the
Naha area, two or three miles south.

The handful who were to survive would fully appreciate the quantity of
American supplies and equipment — and therefore the hopelessness of
their cause — only after seeing stocks of them near their POW camps. But
even now, it seemed to the battalion's remaining fighters that the enemy
had limitless supplies of ammunition, while they were restricted to four or
five rounds a day from each mortar. After a particularly successful engagement, a warrant officer happily reported the results to Kojo. "Yes, but you
expended more rounds than necessary," the captain reproved. A handful of
Japanese ships had risked sailing to Okinawa after the 10/10 air raid, but
none arrived with either replacement soldiers or matériel after L-day, and
the trickle delivered by air stopped after the first week of April. Kojo worried about running out of ammunition during an enemy attack. Like the
drinking water, each shell had to be brought in on the men's backs at night.

They also carried in their food, reduced to hardtack and a single daily
rice ball, about the size of a fist, with a sour, salty pickle inside. Few were
any hungrier than combat Americans, despite weeks of fighting all day
and working much of the night under extreme duress. Still, they burned
so much energy with so little replacement that all became severely weakened on top of their exhaustion. With no rest and — unlike the Americans — no replacements, the undernourished soldiers grew so tired that
some began sleeping straight through the bombardments.

Command of the skies over Okinawa lay completely in the hands of the U.S. Air Force; the Japanese Navy had already been rendered impotent. Thus the fate of the 32nd Army was just a matter of time.
— Saburo Hayashi, *Kogun: The Japanese Army in the Pacific War*

Dark, gloomy days went by and the Emperor's birth drew near.
— Shigemi Furukawa, *The End of Okinawa*

April 29: the Emperor's birthday. The worse it gets for us, the more hope grows among the soldiers.
— Ikuo Ogiso, *Ah, Okinawa!*

Back at 32nd Army headquarters, senior officers' distress over the erosion of the force's strength mixed with worry that limiting it exclusively to defense was undermining morale. Colonel Yahara, still the consummate realist by Japanese standards, tried to stiffen spirits by emphasizing how much strength had been preserved even after a month of severe fighting. No Japanese force on any other island had held out so long. But few found comfort in such "negative" logic. Staff officers grew increasingly impatient to *be Japanese* by striking back.

Many privates at the front also yearned for something, anything, that promised relief from their wretched existence in caves where they were "on the verge of losing our sanity from suffering inside," as a typical dweller described it. The battle's American rich and Japanese poor differed in more than equipment and supplies. The former were mobile. The latter's fetid refuges — which would protect them only until they died there — also kept planning officers from seeing the enemy's moves. When reports were delivered to them after dark — by foot because so few lines of communication remained operable — it was too late to react to battlefield changes, even if the available Japanese forces *had* been mobile. Thus a soldier's complaint that "we donned a new kind of armor and called it a cave, which bound us hand and foot."

The image of an offensive was better than the underground reality of filth, suffocating stench, and the dizziness of oxygen deprivation. One soldier noticed that those "imprisoned" in his "miserable" cave had begun wishing, "agonizingly, for a decisive sortie." Another was "quite pleased" to leave his "stinking, soot-filled" cave for what would probably be his end.

While the fierce Japanese defense was confounding Americans, Japanese soldiers were *more* confounded by the failure of their Air Force and Navy to appear.

We look up at the sky every morning thinking, "Today must be the day!" But all we see overhead are enemy planes, like a swarm of bees.

"They won't come," some soldiers say pessimistically. "No more planes are left in Japan, that's the only reason I can think of for their not coming."

"No, they'll surely be here," others insist. "Planes always come just when everyone gives up."

The approach of the Emperor's birthday, first among national holidays, swelled hope like a rising tide. Thousands of caves lived on thoughts of April 29's promised issue of sweet potato brandy (which most wouldn't get) and of the giant swarm of friendly planes that would appear that morning after having cleverly bided their time. Then reinforcements would arrive to end the "merciless hurricane" of American fire and start the crushing of the brazen enemy. Sweet revenge! A medical corpsman drew strength from visions of the jubilee's "mass" of planes that would signal the "gigantic counterattack" for "turning the tide of the war at one huge blow!"

> So we went to the opening of our shelter to watch the sky — but the day came and went like all others, raining enemy bombs and shells. We saw not a single set of silvery wings bearing the Rising Sun. . . . Our only comfort was in Imperial Headquarters' exaggerated announcement of the results of the [kamikaze] attacks.*

Kojo's surviving soldiers, accustomed to living by starlight, used that morning's predawn hours for their usual brief break before the American bombardment began. They ate their cold, moldy rice balls and assured themselves the Combined Fleet was on its way. Although the decimated Imperial Navy had no such plans, a tense staff meeting was taking place in the headquarters tunnel deep below Shuri Castle.

The advocates of switching to offense had grown disgusted and bold enough for Colonel Yahara to complain that his life had been threatened by some of the "fire-eaters." Predictably, the most fervent deprecation of defense and acclaim for attack came from Lieutenant General Isamu Cho, Ushijima's fiery chief of staff. Rumor had it that the ultranationalist planner of assassinations and unauthorized military forays during the 1930s pleaded with Yahara to accept the need for an offensive. "You have your own ideas, of course, but I beg you — please die with me." Cho's hot tears in the tunnel corridor were said to have wet Yahara's hands and melted his cool reasoning.

If that exchange indeed took place, the two nevertheless clashed sharply at the staff meeting on the Emperor's birthday. The struggle between Cho's passion for action (or romantic self-sacrifice) and Yahara's

---

*Although hope for salvation was soon transferred to Navy Memorial Day, May 27, much of the trust would be gone by the time it arrived.

commitment to rational economy of force (or dreary submission to crushing reality) was again out in the open. Four weeks earlier — two days after L-day — Cho had urged a massive charge against the newly landed and still disorganized enemy, but Ushijima disapproved. Then came the secret signal informing of *Yamato*'s imminent sortie, which included instructions to take advantage of it by counterattacking on the ground, starting April 7, when the great ship was scheduled to arrive off the coast. Cho exulted. The "attack and more attack" that had created the Empire would now save it by smashing the confused Americans. However, Ushijima believed the first week of the battle was still too early for counterattacks, and telegraphed Tokyo with his advice to stop the naval operation. Combined Fleet headquarters seemed to be living in a dream world, ignorant of the enemy's immense strength at sea and in the air.

A very modest counterattack *was* made on April 12, after which emotion swung toward Cho's stance. Now, on April 29, he remained convinced that Japanese resolve could negate the American material advantages, just as Yahara still believed premature preoccupation with "honorable" death was self-indulgent. Cho's basic idea was to create battlefield chaos in order to engage the enemy in the hand-to-hand combat at which the Japanese excelled. He argued eloquently and persuasively that if things kept going as they were, the 32nd Army would soon lose its offensive capacity, then its ability to resist at all. The only hope was to snatch life from the midst of death by taking action while the means still existed. Mutual annihilation was better than the steady attrition that could end only in certain defeat.

Annihilation was inevitable either way, Yahara countered, but an ill-conceived counterattack would hasten it. An attacking force usually needed a 3-to-1 advantage for success in modern battle. Charging a superior force with an inferior one was reckless rather than merely extremely risky. The losses, inevitably greater if the troops forfeited the advantages of their rear-slope positions, would mean failure in the 32nd Army's primary duty of prolonging the battle as much as possible to give the mainland more time to prepare for its invasion.

But a chorus of angry patriots who craved action at any cost all but shouted down Yahara's appeal. Reluctantly approving the staff consensus, the ordinarily amiable Ushijima ordered his chief operations officer to stop arguing in a way that would undermine unity and morale. He scheduled a massive counterattack for May 4. The following day, Emperor Hirohito, who'd been urging his advisers from the beginning to press for something similar, radioed a message from Tokyo: "We really want this attack to succeed."

Five days of intense planning and preparations followed. Kojo's 24th Division would be the main attacking force, the 62nd having been too weakened to participate. A tank regiment and infantry battalion were moved up from reserve and committed for the first time. The spearhead would be in sight of Kojo's position, although other units would make the initial breakthrough. The final objectives were a full five miles north, halfway to the landing beaches, where the first main defensive line, including Kakazu Ridge, would be restored. The men of the 24th Division were ordered to "kill at least one American devil for every Japanese" — an extremely optimistic goal, since their losses had been roughly 10 to 1 until now, even with their underground protection. But the mood was exuberant. *Attack at last! Victory! Honor!*

The Fifth Floating Chrysanthemum was launched to coordinate with the counterattack. On May 3 and 4, kamikazes sank a destroyer and put seventeen other American ships out of action. On land, the Japanese softening up took place during the night of May 3–4. A small banquet, served by attractively dressed typists and clerks, was still in progress in the headquarters tunnel when the big guns began firing, at 0450 hours. As dawn approached, they delivered the most powerful Japanese barrage in the Pacific War so far: half an hour of all-out bombardment, as opposed to firing a precious few rounds then pulling back into hiding. Those first full salvos in the thirty-four days of fighting were a grim surprise to the Americans.

Captain Kojo could not know that, apart from cases of battle fatigue, the barrage caused relatively few casualties because most Americans were dug in "deep and dry." But he and his men rejoiced in the flash and thunder of the Japanese artillery, especially after its failure to support his fighting until then. Cho's argument that attack would greatly boost morale seemed proved.

In Kojo's 22nd Regiment, only the remains of Captain Kiguchi's rifle company would join the initial strike. The other units were assigned to screen the vanguard of two attacking regiments with heavy fire and smoke, then leapfrog ahead of them. Although Kojo knew nothing of Yahara's opposition to the counterattack, his regimental commander had told him he'd be in no hurry to join the advance, and he later learned that Yahara, determined not to doom the command to premature destruction, had confidentially advised some sympathetic officers that not all units need participate.

In fact, the debacle was as bad as he predicted, despite the initial American surprise. Almost a thousand valuable men were lost without purpose when Japanese amphibious units were spotted approaching both coasts. Those who survived destruction in the water by American artillery were slaughtered on the beaches, far from their targets. Navigational errors brought some boats directly into the sights of American batteries, where troops shouting "Banzai!" helped pinpoint the fire on themselves.

On land, Japanese detachments courageously attacked through their own killing artillery fire, most meeting total failure. After small units on both sides moved closer to annihilation by the other's guns, Japanese weakness in numbers and logistics rapidly became decisive. Delayed by faulty transportation, two battalions of the 89th Infantry Regiment, a sister regiment of Kojo's 22nd, were caught in the open by American artillery, which cut down another thousand-odd men in minutes.

Quickly recovering from their surprise, American units used their immense firepower with devastating effect. "The 'all-out' offensive evaporated like a brief dream," a Japanese survivor would lament. "When dawn arrived, our forces, which had taken advantage of darkness to penetrate enemy territory, were exposed on the surface [that is, not in a cave] and cut down by the typhoon of enemy fire from ships, planes and howitzers." Two nights later, a few bloody stragglers from an attacking platoon dragged themselves back to the cave of that survivor to report no gain whatever for the massive losses. All realized the huge expenditure of irreplaceable ammunition had also been for nothing, and "miserable and gloomy days" returned to the cave after its forty-eight hours of hope.

Only one battalion managed to penetrate about a mile to the north. Part of a sister regiment of Kojo's 24th Division, it was commanded by Captain Koichi Ito, who was also twenty-four years old and involved in his first combat after taking command of his battalion in Manchuria. At the Imperial Military Academy, Ito had been an even brighter exemplar of regular Army officer resolve than his classmate Kojo. Since arriving on Okinawa, he'd received a total of one letter and hadn't concerned himself about how many arrived or didn't arrive for his men.

That one letter was from his father, a former naval officer who happened to be friendly with a high-ranking strategist fired for refusing to help plan the war against America. "If you start a war without first equipping the Air Force to match other leading nations," the strategist had warned, "Japan will be in ashes and you will hurtle to hell." But if that rare acquaintance with dissenting views gave Ito an unusual perspective on the war, it didn't weaken his commitment. Before the American landing, he rode his battalion relentlessly and won the highest commendations for digging fortifications, then refused to be sent home on the eve of L-day despite a severe case of dysentery.

Ito's battalion was situated a few hundred yards west and behind Kojo's on Kochi Ridge. Jumping off from there, he alone managed to advance as planned and survive the first day with most of his force intact. The iron captain attacked again at midnight, firing a flare at a hill mass called Tanabaru escarpment, from which Japanese units had been driven almost two weeks before, to show he'd reached his first major objective. But he was so surrounded by enemy guns that he had to keep all heads below ground and communicate with his officers by tossing messages tied to rocks into their foxholes. Just over a third of his six hundred men — down from a thousand before May 4 — were alive when he extricated himself, with supreme bravery and skill against overwhelming firepower, on May 7.

During the previous days, the success of his haggard force with its severely limited armament and support — no tanks, rocket launchers, flamethrowers — suggests what might have been achieved with greater supplies and even partial air support. But Ito was the exception that proved the rule; the counterattack was acknowledged as having collapsed even before his second sally that midnight. On the evening of May 5, the 32nd Army announced it would "temporarily" suspend the attack, claiming that it had inflicted sufficient damage.

If the wording saved face for Cho and the staff officers, Ushijima couldn't undo the consequences of his second major strategic mistake after letting Kerama Retto and the airfields at Yomitan and Kadena fall with almost no opposition. The loss of nearly seven thousand of his best troops was catastrophic. The 24th Division had been disastrously weakened. Japanese artillery was decimated. The exposure of the previously hidden ordnance enabled American forces to pinpoint and destroy nineteen heavy guns on the first day alone. And American casualties, heavy as they were by their own measures, barely exceeded those of the hard days of storming Japanese defensive positions. Instead of the prescribed kill ratio of ten to 1, the Japanese lost up to twenty for every American.

Even Cho now accepted that the 32nd Army could no longer think of offense. When they heard of the decision to abandon the counterattack, angry young members of the staff demanded an explanation. An apologetic Cho did what he could to stem their tearful despair, and Ushijima is said to have summoned Yahara for his own lachrymose promise to be guided by his advice in the future. Staff officers of course carried on, but "a pall of gloom" settled on them, as a scholar described the effect of the May 4 failure, "and it never lifted."

Genuine information came from the front in the person of blood-covered casualties. We were losing ground slowly but steadily. The American advance wasn't rapid but had a frightening assurance. . . . It was no longer a glorious man-to-man fight but a grotesquely one-sided process in which a gigantic organism crushed and pulverized human flesh.
   — A Japanese soldier

I sometimes wonder how we'd have done without our 10-to-1 superiority in combined manpower and maybe more in supplies — without that naval armada and our incredible firepower. I'd have wet my pants if I'd been a Japanese soldier.
   — An American Marine

All our training paid off. Despite the enemy's overwhelmingly superior firepower, my men never panicked. I myself felt truly calm. But our training also included much that was totally irrelevant to modern warfare and blinded us to reality.
— Tadashi Kojo

Intelligence and diligence can stand against even the most extreme technological superiority. But not forever. Ultimately, brave men and overwhelming firepower will always defeat brave men alone.
— Thomas Huber, *Japan's Battle of Okinawa, April–June 1945*

The expenditure of so many Japanese shells reduced each gun's daily allowance from fifty to fifteen. That and the loss of many pieces lessened total Japanese artillery firepower by about half. The depletion of infantry forces required more service and support units to be thrown into the weakening Shuri Line. By American standards, the 24th Division, down to three-fifths of its original strength, was no longer a proper fighting unit.

Although the two days of hopeless gesture hadn't increased casualties in Kojo's 1st Battalion, he now had to face heavier enemy pressure without Kiguchi's help. The junior captain's company was among the units either destroyed to the last man or left with wounded who couldn't make their way back to their lines. Kojo later learned that enemy tanks had massacred most of the men hours after their advance down from Kochi Ridge.

The American units there regrouped and resupplied fast enough to resume their offensive on May 6 (two days before V-E Day). Adding gasoline and napalm to their ordnance, they tried to throw ten-gallon cans over the hill to burn out Kojo's men — who, however, mustered enough fire the following day to force the retreat of two American infantry platoons that had taken part of a small adjoining hill. A cascading rain also helped. Hard as it was on the Japanese, it caused more disruption to the attackers by miring their heavy equipment in impenetrable mud. Kojo's men were now the backbone of what a study by U.S. Army historians would call "the chief obstacle to the 7th Division's advance." It demonstrated, the American account would explain, that the defenses at Kochi Ridge "could not be overrun in a single attack but required a tedious, methodical destruction of individual enemy soldiers and positions."

So the 1st Battalion's casualties relentlessly mounted. "The man who reported the names of his friends who had been killed one day would be among the names reported the following one," a soldier from a similarly besieged unit would recall. One by one, two by two, Kojo's troops dwindled. His unit seemed to be going from a battalion to a company to a platoon.

There were now too few men to continue evacuating the gravely wounded to the regimental tunnel south of Naha, where the medical facility remained. Most treatment was limited to stopping hemorrhages. Ambulatory wounded were given first aid and returned to their posts immediately. The chief medical officer was ordered to join the fighters with all his patients from the tunnel — some two hundred men — who were strong enough to hold a rifle.

The opposite traffic, back to the tunnel, was more pathetic. Some of the gravely wounded tried to crawl there "like night worms," as one saw them. Others preferred to die where their fallen comrades lay. Although saddened by his inability to help them, Kojo took their great bravery as normal and even envied the "lucky" who had departed. They'd won honor and an end to suffering, whereas the living had to keep going until the only relief would come for them too.

The captain's long training for sacrifice enabled him to accept the losses with slight concern. Sustained by *gaman,* the exceptional Japanese patience and perseverance in the face of adversity — and by their regiment's venerable record of valor in combat on top of it — the men from whom he continued to stand apart also accepted their lot without complaint. (Kojo would later speculate that their enormous endurance and sacrifice for the nation was almost a natural culmination of their lives of severe deprivation for protracted periods.) Only one company commander suffered a kind of shell shock. When his casualties reached 90 percent, that reserve lieutenant requested permission to return to the regimental tunnel to hunt for reinforcements. A fierce shout from Kojo interrupted his subordinate's very rare impertinence. "*No!* You will stay where you are!"

Otherwise, he saw no cases of mental breakdown, which he wouldn't have understood anyway: Such weakness wasn't permitted — which probably helped prevent it. But the men had normal feelings. Okinawa's May is like southern Georgia's. When the rain let up, temperatures soared in the airless little caves. Daylong confinement there — with the extreme shortage of clean water — would have been torture enough even without "the smell of blood and sweat [that] mixed with the putrid stench of the wounds to suffocate us," in the words of Private Yoshio Kobayashi, who served in a communications unit.

Kobayashi's duties gave him more relief than most from confinement in his "inferno-like" cave, but only at the price of more exposure to danger. Delivering a message weeks before, he and a fellow communications soldier had had to cross a beach bare of all cover. They clung to a telephone pole for futile protection while a Grumman made four or five strafing runs at them, then ran desperately and collapsed inside a deserted cave. Laden with a heavy radio in addition to their rifles and packs, they set out again after sundown. Hands numb, drenched in sweat, they crossed streams in total darkness because bridges were demolished and kept taking cover because shells and bombs fell on them "as if by signal" whenever they risked using a main road. After more hiding the following day, they resumed their mission in the drizzle of dusk until a sergeant they met in the smoke of a recently leveled village told them their destination was already being overrun by Americans. But to their delight — since most Japanese units had little knowledge about or interest in others — he gave them directions to their company, which had moved in their absence. Setting out again for there, they soon completed their odyssey.

> First we saw dead horses [from other, presumably artillery, units]. Decomposed, emitting the nauseating stench of death. Next came a large crater that must have been made by a 500-kilogram bomb. A soldier lay dead at its bottom, sprawled face up, his shoulder soaked in blood to the chest.
>
> We walked on . . . [to] where we met wounded soldiers retreating from the front. No one looked alive. Some dripped blood from the hip down, some were supported by buddies, their own heads covered in blood. . . . I thought I was going mad. Corpses piled up on both sides of the road, some half-skeletons, others bloated with gas. The stench nearly suffocated me. . . .
>
> Somehow we made it to company headquarters . . . [where] many of our comrades were already dead. Senior Private Homma joked that he was a self-appointed funeral director.

Although some of Kojo's men sustained their black jokes even now, the captain himself was far from anything even faintly humorous. Under fire, he was even more strict than in Manchuria and so remote that the lower ranks, to whom he still rarely talked, hardly considered him a fellow sufferer. His higher noncommissioned officers admired his sterling military qualities and bearing more than ever. The young captain kept his figure as straight and neat as possible in the circumstances, and was so committed to fighting to the utmost that he seemed devoid of all personality. The men had called the major who'd replaced him when he was injured the "Old Man," but they had no nickname for this ramrod who cared only about doing his duty, defending his honor.

As the enemy's regular morning and afternoon attacks intensified, Kojo's men grew so weak that he was surprised the enemy didn't mount a major attack. Kochi Ridge now represented a significant bulge on the map, all territory on both flanks having been taken. But Kojo's line was as thin as a thread. The May 4 counteroffensive's shearing of the 32nd Army's edge had put the men in a kind of shock, deepening the numbness caused by the relentless strain on their undernourished minds, bodies, and nerves.

It in no way detracts from American triumphs over their horrendous hardships to acknowledge that Japanese soldiers endured far worse with more fortitude and many fewer breakdowns. They lived in the same mud, even thicker with blood. They were more infested with vermin, more debilitated by disease, more overrun by maggots feasting on their beloved comrades' rotting corpses. Their rations were not to be compared. And the number of incoming shells exceeded the number they fired at Americans by at least fifty times. If American Army analysts of the Okinawa fighting would ultimately conclude that troops should remain in the line no longer than two weeks, because physical and mental fatigue from the need for constant alertness and "strain of continuous shell fire . . . greatly reduces the soldiers' efficiency," what of the Japanese soldiers in May? Brave to begin with, Kojo's were long past fear, except when they saw small arms about to shoot them. They kept to their duties despite gruesome killings and maimings by mortar barrages that seemed to approach machine-gun fire in intensity. Yet their physical condition after the weeks of fighting on empty stomachs and with only catnaps worried Kojo more than the drastically inadequate supply of ammunition, which still had to be carried on foot from two or three miles south.

At dusk, he left his cave with several young officers to inspect his remaining forces. Twice mortar rounds killed all others in his little group. Miraculously unhit and unhurt, he now allowed the shared pressure of the day-and-night ordeal to slightly narrow his distance from his men. But the Japanese Army inculcated self-sufficiency in its battalion commanders. His discussions with regimental commander Yoshida, still on a hill about a mile behind his, were therefore limited to two or three throughout this period.

Nor did they have the American command's give and take between superiors and subordinates. Kojo reported his situation to Yoshida but never requested help. Superiors were assumed to know who needed reinforcements and when, and the captain maintained his composure in the face of difficulty, the clearest mark of the academy graduate. He did not have to remember his responsibility to present an image of unshakable confidence because he still felt calm and had no idea his resistance was among the most stubborn in the entire campaign. This was war. Emotion had no place in it. His duty was to fight serenely to the end.

Thirty years later, the Marine corporal named James Day who'd become commander in chief of U.S. forces on Okinawa would pay tribute to the "remarkable" enemy. "To have fought so well with no air cover, no naval support and virtually no support whatever required enormous resilience and skill." At the time, however, the American command felt no admiration for that, only frustration. Much of the mighty 10th Army remained stalled, despite the counteroffensive's weakening of the Shuri Line.

On the evening of May 10 — the day after Paul Dunfrey led his scouting party across the Asakawa roughly four miles west of Kochi Ridge — Kojo was ordered to pull back about eight hundred yards to three small hills slightly south of his previous position. The 22nd Regiment's other two battalions had returned from their detached duty to the command of Colonel Yoshida, each with some hundred survivors. Together with Kojo's men, including a dozen from his Headquarters Company, the entire regiment, once numbering some thirty-three hundred men, consisted of roughly three hundred combat troops nearing the limit of fatigue. Kojo's were so spent that the regimental commander reinforced them with fresh men pared from the regimental color guard. That decision spoke for itself about the battalion's condition, since capture of the regiment's colors, which had been presented by the Emperor himself, would be the supreme disgrace.

But it bolstered fighting strength to that of approximately two healthy platoons. Kojo deployed them on the new rear slopes. With Shuri only a few thousand yards behind him, his orders to hold his position to the last man were superfluous. Some of his toughest noncoms, including a few veterans of the China War, continued repulsing the advances of the enemy, who tried hard on May 11 — the day General Buckner launched his general offensive — then seemed to lose energy after his weeks of attacks. Kojo believed he could have held the new hills for weeks with rested men and adequate supplies, but both had dwindled to near nothing. Thirty men were too few to fire the mortars or to carry their shells. The 1st Company consisted only of its commander, a replacement lieutenant. The 2nd Company, commanded by a sergeant, had half a dozen men; the 3rd Company ten. All moved in a permanent stupor. When enemy tanks started up to surround Kojo's position, he and the chief medical officer, the lieutenant who'd been ordered from the regimental tunnel to the front, discussed suicide. Then the rain turned so violent that the tanks pulled back.

The end came on May 16, while the Marines were having one of their worst days on Sugar Loaf, four miles southwest. A nearby hill defended by another unit fell, giving the Americans a clear, short line of fire on Kojo's position — but his observers had succumbed to exhaustion and slept. Blowing them apart with hand grenades at close range, the Americans gave the men slightly to the rear their first touch of panic.

Surprised too, Kojo ran through the smoke of the enemy's phosphorous grenades into a well-maintained cave in the largest of the hills behind him. A handful of his men ran with him. The rest were dead.

Several dozen badly wounded men were already there, moaning in the dark. Kojo whispered an order for silence. Despite the American shouts overhead, he hoped absolute quiet inside might allow them to go undetected until they could sneak out at nightfall. But a first lieutenant who'd run in with him — 1st Company's replacement commander — had no stomach for more. "This is hopeless," he whispered. "I'm going to die here." Kojo too suddenly lost heart. The cave's original users were artillery spotters, who had cut a hatch in its top and built a ladder for access. The American shouting from there grew more excited. Kojo knew there was no escape from the hand grenades or satchel charges they were readying to toss down the hatch. Surrender never entered his thoughts. There was only one way out.

He felt no pain or panic, not even disappointment or nervousness. His training or exhaustion kept him utterly calm, although he'd have liked to let his wife and family know how and where he died.

"I've done my duty," he thought with satisfaction. "I fought with honor and fulfilled my life's purpose. Now it's the end." He put his pistol to his temple and enjoyed a vision of beautiful Emiko during their happy trip to Manchuria.

As he curled his finger around the trigger, something hurtled down the hatch. The explosion of a satchel charge, devastating in the confined space, tore the pistol from his hand.

Kojo did not think of trying again when he regained consciousness. After his last-instant reprieve, some counterforce made him prefer to resume fighting until someone killed him, which would be soon enough.

Badly shaken but apparently otherwise unhurt, he couldn't find his pistol in the pitch dark. The sound of American voices, still overhead, warned him not to try to leave until after they did. Groping for fellow survivors, he found two: the despairing first lieutenant and a courageous senior private who'd fought the entire campaign. Kojo's pep talk to the lieutenant was in vain: The reserve officer remained determined to die where he was. But the private was eager to fight again.

The explosion or subsequent shell fire had sealed the mouth of the cave. Hours after the American voices stopped, Kojo and the private began digging with their hands. Finally, 1st Battalion's two known survivors crawled out and into the night's silence. They wriggled like worms into the shell holes that pockmarked the hill until an enemy sentry spied them about twenty yards from the cave. His shots missed. After huddling in their hole for a time, they resumed their crawling down the slope of the hill, past American silhouettes, and toward the new Japanese line.

They found Colonel Yoshida's headquarters cave toward midnight. The regimental commander knew Kojo's position had been overrun because his young operations lieutenant had ignored the American shelling to check from another observation post. Now he seemed happy to see Kojo alive, although he'd known him less than two months. "I always put you in the most difficult positions," he said. "I had to — but I regret it nevertheless." He put out his hand. "You fought very well. You deserve our congratulations."

Kojo fought back tears. Of course he must show no emotion. But now he knew — and was profoundly happy his regimental commander knew — that his position had held out longest on that front.

20 · Ushijima Abandons the Shuri Line

Behold! What is a bell? A bell is that which sounds far, wide, and high. . . . It will echo far and wide like a peal of thunder but with utmost purity. And evil men, hearing the bell, will be saved.
— From the inscription on a scarred, dented sixteenth-century bronze bell that would be dug from the ruins of Shuri Castle

Naha was a graveyard, its people vanished with its buildings. . . . Nothing moved in this desert of stone and carpet of rubble.
— From a Marine Corps film

A homeland was destroyed.
— From a film of the American Armed Forces Far East Network

Sugar Loaf was taken two days after Kochi Ridge. Neighboring barriers fell almost concurrently. The 6th Marines pressed on to Horseshoe Ridge behind Sugar Loaf, the 1st Marines pushed up through slaughterous Wana Draw below Shuri itself, and the American Army divisions took Conical and Sugar Hills as well as the Wart Hill–Flattop Hill–Chocolate Drop triangle east of Shuri, where the defense network almost equaled that of the Sugar Loaf triangle to the west.

May 11 to 21 could hardly have been more savage at every muddy knob and slope below those barriers. The 96th and 77th Army Divisions together reported 2,271 wounded and 402 killed and missing. The dead below Chocolate Drop struck one observer as a skirmish line lying down to rest. Most of the sixty thousand Okinawan and Japanese deaths so far had come in and around the Shuri Line.

Fewer than five hundred Japanese prisoners had been taken, many unconscious or too badly wounded to resist or kill themselves. There were even fewer prisoners the other way, partly because Americans were convinced, with good reason, that raised hands would court a quick death. Scores of wounded GIs and Marines played dead when enemy soldiers emerged after dark to strip bodies of wristwatches and rations. Those who lived to tell the tale endured kicks to their gaping wounds, fingers poked straight into their eyes, and booted jumps on their testicles. Almost all who failed such tests with a gasp or moan were finished with a bullet or bayonet.

A few prisoners were treated as badly as in the American propaganda about all Japanese. Two weeks after L-day, three airmen parachuted onto Ishigaki Island, roughly halfway between Okinawa and Formosa, whose garrison had suffered casualties in an American air raid the previous day. Two of the three, beaten too badly to walk, were dragged to holes, where a Japanese captain, proud of his skill — acquired in China — neatly beheaded one. When a second executioner, having noisily boasted about being chosen, managed to cut through only half his victim's neck, sailors finished the job. The third man, whose unwillingness to answer questions during his interrogation condemned him to a less honorable end, was tied to a stake and used for bayonet practice. Two other Americans were beheaded on Izena Island, some fifteen miles north of Okinawa, and three shot to death on Ie Shima, where Ernie Pyle was killed.

No such cold-blooded atrocities would become known on Okinawa itself, perhaps because no American prisoners were reported taken at the Shuri Line, where the dead died in combat. But despite their numbers, 10th Army staff members believed they could see the end after the critical ten days that melted the core of the defense. Gleanings from interrogations of the few Japanese prisoners supported the assumption that Ushijima was making his final stand where he'd hurt them most. The Japanese also took it for granted that they'd remain in the rump of their Shuri bastion until the last man was killed by the enemy or by himself. Rumors circulated about a plan to pull in all functioning units from farther south for a last-ditch effort near the 32nd Army headquarters tunnel. On May 22, however, the commander called another conference, this one to discuss new contingency plans with his senior staff and high officers of his fighting units.

With no more than a third of his combat strength to defend little more of the line than Shuri itself, Ushijima knew the full difficulty of his position. Imperial General Headquarters had abandoned the pretense of supporting a decisive battle on Okinawa. A week earlier, while his "land battleships" ringing Shuri were still repulsing their attackers, the ordinarily laconic general had requested reinforcements, warning that the fall of the line would mean the end of his organized resistance. Tokyo's answer was a promise of commando-type raids.

One was actually mounted two days later on Yomitan Airfield, which had been taken on L-day and now teemed with American planes. The Japanese allocated twelve obsolete bombers for the assault, each carrying a dozen paratroops from an elite unit that planned a suicidal attack with grenades and explosive charges. But mechanical trouble kept four of the planes on the ground, and when radar detected the others' approach, seven of the remaining eight were downed by American antiaircraft batteries firing an "almost solid" crisscross.

Riddled with shell fragments, the single surviving plane managed to belly-land at Yomitan, where its crew leaped out together with the dozen commandos, demolition charges tied around their waists. Before being killed to the last man, they destroyed or damaged twenty-seven planes and much aviation fuel and munitions. Happy news of the field's retaking went out to the soldiers of the 32nd Army. In fact, it was cleared of debris and put back in operation the following morning, and the Japanese made no further attempt to land troops on Okinawa, so close to their airfields in China, on Formosa, and on the mainland.

Only the kamikaze raids continued. Like them, that first attempt to put a force on land confirmed to Americans that their enemy was incorrigibly fanatic. Pilot Samuel Hynes was shocked by a raider blowing himself up with a grenade held to his belly. Hynes reasoned the point of the May 24 raid was self-destruction rather than destruction. He was appalled by his own conclusion that "the true end of the war for the men I was fighting against was not victory but death."

Although the May 24 raid was coordinated with the Seventh Floating Chrysanthemum, Ushijima now knew Imperial General Headquarters valued kamikaze operations more for delaying the inevitable invasion of the mainland than for trying to prevent the 32nd Army's certain defeat. Having had no illusions about winning since he lost the 9th Division, he now had none about reinforcements either.

However, he did have options, which was why he called his key conference on the evening of May 22. He'd found a way to forestall the end.

Two evenings later, American spotter planes flew over Shuri Castle to help direct gunfire from several ships led by USS *Mississippi*. Her crew had no idea an earlier battleship of the same name had closed on the same target.

The first was the sometime flagship of the squadron that opened Japan. Astute, arrogant Matthew Calbraith Perry stopped in Okinawa on his way there and back — and dictated severe terms to his utterly innocent, unwilling hosts. "Poor Okinawans!" said appalled members of his party of that first American-Okinawan encounter. An embarrassed clerk on the earlier *Mississippi* called the island "a mouse in the talons of the eagle."

She arrived in May 1853. The commodore gave calculated insult to a welcoming party and announced to its leading official — a courtly elder with what struck one of Perry's men as "the most dignified demeanor" — that he intended to call on the castle. One American thought the Okinawan party looked grave enough to be "going to an execution." With great courtesy and tact, they implored Perry not to make his call. Countering that he expected a reception worthy of his position, Perry gave orders that his men could go ashore wherever they pleased.

On a date he chose for his self-invitation, a sedan chair he'd ordered made for himself bore the vain commodore in his most impressive full-dress uniform along the lovely winding roads from the port to the castle. "I cannot conceive of a more beautiful pageant," he would write. The beauty included two field guns and two companies of Marines, whose presence finally forced unarmed Okinawans to open the symbolically important Gate of Courtesy at the entrance to the castle grounds. Some members of his party watched his gun-toting overbearance in dismay. "It was a struggle between weakness and right, and power and wrong, for a more high-handed piece of aggression has not been committed by anyone," a lay missionary and Chinese linguist who served as his translator would write (managing to escape the censorship Perry tried to impose on reports from Okinawa, lest any contradict his own). "I was ashamed at having been a party to such a procedure, and pitied these poor defenseless islanders."

So it went for the remainder of this visit, as well as most of a second one, when Perry returned after putting his demands to Japan. Grave American insults, including a rape by a sailor, widened the cultural misunderstandings. Officers sent ashore to secure housing forced open locked gates and took possession of what turned out to be a schoolhouse. (When all attempts to repossess it failed, Okinawans brought fruits and vegetables for its squatters.) Other commandeered buildings included a temple, and threats to occupy Shuri Castle itself were supported by maneuvers on ship and shore to display the squadron's overwhelming weaponry.

In a charitable moment, Perry called the Ryukyu Islands "as pleasant . . . as any in the world" and Okinawans "industrious and inoffensive." But he, proud of "interpos[ing] a little Yankee diplomacy" against the natives, displayed immediate force at their every failure to show the deference he felt was due him and his country. The commodore behaved throughout as if Okinawans were as duty-bound to obey as he was entitled to command. Setting out for Japan the second time, he left behind an armed party proclaiming he'd hold the Ryukyus under "limited authority" until he'd secured his objectives in Tokyo.

In Perry's defense, it should be said that the same imperious resolve that abused the gentle islanders seemed necessary for his diplomatic assault on Japan. Commodore James Biddle, his predecessor in trying to negotiate with Tokyo seven years earlier — and sixteen years after Japanese had fired on an unarmed American merchant ship — had been repulsed, scornful Japanese interpreting his conciliatory approach as weakness. Perry waved his big stick on Okinawa partly to warn them America would not again be trifled with. Besides, he was acting in a time of expansionist sea power and self-assertion throughout the West. Okinawa happened to be one of the prizes in the European powers' competition for influence and empire in the carve-'em-up colonialist age, in which the white man hailed himself as teacher. Perry's personal hauteur aside, he was up against old empires that were eager to claim all the rich prizes of trade, prestige, and domination for themselves. He might simply have taken a slice of Okinawa, as the British had taken Hong Kong from China just eleven years earlier and the Portuguese took Goa from India.

But Okinawans felt little gratitude. Perry's instructions for convincing the regent to sign an agreement laid power on the line. "Let the mayor clearly understand that this port [of Naha] is to be one of rendezvous, probably for years, and that the authorities had better come to an understanding at once." Persistence in trying to sustain their own laws and customs — "which they have no power to enforce" — would "surely involve themselves in trouble." The commodore used the same tone when threatening to occupy Shuri with his Marines. "It is repugnant to the American character to submit to such a course of inhospitable discourtesy," he said, referring to the resistance to his landing. His double talk had a twentieth-century ring. Americans, he added, "are always regardful of, and obedient to, the laws of the countries in which they may happen to be."

Such rot rested on implied racial superiority, as if Okinawans hadn't had enough of it from Japan. Before his final departure, Perry demanded a treaty stipulating that Okinawans must in the future service American ships and citizens "with great courtesy and friendship." A preamble stated that the servants were signing voluntarily. When they refused, the Marines were again sent ashore to force them. Meanwhile, a party had planted the Stars and Stripes on an Okinawan pinnacle they named Banner Rock, as if Americans had discovered the island.*

Perry knew why "the simple islanders" didn't want him to come ashore. An English ship had received the traditional native hospitality only thirty years earlier, but since then, the Satsuma lords ordered Shuri to keep foreigners out. The commodore had written the secretary of the Navy that Okinawans, "disarmed, as they long have been . . . have no means, even if they had the inclination, to rebel against the grinding oppression of their rulers." But instead of showing compassion for the semicaptives, he punished them more. Solely concerned with American national interests (in his own expansionist view of them), the high-handed intruder puffed with his own virtuousness and even convinced himself the Okinawans much appreciated him for it. That set the pattern of American-Okinawan relations: severely one-sided exchanges that would take place on the latter's land, at their expense. The island's poverty only tightened the cycle

*See p. 179.

of the powerful and self-righteous extracting concessions from the poor and weak.

Perry rested his actions on "the strictest rules of moral law," America's goodness and wisdom making the justice of his demands "self-evident." Japan's worse aggrandizement grew out of greed for Okinawa's trade and her sense of herself as supreme — without the Christian self-assurance, but with other myths of similar effect. The two powers that held themselves morally superior in their respective ways blithely violated a modest people who made no such claim. At one point before Satsuma's conquest, a Shimazu lord offered to settle a debt with ownership of the Ryukyus, to which he had no claim whatever. No less imperiously, Perry proposed annexing Okinawa as a base for military operations against Japan if his mission there failed. Such were the attitudes of rapacious earlier centuries, as if the twentieth would be easier on the Okinawans.

Now, ninety-two years after the commodore had had his way with the defenseless island, the modern *Mississippi* took aim on the same Shuri Castle, making ready to demolish the sixteenth-century monument and center of national life.

Little was left of the surrounding area. Okinawa had been taking heavier naval bombardment for a longer period than any other battle site in history. Even in the north, buildings were leveled that might have served military purposes, although many didn't. But the island's southern third fared far worse. Except during bad weather, most places even hinting of defensive value there had been under fire from sea and air for almost sixty days. Shuri heights had been a prime target from the first. An expert would calculate that two hundred thousand rounds of artillery alone were fired into the little city of about five thousand houses. Naval shells and hundreds of thousand-pound bombs completed what a native called the "laughter" of metal shrieking through the air.

But the walls of Shuri Castle, built of coral block by ten thousand people three centuries earlier, had withstood the pounding. It was those ramparts, twenty feet thick at their base and towering to more than forty feet, on which *Mississippi* trained her 14-inch guns on May 25. American infantrymen with time to look could see naval shells cooling from white to red as they arced toward the target. Soon *Colorado* joined with her 16-inchers. Cracks began to appear after a second day of almost continuous salvos from both wagons, which moved closer for a third day of work. By the evening of May 27, the huge walls had crumbled and the epicenter of five centuries of Okinawan culture was rubble.

Extolling its loveliness shortly before the war, a Japanese artist called the castle area of about three hundred acres, the size of a large college campus, the most beautiful in Japan. Other castles were grander and other beauty spots more impressive, another Japanese admirer explained in 1938. But Shuri Castle's site, structure, and views — of the sea and gentle, undulating hills — formed a unique ensemble. "How can we find in Japan such a perfect combination of nature and culture?"

Now all was gone. Only stone fragments remained of the fairy-tale little roads that had wound to gardens and ponds. Magnificent ancient trees were stumps, some still smoking. Around them, the city too was cinders, dust, and the stench of rotting flesh. Quaint paper-and-wood dwellings with stone walls and pretty little terraces had been blown to bits or burned to the ground, hardly leaving an ash.

Japanese soldiers who'd occupied the grounds of the old royal residences a week after L-day drove away Okinawan custodians who were trying to bury or otherwise protect priceless treasures, from magnificent gifts of Chinese emperors to ceremonial artifacts of the Okinawan dynasty. By late May, the loss was virtually total. Only a buried Chronicle of the Okinawan People, from the fifteenth to sixteenth centuries, was almost certainly still there, but Okinawans would find it gone when they would be permitted to return to the old capital. (The twenty-two volumes were snatched as souvenirs and smuggled to America. When they were at last located, it took almost ten years of pressure and pleading to convince a naval commander to return them.)

Naha's devastation was also complete, although the Americans needed a few more days to mop up Japanese snipers and mortar platoons concealed in the capital's ruins. On May 23, five days after the securing of Sugar Loaf, Marine troops crossed the Asato River, now swollen and muddy from the relentless rains, and fought their way into the city's northern outskirts. The stench of rotting bodies was so strong that the pilot of an observation plane had to cover his face with his hands, even several hundred feet in the air, and with a fresh sea breeze blowing. Another pilot saw a wall standing — not a single entire building, but "just that one white wall . . . rising uselessly from the ruins." No more concerned with civilians than the average American, he nevertheless also noticed that "all the [neighboring] villages had been destroyed and the people who lived in them killed or driven into camps."

From the ground, a Marine infantryman saw the former city of sixty-five thousand — almost 15 percent of Okinawa's population — as debris. "Naha was a deserted, bomb-leveled pile of rubble without even a passable street." The contrast with Guadalcanal and other primitive or deserted islands Dick Whitaker had seen in the Pacific may have made his imagination richer. In early June, when his company pushed through the largest city ever taken by Marines — and the first Japanese city taken by any Americans — fragments of theaters and other buildings suggested to him that it may once have been a fine liberty town. But other Marines saw only a blackened, smoldering wasteland where "practically not one stone remained on any other stone except for in an occasional piece of a building's facade." Perhaps just because too little of the capital remained to suggest what had been lost, it prompted little American sorrow.

Native sorrow also tended to go elsewhere. Although the Japanese had changed the capital to Naha soon after annexing the island, Okinawans still loved Shuri. For all Naha's commercial importance, it never replaced the seat of their ancient dynasty as the cultural heart and soul. Now nothing remained there either. "The palace was gone, the temples, the great gates, and the ancient gardens of the Shuri gentry," an American historian with long residence on Okinawa would summarize. "Gone too were the ancient artifacts reposed in these places, together with the monuments, manuscripts and historical records." The obliteration of so much of a distinct culture was an incalculable misfortune.

Weary, wary units of both the Army and the Marine Corps entered Shuri two days later. Droves of Japanese and Okinawan corpses and rotting trunks of Army horses lay beside heaps of rubble. The hardiest architectural survivors were the bell tower and concrete walls of a small Methodist church built four years before Pearl Harbor, together with the concrete shell of the two-story Normal School where Masahide Ota, still delivering 32nd Army messages, had studied.

Just two groups of unwanted foreigners had previously forced their way into Shuri during its long history as the capital: the ruthlessly expansionist Satsuma Japanese, who invaded in 1609 to end the island's independence, and Matthew Perry's landing party in 1853. With good intentions and bad, out of callous greed and perhaps unavoidable necessity, brave warriors of the same two nations had now managed to utterly demolish the center. London's blitz, Berlin's blasting, and even Leningrad's blockade caused less proportionate damage to their respective countries' national wealth and heritage than the loss of almost all the symbols of Okinawa's independent past.

More than the desolation, what interested 10th Army staffs was the relatively moderate opposition encountered during the final push into the city. They didn't know it came not from the Japanese 32nd Army making its last stand near the headquarters tunnel but from skeleton rear-guard units assigned to delay and deceive.

For Ushijima had evacuated the bulk of his depleted forces. Announcement of his intention to do so was why he called his May 22 conference, after planning the surprise move since May 18, when Sugar Loaf finally fell. Some of his divisional commanders disapproved. Although the south teemed with caves, few had been converted to strongpoints. Besides, it seemed right to fight to the end in the main fortifications where so much blood had been lost. But Colonel Hiromichi Yahara, the chief operations officer, again criticized their desire to die an honorable death at Shuri as useless sentimentality, and Ushijima overruled all objections. That made Shuri's capture, so long a major goal, less significant than the Americans had expected. It signaled the end of the hardest fighting, but not the greatest killing.

Militarily, the evacuation was a great success. Thirty-second Army headquarters was reinstalled in an excellent, if far less elaborate, position in the far south, just a few miles below the beach where the 2nd Marine Division had feinted a landing on L-day and critics of General Buckner's frontal tactics proposed a real second landing to outflank the Shuri Line. The staff quickly resumed operations from there — but once again, the benefit to Japan, this one even more temporary, was at Okinawa's expense. During the rest of the campaign, and for decades afterward, civilians would pay the heaviest price for Ushijima's skill.

Had 10th Army commanders known of the withdrawal, they probably could have shortened the campaign by weeks, bombing, shelling, and outflanking it into a rout. But the eleventh-hour operation was superbly accomplished because the Japanese had good luck on top of their astonishing ability to persevere despite the hardship of loading and marching all night on empty stomachs. The rear-guard force fought cleverly and skillfully enough to allay American suspicions for several crucial days, the same days whose bad weather helped prevent reconnaissance and intelligence from making sense of the isolated movements of men and equipment that were spied on the roads leading south from Shuri.

The pullout began almost immediately after the May 22 conference, when the rain was still so heavy and ground-level fog so thick that the aeronautical ceiling remained effectively at zero. Concealed last-minute withdrawal was nothing new for Ushijima. He'd used it all along — at Kakazu Ridge on April 24, for example, where he'd fired artillery barrages and taken advantage of a foggy night to fall back from the fortifications there just before his troops were encircled. (If American staffs had learned the lesson of their surprise when they finally took Kakazu, they forgot it by now, a month later.) And although southern-moving Japanese columns spied during a partial clearing on May 26 were bombed and strafed, other columns were reported moving *north*. American intelligence therefore assumed that Ushijima, far from withdrawing, was replacing his wounded and most exhausted troops with fresh reserves from the south. More confusing was that some of the columns appeared to consist of civilians dressed in white. (Many were actually disguised Japanese soldiers. That prompted anguish even among some of the most pro-Japanese Okinawans, who foresaw that Americans, after uncovering the subterfuge, would take less care not to shoot civilians.)

It made sense to the Americans — further misleading them about the clever withdrawal — that civilians were evacuating south from Shuri. Their planes had dropped a deluge of leaflets urging just that, and also the wearing of white for protection from shooting. Those circumstances were largely responsible for misinterpreting the movements on the roads until the rains returned with a vengeance on May 29, 30, and 31, reducing visibility to near zero just when the last major unit of Captain Kojo's 24th Division pulled out.

Thus the massive withdrawal was accomplished with far better order than the Japanese could have expected in their dismal circumstances. Excellent planning under Yahara and stoic execution had extricated the 32nd Army to fight not just another day but almost another gory month. When the skies cleared and intense air reconnaissance resumed, 10th Army staff members were amazed that so much of the garrison had managed to pull out. Still, Americans knew they were over the worst, and many resumed their overconfidence. Even at that stage, they underestimated the Japanese ability to endure hell in order to "die gloriously" killing the enemy.

As for the civilian population, it was neither side's business, or only peripherally their business. Both had all they could do to fight their unprecedentedly demanding war.

21 · South from the Shuri Line

The corpses were like yellow mud in the rain. When it cleared up, they became mummies in the heat. Adult faces shrunk to the size of a child's and turned black, except for the teeth, which shone white.
— Yoshio Kobayashi, one of Captain Kojo's men, about his retreat from Shuri

If anything moved in the mouth of a cave you were blowing, you fired away like you fired at any noise at night. I didn't think twice whether civilians or soldiers were inside. . . . Any remorse about human beings being shot in there disappeared pretty quick because this was survival. I wanted to live. I wanted to go home. And I wasn't going to take chances, no chance was worth it.
— Buzzy Fox, G–2–22

W HEN TADASHI KOJO LEFT the Shuri Line critical days after the general withdrawal, his mental and physical condition reflected the 32nd Army's as a whole. After crawling to regimental headquarters from the observation post where he'd attempted suicide, the captain was in no shape to exercise command even if his battalion had still existed. He spent the next twelve days about half a mile from doomed Shuri Castle — his first relief from the exhausting fighting that had begun for him on April 26, three weeks of continuous tension with almost no food.

Now he rested in the protection of a well-built bunker that served as a signal center, on the rear slope of Shuri heights. He did not wonder why he no longer wanted to take his own life, only told himself that he must die in action. With no replacements, resupply, or possible relief from the American onslaught, that would surely be soon.

His command consisted of 1st Battalion's dozen survivors. While he rested, Colonel Yoshida, the regimental commander, scratched together a few men who'd been left behind around the regimental tunnel near Naha Airfield. More replacements arrived from airfield maintenance crews and other service troops pulled largely from hospitals, some recovered only enough to limp and hobble. Soon the once highly trained and spirited battalion of over a thousand men had a ragtag collection of some forty souls armed with one light machine gun and several knee-mortars. Their morale matched their combat readiness.

It further sagged when Yoshida passed on Ushijima's order for the general withdrawal, which dealt a greater psychological blow than any delivered directly by the enemy. For all the pain of defending the Shuri Line, the cost to Americans had heartened the battalion. Holding the fortifications had been seen as a kind of victory,* now replaced with the anxiety and despair prompted by resort to futile improvisation.

As long as the High Command was in its hold-at-all-costs bunkers on Okinawa's high ground, the fighters had retained enough mental strength and unit cohesion to cope with their staggering losses. Abandoning them was the straw that finally destroyed their faith in eventual (in this case miraculous) victory, a central pillar of morale in every army. The strain on Kojo's survivors drastically increased when the confidence that had held them together collapsed, leaving them without hope for any further fighting. "Americans are chasing us, encouraged and totally motivated. This is not the way to run a war," one said of the forthcoming retreat to hastily prepared or wholly unprepared positions.

The rest of the 24th Division pulled out. Men who'd learned their night driving in Manchuria were at the wheel of its last operable trucks, transporting its remaining equipment and ammunition. But the 22nd Regiment remained at Shuri as a rear guard for the withdrawal. The job fell to Kojo, since all that was left of the regiment was all that was left of his 1st Battalion.

On June 6, they too left, first heading for the little Noha River, some five miles south of Shuri. Some wounded were still too feeble to pick up the weapons of comrades killed beside them on the march. Kojo's rest had been much too short for recovery from his hunger and exhaustion on top of the wounds from the accidental December explosion. His own weakness depressed him as much as that of his force. He'd clung to hope against hope while taking the satisfaction of fulfilling his duty. Although part of him knew everything on expendable Okinawa was intended merely to delay the enemy's invasion of the mainland, from whose defense no precious resources or equipment could be diverted, another part fantasized that Okinawa was part of the final, inviolable circle that would be defended with everything available.

With that fantasy now evaporated, the fight went out of him. He could do little more than stumble on to the dismal end, trying to mask his pes-

---

*Thus there was the slightest hint of truth in Prime Minister Kantaro Suzuki's otherwise outrageous April claim that "we can never tell what a fatal blow the unyielding fighting spirit of Japanese soldiers on Iwo Jima and Okinawa have given the enemy mentally. When we compare the magnitude of that shock to the enemy with what we've lost on those islands, we can conclude we are not losing the war."

simism with a Japanese officer's prescribed serenity. He silently agreed that it was a mistake to leave Shuri, where at least some supplies of food and ammunition remained. A sister regiment in the 24th Division had been sent south weeks before to prepare positions and lay in supplies, but surely murderous chaos awaited the units that hadn't done that. Everything Kojo had previously accomplished in the Army had been grounded in preparation and procedures. Now the officers didn't know the terrain where they were headed, even if there were time to dig. They'd be targets, not fighters.

His new adjutant reflected the change of mood. First Lieutenant Yatsugi, an artillery officer, had come up from long years in the ranks. After his unit was destroyed near Shuri, he was assigned to Kojo shortly before the 1st Battalion took up its position at Kochi. There he buoyed up himself and others with infectious reassurances of triumph when the Combined Fleet would arrive. "When's it coming — today?" he'd ask with a smile during the worst bombardments. Now the cheery chatter was gone. Yatsugi and most of the men held their tongues in Kojo's presence, but they were deeply discouraged, especially, as Private Yoshio Kobayashi put it, because they had no idea where they were going or "what would happen when we got to the unknown destination."

> We moved in silence in the torrential rain, gunfire sounding near and far, through and over corpses whose eyes shone dully in the light of flares. We were ordered to stop to eat at a roadside cave but it was filled with water up to our knees, and floating corpses pervaded its interior with the peculiar stench of death. I managed to bring a rice ball to my mouth but threw up after a bite.

The enfeebled soldiers were ordered to carry as many weapons and as much equipment as possible. They could not also carry the wounded, whose number seemed endless. (The chief medical officer's rucksack served to transport the battalion's entire medical supplies, chiefly some bandaging.) One man with both legs smashed crawled on all fours, his knees wrapped in rags. Few had any more strength or inclination than Kojo to notice hordes of even worse-off civilians who were trying to evacuate: grandmothers tugging at children of three and four who had seemingly forgotten how to cry; a baby screaming on the back of a mother dead long enough to begin to disintegrate.

Once the men had guarded their rifles with their lives. "Any little scratch on them," Kobayashi remembered, "would have got us sent to the stockade." Now the rusty things trailed in the mud. Only the young bearer of the treasured regimental colors retained something of the old spirit, never faltering no matter how close enemy bullets and bombs approached.

Still, slivers of good luck were enough to dispel the exhaustion and demoralization. When the rain "miraculously" let up, the group enjoyed the "incredible" additional luxury of no rain of American bombs and shells, which had broken off for an unknown reason. The sky actually turned blue and the mood picked up enough for jokes — until the bombardment resumed hours later. A detachment from that group enjoyed another moment of relief when they were sent on to the temporary 1st Battalion headquarters and found it after midnight, dodging shells as they dragged themselves through the mud.

The new cave, a former emplacement for destroyed 150-millimeter cannon, was large and sturdy enough to provide a sense of security despite the paucity of ammunition and almost total lack of food. Its protection was much needed during an intense enemy assault on the position the following morning. Toward its end, one of Kojo's burned-out men saw an artillery shell blow American bodies into the air and wanted to dance at the sight.

His joy was brief. The Japanese guns resumed their silence and the enemy approached again in a blaze of automatic fire. Bullets hit fellows' heads. Kobayashi loaded his muddy, rusted rifle, aimed at one of the Americans closing in to kill him, and pulled the trigger. To his despair, he heard a click. Throwing away his "soul of a soldier," he desperately gathered pebbles, rocks, and rags for ammunition. The soldier in front of him screamed, "I'm hit!" and tumbled.

Kobayashi accepted that his turn would be next but dusk fell and the Americans broke off to make their night preparations. After dark, Kojo radioed an order to cease radio communications because he believed the enemy was locating the waves to pinpoint their shelling. He also ordered his communications section to evacuate its cave — a seemingly suicidal task, with the Americans encamped just outside. But a new miracle brought salvation for Kobayashi and the others. They found a rear exit from the cave that opened onto a rocky slope. The wounded stifled all sounds from their fearful pain as they were dragged down the jagged incline. With no idea of where they were and only the outline of flare-lit hills to guide them, the communications unit wandered about in desperation, but finally found its way to Makabe, about a mile short of Okinawa's southern tip.

The battalion's next destination was the same crossroads town of Makabe on which many units were converging in confusion. It was only four miles south of Shuri, but Kojo, unable to walk unaided, couldn't reach it in one night. After dusk on June 8, two of his men gripped him under his arms and the party set out. The night was dark, the downpour relentless. Except for the private who'd survived with him at Kochi, his men were all new; hardly knowing them, he felt himself only their nominal commander. His only support was his duty to behave like an officer, an expression of pride to which he clung as his men half dragged him through the mud to a rest stop.

Too weak to take in others' condition on the roads, he did recognize a new low of anguished desperation at the stop, a field hospital halfway to Makabe. That outpost of mutilated bodies and corpses was disbanding in the face of the enemy advance. Two rice balls, potassium cyanide, and hand grenades were being distributed to those unable to evacuate. Ashen nurses told Kojo that the most severely wounded had already been injected.

A voice cried out as he took in the appalling scene. "Mister Instructor, sir. Please, Mister Instructor!"

Japanese recruits undergoing their difficult adjustment to Army life remembered their training officers no less than American Marines remembered their drill instructors. Despite his strictness, Second Lieutenant Kojo had been a popular regimental training officer in 1940, when he first joined the 22nd Regiment in Manchuria — but the tremulous voice would surely have pleaded to anyone its owner recognized. Kojo made out a former trainee, one of whose legs had just been amputated near the hip. The weeping soldier said he knew what was in store for him because the hospital was disbanding. Even if he knew how to crawl with one leg, he could get nowhere through the deluge of rain and sea of mud. Like many of the grotesquely wounded, he had no idea of his unit's location, and he knew that many despairing Japanese soldiers from other units would give no help to stragglers like him. But his old training officer's providential appearance gave him a surge of hope against hope. Alternately smiling in happiness and grimacing in pain, he begged the captain to take him with him.

Kojo's composure had already been shaken. Perhaps the tears he felt beginning to form were for himself and his hopeless position as much as for the doomed amputee. It took all his willpower to keep himself from breaking down. "I'd like to help you but I can't," he said, regaining his self-control. "You know I'm responsible for my troops and I must catch up to them. But don't give up. There's no reason for pessimism just because things look difficult at the moment. Get back to your unit even if you have to creep."

Dragging himself to a nearby hill, the captain used his sword to cut a makeshift crutch from a stand of bamboo. He would fight tears again much later when he learned the supplicant was miraculously among the 32nd Army's 10 percent of survivors.

* * *

Kojo left the following night for Makabe, again supported by soldiers. When he arrived at the 22nd Regiment's new headquarters, he found the full regiment beefed up to about three hundred troops, most of whom resembled those he'd seen leaving the hospital — gravely wounded men who preferred dragging themselves back to their units to suicide. Many had arrived without weapons, and the regiment had none to distribute. The unit's sole remaining purpose was to delay the inevitable as long as possible. The mess was catastrophic to morale, for as the Americans had shown in fighting on despite heavy casualties at Sugar Loaf — and the Japanese had demonstrated even more eloquently at the Shuri Line — its single most important ingredient, more so even than belief in eventual victory, is the commitment to comrades that overrides commitment to oneself. But the disappearance of almost all the old comrades had taken loyalty and cohesiveness with them.

Although nearly all remaining units were being squeezed into the island's southern tip, organization and communications were so feeble that Kojo knew even less than before about the fate of the 32nd Army as a whole, except that it was disintegrating. Actually, his 24th Division, with some eight thousand shaky men strung out on the west coast, was in far better shape than the once proud 62nd, which was down to about three thousand troops. A few units on southern mountains were fighting almost as at Shuri — but less as an integrated army than as additional testimony to the last reward of dying honorably.

Kojo's knowledge that he could do nothing to make his own band into a fighting unit deepened his demoralization. It was almost a relief when Colonel Yoshida ordered him to take twenty men, together with his new adjutant and one more officer, and defend a small ridge about half a mile away, at Maesato village. The new position was a few hundred yards from the western (East China Sea) coast and just over a mile south of Itoman, Okinawa's fourth largest city, now in debris. "This will be our final stand," he told his men. "We'll die here."

Then he deployed them. The twenty men had half a dozen rifles and many grenades as well as some knee-mortars and light machine guns, but they were stymied by the composition of their naked rise. Americans had found it impossible to dig foxholes in coral even with tools; the Japanese phantoms with none couldn't scratch the surface. When the American advance reached them on June 20, they could only lie on the ground during the mortar barrage, Kojo protected by the only bush in sight. The violation of the first rule of infantry warfare — *Take cover!* — disturbed him more than anything before.

Nor could he communicate with his men during the day without risking instant death. When he checked the first night, fifteen were alive. The next day, some surviving signal troops brought him a radio message from Colonel Yoshida, still in a cave on a hill less than a thousand yards away. "We're being attacked. If possible, return your battalion here." Kojo answered that he'd try as soon as it was dark. He could see enemy guns, tanks, and flamethrowers attacking the general location of his regimental headquarters. That was the end of the 22nd Regiment. Yoshida's last message was the traditional one, promising to fight to the end and wishing Kojo luck.

The fire from [American] ships was coordinating perfectly with [our] artillery. We were slowly reducing what was left of that damn Nip artillery and we were getting less and less shelling from the Japs.
— Joe Fater, 8th Marines

American flamethrowing tanks seared [Okinawa's] hillsides with gallons of liquid fuel, roasting hundreds of Japanese hiding in caves. As survivors ran out, waiting infantrymen fired clip after clip into them.
— William Craig, *The Fall of Japan*

The Japs and their screams meant utterly nothing to me. How can you expect anyone to understand that unless they were there themselves — actually in a foxhole getting bombarded and watching their buddies get killed? All these people who talk war and don't have the faintest idea of the hell it is!
— Evan Regal, Marine flamethrower

I saw a shriveled-up old Jap man [actually an Okinawan] being flushed out of a cave near the bottom of the hill by five Marines. The man stood there obviously scared to death. The five Marines surrounded the man in a circle and each had a .45 automatic pistol pointed at the Jap. It struck me that if he twitched or sneezed, the five Marines would have shot themselves up. However, nothing happened, and two Marines took the Jap to the rear.
— Declan Klingenhagen, D–2–29

General Buckner believed the Japanese evacuation of Shuri, no matter how lucky and skillful, had come too late to confront his 10th Army with more than isolated moments of stiff fighting farther south. Roughly four-fifths of Ushijima's machine guns and nine-tenths of his artillery pieces were destroyed or inoperable. One way or another, a quarter of his remaining troops, ten thousand to fifteen thousand men, had been lost during the withdrawal. Roughly a fifth of the combat forces in place on L-day were in fighting condition, a category that included many with serious wounds as well as the universally exhausted "healthy." Real strength was less than that of a proper division — against the four and a half vastly stronger American ones chasing him. "It's all over now but cleaning up pockets of resistance," Buckner assured correspondents on May 31.

But the big-gun advocate and his well-supplied staff greatly underestimated the misery waiting in the last eight square miles still in Japanese hands. Although no more Shuri Lines lay ahead, the third of the south's three east–west mountain spines rose six miles farther south. Japanese were retreating to almost anywhere they could find, but principally to strongpoints that had been well prepared by units of the 24th Division and the crack 9th before it was sent away.

Every night still belonged to the enemy. More desperate now, the Japanese took greater risks and made many Americans even more trigger happy. A desperado slithered into the foxhole of Dan Maczko, a 4th Marines machine gunner, at about 3 A.M. on June 12. Maczko grabbed his arms as he tried to pull the pin of a grenade, then fought the grenade away. Next, he struggled to wrest away a big club — with which he beat the Japanese before stabbing him with his own Kabar knife. In the words of a chronicler of his platoon, he finally "threw the Nip out of the hole and shot the bastardly Nip." Several nights earlier, Stuart Upchurch had heard an unseen intruder slip in near his foxhole. A sharp-eyed platoon mate finally saw him and threw a grenade. Upchurch heard groans, then the blast of a second grenade — not American, he could tell — and felt bits of flesh blown all over him: The infiltrator had held the second grenade, his own, to his chest. Near midnight, another Japanese penetrated even closer than the first until caught by a 10-gauge shotgun from about four feet away. (Marines loved shotguns and filched all they could from supply depots.) The blast tore off some of the second infiltrator's face, severed a hand, and blew apart his chest. Still later that night, a third Japanese ran back and forth just outside the platoon's line until he was killed by a cascade of grenades.

Japanese persistence puzzled and frightened the platoon. "They'd come to our lines, we'd kill them and that was that." Still, many Americans felt an even greater threat just because the sorely pressed enemy appeared more reckless in the dreaded dark. "At every rise, you never knew," said a Marine whose company took more casualties after than before the Shuri Line — although that was rare. "Every night, you never knew."

Every break was still greeted with relief before the advance resumed. During the first fortnight in June, Army divisions pushed south on the east coast and Marines on the west toward the last mountain spine in Japanese hands. A participant in that fighting on more level, open ground described it as "being in a one-acre park with someone you had to find behind some bush and kill before he killed you." Makeshift

Japanese positions occasionally pinned down units until they were extricated by smoke screens or tanks. An American squad encountered a large rice paddy and knew they'd be "pigeons" when they had to cross it. They ran in single file, ten yards apart and as fast as they could through the watery, knee-deep mud. Sure enough, snipers picked some of them off.

Still, far less effective use of terrain by the Japanese than at the Shuri Line made the going now through the scrubby land much easier. The strain of the daytime fighting was also reduced by the sharp drop in incoming artillery and mortar fire and many fewer machine-gun emplacements. And the weather improved. In June, the mud dried to make inordinate dust. A single car on prewar Okinawa's dirt roads raised a thick cloud of ochre particles. Now each truck, tank, and self-propelled gun in the fleets of them "temporarily blinded you until the slight breeze could clear the air," an Army officer noted. The dust also choked people so regularly near the main roads that one of the principal expert recommendations about equipment after the campaign would be for "goggles and dust respirators [to] be issued to all personnel." But dust was easier to take than mud, as long as there was a steady supply of drinking water.

With less danger creeping, crawling, and tiptoeing to Japanese-occupied caves, the Americans could devote relatively more attention to flushing them out. Although some units liked to skirt as many caves as possible, more tried to miss none in their path, since many surely housed the coming night's infiltrators. Dick Whitaker's second wounding, which earned him an examination on a hospital ship and a night on an actual cot in his regimental hospital, took place in early June. Feeling better for his rest and hot meal, he returned to his company and found his machine-gun squad reorganized in his absence because it had been reduced to shreds on Sugar Loaf. He was made a runner for his company commander, replacing a previous one who'd been shot through the head while standing beside that officer, but when the company was advancing in early June and he had no messages to deliver at a given time, he advanced with the others.*

> You're moving ahead fairly rapidly until you see a buddy's arm go up or you hear a "Get down!" Everyone takes cover instantly and you find out the trouble's usually a cave ahead. You approach it extremely gingerly.

---

*Whitaker liked his new job, apart from having to carry a hated walkie-talkie. When it wasn't in use, he could hide most of it under his arm, but he quaked when he had to extend the antenna, which made him a priority target. And despite his new running from platoon to platoon to deliver the company commander's orders, he generally remained as ignorant of the larger picture as before. The platoons often greeted him with questions about where the hell they'd be going. "In most cases, I didn't have the foggiest goddamn notion."

You cover yourself and your every nerve strains for more information. You can't tell from the mouth how big it is. You don't know who's inside — how many civilians, how many Japs, what they're armed with. It could be dozens getting ready to charge out or shoot from inside. Sometimes you hear somebody in there bellow an order.

Next you hear grenades being tapped on helmets to arm them. But all you can see is a black hole with signs of recent use — and that spells death because you're a perfect silhouette if somebody's got you in his sights from inside that blackness. Besides, there were often tunnels or passageways to other caves nearby. The whole thing was spooky. The whole thing spelled *danger.*

To drive the occupants from where they could deliver return fire, the attacking unit fired heavily into cave mouths and gun ports, with the help of tanks, when available (as they would be at Kojo's final position). Then they usually shouted, *"De-te koi! De-te koi!"* — "Come out! Come out!" — loudly and repeatedly, often with bullhorns. A few linguists added, *"Shim-pachina"* — "We'll give you food and water."

No answer in a reasonable time set the "blowing" party to work. Thousands of caves were "neutralized" by a method so practiced that it would have been routine if not for everyone's knowledge that a second's lapse in concentration could be fatal. Members of a team kept the occupants from peeking out of the mouth by pouring heavy rifle and BAR fire into it while others "mounted" the cave and looked for cracks, crevices, or an airhole — ventilating shafts in more elaborate installations — on top. From there, one of a variety of explosives was dropped inside, or several in combination.

When explosions sounded inside caves before any payloads were dropped, the suicides they signified were welcomed. In that case, valiant or foolhardy American volunteers sometimes entered the darkness, after an appropriate interval of silence from within. At a more or less typical opening in a limestone hill, an interpreter repeatedly shouted the "Come Out!" call from fifty feet away. A woman in faded pantaloons and a ripped blouse eventually appeared at the mouth with a naked baby on her back and a child of about five at her side. Repeated assurances she wouldn't be harmed drew the woman a few steps into the open until angry shouts from inside pulled her back there. Three blasts soon shook the hill, and the woman, now headless, was among ten shattered bodies the Marines found in the cave's wreckage. The others included the two children, their arms almost severed, and another baby. Pieces of infant and parental flesh adhered to the walls: a common sight.

Many American teams entered caves to see families clustered together, their torsos ripped apart or brains blown out by a grenade exploded by a parent who was still clutching the children. But suicide explosions were not relied on for a full flushing, because they often killed only a portion of the people inside. The attackers had to do most of the work themselves.

Experienced cave blowers tried to save their dynamite satchel charges for the largest targets. A demolitions specialist would crawl to a ventilation hole, or sometimes the mouth, with the charge, light it, and wait six or seven seconds to prevent the occupants from tossing it back out, which often happened to inexperienced teams. Then the specialist would run. In other cases, fragmentation and white phosphorous grenades were used. Or gasoline or flamethrower napalm was brought up in drums, poured into the upper openings, and ignited with a phosphorous grenade. Since unaccompanied grenades were rarely effective except in the smallest caves, some Americans used homemade bombs of C-2, an explosive putty packed in a can with a grenade for a detonator. General Buckner called all that the "blowtorch and corkscrew" method, something highly inflammable being the blowtorch and explosives the corkscrew.

Americans liked the white phosphorus grenade for its smoke: partial cover for when they decided to storm caves, the most dangerous method of all. The chemical stuck to the skin and could not be removed by water or any solution available to the 32nd Army, let alone civilians. (Vaseline worked, but "the Okinawans didn't have any — or anything else," an American corpsman noted.) Some likened the light of the blue flame with which it burned to that of massed fireflies. While family members or fellow soldiers vainly scraped at the eerie luminescence, it melted holes in the flesh, often down to the bones. By the time most victims lost consciousness, the mud around them also glowed. Other times American grenades set off munitions stored inside. Although supplies of Japanese shells were scanty in the south, their petric acid sent up an acrid yellow smoke that was more lethal than anything dropped, thrown, or fired inside. It took more lives than the explosions and flames.

Similarly, flamethrowers caused many more deaths by suffocation than by burns, the flames consuming all the oxygen in many of the smaller caves. The weapon that most terrified Japanese soldiers was the new long-range flamethrower mounted on Sherman tanks and adapted to shoot a mixture of gasoline and napalm. Although not the final answer to cave cleaning that the 10th Army planners had hoped for, those tanks — with flexible hosing for use on inaccessible terrain — greatly helped.

Otherwise, ordinary, man-mounted flamethrowers were used, and it was a measure of the universality of fear that the men who operated those symbols of World War II inhumanity themselves trembled each time they waddled toward the mouth of a cave. With ninety-five hugely awkward pounds of equipment and volatile liquid strapped to their backs, the volunteers for that hazardous work couldn't carry a rifle or a carbine — terrifying in itself. They had to take extreme care not to trip and fall, in which case they couldn't get up without help and might easily themselves be incinerated by a bullet hitting their tanks. Unable to crouch or quickly hit the ground, silhouetted against the sky from inside the caves, they were vulnerable targets deprived of the infantryman's first protection of taking cover. "You couldn't see them in there, but they could see you — a perfect bull's-eye without a rifle," Evan Regal would recall, still a little wide-eyed at the memory. "No matter how short of ammunition they might be in there, all it would take was just one round. My heart pounded when I went out — *every* time."

It could take a combat eternity of fifteen heart-stopping minutes to approach a cave and find the necessary stable footing, another factor that made flamethrowers' casualties much higher than among ordinary infantrymen. Knowing their vulnerability and value, the riflemen with whom they worked tried to give them as much cover as possible, but it was always too little. Of sixteen flamethrowers on Charlie Hill, the small strongpoint just north of Sugar Loaf, Evan Regal and three others survived. Fearless on the outside, the tough farmboy quaked within.

> Every time I had to walk up to a hole, I was scared out of my mind because I was a sitting duck. No matter how much fire your buddies laid down in the mouth of the cave, you had no protection at all, which was the opposite of everything you learned about combat. Sometimes you could see their helmets inside, sometimes their eyes staring at you, or you could hear them talking — and you didn't know how many there were, so you were scared shitless. . . .
>
> You pulled the triggers — there were two — just as soon as you thought your flame could reach them. In it went, and all hell'd break loose. You heard the shuffling and the screaming and almost always some would come running out, their hair and clothes on fire, for the riflemen to pick them off. The heat was just too intense for them to stay inside or they suffocated from lack of oxygen. Gasoline could glance off sometimes, just searing them, but napalm stuck to their skin like jelly glue even when they ran. . . .
>
> But it's hot for the flamethrower too, even when the flame doesn't bounce back from real small caves. And once you squeeze the triggers, you're helpless for those five to seven seconds while the flame shoots out . . . so you're as good as dead if lots of them come rushing out and the riflemen miss one. That's why the only thing you think about is killing them as quickly as possible. "Oh God, let me get this job over with fast. And let me get them *all* before I get shot." You have utterly no compassion for their screams because you've seen so many of your own

cut down and you know it can be *you* the next second; if you give them the slightest chance, they'll put a bullet between your eyes. You also know the Japs never took a single prisoner on Okinawa — they killed everybody if they overran one of our positions. . . . All you care about the Japs is that they fry fast.*

The uninvolved tend to recoil from cave flushing as unfair slaughter of the trapped. Those who had to do it were all caught up in the heavy work and deadly risks. "This is all a bloody business," a Marine wrote home about those weeks. "But I'm here and digging my foxholes just a foot deeper than the next guy. I've said enough prayers to write a full-size book and thanked God twice as many times for surviving so far."

For the next two days we were engaged in blowing caves, pouring gas down the ventilating shafts and dropping hand grenades. Finally we called for flamethrowing tanks. . . . We killed the little banks of Japanese that still rallied forth.
— From a Marine's personal history

When Americans called Japanese soldiers to come out of their caves, they'd put hand grenades under their armpits. Outside, they'd get as close as possible to the Americans, throw the grenades and try to fly back into the caves. Not very noble, but there was simply nothing else they could do to resist. Anyway, such tactics only work once. The Americans learned to order us to raise our hands higher.
— Masao Murata, 15th Independent Mixed Regiment

After the explosions, the attackers readied to resume firing on the mouth unless the blasts had sealed it. Nerves remained strained even after all manner of scorching and riddling with bullets. Since no volume of fire or explosive could reach all recesses of the larger caves, each man in sight of an entrance remained a potential target.

When occupants began emerging, natives were often first, sometimes shoved from behind. Almost all Americans tried not to shoot them. A large percentage inevitably failed because they'd learned to fire at the slightest hint of unusual movement from anyone but children and the elderly. Killing civilians was a devastating experience for most, especially when they hadn't known who was inside the blown caves. But although dismembered corpses of women and children deeply shocked teams that peeked inside, they were among the war's costs, like those gunned down

---

*Regal's only moments of remorse for burning humans came after he'd been sent to torch one of the tombs being used as pillboxes on the same Charlie Hill where he'd soon be wounded. He told his officer he couldn't be sure whether an American lying right in the path where he'd shoot his flames was dead or alive, but fire from the pillbox was causing so many casualties that the officer ordered him to proceed in any case. "That job tortured me for months. I mean having to shoot so near one of our own. But never shooting Japs."

as they emerged. Before the blasts, Americans couldn't differentiate between caves sheltering natives and Japanese, or a mixture. After them, they were hard pressed to distinguish among the people stumbling out. A pious Marine found it "pretty hard at first" to accept that "our people were shooting human beings who weren't necessarily military. But after I saw what their people — including civilians — did with their hands up, I worried about us, not them. I wanted to leave Okinawa alive!"

While most of the hands-up tricks were performed by soldiers rather than civilians, some of the former were now wearing the latter's clothes. A portion of them feigned surrender just long enough for a thrust into a loincloth for a final grenade. Small as their number was, it was large enough to implant the lesson into the jittery Americans. "A Jap makes a move to give himself up but lifts his arms at the last minute and out tumble two hand grenades," Evan Regal would remember. "That wasn't talk; I *saw* it. You couldn't trust a single one of them."

That was why all civilians between the ages of roughly ten and sixty were regarded as potential booby traps and why the prime rule was "not to take your eye off the devious gooks for a second" until they could be searched. "If they had anything less than a terrified look on them, fingers tightened on triggers," another veteran would remember. "We were pretty terrified ourselves, and some of us were pretty eager to fire away." "If you didn't feel so goddamn threatened yourself, you might have had tremendous pity for the human wreckage in those underground dungeons," a fellow added. "The specimens who came out were horrific. Starving Okinawan boys in Japanese uniforms. Younger kids in just pitiful shape, and lots of mutilations of all ages. Inside, the caves were simply terrible; I can't describe it. People burned to a crisp, giving off that ghastly smell! But you couldn't have real pity because you yourself were so wound up and concentrating on the danger facing *you*. So if those civilians didn't have that fear on their faces, they were dead."

During the night of June 11, a long line of civilians wrapped in dirty blankets headed toward an American unit from farther south. They had nearly passed the forward positions when a vigilant sergeant sensed something wrong. He and his men raked the line with machine-gun fire, then found that many of the group were Japanese soldiers with grenades and demolition charges under their blankets.

A few days later, Anthony Cortese helped throw a heavy charge into a large cave from which no one had emerged in answer to the usual *"De-te koi"* calls. He might have held back had he known there were many women and children inside, but that wouldn't have solved his problem. "We had to assume Japs were in there too, and what about them? Besides, I'd already done a cave where civilians came out first, then a Jap soldier with his hands up. Suddenly he throws himself on the ground and the man behind him, dressed as a woman, starts firing from a Nambu strapped to the first guy's back. We all started firing the minute he hit the ground and killed over a dozen civilians together with the two Japs — but what could you do? What you *couldn't* do was take a chance."

A barrel-chested Japanese with his hands held high aroused the suspicion of a lieutenant from Captain Owen Stebbins's G–2–22 company. The lieutenant didn't know precisely why he shot him dead with his carbine from fifteen yards, but as he fired, he alerted his men with a great shout of "Fire in the hole!" — which saved their lives by sending them instantly prone. His bullet caused a large explosion. Barrel Chest had wired himself to blow apart as many Americans as possible together with himself.

Much later, a handful of Japanese would express regret for such subterfuge in accounts heavy with sorrow, chiefly for themselves. Kenjiro Matsuki, the first baseman for Japan's first professional baseball team, watched fellow soldiers make a white flag in order to inch within grenade-tossing range of Americans. The veteran sportsman would feel "ashamed" to relate such things, "yet what else could we do at that point?" Perhaps that was a new expression of Japan's old tendency to believe her oppression by foreigners justified any subterfuge.

Dick Whitaker approached caves with typical anxiety. "You'd see a stick peeking out with a white rag tied to it — but what was on the other end? Civilians? Japs trying to draw your fire so they could get in a last shot back? Let's say a woman comes out, then a woman with a baby, then a couple of kids — and then a man. Who the hell is he? If he's a soldier, is he armed? Years later, we learned the Japanese Army had a percentage of Okinawan Home Guard conscripts who took their families with them when they retreated. But we had no clear idea then of the relationship between civilians and soldiers."

By mid-June, lots of the Japs were stripped. Maybe they hoped there was less chance we'd kill them if they were out of uniform. Most had blank faces that revealed nothing whatever, at least to us. Their hands were usually up and some did a lot of jabbering. Maybe they were saying how sorry they were, how sincerely they wanted peace, how they'd have come out of their cave earlier if they hadn't been afraid their own fanatics would kill them. But maybe *they* were those fanatics, telling their buddies, "Okay, *now* give it to them." We just didn't know whether they were some sorry privates who'd had it and truly wanted to surrender or hardcore sergeants who were going to pull another stunt and accomplish their last goal in life of killing you together with themselves.

Infantrymen find some little security in predictability, but it further decreased when units combed fields patched with scrub. The day after Whitaker was made a runner, his new unit was held up atop a slight rise in an area that had been subjected to some preliminary clearing. Privates were rarely told the reason for such delays, this one even happier than most because a welcome sun was shining after the weeks of deluge and mud. It would quickly grow stronger, replacing the hardship of perpetual wet and cold with tropical heat and giving Whitaker one of his indelible memories of June: Japanese bodies so bloated by gas that their skin was about to burst — much like, he thought, a boiled knockwurst. But no Japanese, dead or alive, was in sight at the moment, and a member of the party named Nick Tredemis walked down from the little rise to relieve himself. Living together like a wolf litter and plagued by dysentery, the others took no particular notice of the squatter in his open area — until a friend of Whitaker's named Gene Lewis detected a movement some twenty-five yards away. It was a Japanese soldier sneaking up on him with a bayonet tied to a bamboo pole.

Lewis dropped to a prone position and whispered, "Watch this!" When his rifle was steady, he shouted, "Hey Nick, what's that?" and pointed to the approaching Japanese. The sight of the bayonet caused Nick to cut short his business, pull up his pants and grab his rifle in a single movement. When Lewis shot the intruder a second later, the others howled with the gusto of comic relief.

A similar incident two months earlier might have ended tragically for the group. If Lewis had shouted before setting up for a sure shot, the attacker might have thrown a grenade at Nick. If one of the others had charged down the rise before Lewis fired and the soldier with the bayonet was the point man for a patrol behind him — or bait for an ambush — the charger might have been shot. But before opening the curtain on his little number, Lewis knew exactly what was needed to be certain of a kill, while the others instinctively made no move except to take aim too and survey every bush in sight before they laughed.

What bothered American infantrymen now was that their dearly acquired combat wisdom didn't help during the new, fast-moving advance. The formerly underground enemy was now popping up from seemingly nowhere, requiring unpracticed split-second responses. Some appeared from what Marines called "spider holes" because, as one would explain, "you couldn't believe a human being could fit into such a tiny space." Spider holes seemed to be everywhere. Their openings, covered with leaves or branches, were often undetectable until a Japanese fired and disappeared again.

The enemy soldier after enemy soldier Whitaker's company shot in June did not win its members much sense of security. "You're crossing a field of grass up to your waist, advancing in a good line, when somebody suddenly stands up thirty yards away. Is he armed? Is he bait? Does he have a Nambu strapped to his back? Then another pair of hands goes up and another — and it's scary. It happens very fast, and you better react even faster. A lot of our earlier lessons about the fortifications went out the window because now you never knew what they'd do, surrender, blow themselves up, blow *you* up. Some seemed to switch from one goal to another in a fraction of a second."

On watch at his machine gun as dawn approached on June 11, Melvin Heckt saw a gang of Japanese charge over the sandy ridge where his squad was dug in. Their shouts curdled blood. "Banzai! Marine, you die!" Heckt readied to mow them all down, but the machine-gunner's dream turned to nightmare when sand jammed the gun — and his rifle too. One screaming charger dived straight for him. He was certain his time had come — until other squad members opened up and killed some twenty Japanese as close as five yards from the position. Heckt discovered the man who'd dived at him had no rounds in his chamber, just a bayonet. If he'd had a single bullet, "I wouldn't be writing this [his memoir] today."

Fresh excrement in the scrub put Whitaker's senses under huge strain until he shot its maker or moved out of rifle range. One of his patrols brought him to a Japanese field hospital as hurriedly makeshift as the one where Tadashi Kojo rested during his withdrawal from Shuri. A pathetically emaciated patient lay prostrate on a bunk, waiting for an American corpsman's examination. The picture of defeat seemed too weak to move — until he pulled a grenade from his loincloth, jerked out its pin, and hit it on his fist to detonate it. A member of Whitaker's team shot him before he could throw it, corroborating yet again the detestable dictum that the only good Jap was a dead one. They had never fought in ordinary ways. Now, gouged from their fortifications, they could be counted on only to do something crazy.

> *Medical, veterinary, supply and other personnel were brought in to make good the losses. As a result, the [Japanese] line units consisted of men with a variety of specialties, none of which was combat.*
> — Thomas Huber, military historian

> *Our forces are without planes, warships or tanks. Because we are abandoned, we have no hope other than to die resisting. . . . We have come to our end in this despicable land. How I'd like to return safely!*
> — From a diary on a Japanese soldier

> *Thirty to forty of our soldiers were lying on top of one another and I heard faint groans indicating that many were still alive. There was no way for me to save them. . . . There was nothing to do but retreat.*
> — Kenjiro Matsuki, on his retreat from a key defensive position a mile east of Kochi Ridge

The 32nd Army's "crazy" behavior now was caused by its squeeze between the obligations of the national military ethic and the extremely unequal battle conditions. Over sixty thousand men had been killed in May, in ways much like those that wore down Tadashi Kojo's battalion, whose reduction to the dozen survivors mirrored the losses of most others defending the Shuri Line. The ability of some Wehrmacht units defending Normandy the previous summer to hold out and even counterattack despite appalling casualties deeply impressed Allied commanders. But many German weapons, unlike the Japanese, were better than the corresponding Allied ones. And the panzer divisions that fought with extraordinary skill and tenacity despite their dismal prospects did not nearly match the Japanese feat of endurance now, when most troops were living with their own excrement, drinking muddy water from bomb craters, dying of gangrene. Perhaps only a Japanese army could have sustained some 75 percent casualties — seventy-two thousand in number — in two months of fighting without mutinying. The wonder wasn't that organization and discipline were deteriorating in early June but that they'd remained intact so long.

But the something essential that changed with Ushijima's decision to withdraw from the Shuri Line shook even units less shattered than Kojo's.

Captain Koichi Ito, whose battalion had made the only successful advance in the ill-fated May 4 counteroffensive, was among the regular field officers determined to continue inspiring his men with a display of the old composure and confidence. Pride in being Japanese and self-respect as an Army officer kept the persona of Kojo's haughty academy classmate intact. "When we lost comrades, we were certain we would follow them sooner or later. Of course we held our lives dear, but our deepest wish was not to be captured. The wounded were sometimes killed to prevent that when we withdrew. . . . Some were weak, some dishonorable, as in any human group — but I was determined to give all I had for the sake of Japan and the Imperial Army."

The importance the Japanese attached to their leaders helped keep a relatively high percentage of battalion commanders alive — but many, like Kojo, were too physically and mentally exhausted to radiate the prescribed confidence. And without similar shielding, a great proportion of subordinate officers, including the lieutenants and junior captains serving as company commanders, *weren't* alive. That was extremely detrimental to morale, because a leaderless Japanese unit wasn't considered a unit at all. Thus the 32nd Army's great losses and last-minute reorganizations had a kind of multiplier effect on the plummeting spirits.

Many men were beyond being inspired in any case. No people were more moved by symbols than the Japanese — in this case, the pluck, resolve, strength, and ability to prevail over richer Westerners that was symbolized by holding on to the Shuri Line, which was also some compensation for their enormous losses. The shock and pain of evacuating it stripped many of their moral stamina just as exit from the last of the major fortifications stripped them of their best — as they saw it, their only — protection.

Psychological study would later establish that the critical cause of combat stress is duration, even more than severity. All men, including the best and bravest, eventually break under relentless emotional and physical strain. A solid month of unrelieved combat produced some degree of battle fatigue in nearly 100 percent of American troops. Those who fought on Okinawa needed no research for that, knowing the importance of their withdrawals from the line for rest. It was a shining credit to regular officers like Kojo and to Japanese society in general that so few of the defenders cracked, although they had none. Or it was a condemnation of that society, since far more would have lived if officers and senior soldiers hadn't been blindly loyal.

In any case, their resolve began snapping now. The rarity of friendly artillery's dulcet roar was another dark sign, as well as a tactical deprivation. A few of the 10 percent of Japanese big guns not destroyed or abandoned were broken down into pieces for transport farther south, where they would not fire again. An infantry unit on the dismal evacuation trek came upon a single heavy gun still intact. Its crew was struggling to tug it, inches at a time, through the deep mud of a devastated road in a driving rain — a sight that, again, symbolized to viewers the impoverishment of their inner resources too. The proud Yamato men who had sacrificed so much found the current situation almost incomprehensible. Without necessarily believing the brave would live and the cowardly die, they *had* expected to see some evidence that the *side* of the brave and virtuous would be rewarded.

The decimation of the 12th Independent Infantry Battalion had begun on L-day, near the landing beaches. The bombing and shelling, whose purpose seemed to be to destroy "not only humans but also the last ant," dismayed Private Kenjiro Matsuki. After ten days, 350 of the battalion's proud 1,500 men remained. They retreated, one unit eventually to a vital strongpoint at Maeda, two miles north of Shuri and a mile west of Kochi.

Not long before the last of Kojo's force there was overrun, that unit withdrew, eventually to a shelter from which a group of soldiers made a night attack. Private Matsuki watched them leave under cover of darkness to assault an enemy-held escarpment. After the booming order of "Attack!" he heard machine-gun fire from the American position, then a howling of "whooooah . . ." and "ohweee" — "a tragically heroic" sound that lasted for several minutes while the enemy machine guns continued firing. Most dying soldiers Matsuki had previously seen called for their mothers rather than making the glorious shouts of Army hype. But now he actually heard a chorus of the celebrated "Emperor! Banzai!" "That night, for the very first and perhaps the last time, I heard the brave words . . . seemingly jerked out by some great force." (He would later learn that sixty of the assault's ninety men were killed.)

Then the former first baseman, an independent spirit by Japanese standards, retreated farther with three others, moving at night, hard pushed by the American advance that would resume in the morning, ready to use their hand grenades for suicide. A "blazing" machine gun stopped them on their way, and they hid in a rain-filled bomb crater until the flares lost some of their power near dawn and the "heavenly gift" of a morning mist offered a hint of protection. Matsuki led the way in another dash of some three hundred yards to a possibly more permanent hiding place. The machine gun didn't fire again. "We'd stayed in the crater so long that maybe the enemy got tired of waiting or thought we died there."

> I ran up Shuri Road and flattened myself against the hillside. I couldn't stop grinning when the others appeared too. But . . . [then] American trench mortars started firing, seemingly a hundred at once, into the field we'd just crossed and extending onto the road. They made their weird hissing sound, like escaping steam.
>
> We jumped into a long, tunnel-like trench at the foot of the hill . . . and I nearly fell over in surprise: this was being used for serious casualties. They were lying in twos the full length of the trench, 200 or 300 meters — so many there was no place to step. . . . Noticing us, someone pleaded, as if with his last breath, "Hey, please kill me."
>
> That started a chorus. "Hey, kill me quick. Please!" Some must have been dead already because there was little movement as we picked our way around their heads, but someone grabbed my leg.
>
> "There are rifles in this trench," he said in a fairly strong voice.
>
> "Shoot the ones still alive. We can't stand just waiting to die. Please. *Please!*"
>
> But I couldn't do it, not even to answer their earnest pleas. . . . We left the trench . . . [and] a shell fell right on the road. . . . We'd be trapped by tanks unless we hurried, so we decided to run along the foot of the road — which, when I started down the bank and landed on it, felt like a balloon. . . . It turned out to be a makeshift cemetery, with rows and rows of corpses covered by a thin layer of soil.

If Kojo had to fight tears when confronted by his former trainee with the fresh amputation, such sights understandably shook the nonprofessional soldiers even more. The forced abandonment of masses of wounded during the retreat dealt another great blow to morale.

It struck hardest at veterans of victorious campaigns in China and elsewhere, where they used to dash to injured buddies and carry them back for treatment. But even newcomers to combat were mortified by failing the wounded now. When a flare suddenly ignited directly over four litter bearers carrying a man they didn't know, they dropped their burden and ran. "We didn't feel sorry for the stranger. We didn't think about helping him. We only thought about saving our own lives." A warrant officer lamented that an animal instinct of survival prevailed.

When an older recruit had grieved over his first witnessed death in April, a lieutenant objected. "Hundreds — no, thousands — of you will be blown off the face of the earth," he snapped. "Be resigned to that fate." Still, friends had been able to offer some sort of care during April and May. Now good men were pained and shamed by being reduced to deserting the injured.

Almost all serious wounds made brave men frightened ones, a transformation hastened by the state of the medical care. Although most of the great numbers of wounded left behind did not live to spread their gloom, those determined to join the withdrawal made up for them — and were as likely to receive indifference or coldness as compassion from soldiers of other units.

An actor named Masao Murata had been performing with a respected theater in Japan when he was drafted a second time, after a four-year shift in Manchuria. On Sugar Loaf, a grenade gashed the staunch patriot's back and right hip on May 16, the day before Dick Whitaker was hit in the hand. When Murata's unit was ordered to retreat, he was "abandoned," in his own word, with two dried biscuits. His departing comrades gave assurances they would return to fetch him, but he knew their retreat would make that impossible. Once infected, his wounds became grotesquely swollen. Of course no one returned. The struggle for survival was beginning to extinguish all sense of unity and common purpose.

A colonel on the other side of Shuri from Sugar Loaf made a selection for *kirikomi* — suicidal hand-to-hand combat — at that same time. His picked unit used to shout "Banzai!" going into battle, but now a chatter of teeth echoed in its cave. Most of the twenty men the colonel selected were seriously wounded, therefore chilled with fear — like Murata, who'd thought more about what he owed the Emperor than about his own welfare until his injuries punctured his courage, allowing the most terrifying fear of being left behind to penetrate. While Whitaker's first wound was being treated at the battalion aid station north of Sugar Loaf, Murata crawled down from his hill and wandered alone for three full days.

On the fourth, he met two heavily bandaged soldiers — good luck, because he could ask where they'd been treated. The field hospital they cited — more good luck, for not all soldiers of other units volunteered such information — was a cave dug into the side of a nearby hill. Murata dragged himself there but was turned away because that facility didn't serve his regiment. His bloated hip untreated, he begged through his pain — again in vain. Then an officer happened by who recognized the talented actor from an appearance entertaining the troops just before L-day. Salvation!

The lancing and bandaging of his hip gave Murata great relief. Told to move on when they were completed, he began limping from the cave between rows of softly moaning patients with amputated limbs — who gave the former actor an inspiration. Moaning too, he managed to squeeze in among them and even to get a bowl of thin rice soup.

The next morning, a medical officer told the patients they'd be leaving after dark because Americans were advancing on the cave. The nonambulatory were to take "the appropriate action." But no means for suicide were distributed, and Murata stood at the head of the procession leaving the cave at nightfall. A stick given him by a nurse served as a cane, but his useless right leg caused so many falls in the rain and slimy mud that he soon found himself at the rear, "walking" on his buttocks and hoping the dirt wouldn't finish him off by reinfecting his hip.

Alone again and moving only by night, he took forty-eight hours to crawl three miles to a village midway to his destination. (That was a good pace for the thousands of crawlers, many of whom took three to four nights to cover the same distance.) He kept going another two nights, his mouth now too blistered to touch his hardtack. But of all his tortures, the greatest were thirst and the thought of dying alone.

By now, all medical facilities except a few in the extreme south were in no better condition than those visited by Murata and Captain Kojo. With no means of evacuating the wounded even if a hospital ship had magically arrived, all Japanese casualties had been treated on the island or not treated; some amputated their own limbs. The luckiest reached the Haebaru Army Hospital, where young Ruriko Morishita, worked as a nurse's aide. Medic Ikuo Ogiso was attached to a smaller facility, the 2nd Field Hospital. During its operation in the north, highly motivated Ogiso's diligence and dedication had won him promotion to private first class. Then a wing was moved to below the landing beaches, and now, in June, it was again moved farther south.

Under a blanket of enemy bombs and shells, Ogiso's nighttime search for the designated new cave took him from horror to horror. His despair increased when he managed to find the right one, a foul hole whose walls and ceiling oozed moisture. Two days later, thirty patients were delivered to that "hospital," habitation of which would have been a danger even to men in perfect health.

There were of course no sanitation arrangements. Soon over two hundred gravely wounded soldiers were crammed into rock and mud thick with excrement. The dungeonlike grotto's squalor was lit by the flames of occasional oil lamps that cast weird shadows of stalactites on soldiers "who were lying almost on top of each other, all looking like creatures suffering the torments of hell." Sounds of weeping, groaning, and shrieking — as some wounded became deranged — echoed from the walls and through the "nauseating, suffocating" smell of their sweat, blood, pus, and wastes.

The luckiest patients lay where they could wet their throats by holding their mouths open to catch drops from the ceiling. The others remained racked with thirst on top of their excruciating wounds, swarming with flies and maggots. "Each time the bandages are changed, white maggots as thick as a child's little fingertip dropped from the gaping wounds — hundreds of them, all sucking the bloody pus." Medical supplies were so quickly exhausted that "the word *treatment* became a euphemism. . . . All we could do was to disinfect the wound, place medicated gauze over the spot and bandage it." Soon bandages could be changed only every second day, then every third, although patients whose turns were postponed wept with pain. When the borax ran out, the eyes of a blinded soldier, thought to be a graduate of the prestigious Imperial University, were washed with plain water.

Soon the tiny space held an inconceivable 270 people, jammed side by side. The horror paralyzed the medical officer, a former pediatrician who had gone into a stupor at his first sight of the *unoccupied* cave. Now he lay immobilized there, his eyes closed and body rigid.

In *his* civilian life, Private Ogiso had also been a working actor. Now, with only a medic's sketchy medical training, he became a de facto surgeon, cutting open and sewing up a stream of wounded men because no one else could. Amputation was by saw, without anesthesia or antiseptics. Other wounded begged for admission but, as at other facilities, were turned away unless they belonged to units served by that wing of the hospital. Inside, a partition was constructed beneath the lower bunks for tetanus patients, doomed by lack of serum. "It was worse than a pigsty built over the quagmire of blood and pus." Meanwhile, the untreated gangrene cases "tossed about in unbearable agony" as their limbs turned dark and swelled grotesquely. They screamed for days — "It hurts! Please kill me!" — before going rigid. A patient who blew himself up with a hand grenade also killed the man next to him.

If cave medicine hadn't been one of the battle's dirty secrets, it might have provided the starkest measure of the inequality of the two sides' resources. Ninety percent of the Japanese on Okinawa would die before learning it.

The way of bushido is to die — but in this battle where we and the enemy stand on different dimensions of metal and supplies, it completely loses its meaning.

*Something is now beginning that has had no precedent in Japan's military
history: death without meaning.*
— Shigemi Furukawa

*The road was full of . . . injured soldiers on crutches of sticks, crawling soldiers
with their legs blown off going east and west as they hoped to escape to safety.*
— Norio Watanabe

*I hoped to die instantly. That's what I thought about day in and day out, not
about how to live.*
— Kenjiro Matsuki

As American fire turned caves into crematoria, the nonwounded too
trudged south in a daze, dumb with accumulated horrors, bereft of hope
that any effort now could produce even momentary tactical success. The
remaining goal of fighting to the last man to give the mainland more
time and its people more inspiration had lost much of its meaning. Kenjiro Matsuki sensed that "the battle had virtually ended" and this was
mainly "a mop-up of us remnants." His decimated unit "walked in silence, like sheep heading for a slaughterhouse." The ambulatory patients
of the main branch of Ogiso's field hospital — evacuating "inch by inch"
in the driving rain and thick mud — seemed "the chilling sight of defeat
itself."

A few soldiers comforted themselves with a rumor that they were going
south to be picked up by submarine and taken home to Japan. Others
still talked of the massive Japanese landing, now promised by some officers for late June. But the sight of other units as wasted as their own further unnerved them.

The clearing weather made retreating units prime targets. Salvos from
an American battleship caught a transport company that had set out with
150 vehicles. It arrived with fewer than thirty. The bluish flash of large explosion silhouetted a platoon entering a southern village. When the soldiers of another unit reached the spot, "we saw nothing, nobody — our
fighting men had disappeared from the face of the earth like a dream!"

An exhausted soldier of the 15th Independent Mixed Regiment was
dragging a badly wounded leg on June 1 when he ran into Colonel Seiko
Mita, his regimental commander. The de facto leader of Sugar Loaf's
magnificent defense was walking "as if he'd lost his mind." The regiment
of some five thousand men was down to about twenty, roughly 1 percent
of its fighting strength.

Now the first deserters began slipping away, some in civilian clothes, a
few with the look of "wild dogs," as a frightened soldier saw them. By mid-
June, the worst-off units would be a rabble "skulking in holes and
trenches," in a journalist's words, "wandering the countryside looking for

food and water." Although some twenty-five thousand Japanese, numerically a full division, were still coming, going, and hiding in the remaining patch of friendly land, many from broken units hardly knew their fellow soldiers' names. As they became the loneliest of crowds, some would turn on civilians and even soldiers from other units, fighting them for food and shelter.

The post-Shuri Japanese reorganization had been largely a paper operation. In the field, it was too late for anything but last-minute preparations except for units that settled into installations established earlier — most importantly by the 9th Division in the last high ground two miles short of the island's southern tip. Elsewhere, field commanders lacked the time and resources even to properly provision their new positions.

Apart from that last mountain spine and the ridges leading to it, much of the south was too flat for defensive strongpoints. Although even more caves dotted the limestone and coral than up north, they were too few and raw for the remnants of Ushijima's army, not to mention a far greater number of civilians equally eager for shelter. Men who'd grown to hate the old sanctuaries in and around Shuri remembered them with longing. Even the lesser installations there had drainage, leveled floors, and some ventilation. Schoolteacher Shigemi Furukawa noted the difference, starting with the disappearance of a town that had earlier delighted him.

> The town of bright, red-roofed houses shining beautifully in the sun . . . no longer existed. Instead, there were mountains of rubble, scorched lumber, scorched earth. Our company marched through and went into . . . our last stronghold. This cave sloped down from its mouth. With no drainage whatever, it was a slimy morass underfoot. Worse still, the mouth was the only entrance, so there was no ventilation. Accumulated carbonic acid gas was always on the point of extinguishing the lamp.
>
> Even for soldiers whose sole weapon was endurance, living with the oil, smoke, gas and wet — and with all the odors of human existence — brought unbearable suffering. Life in that cave took us to the brink of insanity. After two or three days, I thought I'd prefer to go out and die rather than remain in such hell. . . . Those imprisoned in the agony of that miserable cave began to long for the sun and some air before we died.

Most southern caves and holes in the ground were equally craggy and creepy. A few days of frantic digging in early June managed to slightly improve a selection of them, but many remained pitch-black dungeons, their fetid atmospheres suffocating their packed occupants. Rank moisture dripped from stalactites that left ceilings too low to stand even when their tips were chopped off. The floors were pools of ooze or coral too jagged for sitting or lying on without pain. But although every surface was wet, drinking water was rarely available or was polluted by the waste of dozens of men who were no longer willing to dash out into the rain of metal, even to relieve themselves.

The new 32nd Army headquarters cave was better, partly because it was on a tall cliff above the village of Mabuni. The long, twisting cave near the summit of Hill 89, as the approaching Americans would name the cliff, had a spectacular view of the Pacific from the mouth facing it. But even it was a far cry from the elaborate tunnel beneath Shuri Castle.

In the field, the shortage of water was even more critical than of ammunition. A soldier wounded near Kakazu felt like a dead man because "I became a slave to the desire for water. . . . I was crazy with thirst." That was in April, and in a medical cave. When the days turned fiercely hot in June and water provisioning became as erratic as all other, thirst became unbearable, especially when the fear of slaughter grew intense. While the great American logistical operation delivered water, however foul tasting, in trucks that drove almost to the front, Japanese were ceaselessly tormented even in sectors temporarily free of fighting.

Hunger was less insistent. Those with rice often had to cook it in the muddy liquid of stagnant puddles, soldiers taking turns blowing at the pine needles that served for fuel until their lungs nearly burst. (Carbon monoxide caused cooks to drop utensils without being aware of it.) The C-rations disdained by Americans represented supreme luxury to soldiers who found the leavings on nocturnal forays. Some lived weeks in their cavities, their mud growing ever thicker with the wastes in which they slept, squeezed together and almost submerged. A number literally suffocated to death. "So this was how we were to breathe our last — trapped in a hole without air, without water, without the space to kneel and pray during one's final moments," an inhabitant would remember.

The shelling of the few square miles still in Japanese hands naturally became more concentrated. Even Americans who blessed each shell thought the dawn-to-dusk bombardment "awesome" — at a time when the word retained much of its original meaning. One of the rare Japanese who now wanted to surrender carefully chose a place that promised the best chance without being hit (or shot by his fellows). But he found it impossible to walk ten steps on the first road leading there. Another was convinced the low-flying Grummans and Chance-Voughts, their pilots now hardly inconvenienced by antiaircraft fire, were "determined not to miss a single ant" with their bombing and strafing.

That was no mere hyperbole of the terrified. Samuel Hynes flew his four 500-pound bombs, eight rockets, and many belts of machine-gun ammunition from the Kadena Airfield Tadashi Kojo had originally been assigned to defend. When his squadron inaugurated night attacks in

May, "any light — a truck's headlights, a fire, a lighted doorway — was to be fired on." One night, he looked around for something to attack, "somebody boiling a pot of tea or lighting his way to the toilet, but I could see nothing." After Hynes's last strike, on June 19, against "some trivial target," he assured the squadron intelligence officer he'd scored a direct hit on a three-hole privy.

Just as Japanese field commanders had feared, their units, virtually unsupported by artillery, were far less effective than at the Shuri Line. When men did sortie from their refuges, they were less skilled at concealment, many making themselves easy targets by running from their makeshift positions when they were shelled by American tanks. Most saw themselves as the objects of a roundup. "This went beyond any concept of war," an analytically inclined gunner observed. "This was sheer one-sided destruction and killing."

The dire conditions and prospects now begat dissension. If fighting Americans still engaged in interservice and even interunit rivalry, it was naturally far more common among the men facing annihilation. Japanese soldiers had to be part of a unit to eat with it. Straggling groups from Kojo's 22nd Infantry Regiment would share none of their food with men from a sister regiment of the same 24th Division. Although only a small percentage were truly demoralized at this stage, an infection of spirit began speeding their inevitable end.

It spread easily in the many caves that housed remnants of several units, then attacked the cohesion that had bound each together as a fighting unit. One man watched his infantry company "disintegrate in morale, discipline and even sanity." Previous losses had been heaviest among the bravest and best. Now the survivors saw the units had "ceased to exist," as one would put it. Some feared fellow soldiers — who, for example, would rage against all cooking because smoke might escape from the mouth of the cave and reveal its position. Cliques exchanged death threats. "There wasn't a shred of law or order among us," a wretched soldier would remember. "No one outside one's little group cared what happened to anyone else."

The inevitability of death did not eliminate fear of it. Even more than the Americans, most Japanese felt they were alive only through a series of amazing reprieves: squatting an inch or second away from a bullet, being shielded by a fellow soldier's body, knowing someone with access to medical treatment. When the field hospital where the former actor Masao Murata's wounded hip had been given its skimpy treatment disbanded, he crawled toward the cliff where he'd waited to crush the feinted American landing on L-day, twelve weeks earlier. Four days later, he was again near collapse, having had no food since the rice soup he'd wangled in the hospital cave. But he drank his fill at a well he found, and there was saved by another stroke of luck: Villagers who came to draw water that night recognized the mud-covered heap. Helping him to a tomb, they fed him horse meat and white rice, "very rare those days." Although the feast after his fast caused severe diarrhea, he savored a day of blissful peace from enemy fire, gazing at a blue sky — until a child reported the approach of Americans. Soon he and the civilians heard their *"De-te koi, de-te koi!"* The civilians hid him behind some urns in a corner of the tomb and spread a kimono over him.

> The Americans called again for us to come out. The Okinawans obediently did. Soon [one of the women] came back and told me the Americans were taking them away as prisoners. "So I'm going," she said. "There's rice in the pot and meat in the bowl — please don't throw away your life."
> Then three American soldiers entered with automatic weapons. I was never, ever so very terrified as at that moment. They were stripped to the waist, their tattoos quite visible. I felt my hair stand on end. . . . My knees started shaking violently. I had to push one down with the other to keep them from rattling the urns. I hadn't quite succeeded in controlling them when my diarrhea started again. . . .

Slashing rice sacks with knives, the Americans twice shone a flashlight into Murata's corner. But they finally left, and he escaped into the hills with a hope of making his way to the north to join a Japanese force supposedly still operating there. The unswerving patriot would continue to believe Japan would win the war until he was taken prisoner and saw American supply depots. But like much of the 32nd Army in June, he could hardly be called a fighting man.

> *Death was no longer for victory but only for the sake of dying.*
> — Shigemi Furukawa, about the same period

> *All [chosen for night attacks] were resigned, yet almost all remained terrified. No matter how accustomed the men grew to the incessant shelling, they turned petrified when death approached close enough to mutilate their friends and announce their own time had finally come.*
> — Kenjiro Matsuki

Murata's terror of a lonely death helped explain the increasing incidence of Japanese frenzy. Extreme stress gripped the many separated from their dead or otherwise departed comrades. In the sense that the desperate loners didn't know what they would do at their final moments, Whitaker's fear of the weak but unpredictable remnants as "maniacal" was justified.

As for the majority still with their units, their central experience was waiting for the onslaught to approach their positions. Many saw their final action shortly before their caves were actually straddled. Sent out to seek hand-to-hand combat with the enemy, some rushed tanks as "human mines" with a dozen or more hand grenades wrapped in a blanket. Their last orders were much like those given near a village some two miles north of the 32nd Army's final headquarters at Mabuni. "Tonight we go out to the top of Gushichan Heights," an artillery officer declared on June 10. "I assume you are ready. The time has come to give your life for the country and the Emperor."

No matter what dangers had been previously faced, very few were prepared for a superior's announcement that the time had come for the inevitable end. Some caves actually echoed with chattering teeth. Older men removed photographs of their wives and children from their belongings and stared at them. Their tears irritated some younger soldiers. "How can you fight in that frame of mind?" The scattering who returned from such sorties sometimes met disgust from their officers. "How dare you come back alive?"

Norio Watanabe's independence of spirit put him among the even smaller number who tried to save themselves by fleeing the battle entirely. The antiaircraft battery of the Osaka photographer who had opposed the war from the beginning had been reduced to nearly nothing. His friends had been pulverized in front of his eyes. Whole gun crews had been blown to bits, in one case so thoroughly that the only residue was a gob of innards hanging from a cave's ceiling support. Escaping from a particularly bloody shelling now, Watanabe climbed a hill near his cave in order to be alone. The military oddball long sickened by the futility and stupidity of fighting was also unusual in having married for love, not by arrangement. But with death so near, it was time to dispose of his personal possessions. He put a match to a letter from his adored wife — the only one delivered to him during his year on Okinawa — and to his own photographs of his cherished daughters. Tears wet his cheeks as flames consumed his treasures. His only consolation was a thought that loss of this "miserable war" was Japan's best hope to free herself of the Emperor cult that had dragged her into it.

The battery was further devastated by enemy fire and suicide charges, but to Watanabe's amazing good luck, his squad leader happened to have attended an American university — and to his astonishment, the unusually broad-minded man revealed he intended to escape. Better to be shot for deserting than to die like a dog fighting for an ugly cause.

Watanabe and four trusted fellow soldiers laid plans to island-hop to Formosa. Some dropped out or were killed before they could start; the others left with an Okinawan guide and crept south in search of a canoe, even more afraid of discovery by fellow soldiers than of American bombardments. They wandered, staggered, fled from terrifying dangers, repaired discarded canoes and saw them stolen, were split up by yet more dangers, and risked several other attempts at surrender. Eventually, a chance meeting with another group planning escape put Watanabe in a canoe in the East China Sea. Yet another miracle saved him after a near typhoon swamped the fragile craft. He landed on Kume Island, some fifty miles east of Naha — the birthplace of Masahide Ota, the fervent member of the Blood and Iron Scouts for the Emperor.

Watanabe's bizarre adventures would continue on Kume, where a handful of other deserters soon landed. But their total number would be tiny. He remained the rare Japanese exception.

Early June's stiffest resistance took place on the Oroku Peninsula, which curves into the East China Sea from just below Naha. That was where the abandoned headquarters of Captain Kojo's 22nd Regiment adjoined the much more elaborate tunnel complex housing the headquarters of the Naval Base Force of some nine thousand troops, including Okinawan conscripts — all but a few of whom were untrained or poorly trained for land warfare. In late May, its commander, Admiral Minoru Ota, complied with a request from General Ushijima to join the general withdrawal.

The naval garrison, reduced by the fighting to roughly half its original size, destroyed most of its equipment and heavy weapons, then trudged some five miles south to a position roughly parallel to the crossroads village of Makabe through which great numbers of Japanese units, including Kojo's, would stagger to their final positions. But its planned emplacements turned out to be so exposed that some of Ota's senior officers pleaded to return to their original fortifications, arguing that they belonged to the Imperial Japanese Navy. Until then, the admiral had been a model of rarely achieved interservice cooperation. No doubt influenced by the general demoralization, he permitted half his troops to return to the peninsula, and accompanied them.

On the American side, 10th Army staff debated whether to take the peninsula by pushing through its hills, as conservative General Buckner wanted, or by an amphibious landing. Fortunately for the troops involved, the more audacious approach was chosen. Units of the 6th Marine Division, including those that had just cleared Naha, landed in the predawn darkness of June 4, Dick Whitaker's 29th Regiment following later the same morning.

The first three days were relatively easy, even for the units assigned to take Naha Airfield (although Whitaker's second serious wounding occurred there, on June 6). Most of Admiral Ota's armament was waiting in hilly areas farther inland: chiefly hundreds of machine guns and light cannon transferred from antiaircraft positions and stripped from wrecked planes. Those guns and a variety of land mines were very effective even for troops scarcely trained in their use. The motley units held up the advance, eventually of eight Marine battalions supported by tanks, for over a week. American casualties mounted to a greater proportion even than at Shuri, although the total, 1,608, was far smaller. That was more evidence of how a better-equipped defense would have rent the Americans, as it was preparing to do on the Japanese mainland.

As it was, the Naval Base Force shared the fate of the rump of the 32nd Army as a whole. Ota's troops, green as they were in combat, would have meted out much more punishment in the same battle before the general withdrawal. Now most of their armament and supplies had been destroyed or dispersed elsewhere. Marines finally forced the survivors of the hill clashes down into an area of mudflats and paddies. When they surrounded them, Japanese-speaking Americans shouted inducements to surrender. Some replied by requesting permission for a cease-fire so that they could kill themselves "in peace." Permission was granted, and Marines applauded the more spectacular performers, including a pair who sat on a large demolition charge and lit the fuse. Scores who couldn't decide what to do were easily cut down, bringing the total Japanese dead on the peninsula to about five thousand.

Ota sent his last message to Ushijima on the night of June 11: "Those at our position will all die honorably. . . . Thank you for your past kindnesses. . . . Wish you a victory." The admiral ordered his senior doctor to make certain that three hundred badly wounded troops suffered no further and had an honorable death. Walking down long rows of wounded, a medical team methodically injected outstretched arms until the only sound was the team's own sobbing.

A Marine unit found Ota's headquarters on June 13. The bodies in the medical center were supplemented by hundreds of suicides in the tunnels and corridors. The admiral and five senior officers lay on sleeping platforms in a room near the center of the complex, their uniforms freshly pressed, their throats neatly slit. Ota's death poem expressed a kind of contentment.

> How could we rejoice over our birth
> but to die an honorable death
> under the Emperor's flag.

Elsewhere in Japanese-held territory, the gravely wounded were also dying by their own or their fellows' hands. The American ratio of ninety-seven saved for every hundred wounded was almost reversed in caves like that of medic Ikuo Ogiso. Its agonies continued until it too was disbanded and patients able to limp or crawl were told to make their way back to their units.

The seemingly catatonic medical officer did not answer Ogiso's questions about what might be done to save their nonambulatory patients. Finally, the private had to assume that duty too. His announcement that those unable to return to their companies must die produced absolute silence. "Then the injured started to stir. One missing a leg crawled out. Another broke apart his cot to make a cane and tottered out. To my astonishment, serious cases who until now were considered immobile demonstrated a frightening tenacity to stay alive by crawling inch by inch toward the exit through the mud of blood and pus on the ground."

Ogiso gave three choices to the remaining eighty-plus. He helped the majority who chose potassium cyanide to lie with their heads pointed north, the customary position for the dead. Gunfire could be heard advancing toward the cave as he administered the injections, one by one. Death was almost instantaneous. "When one was done, the next very gently extended his arm toward me."

Then he carried others who yearned for a last breath of clean air outside the cave to a sky unexpectedly brilliant with stars after May's incessant rain. Their heads were also pointed northward. A jar with a few swallows of water was placed in easy reach, together with three hand grenades because the dampness of the cave had probably spoiled a good percentage of them. Ogiso told them to do what they had to when the enemy appeared.

(Badly wounded patients who declined suicide were sometimes shot. In the village of Gushichan two miles north of the 32nd Army's final headquarters, a noncommissioned officer saw to that as the enemy approached. Even some starkly vivid Japanese accounts of the hardships on Okinawa omit such episodes because their writers felt it would have been too cruel to reveal to families that their men died at the hands of their own superiors.)

With no doubt that the turn of all the living was imminent or that death was the highest virtue, Ogiso felt no misgivings. But decades later he would look at the hands that so faithfully followed his orders "and feel an urge to throw myself on the ground and weep."

In resumed torrential rain, he set out for a new cave, where several scattered branches of what was still called the 2nd Field Hospital reunited. Requisitions for reinforcements for fighting units soon reduced the staff of some 250 medical personnel to about a quarter of that. Others failed to return after their dispatch as messengers to the 24th Division's headquarters cave, two and a half miles away. Ogiso, however, survived his stints of sprinting and crawling under the rain of bombs — until their own cave was surrounded and the chief medical officer ordered him to report their end in a final dash to headquarters. Knowing he'd be shot as he inched from the mouth, Ogiso nevertheless moved to obey when a compassionate superior saved him. He was a lieutenant who, reasoning that division headquarters had already been destroyed, suggested he pretend to have made the trip and safely returned.

Ogiso's experience was as typical as any of the medical service survivors — again, the luckiest few. The 2nd Field Hospital, more a mass tomb than a medical facility by early June, was dismantled just when tens of thousands of gravely wounded most needed care. Not even that, however, prompted significant questioning of the system in which the sufferers were locked.

22 · Civilian Suffering

Wandering and sleeping here and there in mountain caves and riversides, crying and weeping, [the civilian refugees] are near death, overwhelmed by hideous fatigue.
— A Japanese doctor

In the desperation of the enemy's position . . . reports have been received to the effect that Japanese soldiers have been shooting civilians who made efforts to surrender.
— From the 6th Marine Division's field intelligence report, June 17

I was surprised to find that life wasn't cheap in the Orient. I saw the faces of ordinary human beings, people brought up on more hard times than me, and I'd had my share. Ordinary human beings racked by malnutrition and dysentery, carrying even worse-off wounded on their backs. . . . They wanted to live and wanted their children to live — and had to watch them die. Over the years, the pictures of those people have grown and grown in my mind.
— A gung-ho Marine

What on earth is the Emperor doing? Does he have any idea of what's happening to women and children? Why doesn't he make a move to stop this hideous war?
— Norio Watanabe

SOME HUNDRED THOUSAND CIVILIANS remained behind the Shuri Line when the major assault on it was mounted on May 11. Their confidence in the 32nd Army and inability to think of an alternative kept them there even after the strict orders to evacuate to the scarcely defended, little-bombarded Chinen Peninsula on the east coast. The Japanese withdrawal in effect pronounced sentence on them.

That wasn't unexpected. Ei Shimada, governor of the prefecture of Okinawa, attended the May 22 conference at which General Ushijima announced his intention to withdraw. Unlike many Japanese officials sent down from Tokyo, Shimada sympathized deeply with the Okinawan people and begged Ushijima not to abandon his main fortifications. He even called the plan "foolish" because it would condemn untold thousands of noncombatants to death, whatever its military value. After the withdrawal, he went further, accusing the Army of having caused needless slaughter.

Ushijima would reply that his primary mission was to give the mainland more time to prepare for the enemy invasion. It's true that he was admirably following his orders to prolong the battle for that reason by every possible day — and brilliantly, in the withdrawal itself (although Colonel Yahara, his operations officer, did the actual planning). And it's hard to imagine a more impressive display of dignity and composure than Ushijima's in the face of impossible odds. He was a great commander of whom it cannot be said he betrayed the Okinawan people, because Imperial General Headquarters had treated them as expendable from the beginning — "a sacrificial stone," as a distinguished Japanese military historian would put it, "in the game of Go." More than supreme courage, it would have taken revolutionary initiative, the vision of a rebel prophet, for Ushijima to surrender when the Shuri Line was broken instead of prolonging the mutual killing.

But had he found the strength for that, he would have been a greater man and in the long run a greater commander.

Of all candidates who might fail his superiors, however, Ushijima was among the least likely. The exemplary general gave Japan four extra weeks by protracting the efforts of some of his forty thousand surviving soldiers — and causing the deaths of almost three times as many civilians. For decades after his death, it was said on Okinawa and repeated by Japanese and American writers that that filled him with remorse. "The Okinawans must resent me terribly," he was quoted as reflecting in his final moments. But that supposed flash of guilt may well have been invented by a sympathizer of Japan trying to make him nobler than he was, to preserve respect for samurai traditions and Japanese militarism despite the agony they caused. Or the story expressed a wish by someone who grieved for Okinawans, whose suffering might be more bearable if Ushijima had regretted how much his strategy had contributed to it. Current evidence indicates that, for all his good nature and soldierly virtue, the stoic general thought no more about them at the end than at the beginning.

The island remained the stage, not an actor, in his Japanese drama of defending personal honor with sacrificial service. However more likable he was than the long line of exploiters from Satsuma and elsewhere, his notion of right and wrong left no more room for native considerations. The campaign's final stage would now surpass the sum of the island's suffering during the previous three and a half centuries.

*   *   *

Most Okinawan leaders contributed by following their old pattern of docile submission to Japanese authority. Scores of thousands might have been saved had they heeded the American leaflets rained on them: Wear white; keep apart from military units; give themselves up. But the majority, still convinced the bestial Americans lusted for their death, were too bewildered to do more than grope for safety in the same eight square miles where the remnants of the Japanese Army were hiding and charging.

The civilian slaughter predicted by Governor Shimada began within days of the withdrawal. Had the 32nd Army held to its promise and remained in its main bastion for the final stand, it would been destroyed to the last man, but a large number of civilians would have been spared because most were apart from the Army, therefore relatively safe. Now the two streamed together on the roads leading south, seeking cover in the same places.

In the north and center, where many noncombatants were quickly interned and fed, however minimally, their suffering had remained within what might be called expected limits. But there was no way civilians could stay alive after mingling with the troops. Prodigious as it had been before, American fire from land, sea, and air became more so on the compressed target of the southern end: almost seven million shells alone in June, roughly fifty for each surviving Okinawan and Japanese.

Dodging that fire, hordes of desperate natives limped and crawled without the slightest idea of a destination. Older ones who had rarely left their villages were lost in unfamiliar territory. Almost all were hungry, thirsty, and weak enough to bend or reel under the smallest bundles. They scattered in panic when bombardments began, some clawing their way into ditches and brush, but thousands were too exhausted to move.

The army of refugees that choked the muddy ribbons of road was much larger than the shrunken 32nd Army. Their meager belongings — scraps of clothing and a piece or two of pottery — were piled in baskets on their heads or hung on shoulder poles. A schoolteacher on his way from the village of the disbanding field hospital Captain Kojo visited during his evacuation found words inadequate to describe the "utter horror. . . . Dead everywhere . . . everywhere. . . . It was hell."

Almost all of the traveling was still done after dark, in rotting shoes or none at all. The steady deluge of the first nights filled trenches, ditches, and all manner of craters. Occasional car or truck headlights illuminated ghostly faces ravaged by exhaustion and fear. Centuries-old villages were piles of stones and ashes. The flesh and fat of people hit by shells "sizzled in the darkness, emitting now blueish, now reddish flames." Groups without destinations wandered on and off the roads, some turning back north in their confusion. A teenage girl saw women and children disappear among some bushes "only to re-emerge a few moments later, striding resolutely in the opposite direction, as though headed for a new destination."

During the day, the bodies that littered roads and fields bloated under the searing sun that replaced the rain. Elderly couples sat in the mud, holding hands with their last strength while awaiting their end. A Japanese soldier saw a mother and her child squatting in a field, their hands covering their faces until they vanished in the flash and smoke of a shell burst, one of thousands of direct hits on unintended targets. Women screamed watching flames roast their children. A few fathers — most were still in the Home Guard — joined the category of the crazed. Split in two at the hip, one stared in horror at the scraps of his wife and three children left by a naval shell.

Some families lurched to their tombs to join their ancestors there. Children of five and six carried infants on their backs. Others whimpered with exhaustion as they were dragged by adults too weak to lift them. Newly made orphans crouched in terror. Wretched suffering was so ubiquitous that families came to ignore others starving to death before their eyes.

A Himeyuri nurse's aide from the Haebaru Army Hospital noticed a stream of soldiers and civilian refugees watching a native with one leg gone. He'd just emerged from a deep puddle by stretching his other leg ahead and supporting himself with both arms. A small bag hanging by a strap from his neck thumped on his chest with each forward jerk. No one stopped to help. "How many miles had he traveled like that and how many miles had he yet to cover?"

Ever since L-day, what Okinawans saw contradicted everything promised by Tokyo and the 32nd Army. Enemy warships filled the ocean, enemy planes packed the sky, enemy weaponry scorched the land — and the awaited counterattack never came. Still, even the victims of occasional Japanese mistreatment almost universally suppressed their questions while hope of eventual victory made every terrible event bearable. It was rooted in the great defensive line on which so many natives too had toiled. Even more than among the troops, citadel Shuri, the heart of the old kingdom and of the defense, had comforted and inspired. "'As long as Shuri holds, as long as Ushijima and Cho command the Army, victory is ours,' we'd tell one another — and believe it." The evacuation of the never-to-be-surrendered fortress dealt a critical blow to that trust.

Families on the road met other families gripped by the same disillusionment. Hearing of massive civilian deaths in other sectors, they realized their suffering had been in vain. Few ordinary folks had embraced the Emperor cult or esteemed the idea of death for him. Further sacrifice could no longer be justified in any way that made sense to them.

The 32nd Army's condition, now exposed to view, further shocked and demoralized. Troops passing piles of uniformed corpses without making a move to bury them, and others disguised in civilian clothes dismayed Okinawans previously unable to imagine Japanese cowardice. Gravely wounded men who had left the disbanded medical facilities not wanting to kill themselves there were the starkest evidence of the military breakdown, more appalling even than the individual stragglers who also didn't know the location or direction of their units. Many had been crippled in both legs. The strongest inched relentlessly forward, stumbling or crawling or pulling themselves with their arms. The weakest, unable even to sit any longer, lay prostrate, waiting for oblivion.

Civilians saw even unwounded troops succumb to despair. One band sat motionless across a road from a burned-out army truck, although every child knew by then that even wrecked military vehicles were a favorite target of enemy planes. Many such groups seemed beyond caring. Okinawans did not have to know how much Japanese soldiers needed firm leadership to perceive that the army was stumbling toward disintegration. All could see for themselves that some units were collections of ragged individuals — a proportion of whom, knowing they had only weeks or days to live, resorted to rape. (One woman reported to have been raped by American and Japanese soldiers on the same day threw light on the new civilian predicament.)

Sharing their dangers and trust in eventual victory, natives and the army had generally gotten along well before the evacuation. But it was almost inevitable that centuries-old dislike and antagonism would reemerge as the common objectives began breaking down, and that the majority would come to sense (if not yet vocalize) that the 32nd Army that had promised to protect them was going to lose.

The claim that Japan was a divine country, destined to rule the world, was increasingly seen as myth. Competing for food, shelter, and impossible salvation helped civilians lose their admiration for the formerly invincible Yamato men, whose mistreatment of them was growing from isolated instances before the withdrawal to a small but clear pattern. Long-standing prejudice against the "little brown monkeys" surfaced among more and more troops who had lost their leadership. Shorn of the restraints of their community and higher authority, some became savage. Never mind that Okinawans were Japanese citizens; that category of desperate soldiers knew them as racially non-Japanese, therefore inferior.

Whom did the Japanese end up defending, whom did they kill? They killed the very people they were pledged to defend. . . . The first were those with the least strength, the shy, the meek, the quiet.
— Toshi Maruki, *The Hiroshima Murals*

*My condition was so bad after the evacuation — and my men's condition —
that I had no energy even to think about incidents of civilian abuse I saw.*
— Tadashi Kojo

*I saw an Okinawan woman who sought refuge in a well. She gave birth to a
baby, there, standing up. These horrible things happen and our hands did them.
No one is saintly during a war.*
— Fred Baxter

At the same time, civilians cared less about the outcome of the battle and
the war. As they trudged the perilous roads amid the masses of dead and
half living, they could think of little beyond their own survival. Their priorities were safety, water, and food, roughly in that order. When the supplies on their backs were gone, sweet potato leaves became a luxury, like
frogs, toads, locusts, snails, slugs, and lizards. Most families resident in
the far south had a cache of food even after their houses had been leveled. Refugees from elsewhere agonized over whether to steal from their
fields and larders. As the weeks passed, the takers became less troubled
by conscience, and those who couldn't bring themselves to steal became
too weak to care about nourishment.

Nursing children were first to succumb to starvation. When mothers'
breasts ran dry, some melted mashed sweet potatoes in boiling water, but
the babies vomited up the liquid. Soon the "yellow clay dolls" stopped
crying and turned cold. Grandparents were usually next. Families argued
about eating sago palms, which would poison them but only after a few
days. Others debated whether to leave their caves to try to scavenge
something in the fields, the effort of which might kill them faster by consuming their remaining energy.

Water, always scarce in the south in summer, became all but unavailable when May's rain turned to June's heat and drought. Few refugees
knew the locations of springs, most of which had been sequestered by
Japanese units anyway. Some drank their own urine. By mid-June, Ushijima's troops, with and without orders from superiors, commandeered
many areas' hiding places — making safety, the first priority, impossible
for civilians.

After dragging themselves south, all had to find shelter from the typhoon of bombs and steel. The only reliable kind was in the caves that
belonged to local communities no less than the wells. In fact, many caves
were the sites of the wells, the fresh water that had formed them serving
as the only local supply. Living for two months in the caves farther north,
the severely distressed people who had been trying to cling to life in the
enormously overcrowded spaces inevitably got on one another's nerves.
Women stopped menstruating and otherwise lost "the last particle of
their female charms," as a native account put it, becoming "physiologi-

cally identical with men." Ventures outside were made only for food, for which all searched "with the sensitive noses of hungry animals," and for excreting. That function was fraught with distress because it inevitably exposed the performers to shell fragments. Latrine trenches began mere yards from cave exits. Excrement overflowed their walls because the stress on top of a diet heavy with unhulled rice balls made by dirty hands turned stomachs sickly. But the desire to defecate was suppressed "with the utmost effect" even when it filled bodies with yearning "from abdomen to breast."

Those were the good days because now, farther south, soldiers expropriated many of the caves, ejecting natives already there. Refusing admission to new arrivals, they labeled protestors "anti-Japanese," including those who refused to surrender their last supplies of food. Over three hundred families in one Makabe area alone were driven from four community caves in early June, after which they sought the almost useless protection of trees, pigsties, rock walls, and the ruins of houses — or simply stayed in the open. Jo Nobuko Martin set the scene in an autobiographical novel. As a barrage of shells burst around her little party of civilians, they found a hillside cave near a village.

> We were greeted by an officer who had just come out of the cave, sword in hand. He began brandishing the sword at some farmers who had gathered nearby. "Get away from here!" he bellowed. "Dirty, stinking farmers! Are you trying to attract the enemy's attention? They'll smell you! Get out!"
>
> The farmers ran at the sight of the officer's sword. [A friend] and I ran with them, but we promptly returned to the cave. After all, we weren't dirty farmers. Surely some kindly officer would invite us into the cave for safety? While we stood waiting . . . the farmers began coming back too. Desperation had made them bold. It was their cave, after all, and they could no longer stay in the village, where shells were now exploding constantly. The officer reappeared, brandishing his sword. The farmers scattered again, only to return in a few minutes. . . . The village was burning. The fire and the bursting shells were driving these men back to the cave, despite the officer with the sword. How would it end?

The usual Japanese excuse was that Okinawans' comings and goings in search of food would reveal their hiding places. But soldiers who drove them to perish under the bombardments knew the cave mouths would be found anyway, not least because all surrounding vegetation had been charred to nothing. Those who took food intended for children usually justified the action as necessary for the national interest they supposedly represented. "Who's more important, your family or the Emperor?" A small minority of inhuman soldiers began to dominate. Some were starving when they forced villagers to pay in food for "information" about what regions might be safe from the enemy. Others fired into hamlets and looted when their inhabitants rushed away to escape what they assumed were American bullets. And when Americans arrived outside cave mouths, many soldiers turned their weapons on civilians inside, threatening death if they tried to leave, hoping their presence would deter the enemy from using explosives on the caves. Or they raped and killed: "our repayment," a Japanese soldier agonized, for Okinawans' "consistent good will, devotion and kindness."

Needless to say, not all Japanese were cruel. Many kindhearted soldiers couldn't help natives because their officers or comrades shouted them down. But many others did perform good deeds. A student named Momoko Yonaha was one of thousands they saved, in her case by taking the trouble, despite their own desperation, to stop her when she reached for a suicidal hand grenade on the beach at the very southern tip. After the war, a few 32nd Army survivors would return to Okinawa to live among the gentle people who had sacrificed beyond the call to save *them.* Many would grieve for civilians together with their dead comrades; some still grieve, recognizing that Okinawans were "the real victims of this war" who bore the greatest share of its pain.

But most Japanese soldiers remained locked in their ignorance, fear, upbringing, and code of war, all of which tended to make them indifferent to Okinawan suffering even when they weren't adding to it. No doubt mainland civilians would be better treated when the fighting would move there. But it never did. One of the poisoned darts of the war started by Japan was that the only battle fought on supposedly Japanese soil was actually fought on Okinawan. After centuries of Japanese effort to instill Ryukyuans with their own militaristic appetites, the military government in Tokyo caused the island some of the most severe destruction, person for person and house for house, ever suffered by any people. The failure of Ushijima's staff to take account of that disaster followed directly from Japan's colonialist attitudes and policies.

The antagonism that flared up as collapse became imminent also fired accusations of Okinawan "spying." That charge, grounded in a notion that any contact with the hated enemy was betrayal, had begun when the first civilians allowed themselves to be taken to American detention camps on L-day. Even without it, some soldiers shot civilians who tried to surrender, which was considered crime enough.

Brutal torture and executions became numerous after the fall of Shuri: shooting, strangling, clubbing, and tossing hand grenades at natives, including hundreds of women and children, whom Japanese had detected moving toward the American lines with an apparent intention to let themselves be taken. Possession of an American leaflet with instructions about how to do that was often taken as proof of treachery.

It may be said in mitigation that Japanese also killed fellow soldiers who attempted to surrender. American combat diaries had many entries like a Marine's on June 13: "The Japs were offered but refused to surrender and threw grenades at two of their brothers who . . . carried leaflets of surrender." But the murders of civilians were more repulsive. As in their conquests in Manchuria and China, some soldiers seemed more controlled by racial prejudice — obviously no American monopoly — than by any rational motive.

Civilians were the handiest scapegoats for those driven to believe that *someone* was responsible for the military disaster. At least a hundred documented executions for espionage took place, all without any evidence of it, most in spontaneous outbursts of vengeful frustration, even against children. They included beheadings, saber slashings of "traitors" tied to trees, and one perforation — of a feeble-minded female "spy" — with a bamboo spear.

When the little offshore island of Ie Shima was stormed, a third of its forty-five hundred natives died, roughly twenty times the number of American combatants killed there. Many committed suicide to avoid capture. But American soldiers found two badly wounded teenage boys who'd survived the hand grenade blasts that had killed the rest of their families. The pair recovered in a hospital tent, from which they escaped when some Americans pressed them to go to their village and bring back some good-looking girls. Japanese soldiers from a detachment of stragglers later found them and took them to their lieutenant. "You gave the Americans military secrets!" he declared, then shouted an order. Swords instantly dispatched the accused. They flashed again after Americans told six young natives in a detention camp to take a letter to the same lieutenant, asking him to come down from his mountain retreat and surrender. Executed for "treachery," the six died singing a patriotic song. Performed in secret, most of the other killings will never be fully documented.

(Ie Shima's suffering mirrored Okinawa's in being caused by both sides. Three months before L-day, the Japanese forced some three thousand natives to evacuate. Weeks *after* the official end on Okinawa, the Americans removed all remaining civilians to improve security on the island's airfield, already gearing up for the coming invasion of the Japanese mainland. By that time, the surviving population was mainly women and children, some of whom tried to defend their demolished homes with stones and spears. Almost every building was rubble when civilians were permitted to return to their island in late 1945.)

Although the Japanese Ministry of Education would order mention of murders of Okinawans deleted from textbooks, the outlines are known.

Members of the 32nd Army stole food, refuge, and life from tens of thousands of Okinawans, chiefly women and children, whom they had supposedly come to protect. A small but significant number bayoneted, beheaded, poisoned, strangled, drowned, and injected babies to silence them in the caves they'd commandeered.

Atrocities were proportionately greater on lesser Ryukyu islands whose smaller garrisons were commanded by junior officers. Before L-day, Japanese commanders ordered all residents of the Yaeyami Islands, a small chain about 265 miles south of Okinawa, to evacuate to even more remote islands in advance of an American attack that never came. The Yaeyami people had long avoided the almost uninhabited, malaria-infested minor islands to which some thirty-two thousand of them were now sent. About half contracted the disease, nearly four thousand fatally. (Claiming no legal proof exists of its culpability, Tokyo has never paid compensation.)

On Zamami Island in the Keramas, natives were ordered to take their own lives after the American landing the week before L-day. One hundred seventy-one people obeyed, most using razors and knives. Some 150 farming and fishing families used hand grenades distributed by the local policeman on Tokashiki, largest of the Keramas. Some adults there survived, however — until, finally, the strong clubbed the weak to death, the young axed the old, and mothers suffocated their children. Regaining consciousness to see some of his family still alive, a sixteen-year-old boy decided he and his brother must finish them off with their hands, since no grenades remained. "We had to do it because of love. . . . When I was finished, my brother and I looked around us. Our parents and sisters were all dead." Then the brothers marched out with sticks in order to die honorably fighting the Americans — as, they'd been told, all the Japanese soldiers had done. On the way, they bumped into some of those supposedly dead Japanese soldiers!

The mass suicide on Tokashiki claimed 325 civilians; garrison soldiers beheaded at least ten more. Ninety percent of the over three hundred Korean laborers who had worked on the island under Japanese brutality also died, many beheaded for allegedly stealing food.

On Kume Island, Japanese soldiers who'd bragged to admiring natives about how they'd defend them murdered twenty-six, roughly twice the number who would be killed by American units when they landed in late June. The dead included a year-old baby, but a lesson had to be made of "spying" civilians whom Americans sent to try to persuade military units in the hills to surrender. The warriors bayoneted some "traitors" so that they'd bleed to death slowly. (There is some evidence that the same garrison also killed several shipwrecked Japanese soldiers who washed ashore. That would have been due to intensified interservice rivalry as the Japanese cause fell apart.)

Private Norio Watanabe, the Osaka photographer who had fled Okinawa and washed up on Kume, learned of the atrocities there when members of the garrison killed the husband of a young woman who had befriended him. "I couldn't understand the reasoning of the Navy men who were killing villagers as spy suspects. Instead of fighting the Americans who landed, our men, full of . . . anguish to protect their own lives, kill the friendly, cooperative villagers!"

But Watanabe, who had always known the folly of war with America, remained the exception, even decades later, in his grieving for the murdered. Those were the kinds of episodes the Ministry of Education assiduously excluded from the school curriculum, together with the Japanese atrocities in China and elsewhere.

Okinawans too began killing themselves in June, because one facet of Japanese propaganda retained its power: No longer willing to die for a lost military or national cause, most civilians remained morbidly afraid of the immensely powerful enemy who still seemed the monsters Tokyo had described. Some natives so feared their torture that they felt relief when their throats were cut by relatives. While newspapers on the Japanese mainland wrote of Okinawan children "dying gloriously on the battlefield," weeping parents were holding them tight as they exploded a grenade to free the family of the threat, or used kitchen knives, tree limbs, or rocks on their babies. Japanese officers and soldiers sometimes finished off survivors of grenades that had killed the parents.

Still, the majority of civilians did not choose death but were killed by starvation, disease, individual Japanese cruelty — or, most of all, indiscriminate American firing. As a whole, the dying caused more emotional torment than at Hiroshima or Nagasaki because the agony was more protracted.

Fourteen-year-old Shitsuko Oshiro pleaded with soldiers to admit her into a cave. Relenting after she promised to leave at the end of the bombardment in progress, they also admitted an older woman, angrily ordering her to stop her baby's crying. Unable to, she took him out.

"After a while, she came back alone. I don't know what she'd done with the child. . . . She wouldn't say anything and nobody would ask her."

Nineteen people in a cave the size of a small bedroom left not a square inch for a middle-aged mother and elderly woman with two small children whom Japanese troops had forced from another cave. The four looked "awfully tired" even to the awfully tired others. With nowhere to go, they settled under a nearby tree until shell fragments killed both women, leaving the baby still sucking at her mother's breast and the older child snuggling to her body in the pouring rain. A teenage boy who left the stifling cave to relieve himself later found them newly dead alongside their mother. "I felt so bad I didn't know what to make of human lives."

Thirst-crazed Japanese soldiers searching for water entered a village's last standing house, where a cloud of flies feasted on innards oozing from a collection of stinking corpses. "It's the same wherever we'd go, there's no safety anywhere," the remaining residents replied to their question about why they hadn't left. And: "If I die, I'd like to do it in my own home." That would be soon: More shells began falling as the soldiers left.

One of Captain Kojo's men recognized someone in the carpet of civilian bodies bordering a southern road. It was young Yasu, daughter of the farmer in whose house the captain had quartered in his first position at Kadena Airfield. Bleeding to death from a shrapnel wound, once-beautiful Yasu asked about the once-dashing captain.

Near the entrance to a cave at Itosu, a teacher and his wife sat on a rock almost submerged in muddy water. Skin and bone, they nevertheless retained an air of refinement while remaining motionless for days, she with her head split open and full of wriggling maggots, he using his last strength to sustain a flow of comforting words to her. A principled Japanese soldier inside the cave gave the couple the considerable gift of a drink of clean water just drawn from a nearby spring. The teacher tried desperately to raise the soldier's canteen to his wife's lips. When the soldier, unable to forget them, volunteered to rush outside and fetch his unit's water again two days later, the couple were facedown in the mud.

Middle-aged Eishun Higa and his family saw a woman's corpse in a pond near a road leading to a village sugar mill. On her back, a baby girl of about a year was moving her hands and head. When Higa's wife said something to him about the poor dead soul, the woman suddenly raised herself from the water. "I'm not dead, I'm still alive. I was hit by white phosphorus" — she was unaware water was no treatment for that — "and can't see. Please take my child and adopt her. . . . If you see a friendly soldier passing, ask him to shoot me as soon as possible."

Higa told the woman to come out of the pond and try to survive. But she said she wanted to stay where she was and die as soon as possible because her burns hurt too terribly. Just then, a heavy rain of shells began falling at the pond, killing Higa's sister-in-law and just missing his children. They ran to seek cover.

A bullet ripped through the thigh of fourteen-year-old Koei Kinjo the moment he stepped outside to relieve himself. Some of the people packed inside the cave lectured him severely for his recklessness; his father was furious.

Days later, they were joined by a young man with a bad throat wound that leaked water when he tried to drink. The new arrival developed tetanus and bit "anything he could lay his hands on, whether it was a man or a stone. He would groan and squeal in an eerie, melancholy voice — and bite." The men worried that he'd hurt someone and that his wild squealing would give away their position. Since he was beyond saving, they choked him to death in hope of saving the others.

Norio Watanabe tried to convince a wild-eyed civilian with two pitiful daughters to save themselves. "You must have seen [the Americans'] propaganda leaflets," he urged the father. "So give yourselves up, let them take you prisoner."

The father's desperately beaten look suddenly turned to fury. "What a terrible thing for you to say, Mr. Soldier. I'd rather die than become a prisoner." Producing a grenade obtained from another Japanese for use on himself and his children, he declared that he'd just killed a third daughter, his eldest, who had been carrying the youngest of the two surviving ones on her back when a shell fragment ripped off half her face. "She tried to cry but only whistles came out. I lost my mind and strangled her with my own hands. *With my own hands!*" he repeated, thrusting them out and watching them tremble.

Watanabe, with three beloved daughters of his own in Osaka, was stunned. "Who told those people to fight on until death, civilians like soldiers? I wanted to tell the father that the Japanese military men who called Americans beasts were themselves more beastly . . . but Okinawans were naive and I couldn't reason with him."

Leaving his foxhole one mid-June morning, an American sergeant saw the bodies of about eighty Okinawan women at the perimeter of the 7th Army Division infantry company with whom he'd spent the night. In an attempt to find safety — or flee callous Japanese, or help *kind* Japanese — the women had unknowingly touched the trip wire strung around the position and set off the machine guns. Having seen similar results on previous mornings, the soldiers got on with their business. The sergeant got on with his: helping compile the Army's official history of the campaign, for which he made no notes about the women because "it was an Army history, so we didn't include much about civilians."

Sixteen-year-old Mitsutoshi Nakajo got no food in his cave because he was considered an adult. Soon children too got nothing because the soldiers confiscated their parents' supply of rotting rice balls: As they explained, they had to do the fighting. "They said they were going on a surprise attack . . . but we knew they just wanted to live and get back to the mainland."

The next day, they announced they were going to dispose of all children under the age of three in order to keep them from attracting the enemy's attention. Nakajo pleaded with the senior officer to let his

younger brother and niece, who were among the five children in that category, leave the cave with him. Saying that the family would become spies
and give away their position, the officer posted guards at the mouth to
prevent their exit. "Then four or five soldiers took away the children one
by one, including my brother, and gave them the injection."

The following morning, the soldiers told the Okinawans they were
going to dispose of the adults too in order to save them from being
crushed them under the Americans' tanks when they were captured. "We
knew they were going to kill us all just to take our food. We were so
shocked we didn't know what to say."

While they were trying to think of how to prevent their execution,
Americans blasted the cave, freeing the civilian hostages.

When Toyo Gima moved from Makabe's huge Thousand People Cave
to a smaller one, a boy of four or five was crying near the mouth because
he couldn't find his mother. When no one replied to an angry soldier's
question of where she was, he and others took the boy into the cave,
where Gima saw "this unbelievable thing. . . . All the civilians who saw it
were crying. I actually saw them put a string [of ripped bandages] around
the boy's neck, but it was so horrible I couldn't watch it to the end."

Seeking water during a lull in a bombardment of her village, nineteen-
year-old Haru Maeda heard her younger sister and brother calling. She
found both wounded and carried them inside her cave, where they told
her that a Japanese soldier had entered their little house and asked their
mother a question. She tried to answer politely but her Japanese was
weak. The soldier swung his sword. Her head landed in the lap of
Maeda's sister-in-law. Maeda's sister ran away with her younger brother
on her back. Soldiers caught up with them and stabbed her until she let
go of the boy, then slashed a wide cut in his stomach.

Now, in the cave, intestines spilled from both children. Running outside for water for them, Maeda saw the body of another brother, her
youngest, together with two boys from another family. They had been dis-
emboweled. Then Maeda saw her sister-in-law's father. He was sitting
cross-legged against a tree, holding his money and his decapitated head.
She found the bodies of another sister and an uncle at the well.

Returning to her wounded brother and sister, she held their hands
and tried to make them comfortable while they "trembled all over, chattering their teeth . . . trembling and crying loudly with pain." One took
three hours to die, the other four. Before the end, they asked Maeda
what she would do after they died. She told them not to worry; she'd join
them very soon. She tried to do that with a piece of string around her
neck but stopped pulling because "I couldn't kill myself after all. I tried it
three times but quit when the string got too tight."

Then she went to see her mother's body, which the soldiers had dragged a short distance from the house. They said they couldn't help what they'd done because they were in combat.

No sampling of civilian suffering in June can convey its scope, which was far greater than what the two armies bore. And although desperate individuals and small groups committed most of the atrocities, some larger units contributed. On June 19, troops of another battalion of Captain Kojo's 24th Infantry Division made a midnight escape from their menaced cave near Maehira, two miles above the 32nd Army's final headquarters. As daylight and American troops approached and they hurried to complete a transfer to another cave, they used their swords to butcher over a dozen villagers already there, including women and children.

23 · Young Okinawans Hold to Their Duty

What was it that Okinawans were supposed to gain and lose in the throes of war? . . . Who is going to be defended from whom in the "national defense"? . . . The colossal ego of leaders on both sides, who threw thousands of men into an inferno of steel and fire for the capture of a few square kilometers of scorched earth, is too great for the average citizen to comprehend.
— Masahide Ota, well after the war

THE EVACUATION OF THE SHURI LINE left most conscripted Okinawans somewhere between the civilians and the military diehards in outlook. Once the defense was seen as lost, older men tended to turn their attention from the fighting to finding their living or dead families. But many of the unmarried, especially among the elite represented by Masahide Ota and Ruriko Morishita, the nurse's aide nicknamed Miss Victory Day, remained as dedicated as any Japanese soldiers, their youthful energy still driven by desire to prove their patriotism.

Until the general withdrawal, Ota, of the Blood and Iron Scouts, remained based in the cave of the communications soldiers near the 32nd Army's underground headquarters at Shuri. By the last week of May, when the line was finally crumbling, the morale of a few Japanese officers was doing the same. Scavenging for food one night in leveled Shuri's caves and cellars, the starving former Normal School students found a container filled with *awamori*, the Ryukyuan liquor with a greater kick than sake. Although alcohol was strictly prohibited, their platoon had become disorganized and demoralized enough so that no officer stopped them from swilling. (Their own officer, the disagreeable intelligence lieutenant, lived apart, in the headquarters complex.) But Ota himself would not be disheartened. Not even the deaths of more than half his unit, most on the roads during their delivering of messages, weakened the morale of the tough young Kume native.

However, the order to leave their cave deeply saddened the group's remaining members. Whatever the dangers, the conscripted students yearned to remain in Okinawa's heart and the repository of its national treasures, including their Normal School and the 32nd Army's headquarters. But although abandoning sacred Shuri was tacit admission of defeat, they of course obeyed the order, which for them came on May 27, the eve of Ushijima's skillful retreat.

Assigned to help prepare the Army's new headquarters, they were the first boys to leave, but not before Ota was startled by one of the Himeyuri girls who'd been living elsewhere in the same student cave throughout the battle. Although the two sexes were still forbidden to talk, just as before the war, a pupil who'd been one year behind Ota in Kume Island's elementary school now approached him and broke the rule with the first and last words to him from a girl student. "You boys all think it's your destiny to die before you're twenty," she whispered. "But death is the end of everything, so you take care of yourself. Please don't die." Convinced the younger girl shouldn't have talked that way — it was *right* to sacrifice one's life for one's country — Ota felt sullied. But he couldn't help feeling flattered too.

The boys then headed for their new base near the 32nd Army's relocated headquarters on the cliff above Mabuni village in the far south. Weakened by severe diarrhea, probably from drinking contaminated water, Ota couldn't manage the sacks he'd been assigned to carry. When he fell, a Japanese sergeant unsheathed his sword. "Stand up or I'll kill you." The sergeant swung and missed. A classmate shouldered Ota's burden in addition to his own, and both trudged on. (At their destination, the boys would be angered to discover that some of the sacks of "vital documents" they'd been ordered to guard with their lives contained officers' personal effects.)

The sergeant's sword didn't dismay the boys, who believed the tough veteran was motivated by desire to accomplish the evacuation successfully. Later during the march, however, the sight of officers wearing civilian clothes over their uniforms prompted the shocked Ota's first resentment of the Japanese. As always, the enemy's dreaded observation planes flew overhead, particularly those called "dragonflies" because of their looks. Knowing pilots' ability to report every detail of movement on the roads, Ota realized all civilians would become open targets as soon as they saw through the disguise.

Conditions in the far south were so bad that when Ota and a fellow communications soldier delivered a message to a cave and found it empty except for some clothing and other supplies, they indulged a youthful impulse to put on captains' uniforms. Sleeves flapping, discounting the risk of being shot for impersonating an officer because discipline had much broken down, they left the little storehouse to return to their own new cave — and nearly stumbled into the arms of an American band directly outside.

Ota had seen only one live American previously: a pilot who had parachuted from a plane shot down in the 10/10 air raid. Bound to a large tree in the courtyard of 32nd Army's Shuri headquarters, the pilot assured a crowd of gogglers that more American planes would soon arrive to rescue him. News of his capture spread like fire, attracting students eager for a peek at him — who, however, utterly failed to live up to expectations. The dreaded "beast" was disappointingly human, obviously very tired and not much older than the teenage students themselves. Someone ventured a timid "hello" to the helpless young captive. His weak smile in response prompted youthful grins in return and fury in a Japanese guard. "How dare you smile at your enemy? Unpatriotic brats!"

Several onlookers who had approached too near the prisoner were seized and badly beaten. Despite that, Ota's best friend, the Normal School's top pupil and a passionate student of English, resolved to test his knowledge of the language. (Its use had been forbidden for years. Even baseball terms such as *strike* and *out* had been given obligatory Japanese equivalents.) In the dead of night, the two sneaked from the school with food and water for the grateful pilot, who seemed tortured with thirst. Ota's friend exchanged a few words in English with him. The next day, he was viciously lashed by military policemen, then drafted into the Army. The boy would be killed in the fighting on Okinawa. The pilot soon escaped, perhaps with help, but was recaptured and shot.*

Now, eight months after that incident, Ota was far beyond thoughts about the nature of the American people. He simply knew that the purpose of those on the island, beasts or not, was to kill Japanese soldiers — whom they shot like ducks. His terror therefore doubled when he and his friend almost ran into the enemy group outside the supply cave. But the huge, half-naked killers failed to see the self-promoted Japanese "captains," perhaps because they were preparing their camp for the night. The boys tore off their new uniforms and hid in yet another cave — where, to their surprise, they found an old classmate who had deserted his unit to look after his mother and sister, among the refugees. Although the 32nd Army's final collapse was still two weeks away, Ota's classmate, a Normal School karate champion, had seen the light.

"We're going to lose this war so come with us and try to save yourselves. There's no point in still trying to fight."

"What's happened to you?" asked Ota, astonished. "You've gone crazy!"

---

*Another American pilot who parachuted into Naha during a raid the following February was executed by an intelligence officer several days after the fall of Sugar Loaf. A third shot down and severely burned in March, a month before L-day, was beheaded, also in May. Little is known about other American pilots presumed captured. At least one would be killed in Tokyo, where many fellow inmates of POW camps were also executed, some in savage reaction to the Emperor's surrender proclamation in August 1945.

He and his friend made their way back to Mabuni, from where their unit's survivors continued delivering optimistic reports to towns and villages not yet in American hands. Approaching one such cave as an artillery barrage began tearing the area, Ota was warned by Japanese soldiers to scram or they'd shoot. But civilians called from inside the entrance, "This is *our* cave, not theirs. Come in!" Certain the shells would kill him in minutes, Ota needed no further invitation.

When the enemy approached the cave's mouth before evening, the soldiers told the civilians to pay them no attention. "We'll kill them, nothing to worry about." One by one, they crawled out of the cave and were shot dead, but the last of them sustained the reassurances. "I'm the only one left but don't worry; I'll make sure you're safe." Shot too the moment he put his head outside the cave, he crawled back in, spurting blood and moaning.

Suddenly, he raised his head and shouted, *"Tenno hekia, banzai!"* — Ota's first hearing of the call for the Emperor to live ten thousand years, supposedly made by all dying servicemen. It filled Ota with such powerful admiration and hope that he had to fight an overwhelming urge to weep. Then, just as suddenly, the bloody man switched back to his fearful despair, whispering an offer of money to the confounded Ota if he'd help him, *please* help him. "I have a bankbook, a bankbook! Please!" Then the thrillingly defiant *tenno hekia, banzai!* again — but weakly. He died minutes later.

Ota stayed put until the dark of the night, then slipped from the cave and through the American lines. In late June, he was in a forward section of the last 32nd Army headquarters cave where Generals Ushijima and Cho were still in command, deeper inside. It was packed with bleeding, half-crazed men milling about in confusion and despair. Forcing himself not to acknowledge the implications of the unholy scene, Ota noticed several women, Okinawan or Korean, some ten yards deeper inside, near General Ushijima himself. Several staff officers were there changing into civilian clothes, evidently hoping to save themselves or infiltrate to the north to fight again. A captain sprawled on the ground grabbed his ankles. "I'm going to die here but please let my family know about me, please *tell* them." Never having seen the officer before, Ota asked his name. The captain was unwilling or unable to answer. The demoralization was such that no one else seemed to notice his display of broken nerve.

But Ota sustained his own nerve. After all, he assured himself, this was only a battle. The rest of the war still lay ahead; glorious Japan would never be defeated.

Leaving the new headquarters cave, he realized he was now on his own. His Blood and Iron unit no longer existed, and individual Japanese soldiers had no more power over him except the power of their bullets. Like fishermen's nets, American tanks, planes, and troops were sweeping everyone toward the island's southern tip. Something like submission to destiny took command of the youth as he waded into the water and began swimming. He had no destination or plan except to escape from the enemy. Soon the end seemed to come by itself. He slipped under the water and blacked out.

When he woke up lying on some rocks, hundreds of Japanese bodies, some lashed together, many bloated like jellyfish, bobbed on the sea and covered much of the beach. He had no idea what had washed him ashore or when, although it seemed days since he'd gone down when trying to swim. Maybe a lucky wave saved him, or a passing soldier — but none paid him any attention now. He crawled a few yards, the limit of his capacity. Although he was certain he couldn't live long in his condition, he existed for weeks. Hiding with packs of dazed, crazed soldiers between giant boulders strewn along the beach, he slept during the day or watched arrogant enemy soldiers at work — or, as it seemed to him, a terrible kind of play. Stripped to the waist, Americans on the cliffs above (almost certainly replacement troops, since those who'd fought the battle were being evacuated for rest and rehabilitation during that last week of June) took their time picking off the mutilated rabble below. Famished, half-dead Japanese played target in that victors' sport by not waiting until dark to crawl from the protection of their rocks to hunt in the sand for a shellfish or clam. Ota himself was starving.

Ruriko Morishita, the sixteen-year-old nurse's aide, also refused to accept the evidence of defeat and demoralization. The high ridge into which her Okinawa Military Hospital's caves were cut was a blackened lump around which hardly anything green was left for hundreds of yards. The ravages of Okinawa's typhoons seemed trifling in comparison to the reddish mud churned into craters by the deluge of shells.

When key strongholds in the Shuri Line began falling, the administration sent scouts south to compete with those from fighting units searching for new sites. They secured caves for each major ward, none large enough to accommodate the three together. The first group left on May 20, a week before the general withdrawal. Miss Victory Day followed five nights later with the last group.

The thought of being left behind was enough to drive some of the seriously wounded to join the exodus. One soldier with paralyzing lockjaw used all his strength to plop from his bunk — a shelf cut into a wall of his cave — into a litter elderly Okinawans happened to be carrying along a tiny passage below. Although surprised, they carried him from the cave without complaint. However, the shock of falling onto the stretcher put the soldier's body into a violent tremble. Gesturing a prayer with his functioning hand, he begged heaven for help.

Nothing mechanical was available. Promised trucks failed to arrive for the patients and residue of medical supplies. The army of broken bodies set out in their rags, some expecting death, others still fantasizing about victory. The shelling and recent downpours had turned the dirt roads into a crazy quilt of quagmires. Some of the young nurse's aides tried to carry patients on litters or on their backs, but since the weight would have been too much even for healthy girls on a paved road, there was nothing to do but set down the burdens after a few gasping hours and stumble on without them. Groaning men struggled to push their crutches through the mire. Even the few who knew the way became lost in a torrential rain that made the night impenetrable. Others gave up when their strength was exhausted, and all had to stop at dawn to find a hiding place for the day. Some groups took three phantasmagoric nights to complete the six-mile trek to the new caves.

Ruriko Morishita worried less about the wrecks she was helping or the hundreds who expired during the evacuation than about the two-thousand-odd gravely wounded patients left at Haebaru. A military medic had assured her trucks would soon be sent for them. "Don't worry, we'll get them to you when we find safe caves for them." Believing that as firmly as what she was told about the war in general, enfeebled Ruriko nevertheless continued to worry.

Actually, Ward Three had received a supply of potassium cyanide to solve the problem more simply and honorably. But the Okinawan pediatrician serving as its chief doctor ignored his oral order to administer it.* As for Ruriko, only when rumors of poison being handed out and administered to patients in Wards One and Two would reach her new cave would she guess that hundreds had killed themselves or been killed. By that time, however, her more immediate difficulties would make Haebaru's seem less devastating.

Ward Three's new cave lay half a mile below the crossroads village of Makabe, about a mile and a half north of the southern tip and three miles east of Mabuni and Hill 89, site of the cave of the 32nd Army's last headquarters. Centuries of rainwater had carved a vertical hole in the ground, then a relatively large chamber at the bottom with wings like the tentacles of an octopus. The Cave of the Virgins, as it would become known, was among the area's best.

---

*Although there is no reason to doubt his quiet, dignified statement that he refused to kill his patients, there must be some skepticism about the claims of the surviving Japanese Army doctors that they did the same. Doses of poison were also provided for critically wounded medical personnel, including young aides.

Twenty-four medics, thirty-six military nurses, and thirty student aides — the virgins, including Ruriko — arrived there after completing the horrific evacuation that had taken many more lives. If no medical supplies remained, the new "ward" had no accommodations for the wounded either. Nor, for that matter, for the ninety members of the staff, inasmuch as that cave, like all neighboring ones, was jammed with local civilians — whom Ward Three's senior medics now ordered to leave. "Military units have priority. We need this place for ourselves." The head military nurse, who had joined the 32nd Army after her public health offices were destroyed by the 10/10 air raid, would have years of nightmares about her role in helping "murder" fellow Okinawans, who obediently crawled out to their imminent slaughter.

With no wounded to care for, the medical staff turned to thoughts of their own unlikely survival. Perhaps because there were no duties to attend to, exhaustion suddenly overwhelmed them, striking down even Miss Victory Day, who with her fellow aides slept in a wing separate from the military nurses'. Most ran high fevers; all were painfully weak. Although the underground dankness nurtured incipient tuberculosis, they ventured outside the cave only when ordered by the Japanese medics, chiefly to fetch water. Ruriko began wondering whether all its inhabitants shouldn't share that risk. Weren't they all Japanese, after all? But her unspoken disappointment in her immediate superiors led to no questions about the war's rights and wrongs, even when caustic Japanese medics lectured the aides about their own importance. "We're here protecting you Okinawans, so of course it should be your job to bring our water." At night, the aides were also ordered out to hunt for sugarcane, weeds, anything to assuage the constant hunger — and to sneak to other caves, search for unexpelled civilians there, and requisition their food.

The 32nd Army disbanded all civilian corps on June 18, about three weeks after Ruriko's arrival in the new cave. Ninety-six people were in the Cave of the Virgins when messengers delivered the order — "Henceforth, act on your own" — the following evening. Each aide was given about a pint of brown rice and two bags of hardtack. One enlivened their farewell party by chanting *naniwabushi*, highly popular stories performed in a singsong voice. A teacher displayed his dancing skills, and there were many choruses of school carols and songs of good-bye before the gathering ended in the old pledge: "Whether I float as a corpse under the waters or sink beneath the grasses of the mountainside, I will willingly die for the Emperor." While soldiers cleaned a machine gun in preparation for fighting their way out, the aides too made ready to exit and disband — some, like Ruriko, convinced that Japan would soon rise again.

At dusk the next day, they heard American voices. The clearest, which sounded female, called, *"De-te koi, de-te koi!"* again and again. The silence in the cave was laden with tension but not fear. All had seen too many corpses to be terrified by death. Ruriko was only slightly surprised to feel so little emotion — and to hear a voice outside speaking Japanese.

"Are there any civilians in this cave? If so, cease your useless resistance and come out. Otherwise, we'll throw bombs in there."

The minutes seemed like days. Ruriko tried to coax two friends to retreat to the cave's even more uncomfortable innards. Suddenly a Japanese nurse moved toward the exit, having decided at the last moment that she must find her father, an Army doctor serving elsewhere on the island. A student aide also wanted to leave. Ward Three's former Okinawan pediatrician had earlier darted to a cave that housed the hospital administration, leaving in charge a Japanese Army doctor and senior medic, who now ordered the errant women to stay put. Posting an armed guard at the entrance, they repeated that no American promises of safety could be trusted. The beastly enemy would rape all women, cut off ears and noses, draw and quarter everyone.

A shattering explosion interrupted their angry words. Thick white smoke — impenetrable, suffocating — filled that part of the cave. Terrified voices cried, "Gas! Poison *gas!*" Scores died in minutes. Others screamed desperately for water. "Mother! Father! Help me, please!"

Ruriko couldn't breathe. A wounded orderly told her to urinate on her trousers and hold them to her mouth — but that protection against the "poison gas" of course provided no oxygen. (Almost all the dead, including the aide who wanted to find her father, were apparently killed by suffocation rather than the explosion itself, which was probably of white phosphorous hand grenades.) The cave resounded with even more desperate screams of "Mother! Father!" Ruriko's best friend lay beside her, moaning about herself and her poor parents, who, she now realized, had probably died in the same unbearable pain. "Sisters, I'm going now — before you do." Gasp. "Oh, how it hurts." Gasp. "Long live the Emperor!"

Those words somehow told Ruriko not to expire in that terrible place. But although she resolved to leave so she could breathe real air, she found she couldn't move. A giant force strangled her until she lost consciousness, terrified yet happy that the agony was over.

When she came to — probably saved by her urine-soaked trousers — she discovered she could produce no sound whatever from her mouth. A fellow aide named Yoshiko also regained consciousness to find her hand tightly held by a third friend. Moving it up and down, Yoshiko called the third girl's name but got no answer. It took her some moments of hard staring into the darkness to see the hand she was clasping belonged to a headless corpse. Yoshiko struggled to her feet and looked down at the nearest bodies — where something moved. "Someone's alive!" she tried to shout, but she too now lost her voice. Soon she recognized the living person as Ruriko, who felt "no sadness, no emotion — only numbness."

During the following two days, more friends joined the heaps of dead ones, agony twisting their faces. On the third, four of the thirty nurse's aides remained alive. The stench of rotting flesh drove them out that evening.

Led by a teacher who'd also cheated death, they dragged themselves outside the cave, where American fire quickly killed the teacher and two girls as they tried to crawl away. Escaping the bullets, Ruriko took shelter in another cave, which she left four evenings later with another handful of survivors. None knew that the Americans had declared the battle over, the island secure. In fact, they saw no Americans at all. Apart from flares that lit up the night, their island seemed empty.

Still dazed from the explosion in the Cave of the Virgins, Ruriko crawled about — not very far, in her condition — in the flat area that lacked outcroppings of coral and crops (the fields were totally scorched) for cover. Separation from others alternated with merging with still others for protection and sanity. Occasionally, the prey fell asleep in midstep. Shot three times, Ruriko would later — after treatment by 10th Army medics and a realization that she'd been a dupe of Japanese militarism — assume the shooters had aimed at her legs because they'd won the battle and weren't hunting for more lives. (It couldn't have been because they took pity on a female: The gender of the filthy refugee in her ragged military uniform was impossible to discern.)

When she woke up the last time, American soldiers were standing over her little cluster of fugitives. A girl who pulled the pin of a hand grenade to save herself from them was near enough so that Ruriko, very weak from her wounds and malnutrition, knew she'd surely die at last. She waited with closed eyes. The grenade was a dud, leaving her also among the lucky: 123 of the 155 Himeyuri girls would soon be dead, together with scores of aides from the five less prestigious high schools. And some thirty-seven hundred soldiers and thirty-eight hundred civilians died in and around the village of Haebaru, "meadows of the southerly wind."

24 · Mopping Up

In every case, the goal was to get rid of the Japs. They were simply capable of too much, too many devious ways and tricks. We were professional killers who knew not to take a chance.
— Norris Buchter

Did I tell you about the Nip who ruined our swimming hole by playing tap-tap on his head with a grenade?
— Buzzy Fox, letter home, July 5

All the beautiful white hospital ships — Solace, Relief, *and* Comfort *— were gone. There were just too many wounded men; they couldn't handle the casualty traffic. So I sailed off for Saipan on an APA. Goodbye Okinawa, and up yours.*
— William Manchester after his severe wounding

Okinawa's third mountain spine traversed its width some three miles from the south end, two miles from General Ushijima's new headquarters on the cliff facing the Pacific. The 32nd Army's last strongpoints were manned by fresh units or survivors of battles farther north who'd had four or five days for frantic preparations before the Americans arrived.

The ragged heights presented another forbidding barrier to attackers, especially two mountains in the center called Yoza-dake and Yaeju-dake. Between those towering island formations, massive escarpments with hills and ridges made the terrain almost as formidable as at the Shuri Line. Although lack of water kept defenders from establishing positions on the peaks, sister regiments of Kojo's 22nd used protective formations lower down, still with excellent lines of sight on the approaches. As at Shuri, efficient defense systems with interlocking fire awaited the Americans. The last of the Japanese antitank guns and heavy artillery zeroed in on the open ground and passes where the attackers, including large numbers of green replacements, were most vulnerable. Although the defenders were far too few and too depleted to stop the tank-supported advances, they had more than enough arms to rip apart unlucky units assigned to take the hardest objectives.

Also as before, the Army divisions faced some of the most difficult mazes of hills, in this case on the Pacific half of the buttelike barrier protecting Ushijima's new headquarters. Many were so steep that they had to be scaled by cargo nets under cover of darkness. In the sectors where Japanese newly arrived from the Shuri Line were too disorganized and discouraged to fight with a fraction of their previous tenacity, the unfortunates were mowed down and burned out with relative ease. But defenders elsewhere used combinations of cliffs, steep slopes, and hundreds of crags, crevices, and niches in the coral and rock to resist for days. Faces stiff with exhaustion, heads bound in bands emblazoned with GOT TO WIN!, many Japanese still fought superbly. One company of the American Army's 96th division lost seventy-five of 175 men in a single day on Yoza-dake. A Marine company lost seventy men and all its officers taking one hill. The survivors of a group that tried to crawl away from an ambush of intense Japanese fire succeeded on the eighth night of consecutive attempts.

The loss of old comrades dismayed Americans even more than before. To be hit so late in the game, having survived so much, seemed the cruelest fate. Yet the day-by-day chance of being killed or wounded actually increased. Having dropped significantly after the taking of the Shuri, American casualties grew again at the last barrier, where a properly supplied and reinforced 32nd Army would have built another Shuri Line.

The hardest fighting took place at Kunishi Ridge, half a mile to the west of Yoza-dake and one mile in from the East China Sea. The two-thousand-yard-long outcropping was smooth and steep enough to have been constructed to the defenders' specifications. On June 9, units of the 1st Marine Division forded a little stream that marked the start of the assault on the ridge. As at Sugar Loaf, they then had to cross an open area to reach the objective, which was serviced by a single road covered by defenders — also from a sister regiment of Kojo's 22nd — who were dug in at all the best places with more surviving armament than any other unit, together with a detailed fire plan for the exposed areas that had to be crossed. After making no progress the next two days, the Marines had to bring up reinforcements in tanks. Twenty-one were destroyed during assaults and counterassaults similar to those at the Shuri Line. Progress up the hillsides was yard by yard against intense fire from concealed guns and mortars. It took three more long, hard days — five in all.

So it went at the other strongpoints in the last line, on and off the twin peaks of Yoza-dake and Yaeju-dake. The approach to the latter was blocked by a large mass called the "Big Apple," from which the artillery fire was deadly. The fierce battles for Hills 69 and 95, the western and eastern anchors of that last mountain barrier, were sagas in themselves. Ushijima had ordered the positions defended to the death.

Back at our holes, we "saddled up," ready for the daily patrols and daily killing.
— Stuart Upchurch

The 1st Division was understrength both in numbers and in physical
constitution, while Mezado [Maesato] loomed on its right flank, an obstacle as
formidable as any yet faced.
— Fletcher Pratt, *The Marines' War*

For Marine units, the action in the far south was spotty. The unlucky ones continued taking heavy fire from steep coral formations as they crawled ahead or inched around to rake the hidden enemy with their own armament. Others drove toward the southern coast almost unopposed. But nighttime's nightmare became worse because more dislodged Japanese prowled from dusk to dawn — many hunting for food and water rather than for the enemy, but Americans didn't know that.

When an infantryman named Charles Leonard threw his last grenade into a shallow cave, a great cloud of smoke gushed out, together with some burning white phosphorus. A gob landed on his sleeve, melted through it in an instant, and emitted a nauseating smell as it burned into his flesh. Yanking the bayonet from his rifle, he scraped furiously at the phosphorus, while out from the cave from which he'd turned his attention charged a Japanese soldier with *his* bayonet. Leonard managed to kill him with four quick rounds and only superficial wounds to himself from the enemy blade. The dead body slumped to the ground. Leonard shot it four more times and continued jerking on the trigger even after his clip had ejected.

Manifestations of camaraderie and of bad luck also continued. A platoon leader wounded on Sugar Loaf badgered hospital personnel to discharge him. He needn't have gone back to the line, maybe even *shouldn't* have in his condition, but his men were still there. The night after he resumed command of them, a hand grenade and coral fragments smashed his face to pulp.

On the morning of June 19, a fourteen-year-old Okinawan named Shin-ichi Kuniyoshi was in a hillside cave above the leveled hamlet of Asato, a mile north of the last mountain barrier, near the site of the decoy American landing on L-day. Shin-ichi had been so hungry so long that his skinny body looked like a child's, while his dirty face, aged by the fighting, might have belonged to a thirty-year-old.

Before the battle, the boy stood out because his father, who had come to identify with Japanese ambitions and discipline while working on the mainland, imbued him with his own pride in having served in the Imperial Japanese Army at a time when it was still rejecting four of five Okinawan draftees. On top of that, the Army's exploits during the war's early years enthralled Shin-ichi and his inseparable friend Miyagi, who dreamed of becoming officers. Shin-ichi's father was called up again, this time as one of the Home Guard's twenty thousand. His oldest brother, a soldier in Manchuria, would be captured by the Soviet Army when it entered the war a week before its end and kept for five years of Siberian slave labor. A second and third brother, one a sailor in the Imperial Navy and the other a kamikaze pilot, would soon be killed in action. His mother wept and pleaded to Shin-ichi, her only son still at home, but she lost to the exciting game of war. A month before L-day, he and fellow ninth-grader Miyagi volunteered to serve with the 32nd Army, vowing to die for Japan.

Their perilous work delivering messages in a less prestigious unit than Masahide Ota's could not dim their patriotism or devotion to the Imperial Army. Only one incident was troubling. In May, Shin-ichi found himself with a unit kept without water for several days by extraordinarily intense American shelling. Although Shin-ichi instantly obeyed a soldier's order to dash to a nearby well, he felt the soldier himself should have taken that great risk. However, his own unit was like a family, its gentle sergeant named Inagaki serving as a surrogate father to the forty-six boys. On nights when Inagaki considered the shelling too terrible, he risked his own life — in failing to follow a superior's orders — by not dispatching them with their messages. Still, only six survived their racing or creeping from cave to cave, or charges at American troops and tanks.

Now Shin-ichi and Miyagi crouched in the relatively solid Asato cave with a group of lost soldiers they barely knew while the Americans assigned to that sector of the last mountain line were about to approach. There was something admirable as well as terrible in the methodical advance of their tanks and soldiers, which were clearing the entire hill. They did their grim work cave by cave, job by deadly job. Survivors of some nearby caves that had already been blown had taken refuge in this one, doubling its inhabitants to fifty or sixty soldiers. They had small arms, grenades, and a light machine gun for use against the enemy's flamethrowing tanks, everyone's greatest worry — whose roaring exhaust announced the time had come at about 6:30 A.M.

But they missed the cave's well-concealed, almost hidden vertical mouth and continued up the hill. Squeezing in with soldiers directly under the entrance shaft, Shin-ichi tried to keep his body covered while awkwardly firing up at the legs of American infantrymen who were following the tanks. The return fire down into the cave was as effective as their own was futile, because of the angle. Corpses piled up under the entrance. Brave men crawled from the cave's farther reaches to replace them.

At seven o'clock, they heard "Okay!" in an urgent American voice. A minute later, a blinding explosion knocked them flat. When Shin-ichi came to, his eardrums felt shattered and his arms were pinned in excruciating positions by a terrible weight pressing on his chest. Facedown and unable to move, he guessed six or so corpses were in the pile crushing and suffocating him. Miyagi's moaning pleas echoed from the walls along with others, but he could do nothing to help his friend, whose voice lasted longest. When it went silent, Shin-ichi himself began to moan, perhaps hoping a human sound might dispel his infinite despair. Neither arm could be freed for using his hand grenade on himself, but he supposed the weight of the bodies would kill him soon.

Hours later, a voice from deep in the cave asked who was calling for help. Soon the relief that the voice bestowed from utter gloom was reinforced by the miraculous sounds of steps inching unsteadily toward him. At last the terrible weight on his body was very slowly lightened. Finally free to roll over, he saw the unit's gangling young commander above him, both eyeballs hanging low on his cheeks and the metal fragment that had forced them out wedged in his forehead. Dripping blood and exhausted from his effort, the lieutenant dropped to the ground. "You can still fight so take my pistol," he wheezed. "It's got three rounds. Use two against the enemy and the last one for yourself. But first try to get to headquarters and report what happened to us here."

When the lieutenant died, it was Shin-ichi's turn to feel his way in the dark. The corpses had apparently saved him from more than cuts and bruises. He found Miyagi's body and tried to stifle his weeping. "I'll get back at them for this, I promise on my life. I'll kill as many as I can." Then he climbed over the piles of decomposing flesh at the cave's mouth. Although the front line had pushed well south of it, the sight of enemy soldiers nearby, stacking ammunition, prompted him to return to the dark and wait with the bodies.

Sneaking out again after dusk, he encountered more Americans almost immediately, some in foxholes, others pitching tents to radio music. But the sentries patrolling every fifteen yards or so failed to see him. The headquarters cave the lieutenant had cited in his last order was on Yoza-dake, about a mile and a half due east. With the enemy shells pounding it as his guide, Shin-ichi believed he could find his way even at night. First he had to pick the safest spot to slip through the enemy line, then the safest trail. On his belly, dragging himself by his elbows, he made about a yard a minute. The first streaks of dawn found him exhausted — and in the middle of an American encampment.

The only consolation was that it was of course free of enemy shelling, bombing, and strafing. But he knew he was finished unless he found cover immediately. Raising his head just enough to look around, he saw clusters of Japanese corpses in a drainage ditch. Inching there, he covered himself with bodies, completing his camouflage before full light. All he had to do was look like another corpse until sunset, in about sixteen hours.

Larger problems kept him from dwelling on the appalling stench of the real corpses roasting in the sun. The hardest was to fool the beasts by not moving a single muscle. Daylight temperatures of course rose higher than Okinawa's late-June mean of over eighty-five degrees, especially here in the far south. The abnormally hot sun of *that* late June on that particular plateau — long known for its lack of water — scorched him unmercifully. Involuntary pleas for his mother sounded in the adolescent's head. He hadn't eaten or drunk for days. The agony of his thirst exceeded that of maggots wriggling from the corpses into his fresh cuts, nostrils, mouth, and anus. But he didn't move for the full sixteen hours — and triumphed.

When it was dark enough to resume, the stunning bombardment of Yoza-dake kept him headed in the right direction through all detours around enemy positions, animal instinct alerting him to their breathing and body heat. Only the unrelieved thirst became unbearable, but he continued crawling until something suddenly landed on his back, frightening him almost literally out of his mind. *"You carry me to Yoza. On your back."* One leg of the Japanese soldier who hissed those frantic words was a mushy stump of raw flesh and crushed bone.

The lad of under five feet and less than a hundred pounds had no choice but to obey, even knowing he'd now never make Yoza. It was a sentence to death from an enemy rifle because he'd have to stand or slouch to try to manage his burden. However, the order had come from a superior — who pointed a pistol at his head for good measure.

The deadweight buckled his knees. After twenty yards in a field littered with Japanese corpses, the famished boy could not take another step. "Sir," he whispered, "I have to go. I have a bad case of the runs." His pistol unmoving, the soldier ordered him to "take care of your business right here." Setting down the millstone and making as if to open his own trousers, Shin-ichi tried to calculate how much the missing leg would slow his tormentor's movements and whether he'd be willing to bring on his own certain death by firing. He held his breath, raced away, and dived to the ground — saved once more.

Finding his way again, he headed for the flares lighting Yoza-dake "like a hundred moons." Aware that his thirst was more likely to finish him than exhaustion, he nevertheless reached the mountain before dawn, and his luck held long enough so that no shell hit him on his crawl to the headquarters cave. Some thirty soldiers inside, hardly believing the boy had managed the odyssey from enemy-held Asato, praised him generously. As if that weren't enough, they treated him to as much as he wanted of all they possessed. Dizzy with pride and happiness, he drank his belly full of water, feasted from their bags of hardtack, and could ask for nothing more.

25 · American Atrocities

We were not in favor of giving the Japs a chance to surrender, but orders are orders.
— A Marine in a letter to his parents

It got to the point — I shouldn't say this — that Japs wouldn't surrender to Marines. . . . Ninety-nine percent would shoot them, and that includes me.
You know why? You hated them for what they did to your buddies, so many of them. Besides, they tried to pull so many dirty tricks with their hands up — you could never trust them. So they weren't worth the really great risk, which you didn't want to take anyway. I didn't.
— Another Marine, forty years later

Nobody wanted to take prisoners to begin with — nobody who had had a buddy killed, which was almost everybody. And nobody wanted to go somewhere to do it — leave his living buddies to walk the prisoners back behind the lines. Why take the risk? When they first started surrendering, we shot as many as we took.
— A third Marine, also later

IN MID-JUNE, a week before the campaign's official end, Japanese began surrendering in sizable numbers. Until then, the average had been four men daily, most physically or mentally disabled by explosives. Many American companies fought for eight or ten weeks without taking a single prisoner. But when the 32nd Army's teetering morale began going over the edge in some units lacking all communications with others, white flags, or substitutes, became a relatively common sight.

On June 12, the day after Admiral Ota's farewell message to General Ushijima, a stunning 159 members of his Naval Base Force surrendered from among those who hadn't killed themselves before the Marine spectators on the Oroku Peninsula. The daily average rose from mid-June's four to fifty during the third week of the month, soaring to 343 on June 19 alone, a huge number by Japanese standards. One four-man patrol captured 150 prisoners after their officers bowed, shot some Okinawan women who'd been accompanying them, and killed themselves. In all, almost three thousand Japanese were taken prisoner during the second half of June, about a third of the number killed during the same period.

The final count would come to seventy-four hundred, somewhat less astounding than it seemed because about half were conscripted Okinawans. Still, it was more than during all the rest of the Pacific War, and many Americans, having seen no enemy soldiers at all apart from dead ones, were justifiably frightened by sudden appearances of droves of living ones. A Marine fire team approaching the cliffs above the southern coast in late June was startled by four enemy soldiers who emerged from the bush carrying two wounded ones on stretchers. They gestured for the four to drop their gear and strip. When they were in loincloths and little able to work a trick, the Americans approached with C-rations, water, and smokes. Suddenly, up to a hundred more poured from "nowhere" and surrounded the Marines — who included eighteen-year-old Lenly Cotten. Having seen Japanese blow themselves up with grenades held to their chests, Cotten thought that the well-armed crowd would see to his end. "There we were, completely surrounded; they could have finished us like Custer. They didn't seem to know what they were going to do, and *we* sure as hell didn't know, only that dying was their honorable thing and taking an American along was even better. But they'd probably sent out those first six to test us, see whether we'd torture them. After an age, they gave themselves up, the whole bunch."

Such surrenders were new in Japanese history. Although the percentage remained very slight relative to those killed in action, the absolute count leaped to nearly a thousand — probably half of them conscripted Okinawans — on June 20 and 21. That was the number of prisoners taken. The number shot will never be known.

Some Americans believe it was many. "You had no mercy for them whatever by the end of the campaign," one would explain. "Nine Marines in ten would shoot them. If you saw a Jap trying to surrender, you'd let him have it fast." Other participants have disputed that. Another infantryman remembered his outfit as "pretty damn tough; it was all hate and kill. But when we took a prisoner, he stayed alive." The truth between the extreme claims can't be measured except to say that the killing of prisoners was widespread in at least some of the units.

Many officers condoned and even suggested it, until the multiple surrenders near the very last days. "Your company commander would say, 'Take these people [Japanese prisoners] to regimental headquarters and be back here in five minutes,'" a third infantryman would explain. "Regimental headquarters was thirty minutes away. He was telling you to get rid of them." "We gave our prisoners every excuse to run so we could finish them," another veteran would add. "Nobody wanted to escort them five hundred yards through scary terrain where he could be shot. Nobody wanted to go *five* yards with them. For what?"

A weary platoon of Owen Stebbins's G–2–22 company was cleaning out a sugarcane field south of Naha in early June. One of its combat veterans was calculating whether to jump across a little brook or get his feet wet when a young replacement's terror-frozen face instantly sent him into a higher level of alert. The veteran, Irving Oertel, shot at almost the same instant as he looked down and saw a Japanese arm reaching through some reeds to grip the replacement by an ankle. No one will ever know whether the wretched man was trying to hurt the American or surrender or both. "Later, I realized that's what the Jap might have been trying to do, surrender. But what I did then was what anyone with experience would have done: shot him that second. Killing was instinct by that time. You were shot if you didn't shoot. You killed and didn't think twice about it."

"When they started surrendering," another man would remember, "we were supposed to take them back to . . . the command post or to some guys who came up from regimental headquarters. But we never took a lot of them back. We shot them — me too. We did it because . . . what we'd all been through all that time, understand? It was that terrible combat. It was Japs pretending to surrender so they could shoot *you.* One dressed in civilian clothes suddenly whips a pistol from behind his back and tries to get us with it. I saw plenty of things like that, but one was enough for everybody. So not many prisoners arrived back at command posts until the very last days."

A member of an Army transportation company encountered a group of Marines who counseled him to shoot the prisoner he was escorting to the rear. The soldier took the suggestion but his carbine jammed, whereupon the Marines advised him to take his time and clean it — which he did, then fired. The same soldier, perhaps remembering how casually he'd been urged, assumed a truckload he saw of Naval Base Force prisoners was being driven to a convenient place for shooting. They seemed white with fear.*

I shot one in the back as he was trying to escape. One day, I shot one who was trying to surrender.
— A Marine who would dedicate much of his later life to reconciliation

We had barbaric people too. You don't make a bracelet of Jap teeth without ripping them out of Jap heads.
— Another Marine, 1983

*It's worth repeating that Japanese who wanted to capitulate probably faced a greater risk of being killed by bullets from fellow Japanese than from Americans, who came to realize that when they saw Japanese throw grenades at others who carried surrender leaflets. When a Japanese lieutenant who'd graduated from an Ivy League college gave himself up with one of his sergeants, a sniper apparently aimed his fire more at them than at the Marines to whom they surrendered. The pair seemed fatalistic about it until one of the Marines told "you dumb bastards" to take cover, whereon they did and were saved.

Okinawa was a killing field. In the 82 days of battle for that island, an average of about 2,500 people died every day. Under those conditions, with death everywhere, I seemed to have gone into a sort of trance. It was as if I had left my body and was looking at myself in a movie. I just did not feel anything.
— Peter Milo

Shooting a man who had his hands up or may have wanted to put them up wasn't necessarily an atrocity. No American infantryman, whatever his previous moral tenets, had any question that unless every Japanese who prompted the slightest doubt about his intentions was killed, he would kill Americans. That cliché expressed an unrelenting reality on Okinawa. It did not necessarily reflect racial hatred or any other kind; many simply knew the job had to be done. On top of that, however, most riflemen were exhausted, frightened, and full of grief for their own losses when they pulled their triggers on the unarmed, or seemingly unarmed, men.

Some felt ambivalent about the enemy. Some had twinges of respect, admiration, perhaps sympathy. William Manchester was among those who hated other people more, including Frank Sinatra and everyone else who was free of danger and actually enjoying himself, "whereas the Japanese were right where we were, in the mud and shit, getting pounded by artillery." But most of the time, the feelings of virtually all Americans in the line were clear: The bond with their comrades in arms prompted loathing for those who shot and shelled them. "I didn't hate Japs before," one would remember. "It came the minute I saw my first buddy lying there in parts — the guy I lived with every day, the guy I loved. I started hating the bastards, and I feel it to this day. *I saw my buddy get killed!*"

It made no difference that killing was a primary and intrinsic goal of both sides and that there was nothing personal in it. Despite that logic of war, the death of friends was a shattering personal tragedy for all Americans (as, of course, for all Japanese). Flamethrower Evan Regal knew most of his company's sixty-nine KIAs (of its original 256 men). "The Japs had to be killed anyway because of how they fought; there was no other way. But what made you *want* to do it was your friends. When you saw their corpses day after day, your hatred — oh God, *hatred* — built day after day. By June, I had no mercy for a single Jap who wanted to surrender."

Any inclination to be merciful was further reduced by the aspiration to emerge whole: hidden hope that rose in proportion to the approach of victory. When the ocean below the southern coast became visible from the high ground, Americans had a real chance to "make it," and many resolved to do so, to beat the casualty odds no matter what. That was just when the number of Japanese prisoners surged, along with the pressure for their quick disposal.

To escort a prisoner to the rear was to expose oneself to very real extra danger. No one wanted to gamble on leaving the security of his unit for a single step through land dotted with hidden caves and spider holes. Such risk was taken to help a buddy back to an aid station, but not for a Jap whose fellow Japs had killed so many of yours and who was aiming to add you to his count. Not for a sneaky rat who, even at this stage and even after being searched, might die happily by pulling a grenade from an orifice and blowing you up along with himself. Every combat American had seen or heard of killing performances of the final duty. Their goal was to dispose *quickly* of everyone who might try. Ordinarily mild Norris Buchter had learned "they were simply capable of too much, too many devious ways and tricks. You didn't want to get within grenade-throwing range of them, so you sometimes shot them as fast as you could."

There were also sound practical reasons for torching Okinawan huts, as Americans continued to call native houses. Since enemy snipers hid in some, no regret or guilt was felt burning large numbers to the ground. And there were provocations for many unreported incidents of cruelty. In early April, a Marine fire team used cigarettes to burn USMC on the chest of a dazed Japanese soldier they'd captured, then broke his leg by dropping the stretcher on which they were carrying him to the rear. The group had found the "sonofabitch" next to a woman he'd raped before slitting her throat and murdering two children.

Beyond that, there was the Japanese way of fighting. People who charged through their own artillery fire on their way to American positions showed they cared less for themselves than for their Emperor, and were willing to spill any amount of blood for their own satisfactions as well as for him. In the third week of June, a Korean laborer emerged from a cave near the southern tip and told the American team that had blasted it a dead Marine was inside. Reluctant to enter in case some of the Japanese were still alive, the Americans gave the Korean a wire to tie to the corpse. When they pulled it out, one of the team saw an old prewar friend who'd also trained with him on Guadalcanal. His ears and penis had been cut off, his face smeared with excrement. Maybe an angel wouldn't have wanted to take revenge against such barbarity.

The Marines suspected of driving the truckload of Naval Base Force Japanese to possible shooting had just taken some territory where American captives had evidently been shot. "Okay," one of them said, "the Japs don't take prisoners and we won't either." Some Americans sprayed cave mouths with full submachine-gun magazines after promising safety to all who came out with their hands up — but even they weren't necessarily war criminals (although not all other Americans considered them fully normal either).

But if some of the brutal acts could be rationalized, others couldn't. War spawned many unqualified atrocities on Okinawa, as it almost always does. "Once you kill somebody, the first one, it's much easier after that," Ed Jones would remember. "When they came out of the caves, it was like target practice, like a turkey shoot." Some of the most revolting acts involved the enemy dead. One machine-gun squad moved about with a makeshift little pipe for directing their urine into the mouths of Japanese corpses.* "I like to think we went to Okinawa with American standards and morals," a man in that squad would remember in shame and disgust. "But it was a crazy world there and we did crazy things."

On one of the last days of the official campaign, a platoon leader asked for volunteers to clean up a cave that had been vainly showered with surrender leaflets. Noises disclosed that enemy soldiers were still inside, but Lenly Cotten, "one of the 'crazies,'" in his own description, was "looking for a little more excitement now that the real fighting had dulled down." He and other volunteers lowered themselves into a theaterlike cavern that fronted the cave. While taking prisoners there, Cotten saw a Japanese fail to raise his hands. He fired a burst of his BAR at his feet and saw the man dash deeper into the cave. Just after Cotten called for a satchel charge, he heard the pin of a Japanese grenade being driven in and turned to race away, but couldn't move fast enough over the coral. Exploding precisely where he'd had been standing, the grenade sent fragments of steel and coral into most of his body. (He would spend eleven months recovering in hospitals.)

When the satchel charge was thrown and the dazed Japanese emerged from hiding, probably with ruptured eardrums, another volunteer fell on him with his Kabar knife. "He was a buddy," Cotten would remember. "He'd lost one friend after another since April, and he himself had had a dozen minor wounds. I felt pretty happy when I heard the Jap had been slashed to death. 'Nice going, they got that sonofabitch.'"

Later, Cotten's happiness would be replaced by memory of the "poor bastard" and regret for war's madness and cruelty. He was one of the vast majority on Okinawa who killed frequently without becoming killers,

---

*An officer who took pleasure urinating directly into the mouths of dead Japanese once pulled down a corpse's trousers so that he could shoot off the head of its penis. As he took aim, Eugene Sledge "turned away in disgust. . . . Mac was a decent, clean-cut man but one of those who apparently felt no restraints under the brutalizing influence of war — although he had hardly been in combat at that time."

That incident also illustrates that most Americans, although they rarely protested, were revolted by such acts even after combat's brutalization. And that a disproportionate number of the vile acts were performed by new replacements or noncombatants, as opposed to bone-weary infantrymen who'd seen too much horror during their stints in the field. The soldier who cleaned his carbine at the suggestion of Marines in order to shoot his prisoner a second time was an artist who continued feeling so bad about it after returning home to Flushing, New York, that he made a lithograph of the scene.

whose killing was sane, not sadistic. But almost inevitably, a small percentage of Americans was as thrilled by the act of killing as by winning the battle. Almost inevitably, too, the percentage of disturbed psyches grew during the campaign. Every combat infantryman knew men — sometimes heroes — who took unnatural pleasure in the pain it was his duty to cause.

> *I've a Jap Imperial Marine coat, one for myself and one for [Uncle] Eddie. We captured a Nip Q[uarter] M[aster] dump and they are brand new so Eddie doesn't have to worry about any stink in them.*
> — Buzzy Fox, letter home, June 15, 1945

> *The place [up north, after its capture] was loaded with hundreds, maybe thousands, of the Nip Marine insignia. So this enterprising officer dug up some sewing machines, got some cloth and put everyone he could find to work making Japanese Imperial Marine battle flags. . . . Then he took the flags out to some of the hundreds of U.S. Navy ships off Okinawa. My God, did he clean up!*
> — Lee P. Stack, a tank officer

There was also the strange lust for souvenirs. If the Japanese determination to die defied explanation to most Americans, their own passion for largely worthless Japanese artifacts also bordered on the bizarre. In a campaign that demanded every ounce of energy to stay alive, every infantryman knew one of the most perilous things he could do was go on a souvenir hunt. A disproportionate number who left their units for that sport — usually in twos and threes, often without informing their platoon leaders — were later found with their torsos riddled or throats slit. Some were killed by souvenirs that had themselves been booby-trapped: grenades fixed behind pictures on "hut" walls, Japanese rifles wired to explode when picked up. Yet no amount of risk deterred multitudes from violating fundamental rules of the combat wisdom they'd acquired with such pain.

Veterans of previous campaigns launched the competition for trophies as early as L-day. When the unknowing Zero landed at Yomitan Airfield that afternoon, Marines rushed to strip the pilot the moment they shot him, and the game of "collecting" — often, as one observer put it, "before the enemy hit the ground" — was on.

Samurai swords led the list. Other prized items included Japanese battle flags and waistbands made by loving mothers who solicited contributions of a stitch each from a thousand women in the soldier's neighborhood, a favorite of kamikaze pilots on their final flights. But terrible risks were also taken for the most doubtful treasure: letters, teeth, belts, bones, underwear, yellowed snapshots, dirty caps, watches, rifles, combs, rice bowls, ears and fingers for pickling, *anything*. Infantrymen who traveled light and lean would proudly proclaim, "Got me a souvenir!" then unwrap something from their packs to show around: an ear. It did not have to be military. Booty was also taken from the most humble Okinawan home, often family photographs on the walls. One man grabbed two photograph albums, a track suit, and a pair of shoes — of an Okinawan track star, it happened — from the rubble. (The albums would lie unopened under his bed for nearly four decades before he returned them.) Others looted Okinawan offices of documents for which they had no conceivable use.

Dedicated collectors removed leg wrappings from reeking corpses. An otherwise admirable married man complained in a letter home that a wedding ring he'd taken turned out to be brass and "tarnished my whole finger." An officer observed a soldier searching the body of a Japanese he'd just killed. A wallet was among the items that tumbled out when he slit his pockets with his trench knife. Examining it, the looter found, much to his surprise, that it contained some American identification cards and several snapshots of an American girl. "Why those dirty bastards!" he cursed. "They even rob our dead!"

The passion for loot derived partly from life assertion. To the displaced, frightened young "collectors," the objects were proof of their survival in the netherworld of combat against the "fanatical" Japanese. But it also derived from a view of those Japanese as less than fully human. The otherwise worthless souvenirs had the value of being from another species, another planet.* "It is inconceivable to me that Americans in Europe would value some old sock or filthy cap just because it had belonged to a German, yet that is what is regularly done with Japanese souvenirs," wrote Donald Keene, a naval officer who would become a distinguished scholar of Japanese literature. "The curiosity attached to the Japanese prisoner is such that many Americans are amazed to find that some of them are reasonably well built, that others have had enough education to say 'Thank you' in English (which is usually interpreted as 'He speaks fluent English!'). . . . I think the answer . . . is that the Americans are unable as yet to appreciate the Japanese as human beings."

A good proportion of American letters home was devoted to the booty and to resentment when it was confiscated. "You risk your life getting the darn things," a veteran complained, evidently oblivious to the folly he was revealing, "and then some jerk takes them away from you." Some

---

*While fellow servicemen in Europe collected Nazi items, the thirst for them was less acute. Their current high value for a scattering of Americans — such as members of the KKK and other far-right groups — even as interest in Japanese materials has much declined seems to strengthen the explanation of the combat fascination for the latter as being driven by the perception of Japanese as subnormal. For that decline went hand in glove with the growing American acquaintance with and acceptance of Japanese, while other factors have given the Nazi loot its new shine for extremists.

items were confiscated as contraband firearms, others because they were
evidence of the officially prohibited mutilation of corpses, as when infantrymen rushed from their foxholes at first light to yank gold teeth
from the enemy infiltrators killed during the night.* Here too, letters
home revealed an almost innocent greed, as when a machine-gunner informed his mother of his rights to a Japanese corpse he'd shot.

> I waited for daylight because that Nip was "my man" and whatever he
> had on him belonged to me. . . . When light came I pounced on him
> [but] all the son of a gun had was a flag and a fountain pen and of
> course a grenade but I let him have that. . . . That same night my buddy
> in the next hole got a Jap doctor and he got a pistol, saber and watch. I
> already had my saber and 2 watches so I wasn't envious.

Souvenirs were also solid currency for obtaining cigarettes, fruit juice,
and other valuables, including pornographic photographs. (The latter
were supplied mostly by Navy photographers who had access to negatives
in a rear base. In mid-May, a sailor traded a dozen dirty pictures for a
stained little Japanese flag and what a witness to the transaction took to
be a small quantity of opium.) As soon as their fighting finished, infantrymen hitchhiked to other units to sell or exchange some of their acquisi-
tions. One who'd "relieved" a Japanese doctor of his sword — "which
goes big out here and it's a mighty proud thing to own" — hoped to sell
enough prizes to buy a little car when he returned home. At that point,
he also had three rifles, two of which he would give away or trade and
one he'd sell for fifty dollars, just under a month's salary. A fourth rifle
was stolen, although he'd taken the precaution of sleeping with it to
guard against that.

Trophy hunting merged with sadism when gold teeth were pried not only
from corpses but also from those badly wounded, who were first stabbed,
bayoneted, or shot as they lay on the ground. In general, the most zealous
collectors of ears and skulls were the most likely to commit atrocities.

Ernie Pyle prettified souvenir hunting like the rest of combat. "One of
these days, Mrs. Leland Taylor of Jackson, Mich., is going to be the envy
of all her friends," he filed in April. "For she is about to come into possession of four pairs of the most beautiful Japanese pajamas you ever
saw. . . . Mrs. Taylor's husband, who is a Marine corporal and known as
'Pop,' found these pajamas in a wicker basket hidden in a cave. . . . Pop
carries the basket around on his arm from place to place until he gets a

---

*More than one factor kept the majority of Americans from joining such activities. On
Guadalcanal, a platoon sergeant who worked over every corpse he could find showed a bag
of gold teeth to a captain. "How in the name of heaven," the captain reacted, "can you put
your hand into a stinking Jap's mouth?"

chance to ship them home." As usual, the supply of supposedly charming detail concealed the real story.

Several days after the "comic" incident of a Japanese sneaking up on Dick Whitaker's buddy while he was relieving himself, members of the company, still on the Oroku Peninsula, came upon a little house that promised some comfort for a night after its rice-paper door and windows were knocked out to provide clear fields of fire from inside. Toward morning, Whitaker lay half awake on a mat, calculating whether it was safe to light a cigarette. Once again, he'd gotten little of the sleep his body craved, now less because of fear of an intruder cutting his throat than because he'd spent much of the night standing watch.

His assignment as a runner for the company commander being still quite recent, he hardly knew Charles Oates, the man now on watch. He did know that young Private Oates himself had been a runner for the previous company commander, Captain Robert Fowler, and that Fowler's death had deeply upset him, with good reason. Difficult Oates was thought to have gone "a little Asiatic," meaning sadistic or willing to court too much risk in his eagerness to kill. (The irony in that tag for fellow Americans with a penchant for brutality was apparently unintentional.) Then Fowler took him under his wing, and Oates, who'd bucked orders from everyone else, settled down under his surrogate father — until the captain bled to death from a wound in the spleen.

Now, in the dark of the house, Oates touched Whitaker and turned back to stare at something outside. Without so much as a whisper, Whitaker silently crawled to a knocked-out window, from which he made out three Japanese soldiers approaching with extreme caution through a thick morning mist rising from a nearby canal. When they were a hundred yards away, Whitaker saw they were in loincloths, apparently unarmed and possibly intending to give themselves up. Shuffling forward in half steps, they soon saw Oates in the doorway, who gestured for them to keep coming. Then Whitaker noticed he was holding behind his back Captain Fowler's gift to the stricken, grieving problem kid as the former lay bleeding to death. It was a chrome-plated Colt .44.

Whitaker knew Japanese who stripped almost naked could be signaling a wish to surrender, but also that loincloths could conceal grenades. Either way, he also knew never to trust a pistol alone. Again without a word, he slithered to his mat, picked up his submachine gun, and covered the three unknowns while they continued inching forward to the beckoning from the doorway — until they were twenty yards away, when Oates dropped to a crouch and fired as if in a Western movie.

The sprawled bodies meant nothing to Whitaker at the time. He and his buddies had seen "so much death in so many ways" that three more

weren't worth thinking about. If he *had* thought then, he'd have reckoned they were Japanese who deserved to die. What stayed with him was
only how Oates saw to it. The rules would have had him stop the Japanese
and search them, awakening the others in the unit in the process. If he'd
preferred killing them, he could have done that too without objection by
the other Americans. But in order to avenge the death of the captain he
loved, the "Jap killer," as he became known after Fowler's death — a significant term among Marines, who were all Jap killers — had to do it with
his prized gun.

That was different from the nasty *job* of killing. Within a week, Oates
was missing from his unit. Nothing was heard of the violator of combat
wisdom until a flamethrowing tank found his body several days later.
Whitaker and the others guessed he'd died on a private, extracurricular
mission to kill more Japs.

Atrocities against natives shouldn't be mentioned without stressing the
10th Army's overriding respect for the Geneva Convention, and specifying that most units were frequently told — in some cases constantly admonished — to try to save innocent lives. For most troops, such lectures
were superfluous. They didn't *want* to kill unarmed civilians. In many
cases, they risked their lives not to — by throwing smoke instead of
phosphorous or fragmentation grenades into caves, for example. That
consideration for the possible native families inside allowed any Japanese
soldiers mingled with them a chance to shoot back.

It also merits repeating that many Americans were humane far beyond
the Convention's requirements. Voluntary mercies and kindnesses to
civilians abounded, from individual fighters emptying their packs to feed
children, to units adopting older children as mascots, to corpsmen — the
same ones who saved Japanese wounded — delivering Okinawan babies
under extremely difficult conditions. And not only corpsmen. Sergeant
J. R. Aichie, a machine-gunner never trained in obstetrics, delivered or
helped deliver five babies during the campaign, all of whom he'd see on
postwar trips back to Okinawa.

The photographs of GIs and Leathernecks passing out candy bars, cigarettes, and cans of food didn't lie, nor was the American public wrong to
be convinced of their men's instinctive magnanimity. An Okinawan kid
hiding in a cave watched the approach of two enormous shoes worn by a
"giant" flamethrower. He said a trembling good-bye to his parents. The
giant handed him a Hershey bar. Another kid in a nearby cave with his
mother and grandmother hadn't eaten for four days, but they wouldn't
let him slip out to scavenge for food out of terror of the approaching
Americans. When they actually appeared and called from the mouth
of the cave, the civilians finally went out expecting to be tortured and

killed. The boy's mother begged him not to eat a can of food offered him by a Marine, but he was too hungry to listen. Forty-five years later, his voice still broke when he told the story.

In June, Marines told another boy they'd found in a Japanese uniform he'd surely be killed unless he took it off immediately. He happened to be not the Okinawan they took him for but a petite Japanese soldier. Gullibility aside, American bravery helped many Okinawans. While some soldiers and Marines used grenades to ignite the napalm they'd poured into caves, others — or sometimes the same men — risked their lives to get civilians out when they realized whom the inferno was burning.

If a balance sheet between atrocities and generosities is ever drawn up, an outsider who never suffered the pressures of combat won't be fit to do it. But ignoring the shameful acts completely, as virtually every military account does, is too good to war and its phony legends. If Secretary of the Navy James Forrestal could "never again see a U.S. Marine without experiencing a feeling of reverence," as he said after watching a film of the 1944 landing on Saipan, Okinawa fighters themselves knew better.

It was no atrocity to steal natives' chickens, pigs, and cattle, even if that was prohibited. Men who'd been withdrawn from the line for a brief rest couldn't be expected not to grill some fresh meat instead of trying to swallow more C-rations. It also wasn't an atrocity to throw phosphorous grenades into occupied caves, although they were terrible weapons. "The thing about a phosphorous grenade is that you can't get it off the skin, so it just keeps burning into a person," an American medical corpsman who treated many Okinawans would lament. "Mostly I remember the women burning. To me, phosphorous weapons are dirtier than napalm and they should be banned, it's just too cruel a way for civilians to die." However, they weren't banned, and the Americans knew their own lives were at stake from enemy soldiers hiding in the caves together with civilians.

The grenades would prompt some Okinawans, including honorable civic leaders who weren't anti-American, to charge that the poison gas used on some caves was in violation of the Geneva Convention. Well after the war, still haunted by the huge number of civilian deaths, they'd ask interested American visitors to investigate. They did, and discovered what had actually happened: American explosives unintentionally *released* poison gases that caused thousands of agonizing deaths in the confined cave spaces. The most lethal was an acrid yellow smoke from the petric acid used in Japanese munitions stored there.

However, rape does qualify as an atrocity, and there was much of it, even if most fighting units had no knowledge of it whatever. Some fully believed their officers' warnings that "anyone who touches an Okinawan woman will be shot on the spot" — or needed no such threats. But other individuals and groups behaved differently, and American military chronicles ignore their crimes.

On April 7, six 6th Division Marines entered the house of a village on the coast of the Motobu Peninsula. A mother and her fourteen-year-old daughter were hiding beneath the house, as most women except for the very young and very old hid from the invaders whenever possible. The "red giants" and "red ogres," as the two perceived the loud, sunburned Americans, dragged them into a little yard and took turns.

Later that month, eight Americans took four women from the tiny off-shore island of Aka to sea in a little landing craft and gave them the choice of succumbing or swimming. After they yielded, the men threw them overboard anyway. Those eight, who were black, helped give blacks in general a reputation among Okinawan women as the most persistent rapists, "who never gave up no matter how you ran," as one would put it. But fear of whites was only marginally lesser, especially in some northern villages whose few hundred inhabitants reported scores of assaults.

Shame and disgrace, together with the Americans' role as victors and occupiers, kept the reported cases to fewer than ten by 1946, almost all accompanied by severe bodily harm.* The vast majority of probably thousands of incidents in all were not in the south, where most Americans were too busy and exhausted to think much about women, but during and after the far easier northern campaign, especially by troops landed for occupation and mop-up duty while the bitter southern fighting raged in May and June. The easiest prey, with the least opportunity to lodge a complaint, were evacuees from central and southern areas, such as the Sonans. The silence of almost all victims kept it another dirty secret of the campaign. Few revealing pregnancies occurred, stress and bad diet having rendered most Okinawan women temporarily infertile. Many who did become pregnant managed to abort before their husbands and fathers returned. A smaller number of newborn infants fathered by Americans were suffocated.

Other episodes were more mistakes than atrocities. A medical corpsman spied movement in the darkness of a night he'd never forget. "Hey, there's bushes out there that weren't there before!" The squad threw dozens of hand grenades and heard a chorus of moaning until dawn, when they discovered that all the dead and dying were women, one very

---

*That echoed the rare reporting of previous rapes by Japanese soldiers, the victims being intimidated by the mood of national emergency as much as by the perpetrators themselves. Japanese veterans of the Manchuria and China fighting were considered expert rapists. But many Okinawan women accepted that once war came to the island, they'd inevitably be next in line, first for abuse by the dominating Japanese, then by the victors seeking spoils.

beautiful. One of her arms had been blown off and both legs were dangling on small pieces of skin. "She was still alive, somehow hanging on — but there was no hope for her. She was mercy-killed."*

It was sometimes a short step from that confused picture to the grimmer one of random killing. One infantryman would remember pumping bullets into "straw houses" on the northern edge of otherwise leveled Naha. "There was some return fire from a few of the houses, but the others were probably occupied by civilians — and we didn't care. It was a terrible thing not to distinguish between the enemy and women and children. Americans always had great compassion, especially for children. Now we fired indiscriminately."

On the other side of Naha, an infantryman bet a mortarman he couldn't put a round down the chimney of a little house about five hundred yards ahead. "We bet a dime and I gave him three tries. His second round went straight down that chimney and exploded, *wonk!* We didn't know if anybody was inside and it didn't matter anymore, just didn't matter."

Several medical corpsmen used their carbines to force a family into another little farmhouse before setting it alight, then fired round after round into its windows and doors while it burned to the ground. Another corpsman from the same unit didn't know whether the civilians had done anything to provoke the atrocity, "but those men never needed provocation for their brutality. They were the worst kind of redneck, bullying everyone, always looking for trouble — and so tough that even our officers feared them."

Those particular officers — civilian doctors before the war — weren't forceful military leaders. The horrified corpsman who witnessed the intentional burning was confident nothing so blatantly evil could have been done in combat units, which had better discipline and much less need for "excitement." Not everyone in those combat units who killed a civilian unnecessarily was sadistic; most simply no longer cared. Eugene Sledge and others were infuriated by the death of an old woman in a hut who had used sign language to beg Sledge to shoot her because she had a large, gangrenous wound in her abdomen. Sledge would do no such thing, but another Marine pulled his trigger. Even in the throes of battle, the others felt passionately that their job was to shoot Japanese, not old women: "Japs shoot back!" But far from everyone could still make that distinction.

---

*The bombs that badly damaged a leper colony on offshore Yagaki Island were also probably a mistake. It stood near Japanese pens for suicide boats, and Americans who discovered the installation probably assumed its easily visible Red Cross markings were another Japanese trick.

Days before the campaign's official end, many Okinawans were sheltering in caves about three miles above the island's southern tip, together with some of the remnants of the 32nd Infantry Regiment, a sister of Captain Kojo's 22nd. Native historians recorded testimony that on June 18, 19, and perhaps 20, some sixty civilian men who'd been flushed from those caves were separated from the women and children and killed; at any rate, never seen again. The perpetrators' identification as Marines is suspect because terrified Okinawan civilians didn't distinguish between American servicemen of the various branches.* And no independent confirmation of murders has been made, although that *has* been done, very recently, for other civilian accusations of brutality long disputed by the services. But even if the allegations about June 18–20 were fabricated or twisted, the record of willful atrocities against unarmed natives is large enough, even if small in proportion to the number of man-hours spent under battle pressures that easily unhinge the bravest.

And although they remained far fewer than those committed by Japanese, troubled observers recognized the pitfall. One self-described green replacement watched a veteran run the blade of a knife through "a sweating Jap's throat" he was interrogating. He didn't know why, "but after I fought for a while myself, I realized there was no reason for that kind of crap. Well, there was a reason but it can't be accepted. Because the minute you do accept it, we become like Japs or Nazis and there are no winners, just all losers." Beyond that, a Marine infantryman's later reflection that war itself is an atrocity may one day be accepted as obvious. Meanwhile, the notion that civilian suffering was "accidental" needn't be swallowed, since the barest knowledge of war attested to its inevitability. Although American firepower wasn't intended to cause the greatest civilian pain, the commanders knew it would.

*Those historians speculate they may have incited by an event on the afternoon of June 18, described in the following chapter.

26 · The Military Toll

This morn we are packing sea bags, hammocks, etc. We received fresh eggs, potatoes and butter. What's the Corps coming to?
— From Melvin Heckt's diary, June 18

All along the beach all you could see were Nip shoes and clothes. They must have discarded them when they were forced to swim — where to no one knows. But they figure drowning was better than to be captured by the American "cannibals."
— Buzzy Fox, June 25

GENERAL BUCKNER HAD WRITTEN General Ushijima on June 10, two weeks after his evacuation from the Shuri Line. Dropped by air, the message took seven days to reach the 32nd Army's transferred headquarters in the cave high on the cliff above the Pacific.

The forces under your command have fought bravely and well, and your infantry tactics have merited the respect of your opponent. . . . Like myself, you are an infantry general long schooled and practiced in infantry warfare. . . . I believe, therefore, that you understand as clearly as I that the destruction of all Japanese resistance on the island is merely a matter of days.

Buckner's invitation to end the useless bloodshed — useless, of course, in American eyes — is said to have prompted laughter from Ushijima and Cho, who found the notion of surrender hilarious.* But both officers knew "matter of days" was no figure of speech.

Cho busied himself writing cables to bolster the mainland's defense with lessons learned about the latest American tactics and methods, then tried to arrange for staff officers able to teach those lessons to smuggle

*Although no one seriously expected them to agree, the 10th Army staff hoped the open message might prompt surrenders by less resolute Japanese. Tens of thousands of leaflets dropped on enemy territory the following week focused on Ushijima's refusal to negotiate and appealed to his subordinates to give themselves up rather than become victims of their commander's selfish intention to doom his entire army to destruction.

themselves back to Tokyo. Ushijima's more ceremonial final duties included a farewell cable to his direct superior on Formosa, the commander of the 10th Army Area (not to be confused with the American 10th Army opposing him on Okinawa). He reported that the "overwhelming tide of the enemy's material strength, which won control of the land, sea and sky," had brought the battle to "the brink of total disaster." The commander also confessed that his lack of wisdom and virtue was responsible for the failure, despite "superhuman" efforts from every soldier and "devoted cooperation" from the natives.

> For the Emperor and people of Japan, I have no adequate words of apology for the state of the fighting. It has come to the point where we are about to deploy all surviving soldiers for a final battle — in which I will apologize to the Emperor with my own death. Yet the regret for not having accomplished my enormous responsibility will torment my soul for thousands of years to come.

Ushijima also promised that those facing the final mortal combat were fully determined to join the heroic spirits of tens of thousands already fallen on Okinawa. "We shall, all of us, transform ourselves either into demons to protect the nation and destroy the enemy who is attempting to invade our mainland or into a Divine Wind to ride the skies and join the battle for ultimate victory."

Finally, the general expressed profound gratitude to higher authorities and other units for their cooperation and guidance (of which he'd had so little). Although high-ranking samurais' tradition of leaving behind a poem or two was not always observed in the pressure of the various national crises, Ushijima took the time to compose two *jisei*.

> Even as I expire, bullets and arrows depleted,
> Dyeing heaven and earth [with blood],
> My soul will, my soul will
> Return to protect the holy nation.

and:

> The island's green grass,
> Wilting without waiting for autumn,
> Will revive with the return
> Of the holy nation's Imperial spring.

The day after Ushijima's and Cho's reportedly laughing dismissal of General Buckner's surrender proposal, he visited forward positions for a firsthand look at the progress of his forces. Kamikazes were still crashing into ships, although the Floating Chrysanthemum operations had been considerably reduced in order to conserve planes and pilots for the mainland campaign. And American casualties remained severe in the faster but still deadly advance on land: almost three thousand that very week, to be followed by even more the following one. June casualties alone, when the battle was supposedly over except for the mopping up, would be a third of Iwo Jima's heavy total. Weaker than ever with skin and stomach problems, nervous strain and cumulative exhaustion, sweaty infantrymen knew each terrifying day might be their last. But after seventy-eight of them — forty-eight more than the number originally estimated for the job — the end was in sight, especially to the commanders. Buckner had just told another press conference that most of what remained to do was mopping up. At last his optimism was justified.

That afternoon of June 18, he chose to observe a component of the 2nd Marine Division that had been withdrawn for seven weeks to Saipan after making its feinted landing on L-day. Its fresh 8th Regiment, recently returned to Okinawa, was spearheading one thrust of the final push: a kind of coup de grâce for the spent defenders. But isolated Japanese artillery units in that area were still unloosing sporadic fire.

Fit, tough Buckner had ignored urgings to postpone a visit so close to the fighting. Accompanied by the newly committed regiment's commander, he came up to a forward observation post easily in sight of the major ridge where Tadashi Kojo's men were about to spend their final hours as an organized force, then the cliffs at the island's southwestern tip.

The observation post, like most, was a few square yards cleared of scrub, this one on Maesato Ridge. Artillery spotter glasses, supplemented by a second pair captured from the Japanese, had been positioned between two large boulders roughly a yard apart — protection against the remains of the Japanese 1st Heavy Field Artillery Regiment on the next hill farther south, which had taken typical punishment on its retreat to there. In previous positions, that battery had sent puffs of smoke from empty caves in order to deceive American naval and artillery gunners. Still, day after day of concentrated fire terrified the men and destroyed their guns, the pride of the 32nd Army — some before they had fired a round. Now only one of a dozen was left — "miraculously spared," as one of its crew saw it, and maintained by parts salvaged from the wreckage of the other eleven.

Just after 1 P.M., one of the skeletal survivors scanned the hill to the north and focused his binoculars on the surprising sight of some apparently high-ranking enemy officers who, using *their* binoculars, seemed to be looking in the direction of General Ushijima's headquarters on the opposite coast. After almost an hour at the vantage point, confident, hardworking General Buckner told the others that he was ready to move on to observe another unit. Before he'd completed his good-byes, an expert Japanese artillerist ordered the remaining gun to fire at the tempting target of American brass. Spare members of the battery, "knowing very well we'd get a 'return gift' of a thousand shots back from them for every shot from us," hurried into their cave.

Since heavy artillery usually required considerable adjustment on a target, American officers were surprised by the accuracy of the gun's five rounds. One hit one of the protective boulders, flinging a shower of metal fragments and splinters of coral or rock into Buckner's chest.

> *Heads were bandaged with bloody gauze and faces were hardly recognizable. Almost every type of wound imaginable was evident. . . . What do those men have to gain amid all this misery while others sit back and reap huge benefits or perhaps complain because of the lack of some pleasure or convenience?*
> — Kenneth Cecil, observing the treatment of Army casualties on May 21

> *The absence of screw-ups wasn't as remarkable as the absence of cowardice among the fighting men, but maybe both came from the same source.*
> — Hospital Apprentice First Class Edmund Shimberg about his field hospital

The odds favored the commander's recovery. American battlefield medicine was as good as anything in the campaign, distinctly better than the general's intelligence and strategy. Thousands hit just as badly had already been saved.

Seven hours of fierce fire kept Paul Dunfrey, the first lieutenant who'd scouted south of the Asakawa for the major assault of the Shuri Line, from being evacuated after the bullet or bullets had severed his bowel and driven fragments of his belt buckle into his intestines. He was spared when doctors on a hospital ship used a new technique, later described in a book titled *Miracles of Surgery*, to fuse his bowel. (After his long hospital recuperation, a doctor, necessarily ignorant of the operation's long-term effects, told Dunfrey's wife to take him home and have a good time because he had maybe five years to live. Dunfrey would be in vigorous shape forty years later.)

Young Forest Townsend, a self-described "country green kid," was hit by a Nambu light machine gun as he dashed across a field outside Naha. He lost consciousness in his rain-filled shell hole but briefly came to in a battalion aid station, then in what he took for a field hospital tent, where he was given only a wet rag to suck for his desperate thirst. When he awoke a third time on a hospital ship, he had great trouble breathing. His surgeon came from near Philadelphia's Main Line, not Townsend's territory. The eighteen-year-old would remember that savior's hands the rest of his life. "They were the most gentle I ever knew, with real healing power, honest." He would tell Townsend that with his kind of hit, "I'd say you were one in ninety thousand to live"; his heart must have moved a fraction of an inch when the bullet struck. "Miraculous."

But of course Townsend's recovery was more the result of surgical skill and the general quality of care than any miracle. Much would later be made of how earlier island fighting served to heighten the ferocity and deadliness on Okinawa. Analysts attributed the enormous mutual cost to both sides' application of lessons learned along the way. That was only partly true, since combat required as much improvisation on Okinawa as elsewhere. In medicine, however, lessons had indeed been learned and great progress made in lifesaving techniques. Special landing craft equipped for surgery delivered the wounded to hospital ships. New penicillin and sulfa powder worked wonders, as did the sterling collection of specialists in burn treatment, internal medicine, and every branch of surgery. Refrigerated whole blood, much better than plasma for reviving bodies in grave shock from the loss of most of their own blood, had first become available on Iwo Jima two months earlier. Over fifteen thousand gallons were flown from the States to Okinawa in a matter of days. The new techniques helped reduce the mortality rate of the wounded to half that of previous Pacific battles, approaching Europe's rate.

The exceptions came when dire cases couldn't be delivered to doctors in time — a terrible moment for their friends. John Townsend delivered a Marine badly wounded by machine-gun fire to a battalion aid station and was told to place him with a dozen others under a tree. Townsend, who'd never heard of triage, protested mildly. "Sir, if you leave him there, he'll be dead in thirty minutes." A doctor explained that since there was no hope whatever of saving him, he had to work on others. Like young Townsend, many infantrymen five minutes from the strain of battle took that explanation badly, especially when the wounded men were buddies. A few exploded and threatened to shoot the doctors. But such episodes were rare, partly because the majority of cases met the opposite response from medical personnel.

Some wounded were frighteningly disfigured. Okinawa produced World War II's first American "basket case," a master sergeant shorn of all four limbs. The sergeant was walking ahead of his men to spot mines when he stepped on one. But even he survived, because he was quickly carried to a hospital. (Still slightly deaf and suffering from shock when he was returned to the States a month later, he thought he'd make "an excellent propaganda photo to end all wars.")

Unless the wounds were nearly fatal to begin with or enemy fire prevented corpsmen or fire-team buddies from starting the usual speedy delivery to emergency treatment, hit men had an excellent chance to live. The sequence of care began right on the line, where medical corpsmen, one in each platoon, applied first aid. They carried bandages and gauze, packets of infection-inhibiting sulfa, vials of morphine in self-contained hypodermic needles, and little bottles of blood plasma and brandy. The next step was the battalion aid station, often only two or three hundred yards back from the front, but beyond small-arms range. It was sometimes a tent with better-supplied corpsmen or occasionally doctors who patched minor wounds, after which many men went straight back to their units. But aid stations overflowed during intense fighting and shelling. A short film of the youthful chests rent with deep gashes, limbs torn off, intestines spilling out, eyes wide with agony, and teeth gritted to stop moans would have educated the home front about the campaign's real nature.

In any case, quick delivery to an aid station was crucial. If that could be done for General Buckner, his chances were good. In a month or more, he might even be able to assume the still-larger command for the mainland's invasion that would surely be his if recovery went well.

The seriously wounded were next delivered to a better facility. They were carried or transported to their division's collecting and clearing company, and from there to a field or portable surgical hospital, or to a splendidly equipped white ship with a comforting name such as *Hope, Relief*, or *Solace*. Many were still in shock, bodies slumped and faces twisted with battle tension, but conscious patients saw the floating hospitals as vessels of great beauty. Their hundreds of beds were full throughout the hardest days on the Shuri Line, when other wounded were airlifted to base hospitals in Hawaii or the States. A veritable bridge of planes also transported hundreds of patients to Guam.

The outward journey of Emil Rucinski was as typical as any. When the gunnery sergeant's platoon dug in for a long night of heavy mortar fire at the Shuri Line, he was its new leader, the lieutenant having been hit in the morning and the platoon sergeant in the afternoon. As that third platoon leader in fifteen hours crawled toward his company commander for instructions after many members were hit, he too fell. Rucinski felt as if a baseball bat had whacked him to the ground, but remembered his training and remained calm, calling for a corpsman. A sniper's bullet had entered the left side of his chest, shattered a rib, ripped his diaphragm, and badly mangled his kidneys and lungs. After a corpsman's doses of plasma and morphine, stretcher bearers brought him back to his battalion aid station, from where a jeep took serious casualties to a landing craft. They were hoisted onto a converted transport ship that had fought off kamikaze attacks while waiting offshore. Treating Rucinski at sea, the ship's medical services delivered him, after stops at Guam and Honolulu, to a medical receiving station in San Francisco. Later he was sent to a hospital in Virginia — the nearest suitable facility to his Massachusetts home — until his discharge in January 1946, seven months after his wounding. By the end of the campaign, almost thirty-one thousand men, 80 percent of all battle casualties, would be evacuated similarly, half by ship, half by air.*

(Decades later, a man who'd seen the prostrate, blood-soaked Rucinski when he seemingly hadn't the slightest chance to live turned white when a grinning apparition who looked uncannily like him walked into a Marine reunion. The observer had to be convinced it was indeed the "dead man," alive and well.)

When Joseph Bangert was rushed in to replace a just-killed corpsman on Sugar Loaf, his platoon had to shout the dangerous "Corpsman!" instead of "Bangert!" because no one knew his name. Bangert also knew no names and had trouble learning any during his baptism under fire because his platoon kept getting replacements for "guys shot bad, guys shot worse, guys killed. There were bodies everywhere" — including one with half a head, although the man was still alive. Some tried to joke about getting their "lucky ticket home"; a much smaller number asked to be shot. "Don't let me go out like this, Mac. Put me out of my misery." But even some of those cases survived, to their own surprise.

Field hospitals were clusters of tents serving as a combined evacuation center and early-day M*A*S*H. Hospital Apprentice First Class Edmund Shimberg, a nineteen-year-old from the Bronx serving as a dogsbody in Corps Evacuation Hospital Number 2, had arrived on Okinawa somewhat skeptical. "Before we started functioning as a hospital, we were a running joke for ourselves. 'This screw-up outfit will never be worth a dime.' But everything came together when it had to." The facility's neurosurgeon and urologist were world class. The surgical group as a whole was excellent by every current standard, and expense was "simply never considered."

Shimberg stopped swabbing floors and changing dressings to assist with surgery when it was performed throughout the night. Trauma teams working under extreme urgency gave the tents the look of a city hospital's emergency ward after a natural disaster. "If men were brought back to us alive, their chances were very good because the medical practice was superb."

In the end, ninety-seven of every hundred wounded Americans would live — including even First Lieutenant Dale Bair, the replacement for Captain Owen Stebbins who was seriously hit three times during the first assault on Sugar Loaf. That figure more than reversed the Japanese one of nine in

---

*On some ships, wards packed with gravely wounded were shown a selection of the films then entertaining the American public and giving them their phony images of the war. William Manchester's ward in Hawaii was treated to a visit by John Wayne, star of the gung-ho *Sands of Iwo Jima*. Wearing a fancy cowboy outfit, down to spurs and pistols, the celluloid hero greeted the wounded with a self-satisfied "Hiya, guys!" — which was greeted by a stony silence. Then someone booed. "Suddenly everyone was booing." Hollywood's mythologies, prominently conveyed by Ronald Reagan too, were exceeded only by those of the Japanese, with their crude, ugly fairy tales of Japanese good and American bestiality.

ten dying. But General Buckner was about to join the 3 percent. Bleeding heavily, he couldn't be evacuated to an aid station. Despite the desperate efforts of a medical corpsman in his entourage, he died within minutes. The footsloggers who'd known all along that nearness to the campaign's end was no protection from death took his as confirmation.*

When the news reached the 32nd Army headquarters cave by radio from Tokyo, Cho and the young staff apparently cheered. Only Ushijima, reportedly perplexed by their glee, remained silent and later supposedly said a prayer for his opposite number — although that may be rumor spun into myth. What is certain is that Buckner was the highest-ranking American killed in action during World War II. With so much death everywhere, his seemed to some "not inappropriate." None of the officers standing feet or inches from him had been scratched. Like so many of his men, the commander had been dealt a dose of combat's vast store of random bad luck.

> *Our strategy and tactics were all utilized to the utmost and we fought valiantly; but they had little effect against the enemy's superior material strength.*
> — From Mitsuru Ushijima's last message to Imperial General Headquarters

> *A simultaneous shout and a flash of a sword, then another repeated shout and a flash, and both generals had nobly accomplished their last duty to their Emperor.*
> — A self-claimed eyewitness to the deaths of Ushijima and Isamu Cho

> *The hill, shrouded in the smoke of battle, was burning like an erupting volcano, red in the setting sun.*
> — An Okinawan schoolteacher describing Hill 89 the following day

Buckner's death occurred within hours of Ushijima's apology for failing to accomplish his mission. The reply of the Japanese headquarters on Formosa came the following day: a letter of commendation extolling the 32nd Army's great efforts and extraordinarily brave fighting. Ushijima issued a general order to his army that same June 19, its typically vague phrases essentially calling on all to sacrifice themselves.

> I appreciate and congratulate your brave efforts for the past three months in carrying out your duties. But now we face the end, as it has become extremely difficult to continue our efforts. Each of you should

---

*However, desire for revenge may possibly have been responsible for some of the subsequent alleged atrocities against civilians. The sixty-odd alleged murders on June 18, 19, and 20 came immediately after Buckner's death on the eighteenth. All were in the same vicinity, some right in Macsato, directly below the observation post. A company commander who witnessed Buckner's death would write that it prompted his regiment to throw caution to the winds. "We . . . rushed to smash those who had killed our commanding general" — not civilians, but perhaps the anger of a few extended to them.

follow the orders of whoever is highest in rank in your group and continue to resist to the very end, then live in the eternity of our noble
cause.

The cliff containing Ushijima's cave, Hill 89 to the Americans, stood
about four hundred yards south of the village of Mabuni. That was just
over a mile south of the last Yoza-dake–Yaeju-dake–Kunishi Ridge mountain line and two miles from the island's southern tip. By the next day,
June 20, the hill and village — to which headquarters guards were sent as
final combat troops — controlled only a small pocket, into which much
of the entire remains of the 32nd Army had been squeezed. Stretching
some five miles along the Pacific coast, it was only a few hundred yards
deep along most of that distance. Now the American Army's 7th Infantry
Division attacked it from the north. First to encounter the outer edges of
the first massive Japanese line south of L-day's landing beaches, the 7th,
with rest periods, had been fighting since then. Now, a month after its
hardest work at the Shuri Line, so little was left of Japanese territory that
Army commanders hesitated to call for the usual massive concentrations
of air and naval gunfire support for fear of hitting their own men.* The
weary soldiers had to eliminate the last resistance with flame, explosives,
and tanks, breaking up the pocket into smaller ones and eliminating
them one by one like, a historian would write, "a man stamp[ing] out so
many snakes, until there were no more Japanese to kill."

On that June 20, a brave soldier delivered Ushijima his last message
from 24th Division headquarters, which was still holding out about a mile
northwest. Meanwhile, units of the same 7th Division fought their way up
Hill 89, a coral formation that rose over two hundred feet almost straight
from the sea. Its jagged pinnacle was studded with crags and crevices:
perfect protection for Japanese snipers, mortarmen, and a few machine-
gun squads with operable guns. Desperation stiffened their resistance.
Flamethrowing tanks used nearly five thousand gallons of napalm to
burn them out. When the summit was finally taken on June 21, only the
area around Ushijima's headquarters remained.

The large cave had two entrances, one facing land and the other the
sea, both slightly below the fairly level summit. A Japanese prisoner of the
7th Division agreed to deliver a last surrender appeal to Ushijima. When
he approached the landward mouth calling out the American message, it
was sealed by an explosion from inside. A subsequent explosion, set off by

---

*A Marine battalion that had fought to the southern end watched an Army unit advanc-
ing toward the same coast, flushing out and shooting Japanese soldiers singly and in small
groups. The Marines grew tense as doggie mortar shells landed nearer and nearer. Finally, a
furious officer told the Army officer in charge that his big mortars would go at their troops
unless the dangerous fire stopped immediately. It did.

Americans who found an air shaft, killed ten officers and men: the first major casualties among the 32nd Army staff, who had been drafting orders while an average of over twenty-five hundred people were being killed on the island during each of the eighty-two days since April 1.

> *The commanders of the Okinawa Defense Forces ended their lives as warriors but could not escape criticism for dragging not only their line soldiers but also the unfortunate civilians into the war. It did not matter to others that they had acted "under orders."*
> — Masahide Ota, well after the war

Ushijima received a farewell message that day from the minister of the Army and the chief of the general staff. He sent a last report to Imperial General Headquarters and broke off radio communication. That evening, American grenades exploding overhead rumbled the cave during a farewell party for surviving members of the staffs of the army and of the demolished field units. Ushijima wore his full-dress uniform, Cho a white kimono. They toasted their guests with sake while dining on miso soup, fish cakes, canned meats, rice, cabbage, potatoes, pineapple, and tea.

The two generals also savored the last of a bottle of Black and White that Cho, his affection for Scotch intact, had brought with him from Shuri. Deeper inside the long, twisting cave, headquarters personnel sang "Umi Yukaba," a solemn ancient poem about sacrifice for the Emperor.

At three o'clock, just before moonrise, most of the officers left with most of the remaining men for a final "die in honor" attack. A more realistic assessment of the American strength all around them had forced abandonment of a plan for the generals to die at the summit while watching those last units push the enemy off and down the hill, then retake Mabuni village below. An hour later, just after four o'clock, all was ready for a shorter sortie by the two generals. "Well, Commanding General Ushijima," the junior said, "as the way may be dark, I, Cho, will lead the way." "Please do so," came the still professionally serene answer. "I'll take my fan since it's getting warm."

The generals rose, Ushijima picking up an Okinawan fan. Colonel Yahara was notably absent, the chief operations officer's request to join his commanders in their final act having been denied. Instead, Ushijima and Cho ordered the sober strategist to escape and make his way back to the mainland to inform Imperial General Headquarters about American tactics and techniques. "If you die, no one will be left who knows the truth about the Battle of Okinawa. Bear the temporary shame but endure it. This is an order from your military commander." (Soon captured by American forces, Yahara would face severe criticism for failing to die honorably, despite his orders.) Reversing his lifelong romanticism, Yahara's old antagonist Cho was particularly eager for young staff officers not to deprive Japan of the benefit of their experience and potential as leaders of guerrilla warfare on Okinawa by killing themselves. Although some staff officers nevertheless remained with the commanders now, two dozen or so had already obeyed Cho by sneaking from the cave.

While attempts were made to distract the Americans above, the two generals left the cave's unsealed mouth. Ushijima imperturbably fanned himself as they walked a few yards to a small ledge overlooking the Pacific Ocean. "These are calm minds facing death," a witness would report. "The generals . . . have the air of immortals passing by." A sister-in-law of an Okinawan major, one of the few native officers of higher rank, had prepared the required white sheets. One was placed over a quilt on the ledge. Ignoring American grenades lobbed in the small party's direction, Ushijima and Cho bowed toward the eastern sky. Then, as James and William Belote complete the story, "both knelt on the sheet, facing the ocean since room was lacking on the ledge to perform the ceremony facing north toward the Imperial Palace."

> Silently each opened his tunic, baring his abdomen. At General Ushijima's side stood his aide, Lieutenant Yoshino, holding two knives with half the blade wrapped in white cloth. The adjutant, Captain Sakaguchi, stood on Ushijima's right, saber drawn. Yoshino handed a blade to Ushijima, who took it with both hands and with a shout, thrust. Simultaneously Sakagushi's saber fell on his neck as prescribed, severing his spinal column. Ushijima's corpse lurched forward onto the sheet.
>
> Then General Cho took his turn and the ceremony was repeated.

That, at least, is more or less how most chronicles record the deaths, perhaps owing something to imagination. The traditional account, passed from writer to writer, relies heavily on the testimony of a Japanese military policeman who later admitted he wasn't where he claimed to be but heard the story from others. The cook who prepared the bountiful final meal supposedly watched from the cave mouth, where he was reported as having heard pistol shots, possibly the source of the blood at the temples seen in photographs of the corpses taken several days later.

Shooting would have violated the samurai code, the notion of which enraged some Japanese officers after the war. "You sonofabitch, you've demeaned their families and insulted the samurai way," one would scream to an Okinawan whose research led him to question the conventional version of the suicides. Some who uphold that version insist the death photos proved nothing because Americans had faked them. After all, a multitude of high-ranking Japanese officers elsewhere committed *seppuku* exactly as described on Hill 89. And the shots may have been fired by seven staff officers — some accounts say nine — who "blew their brains out" at the same time. Still, some knowledgeable students of the campaign suspect that Ushijima's serene end may have been prettified to bring honor to his death and the samurai code.

Definitive answers will probably never be found. Too many of the extant accounts derive from tainted sources and too many offer contradictory details, even about what the principals were wearing; some put Cho also in full-dress uniform rather than the white kimono. They differ on whether moonlight was shimmering over the sea during the farewell meal or whether the moon hadn't yet risen — perhaps because even the date is uncertain. Americans believe the suicides took place in the early morning of June 22, but some Japanese place them on June 23.

It *is* known for certain that soldiers of the American 7th Division found the corpses several days later, where orderlies had buried them — but was that in shallow graves below the ledge or in the headquarters cave? This too is disputed. (Yahara had planned for burial at sea because the cave floor's coral was too hard for digging graves.) Cho had written his own epitaph on a silk mattress cover. The founding member of the Cherry Blossom Society declared that he was departing "without regret, shame or obligations." The war launched with much aid by his savagely nationalist society had taken more than sixteen million lives and brutalized hundreds of millions more, with a prospect of embracing a huge increase during the coming invasion of the Japanese mainland. The patriot was satisfied his honor was intact.

At General Buckner's solemn funeral in an Army cemetery, his three-star personal flag flew alongside the Stars and Stripes. Riflemen fired a volley, and a commemorative artillery barrage shook the ground. Although Ushijima was given no such honors, Japanese prisoners were permitted, soon after the battle's end, to spend a few moments paying respects at his and Cho's graves. A year later, the commander was posthumously promoted to General of the Army, the second and last in Japanese history. The first was the revered soldier-statesman of the Meiji era to whom he'd often been compared: Saigo the Great, of Kagoshima.

In the only Pacific campaign to take the lives of both sides' commanding officers, close subordinates kept falling. The day after Buckner's death, a sniper killed a Marine colonel who'd warned the commander not to come to the front. That same June 19, Brigadier General Claudius Easley, assistant commander of the Army's 96th Division, was pointing toward a Japanese machine gun when two of its bullets hit him in the forehead. For once the losses at the top reflected those at the bottom. Total 10th Army casualties would be 35 percent of the troops engaged, stunning by American standards. The 3,430 Marines killed represented 14 percent of all who died in World War II. Taking the island's .6 percent of total

Japanese territory cost more than 1 percent of World War II's total American casualties. The full number would come to over seventy-two thousand — nearly as many as the 32nd Army's Japanese soldiers (excluding the Okinawan conscripts). Of those, 7,613 were killed and missing in action, and the remaining sixty-four-odd thousand were almost equally divided between those wounded seriously enough to be out of action more than a week and nonbattle casualties, chiefly victims of battle fatigue. Secondary sources often state that the one hundred thousand Japanese killed and captured indicated a highly favorable American loss ratio of 1 to 17. However, the overall impact, not including the Navy's unprecedented losses of nearly five thousand killed and roughly the same number wounded, was less triumphant than those figures imply.

Measured by the casualties they inflicted, Ushijima's forces performed brilliantly, but only at the cost of ten times more KIAs of their own. The 10th Army estimated it killed two thousand Japanese on June 19, the day after Buckner's death, three thousand on June 20, and four thousand on June 21: figures hard to imagine except from death camps. The equivalent of half a combat division died during those three days, not including many of the Home Guard's last-minute, barely trained Okinawan teenagers. The number was also nearly half the total Japanese dead during the thirty-six hellish days on Iwo Jima.

When the fifty-six hundred men of the 44th Independent Mixed Brigade went to the bottom with *Toyama maru* the previous June, the disaster seemed enormous. The ship's terrified soldier-passengers could not have imagined that a greater percentage of them would survive than the proportion of the 32nd Army on land.

Book IV

27 · Expiration of the 32nd Army

Torrential rains and difficult terrain, together with stubborn opposition by a fanatic enemy fighting from an intricate cave system, contributed to make this campaign one of the most severe in the history of the United States armed forces.
— From the confidential report "Principal Lessons Learned in the Okinawa Operation"

The strength of willpower, devotion and technical resources applied by the United States to this task, joined with the death struggle of the enemy, places this battle among the most intense and famous in military history. . . . We make our salute to all your troops and their commanders engaged.
— Prime Minister Winston Churchill to President Harry Truman, June 22, 1945

T HE FALL OF KUNISHI RIDGE initiated an open season on the more than ten thousand diseased, partially armed Japanese burrowed in the trenches, ditches, and caves of the far south's flat sectors. Like the teeth of a comb, infantry platoons walking at arm's length across fields or scrubby rises cleared them out like animals, as a Marine would remember.

They had no reason to know or care that many of the enemy soldiers who popped up from tiny holes had been there for days, often without food or water. Or that they were terrified of their approaching death. If they'd been demoralized and desperate before, now many were frenzied, and what Americans *did* care about was that the cornered "animals" were still trying to kill them. "We knew we were coming to the end, of course. But in a way, that only made you more eager to live — to do anything to make it to the end after coming that far. Every day you hoped like hell it was the last one. Thirty days was like three years."

Flushing out a cave, Ed Jones thought he saw a Japanese who'd been behaving "funny" reach into his loincloth and pull out a grenade. Jones blew his head off, together with that of a nearby fellow soldier: a typical incident during the 32nd Army's terminal days, when bullets from almost every American or his buddies stopped sudden charges of isolated Japanese.

Some attacked with knives or sticks. Combing out a cornfield, a friend of Dick Whitaker's was in the team's point position when a Japanese stepped from behind a tree and hit him hard in the head with a scabbard. If he'd had the sword, his friend might have been beheaded. As it was, the frantic

Japanese grabbed a shotgun and raced away with it, his obvious terror yet more evidence that the Japanese were capable of anything.

Mopping up in another field of high grass, the same company was near enough to the southern coast to hear ships' public address systems urging surrender. John Senterfitt, the man with whom Whitaker had crawled down from Sugar Loaf, was five yards to his left. A sudden explosion there prompted a cry of "I'm hit!" Rushing to the drainage ditch into which Senterfitt had fallen, Whitaker saw a tangle of bloody flesh for his buddy's left arm. But Senterfitt struggled to his feet, and the corpsman who hurried over found nothing wrong with him. The explosion had come from a Japanese blowing himself up as the patrol passed the ditch — and spraying his blood so hard on the shocked Senterfitt that he thought he'd been wounded.

He and Whitaker didn't laugh at the time because "we were all so strung out." The tension might have been even higher now because "it'd be crazy to get killed in those last days." And even more bizarre things were happening even more unexpectedly.

> The Japs were in a kind of frenzy under their incredible pressure. They were squeezed into the last pockets before the ocean, where they could kill themselves or make a banzai charge. I saw some rush out absolutely determined to kill one of us with a last grenade. And since we were skinny and exhausted — no real sleep for about twelve weeks — and a little hyper about the end, we were still very nervous.

The mutual killing continued. On June 17, two Marine colonels used a tank to reconnoiter a hilly sector where mortar, machine-gun, and artillery fire had stalemated the advance. The tank commander, who also commanded the battalion, instructed his guest on how to use the vision cupola to pick out targets, but the latter cracked open the turret hatch about three inches for a better view. A grenade from a Japanese knee-mortar concealed in nearby rocks entered that opening and ripped him apart. He emitted a single gasp as he died, one of 250 Americans during the final week.

General Buckner's command passed to Major General Roy Geiger, his deputy and, until then, commander of the 10th Army's Marine contingent. But a Marine would hold that position only until Lieutenant General Joseph W. Stilwell of the U.S. Army — astute Vinegar Joe, famed for his role as adviser to Chiang Kai-shek — would be appointed the new force leader days later, after the campaign's official end.*

---

*One of the American Army's least orthodox and most capable generals, Stilwell would surely have fought a much more imaginative Okinawan campaign than Buckner.

Geiger declared the island secure on the afternoon of June 21. The following day, a small detachment from Stebbins's G–2–22 company raised a flag — the same that had been used at the northern end two months earlier — on a tree limb at Ara Saki, the extreme southern tip. One of its members was Medical Corpsman Joseph Bangert, who guessed the group was picked for having survived the full eighty-three days since L-day. Bangert believed the 10th Army's public relations staff members were trying to repeat the success of the famous flag-raising on Iwo Jima, which was already a national symbol. No doubt that earlier image explained the home front's reaction to the Okinawa photos as old news and helped explain why the campaign as a whole remained sorely underreported. Naturally, no photos showed the bloody clothing that littered Ara Saki, abandoned by Japanese soldiers and civilians who'd jumped from the cliff or swam off without a destination.

While the American public chalked up another victory somewhere in the Pacific, infantrymen wondered why territory so dangerous had been declared secure. Perhaps headquarters staff truly believed that only mopping up was needed now; perhaps the brass wanted to boost their standing — but in the field, relaxation of caution could still be fatal. Dick Whitaker's company commander, for whom he was still a runner, was a former enlisted man whose promotions had come when his superiors kept getting eliminated. But although that certified survivor's experience and skill probably helped him become the sole company officer not killed or wounded badly enough to require evacuation, he grew careless enough to open a map as his team was advancing on a dry strip between rice paddies the day after the official "securing." A Japanese soldier's appearance from nowhere with a hand grenade scattered everyone wildly, the map reader into a ditch, where he remained unhurt. His luck held again later, when he approached Whitaker unannounced from behind and Whitaker, with the usual spurt of adrenaline, spun around, stopping his trigger squeeze an instant before it tripped the hammer on his Thompson.

A New Jersey Marine named Red Burdett was about to relieve himself the morning after the flag-raising when he almost bumped into a Japanese soldier. The two ran opposite ways around a huge boulder, and the Japanese shot Red dead when they met again near their starting point. Later that day, when Buzzy Fox of the same state was cautiously advancing near a tank across a scrubby tract, a nearby tank hit a mine and flew into the air. "I felt so sorry for the crew. To have come so far and no farther. Every moment was crazy."

But of course vastly more Japanese than Americans were killed during the 32nd Army's last days. Even the units that had had enough cohesion to fight well on Kunishi Ridge and the final mountain line's other strong points disintegrated into confused little bands more absorbed with putting off destruction than fighting back.

When the last Japanese were compressed into a small pocket at the south end, the great "turkey shoot" began. . . . I suspect there were as many American casualties as Japanese with all those bloodthirsty people looking for targets.
— Thomas Hannaher

Just before the flag-raising on the southern end, we were sitting on cliffs about 150 feet high, shooting at Japs in loincloths. They were either trying to swim around to attack us from the rear or trying to save themselves. There were bodies all around. It was target practice.
— Irving Oertel

I always wanted to live, no matter what. To be captured, to be sent to heavy labor in America, never to go home again — even that would have been all right. But of course I never told that to anyone.
— One of four Japanese survivors in a unit of 169 men

Return American fire virtually obliterated the remnants of the heavy artillery battery whose "lucky shot" had killed General Buckner. The next morning, the exhausted survivors were ordered from their last cave on Yaeju-dake Mountain to an east coast village. Since leaving the cave, let alone reaching the village, was nearly impossible, "the order was very cruel. It was tantamount to 'Kill yourself!'" — and many indeed died, some by their own bullets after they'd been seriously wounded. Fleeing to a pine grove, Senior Private Hiroshi Uchihata and three others took refuge in a hole so small they could scarcely move. They covered it with branches and set up their last weapon, a machine gun.

Squeezing out to draw some muddy water for the group at twilight, Uchihata heard a sharp *psssst* and felt a hot stab at the back of his left knee. A chunk of metal, perhaps from a tank shell, had disabled him: a dreaded wound, because it would keep him from moving with his fellows. Since the American flamethrowing tanks that had already burned part of the pine grove would surely return in the morning, he decided it was time to lift a burden on the others.

He crawled back to his hole, then out again with four grenades. While he was looking for a place to end his struggle before it grew fully dark, a soldier named Hayase appeared and asked what he was doing. Uchihata added to his explanation a wish for a last drink of clean water from one of the springs that bubbled up at Mabuni beach. Hayase, his superior, asked to join him, perhaps hoping Uchihata, who'd learned his way around while serving as a regimental messenger, might lead him not only to clean water but also, somehow, to safety.

The nearest cliffs were very near 32nd Army headquarters. Making their way there, they found a steep path leading to the sand, rock, and jagged coral at the shore below. But torrential rain drove them to the fragmentary shelter of a lone still-standing palm tree, where Uchihata intoned a chant of the Nichiren sect believed to have protective powers. Despite his decision, he wanted to live. Asking the gods for help as never before, he refrained from mentioning the possibility of surrender to Hayase, although he couldn't put it from his thoughts.

When the cloudburst eased, they used vines to descend the cliff, Uchihata in agony from his leg. Entering the sea, they alternately swam and crawled the reefs vaguely northward, Uchihata leaning on Hayase for support. They'd worked and fought in the dark for so long — Uchihata driving on pitch-black nights before all his unit's trucks were demolished — that it wasn't difficult to see in the midnight ocean. Without specifying their destination, they agreed to seek somewhere safe.

Hayase disappeared during the course of a swimming leg an hour or so later. Since the two hadn't mentioned suicide again and no rifle shot had sounded from the American-controlled beach, Uchihata assumed he'd drowned.

On land again, he found a stick and used it to limp among ragged groups of soldiers also struggling north on a "passport route" along the shore. A rumor was circulating that Americans waiting at a break in the cliffs weren't shooting men who approached with their hands held high. Still wondering what he'd do when the time came, Uchihata was gladdened to recognize a corporal named Yamazaki, next to whom he used to bunk in Manchuria. But Yamazaki immediately asked for one of his grenades. Uchihata refused, because he himself might need them ahead. Besides, he didn't want to assist a friend's suicide, although he still thought he himself might resort to it at any moment. Yamazaki disappeared without further conversation. Never to see him again, Uchihata would assume he found other means of suicide or was shot, like most of the others.

After dawn, he heard a shout from atop a cliff. The sight of a lone enemy soldier there reminded him of an old prediction of an acquaintance who'd lived in America that Japan could never win against her might — and also his assurance that Americans were gentlemen. But although the enemy rifleman up there indeed refrained from shooting the rabble of soldiers and civilians on the beach below, Uchihata couldn't bring himself to surrender.

Feverish now, his wound throbbing, he hid behind a huge rock, watching bloated bodies wash up on the beach and half-living Japanese scavenge for food. Knowing he'd soon starve in his condition, he agonized over his decision one more day, then pulled himself up and, supported by civilians, "allowed himself to be rescued" — the straight words *surrender* and *prisoner* crossed no one's lips — by continuing toward "passport point." He would remain convinced he'd never have done that if not for his wound.

> *I saw so many caves blown, I couldn't remember any except for this huge one just north of the final ridge. It was the size of a large ballroom with tunnels branching off — probably held hundreds. After we thought all the civilians were out, we heard the soldiers singing their heads off and getting all sake-ed up. Then the grenades started going off down there. We thought the Japs had been under such terrific bombardment they must have been kind of nuts anyway. We waited a couple of hours before we ignited the gasoline. By that time, they were probably all dead anyway.*
> — James Burden

> *"There he goes, shoot him," one soldier shouted excitedly. "Shoot him yourself," another remarked. "I don't want to clean my rifle today."*
> — From the notes of a lieutenant colonel observing the action on June 19

> *The Jap corpses were all bloated, with juices dripping down and maggots crawling into the mouths, nostrils, ears. . . . They reminded me of turkeys and I couldn't eat turkey for four years.*
> — Ed Jones

Americans heard more and more drunken singing in caves before they tossed in their explosives. For those inside, the dreaded indication that the enemy had actually appeared was usually the repeated *"De-te koi."* Others heard movements of boots or wheels, coughs, voices speaking unintelligible English — or nothing at all until a grenade exploded inside, or a flamethrower's napalm seared. Some quickly died of suffocation or, in some cases, heart failure. But first blasts rarely killed all the occupants of the larger caves.

The survivors moved farther to the interior while more explosives were tossed in, sometimes over the course of days. Some who'd survived the worst of combat, even the reduction of their units to skeletons, now went berserk. American veterans who rightly called battlefield horrors "incomprehensible" — even to infantry school graduates — would themselves have been hard pressed to comprehend the experience here. Deranged men "would suddenly start screaming with their eyes unfocused, jabbering. They would either run out of the cave or deep into its interior, never to return in either case."

The doomed increasingly preferred their own grenades, used on themselves. Increasingly, too — with enemy fire so much reduced — Americans outside stubborn caves called not for single barrels of gasoline but for dousing by trucks that moved up, or for bulldozers to seal their mouths with the occupants inside. More Japanese officers deliberately stood up in the line of fire of American machine guns directly outside their shelters.

The moments of comic relief would be vividly remembered. At a large cave where bullhorns blared with the usual insistence that no one with his hands up would be hurt — "We're sorry for you civilians, so please come out right now" — some civilians finally did emerge from the mouth, which lay below a small plateau. Gripping his weapon in one hand, a Marine Hercules stood above it to snatch skinny women, children, and old men with the other, then lift them, one by one, to the level ground above. "Up you go, Mac . . . that's right, Mac, out you come." When a Japanese soldier appeared at the mouth, American fingers instantly tightened on their triggers. "Easy, Mac," cautioned Hercules. "No trouble, okay?"

"My name's not Mac," replied the Japanese soldier in startlingly clear English. "My name's Yoshio and I'd rather be in Texas, where I ought to be."

To the astonishment of the watchers, who included General Lemuel Shepherd, commander of the 6th Marine Division, Yoshio explained that he'd traveled from his San Antonio home to visit Japanese relatives in 1941, when he was stranded and drafted. This was his first friendly contact with Americans since Pearl Harbor.

Other caves housed a few Okinawan-American teenagers prevented by Pearl Harbor from returning from a visit to *their* relatives. Their war had been especially unhappy, beginning with years of pressure not to reveal that half their hearts as well as half their families remained in the States. Then battle itself, with its fearful American damage to the home island they also loved, tore even harder at their allegiances. Okinawans with no American ties were also stunned by the slaughter of individual Japanese soldiers they knew and liked. Most of the ordinary, unassuming Japanese "Macs" with whom they'd been living or serving had become heaps of filthy corpses.

If all combat seems beyond the pale of human life, the campaign's finale drove the Japanese survivors even farther beyond. A few days after the deaths of Ushijima and Cho, about a third of the forty to fifty soldiers in a large cave nearby began blowing themselves up with grenades while fellow soldiers yards away continued trying to dry their wet uniforms. Meanwhile, more evidence of the catastrophe accumulated at the beaches. Long stretches at the island's far southern end where Hiroshi Uchihata crawled and hobbled were fringed by razor-sharp coral extending a hundred yards seaward. Two steps on the poisonous spikes that slashed the soles of boots and feet were torture. Now thousands of

Japanese were trying to escape — anywhere — along the half-submerged fangs, or to hide somewhere like crabs. Hundreds were picked off by Americans on the cliffs above who, unlike the sentry Uchihata observed, did shoot the tottering targets.

At night, a steady succession of flares lit the coast brighter than a full moon, as a terror-stricken Japanese saw it. By day, the crisscrossing dregs on the beach and farther inland were bewildered without the authority, clear-cut duty, and group allegiance that had formed and nourished them since infancy. The minority willing to give themselves up wandered for days with no idea how to do it. Even Norio Watanabe, the dissident Osaka photographer, felt the surrender for which he'd long yearned would stamp him with dishonor that "must remain all my life." Kuni-ichi Izuchi, who'd been carrying the bones of his friend's cremated hand to return to his family, happened to be his unit's highest-ranking man of about a dozen remaining after June 18. He believed he might be able to save those few if he could muster the courage to suggest they give themselves up, but the idea was "unthinkable, one simply doesn't say such a thing in the Japanese army. The slogan 'Better to be smashed into pieces as a precious stone than survive as a roof tile' was etched deep into us."

Still, Izuchi did include surrender among four choices he put to the survivors. His others were to try to reach the north by breaking through the Americans swarming over the last pocket at Mabuni, to kill themselves with hand grenades, or to try to reach the Chinen Peninsula by swimming out from Mabuni. "Chief, I can't become a prisoner, it's too frightening!" went the very first response. Knowing the fear wasn't only of dishonor but also of "slaughter" by outraged fellow soldiers, Izuchi didn't argue.

The worst wounds of Kenjiro Matsuki's months of miraculous escapes from seemingly hopeless situations were six deep holes in his left leg and hip from a mortar shell. The former professional baseball player dragged himself to a cave where a dozen other soldiers were joined by twenty-one Okinawan nurse's aides. When one of them volunteered to go for water and was hit almost immediately by the rain of shells outside, she used a grenade to blow up two seriously wounded Japanese soldiers together with herself.

The other twenty young women all decided to escape rape and disgraceful death by following her example. No one tried to stop them until Matsuki finally revealed he'd visited Hawaii and could promise the enemy wouldn't abuse them. "You're not soldiers. Please surrender."

After convincing the girls, he secretly tried to persuade a lieutenant to lead them out because the officer, hideously burned by a flamethrowing tank that incinerated the rest of his mortar platoon, couldn't last long without medical help. Even without suggesting surrender, a private daring to address an officer on his own initiative — even one from the same region of Japan, as those two were — testified to how much discipline had crumbled. The lieutenant's eventual agreement perhaps spoke of his background as a teacher and the excruciating pain of his swollen, purple face. Still keeping their plan from the others, Matsuki made a white flag from a piece of cloth and prayed for the girls. Yet he himself, the one Japanese in ten thousand who disbelieved the anti-American propaganda, couldn't bring himself to leave with them and the lieutenant. "To die rather than be captured was central to our education and national life. No matter what I thought personally, I didn't have the courage to go against that or what the old soldiers would have thought of me."

He eventually tried to swim around the enemy lines but was too weak, and the American positions, now armed with nets in the water as well as machine guns overlooking the beach, were too strong. Back on land, he fell asleep making plans for a breakthrough and awoke to half a dozen American rifles pointed down at him. If his last grenades, one for the enemy and one for himself, hadn't been out of reach, he too, the gregarious first baseman who'd played against major-league all-stars, would have killed himself rather than surrender.

Tadashi Kojo didn't know that the evening of June 17, when the commander of the 22nd Regiment sent him the traditional last message of good-luck wishes and a promise to fight to the end, marked the effective end of the 32nd Army, although it would be two more days before Commander Ushijima would make that official. But after the enfeebled captain saw the coordinated attack by American planes, artillery, and tanks on the 22nd regimental headquarters cave less than a thousand yards away, he ordered his radio section to destroy its equipment, then attack the enemy. Six radiomen obediently smashed the set they'd guarded and maintained with scrupulous care since Manchuria, then shook hands in silence, without even the usual "see you soon." "Only our eyes, boring into one another's, conveyed our farewells." Leaving their cave in the darkness of night, the six had no idea of what to "attack." When a small enemy ship just off the beach sent them "a torrential rain of machine gun fire," they fled with their remaining strength.

They were running blindly in a field lacking all cover when a heavy barrage of shells burst almost on top of them. Neither scores of previous shellings during their twelve weeks of battle nor the knowledge that they would surely die within days or hours diminished their terror; it was as if their initiation to artillery bombardment came only now. Private Yoshio Kobayashi was no better at running than as a boy. "Even in desperation, even under the threat of death, slow runners are slow." But he escaped yet again* — and hours later gazed at the sky from a shallow foxhole. It

---

*Running back across the same field at dusk the next day, he was surprised to see a soldier sitting there, arms crossed, legs lazily stretched out. What a brave or stupid man to rest in such a deadly place! Then he saw a face split in half like a watermelon.

struck him that his beloved home in Hokkaido lay under the same stars. What were his parents doing? Thoughts of the strawberries that were at their peak back there thrust him deep in nostalgia.

He and his five companions wildly hoped to somehow infiltrate to the north. After dark the next day, they found the remnants of Kojo's force in two small caves at Maesato, one designated battalion headquarters. Outside, corpses of a unit that had previously occupied the position filled the nine or so yards between two huge rocks. Some of the bodies were still smoking, for although the boulders protected them from most artillery fire, mortar shells had landed between them.

Captain Kojo was there with his fifteen men, of whom more were killed by mortar fire in the morning. American tanks followed, their roaring exhaust announcing they were driving directly up to the caves. The shape and size of the mouth of Kobayashi's protected the interior from direct hits, but its walls were thin. The shells that blasted the surrounding rock from noon until evening seemed like a giant club relentlessly pounding on metal buckets over the men's heads. Kobayashi felt he was losing his mind from that bludgeoning and the acrid smoke that drifted inside, from which it — like the men — had nowhere to escape.

Wounded messengers from nearby caves crawled in that night with news that their units had been reduced to a handful of men or entirely annihilated. Kojo, torn by conflicting concepts of duty, had no orders to leave his position, and now there was no one to give them. But he could neither feed his men nor supply them with arms, water, or even proper cover, a deeply painful admission. Exposed as they were, the ragged survivors could serve only as targets, unable to fight back when dawn — surely their last — would arrive. For the first time in his military life, the quintessential academy graduate made an unauthorized decision — with great difficulty but also conviction. "I can do nothing for my men any longer. Therefore, I'm right to release them from my command, even without orders."

He summoned his messengers, announced he was disbanding the unit, and told them to pass the word that the remaining men were to pair off and exit at midnight for a hand-to-hand attack. Any survivors were to try to break through the enemy lines and find their way north — specifically, to the battalion of academy classmate Captain Tsuneo Shimura, which had been bypassed during the American advance. Kojo had seen reports that Shimura's battalion — of his 24th Division's sister 32nd Regiment — had been unable to join the withdrawal from Shuri because it was surrounded. But it apparently managed a short advance to some high ground roughly three miles north of the old capital, where it continued to hold a pocket. (The reports were generally accurate: Some four hundred officers and soldiers of Shimura's force were indeed alive.) The captain distributed the last of the hardtack, then gave each pair of men two hand grenades, which left one for the final pair, his adjutant and himself. "So this is it," thought Kobayashi, listening to his commander's last order. "This is the end of me." The private gave the captain a final salute and darted back to his own cave to spread the word. Kojo watched the men leave, two by two. His duties as a field officer had ended.

Yoshio Kobayashi managed to escape to the beach after Kojo's order to disband. Three days later, when the American flag was raised at Okinawa's southern tip, he was two miles from there, huddled in a cave with some civilians and soldiers from various units. The thunderclap of a white phosphorous bomb exploding in the dark brought shrieks from women and children while he inhaled poisonous smoke with his uncontrollable coughs. Covering his face with a wet rag and gripping one of the four grenades he'd managed to acquire, he thrust his head into the slime of the cave floor and endured the "slow torture" of Americans approaching, their caution stretching his self-control "beyond limit." "The core of my head freezes in the face of certain death. *Now! Now?* The feeling is beyond my power to describe. Time crawls, yet there's not enough. . . ."

The ray of light inching toward him from behind a curve in the cave was surely from an American flashlight. *Soon now!* Japanese soldiers crept farther into the interior, but he knew it was futile. Now the enemy soldiers were directly in front of him, shouting and beaming their flashlights "like a spotlight on actors." The din of their grenades and automatic fire again rent his ears. His mind blank, he sat up and threw a grenade, whose explosion forced a terrible scream from an enemy soldier. A fragment hit Kobayashi himself in the chest, making each breath excruciating, although they weren't really breaths; he could only pant "like a dog in August" while blood poured down his mud-covered front. "Oh it hurts, it hurts," he chanted, half in delirium. But the light beams disappeared, perhaps thanks to his grenade. The Americans appeared to retreat from the cave.

There was no antiseptic or medicine, but a comrade came to help. Although the bandage Senior Private Maruyama tried to place on the wound in total darkness was a triangular smidgen, contact with his uninjured body provided a surge of comfort — as when Mother takes a sick child's hand, Kobayashi felt.

His dread of being alone surpassed his physical agony. The others' plan to sneak from the cave that night and strike out for the north meant a final parting from them: He was too badly hurt to join. When his last hours with his friends had passed and the time for his abandonment arrived, a flood of sorrow and terror seemed to wash him from the face of the earth. Still, he urged Maruyama to go, and the senior private, although dismayed to leave him, had no alternative. Offering him two of his remaining three grenades, Kobayashi asked that his last one be placed in his hand: "One's enough for me." Repeatedly entreating him not to be "hasty," Maruyama answered that he would return and wanted to find him alive.

When the others had gone, Kobayashi dragged himself around the cave on all fours, hurting as much from his "overwhelming sense of desolation" as from his wound. In mud to his hips, lapsing in and out of consciousness, he supported his torso with his hands, face upturned to endure the suffocation and excruciating pain. Civilians were alive deeper in the cave, but here, where his injuries held him captive, the only sound was a whooshing of bats.

Unconscious, visions of his buddies returning and expressing their delight in finding him alive made him ecstatic. Conscious again, he slithered in circles, comforting himself with the knowledge that when he could endure no more, relief would arrive four seconds after pulling the pin of his grenade. Then he realized that salvation was *missing from his hand!* Gasping with madness, groping for the metal sphere in the blackness, he nevertheless remained terrified by every new noise, as if his life were still precious. He didn't know that over twenty-four hours of near delirium had passed when a native girl returned to the cave and reported that his fellow soldiers had all been killed attempting to break through the American lines. (Caught herself as well, the girl had promised to lead the Americans to Japanese soldiers but ran away from their truck when it stopped.)

Devastated by the death of his last friends, Kobayashi managed, with the girl's help, to crawl deeper into the cave, where civilians were cooking. The sight of them brought immense relief at no longer being alone. An elderly man helped reposition Maruyama's filthy bandage on his chest. The generosity of an elderly woman's gift of a rice ball astonished him until he learned that Maruyama had left her some rice on her promise to feed him after he, Maruyama, had slipped from the cave — to his death, Kobayashi now knew. Sharing his rice ball with the adolescent girl, he couldn't restrain his tears.

28 · The Civilian Toll

We saw civilians who didn't utter a cry with absolutely terrible wounds and maggots crawling all over them. What they endured! Such stoicism!
— Arthur Cofer

The civilians were in just terrible shape — wounded, starving, terrified. You never saw such fear on faces. But we still couldn't trust them because of the gung ho ones mixed in.
— Buzzy Fox

The old were particularly pitiful. Half starved, utterly exhausted, harried from pillar to post during the 80-day-old campaign . . . their faces were solid in misery.
— Major Roy Appleman, a prominent Army historian of the battle

SHORTLY BEFORE OR AFTER Tadashi Kojo had disbanded his command, a much-depleted Company F–2–29 advanced along the same western coast. Some men took a moment to admire the blue and green of the East China Sea shimmering in the sun. LSTs patrolled the coast down there, loudspeakers blaring appeals in Japanese. "The battle's over! Come out with your hands up! You'll be given food and water." Planes dropped yet more leaflets with the same message. The company pushed ahead slowly, rooting out Japanese from ditches, culverts, fields, caves, and demolished houses. The look of the haggard Americans, who were still taking occasional sniper fire and suicide charges, didn't suggest the end was in sight. All were exhausted. "Tense, anxious, jumpy, wasted away," Dick Whitaker would remember. Nights were still a physical and mental ordeal. Noises in the dark would set off a cascade of fire, and new collections of dead "Japs, goats, women, children" would be found in the morning.

The men of the company's point patrol had stopped at the edge of a cliff and were focused on something in its unseen face, facing the sea. When Whitaker reached them, he was told of a large cave mouth there, from which small-arms fire was trying to reach an LST close ashore. Still broadcasting in Japanese, the little ship was also using radio to report the mouth's location and activity to the Marines.

Finding some air vents into the cave from above, the men threw in phosphorous, smoke, and fragmentation grenades and called for napalm, then sprawled on the ground until a fifty-five-gallon drum arrived on an amtrac. The liquid was poured into the vents and set off with another phosphorous grenade. More screams than usual followed because the cave — like many in the far southern end, where some extended ten or more miles — was huge, and civilians from the north had been pouring into it as if from funnels. The Marines were enveloped by the familiar smell of white phosphorus and burning human flesh. The LST radioed that soldiers and civilians, many hardly able to move their ghostly bodies, were teetering from the cave mouth and down the steep cliff. The ship moved in to pick them up from the beach, where other Marines waited to help. Fox Company resumed its advance, and civilians continued to be saved or killed.

Farther south, another company took the last hill and came to a cliff from which civilians were leaping, as at Saipan. Some jumped alone, some in pairs and small groups; a few pushed one another. A platoon leader who'd fought straight through from L-day watched in mixed relief and caution.

> It was like ants when their nest has been dug up. . . . Civilians running here, running there, looking for a place where their fall wouldn't be broken on the way down, for a rock down below where they could hit full. Women too. It was the end of a long rabbit hunt: you'd been flushing them out and they kept running for new cover ahead of you. Now you flushed them out again and they were trapped, so they dove onto the rocks. . . . We didn't shoot them but we didn't try to stop them either. Seeing civilians do all that didn't bother me one bit, not one iota. Maybe I was half crazy myself by that time, I don't know — but I had other worries. I'd seen a lot of horrors by then, including one of my own men killed only a few hours before. What I was worried about was whether one of those milling ants would turn around and try to blow us up.

Actually, virtually all the blowing up civilians attempted was of themselves, not Americans. Until the last day or two, the goal of most families had been to find refuge from the enemy advance. Now it was to avoid capture and agonizing death.

The overwhelming majority remained convinced that surrender would lead to fatal torture. Accounts of relatively humane treatment in the detention camps circulated widely but were so mixed with rumors and wild falsehoods that the desperate refugees had little reason to believe anything good about the hairy, sunburned Americans with their indiscriminately ferocious firepower. More than ever, civilians were on their own, each depleted family responsible for itself. Some Japanese soldiers, especially those who'd been abroad, tried to persuade them to let themselves be captured. But a larger number continued warning to expect American atrocities, and a small number continued shooting "spies" and "traitors" who tried to surrender. "Don't be discouraged," a lieutenant told a group of terrified civilians. "Although Okinawa has fallen victim to the enemy's hands, we haven't come to any decisive, fatal pass."

Those who'd been issued or otherwise obtained hand grenades were envied. "I was in high spirits from the moment I held it in my hand," one would remember. "I could kill myself in a moment. The thought made me shudder with joy." But even when families squeezed together in small caves, the explosion often left a badly wounded survivor or two. Japanese soldiers sometimes finished the job with rifle butts, sticks, or rocks. Okinawans themselves used knives, rakes, hoes, and rocks on family members. Killing women and children with makeshift instruments wasn't difficult, but most people in their severely weakened condition found killing *themselves* nearly impossible. Many parents had to find other methods, including hanging, after dispatching their children.

Two women trying to drown each other on a southern beach by forcing their heads under the water seemed to a Marine "like a pathetic comedy after seeing all that death." A buddy finally waded out and brought them in.

The physical difficulty of accomplishing suicide by other means increased the number who chose cliff jumping. Below them, civilian clothing and shoes were mixed with the uniforms strewn along the beaches "as if people had gone in for a swim," an American observed. "Except that the clothes and shoes were bloody."

All around the island's southern tip, clusters of living Okinawans hid in nooks under cliffs and behind boulders above the water's edge. Now many soldiers appeared willing to surrender, but commanders of still-functioning units ordered final banzai attacks. Those without rifles were instructed to use bamboo spears; those without spears, to gather stones. When attacks were actually launched up the steep cliffs, American fire from the top sent corpses tumbling down to join those decomposing on the beach. The approach of Japanese soldiers faced with such prospects especially frightened the civilians with children. The ferocious ones who demanded rice from their tiny stores and warned of orders to kill all "nuisances" to "military operations" naturally made a sharper impression than the kind and the gentle ones.

While a relatively well-groomed woman emerged from a cave at southernmost Kyan Point ("Suicide Cliff") and tried to strangle herself with her kimono sash, other civilians reasoned that killing oneself because other family members were already dead would leave no one to remember their tragedy. But even those who argued that although death from one side or the other seemed inevitable, people must try to stay alive every possible moment quaked when Americans reached their groups to herd and help them back up the cliffs — where, many were certain, waiting trucks would take them to tanks that would crush their bones.

Some members of the Okinawan elite insisted the "temporary" setbacks changed nothing important. The Kadena chief of police was among those giving assurances that the 32nd Army was strong enough to carry on and that Ushijima's air officer had escaped to Tokyo to lead the air assault that would precede the Japanese counterlanding. (Lieutenant Colonel Naomichi Jin was indeed among the staff officers ordered to escape instead of killing themselves.) Meanwhile, patriotic young Okinawans shouldered on. After delivering his message to the Yoza-dake cave, Shin-ichi Kuniyoshi, the fourteen-year-old communications soldier who hadn't moved a muscle while maggots ate into his orifices during his sixteen hours of hiding among corpses, was told his unit had moved farther south. Picking a route through territory still in Japanese hands, he climbed down the mountain and walked the three miles in several hours.

The new position was on Hill 89. Not knowing of Ushijima's and Cho's suicides there, Shin-ichi was happy to find five or six classmates in his cave, survivors of their original group of forty-six. They were surprised by the excellent Japanese of the surrender appeals broadcast by an American flotilla patrolling some three hundred yards from the beach below. "Japan has lost so cease your useless resistance. Come out now with your hands up and you won't be harmed." *"Won't be harmed,"* snorted Shin-ichi, knowing he could expect nothing as good as a swift death from any American. But disturbing talk about Japanese soldiers who were sharing the same large cave reached the boys on the morning of June 23, the day the 10th Army brass would declare Okinawa secure. Shin-ichi reasoned that even if their traitorous talk about Japan losing the war were true, it couldn't answer the question of what he, *a Japanese soldier,* should do.

Below Hill 89 and the adjacent cliffs lay a strip of junglelike vegetation, then massive boulders interspersed with pockets of coral and sandy beach bordering the sea. Shin-ichi watched Japanese soldiers making their difficult way down the cliff, through the dense growth, and into the water. Some swam out toward the American ships, others only far enough to drown themselves. More remained on shore, saving their honor by shooting the swimmers who betrayed an intention to surrender.

Back in the cave, some of his little group wanted to save themselves, however slim the chances, while others insisted on obeying their final order to infiltrate to the north and fight to the last. Remembering his vow to his dead friend Miyagi, skeletal Shin-ichi didn't want to swim anywhere or even think of surrender. But his desire to continue fighting had drained away, together with his energy. He decided to join some of the boys and a dozen Japanese who, led by an unusually trustworthy and decent soldier, indeed went north, toward the spot where Japanese units were supposedly still strong and in high spirits.

Lacking a destination, most civilians stayed put during those final days. On June 24, a high school teacher who'd believed the Japanese propaganda as staunchly as most had a sudden change of mind. No one, he now reasoned, could be as cruel as Americans were painted. Human beings were human beings, after all, and it wasn't their nature to kill. Using all his powers of persuasion on himself and a dozen female students who were sitting in a tight circle so their three hand grenades would kill them all, he managed to stop them from detonating the weapons at the last moment.

Two days later, a Japanese soldier in a cave urged a forty-one-year-old man to make ready to die. Doing that, then tossing aside his last bag of rice, the latter left the mouth, where souvenir-happy Americans merely searched him and relieved his pockets of their paltry contents. The same day, after phosphorous and fragmentation grenades burned and blasted two families to death in a tiny cave a mile up the coast from Mabuni, an infant's cries stopped the American team just before it proceeded to the next cave. Then they rushed a burned, blackened, wormy orphan to treatment and survival.

On the day of the southern flag-raising, a five-year-old with large areas of skin seared off by a flamethrower sought relief by running toward the sea along the razor-sharp coral. Slightly smaller and younger than the napalmed Vietnamese child whose photograph would become one of that war's starkest symbols of native suffering, this one was no less horribly burned. He was one of up to one hundred thousand civilians — the number merits repeating — who perished in June, most during the last ten days. Fifty years later, native experts would still disagree about a precise figure and predict it would never be known due to the total demolishment of so many registry offices, together with all inhabitants of villages who would have remembered their neighbors. But it's fairly certain that almost as many died as survived — more than servicemen of both sides combined.

Before the survivors stopped expecting anything like equal treatment, Okinawans used to wonder why so little attention was paid to their numbers. They felt it altogether right for mainland Japanese families to stream to the island to hold memorial services for their dead and to search for the bones of the missing. The annual expressions of international grief on the anniversary of Hiroshima's losses were also right and good — but how to explain the scant interest in the larger Okinawan ones?* While the atomic victims were categorized in minute detail by age, sex, occupation, distance from the epicenter, and other indices, the Okinawan dead remained almost secret. And in general, the enormous torment of the bombs for the Japanese cities was less tragic for Japan than the months of fighting for Okinawa, which bore far less responsibility for having started the war.

Fifty-five years after Hiroshima and Nagasaki, their precise death tolls are also unknown. Estimates vary between a 1967 United Nations figure of seventy-eight thousand in Hiroshima and twenty-seven thousand in Nagasaki to more than thrice that in later Japanese accounting. Some experts take 140,000 and 70,000 as a best final estimate: a combined total some 25 percent higher than on Okinawa, where final guesses put the figure at about 150,000 civilians. Of course the Okinawan deaths — and those of an additional ten thousand Koreans brought in to perform heavy labor and camp services for the 32nd Army — were caused by conventional weapons, a crucial difference for some thinkers. But if one innocent life is as sacred as another — if what shocks and dismays about Hiroshima and Nagasaki is their appalling numbers — the comparison with Okinawa must be pursued. The American forces alone fired 7.5 million thirty-seven-millimeter to eight-inch howitzer rounds, 60,018 five- to six-inch naval shells, 392,304 hand grenades, 20,359 rockets, and just under thirty million machine-gun, rifle, and pistol rounds into the island. Together with the Japanese contribution, that staggering weight of metal lacerated almost as much Okinawan flesh as the two atomic bombs seared Japanese. And the greater number of civilians slaughtered on Okinawa than in either Hiroshima or Nagasaki more often died in days or weeks rather than minutes, with that much more time to witness their families' agony. A third of all Okinawans were probably killed, and most of the island's national and cultural artifacts were demolished. Few peoples have suffered such a catastrophe.

The Japanese rightly feel their war losses were calamitous. Only in comparison with Okinawa's can they seem less so. "Look at it this way, the way the Japanese never seem to and Americans have never thought of," said a long-term American resident of Okinawa in 1990. "The relatives of Japanese soldiers killed and missing in action here have been visiting the

---

*Native estimates may be more reliable than Japanese or American because the Okinawan tendency to exaggerate is probably less pronounced than the former belligerents' tendency to underestimate. Washington's record in coming to terms with the hardest truths of the war has been less dismal only than Tokyo's. But some of that failure is due to "innocent" rather than intentional ignorance. Not even American fighters on the island who witnessed a portion of the destruction had any way to appreciate the total. Until he was properly informed forty years later, a general in command of a fighting division believed twenty-two thousand civilians died in all.

island for decades, expressing legitimate grief over what their poor men endured. What they never seem to realize is that every Okinawan family was devastated far worse. No matter what happened to Japan, it was easier than what happened to Okinawa. Many Japanese talk about the atomic bomb with deep, moving pain while they're here, never thinking that Okinawans lost much more than two cities — just about their whole island."

The imprecise casualty figures make much of this speculative, like the estimates of the psychological damage to the "unwounded." Trekking south with her family in June, an eleven-year-old passed infants sucking at dead mothers' breasts and beheld an aunt standing at her side ripped apart by a shell. Through all of that, she clutched her prized report cards as her school's top student, as if they were her connection to the sane world of *before*. In the end, however, the extended trauma of explosions and carnage destroyed her ability to read and write. So it went for lucky survivors — and the tragedy would continue *after*, when a world well informed and regularly reminded about the atomic deaths would scarcely hear of the Okinawan.

29 · The Atomic Bombs

The U.S. Army is sure to attack and indeed has the power to do so. The sooner the enemy comes, the better for us, for our battle array is complete.
— Radio Tokyo, June 28, on the loss of Okinawa

The immense cost of capturing the island, in human and material terms, did undoubtedly have a considerable influence on the decision to use atomic weapons. American leaders were left in no doubt that the losses in American lives increased dramatically the closer they came to the Japanese homeland. The experience of Okinawa . . . the most brutal military engagement between American and Japanese forces in the war . . . convinced them that invasion was too high a price to pay.
— Ian Gow, military historian

I lived through Okinawa somehow, but the great battle of the mainland lay ahead. How long could my luck hold? Then the dropping of the A-bomb put a brand-new light in my life. I'd be going home, after all. And I did!
— Thomas Hannaher, American artilleryman

THE EMOTIONAL END FOR THE AMERI-CANS who fought the campaign came not when they were shipped out but a month later. Crammed into LSTs and troopships for another rough voyage to rear bases for rest and retraining, the exhausted units, composed mostly of replacements for the casualties, were too spent to contemplate the warning of the 6th Marine Division's commander that they'd completed merely "a prelude" to the fighting ahead. Norris Buchter's combat friends, all "too tired and too tense to think of the future," were typical. "We'd never really slept during the months on Okinawa, even when we supposedly slept. After those months constantly on edge, all we could think of was the relief of getting off the island to anywhere we could sleep a whole night through."

The trip to the largest rear base on Guam took a week. Skinny, nineteen-year-old Corporal James Day, winner of a Bronze Star for heroism on Sugar Loaf, spent a month on a work party there, loading ships for the planned landing on the home islands. Then he heard the news about Hiroshima, and his elation was immense. Also on Guam, Dick Whitaker, still a company runner, spent most of his time happily cooling his heels in the Quonset hut of battalion headquarters or delivering messages from there instead of training in scorching fields for Operation Downfall, the forthcoming invasion of invasions. Whitaker had felt and seen no joy when the Stars and Stripes was raised on Okinawa's southern tip because the ceremony wouldn't free him or his mates from further fighting. But all erupted wildly when "the poop" about the odd thing called the atomic bomb was translated into the single essential fact for them. "It was instant pandemonium. We whooped and yelled like mad. We shot bullets into the air and danced between the tent rows, because this meant maybe we were going to live, and not as cripples."

The jubilation was universal. "Everyone knew [Okinawa] was just the last stepping-stone to the really terrible stuff waiting on the Jap home islands," a wounded comrade would agree about the lack of relief when that campaign ended. "Everybody knew if he hadn't been hit so far he soon would be because we were going from the Oki slaughter to a much worse one." For them, Hiroshima "lifted a great blanket of impending doom," as an Army sergeant named Donald Dencker would remember.

Operation Downfall's general concept had been approved in the autumn of 1944, roughly when Okinawa was chosen over Formosa as that last stepping-stone. Two days after L-day, the Joint Chiefs of Staff instructed General MacArthur to begin detailed planning for the suboperation titled "Olympic," the initial landing on southernmost Kyushu. President Truman gave it final approval on June 18, the day of General Buckner's death. Although few on Guam knew the new D-day was set for November 1, eleven weeks after the Hiroshima bomb, its imminence was common knowledge. It was no secret that the stream of bombers taking off from Guam's airfields was softening up the landing areas. (Prelanding naval bombardments of the Japanese coasts, most notably by three of America's four *Iowa*-class battleships, and by the Royal Navy's *King George V*, also started in mid-July.) It was no secret either to veteran infantrymen that all the bombardment in the world wouldn't keep their blood from pouring in a confrontation with a defense bound to be much stronger than Okinawa's. The news came to one man when he lay badly wounded in a San Francisco naval hospital. "My whole body shouted, 'Thank God for the A-bomb!' Because otherwise I'd have been sent out to more combat as soon as I was patched up — and killed sooner or later. Those were the odds. I was overjoyed."

Okinawa veterans' sympathy for the atomic victims was greatly lessened by their conviction that the alternative would have been their own deaths or crippling injuries. Certain of that, they'd feel pity, contempt, or anger — most of which would turn to resignation over the years — for noncombatants who later branded the bomb's use as unnecessary and immoral. Their gut told them there was no other way but to kill the Japanese, that all the rest was talk, that no one could understand — because it was otherwise incomprehensible — unless he'd fought the singular enemy.

Although they, with their profound self-interest and severely limited perspective from foxhole lips, weren't necessarily right about "the beautiful bomb," they weren't necessarily wrong either. Virtually every American who fought in the Pacific saw the awful weapon as a "miracle of deliverance," as Winston Churchill poetized for them. Eugene Sledge, the devout private who'd been sickened to the depths of his soul by the horrors on Okinawa, noted that those still more or less whole afterward viewed the next phase "with complete resignation that we would be killed." Frazzled veterans of all island battles wondered why they'd survived so far only to have to die on Kyushu or Honshu, sites of the first and second mainland landings — the latter just below Tokyo, planned for the following March.

That's why the end of the fighting on Okinawa produced the scant American emotion — not even a beer ration — while news of the atomic bombs caused the euphoria. Some of the toughest veterans broke down and cried with relief.

Their joy obviously doesn't resolve the ethical questions about using the appalling weapons. Nor can that be done on these pages — or, probably, *any* pages. Certainly the libraries of previous writings haven't done it. All that *can* be done here is to ask whether the Battle of Okinawa can throw any light on the tortured question, remembering that the sum of its civilian and military deaths probably exceeded those in Hiroshima and Nagasaki combined, and that the cultural devastation was greater and longer lasting.

Nor, however, does that comparison supply the answer, since no amount of previous death and destruction can justify the bombs' hideous devastation if they were unnecessary. Still, the Okinawan tragedy may help clear some of the historical haze in which the later Hiroshima and Nagasaki ones are commemorated. Their ghoulish images of seared, irradiated civilians understandably blurred perception of larger realities in Asia. The new weapon produced far more graphic ruin than anything previous and did it in two stunningly dramatic events, each with one plane, one bomb, and one obliterated city. It posed a greater threat to the future than the heaviest concentration of bullets, mortar shells, torpedoes, and conventional bombs had done. Here was stark evidence of humanity's ability to mutilate itself. Still, those images convey only a fragment of the Pacific War's misery — which must figure in the debate about whether the A-bombs ultimately increased or diminished it.

* * *

Pro-bomb American politicians long denied that their real or chief purpose was more to frighten Moscow than to hasten the end of the war. Not for the first or last time in our relationship with the scheming Soviet Union, that was a lie. It's now beyond dispute that some high administration officials, led by Secretary of State James F. Byrnes, were indeed eager to demonstrate American power to Stalin — who, after Germany's surrender, was already busy dividing Europe into East and West. Still, most decisions are made for more than one reason, so this doesn't invalidate the conventional wisdom that Harry Truman made his untroubled choice much under the influence of the unexpected duration and ferocity of Ushijima's defense. At least that much is true. From the time the new president took office in mid-April, the casualties on Okinawa almost equaled those of the previous three years in the Pacific, ever since, and including, Pearl Harbor. Dreading "an Okinawa from one end of Japan to the other," Truman — an Army veteran who'd seen some of World War I's carnage with his own eyes — was shocked by answers to his pointed requests for the final count of dead and wounded.

But whether or not the old artilleryman knew the full impact of combat suffering — he almost certainly knew little about the civilian tragedy — isn't the point. Since bad decisions can be made for good reasons, the question is less why this one was made but whether it was right.

The servicemen who never had the slightest doubt to begin with quickly confirmed their own answer. The occupation force sent to the Japanese mainland after her surrender included the 4th Marine Regiment, reconstituted after its near annihilation in 1942. Following an emotional meeting with gaunt prisoners who'd surrendered on Bataan and Corregidor, its current members saw what one called the "unbelievable concrete and firepower" that would have faced them in the second phase of the aborted invasion, at Tokyo Bay.

High seawalls backed by gun-bristling fortifications more formidable than the Shuri Line's silenced Americans in other units of the occupation force who visited their planned landing sites. One insisted that clusters of dreaded heavy cannon now flying white flags from their barrels would have "blown us out of the water."

Hyperbole aside, inspection of the weaponry prepared for *Ketsu-Go,* the operation to crush the American landings, corroborated that casualties were certain to be much higher against Japanese defending the familiar terrain of their sacred home islands than they'd been on distant possessions and conquered territory. "I don't think many of the Oki vets would have been around to talk to you without the beautiful bomb" was scant exaggeration. Robert Stewart saw plans that made his 2nd Marine

Division — the one that had gone into reserve after making the decoy landing on Okinawa — one of the invasion's spearheads. Those plans made no mention of the unit after D-day plus 4. "In other words, our losses would have been so great my division would no longer have been a serviceable division after the fourth day," Stewart would observe.

One infantryman noted that his canceled landing site near Nagasaki, eighty miles northwest of Kagoshima, had "enough ammunition to keep its hundreds of guns firing for months." But more than heavy coastal artillery and unprecedented stocks of shells chilled Okinawa veterans. The potential killing grounds also held large supplies of bamboo spears with knives tied to their ends. Since all men of fighting age were gone from the area, the observers supposed women and children would have used the makeshift weapons. "Who the hell could have shot those women and kids?" asked one. He paused. "I guess we'd have had to."

The speculation about the spears was also correct. The day after the southern flag-raising on Okinawa, the Imperial Army took command of the volunteer corps operating in mainland residential neighborhoods and workplaces. The members of that "final people's movement" were chiefly civilian men under sixty-five and women under forty-five, but students were also mobilized into fighting corps — great numbers of them because so many war plants previously employing student labor had been bombed out or idled for lack of raw materials. The calls for the hundred million to "die proudly" were more insistent than ever. (Mainland Japan's population was actually closer to seventy-five million in 1945; the commonly used hundred million figure included citizens living in colonies.)

Never mind the absurdity of bamboo. As with the kamikaze pilots, sacrifice in a futile cause was part of the goal and reward. Drilling with carpenter's awls, high school girls were told "to guard their honor like samurai" against invading troops. When the Americans come, a teacher instructed, they must be ready to "settle" the war "by drawing on our Japanese spirit and killing them."

> Even killing just one American soldier will do. . . . You must aim at the enemy's abdomen, understand? The abdomen! If you don't kill at least one enemy soldier, you don't deserve to die!

A fifteen-year-old who confided to her diary that they'd have looked ridiculous facing American flamethrowers and machine guns with such tools dutifully took part in the drills nevertheless. "One reason for persisting . . . was that no one wanted to be blamed for quitting. Another was that people weren't fully aware of the grim situation in Okinawa, the Pacific or even the Japanese cities unless they happened to be there."

Of course the principal resistance would have been military. The Japanese war machine that critics of using the bombs would pronounce finished had four million men under arms. (Ushijima had had about ninety thousand, not counting the Okinawan Home Guard.) Although saving their honor by fighting to the end couldn't possibly have achieved anything more than inflicting damage before they died, that damage would have been terrible. Thousands of planes were intact — the tallies vary from three to sixteen thousand — many of which were carefully hidden and designated for kamikaze use. Some five thousand additional pilots were being trained to fly them. Had they been sent up, with their shorter distances to cover, the toll inflicted would have been stunning, and supplemented by a panoply of old and new suicide weapons. (The radio commentator who said he looked forward to an early landing "just to sense the thrill when we strike a deadly blow to the enemy" and promised "worldwide amazement" at Japan's array of "special attack" weapons wasn't entirely bluffing about the latter.) Allied naval brass, knowing the Japanese had been concentrating on the mainland's defense for months, braced for much more intense kamikaze attacks than those at Okinawa.

Unlike the earlier concentration on warships, the chief targets this time — in an effort to shatter the invaders' morale with the maximum possible casualties — would have been the troops wading in to land. However, the greatest toll would have been farther inland, where "the incomparable Japanese infantry," as an American analyst later assessed it, would have been supported by vastly more artillery than on Okinawa. American anticipation of the cost was evident in the forty-two divisions allotted to the invasion. Seven had fought on Okinawa.

The often cited total of a million American casualties is fanciful. That figure appears to have made its public debut eighteen months after the fact, in a magazine article by Secretary of War Henry Stimpson, although other writers would claim the source was General MacArthur, whose casualty estimates in previous battles had been uncannily accurate. MacArthur did make a careful study of the mainland operation at President Truman's request, but his prediction was much lower.* Although

---

*Winston Churchill nevertheless seized on the round-figure estimate. "Up to this moment," he would write about the Potsdam Conference in late July, when Truman informed him of the results of the final test of the atomic bomb in Nevada, "we had shaped our ideas towards an assault upon the homeland by terrific air bombing and by the invasion of very large armies. We had contemplated the desperate resistance of the Japanese fighting to the death with samurai devotion, not only in pitched battles but in every cave and dugout. I had in my mind the spectacle of Okinawa Island. To quell the Japanese resistance man by man and conquer the country ward by ward might well require the loss of a million American lives and half that number of British — or more if we could get them there: for we were resolved to share the agony."

several other agencies conducted studies then and later, no one can say how good their estimates were, because it was impossible to know how much more fighting would be necessary to overrun the entire mainland or compel a surrender. Those were the crucial questions, on which Japanese attitudes at Okinawa surely bear.

> *The entire population of Japan is a proper Military Target. . . . THERE ARE NO CIVILIANS IN JAPAN.*
> — 5th Air Force intelligence report, July 21, 1945

> *How the hell are you going to storm a country where women and children, everybody would be fighting you? Of course we'd have won eventually, but I don't think anybody who hasn't actually seen the Japanese fight can have any idea of what it would have cost.*
> — Austin Aria, American infantryman

The predictability of the veterans' renewed love for the bomb when they saw what it saved them from is no reason to dismiss arguments for its use. Of course it killed many people, but the equation, if there is one, must include those it saved, to the extent that saving now seems established and the number can be estimated. Although the American fighting men who cheered Little Boy and Fat Man for bestowing them with survival cared virtually nothing about the Japanese losses, they, the enemy deaths, must of course be taken into consideration — but not simply the gruesome ones at Hiroshima and Nagasaki.

The ratio of Japanese combat deaths to American was over 10 to 1 on Okinawa. It might have been marginally lower if fighting had proceeded to the enemy's heartland, where reinforcements would have been more easily available than to the Japanese garrisons on the cut-off islands. However, civilian deaths from conventional combat surely would have been much higher, if only because the mainland had many more civilians who were committed to die for Emperor and country. The best estimates of total Japanese deaths in a conventional mainland campaign are five to ten million. If civilian suicides and suicidal resistance had generated hysteria — a likely prospect in light of the experience on Guam and Okinawa — the toll might have been higher.

The country would have been leveled and burned to cinders. New information confirms that Stalin was preparing to land troops on the northernmost home island of Hokkaido (home to many of Captain Kojo's soldiers). If the Red Army had seized it, Japanese casualties, extrapolating from the number of POWs who died in Soviet camps, would have reached four hundred thousand. That would have been just a part of the loss if, as a full Allied partner during ground combat from 1945 to 1946 or later, Stalin insisted on dividing Japan, like Korea and Germany.

All postwar life, starting with retarded economic recovery, would have suffered heavily.

Any estimate of the savings gained by the atomic bombs must also include hundreds of thousands of combatants and civilians in China, Manchuria, and other territories still occupied, often viciously, by Japan. The Pacific War had already claimed at least sixteen million lives, three million of which were Japanese. (The American figure in both the Atlantic and Pacific theaters was roughly 290,000.) In China alone, only three more months of it would probably have cost a hundred thousand more. In addition, tens of thousands of British soldiers would have been killed and wounded among the two hundred thousand scheduled to invade the Malay Peninsula on September 9, a month after Nagasaki. Six divisions, the same number as at Normandy, had been assigned to that operation, which was expected to take seven months of savage fighting, over half the time required to defeat Hitler's armies in Europe.

The savings must also include European and Eurasian prisoners of the Japanese, chiefly from English and Dutch colonial military and civil forces. After the fall of Okinawa, Field Marshal Hisaichi Terauchi directed his prison camp commanders to kill all their captives the moment the enemy invaded his Southeast Asia theater — which would have been in September, when those two hundred thousand British landed to retake Singapore. There was a real chance that some or many of Count Terauchi's subordinates would have carried out his order, in which case up to another four hundred thousand people would have been massacred.

Even more were doomed to soon die of "natural" causes. Japanese treatment of their prisoners grew more brutal as the military situation worsened and their hatred swelled. Dying daily in droves throughout the summer of 1945, even more would have perished of disease and starvation during the following winter. Laurens van der Post, who'd been a prisoner for more than forty months, was convinced the majority of the half-million captives in the hellish camps couldn't possibly have survived the year 1946.

Those numbers might justify Churchill's use of "deliverance" for the atomic bombs, even knowing the cost was the hundred thousand or more horrible deaths of men, women, and children. The natural wish to dismiss that price as too dreadful can be satisfied only by denying the more dreadful military and political realities of 1945.

On the other hand, the figures are an eternal indictment if an invasion was unnecessary. Once again, that is the real question. Did even those hundred thousand have to die at Hiroshima and Nagasaki? Wasn't Japan already beaten?

Japan was finished as a warmaking nation [but] . . . Japan's leaders were
going to fight right on. To not lose face was more important than hundreds and
hundreds of thousands of lives. . . . To continue was no longer a question of
Japanese military thinking, it was an aspect of Japanese culture and psychology.
— James Jones, *WW II*

The cabinet expected the volunteers to be home-front equivalents of the kamikaze
pilots, who went into battle with meager weapons fully prepared to die. . . .
Civilians may have been fed up and the volunteers may have felt foolish
training with spears and awls, but nearly everyone on the home front kept up the
fight to the very end.
— Thomas R. H. Havens, *Valley of Darkness: The Japanese People and World War*
Two

The country's woeful condition before the bombs were dropped was
hardly secret either. Virtually her entire merchant marine and Navy lay at
the bottom of the Pacific, while America alone, without the Royal Navy,
had twenty-three battleships, ninety-nine carriers, and seventy-two cruisers on hand in August. The Imperial Navy's corresponding numbers
were one, six, and four — and it had fuel enough only to sustain a force
of twenty operational destroyers and perhaps forty submarines (supported by suicide boats and other small craft) for a few days at sea. Nor
was sufficient food available for civilians who showed their ration cards in
the shops that still stood. Relentless saturation bombing, easier than ever
with the new bases on Okinawa and the feeble opposition from Japanese
interceptors, was leveling Japan's cities.

The average adult existed on under thirteen hundred calories a day. As
many as thirteen million were homeless. Malaria and tuberculosis were
rampant, especially in the shantytowns rising in the urban ashes. Schoolchildren, barefoot in winter as well as summer, rooted out forest pine
stumps for the war effort. The trees themselves were long gone. In
Tokushima, home city of many of the six thousand troops lost on *Toyama*
maru, metal was so scarce that the bells of shrines were melted down, together with charcoal braziers, the sole source of heat for the remaining
wood-and-paper homes. While huge numbers of Red Army troops mobilized to attack Manchuria — just as Tadashi Kojo had feared a year earlier, when his regiment was shipped from there to Okinawa — there was
no hope of supplying the defenders even if the merchant fleet hadn't
been destroyed and the country's industry wasn't in shambles. Exhausted, slowly starving Japan was in no shape for further fighting.

Many in high positions knew that, of course. The cabinet of Hideki
Tojo had resigned on the day the fall of Saipan was made public, eight
and a half months before Okinawa's L-day. Everyone who knew the ellip-
tical statements of Japanese politics understood that such a change of

government after a military blow of that force was an admission of defeat and of desire to end the debacle.

Tojo's successor, Kuniaki Koiso, wanted a truce and tried to obtain it, partly with a flimsy attempt to negotiate with Washington and London through Chiang Kai-shek. *His* replacement, an elderly baron named Kantaro Suzuki, tried harder. The partially peace-seeking cabinet of the third wartime prime minister was installed the day after *Yamato*'s sinking. Suzuki's necessary noises would soon include the proposition that Okinawa's loss had *improved* Japan's strategic position while dealing a crushing spiritual blow to America: "Now is the time for every one of the hundred million . . . to become glorious shields for the defense of the national structure." But the clearest signal of his real intentions was the appointment of career diplomat Shigenori Togo as foreign minister. Disgusted by the Pearl Harbor trickery, Togo went on to become one of Japan's most forceful critics of the war and the military establishment.

Until recently, the Emperor, a little like Tsar Nicholas II during World War I, had been more concerned with preserving his imperial prerogatives than with ameliorating the suffering of his people. Like his Army leadership, he firmly believed that the "decisive" battle would take place in the homeland, and did nothing to encourage responses to American peace feelers in May, while the Shuri Line held. (No response was made.) But by the summer, his earlier satisfaction in the expanding Empire was gone. As he'd reveal soon after the war, the smashing of the 32nd Army convinced him that Okinawa must be the final battle; there was now "no choice but unconditional surrender." On June 22, 1945, the day before the southern flag-raising, he summoned the Supreme War Council to the Imperial Palace. Expressing deep concern about the state of the war, he apparently suggested that diplomatic feelers should be made to try to end it. In other words, he'd become a supporter of the peace faction, inasmuch as the scattered individuals it comprised deserved to be called a faction and his guarded hints could be construed as substantive support.

Now the government renewed earlier efforts to persuade Moscow to use its good offices for negotiations with the Allies. Since Stalin was already moving huge forces from Germany to join the struggle against Japan, however, those efforts had not the slightest chance for success. Still, the unknowing Japanese peace advocates pursued Moscow more and more urgently while Hirohito sought to encourage talk of peace in confidential meetings with former prime ministers. The *jushin,* as that small group was called, were in tacit alliance with other elder statesmen — even a few military leaders such as Admiral Mitsumasa Yonai, the minister of the Navy who hadn't opposed *Yamato*'s sortie as vigorously as he'd wanted to because he was already preoccupied by the larger question of how to stop the war.

The sprinkling of peace advocates included Marquis Koichi Kido, the Lord Privy Seal and Hirohito's closest political adviser. Among their other efforts were three probes in Sweden and Switzerland. While those were being pursued, cabinet members marshaled evidence that continued fighting was impossible and the Emperor's confidential advisers urged more directly, and to ever more receptive ears, that the war was lost and must be stopped. The forbidden word *peace* was even pronounced in (restricted) public. How, then, can the slaughter of Hiroshima's and Nagasaki's civilians possibly be justified? Didn't American policy makers know that Japanese slogans in the summer of 1945 — "The sooner they [the Americans] come, the better. . . . One hundred million die proudly" — were ritual bleats by the vanquished and humiliated?

> *The atomic bomb attacks and the Soviet entry into the war, thus deteriorating our position, shocked us. But we can take some countermeasures. . . . We still have enough fighting strength remaining. Furthermore, don't we have large army forces still intact on the Chinese continent and in our homeland? It might be the view of some clever fellows to surrender with some strength left instead of being completely destroyed. . . . But those fellows advocating that idea are nothing but selfish weaklings who don't think seriously about the future of the nation and only seek immediate benefits.*
> — August 11 diary entry of Admiral Matome Ugaki, commander of the 5th Air Fleet on Kyushu, which carried out kamikaze and conventional attacks on the American fleet off Okinawa

> *This is a great problem for me. . . . Although an Emperor's order must be followed, I can hardly bear to see us suspend attacks while we still have this fighting strength. I think many things remain to be done after consulting with those brave men willing to die.*
> — Ugaki on the possibility that Japan might surrender after the destruction of Hiroshima and Nagasaki

The atomic killing can be justified only if the growing opposition to the war by the Imperial household and elements of the government and the military were irrelevant because they were totally doomed to fail. And the evidence — although it can never, by the nature of things, be wholly convincing — points in that direction. For example, the Japanese ambassador in Moscow believed the peace overtures to Stalin were "ridiculous" because they claimed too much for Japan. At that point, even the Emperor preferred waiting for a more "favorable moment" to offer serious concessions, meanwhile keeping up the fight to show the *Americans* "the disadvantages of continuing the war." More to the point, the government wouldn't accept Washington's demand for unconditional surrender because the military still controlled it.

How solidly? Those who wanted to end the war were frightened, no matter how high their positions. Prime Minister Koiso had undertaken his peace initiatives in great secrecy, probably in fear for his life. Even Prime Minister Kantaro Suzuki, an admiral and hero of the Russo-Japanese War of 1905 as well as a baron, could not make direct approaches for negotiation without courting another attempt on his life. (The first had been in 1936. The seventy-eight-year-old Grand Chamberlain was weakened by a bullet still lodged in his heart from the time of the extreme ultranationalists' most ambitious coup attempt.) Besides, all the would-be peacemakers were on the periphery of real state power. Japan remained dominated by the Supreme War Council's die-hard faction, the very kind of "Manchuria Gang" activists and sympathizers who had terrorized and assassinated opponents in the 1920s and 1930s and helped push the country into her wars. Even the civilian leaders who'd begun whispering the hitherto blasphemous thought that the fighting had to stop had scant hope it would. The Lord Privy Seal put it in a nutshell in early June, when the 32nd Army was facing its annihilation on Okinawa. In a secret memorandum to the throne, Marquis Kido ventured that Japan had lost the war, "regrettable though it is." Nevertheless, the overriding determinant was the military leaders' will to "fight to the death." Therefore, he had to advise the Emperor that any peace move was "almost impossible."

The public record is long and full on the real rulers' refusal to consider negotiation until after a "decisive" Tennozan on the mainland. So far, the old guard insisted, the war had been a series of indecisive skirmishes; now was the time to lure the Americans to their annihilation in the final battle on Japanese soil required for preservation of the national honor. Some 150,000 dead Okinawans were proof of their determination to continue sacrificing any number of civilians to that resolution. "Even if the Japanese people are weary of the war," Commander of the Combined Fleet Admiral Soemu Toyoda insisted, "we must fight to the last man." And scarcely any of those "last men" themselves — the cannon fodder — made the slightest sign of opposition, let alone protest, no more than did Captain Kojo's doomed men. Most Japanese, including civilians, still couldn't conceive of any other end to the war than victory or death. Just before the Emperor's August 14 broadcast telling his people to accept defeat, Tokyo shopkeepers sharpened knives, expecting an order for the entire nation to commit suicide.

But the decisions lay with the military diehards, and fighting to the death was indeed what they were utterly resolved to do. To men such as Toyoda and War Minister General Korechika Anami, death for honor and Japan was more than ever life's purpose. That same August, Captain Kojo, who'd known for months of his Emperor's order to capitulate, didn't do so, even though he had no men to command and no military function whatever. No thought of surrender ever entered the conscious thoughts of the desperate straggler on Okinawa because he yearned for *his* war to end in his death, just as thousands of otherwise admirable kamikaze pilots had sought personal rewards, not military advantage, from their gestures. Although the political generals in Tokyo could not have entirely avoided mention of surrender, it represented to them the worst conceivable eventuality, incomparably worse than expiration.

Little of the military affirmation was bombast. None of it changed until the atomic bombs, both of them. Even then, some of the key generals insisted the fighting should continue in the ashes. And the resolution of even the less fiercely committed decision makers ebbed so slowly, with such distant prospect of the eventual acceptance of common sense over *bushido*, the Way of the Warrior, that continued resistance was all but inevitable. Their relegation of other considerations — such as the desire to continue living — to secondary importance much diminishes the significance of the evidence of Japan's weakened condition and the small but waxing peace faction.

That situation wouldn't have gone on forever, but surely for the remainder of 1945, to make an optimistic estimate. Since the commanders of the Army and the nation were almost certain to prevail, if necessary by assassinating any "weaklings" who dared speak openly about ending the war, the documentation of the country's wretched condition after the defeat on Okinawa is indeed largely irrelevant: It demonstrates that further fighting was senseless in *Western* perception, but not that of the ruling Japanese. The handful of leaders who wanted to negotiate peace had an extremely slim chance of performing the unprecedented feat of convincing the Imperial Army diehards to abandon the powerful code and passionate ethic under which they had striven until now.

That they'd have had utterly no hope of victory in the "decisive" battle wasn't the point for the Manchuria Gang, even less than it had been for the admirals who had sacrificed *Yamato* in their war for honor. Many areas of the mainland much resembled Okinawa in terrain; Kyushu in particular was even more riddled with caves. As for supplies, Japan's armory had enough for more years of suicidal delaying actions on this mountain and at that escarpment. Superior American firepower would have provoked more murderous savagery on both sides, and deeper cultural devastation of Japan. Calls would have been made for ever greater sacrifice, although they already specified that every life must be given for the country.

That's why many Japanese civilians as well as American infantrymen cheered the bomb. Not surprisingly, the Japanese kept their approval to themselves. Even half a century later, few feel able to voice their belief that the terrible weapon liberated them. But nonmilitarist Japanese, of whom there were surely millions, now and then do whisper a confession that they believed they were doomed before Hiroshima and Nagasaki saved them.*

Conservatively put, Okinawa demonstrated the extreme unlikelihood of surrender by the Japanese who held the country in their grip, no matter what the odds against successful defense. The foregone outcome of the battle for the island neither made the Japanese fight less resolutely nor diminished the casualties on either side, or among Okinawan civilians. And the capitulation that was inconceivable to the Mitsuru Ushijimas and Tadashi Kojos was equally so to those military leaders in Tokyo, whose education and attitudes were identical. As we're about to see, the high commanders were extremely reluctant — and in some cases simply unwilling — to consider surrender even after Hiroshima and Nagasaki.

A stronger case can be made against the second bomb, especially its dropping so cruelly soon after the first. The Supreme War Council's minutes reveal that Hiroshima's destruction made no real dent in its thinking. After acknowledging that an awesome new weapon had caused it, the members essentially proceeded directly to their outstanding military concerns. Nevertheless, three days gave them too little time to assess the damage and the nature of the weapon that produced it, let alone to reflect on the larger consequences. Besides, the American decision to destroy Nagasaki on August 9 was made for all the wrong reasons — worries about logistics, weather, and other relatively trivial matters rather than about a massive number of human lives or other civilized concerns. And this was only the last of the callous and stupid considerations that influenced American judgment about the momentous issue. The ancient Japanese capital of Kyoto had been removed from the target list at a late moment only because Secretary of War Stimpson happened to know its enormous cultural significance. Before that, petty and even selfish motives played their customary parts in the drama. The Army generals who supervised the atomic project pushed for employing its yield partly to advance their own reputations and to fulfill an obligation to thrift: Not to use a product whose development had cost so much time and money would have been a "waste." Whereas the waste some foreign policy direc-

---

*A highly intelligent but otherwise fairly typical young woman living in a village near Nagasaki never thought of surrender until then because it was unimaginable. (Failure to attend her school's special class in the use of the bamboo spear would have been to court arrest.) Although deeply grateful to the bomb for "doing the trick" of saving her, she could not express that because she lost many friends in Nagasaki and it would have "looked indecent." But she had no doubt that the atomic bomb gave her leaders a way out. Now she could hope that "maybe there was a future of a kind instead of no future. . . . Thank God!"

tors wanted to avoid was, as mentioned, of the opportunity to unnerve Stalin, who was turning the countries liberated by the Red Army into Soviet satellites.

But although it can never been known whether the Japanese in control would have abandoned their commitment if given just a week or two more to consider Hiroshima's significance, the indecent haste with which Nagasaki was demolished so soon on its heels apparently made little difference to them. The Supreme War Council's minutes also reveal that the generals were nearly as determined to continue after the second bomb as after the first. (The destruction of the cities appeared to have troubled them less than it did Truman.) They were stopped only by the Emperor's unprecedented cabinet pronouncement, after decades of outward silence about decisions made in his name. Even after His Majesty expressed his wish to prevent further slaughter by "bearing the unbearable" of surrender, it was touch-and-go during the five days after Nagasaki whether hardliners would prevent him from making his very first broadcast to the nation — the surrender resolution — as some were utterly determined to do. A good number of those resolved to continue the war planned assassinations and a coup, their trusted methods for furthering the Emperor's purported "real" wishes and the country's "fundamental" values. High officers *did* commit murders and mutinies, although not enough to prevail.

Those circumstances also weaken the argument that a demonstration bomb dropped off a Japanese coast before resort to the deadly ones might have been enough to achieve surrender. From the perspective of the twenty-first century, conscience probably did require such a warning, even though only two atomic bombs had been made, and the military diehards' grip might have been further strengthened by a demonstration bomb that failed to explode. (None of the makers was certain the triggers would work over a target, as opposed to at the test site.) Still, the same evidence of the persistence even after Hiroshima and Nagasaki suggests it would have changed none of the relevant minds.

No shining wisdom lit a road through the thicket for Truman and his advisers. Some of their ignorance was excusable, because no one knew or *could* know much about the never-used atomic creation; many facts that became known after it was unleashed weren't known before. The military chiefs, for example, were convinced an invasion would be necessary even after the bombs were dropped, and they continued planning for it while the arrangements for the bombings went ahead. Nor could they know much about the effects of radiation, since the scientists were uncertain about it. (A few predicted disaster, and a sprinkling warned that a catastrophic chain reaction might endanger the entire world, but the great majority disagreed.) Nevertheless, the American leaders were characteristically uninterested in the nonmilitary aspects of the new munitions, to which they devoted scant consideration or discussion. Nor was any serious proposal *not* to use the bomb made or entertained.

Time has shed new light on those lapses. During the half century following the advent of the new bomb, it took on much symbolic weight that wasn't felt at the time, when it was perceived essentially as merely a much more powerful weapon. Knowing what was *then* known under the then-enormous pressures to end the awful war — as opposed to enjoying the luxury of retrospective judgment — only some higher order of human being would have made different decisions, or agonized about them much more than Truman did. And even now, very few commanders in chief are much concerned about limiting casualties apart from their own. Still, the president and his advisers knew far too little about Japanese history and culture (just as they did about, one might add, nonwhite-male Americans, such as women, blacks, and Native Americans). They cared far too little for the Japanese people. (It was almost cynical to have expected Hiroshima residents to take action on the leaflets warning them of impending destruction.) Consciously or otherwise, they, like the country as a whole, were steeped in racism. Their concern barely extended beyond winning the war and saving *American* lives.

However, that too misses the point, since the question, once again, is not about them or why they chose to do what they did, but the consequences. Their failures — the selfishness, narrow nationalism, unwillingness to grapple with the full significance of their decisions — didn't change the situation in Japan. Even if the feeble peace "faction" did manage to turn tables on the militarists, the improbable relief would have come only months or years into the invasion of the mainland, when millions of lives would have been lost. Yes, more willingness to negotiate and a better grasp of the enemy's sensibilities might have coaxed an earlier surrender — but that can be said of any war. And no enemy coaxing had less chance of success than with the commanding members of the Supreme War Council. If Ushijima's laughter at Buckner's surrender proposal was apocryphal, his rejection was no less absolute for that.

I was aware of the peace offerings Japan was making to the Russians in the summer of '45. But the Japanese Prime Minister was unable to control the Army. The Army was dominant in these matters, and they could only apparently be slugged into submission.
— George C. Marshall, American chief of staff

Truman made no decision because there was no decision to be made. He could no more have stopped it than a train moving down the track. It's all well and good to come along later and say the bomb was a horrible thing. The whole goddamn war was a horrible thing.
— George Elsey, naval intelligence, decades later

Not everyone who knew how the Japanese fought approved the use of the bomb. Admirals Ernest King and William Leahy argued that a more hermetic maritime blockade than the one in place during the summer of 1945, coupled with more intense bombing and naval gunfire, would have forced surrender within a reasonable time. Leahy called the atomic bomb "an inhuman weapon to use on a people that was already defeated and ready to surrender. . . . [We Americans] had adopted an ethical standard common to the barbarians of the Dark Ages." A scattering of high-ranking officers — none from infantry units — agreed. A few maintained there was no need for atomic bombs *or* an invasion: Deprived of supplies and food, Japan would have surrendered sooner or later. Most of that sprinkling spoke out only after the war, when evidence became available of just how severely American submarines had crippled Japanese industry. They apparently didn't notice that their argument also applied to the Palau Islands, the Philippines, Iwo Jima, and the other murderous stepping-stones. If blockades could have done the job, weren't the deaths there and at Okinawa also logically unnecessary?

Either way, their voices were rare exceptions among the fighting men. Otherwise, an almost visible line separated those who judged Japanese intentions through the prism of combat experience from people further removed, military as well as civilian. Complaints about the atomic bomb's inhumanity in particular increased in proportion to their makers' distance from the hell to which the weapon had put an end. "In general," Paul Fussell summarized, "the principle is, the farther from the scene of horror, the easier the talk."*

To report that the less one knew about the island battles, the more likely one's disapproval is not to say combat participation was essential for reaching solid conclusions about the bomb, only that the very persuasive arguments *against* usually leave unmentioned the mortal costs of the alternatives, ignorance of which was likely to strengthen moral opposition. In any case, most of those with actual experience of Japanese behavior during the war — as opposed to those who reckoned what it *ought* to have been — were certain blockade and bombing couldn't work.

Actually, they might have. The Stars and Stripes and British ensign flew from nearly a thousand destroyers and destroyer escorts in August, and American yards were launching more every week. Stationed within sight of each other, they and the capital warships, supplemented by thousands of planes, could have sealed off the home islands. But it's hard to understand how that would have saved more lives or otherwise been more humane. On the contrary, it's almost certain the majority of Japanese would

---

*The single veteran of Okinawa I encountered who questioned the use of the bomb had arrived after the fighting was over.

have voluntarily or compulsorily — in either case, agonizingly — persisted in rejecting surrender even after mass starvation. As Richard Frank concluded in his admirably restrained *Downfall: The End of the Imperial Japanese Empire* — a 1999 study based on archival research that makes many of the old arguments sound like uninformed ranting — "Alternatives to the atomic bombs carried no guarantee that they would end the war or reduce the amount of human death and suffering." In particular, a blockade, which also wouldn't have distinguished between military personnel and civilians, would probably have been *more* barbarous because it would have taken more lives, probably many more, by pervasive famine spread by the destruction of the transportation system.

It's even harder to imagine that conventional air attacks would have been halted during the process. Wars don't work that way, which may be partly why not even the blockade's handful of advocates suggested the bombing be suspended. Civilian casualties in the eighty-odd Japanese cities firebombed by early August were already three to four times larger than those at Hiroshima and Nagasaki combined. On August 1, to take just one example, the secondary target of Toyama, a city of 130,000, was 99 percent burned to ashes, as one report specified. Saturation raids were reaching down to cities of 55,000 inhabitants because too little was left of Tokyo, Nagoya, Kobe, Osaka, Yokohama, Kawasaki, and other industrial centers to make additional mass attacks on them worthwhile. A key aide to General MacArthur would call those conventional raids "one of the most ruthless and barbaric killings of noncombatants in all history." Radio Tokyo's term was *slaughter bombing*.

Critics of using the atomic bombs would stand on firmer moral ground if they also protested the incineration of those cities. Their horror at the barbarity of Little Boy and Fat Man would hit harder if it included the killing of so many *more* hundreds of thousands of civilians by conventional weapons — and acknowledgment that it was certain to continue under the command of the passionately committed Curtis LeMay, the Air Force general who'd promised to beat Japan back to the Dark Ages. (On the eve of the March firebombing of Tokyo that killed nearly two hundred thousand, the general wired a colleague to be ready for an "outstanding show.") If every human life is equally sacred, how can the war's prolongation by more than a month be thought to have been better than a resort to nuclear destruction?

And even if LeMay could have been restrained, starvation, exhaustion, and disease would have taken many times the toll of the two atomic bombs. That pertains to Japanese lives only. During the months or years of blockade and bombing, hundreds of thousands or millions of non-Japanese would have died, chiefly on the Asian continent, including those Allied prisoners of war whose numbers alone would surely have exceeded those of the atomic victims.

The Supreme War Council, up to the time the atomic bomb was dropped, did not believe Japan could be beaten by air attack alone. . . . [It] had proceeded with the one plan of fighting a decisive battle at the landing point and was making every possible preparation to meet such a landing . . . until the Atomic Bomb was dropped . . . at [which] point they decided it would be best to sue for peace.
— Prime Minister Kantaro Suzuki, December 1945

If the defense of the Japanese home islands, with their immensely greater area and enormously greater population, was going to take on the character of the defense of Okinawa, where and when and at what cost was it going to end?
— James Jones

Of course Japan *did* capitulate, prima facie evidence that all the predictions about her refusal to do so was so much talk. On the other hand, how it was achieved strongly suggests that only the atomic bombs could have done it without the years of "decisive battle" or mass starvation. For surrender was (barely) accepted only when the Emperor spoke up, and that moment came only five days after Nagasaki. It was the terrifying atomic devastation that prompted his startling intervention, then tipped the balance among military commanders in favor of obeying him.

Concluding an imposing study of the Pacific War, the historian Ronald Spector pronounced himself "unable to demonstrate how the Japanese high command might have been induced to surrender without the *combined* shock" of the bombs and the Soviet entry into the war on August 8. But while the Red Army's massive power was indeed an added factor, all available records of the thinking of the military leaders and of the Emperor suggest it was no more than that. The latter's Imperial Rescript, the unprecedented broadcast that summoned the nation to surrender, made no mention of expected Soviet offensives in Manchuria, perhaps because the Army had already written them off, but spoke only of the crucial determinant: the "new and most cruel bomb, the power of which to do damage is indeed incalculable."

Incalculable went well beyond the Emperor's "toll of many innocent lives." The "apparition of this almost supernatural weapon," said Churchill, gave the courageous Japanese people "an excuse [to] save their honour and release them from their obligation of being killed to the last fighting man." (He omitted nonfighting men, women, and children.) Perhaps some other shock might have accomplished the same, but in the end, it was the bombs that provided the face-saving opportunity. The spectacle of the immense American fleet at Okinawa, among the most graphic displays of conventional weaponry in history, had done nothing to reduce General Ushijima's 32nd Army's obligations to code and country. The troops loathed the American planes that pulverized them with virtual impunity from return fire, but fought on defiantly without thought of surrender. They took unimaginable punishment from every available weapon without cracking until the pitiful 5 percent of survivors had been deprived of supplies, fortifications, and leadership. Brother soldiers would surely be even braver and tougher on the sacred home islands with their immeasurably better preparation. No accumulation of bombs, shells, and bullets was likely to free them from their commitment.

The chief of the Imperial General Headquarters' Operation Section recorded that "the geographical advantages of the homeland were to be utilized to the highest degree" in that "first and only battle in which the main strength of the air, land and sea forces were to be joined." Even if that too was empty bragging, the mainland fighting would surely have been more ferocious than Okinawa's — more like the even harder struggle (*far* harder) if the 32nd Army hadn't lost its best unit, the crack 9th Division. Or it would have been worse yet, for the Japanese had guessed the American landing sites with terrible precision and the invasion force wouldn't have had a 2-to-1 advantage in numbers, as at Okinawa; on the mainland, the opposing sides would have been roughly equal in size. An analyst of "Olympic Miscalculations" would conclude that it would have been "a nightmare for both sides" because far more Americans would have landed on Kyushu than the Japanese expected, and many more Japanese would have been waiting on the beaches, primed to counterattack with everything they had, than the Americans anticipated. It turned out that American intelligence, even with its code-breaking advantages, grossly underestimated the Japanese strength throughout the mainland. (There was nothing new in that.) The Army was still expanding; deployments discovered later were dismaying. As on Okinawa, the defenders managed to muster more and better-equipped forces into critical strongholds than the Americans believed.

Again, however, the crucial factor was resolution, not numbers. The Japanese leaders, especially War Minister Anami, had no incentive to surrender because they were fighting their different war — for face and honor, not victory. They were also confident of inflicting enough damage to break the enemy's morale, evidence of which they saw in every American attempt to propose surrender terms. So the military casualties alone, even if exaggerated by some postwar estimates, would have been immense. If the Battle of Okinawa dwarfed the Battle of Britain, the ultimate Tennozan would have been the most ambitious project in peace or war ever undertaken by the United States, involving thousands of ships, tens of thousands of planes, and more than five million men. History's greatest combat sausage machine might have ground up more American bodies than the entire war until then, in both the Atlantic and Pacific theaters.

Everything rested with the six members of the Supreme War Council, most of whom essentially *didn't care* about the odds against them. "They were psychologically blocked, capable only of stumbling forward," the distinguished historian John Dower concluded. Something was needed to free them from their trance. Hardship alone, no matter how severe, wasn't enough. The something had to be qualitatively different from the current mix of conventional arms and strategic pressures — and perhaps it wasn't accidental that the people whose Emperor was descended from the Sun Goddess, and whose word for their nation, Nippon, is written with characters that mean "origin of the sun," saw the atomic blasts as "brighter than a thousand suns." They signaled more than a new weapon. Their explosions represented more than the equivalent of ten thousand tons of TNT. They announced the appearance of another order of force, greater and more authoritative — and a way out for the land of the Rising Sun.

Perhaps paradoxically, the way out may be seen as supporting an old Japanese belief that mercilessness is the swiftest route to a merciful peace. Japanese hatred of her white enemies was certain to have swelled as their conventional bombs and shells destroyed the country. Were the atomic bombs humane in the long run by quickly ending the war and curbing that? Didn't the Vietnam War's years of peace negotiations take many more lives?

All that is of course speculative, and nuclear weapons may yet become the scourge of humanity by fatally contaminating the planet, if not demolishing large parts of it. But until then, if and when that happens, Okinawa's caves, killing grounds, and anguish should be remembered, together with the total of deaths there, which was greater than in Hiroshima and Nagasaki combined. The ambivalent human record suggests that the first atomic bombs probably prevented the homicidal equivalent of scores more of the same: the five to ten million Japanese deaths if invasion had been necessary, in addition to all the others, Western and Asian.

It's difficult to comprehend such figures and to remember the strains of 1945. Focusing repulsion on the bomb is easier. But if a symbol is needed to help preserve the memory of the Pacific War, Okinawa is the more enduring one.

30 · Aftermath

We went to Guam and the A-bomb was dropped, ending the war and avoiding a landing on Japan that would have killed most of us. . . . And the privates of this war will rule the world.
— Thomas Hannaher

Okinawa seemed like a bypassed island. Thousands of men, hundreds of planes and shiploads of equipment were sent there to do the biggest job of the war. Then suddenly the job was called off and now nobody gives a damn what happens. The big shots and many little ones are running off to China and Japan for sightseeing and souvenirs. Those who cannot do so well for themselves are just taking it easy, except for a conscientious few who struggle on with their jobs in the face of general confusion and corruption.
— Donald Keene in September 1945, six weeks after Japan's surrender

GENERAL STILWELL, the new American commander, announced the campaign's official end on July 2, nine days after Okinawa had been declared secure. When a final surrender ceremony was held two months later, almost all the fighters were gone. The Marine divisions had been relieved by Army troops within days of the June 23 flag-raising and shipped out, some savoring a fairly silly rumor that they were going home.

In fact, most went to Guam for rehabilitation and retraining, as mentioned, then to occupation duty on the Japanese mainland and the Asian continent. Emperor Hirohito's surrender broadcast, nine days after the ruin of Hiroshima, flooded Guam with delectable new chatter: home by Thanksgiving, by Christmas, by Easter — but not Dick Whitaker. In October, his regiment was shipped to China to help repatriate Japanese forces there. After the "sweet revenge" of watching officers humbly stack their swords, his battalion proceeded to other pleasures. Quartered in the port city of Tsingtao, it had the regiment's highest rate of venereal disease.

Demobilized after eight months in China, Whitaker returned to Saugerties on Memorial Day 1946, in time to watch Main Street's parade. He was still in uniform. There was little defiant trumpeting that the country was number one but much affection for "our boys." Friends hugged him. His hand was pumped for hours. "It was," he'd remember, "a good day to come home."

The spectators dispersed after the parade. His parents walked home, Dick to George Broome's saloon. George looked the same and the bar stool felt the same. The first beer was on the house, the next was his. "The war was over. The circle had closed."

It had closed almost completely to those ignorant of battle, for the happy twenty-year-old who'd never written home about its real hardships found himself still unable to talk about them now. Combat veterans didn't know how to do that. They didn't want to brag to listeners who lacked the means to comprehend. "What's the point?" gregarious Whitaker would ask in explanation of his near silence about his life's emotional apex and nadir. "How can anyone *know?*" Paul Fussell suggests another reason for the fighters' unspoken conspiracy of silence. They'd participated in an event that smeared a monstrous blot on the human race. The appalling outrages to decency so soon after those of World War I left them with a sense of shame for the species supposedly created in God's image. They were happy to forget them.

Only other combat infantrymen knew, and none needed reminding, which is partly why veterans preferred swapping funny stories about the screwups to revisiting the horror. "The funny thing is," they'd say one way and another, "I remember more of the amusing incidents than the blood and the gore." Meeting others who *did* know would give them an infusion of battlefield camaraderie's unique intensity as long as they lived, but their glow needed no extra stimulus then, in 1946. Although Whitaker was saddened to see many more gold stars on the yellowing honor roll over Broome's fireplace, some signifying the deaths of friends, his own name there generated deep satisfaction. After months of beers and laughter, the saloon doors stopped swinging with the newly demobilized; all who had made it through the war were home. Now the party too was over, but Whitaker remained proud.

So did almost every American who returned from the edge without crippling injury. He had a lifelong reservoir of pride and self-confidence, even if outsiders would never know what filled it. Marc Jaffe, a first lieutenant who'd broken down with shock during his first fighting on an earlier island but returned to win a Bronze Star for gallantry below the Shuri Line, knew his life had been irrevocably changed. "Whenever I ran into physical or psychological hardships later, I thought of Okinawa. I knew if I could survive that, I could survive anything."

Jaffe and the others talked as little about the highs as the lows, but they'd never forget. Would they do it again, even with the excruciating fear and misery? You bet they would, especially when asked while basking in their neighbors' grateful admiration and savoring the knowledge that they'd never *have* to do it again.

"That was the peak."

"My proudest moments."

"I can't explain it but they were the best days of my life — when *I* was best."

> *The battle is over but Japan is still fighting. If we can decrease the enemy's power by even one or two men, that is our duty.*
> — A Japanese straggler on Okinawa

While the band that greeted Whitaker's troopship in San Diego banged cymbals in the hearts of her thousand passenger-veterans, no music played on the wrecked Japanese piers at which a trickle of Japanese ex-soldiers arrived from Okinawa in wretched defeat. Family members, themselves physically and spiritually traumatized by the ruinous war, welcomed their own with joyful pity, but many held the once vaunted Army as a whole in scorn. (The memory would remain hateful to most Japanese. In 1963, eighteen years after the surrender, less than 1 percent of all surveyed by a television station remembered the war as the best period of their lives. The exceptions were presumably superpatriots and ex-officers, now in the cold of Japan's powerful postwar antimilitarism.) Moreover, most Okinawa veterans felt scarcely human at the time of their homecoming — which was still far off for a good number. The war that was over for Whitaker and his fellows dragged on for the 32nd Army's stragglers. For those thousands during the first months after the collapse of organized resistance, the American flag-raising and surrender ceremonies might as well have been on the moon. Even if the desperate fugitives had heard of the 10th Army's designation of the island as secure, it would have meant nothing to them. "We shot three more Nips last night," a Marine laconically recorded in his diary a week later.

When the 32nd Army dissolved, few of its members were alive without some freakish act of providence, perhaps supplemented by their temperament. The surviving 10 percent probably had a higher-than-average quotient of initiative and individuality, qualities that would now count even more — as with the inhabitants of the last cave of medic Ikuo Ogiso, the actor turned de facto surgeon. More skeletons than soldiers, the macabre creatures had sunken eyes, uniforms stiff with mud and excrement, and no direction other than their own.

When the cave was surrounded, the unit's chief medical officer ordered his twenty-five nurse's aides to exit and surrender. Calling themselves *Yamato nadeshiko* — proud and virtuous Japanese women — those erstwhile students from a less prestigious high school than Ruriko Morishita's pleaded for permission to remain and die with the soldiers or to join them on a breakout to the north. But the officer remained adamant and the girls obeyed. (Ogiso would later write with relief that his commander, although a major in rank and a China veteran, saw his "true mission" as a medical doctor concerned with preserving life rather than a professional soldier who takes it. Thanks to him, twenty of the girls were eventually saved — "twenty precious lives, mothers who now enjoy a peaceful life.")

The eighty-odd men who remained after the aides had left survived remorseless satchel charges and phosphorous bombs, but fear of death drove some to get it over with by running from the mouth. The others burrowed deeper into the vast cave, which was near the southern village of Itosu. In accordance with divisional headquarters' last order to continue fighting, passed down from General Ushijima's final message, Ogiso's chief instructed his men to form groups for sorties from the cave. The major then dissolved cyanide in the last of his alcohol and swallowed it — or was injected by an aide, as some near him believed; the cave was too dark for Ogiso to see.

Leaving for their final attacks several nights after the 10th Army's declaration of the end of organized resistance, the first groups felt as if a bad dream were animating their limbs. While the "human bullets" inched toward American positions until they were hit by conventional ones, six of the most respected and resourceful doctors and senior staff members remained in the cave. They had decided to wait until the enemy's guard went down, and invited the conscientious Ogiso to join them.

The modern cavemen devised ways of preserving fire in the eternal wet — "the most precious commodity in the world for us." One of the best methods employed cartridge powder, empty cans, and abandoned medical bandages woven into a slow-burning rope. Every flame was tended reverently, in fear of insanity without it. A supply of rotting rice gave the group several days of unhurried nostalgia and lice picking between continued American explosions. Ogiso's cave was one of the prodigious southern ones that wove and twisted for mile after unexplored mile. Forced by American probes to move deeper into it, the gasping, tottering seven explored huge reaches of treacherous swampland, jagged "mountain" ranges, and secret passes unknown even by local Okinawans: a supernatural universe of eeriness and dread. Ogiso supposed the primal fear he felt in the perpetual darkness resembled that of human beings thousands of years earlier. "The darkness and thick, sticky air coil around your skin . . . while a weird aura rises from the grotesquely shaped stalactites and water's slimy surface. . . . To live shut up in that darkness all alone was beyond a normal human being's endurance."

The subterranean existence was fashioning a new order of human experience, combining elements of *Robinson Crusoe*, *The War of the Worlds*, and Dante's *Inferno*. Other Japanese encountered in the menacing vastness — for the bands remained almost totally apart, as if belonging to separate tribes — looked like a prehistoric subspecies. Accumulated spectacles of suffering in the gargantuan dungeon finally corroded Ogiso's training and self-discipline. A demented soldier's shriek of "Banzai to the Emperor!" as he flung himself to a watery death filled the patriot with deep anger at the once revered deity. *"Emperor, do you really know?* In your name, in places like this, men are dying unnatural, violent, miserable deaths." Yet the survivors sought to reassure themselves that they'd serve as guides for the forces who would soon arrive to liberate Okinawa. With ships like *Yamato* leading her superb Navy, how could Japan lose?

Months in the utterly sunless damp also bred physical affliction. To end the unbearable pain of a stomach disease, Ogiso armed a grenade and pulled the hissing metal to his chest. A doctor in the group kicked it away just in time.

When the survivors finally emerged two months later, they joined a small army of stragglers who returned to underground refuges throughout the day but spent nights careering through the countryside. Most began by trying to obey the order to penetrate to the mountainous north. One of the most persistent rumors was of units supposedly intact in a heavily forested area near the island's northern tip. Its name, Kunigami, was whispered as if it meant "deliverance" or "secret superweapon."

Shelling had so altered the landscape that finding their way would have been difficult in the darkness even with a map. The North Star was the primary beacon to the mythical forest holdout with its vividly pictured food, weapons, and clean water. When band after band was slaughtered attempting to reach it by snaking through the American lines, some thought of swimming there with baskets of debris on their heads intended to blend with the battle's heavy flotsam in the water — or floating to the mainland on rafts. American sentries on beaches leisurely picked them off.

But the majority of stragglers simply existed, their goal reduced to staying alive until their rescue by the imagined Japanese counterlanding. The more principled groups agreed among themselves that individuals discovered by an enemy patrol or injured too seriously to carry on would unburden the others by killing themselves. But those who kept that promise delivered a fearful blow to their friends, of whom ever fewer were left. The still-living roamed fields smelling of the earth, whose fragrance they might be savoring for the last time, and of the decaying corpses they'd perhaps join before dawn, for they lived in constant dread of being shot at any second. "Thank God American sentries speak loudly even on duty," one man noted. Fleeing their bullets, slithering back and forth, losing their way in villages whose every landmark had been destroyed, the human wrecks wormed from their caves and burrows every night to haunt southern Okinawa, inadvertently crunching rotting skeletons in the dark and passing cave entrances eerily glowing from the phosphorescent explosives tossed inside. They met, scattered, exchanged rumors, scavenged, and watched their numbers inexorably decline.

The nightly activity lasted three or four hours, from when the Americans fell asleep in their tents to the first suggestion of dawn. Failure to return to a burrow or find a new one, even if it reeked with decomposing bodies, was a virtual death sentence. "I wanted to grab the sun and smash it down," a straggler forced to endure the terror of several days above ground would remember. American leaflets proclaiming further resistance useless because Japan had capitulated were half believed. Some wept reading reprints of the Imperial Edict of Surrender. Others predicted that anyone who followed the American instructions for surrender — discard all arms; appear on specified beaches holding up a leaflet — would be tortured to death.

Although the majority had lost all desire to keep fighting and used their remaining weapons only to save their lives, they lacked the will to free themselves from their new form of enslavement. Others — or the same men at different times — became determined to kill at least one of their monster hunters before the end. Chased into fields by American "pacification" units, some groups threw their last grenades at them and were filled with frustration when they didn't explode or with satisfaction when they heard enemy screams. Others tossed grenades into audiences at outdoor movies or ambushed squads searching for them. The most daring crept into tents and massacred the sleepers — or, more often, stole food and weapons with growing expertise, sometimes even taking time to search for cigarettes. One team made off with a portable USO phonograph and records of the current American hit songs. Others interrupted their forays to enjoy moments of the open-air movies without trying to disrupt them.

The victors lit grass fires to chase the desperadoes into walls of automatic fire. A straggler who returned alive from a pass covered by a machine gun reported seeing "a red river" of Japanese blood. When American dogs missed a man despite coming close enough for him to hear their panting, the trembling prey wondered whether it was because his months of bestial life had changed his smell from human to something else. Other terror-stricken groups sniffed the cigarette smoke of search patrols almost on top of them.

The Army's rigid class system and class consciousness collapsed. Similar aim and outlook were now what drew together the clusters that formed, and they were led by men of ability rather than rank. One straggler observed that unthinkingly obedient Japanese soldiers had become "naked human beings who came together and dispersed by the force of human attraction and repulsion." Officers insulted to their faces by privates nevertheless begged them for admission into their groups. Exclusion or expulsion was a terrible fate, usually leading to starvation as well as the anguish of isolation, that state so achingly contrary to Japanese instinct. Some men joined groups headed for almost certain death at passes covered by machine guns, not out of nonexistent hope but for the last comfort of numbers. Friends promised each other to stay alive, but weaker ones gave up the exhausting work of hiding and allowed themselves to be killed. Other friends swore to each other never to separate under any circumstances, but of course did when bursts of enemy fire scattered them in terrified chaos or they simply lost touch in the dark.

It was great credit to them that a semblance of civilized behavior survived. The most seriously wounded men sometimes begged to be killed for the sake of the others. Some of those unable to join the forays for food would accept none, believing they had no right to it. But although acts of generosity and self-sacrifice were not uncommon among the newly made comrades, most bands regarded all others as rivals, sometimes quarreling savagely over hiding places and tactics. While some members hated "the gigantic Japanese military power that thrust us into this utter misery" with all the intensity remaining in their frail bodies, others threatened to kill anyone who mentioned surrender.

Few of either stripe could keep themselves above the struggles over food. By September, an outsider who stole a morsel from a group's supply risked instant death. (One ring cautiously dug up a portable safe their unit commander had buried before killing himself. They were ecstatic to find bundles of thousands of 100-yen bills stacked inside, because the paper on which the fortune was printed was enough to cook a canteen of rice.) Some groups fought others like bandit gangs for a cache of anything edible, sometimes with swords and to the death.

Food included wormy sweet potatoes and worms themselves. Arriving at new caves, starving survivors rummaged feverishly among decomposing corpses. The rucksacks still on the backs of the bodies were putrid with rotting flesh, but the men managed to swallow hardtack that had dried rocklike after its soaking in blood. Perhaps the unluckiest Japanese of all were those who suspected the truth about the end of the war but feared retaliation by others, mostly noncommissioned officers, who were convinced their duty was to stay ready to join the Japanese counterlanding. Whatever the 32nd Army had suffered before, the surviving stragglers endured more — and by this time for longer than the campaign itself.

In the later stages of the campaign, I was assigned to guard a large compound of prisoners. The inmates were behind barbed wire. Most were civilians but it was hard to tell. One of them blew himself up with a hand grenade.
— Thomas Hannaher

By early 1946, the several hundred Okinawan soldiers who remained loyal to the Imperial Army lived in the same predicament as the fair percentage of Japanese survivors who wanted to surrender but didn't know how. Although some used the same caves for rest stops, the two nationalities usually remained separate unless engaged in barter.

Shin-ichi Kuniyoshi, the native boy who repeatedly defied death to deliver the message to Yoza-dake, shared the life of desperate fleeing and hiding. Now fifteen years old, he was approaching collapse from exhaustion and the pain of maggots eating his flesh at every cut and scratch. As much as he was able to think at all, Shin-ichi realized he wanted to continue living, but he had no idea how to give himself up. Masahide Ota was slightly more committed. After his failure to escape by swimming and inexplicable washing ashore, he made his way inland to pursue the instinct for survival, but with no real hope of ending alive. (A good half of the Normal School's four hundred students would survive, but only about a quarter of his class of 128.)

The starving twenty-year-old ran into a fiercely patriotic Japanese second lieutenant formerly assigned to guard duty at the 32nd Army's Shuri Castle headquarters and now furious at the "traitorous" Okinawans whose "betrayal" had cost Japan the battle. Declaring that "locals" had no right to be in that sensitive area, he prepared to protect Japanese interests, and vent his revenge, by shooting the trespasser. Ota saved himself by thinking quickly enough to produce an old document certifying his assignment to intelligence operations. The tattered scrap in his pocket was miraculously still readable after his time in the sea and crawling in the fields.

He sustained himself largely from American garbage dumps and the occasional tent into which he tossed a grenade to flush out its occupants before racing in to grab what he could. For companionship, he found an idealistic Japanese private named Shirai, a student of English literature, who, in defiance of everything, had carried a *Webster's* dictionary with him throughout the battle. When one night's booty from an American tent included a copy of *Life* magazine, Ota was surprised at how easily his upright older friend was able to read an article accompanying photographs of bomb-ravaged Japan — and amazed when he reported the war was over. Shirai, begging him not to repeat the news to other stragglers — some of whom would kill anyone who said such a thing — implored the youth to surrender. "You're a student, not a soldier. If you can survive and get out of this mess, you must study English. Come to Tokyo. I'll help you if I'm alive."

Those fervent words would remain with Ota the rest of his life. They prompted a realization that he'd been a fool who didn't even know the supreme fact that the war was over — and wouldn't have believed it from anyone else's lips. Realizing he'd have remained a prisoner of his false beliefs without Shirai's knowledge of English, he suddenly knew he must stop fighting and start studying.

In the end, some surrounded Japanese stragglers agreed to be disarmed, but not to be called prisoners. A sprinkling avoided the disgrace of capture by mingling with Okinawans and learning their ways well enough to avoid detection by the natives employed by Americans to weed them out. After a year, search teams found fewer and fewer stragglers. One discovered in 1972, nearly twenty-seven years after the formal surrender, was almost certainly the last.

Almost everyone taken alive in 1945 and early 1946 very quickly considered himself lucky. Jittery, angry Americans continued shooting a few with their hands up, but most of the defeated men ended safely in prison camps, where they weren't tortured but treated to what they took for unimaginable kindness and generosity, and looked back at their straggling days as their grimmest payment for believing Yamato propaganda.

The greatest volume of surprise had come in late June 1945, when the greatest number of Japanese surrendered. Loaded onto boats in the south, many regretted not having killed themselves before being taken out for drowning, as they were convinced would happen. But when they reached large camps in the north, hundreds of stripped Japanese blinked in wonder at offers of water and cigarettes from the "demons" and "beasts." One soldier asked for what he believed would be a final cigarette and got six, which he smoked in a row after his long tobacco deprivation. Kuni-ichi Izuchi, the proudly patriotic artist, had killed many Americans and was certain he'd be hated as he hated them. But he was amazed by the captives' treatment "as human beings rather than enemies." He even sensed a bond with his captors, inconceivable until then. They seemed to understand that he'd fought for love of his country just as they — a sudden revelation — loved theirs.

The 22nd Regiment's chief medical officer, the lieutenant who'd grown close to Captain Kojo during the unit's annihilation, was among those astonished by Americans' "humanistic" behavior. One group of a hundred or so prisoners waiting to be crushed by nearby tanks included Kenjiro Matsuki, the former first baseman. They could barely understand when the wounded among them were asked to come forward for trucking to a hospital.

Others scarcely believed the rations they were fed, far better than their own during the fighting. Many were reduced to tears at the sight of enemy medics trying to save their dying comrades: American doctors treating maggot-infested *Japanese* wounds! A surgeon in a hospital tent cut open a cast on the arm of a warrant officer in Tadashi Kojo's battalion and ordered a medic to make a new cast with the wrist up instead of down — because, the doctor explained to the medic, the Japanese held their rice bowls palm up. The warrant officer was "unforgettably" moved by the surgeon's seemingly immense concern for human life. Izuchi was equally moved by distribution of quinine "as generously as if to American themselves" to malaria-stricken Japanese from Ishigaki Island (where the American pilots had been beheaded).

During the first days in POW camps, where minimal rations were received as startlingly generous and normal behavior toward captives seen as magnificent, the invariable Japanese astonishment led to the first serious questioning of their indoctrination, then anger at the authorities responsible for it. Man after man found life as a prisoner of the hated enemy better than as a soldier of the Empire, with kinder treatment from their new superiors.* But those who hadn't had that revelation because they were still outside the camps clung to their old attitudes and habits, enforced by the diehards among them. Although talk of the benefits of surrender spread among the stragglers, most remained captives of Japanese militarism.

Tadashi Kojo had disbanded the last of his battalion on June 21. In the dead of night, he crept down to the west coast beach with his sword, his adjutant, and their single grenade. Small craft patrolled with loudspeaker messages and machine-gun volleys. The two hid behind bushes and boulders, living on hardtack and watching ragged groups flee every which way. Abandoning caution as useless, a few even lit fires to cook sweet potatoes. Kojo's plan was still to smuggle himself to the battalion of a sister regiment in the 24th Division that had reportedly been bypassed by American forces above the Shuri Line: Now the remnants, joined by other Japanese from service and airfield maintenance units and still commanded by Captain Tsuneo Shimura, his academy classmate, were supposedly holding out not far from Kojo's former position at Kochi.

Not all appeared lost to Kojo in the strange quiet following the disbanding of his own command. When the Americans stopped firing their big guns, they seemed to pull most of their ground troops inland — unbelievably, for Japanese forces in that situation would have combed the beaches to completely finish off the enemy. Still, the captain's probing

---

*A former orderly to Japanese officers who tested his judgment by contriving to become an orderly to Americans found confirmation that many of the latter were more charitable to Japanese soldiers than the former had been. The Americans, although forbidden to give the prisoners gifts, threw away barely used shirts and razor blades where they'd be easily found. And Norio Watanabe, the Osaka photographer who'd fled Okinawa in a canoe, was startled to be paid nine cents, then a princely sum to a Japanese, to take identification photos in his camp.

established that enough sentries and patrols were operating to make it almost impossible to sneak through to the north. He reckoned it might be safer for his adjutant and him to round the southern tip and work their way up the east coast.

Pressed against the base of the cliffs or burrowed under boulders, hundreds of maimed Japanese hid along miles of shoreline or scurried on the beaches. The captain offered them occasional encouragement, but years later would be most proud of his advice to a young teacher with five schoolgirls he spied huddled behind some rocks just as a patrol began "cleaning" the area with bullets and flamethrowers. When the frightened teacher asked for a grenade, Kojo asked why he wanted it, although he of course knew the reason.

"We must kill ourselves. *Please.*"

The captain postponed his flight from the patrol in order to formulate a persuasive refusal. He and his adjutant needed their one grenade for themselves, he said — and teachers had no need of them anyway because unarmed civilians unquestionably wouldn't be harmed. Although he actually believed Americans probably *did* rape and torture, he nevertheless wanted the little group to try to survive. "So you must go up to them and surrender yourselves," he pronounced solemnly. "You aren't military people and you have no obligation to die for your honor. Do as the loudspeakers say."

The enemy edged closer. When their hand grenades joined their bullets and flames, Kojo scurried in one direction, the teacher and pupils in another, not to be seen again. In a moment, something else gripped the captain's attention: the sole of an American boot appearing between two rocks directly above him. But its wearer's bullets missed from near point-blank range.

His adjutant was First Lieutenant Yatsugi, a trusty mustang who'd been commissioned during combat in China, then joined him as a replacement during the Kochi fighting. Climbing down a cliff several nights later, the two foraged for sweet potatoes until Kojo hit a trip wire and flares revealed Japanese corpses caught there hours earlier and still bleeding from bullet holes. Enemy soldiers surrounded them as they tried to crawl away. A last-second dash took them back to the cliff, but they lost the trail and couldn't climb up. Enemy rifles approached, glinting in the starlight. This time, there would surely be no way out. Between his wild pantings, Yatsugi asked for the grenade.

"What for?" Kojo asked again.

"This is the end, Captain Kojo. I have to kill myself."

"And what about me after you use it? Stop blabbering and follow me."

His angry tone belied a calmness grounded in trust that instinct would dictate whether to use the grenade on Yatsugi and himself or on the enemy. The adjutant did follow him to an even more miraculous escape from the cliff, but extreme danger reappeared nights later in one of the breaks between the cliffs where machine guns completely covering stretches of beach chattered throughout the night at the human crabs stealing east and west. This one was in sight of Mabuni beach, below Ushijima's suicide ledge, where Kojo wanted to make his penetration inland and north. He and Yatsugi swam seaward to circumscribe its fire, but Kojo had been a weak swimmer even before the grave, still-unhealed wound behind his ear, then his further enfeeblement at Kochi and afterward.

"We won't make it, let's go back," he shouted to the lieutenant.

"No, Captain, I'm going to keep trying."

Kojo never saw Yatsugi again. He would guess that his companion may have intentionally drowned.

Alone now, the once haughty elitist joined the anonymous nocturnal creatures forming and leaving bands on their intuition about whom to trust. Thirst tortured them even more than in June. Although his seemed as vast as the ocean that blazed all day in the midsummer sun, he learned to avoid the springs that bubbled up from the foot of the cliffs at low tide. Most were littered with corpses over which the weaker-willed Japanese kept crawling in demented craving. American snipers up on the cliffs seemed to prefer the more challenging targets who made desperate dashes.

Waiting beneath the same Mabuni cliff several nights later, Kojo strained for sounds of American patrols above.* Hearing none, he finally climbed the nearly vertical rise. That feat, nearly inconceivable even if he hadn't been so weak, inaugurated a two-month crawl in search of the enclave of his fellow battalion commander, twenty miles north as the crow flies. He ate almost anything. He slept in caves, in tombs, and in the open, occasionally on steep slopes, his feet braced against tree stumps to keep from falling: The sharper the incline, the less chance an American patrol would find him and shoot. One night, yearning for a cooked meal prompted him and some temporary companions — they'd been forcing themselves to swallow raw rice and sweet potatoes — to attack a jeep for matches. Bullets sought them out night after night, "like rabbits during a hunting season." Enemy rifles fired from so close he could feel their muzzle blasts. Unlike the time with Lieutenant Yatsugi, he trembled violently while waiting for certain death. He tried to decide whether to use a pistol he'd found, knowing the return salvos after a single shot at an American would finish him in a second.

The fearful tension of those episodes suppressed even his boundless hunger and thirst. Hours afterward, he remained too drained to open his

---

*The Peace Park dedicated in 1995 to mark the fiftieth anniversary of the battle's end, lies below the cliff's other, gentler face, facing toward the land. See p. xix and p. 462.

mouth for a word to a fellow straggler. Nor did his escapes help him penetrate north of the Shuri Line, along which he kept crawling until his sweat turned unrecognizably greasy, probably after so much stress with so little nourishment and sleep. The lights of a plane above a field where he wandered alone prompted fantasies of becoming a bird that could fly to his wife and parents to tell them he was alive. He had no explanation for the wild shooting from thousands of enemy guns one mid-August night, tremendous volleys that lit the sky with tracers (no doubt after Emperor Hirohito's surrender message, which was broadcast on August 16). But the subsequent cessation of kamikaze attacks, until then the targets of a huge volume of antiaircraft fire from American ships, was ominous.

Japanese encountered in the dark challenged *yama* (mountain) and were answered with *kawa* (river); other passwords were *chu,* loyalty to the Emperor, and *koh,* devotion to the family. Some reported that the bypassed battalion he was trying to reach was still operational, inspiring news because its commander, Tsuneo Shimura, was an old drinking friend from Manchuria as well as an academy classmate. Kojo waited out the severe late-August typhoon that delayed the formal surrender ceremonies by battering American ships en route to Tokyo Bay. Although he still had visions, no matter how absurd, of the arrival of the Combined Fleet, he believed he had no further duty or right to command anyone but himself. All he wanted was to keep going so he could die a warrior, an honor that beckoned much more brightly than life. The noble ideals absorbed during his Satsuma childhood bolstered his will when exhaustion had seemingly destroyed his body. It took enormous patience and cunning just to learn that his classmate's cave was on some high ground about five miles north of Shuri. Visions of it as the answer to everything sustained him despite all else.

The September night when he finally reached the cave and contrived to safely enter it in the dark seemed a sanctified end to his stinking, terrifying odyssey. Overjoyed to see each other alive, the twenty-four-year-old captains held hands and luxuriated in their wonderment and even sense of fulfillment — until Shimura announced *he was going to surrender the very next morning!* The war, he explained, was over; Japan had been defeated.*

Dangerously weakened Kojo went into shock. Staring at his treasured comrade, he thought of his months of hunger, misery, and near delirious

---

*Shimura had been convinced of that days earlier by Koichi Ito, another academy classmate, who'd commanded the only unit to achieve significant results during the ill-fated May 4 counteroffensive (see p. 279). After the 32nd Army's dissolution, iron-willed Ito had, like Kojo, disbanded his broken battalion and kept going on his own, despite severe dysentery — until his regimental commander, also a straggler, ordered him to investigate whether the war was over. American officers took Ito to a POW camp to see Colonel Hiromichi Yahara, Ushijima's captured operations officer, after which he informed several Japanese enclaves, including Shimura's, of the Imperial surrender order.

efforts to stay alive in order to reach him — while Shimura quietly elaborated that he felt the Emperor's will must be obeyed. "You're right," the reeling listener finally managed to reply. "You have three hundred men to feed and you *should* surrender. But I'm responsible only for myself. I'm going on alone." The part of him that couldn't accept Japan's defeat was stronger that the part that believed in it.

To be gone from the cave when the unit surrendered, the exhausted shell of a man set out again before dawn with a naval warrant officer, a private met along the way, and some pistols and fervent good-luck wishes from Shimura. He didn't question why he wasn't obeying the Imperial order; he simply knew that *his* war had to end with his death. Inability to surrender had become an entirely personal matter, unrelated to national concerns. What point could there be in denying the entire meaning of his life by staying alive?

The new group wandered to the former headquarters of Kojo's 22nd Regiment below Naha Airfield. From there, they dug through the rubble blocking the entrance to the elaborate adjoining tunnel of the Naval Base Force. Although the corpses covering the floor were beyond the bloated stage, they emitted a corrosive gas at each touch, and the group couldn't move in the dark without trampling them. The smell and flies were worse than everything previously endured. Lighting a precious match, Kojo saw the bodies of radiomen and operations personnel slumped over their transmitters in spaces he'd visited before leaving for combat in April.

New slogans summoned from the blood-splattered walls: JAPAN WILL NEVER BE DESTROYED! JAPAN WILL RISE UP LIKE A PHOENIX! Their senses disabled and degradation almost complete, he and the others rummaged for food.

More months passed in the dark of a succession of caves. When Okinawan civilians freed from their internment ventured into one of them later in the autumn, Kojo almost shot them for trying to persuade the stragglers to surrender, then realized other civilians would report them sooner or later. Sure enough, a jeep appeared before he'd had time to find another hiding place. The pacification unit consisted of an American driver, two Nisei interpreters, and a Japanese officer using an assumed Okinawan name. Their talk about the end of the war and the folly of further resistance was friendly in tone. Kojo stood apart when a second visit convinced most of the cave's inhabitants they wouldn't be killed if they submitted. However, he said to himself, while everyone had an absolute right to surrender, he had his own code.

Nevertheless, something intrigued him about an enemy who lacked the slightest hint of a victor's hauteur or display of superiority, even in weaponry. Yes, the truck that accompanied the jeep might well be hiding a machine gun, but the curiously relaxed Americans didn't carry even pistols. Kojo had never seen a "blue-eyed devil" outside of combat and the parties that had been hunting him. Could his image of arrogant murderers be wrong? A voice told him to put an end to further thought by killing himself *right now;* the time had come again. Another voice observed that he alone was still trying to be a warrior. The enemy seemed to have moved on to new goals, apparently related to an entirely different kind of life.

He'd been prepared for Americans flourishing guns and for insults to his honor. He'd have shot anyone like that who entered the cave, then shot himself — but would such a display make sense now? The first party had asked the stragglers to please prepare to give up their weapons. Some now did; others had buried theirs. Telling himself it was the responsibility of the senior Japanese present to observe carefully, Kojo inched closer. Then, in a kind of trance, he handed his pistol to an American lieutenant — which the latter returned, asking how to unload it. Was he an enemy or a wiser man? Kojo's realization of how easily he could have shot the lieutenant forced him to accept that the war had ended. He returned the pistol to the American, who invited him into the jeep. After five months of nocturnal existence, the sunlight blinded. When the men had been loaded into the truck, they were driven to a military police post and given cigarettes, then to a POW camp in the north.

The last substantial group of Japanese POWs was repatriated in the spring of 1947, two years after L-day. Kojo had had the luck to be released a year earlier, in late March 1946. He returned to bombed-out Tokyo and by train to leveled Kagoshima, where he spent almost a year in immobilized depression in a corner of his parents' house. Throughout the country, returning soldiers — those losers in their often terrible physical condition — were despised. Many became outcasts. In addition to the battle and the war, Kojo in particular had lost his beloved wife, Emiko, whose parents were influenced by the severe social changes that turned Imperial Army officers from figures of admiration to objects of contempt.

He himself shared the new antimilitarism. His first job — obtained with a fake résumé to conceal his military profession — was as a laborer at an American air base. When he became a driver for an American high in the occupation administration, he resisted the influential lawyer's attempts to persuade him to join Japan's new Self-Defense Force. Although he badly needed a better-paying job to support a new family, memories of Okinawa kept him a driver, even as his mental and physical strength slowly returned. "Japan doesn't need an army," he replied. "Japan must never fight again."

Eventually, however, he did join the Self-Defense Force, and in time advanced to captain again, before retiring in 1970. Fifty years after his fighting, the scrupulously neat ex-soldier walked with some of his old ramrod straightness. One of the smaller postwar ironies is that the average Japanese survivor of the battle — that relative handful — is in better physical condition than the average American. Many also appear more prosperous, but not Kojo, who ignored friends' urging to apply for a pension for his war wound, the permanently damaged hearing. "No, I can't sell my ear to my country," he answered. "I must feel I did my duty." (Postwar Japanese politicians who awarded themselves honors and rewards gave nothing to the veterans who returned half alive from Okinawa.)

Kojo is among the probable majority of ex-POWs who never lived down the stigma of captivity, although his came only after the destruction of his battalion, Japan's surrender, and his grueling months as a straggler. The old samurai in the Satsuma son lived on in devotion to the memory of General Ushijima, Colonel Yoshida — commander of his 22nd Regiment — and "all who fought to the last and died in the fields or in the water in order to defend Okinawa." His loyalty was coupled with resentment of "those who refer to the Imperial Army in flippant tones" and indignation that "the superb conduct and sacrifice" of "our great Army" and the special attack forces at Okinawa are less celebrated than "the tragedy of Okinawan civilians represented by the [Princess] Lily Brigade or well-publicized atrocities committed on Okinawans by a few desperate soldiers." Antimilitarists who "insinuate that Okinawans are the only victims" disturb him particularly. "'That's enough!' I'd like to plead. 'It's time to stop!'"

Yet the war changed Tadashi Kojo radically, starting with liberation from the narrow focus of the Imperial Army officer. The once feared battalion commander now takes great interest in the outside world. He has also returned to his boyhood literary interests, using the English he taught himself after the war to work as a translator after retiring from the Self-Defense Force. From his present peaceful life, the articulate, attractive eighty-year-old looks back in horror and wonder at his former one as a rigid officer whose entire being was devoted to battle for honor and the Emperor.

> *I shouted in my heart: let no trees grow, no grass sprout on that hill [the site of Shuri Castle] until all the peoples of the world have seen this ruin wrought by the Battle of Okinawa.*
> — Seizen Nakasone, Okinawan schoolteacher

> *Washington virtually lost sight of the Ryukyus. . . . An appalling indifference blanketed [Okinawa]. . . . The island became an immense, neglected military dump, strewn with the war's debris. Towns and villages were rubble heaps; tens*

of thousands lived in caves, tombs and lean-to shacks, or took shelter in relief camps established by the military forces. They were expected to live at subsistence level until a formal peace should restore them to Japanese administration and permit American withdrawal.
— George Kerr, historian

When Okinawans look back, it's with little hope others will ever appreciate the battle's impact. Clarence Clacken's *The Great Loochoo* ventures the illusion that the resilient people "showed remarkable ability to stand up under physical and mental strain," the survivors having "suffered little physical deterioration except for filth, disease and lice infestations." In fact, their cataclysm, if it didn't surpass Hiroshima's and Nagasaki's, lasted far longer. After most of the battle's explosives had fallen on them rather than the two armies, decimated families clung to life as if by their fingernails. Perhaps the point is made by the fact that the civilians who visited Tadashi Kojo's cave in November 1945 came in search of food from the wretched Japanese stragglers inside, who were themselves barely alive. Okinawans ate almost anything in 1946 and 1947, including dogs.

As in postwar Germany, their condition generally worsened yet further from what it had been during the fighting. With virtually every settlement in ruins, they had only scraps from the rubble for building shelters. Tens of thousands lived in cartons, tar paper, and other American refuse — but no nearer than a mile to the bases and billeting areas, whose security and health were protected by prohibiting them from coming closer, never mind that it was their land.

Meanwhile, they blinked at their occupiers' construction. Even during the battle, their admiration and dismay at the enemy's ability to alter nature with his explosives had been deepened by their first sight of "instant" roads and airfields. The American works, massive in terms of the island's history and scale, were inaugurated the day after L-day, when young men jumped into huge construction machines as soon as areas behind the lines were judged relatively safe from Japanese artillery. Even in April, a pilot reported that much of the captured land "looked more like a construction site or highway project back home than a battlefield."

By June, Army engineers and Navy Seabees were well advanced in their transformation of selected areas into a "little America" and an arsenal for the invasion of the mainland. A prewar project to build a north-south highway the length of the island had been estimated to require ten years. Emerging from underground, natives gasped when they saw American know-how and machines had already completed much of the job. However, the spectacular blasting and bulldozing were done with no notice of their concerns. Village remains were knocked flat to accommodate military projects, their rubble added to the new roadbeds. Entire hillsides of tombs were destroyed and paved over without a word of protest, since no native aware of the sacrilege was anywhere in sight.

Too poor to return to traditional styles when they themselves at last began building anew, the desperately ill and unhoused Okinawans turned instead to the cheapest, most accessible alternative: American military base design. A proliferation of stark concrete squares, cheap and fast to pour, spread over the south like a Marxist nightmare of proletarian hovels. Soon the valleys of some of the world's most graceful architecture were cursed with some of ugliest, a sprawl of garages, cheap shops, and instant slums. Perhaps Okinawan culture was in any case destined to be submerged in Japanese and American, in the "ordinary" twentieth-century way. But the obliteration of almost all the old, important, and beautiful greatly hastened and expanded the process.

The destruction of tens of thousands of family tombs was especially damaging. The 32nd Army's fortification of a selection of them had disturbed some natives more than anything else in the defensive preparations. Since those little homes where the living would join their ancestors' spirits were built and maintained in order to fulfill life's purpose, they viewed their use for military functions as profoundly offensive. Their subsequent devastation during the fighting was inevitable: Once American infantrymen learned some were serving as pillboxes and machine-gun emplacements, they used the full range of their weaponry to demolish thousands in their path. The "poor Okinawans," General Stilwell put it with characteristic bluntness, "have had even their ancestors blown to pieces." Not only blown but also tossed into the mud like used rations. The little structures could provide a "sensational" dry night while rain soaked everything outside — what Thomas Hannaher called "living with the dead to stay alive." However, those dead were often disposed of. Seekers of souvenirs as well as shelter removed their beautiful ceramic urns, often dumping and scattering their bones in the process.

Although Okinawans' uncommonly strong family and spiritual life did help the survivors get through with remarkably few nervous breakdowns, mental illness soon soared to a higher rate than anywhere else in the Pacific. Psychiatrists believe a significant cause was the destruction of the tombs that had remained at the core of native culture and belief until the battle. People whose emotional health had been nourished by the security of ancient family roots could neither pay tribute to their ancestors nor complete their own lives by joining them. With so many tombs smashed and so many parents and grandparents killed, younger generations grew up unable to find their homeless family spirits, a shocking condition for both living and dead.

*   *   *

The occupation of the island that would endure until 1972 — fully twenty years longer than the mainland's — was characteristically American: often generous in personal ways and in response to individual cases of hardship, usually ignorant of and insensitive to native ways and needs. When Commodore Perry had compelled Okinawans to satisfy his "reasonable" demands almost a century earlier, he was certain they'd appreciate American "lenity and humanity." Now Americans who paid wages to civilian laborers and distributed free rations — the only antidote to mass starvation — were similarly convinced of their traditional magnanimity, especially after billions of dollars began flowing into the economy in support of operations for the Korean War and other anti-Communist operations. But although the selective medical assistance and scholarship grants were indeed admirable, the twenty-seven years of occupation brought far more shame than honor to the Pentagon and the men in the field who, again like Perry, tended to ignore official noises of good intentions from Washington.

Japanese-speaking naval officers, some trained in Asian studies and civilian administration, did good work during the occupation's initial year or so. ("Without doubt," reported a Navy-commissioned study of the impact of the invasion and occupation in February 1946, "our military operations in Okinawa have caused far greater disruption, destruction and casualties than any previous violent historical episode in the archipelago, and cannot be regarded by the people as anything but a calamitous disaster.") But its quality and integrity plunged when it was taken over by the Army, most of whose senior officers knew nothing about their jobs and hardly cared to learn, since they were considered a detour from line command and its promotions. After Masahide Ota became a scholar and journalist, he'd rightly conclude that the military government was "dominated by officers who felt little sympathy for scourged Okinawa's 'moonscape' or for her ruined people." They resented their assignment to "a now blackened, desolate island instead of the far more interesting [Japanese] mainland. . . . To put it simply, they neither liked their work nor had a professional understanding of it."

Even the exceptional local commanders with the ability and inclination to learn about native traditions and concerns hardly had time, because the Army rotated them almost annually. No fewer than twenty-two generals governed during the twenty-seven years of American rule, and Pentagon officials changed almost as rapidly as the come-and-go occupation personnel. As Ota charged, Okinawan duty was considered undesirable enough to be threatened as punishment for "goof-ups." The island became notorious as a place of exile from the Japanese mainland — a veritable Siberia, as George Kerr called it, otherwise known as "the end of the line" or "Botany Bay" for incompetent colonels and civilian bureaucrats, in much the same way as Tokyo had sent down second-rate admin-istrators during its 1879–1945 rule.*

Soon only a few overseas eccentrics gave a damn about the remote pos-session. Back home after the campaign, the combat veterans whose unin-tentional shooting of women and children had given them their inkling of the civilian calamity wanted only to forget their nightmares. Resuming their civilian lives in the postwar boom, they knew nothing about the abysmal conditions on the island — and couldn't know because "the dra-conian control of the United States," as John Dower called it, was accom-panied by censorship and secrecy. "Throughout the occupation, and indeed until 1955, no news reports or commentaries about Okinawa were published in the press, making the image of that virtually invisible prefecture as a penal colony seem perfectly reasonable."

The vacuum of public interest and accountability allowed the gener-ally negligent and substandard occupation to go unnoticed. The force was composed not of combat troops who'd seen at least some of the bat-tle horror but of "callow youth," as one of their officers called them, who "demanded [their] creature comforts from the armed services." And from the Okinawans, just under a hundred of whom they robbed, raped, otherwise assaulted, and murdered during the first six months of 1949 alone: predictable distractions of occupation troops banished to an im-poverished backwater.

Those youths felt condescension or scorn for the primitive "gooks" who eked out their existence without commerce or currency. Especially during the first postwar years, when family land was the sole source of self-support and the Army paid no compensation for what it seized, scav-enging natives lived in miserable poverty, some in areas ravaged by malaria, all in deep shock and bewilderment. "One must face the fact," wrote the naval officer who studied the island's condition, "that our op-erations and base developments have reduced seriously and permanently the future capacity of Okinawa to support human life by agriculture."

But the fact was ignored. In 1947, an American soldier with the Corps of Engineers described Naha as "just piles and mounds of stone and con-crete fragments . . . divided into large sections by what appeared to be roadways that had been bulldozed through the ruins." "This looks exactly like the Somme," said a visiting British official about the material and human debris while bulldozer flotillas were leveling the remains of tombs, cemeteries, and other hallowed sites for bomber runways. The "dumping ground" for Army misfits, to quote Ota again, served the same

---

*John Dower, the eminent historian of postwar Japan, called it "an American version of exile to the gulag, where U.S. policy eschewed reform and focused instead on turning the war-savaged archipelago into an impregnable military base."

function for war surplus and junk. The transitory occupation commanders were so little interested in native needs and so high-handedly auton-
omous that a witness described an assistant secretary of the Army as
"flabbergasted with what he saw" during an unannounced visit in 1949.

Although some of the worst outrages were remedied, native hardship
remained severe until the late 1950s. One of the war's enduring ironies is
the far more generous treatment of the aggressive Japanese home islands. While they were gearing up for their impressive economic recovery, Okinawa remained in deep poverty, partly owing to the unconcerned
generals who conducted their occupation more repressively than on the
mainland. After all, their real business was operating America's defense
installations, not caring for natives. Thus was the hardest punishment administered to peace-loving Okinawans who'd been least responsible for
the war that hurt them most.

The unsupervised Pentagon's freedom to run "the rock" like one big
military complex was hardly accidental. On the contrary, it resulted from
traditional attitudes and conscious calculations by the powers that had
devastated it. Shortly after the Meiji government had fully seized the
Ryukyu archipelago in 1879, it offered to divide it and give half to China.
Tokyo's motive in 1945 remained the same: benefit to the Japanese mainland. Once more, it used Okinawa as a bargaining chip, now in negotiations with Washington. Having gambled that the massively costly struggle
for the outpost would deter or delay an invasion of the home islands, it
sacrificed Okinawa again. This time the purpose was to save the mainland from further disturbance and disgrace if it hadn't been able to sever
the incinerated battlefield from Japan — a dishonest legal maneuver —
and help send the bulk of American forces to its silenced territory.

The plans and purposes of the mainland's occupation were drawn by
American civilians. For Okinawa, however, the task was left to the combat
forces that waged the battle. The difference was crucial. As intended, it
gave overwhelming preference to military considerations. For its part,
Tokyo didn't object to placing its most shell-shocked citizens under foreign military rule for nearly thirty years. On the contrary, it volunteered
to donate the island to the United States, like a bone thrown to divert the
victors from larger demands on those sacred home islands. The same
government that had tried to cajole traditionally peaceful Okinawans
into joining the frantic wartime sacrifice by hawking racial unity now
reverted to its old, deep-rooted view of them as inferior and dispens-
able. Their voting rights were abolished. Stripped of the protection of
Japanese laws and postwar agreements with Washington, the characteristically pliant and now-prostrate people could only submit. The unham-
pered American occupiers needed only occasional resort to bayonets

and bulldozers to "lawfully" expropriate the land they wanted for their new installations. That made perfect sense to them, because while they never saw the Japanese mainland chiefly as their military outpost, Okinawa was "basically strategic," as General Douglas MacArthur confirmed — that same supreme commander whose Tokyo headquarters dubbed the Emperor "the first gentleman of Japan" and was entertaining members of the Imperial household. More than that, he called the Ryukyus America's "natural [!] frontier."

> *Okinawa lies in the midst of military bases.*
> — Okinawan quip of the 1970s

> *What, again, is Okinawa designed to defend — and for whose benefit? What do we really mean when we say, "to defend the country"? Who is defending whom and from whom?*
> — Masahide Ota

No one in Washington objected to the relentless militarization of Okinawa by the same Far Eastern command that was implementing its antimilitarist reforms on the mainland. (It's not too much to say that Japan's postwar Constitution, with its celebrated renunciation of war and its means, *rested* on the severed island's militarization.) American installations — among the largest and most important concentrations outside the continental United States — soon occupied a fifth of the chronically overcrowded island, including much of the most desirable (flat) farmland in the central and southern areas. Just because the pacifist people's holocaust had gone virtually unknown, they who'd suffered more grievously than almost any other during the war were made to suffer more.

On went the largely single-minded military rule for decades. By 1971, Berlin was the only other major area under occupation as a residue of World War II — while Okinawans looked back at the war as confirmation that the island's salvation lay in their pacifism. Not every last one of them regretted having fought for Japan, especially among the young and the elite. But the handful of exceptions proved the rule of enormous regret and corresponding mistrust of everything involving war. If most Japanese turned fervently antimilitarist after the war, an even greater proportion of Okinawans did so even more passionately. Still deep in devastation, people remembered prophetic warnings that the militarization would invite attack by Westerners with whom they, the inhabitants, had no quarrel. Their overriding lesson from the battle was that far from protecting them from anything — as the Japanese Army loftily promised it would from bestial American invaders — military bases on their land *invite their destruction*. And that it would be greatest right there, not at the command centers of the foreign powers that maintain the installations. And that civilians would suffer most.

That was their chief reason for voting to revert to Japan in 1972. They'd been encouraged to believe that after twenty-seven years of an occupation configured to Pentagon blueprints, the bases would be eliminated or much reduced. Instead, a Japanese-American Defense Treaty of the same year — drafted and signed without consulting them — assigned the United States rights to their extended use. Maintenance of those bases was the key to the entire reversion bargain, which included additional secret arrangements for the two powers to trade Okinawan favors. Japanese officials promised Washington its commanders would continue enjoying far greater freedom of action there than on the mainland — which they did, and still do.

American veterans who returned in 1987 were surprised to find skyscrapers, choking traffic, and a crazy quilt of stores and shops on the pre-industrial landscape they'd left forty-two years earlier. Some made the trip largely to visit cemeteries. James Hall found the grave of a buddy killed in April 1945. "I visited my fallen comrade and it was as if time stood still. I can only . . . [say] that something that has been a part of my life for all this time has been put to rest." But the chief purpose of the mass visit was to attend the unveiling of a joint monument to the dead of the 32nd Army and the 6th Marine Division. "We hope, as at our Gettysburg, our wounds will be healed by recognizing gallantry on both sides," wrote Edward '(Buzzy)' Fox, organizer of the American fund-raising campaign. He was justly proud of the "international beacon to the world showing that peace is possible; war a waste."

The climactic moment came at a banquet, when the Japanese and American contingents, which had previously sat apart, were asked to shake hands. That was very hard for some, especially those who'd forced themselves to return to the place of their deepest misery. But many who did take a giant step toward reconciliation by reaching out to touch the former enemy felt great relief. A few embraced men whom they'd only wanted to kill, kill, kill. "I should have done this years ago," said one. "I have lived a life full of needless hate. It is gone now and I feel at peace with myself and the world."

American participants were buoyed with a feeling of purification and even joy. It wasn't simply that "it's better to eat together than to fight each other," as one put it, but the fulfillment of an inner yearning to make peace and cast off hate. A man who'd lost his right leg and his best friend during the battle drank and laughed with Japanese veterans who were also missing limbs. "This was a wonderful event and I am so happy I could be there."

William Manchester was among the veterans who had bitterly opposed the blasphemy of a joint memorial with the detested "Japs." After Stuart Upchurch made the trip with a replacement he'd looked after when the latter was wounded just after Sugar Loaf, the tough former machine-gunner penned an open letter to the distinguished writer who could never forget Japanese atrocities.

> Mr. Manchester speaks of atrocities. Atrocities were committed by both sides. This subject should best be left alone. The burning of Tokyo was taking war to innocent civilians. . . . At Okinawa, who demolished the capital city of Naha that was never a military object? Who killed 150,000 Okinawans? We had the big guns and the ships and the planes. I don't think we ought to compare atrocities. War is an atrocity unto itself. . . . The war is over. . . . The hostilities caused by the politicizing on both sides have ended. Let the hate sold by the propagandists die. You served your country well, Mr. Manchester, but I think you've served yourself ill. The [memorial monument] is a fine idea. It is clean and pure. It was for remembering your friends that should have drawn you there. You would have felt closer to them than ever. I know I did. Let go the hate. The teachings of both Christ and Buddha were represented at the ceremony. Both teach the fine art of brotherly love. And that's really what this world is supposed to be about, isn't it?

Some men of both nationalities wept silently, and a few even openly. If only they — and their people, their governments — had known forty years earlier what they now knew!

The monument's third side is dedicated to the Okinawan dead. "As it is in all wars," said an American contributor, "the soldiers are paid to fight and die, but the hapless island people were total victims." Recognition of the scope of the civilian tragedy came late and only partially to veterans of both armies. Some began glimpsing it in the late 1980s when they, approaching their seventies, grappled with thoughts of their own mortality. By 1990, when only two of the flag-raisers on the southern tip were alive, veterans' associations were spending a fair part of their time returning souvenirs, many members regretting their youthful appetite for them. Okinawan families who'd lost everything during the battle were profoundly grateful for the smallest scraps. Forty-two years after the battle, an ex-Marine sent back a postcard that a soldier serving in Manchuria had mailed from there to a buddy's five-year-old daughter back on Okinawa. The card said the father had died bravely and often spoke of the daughter, who, forty-eight years old when she saw it again, was overcome.

It took the Virginia Military Institute longer to give back its booty; pressure had to be applied by highly placed veterans before a fifteenth-century Buddhist bell, which a Marine general had given the school as a trophy of war, was returned in 1991. A few other irreplaceable national treasures — of the handful of undamaged ones — continued to serve as decoration for American homes and gardens. But individual Americans, increasingly preoccupied with their moral record as they approached the end of their lives, were more eager than institutions to put things right. One of the matters that most troubled Joe Bangert, the iconoclastic medical corpsman, was shooting a stand of "moving trees" that turned out to be not Japanese soldiers but Okinawan nurses. Bangert's wife realized how much the incident had been on his mind for over forty years. Just before he died, he told her he knew war was hell "but he never thought he'd kill a woman. It bothered him terribly."

One of the unveiling's speakers was James Day, the corporal who'd fought on Sugar Loaf and went on to assume command, well in the postwar period, of all American forces on the island. An uncommon friend of the Okinawan people, Day noted that compared to the civilian deaths, the military losses in history's "largest and longest major battle . . . almost pale in significance. It is a stark documentary to the folly of mankind. It is a stark documentary to the foolishness of war."

Such confirmation from a general might seem to have provided a decent ending to the Okinawa story, if not yet to the "foolishness of war." However, little justice or fairness is yet in evidence. For all the recent decline in overt racism, for all the growing recognition that all nationalities live in one world where what's bad for *them* must in the long run also be bad for *us,* some of the Pacific War's underlying causes endure. Americans still cherish their sense of moral superiority, recently reinforced by the assumption that their military supremacy is conferred by a kind of divine right. For her part, Japan nurtures an equally firm conviction of *her* superiority, and the "Japanese fighting spirit," although no longer directed to conquest, remains central to the national ethic. And neither superior nation has yet done right by Okinawa after doing so much wrong.

During the twenty-nine years since the island's restoration to Japan, many pledges to shrink the bases have been made, the most notable in response to native protests after a 1995 rape of a twelve-year-old schoolgirl by three American servicemen. But American installations continue occupying almost one-fifth of the now even more overcrowded island (whose population has almost tripled since 1945, to 1.3 million). Some three-fourths of our bases and more than half our troops stationed in Japan crowd its .6 percent of her national territory.

Mile after mile of base fences flank the major roads. Vast airfields and military housing complexes occupy the choicest sites. At least 15 percent of the most fertile farmland is buried under runways. "Even if some of the airfields or roads are abandoned after having served their purpose, there will be little prospect of restoring fertility to the hard coral-filled strips for many years," one sympathetic American analyst warned in 1946. Rather than abandoning the airfields during the next forty-five years, however, the military authorities lengthened them and thickened the concrete. Picture the reaction if something similar were imposed on the good people of, say, Long Island or Dade County.

The Land of Constant Courtesy, with its long history of toleration, compromise, and peaceful relationships with its neighbors — a history in sharp contrast with those of mission-bent Japan and America — lives with inescapable daily intrusions. They take place on the ground, where our servicemen, according to the Okinawan police, have committed nearly five thousand crimes — including mugging, molesting, and murdering — since the reversion, and far more during the arguably illegal American occupation. (The widely reported 1995 and 1997 rapes were but the last of many hundreds, about which the American public never heard a whisper. The numbers were greatest during the late 1940s, when almost all Okinawan women were hungry, defenseless, and intimidated.) They also take place in the air, where screaming jets, operating with a freedom decreed by imposing severe restrictions on airspace allocated for civilian use, produce one hundred decibels from early morning to late evening. And they take place in the sea, where poisonous chemicals are secretly dumped.

Muggings, taxi robberies, sexual misconduct, and other delinquency by base personnel of course continue. Seedy "night business" still surrounds some bases. Live firing exercises still cause brush fires, bullets ricochet from ranges into adjoining civilian areas, errant parachute drops damage property, and sugarcane fields are scarred by emergency landings of warplanes that benefit Okinawans as much as the Great Wall of China does. American domination of precious water resources has of course ended, but hillsides pockmarked by artillery fire and ridges sliced for helicopter landing pads continue sending streams of red silt into the sea.

However, Okinawa's aversion to the military presence comes from something deeper in its soul and stronger than nostalgia for its long history of nonaggression. The shiny jets that American airmen park at their base gates with understandable pride make natives shudder. The prized military hardware provokes insecurity *on their own island.* A dissenting American recently called the transformation of a profoundly antimilitarist island into a kind of supercarrier for a foreign power a "long-term rape of the entire island culture." Japanese and American veterans who return as tourists often gape at the Rising Sun and Stars and Stripes flying side by side from tall flagpoles. Okinawans see them less as ironic than as symbols of their centuries-old subjugation. The American participation began in 1853, when Matthew Perry pointed his big guns at the utterly inoffensive islanders and made his brazen, unprovoked demands. Determined to secure a military base there, Perry even claimed suzerainty over the Ryukyus. By the time his report of that reached Washington, a new president ordered it to end because he was convinced it would require congressional approval. Still, the commodore compelled the captive Ryukyu monarchy to sign the flagrantly unjust "friendship" treaty that established a "permanent anchorage" for the United States — a proclamation of American "needs" that scarcely changed when General MacArthur reasserted it. The United States *had* to maintain dominion over the Ryukyus, the Supreme Commander insisted, because they were "absolutely essential to the defense of our Western Pacific Frontier. . . . In my opinion, failure to secure it for control by the United States might prove militarily disastrous."

To avoid association with nineteenth-century imperialism, the defense of that "frontier," six-thousand-odd miles from the actual one, is said to greatly benefit Okinawans too, just as Japan claimed throughout her much longer mistreatment of the island. Pentagon strategists maintain it still needs our protection, now against latently expansionist China. They see Okinawan bases as "the linchpin" of America's Far East strategy for countering that.

Some military experts doubt they're a right or necessary linchpin, or that Okinawa is suitable for training troops; Hawaii or Guam, both apparently willing to accept a transfer, would be better. More than that, they argue that withdrawing our installations from the island, "dangerously vulnerable" to missile attack, would *enhance* our Pacific defenses by freeing us from an obsolete Cold War stance that also impedes the rapid deployment of the highly mobile forces demanded by current crises. But whatever the rights and wrongs of that dispute, world powers' pursuit of their own strategic interests is precisely what has long tormented Okinawans. They might consider the burdens less onerous if they could understand their benefit to them. Even before the Soviet Union's collapse, some were emboldened to ask what the bases were protecting them *from*. Never having had an argument with Moscow and not now having any with Beijing, the majority fear them far more than any imaginable foreign threat. That is to say, the purportedly "protecting" installations, with their dangerous equipment and potential as targets, represent more menace than any conceivable enemy.

Not *all* are troubled. A minority, conspicuously including those who benefit most directly from ground rents, bar sales, and retail income, want our twenty-seven thousand servicemen to remain. The number of hypocrites making profit and political hay from the American presence is no smaller than that of the champions of Japanese nationalism and militarism before the war. Others fear a reduction in subsidies from the national government, which also pays the base rents for Washington. The poorest of Japan's forty-seven prefectures, whose people tend to stroll in a southerly manner rather than dash to work in the morning, has grown accustomed to those subsidies.

The question is further complicated by the hugely disproportionate share of the Japanese Self-Defense Force they also unwillingly host, causing many even more anxiety than does the American behemoth. Not long ago, a British writer lamented that after many years living and traveling on the home islands, he could "count on the fingers of one hand the Japanese who reacted to me as just another human being." But although that experience is common for *gaijins* there, where even the most polite receptions seem stiffened by inhibition, foreign visitors to Okinawa are treated to a markedly easier, warmer atmosphere.

The casually hospitable natives attach far less importance to nationality — except, paradoxically, in the case of their fellow citizens from the mainland. Statistical evidence supports travelers' observations that many feel more comfortable with Americans than with ethnic Japanese, some of whom continue to treat them as racial inferiors. (A survey in 1982, ten years after reversion, found that over 40 percent of Okinawans felt awkward with Japanese from other prefectures; less than 5 percent had formed friendly relationships with them, although that figure has surely increased since then.) *We like you,* they tend to tell us. *We just wish you'd take your weaponry elsewhere.* But if the bases must stay, many quietly prefer them to remain in American hands than to be given over to the Japanese.

However, distrust of mainland intentions hasn't changed a clearly expressed wish for relief from the huge military establishment. Polls reveal that the great majority, an unusually consistent 80 percent since 1982, want the installations eliminated or sharply diminished. Japan's recent economic troubles, which are particularly severe on tourism-dependent Okinawa, have softened that position, but not by much.

Despite that, our policy makers continue claiming that the bases afford the island great economic as well as security benefits. Adjusted for political correctness, they echo the U.S. high commissioner who, shortly before the reversion, admonished that a base-deprived Okinawa would "revert immediately to a barefoot economy, dependent on sweet potatoes and fish." That argument flies in the face of the experience of the Philippines, where military spokesmen also predicted bankruptcy when Manila demanded the closing of even larger U.S. bases at Clark Field and Subic Bay — whereas new commercial ventures on the vacated sites in fact sparked an economic spurt in the early 1990s. But on goes the old canard about "economic ruin" while the speck of others' land remains captive to our global objectives.

Elderly 10th Army veterans who oppose "losing" the island where so much of their blood was spilled tend to relent when informed of the vastly greater volume of Okinawan blood that soaked the same land. But when other objections fail, American spokesmen usually fall back to another, supposedly decisive argument. *We have a defense treaty with Japan. Besides, the Japanese want us to remain on Okinawa.* Their Japanese counterparts like to end the debate with the complementary "clincher." *We have a treaty with America. And it requires us to accommodate her military needs.* But that treaty was the one conceived twenty-nine years ago, in the tension of the East-West struggle, and forced on Okinawa without consultation. Why shouldn't it be rewritten?

The test for the fairness and decency we like to claim is even simpler than asking what we'd want if we were in the Okinawans' shoes. It's to ask what they themselves want. Yes, the national government in Tokyo has legal sovereignty over the island — but could Washington compel the people of, say, Oregon or Michigan to maintain an immense, unwelcome military establishment on their best land? How long would Americans of any state tolerate that? How long would Congress persist? Yet these ten years after the evaporation of the global Communist menace, the Pentagon that undertook to make significant changes in that eventuality still wants its outpost, and the Japanese government continues shunting the unwanted installations to the disposable land of the "little yokels," nine hundred miles south.

With the promised "peace dividend" still unseen, more and more Okinawans are overcoming their traditional reluctance to assert themselves. During the summer of 2000, twenty-seven thousand held hands to encircle the giant Kadena base — site of Tadashi Kojo's original position — in protest, while other residents pursued suits against Washington and Tokyo for harming them with, among other things, massive air and noise pollution. Although their antimilitarism hasn't yet advanced to insurgent anti-Americanism, the swelling exasperation is less likely to disappear than to one day cost more than their strategic bargain is worth. Why they remained docile so long is less important than their waxing resentment of the exploitation that continues into the new millennium. Their seemingly immutable occupation, which is essentially what our overpowering military "presence" amounts to, keeps them haunted by the ghosts of the war that sent them to their inferno. After that catastrophic illustration of fortifications bringing death rather than the promised salvation, they now fear that the present bases may again engulf them in war — which reflects as much wisdom for *their own land* as do the global calculations of the Pentagon and White House.*

---

*American military leaders' unwillingness to accept that surfaced yet again early in 2001, when someone leaked an internal e-mail message from the commanding general of U.S. forces on the island. He called high native officials "all nuts and a bunch of wimps" for pressing for base reductions.

Okinawa was actually supposed to be defended by three divisions. I was
concerned . . . but . . . there was no longer any means of transporting
[reinforcements] there.
— Emperor Hirohito, commenting on the defeat and making no mention of
Okinawans in his regrets about the Japanese losses

As for the Japanese, a few visionary veterans took the lead in building the
1987 memorial and reconciling with their former American enemies.
THE YEARS HAVE FLOWN — HALF A CENTURY, reads the inscription on their
side of the monument. AS WE REMEMBER OUR FRIENDS LONG GONE, LET US
RING OUT THE BELL OF PEACE! But for all the generosity of that small corps
of internationalists, for all the Japanese sentiment for their dead, especially among those who visit Okinawa, the government's continued
shunting of American military activities to the island gives living Okinawans little peace. As we've seen, the native hope that reversion to
Japan would bring a significant reduction in the size and number of the
bases "so that the island would become . . . a little better to live in" remains ignored.

Japan isn't primarily to blame for Okinawans remaining the nation's
poor relatives. (Although per capita income increased from 60 percent
of the mainland's at the 1972 reversion to 75 percent since then, Okinawa Prefecture remains the poorest of the forty-seven, with the highest
unemployment rate.) But Tokyo's continued concentration of the defense establishment on the racially non-Japanese island prolongs the old
imposition of its will on the former colonials, and it includes continued
banning of the kind of foreign investment that helped ignite prosperity
elsewhere in Asia. Okinawa's .6 percent of Japanese territory is, remember, crammed with almost 75 percent of the regular (as opposed to contingency) American-used bases and installations in all the forty-seven
prefectures, and is staffed by almost three-quarters of all American personnel. That, together with the extremely lopsided share of Self-Defense
Force installations, is forced on a people whose museums display
weapons only in antiwar exhibits. On it goes, the old pattern of using the
island as an expendable or sacrificial outpost, a stepping-stone, a dumping ground.

The present impositions are far less oppressive than Satsuma's and
lack the naked presumption of the Perry party that planted Old Glory as
if they'd discovered the island. But the old mentality endures in Japan
even more than America. Although the three-month delay of American
forces on the island saved the mainland from stupendous destruction, its
people, who should feel the greatest need for restitution, are still exploit-
ing the weakness that enabled their predecessors to make a pawn of Okinawa since the early 1600s. Actually, the typhoon of steel and bombs
wedged the pawn more firmly between the rock and hard place of Japa-

nese and American imperialism, with their goals that are alien to Okinawa's nature and destructive of her land.

But if the smoke and smell of World War II's last dirty deal darken the island, other aspects are bright. Tourists who arrive expecting a more southern Japan quickly sense they're in a different culture altogether, with a much softer ambience. The difference is palpable the moment they step from the plane and find themselves at home amid the easier smiles and more rhythmic gaits in the old Kingdom of the Ryukyus. Whereas economic achievements are less impressive than on the mainland, the hospitality and happiness quotients are noticeably higher, and it matters little to most natives whether or not the people they make room for in their bars are foreign.

Okinawa continues to have many of the troubles of island communities dominated by a richer, more powerful neighbor, including a mixture of dependence and resignation to inferior status, punctuated by ineffectual talk and rare flashes of resentment. But to the extent that any generalization of this kind is valid, it is again a sunnier, emotionally healthier place than either of the powers that still dominate its economy and fate. Its passionate clusters of resident Japanese and American admirers are held there not by sadness over the destruction but by love of the tolerant, artlessly welcoming social climate, the innate sense of human community that puts them at ease. Where the scars have healed and the tawdry postwar sprawls are not in view, it is a beautiful as well as a friendly island. Despite the predictions of Americans who observed the devastation in 1945, Shuri Castle was rebuilt. More precisely, a reproduction was constructed for the fiftieth anniversary of the battle's end, and the loving creation affords a glimpse of the old harmony and beauty.

Masahide Ota, the fervent member of the Blood and Iron Scouts for the Emperor whose revelation came when the friendly Japanese soldier read to him from *Life* magazine, gave himself up in late November, five months after the battle's official end. In his internment camp, he whittled a bamboo stick into a "pen" and used his morning coffee as ink to write and rewrite *shinsei*, "a new birth," and *saisei*, "rebirth." Following that self-admonition and his sudden passion to learn English, the former Normal School student worked his way into Tokyo's Waseda University, then to graduate study at Syracuse University.

He went on to become a professor at the University of the Ryukyus, a prolific writer in Japanese and English, a forceful critic of the battle tactics that caused the terrible damage to the island Japan claimed to be defending. Challenging the notion that 1945 was "a nightmare of the past," the ardent promoter of Okinawan identity insists its lessons are totally relevant to the present. More than anything, he sees them in the indoctrination that deceived him and in illusory national needs that crush bodies, spirits, and human interests in the name of "empty words such as 'the will of the state' or 'in the interest of the state.' . . . Every one of the Okinawan people learned the preciousness and dignity of human life through the terrible consequences of the battle."

That attitude had much to do with making certain the 1995 memorial honored the dead of *all* nationalities. (It was the Peace Park's stand of marble walls that prompted the American journalist to compare it to Washington's Vietnam Wall, in turn prompting Ota's "but there are no Vietnamese names on the Vietnam Wall.")

Elected governor of the prefecture in November 1990, Ota served two terms, through 1998. Although he enjoyed the company of Americans and often visited the United States, his platform focused on antimilitarism in general and the drastic reduction of the American bases in particular. The Okinawan worldview, he wrote, "gives supremacy to human life and dignity; it gives value to friendly trade with neighboring countries, to hospitality based on mutual understanding, to peaceful coexistence." That self-advertisement is essentially accurate, perhaps because natives continued to think of themselves as Okinawan whether they were governed by Japan or America. Their attitudes are of course changing, as all do, especially with increasing globalization — but to a great degree, they remain rooted in old island ways rather than in the presumption that underlies the American and Japanese calling to perform world missions.

Maybe their fundamental virtue is simply being unable to dictate to others. Littleness can be a blessing in a world shaped by ambitious giants. A week or two in their amiable company raises questions about the wisdom of "bigger" peoples burdened by believing they've been chosen to shape others in their image.

Bibliography

TRYING TO STUDY a military campaign, one is quickly struck by the difference between the reality of close combat and most books about war. The books are of course indispensable for many facets of the study, such as strategy, historical and social background, and analysis of the warring sides' philosophy of training and operations. But apart from novels, few contribute much to the understanding of what individual men think and feel while fighting. Since my principal interest was daily life at the front, together with the fate of civilians caught in the battle, most of my research was more journalistic than scholarly. More of my information, in other words, came from interviews with Japanese, Okinawan, and American survivors than from written sources.

My greatest fear was and remains joining those who don't know the difference between combat and talking or writing about it: "armchair warriors," as John Bayley recently called them, who never performed feats of fighting but who "nonetheless become connoisseurs of them at second hand." To some degree, my worry is muted by the near unanimity of the people with whom I talked. For if it is hard to acquire a sense of the duress of combat from books, it is also hard not to see and feel the power of the memory while listening to the fighters. All my previous journalistic work convinced me of the truth of the conventional wisdom about no two people having the same memory of an event they witnessed together. But probably because battle is such a terrifying form of human conduct, subjecting the parties to such extreme pressures and pain, the survivors of the Okinawan campaign spoke with almost one voice about their experiences. That is to say, the recollections of the various categories and subcategories of participants — Japanese, American, and Okinawan; Marines and soldiers, artillerymen and infantrymen, men and women — were remarkably consistent. This seemed to be true even of people with sharply disparate social and educational backgrounds. It was also true that the least educated foot soldiers were often as eloquent as high school and university graduates, for what they said came from the gut rather than the intellect.

On and off, I questioned them for eight years, throughout the time I worked on the book. My introduction to stories of the fighting began about a year earlier, when Dick Whitaker, my closest neighbor on a lonely dirt road in northwestern Connecticut, mentioned some incidents he had witnessed and experienced during his tour on the island. (Whitaker began talking about the hardships and savagery only after years of cutting and splitting firewood together.) In all, I interviewed some forty Marines; a similar number answered a brief questionnaire I mailed to veterans of the 6th Division. In between, I made two trips to Okinawa and Japan for interviews and research there. I spoke to many Americans, especially at reunions of veterans, without taking notes. But the notes and tapes of most of my substantive interviews, together with some diaries and letters, are in my possession and available for review. As I said, they constitute the major part of my research.

Some books were also extremely helpful. I have already mentioned the most impressive, E. B. Sledge's *With the Old Breed at Peleliu and Okinawa* (Novato, California: Presidio Press, 1983). This memoir, undertaken so that the writer could leave his grandchildren a record of a Marine infantryman's experiences, rightly became an instant classic, much admired on Okinawa as well as among American veterans. Nothing I know comes as close to off-the-record observations and memories of combat in the Pacific. Samuel Hynes's *Flights of Passage: Reflections of a World War II Aviator* also belongs to the small category of war memoirs that ring utterly true. And William Manchester's *Goodbye, Darkness* offers vivid glimpses of combat's fear and filth; the book's puzzling inaccuracies do not invalidate some of the best descriptions in English of the fighting on Okinawa and in other Pacific campaigns.

Among the contemporary writers about war I encountered, the most successful in conveying the truth about combat — which necessarily includes debunking the myths and deceptions about glory in the bulk of war literature and cinema — include John Keegan and Paul Fussell. I did not read Japanese books similar to theirs, not because they do not exist — no doubt they do — but because I do not read Japanese at all; all the written materials I did examine were translated for me by Tamako Yorichika. The memoirs interested me most. Many are excellent, among them those by Shigemi Furukawa, Kuni-ichi Izuchi, Yoshio Kobayashi, Kenjiro Matsuki, Ikuo Ogiso, and Norio Watanabe. Mitsuru Yoshida's extraordinarily moving *Requiem for Battleship Yamato* may be the best record of the monstrous waste, pain, and horror of the fighting, perhaps because it makes no attempt to chronicle them but records flashes of observation and thought in a kind of impressionistic poetry.

As for Okinawa itself, America's almost resolute lack of interest in the land where she fought one of her hardest, proudest battles and now maintains her largest foreign military establishment helps explain why so much Okinawan suffering has gone unknown. But the few books about the island in English include George H. Kerr's *Okinawa: The History of an Island People,* a labor of love that is among the best products of the postwar occupation.

The following is not an exhaustive bibliography but a selection from books, articles, and other written materials read and consulted.

After the Battle (Okinawa, a Marine Returns). London: Battle of Britain Prints, 1984.

Agawa, Hiroyuki. *The Reluctant Admiral: Yamamoto and the Imperial Navy*. Tokyo: Kodansha International, 1979.

Appleman, Roy F., James M. Burns, Russell A. Gugeler, and John Stevens. *Okinawa: The Last Battle*. Washington, D.C.: Department of the Army, Historical Division, 1948.

Bailey, Thomas A. *A Diplomatic History of the American People*. New York: Appleton-Century-Crofts, 1964.

Baldwin, Hanson W. *Battles Lost and Won: Great Campaigns of World War II*. New York: Harper & Row, 1966.

Barker, A. J. *Okinawa*. New York: Gallery Books, 1981.

Belote, James and William *Typhoon of Steel: The Battle for Okinawa*. New York: Harper & Row, 1970.

Benedict, Ruth. *The Chrysanthemum and the Sword*. Boston: Houghton Mifflin, 1946.

Bennett, Henry Stanley. "The Impact of Invasion and Occupation on the Civilians of Okinawa," *U.S. Naval Institution Proceedings*, vol. 21 (February 1946).

Berry, Henry. *Semper Fi, Mac: Living Memories of the U.S. Marines in World War II*. New York: Arbor House, 1982.

Bix, Herbert P. *Hirohito and the Making of Modern Japan*. New York: HarperCollins, 2000.

Blair, Clay, Jr. *Silent Victory: The U.S. Submarine War Against Japan*. Philadelphia: J.B. Lippincott, 1975.

Boei, Cho, Kenshujo Boei, and Shitsu Senshi (compilers) (Defense Ministry, Defense Research Institute, War History Office). *Okinawa homen kaigun sakusen* (Okinawa Region Navy Operation). Tokyo: Asagumo Shinbun Sha, 1968.

———. *Okinawa homen rikugun sakusen* (Okinawa Region Army Operation). Tokyo: Asagumo Shinbun Sha, 1968.

———. *Rikugun koku sakusen* (Army Air Operation). Tokyo: Asagumo Shinbun Sha, n.d.

Braddon, Russell. *The Other Hundred Years War: Japan's Bid for Supremacy, 1941–2041*. London: Collins, 1983.

Brooks, Lester. *Behind Japan's Surrender*. New York: McGraw-Hill, 1968.

Burnham, Alexander. "Okinawa, Harry Truman and the Atomic Bomb" in Burnham, Alexander (ed.), *We Write for Our Own Time*. Charlottesville: University Press of Virginia, 2000.

Buruma, Ian. *Behind the Mask: On Sexual Demons, Sacred Mothers, Transvestites, Gangsters and Other Japanese Cultural Heroes*. New York: Pantheon, 1984.

Bywater, Hector C. *The Great Pacific War*. New York: St. Martin's Press, 1991.

Cary, Otis (ed.). *War-Wasted Asia: Letters, 1945–46.* Tokyo: Kodan International, 1975.

Committee for the Compilation of Materials on Damage Caused by the Atomic Bombs in Hiroshima and Nagasaki. *The Physical, Medical and Social Effects of the Atomic Bombings.* New York: Basic Books, 1981.

Congdon, Don (ed.). *Combat: The War with Japan.* New York: Dell Publishing Company, 1962.

"The Contribution of the British Pacific Fleet to the Assault on Okinawa, 1945." Supplement to *The London Gazette,* June 2, 1948.

Coox, Alvin D. *Nomanhan: Japan Against Russia.* Stanford: Stanford University Press, 1985.

Cortesi, Lawrence. *Valor at Okinawa.* New York: Zebra Books, 1981.

Costello, John. *The Pacific War.* London: William Collins & Sons, 1981.

Craig, William. *The Fall of Japan.* New York: Dial Press, 1967.

Dictionary of American Naval Fighting Ships. Washington, D.C.: Naval History Division, Department of the Navy, 1976.

Dillaway, Newton. *The Lesson of Okinawa.* Wakefield, Massachusetts: Montrose Press, 1947.

Dower, John W. *Embracing Defeat: Japan in the Wake of World War II.* New York: W. W. Norton, 1999.

———. *War Without Mercy: Race and Power in the Pacific War.* New York: Pantheon, 1986.

Dower, John W., and John Junkerman (eds.). *The Hiroshima Murals: The Art of Iri Maruki and Toshi Maruki.* Tokyo: Kodansha International, 1985.

Dull, Paul. *A Battle History of the Imperial Japanese Navy.* Annapolis: U.S. Naval Institute Press, 1978.

Evans, David C., and Mark R. Pealtie, *Kaigun: Strategy, Tactics and Technology in the Imperial Japanese Navy, 1887–1941.* Annapolis: Naval Institute Press, 1997.

Fallows, James. *National Defense.* New York: Random House, 1981.

Fane, Francis Douglas. *The Naked Warriors.* New York: Appleton-Century-Crofts, n.d.

Feiler, Bruce S. *Learning to Bow: An American Teacher in a Japanese School.* New York: Ticknor & Fields, 1991.

Fosco, Maraini. *Meeting with Japan.* New York: Viking, 1960.

Frank, Benis M. *Okinawa: Capstone to Victory.* New York: Ballantine Books, 1970.

———. *Okinawa: The Great Island Battle.* New York: Elsevier-Dutton, 1978.

Frank, Richard B. *Downfall: The End of the Imperial Japanese Empire.* New York: Random House, 1999.

Furukawa, Shigemi. *Okinawa no saigo* (The End of Okinawa). Tokyo: Kawade Shobo, 1968.

Fussell, Paul. *Thank God for the Atom Bomb and Other Essays.* New York: Summit Books, 1988.

———. *Wartime.* New York: Oxford University Press, 1989.

Fussell, Paul (ed.). *Modern War.* New York: W. W. Norton, 1990.

Gilbert, Martin. *The Second World War.* New York: Henry Holt & Company, 1989.

Glacken, Clarence J. *The Great Loochoo: A Study in Okinawan Village Life.* Berkeley: University of California Press, 1955.

Gow, Ian. *Okinawa, 1945.* New York: Doubleday & Company, 1985.

Hara, Tameichi. *Japanese Destroyer Captain.* New York: Ballantine Books, 1961.

Haraguchi, Torao. *The Status System and Social Organization of Satsuma.* Tokyo: University of Tokyo Press, 1975.

Havens, Thomas R. H. *Valley of Darkness: The Japanese People and World War Two.* New York: W. W. Norton, 1978.

Hayashi, Saburo. *Kogun: The Japanese Army in the Pacific War.* Westport, Connecticut: Greenwood Press, 1959.

Hersey, John. *Hiroshima.* New York: Random House, 1989.

Hough, Frank. *The Island War.* Philadelphia: J. B. Lippincott, 1947.

Howarth, Stephen. *Fighting Ships of the Rising Sun: The Drama of the Imperial Japanese Navy.* New York: Atheneum, 1983.

Hoyt, Edwin P. *Closing the Circle: War in the Pacific, 1945.* New York: Van Nostrand Reinhold Company, 1982.

———. *The Kamikazes: The Dramatic Story of Japan's Desperate Suicide Missions.* New York: Jove Books, 1984.

Huber, Thomas M. *Japan's Battle of Okinawa, April–June 1945* (Leavenworth Papers, No. 18). Ft. Leavenworth, Kansas: U.S. Army Command and General Staff College, 1990.

Hynes, Samuel. *Flights of Passage: Reflections of a World War II Aviator.* Annapolis: Naval Institute Press, 1988.

Ienaga, Saburo. *The Pacific War: World War II and the Japanese, 1931–1945.* New York: Pantheon, 1978.

Ikemiyagi, Shui. *Senjo ni ikita hitotachi: Okinawasen no kiroku* (Those Who Lived Through It: Records of the Okinawa Battle). Tokyo: Saimaru Shuppan, 1968.

Inoguchi, Rikihei, and Tadashi Nakajima, with Roger Pineau. *The Divine Wind: Japan's Kamikaze Force in World War II.* Annapolis: U.S. Naval Institute, 1958.

Ito, Masanori. *The End of the Japanese Imperial Navy.* New York: W. W. Norton, 1962.

Izuchi, Kuni-ichi. *Okinawa ryoshuki* (The Diary of a Prisoner on Okinawa). Articles serialized in a provincial Japanese newspaper, June–August 1984.

———. *Waga Okinawa senki* (My Tale of the Battle of Okinawa). Articles serialized in a provincial Japanese newspaper, date unknown.

The Japanese Navy in World War II. Annapolis: U.S. Naval Institute, 1969.

Japan's War: The Great Pacific Conflict. New York: McGraw-Hill, 1980.

Johnson, Jesse J. (ed.). *Black Armed Forces Officers, 1793–1971.* Hampton, Virginia: Hampton Institute, 1971.

Jones, James. *WW II: A Chronicle of Soldiering.* New York: Ballantine Books, 1975.

Karnow, Stanley. *In Our Image: America's Empire in the Philippines.* New York: Random House, 1989.

Keegan, John. *The Face of Battle.* New York: Viking Press, 1976.

———. *The Mask of Command.* New York: Viking Press, 1987.

Kennedy, M. D. *The Military Side of Japanese Life.* Westport, Connecticut: Greenwood Press, 1973.

———. *Some Aspects of Japan and Her Defense Force.* London: Kegan Paul, Trench, Truber & Company, 1928.

Kennedy, Paul. *The Rise and Fall of the Great Powers: Economic Change and Military Conflict from 1500 to 2000.* New York: Random House, 1987.

Kerr, George H. *Okinawa: The History of an Island People.* Rutland, Vermont: Charles E. Tuttle Company, 1958.

King, Norman H. "Civilian Casualties in the Battle of Okinawa, 1945." Ryukyu Islands Project, Research and Information Papers, November 1972.

Kobayashi, Yoshio. *San! Okinawa sen* (Alas, the Battle of Okinawa!). Tokyo: Ashi Shobo, 1985.

Kogun, The Japanese Army in the Pacific War. Quantico, Virginia: Marine Corps Association, 1959.

Krulak, General Victor. *First to Fight.* Annapolis: U.S. Naval Institute Press, 1984.

Leckie, Robert. *Delivered from Evil: The Saga of World War II.* New York: Harper & Row, 1987.

———. *Strong Men Armed: The United States Marines Against Japan.* New York: Random House, 1962.

Lee, Ulysses. *The Employment of Negro Troops.* Washington, D.C.: U.S. Army, Office of the Chief of Military History, 1966.

Lensen, George Alexander. *The Russian Push Toward Japan: Russo-Japanese Relations, 1697–1875.* Princeton: Princeton University Press, 1959.

Livingston, Jon, Joe Moore, and Felicia Oldfather (eds.). *Imperial Japan, 1800–1945.* New York: Pantheon, 1973.

Lorry, Hillis. *Japan's Military Masters: The Army in Japanese Life.* Westport, Connecticut: Greenwood Press, 1973.

Makiminato, Tokuzo. *Tetsu no Bofu* (The Metal Typhoon). Naha: Okinawan Times Publishing Company, 1970.

Manchester, William. *American Caesar.* New York: Little, Brown, 1978.

———. *The Glory and the Dream: A Narrative History of America, 1932–1972.* New York: Bantam, 1974.

———. *Goodbye, Darkness: A Memoir of the Pacific War.* Boston: Little, Brown, 1980.

Maretzki, Thomas W., and Hatsumi Maretzki. *Taira: An Okinawan Village.* New York: John Wiley & Sons, 1966.

Martin, Jo Nobuko. *A Princess Lily of the Ryukyus.* Tokyo: Shin Nippon Kyuku Tosho, 1964.

Matsuki, Kenjiro. *Matsuki Ittohei no Okinawa Horyoki* (Pfc. Matsuki's Tale as a Prisoner on Okinawa). Tokyo: Kobun Sha, 1974.

Miller, Don Ethan. "Brick Breaker," *Atlantic Monthly,* April 1987.

Millot, Bernard. *Divine Thunder: The Life and Death of the Kamikazes.* New York: McCall, 1971.

Minami, Hiroshi. *The Psychology of the Japanese People.* Tokyo: University of Tokyo Press, 1971.

Minear, Richard H. (ed.). *Hiroshima: Three Witnesses.* Princeton: Princeton University Press, 1990.

Morison, Samuel Eliot. *History of United States Naval Operations in World War II,* vol. III: *The Rising Sun in the Pacific, 1931–April, 1942;* vol. IV: *Coral Sea, Midway and Submarine Actions, May 1942–August 1942;* vol. XIV: *Victory in the Pacific, 1945.* Boston: Little, Brown, 1975.

———. *"Old Bruin": Commodore Matthew C. Perry, 1794–1858.* Boston: Atlantic Monthly Press, 1967.

Morris, Ivan. *The Nobility of Failure: Tragic Heroes in the History of Japan.* New York: Holt, Rinehart & Winston, 1975.

Morris, Ivan (ed.). *Japan, 1931–1945: Militarism, Fascism, Japanism.* Boston: Heath, 1963.

Morris, Morton D. *Okinawa: A Tiger by the Tail.* New York: Hawthorn Books, 1968.

Morton, William Scott. *Japan, Its History and Culture.* New York: Crowell, 1970.

Moskin, J. Robert. *The U.S. Marine Corps Story.* New York: McGraw-Hill, 1977.

Nagatsuka, Ryuji. *I Was a Kamikaze.* New York: Macmillan, 1974.

Naito, Hatsuho. *Thunder Gods: The Kamikaze Pilots Tell Their Story.* Tokyo: Kodansha International, 1989.

Naka, Shohachiro, and Kenich Tanigawa (compilers). *Okinawa no shogen* (Okinawa Testament). Tokyo: Chuo Koron Sha, 1971.

Nakasone, Seizen. *Himeyuri no toh wo meguru hitobito no shuki* (The Himeyuri Monument and Friends — Notes). Tokyo: Kadokawa Shoten, 1980.

———. *The Tragedy of Okinawa.* Tokyo: Kacho Shobo, 1951.

Nalty, Bernard C. *Strength for the Fight: A History of Black Americans in the Military.* New York: Free Press, 1986.

The New Yorker Book of War Pieces. New York: Schocken Books, 1988.

Nichols, Charles S., and Henry I. Shaw. *Okinawa, Victory in the Pacific.* Rutland, Vermont, and Tokyo: Charles E. Tuttle Company, 1955.

Nichols, David (ed.). *Ernie's War: The Best of Ernie Pyle's World War II Dispatches.* New York: Random House, 1986.

Nitobe, Inazo. *Bushido: The Soul of Japan.* Tokyo: Charles E. Tuttle, 1969.

Norman, Michael. *These Good Men: Friendships Forged from War.* New York: Crown, 1989.

Oechsle, Rob, and Masatoshi Uehara. *Aoi me gamita Dai Ryukyu* (Great Lewchew Discovered: 19th-Century Ryukyu in Western Art and Illustration). Naha: Nirai Sha, n.d.

Ogiso, Ikuo. *Ah, Okinawa!* (Ah, Okinawa!: A Secret Record of the Bloody Battle of Derangement and Bitter Resentment). Tokyo: Kobun Shuppan Sha, 1968.

Okinawa. Washington, D.C.: Department of the Army, Historical Division, 1977.

Okinawa kenshi: Okinawasen kiroku, 2 (History of Okinawa Prefecture: Records of the Battle of Okinawa, 2). Compiled and published by the Education Committee of Okinawa Prefecture, 1974.

Okinawa: The Last Battle. Okinawa: Senkiroken Shashin Kanko-kai, 1948.

Okuda, Koichiro. *Okinawa Gun Shireikan: Ushijima Mitsuru* (Mitsuru Ushijima: Commander of the Okinawan Army). Tokyo: Fuyo Shobo, 1985.

O'Neill, Richard. *Suicide Squads: W.W. II, Axis and Allied Special Attack Weapons of World War II: Their Development and Their Missions.* New York: St. Martin's Press, 1981.

An Oral History of the Battle of Okinawa: Survivors' "Testimonies." Naha: Okinawa Prefectural Government, 1985.

Ota, Masahide. *The Battle of Okinawa: The Typhoon of Steel and Bombs.* Okinawa: Kume Publishing Company, 1984.

———. *Okinawa-sen to watashi* (The Battle of Okinawa and I). Tokyo: Iwanami Shoten, 1972.

Ota, Masahide (ed). "A Comprehensive Study of U.S. Military Government on Okinawa (An Interim Report)." Ginowan, Okinawa: University of the Ryukyus, 1987.

Pacific War Research Society. *Japan's Longest Day.* Tokyo: Kodansha International, 1968.

Perret, Geoffrey. *There's a War to Be Won: The United States Army in World War II.* New York: Random House, 1991.

Pfuhl, Richard. *Chasing the Sun.* St. Louis: Ten Square Books, 1979.

Piggott, Juliet. *Japanese Mythology.* New York: Peter Bedrick Books, 1983.

Pineau, Roger (ed.). *The Japan Expedition, 1852–1854: The Personal Journal of Commodore Matthew C. Perry.* Washington, D.C.: Smithsonian Institution Press, 1968.

Poolman, Kenneth. *Illustrious.* London: William Kimber, 1955.

Potter, E. B., and Chester Nimitz. *Triumph in the Pacific: The Navy's Struggle Against Japan.* Englewood Cliffs: Prentice-Hall, 1963.

Pratt, Fletcher. *The Marines' War.* New York: William Sloane Associates, 1948.

Pyle, Ernie. *Here Is Your War: America's Favorite Correspondent Tells the Story of Our Soldiers' First Big Campaign.* Chicago: Henry Holt, 1943.

Rabson, Steve. *Okinawa: Two Postwar Novellas.* Berkeley: University of California Press, 1989.

Rand McNally Encyclopedia of World War II. Chicago: Rand McNally, 1977.

Reischauer, Edwin O. *Japan: The Story of a Nation.* New York: Alfred A. Knopf, 1974.

Reischauer, Haru. *Samurai and Silk.* Boston: Harvard University Press, 1986.

Rhodes, Richard. *The Making of the Atomic Bomb.* New York: Simon and Schuster, 1987.

Rooney, Andrew A. *A Few Minutes with Andy Rooney.* New York: Atheneum, 1982.

Ross, Bill D. *Iwo Jima: Legacy of Valor.* New York: Vintage Books, 1986.

Ryokan, Yoshiaki (compiler). *Hikoku — Okinawa sen (Showa no senso — Jaanarisuto no shogen, v. 5)* (The Tragic Tale of the Battle of Okinawa — War in the Showa Period Series: Journalists' Testaments, vol. 5). Tokyo: Kodansha International, 1985.

Sakakibara, Shoji. *Okinawa: Hachijyu-yokka no tatakai* (Okinawa, the 84-Day Battle). Tokyo: Shincho Sha, 1983.

Sheehan, Neil. *A Bright Shining Lie.* New York: Random House, 1988.

Shukyo Jijo Kenkyu-kai (Religion in Japan). Tokyo: Foreign Press Center, 1980.

Silvera, John D. *The Negro in World War II.* New York: Arno Press, 1969.

Smith, Peter C. *Task Force 57.* London: William Kimber, 1969.

Smith, Stanley E. (ed.). *The United States Marine Corps in World War II.* New York: Random House, 1969.

———. *The United States Navy in World War II.* New York: Random House, 1968.

Spector, Ronald H. *Eagle Against the Sun: The American War with Japan.* New York: Free Press, 1985.

Spurr, Russell. *A Glorious Way to Die: The Kamikaze Mission of the Battleship* Yamato, *April 1945.* New York: Newmarket Press, 1981.

Statler, Oliver. *Japanese Inn.* Honolulu: University of Hawaii Press, 1961.

Stein, R. Conrad. *Battle of Okinawa.* Chicago: Children's Press, 1985.

Storry, Richard. *The Double Patriots: A Study of Japanese Nationalism.* London:

Chatto & Windus, 1957.

———. *A History of Modern Japan.* New York: Penguin Books, 1960.

Tasaki, Hanama. *Long the Imperial Way.* Westport, Connecticut: Greenwood Press, 1970.

Tetsu No Bofu: Okinawa senki (The Typhoon of Steel: A Record of the Battle of Okinawa). Naha: Okinawa Times, 1950, 1980.

Thomas, Lewis. *The Youngest Science.* New York: Viking Press, 1983.

Thorne, Christopher. *Allies of a Kind: The United States, Britain and the War Against Japan.* London: Hamish Hamilton, 1978.

Togo, Shigenori. *The Cause of Japan.* New York: Simon & Schuster, 1956.

Toland, John. *The Rising Sun.* New York: Random House, 1970.

Tregaskis, Richard. *Guadalcanal Diary.* New York: Random House, 1943.

Tuchman, Barbara W. *Stilwell and the American Experience in China, 1941–45.* New York: Bantam Books, 1972.

Ugaki, Matome. *Fading Victory: The Diary of Admiral Matome Ugaki, 1941–1945.* Pittsburgh: University of Pittsburgh Press, 1992.

Urasaki, Jun. *Okinawa no gyokusai* (Okinawa's Fight to the Last Man). Tokyo: Nihon Bunka Sha, 1972 (Bunka Shinsho series).

U.S. Army Assessment Committee. *Japanese Naval and Merchant Shipment Losses During World War II.* Washington, D.C.: Government Printing Office, 1947.

U.S. Army Forces in the Pacific Ocean Areas. *Participation in the Okinawa Operation* (declassified July 25, 1990).

Chronology

1452	First mention of Shuri Castle in Okinawan chronicles.
1853	Commodore Matthew Perry "opens" Japan, stopping at Okinawa.
1871	Tokyo claims Okinawa as Japanese; China responds by declaring it hers.
1875	Tokyo imposes sovereignty on the Loochoo Islands, changing their name to Ryukyu.
1879	Japanese troops occupy Shuri Castle, abolish monarchy, and annex the islands.
1931	Japanese forces stage an anti-Japanese incident, strike immediately in supposed retaliation, and go on to conquer Manchuria.
1937	Japanese forces stage another incident as a pretext for invading China; Tadashi Kojo enters the Imperial Military Academy at age seventeen.
1940	Kojo graduates and is assigned to the 22nd Regiment in Manchuria; briefly returns to Chiba, near Tokyo, for a combat engineering course.
1941	Sixteen-year-old Masahide Ota of Kume Island enrolls in Okinawa's Normal School.
December 7	Attack on Pearl Harbor.
December 11	United States and Britain declare war on Japan.
April 1942	Japanese forces conquer much of Philippine Islands; Bataan Death March.
June 4–6	Battle of Midway.
1943	First Lieutenant Kojo completes school for battalion commanders, returns to Manchuria, and is promoted to captain and the regiment's youngest battalion commander.
March 1944	Imperial General Headquarters activates the 32nd Army for defense of Okinawa.

April	First large shipments of Japanese equipment and supplies arrive on Okinawa. Kojo marries.
June 29	Sinking of the *Toyama maru,* with loss of almost the entire 44th Independent Mixed Brigade.
July	Dick Whitaker enlists in the Marines and is sent to boot camp on Parris Island; Kojo's 22nd Regiment withdraws from Manchuria and is shipped to Okinawa via Japan; General Masso Watanabe spends his last days in command of the new 32nd Army on Okinawa.
July 19	Prefectural government orders young and elderly Okinawans to evacuate.
August	General Simon Bolivar Buckner Jr. assumes command of the American 10th Army; General Mitsuru Ushijima takes command of the Japanese 32nd Army. Kojo's 22nd Regiment arrives on Okinawa.
August 21	Three ships bearing some six thousand evacuees from Okinawa depart from Naha for Kagoshima. One is sunk by an American submarine; 1,845 women and children die.
October 3	U.S. Pacific Fleet admirals choose Okinawa over Formosa as next and last stepping-stone to the Japanese mainland.
October 10	10/10 day — first American air raid on Okinawa.
December– January 1945	Accidental explosion wounds Kojo; despite severe ear infection, he waits a month before being taken to a hospital.
February	American forces land on Iwo Jima.
March 9–10	Great Fire Raid on Tokyo by American incendiary bombs.
March 15	Fleet of American warships closes on Okinawa.
March 26	Beginning of final week of bombardment prior to invasion of Okinawa. Kojo rejoins his battalion, although he is still weak and ill.
March 30	Emperor Hirohito meets with Admiral Oikawa, Imperial Navy's chief of staff.

April 1	L-day: U.S. landing on Okinawa; Dick Whitaker goes in on third wave; Masahide Ota, drafted as a communications soldier for 32nd Army intelligence, watches from Shuri Castle, near General Ushijima.
April 6	Start of Operation Heaven Number One; destruction of the battleship *Yamato* the following day.
April 6–7	First Floating Chrysanthemum (mass kamikaze attack).
April 12	Death of U.S. President Franklin Delano Roosevelt.
April 12–13	Second Floating Chrysanthemum.
April 15–16	Third Floating Chrysanthemum.
April 16	Yae-dake, highest peak in the north, taken by Americans.
April 18	Death of journalist Ernie Pyle.
April 20	Commander of American operations in Okinawan north declares it secure.
April 24	Americans take Kakazu Ridge.
April 26	Kojo resumes command of his old 1st Battalion and joins the fighting on the Shuri Line.
April 27–28	Fourth Floating Chrysanthemum.
April 29	Emperor's birthday. At a staff meeting in 32nd Army headquarters, General Cho's argument for offensive attack wins out over Yahara's defensive strategy.
May 3–4	Fifth Floating Chrysanthemum.
May 4	Ushijima schedules massive counterattack; Kojo's 22nd Regiment assigned to screen advances of two attacking regiments, then join the advance.
May 5	After heavy casualties, the 32nd Army announces "temporary" suspension of the counteroffensive.
May 8	Germany surrenders; V-E Day in Europe.
May 9–10	Units of 6th Marine Division cross the Asakawa.

May 10	Kojo ordered to pull back slightly from his position at Kochi, in the Shuri Line.
May 10–11	Sixth Floating Chrysanthemum.
May 12–19	Battle of Sugar Loaf Hill.
May 16	Kojo's 1st Battalion is decimated; he is preparing to kill himself when an American satchel charge rips the pistol from his hand. Kojo and a senior private make their way to Colonel Yoshida's headquarters cave; Kojo spends next twelve days in unofficial reserve in a signal center near Shuri.
May 17	Dick Whitaker's platoon charges Sugar Loaf and retreats. Whitaker is wounded on May 18.
May 22	Ushijima calls a conference with senior staff and highest field officers.
May 22–31	Massive withdrawal of 32nd Army from the Shuri Line.
May 23	First American troops cross the Asato River.
May 23–25	Seventh Floating Chrysanthemum.
May 24	Japanese raid on Yomitan Airfield.
May 25–27	USS *Mississippi* destroys Shuri Castle; Naha also destroyed.
May 27	Eve of Ushijima's retreat. Students from the Normal School, including Masahide Ota, ordered to evacuate; he and his classmates head for their new base near the 32nd Army's relocated headquarters in the south.
May 27–29	Eighth Floating Chrysanthemum.
June 3–7	Ninth Floating Chrysanthemum.
June 4	Whitaker wounded again.
June 6	Remnants of the 22nd Regiment retreat to the far south.
June 10	General Buckner writes to General Ushijima inviting surrender; dropped by air, the message takes seven days to reach the new 32nd Army headquarters cave.

June 11	Admiral Minoru Ota sends farewell message to Ushijima.
June 12	159 members of the admiral's Naval Base Force surrender.
June 13	Marine unit discovers Admiral Ota's headquarters, filled with hundreds of bodies of suicides.
June 18	General Buckner killed at the front. The 32nd Army disbands all civilian corps.
June 19	Ushijima gives final orders to resist to the very end; troops of another battalion of Kojo's 24th Division slaughter over a dozen civilians in an apparently unpremeditated raid.
June 20	American advance reaches Kojo's dwindling 22nd Regiment at Maesato village; the regiment makes its final stand; Ushijima receives his last message from 24th Division.
June 20–21	Nearly a thousand Japanese and conscripted Okinawans surrender.
June 21	American 7th Division captures hill of Ushijima's headquarters cave. Island declared secure; Kojo disbands the last of his battalion.
June 21–22	Tenth Floating Chrysanthemum.
June 22	Emperor Hirohito summons six leading members of the Supreme War Council to discuss possibilities for peace.
June 22–23	General Mitsuru Ushijima, commander of the 32nd Army, and Chief of Staff Isamu Cho commit *seppuku* on ledge outside headquarters cave.
June 23	American flag raised on southern tip.
July 2	General Joseph Stilwell, Buckner's replacement, announces the campaign is officially over.
August 6	A-bomb dropped on Hiroshima.
August 8	USSR declares war on Japan.
August 9	A-bomb dropped on Nagasaki.

August 15	Emperor Hirohito surrenders. Message is broadcast on August 16.
September 2	V-J Day. Japan signs surrender terms aboard the battleship *Missouri*.
October	Whitaker's regiment is shipped to help repatriate Japanese forces in China. Masahide Ota surrenders and resolves to achieve a rebirth in learning, pacifism, and individualism, as opposed to serving state interests.
Late autumn	Kojo surrenders and is sent to POW camp.
March 1946	Kojo returns from Okinawa to his native Kagoshima, where he spends close to a year in severe depression. Finally lands a job as a laborer, then as a driver for an American in the occupation force. He will join Japan's Self-Defense Force as a captain in 1954.
Memorial Day 1946	Whitaker returns home to Saugerties, New York.
1947	Opening of first full store in Naha amid rubble and wreckage left by the campaign. Most Okinawans continue to live in severe poverty.
1949	Vickery Report to the U.S. Department of the Army suggests appalling condition of Okinawa under American occupation.
1972	American occupation ends; Okinawa reverts to Japan (the large Okinawan majority in favor of reversion will shrink as its promises fade).
1987	Unveiling of memorial to Okinawans, Japanese, and Americans killed during the campaign.
1992	Unveiling of reproduction of Shuri Castle.
1990	Masahide Ota elected governor of the Prefecture of Okinawa; serves until 1998.
1995	Unveiling of Okinawan memorial of the dead of all nationalities to mark the 50th anniversary of the battle's end.
	Rape of a 12-year-old schoolgirl by three American servicemen attracts international publicity.

1997   Another well-publicized American rape of an
                Okinawan.

2000   Japan has Okinawa host the G-7 economic sum-
                mit, largely to seek acceptance of the status quo
                on the base issue; President Clinton promises to
                reduce the American "footprint" on the island.

2001   The commanding general of U.S. forces apolo-
                gizes for calling Okinawan officials who urge base
                reductions "all nuts and a bunch of wimps." Also
                apologizes for a Marine arsonist who set fire to
                civilian property; another Marine is convicted of
                molesting an Okinawan girl.

Index